TUTORIAL
on Software Restructuring

ROBERT S. ARNOLD

IEEE Computer Society Order Number 680
Library of Congress Number 86-80071
IEEE Catalog Number EH0244-4
ISBN 0-8186-0680-0

IEEE COMPUTER SOCIETY

THE INSTITUTE OF ELECTRICAL
AND ELECTRONICS ENGINEERS, INC.
IEEE

COMPUTER
SOCIETY
PRESS

Published by IEEE Computer Society Press
1730 Massachusetts Avenue, N.W.
Washington, D.C. 20036-1903

Ada is a registered trademark of the U.S. Government/Ada Joint Program Office.
UNIX is a trademark of AT&T Bell Laboratories.
VIA/INSIGHT is a trademark of VIASOFT, Inc.
RECODER is a trademark of Language Technology, Inc.
SUPERSTRUCTURE is a trademark of Group Operations, Inc.
SCAN/COBOL is a trademark of Group Operations, Inc.
Structured Retrofit is a trademark of Peat, Marwick, Mitchell, and Co.
PATHVU is a trademark of Peat, Marwick, Mitchell, and Co.

COVER DESIGNED BY JACK I. BALLESTERO

IEEE Computer Society Order Number 680
Library of Congress Number 86-80071
IEEE Catalog Number EH0244-4
ISBN 0-8186-0680-0 (Paper)
ISBN 0-8186-4680-2 (Microfiche)

Order from: IEEE Computer Society   IEEE Service Center
Post Office Box 80452   44 Hoes Lane
Worldway Postal Center   Piscataway, NJ 08854
Los Angeles, CA 90080

 THE INSTITUTE OF ELECTRICAL AND ELECTRONICS ENGINEERS, INC.

Acknowledgements

I thank William E. Perry of the Quality Assurance Institute for sparking my interest in software restructuring techniques. Tom Reid of the MITRE Corporation; Walter Mahan, a consultant working at Morino Associates; and an anonymous reviewer selected by the IEEE Computer Society, provided valuable comments on earlier drafts of this Tutorial. Thanks also to Mark Weiser and Ben Shneiderman of the University of Maryland, and to Gavriel Salvendy and John Wiley & Sons, for allowing the paper on human factors to be published here prior to its publication as a chapter in the *Handbook of Human Factors/Ergonomics* (G. Salvendy, Editor). Margaret Brown and Chip Stockton of the IEEE Computer Society gave welcome assistance and encouragement to me in completing the Tutorial.

Preface

This Tutorial is devoted to putting structure back into software, whether the lack of structure results from software maintenance or from software development.

With continued change, programs tend to become less "structured." This is manifested by out-of-date documentation, by code that does not conform to standards, by increased time for programmers to understand code, by increased ripple effect of changes, and so on. These can—and usually do—imply higher software maintenance costs.

Software restructuring is an important option for putting high software maintenance costs under control. The idea is to modify software—or programmer's perceptions of software structure—so one can understand it and control it anew.

There are many reasons why software managers and programmers should be aware of software restructuring:

- Implementing standards for software structure
- Regaining understanding of software by instilling software with known, easily traceable structure
- Extending system lifetime by retaining a system's flexibility through good structure
- Preparing software for conversion

(This list is greatly expanded in Part I of this Tutorial.) Software restructuring is an integral part of achieving many goals in software maintenance and in corporate planning for software change.

The Tutorial's goals are to acquaint the reader

(1) with the available technology for software restructuring, and

(2) on how to apply this technology on real-life software restructuring problems.

This book is intended for software engineering practitioners and researchers. Among practitioners, software maintenance managers will be interested in the range of options, and relative costs, for performing software restructuring. Software maintenance programmers will be interested in techniques designed to make their job easier. Even software developers will be interested in software restructuring—to see how certain ways of building software tend to lessen the need for restructuring software later on.

For software practitioners, this collection of papers presents a sound basis for understanding and dealing with software restructuring problems. The notion of software "structure" is discussed and its practical importance illustrated. A wide variety of software restructuring approaches is presented. The approaches range from those that do not modify software at all, to approaches that emphasize manual software changes, to some commercially available restructuring tools, and to automatic rule-based transformation systems.

The Tutorial also presents decision rules for deciding if restructuring a given piece of software will be cost-effective. In today's world of high-budget software maintenance, cost criteria generally enter into any decision for adopting new technology.

For researchers, this Tutorial collects a substantial body of software restructuring literature. This book does not contain all known work on software restructuring, but it does contain many seminal works on software restructuring. Any work not contained here is likely referenced in the Tutorial's annotated bibliography.

Why This Tutorial?

One sign of a maturing field is the emergence of specialty fields. The need for software restructuring grew out of software maintenance practices that made software progressively harder to understand and reliably change. But software maintenance by no means corners the market on producing poor software structure. Poor structure may also result from software development.

Software restructuring differs from software maintenance in at least two ways. First, as just indicated, software restructuring can apply to software development as well as to software maintenance. Second, software maintenance programmers normally spend their time creating functional software enhancements and in fixing software bugs. Restructuring is given relatively little attention.

The reasons for this neglect are in part economic. Few people are aware of how to quantify the benefits of software restructuring. Among software maintenance programmers, software restructuring is often viewed as a dispensable luxury. "Who cares if restructuring may save money in the long run? I'm rated by my productivity *now*. That means getting my assigned changes done on time. Boy, do I have a lot of changes!"

The benefits of software restructuring often appear in the long run, across generations of maintenance programmers and across strategic plans for software systems. Software restructuring seeks to recover, preserve, and even extend a software system's asset value to an organization. This translates to extended system life, higher reliability, and higher flexibility. It also means maintenance changes may cost more, and take longer, owing to procedures instituted for preserving software structure once that structure is achieved.

Tutorial Organization

Part I, "An Introduction to Software Restructuring," gives a tutorial introduction to software restructuring. The reader should read this first to understand what "structure" is, software restructuring's role in software engineering, and the 30-plus currently known approaches to software restructuring.

Part II, "Perspectives on Software Structure," presents ways to characterize software structure. These range from software metrics which directly measure software characteristics (e.g., the number of decisions in the control structure), to indirect software characteristics (e.g., software understandability), to programmer characteristics (e.g., experience with programming in a given language).

Part III, "Origins/Effects of Poor Software Structure," shows how poor structure can appear in code in the first place. One seldom forgets lessons from software structure horror stories.

Part IV, "Strategies/Tools for Recognizing Structure," concerns the means for programmers to detect software structure. Sometimes being able to recognize good (or bad) structure is sufficient for a programmer to take further action. After experience is gained, the recognition tools form a part of the programmer's view of structure.

Part V, "Infusing Software with Structure: Code Level Approaches," presents several code level approaches for restructuring code. These range from a manual approach based on a theory of structured programming, to an approach based on programming style, to commercially available tools for restructuring code.

Part VI, "Infusing Software with Structure: System Level Approaches," presents system level approaches for restructuring code. These approaches differ from those of part V in that the software's specification or design play a bigger role in restructuring. The approaches range from recapturing specification information about a system, to an approach that restructures software engineering practices in addition to the software, to principles for structuring (and restructuring) maintainable systems, to restructuring with a view to supplying reusable code modules.

Part VII, "Restructuring Criteria and Cost Models," presents factors that can motivate restructuring and gives models for calculating the time frames and payoffs of software restructuring. These are practical issues that influence (1) the technology transfer of software restructuring (e.g., using cost information to sell management on trying software restructuring and (2) the timing of software restructuring (i.e., what aspects of software structure motivate to consider using a restructuring approach).

Part VIII, "Rule-Based Restructuring Systems," concerns the use of automated rules, or transformations, in performing restructuring. Although still undergoing research, rule-based systems offer several ideas that improve the flexibility of a restructuring approach and allow the user greater control in deciding what aspects of structure are relevant.

The Tutorial concludes with an annotated list of references to the software restructuring literature.

Robert S. Arnold
February 7, 1986

Table of Contents

Part VIII. Rule-Based Restructuring Systems

I. An Introduction to Software Restructuring

Robert S. Arnold

1. In a Nutshell . . .

Software restructuring won't always save money, but it is worth checking out before releasing a poorly structured system to maintenance, resigning oneself to high maintenance costs or maintained software which regularly "bites back," or prematurely retiring a software system undergoing maintenance.

With continued change, programs tend to become less "structured." This is manifested by out-of-date documentation, code which does not conform to standards, increased time for programmers to understand code, increased ripple effect of changes, and so on. These can—and usually do—imply higher software maintenance costs.

Software restructuring is an important option for putting high software maintenance costs under control. The idea is to modify software—or programmer's perceptions of software structure—so one can understand it and control it anew.

There are many other reasons why software managers and programmers should be aware of software restructuring:

- Regaining understanding of software by instilling software with known, easily traceable structure. This has the side benefits of
  - easier documentation,
  - easier testing,
  - easier auditing,
  - potentially reduced software complexity,
  - potentially greater programmer productivity,
  - reducing a maintenance department's dependence on individuals who alone understand poorly structured software, and
  - greater programmer job satisfaction due to decreased frustration in working with poorly structured software.
- Creating software whose structure more closely resembles the structure taught to newer generations of programmers
- Reducing the amount of time needed for maintenance programmers to become familiar with a system
- Upgrading software along with upgrading software engineering practices
- Implementing standards for software structure

- Making bugs easier to locate
- Extending system lifetime by retaining a system's flexibility through good structure
- Preparing software as input for software analysis tools
- Preparing software for conversion
- Retaining software's asset value to an organization

Software restructuring is an integral part of achieving many goals in software maintenance and in corporate planning for software change.

1.1 A Definition

Software restructuring is the modification of software to make the software (1) easier to understand and to change or (2) less susceptible to error when future changes are made. "Software" includes external and internal documentation concerning the code, as well as the code itself.

This definition excludes software changes for other purposes (e.g., code optimization). Code optimization does imply "restructuring" in some sense, but normally does not concern the key element of software maintainability.

For this Tutorial, software restructuring is more for the programmer's benefit than the computer's. The purposes of software restructuring are to decrease the programmer effort needed to modify code and to reduce software defects. Given that programmer costs far exceed hardware costs, software restructuring appears as a plausible way to trade programmer time for computer time. We will see, however, that this cost savings often only appears in the medium to long term (months to years) after restructuring is applied, rather than in the following days or weeks. Introducing a restructuring approach can require initially *more* programmer time.

1.2 What is Software Structure?

Software structure is a collection of software attributes that "make sense" to the perceiver. This says software structure is composed of a set of software attributes, the elements of which depend on the person. Software structure, like a scientific theory, is a subjective artifact.

The definition does *not* imply that none of these attributes can be objectively defined and measured. For some people, software structure attributes can be objectively defined and measured, though other people will dispute whether these attributes constitute meaningful aspects of "structure."

Unfortunately, few authors—anywhere—define their notion of software structure in their papers or books. This applies to most of the papers in this Tutorial. The reader should realize that the "structure" in restructuring is often implicit, with the discussion context hinting at what structure is intended.

1.3 Software Restructuring and Software Maintenance

Software restructuring is most often applied to software undergoing maintenance, for this is where the lack of software structure becomes most evident (and expensive). Throughout the Tutorial, software restructuring will be considered in the context of software maintenance.

However, software restructuring is also applicable during software development. This occurs especially in those developments where the activities tend to resemble "traditional" software maintenance (i.e., no quality assurance, deadline-driven, little if any testing, no code reviews, etc.), and code becomes less structured.

To take a plausible example, in a large software project that has little reused code, takes several calendar years to build, and has little quality assurance, the potential for unstructured software toward project end can increase. The development activities prior to delivery could center on corrections to errors uncovered by tests and on enhancements requested by users due to changed needs since the system was contracted. If development is deadline-driven, the changes may be hurried and resemble patches, which can lead to worse software structure. In this situation, software restructuring might be advisable before the system is accepted for maintenance.

1.4 Goals of Software Restructuring

A major goal of software restructuring is to preserve or increase software value. Software value can be measured externally or internally.

External software value is the cost savings the software provides to the user community, relative to other, non-software means of satisfying user needs. For users, successful software maintenance is typified by few—preferably no—visible bugs in the software and rapid response/implementation of user requests for system change. Systems undergoing maintenance often become progressively more difficult to change (Lehman [80]). If this progressive software ossification ever begins affecting the user's expectation of delivered software capability, the external value of the software may decrease.

Internal software value involves at least three kinds of cost savings: (1) the maintenance cost savings that the software form provides relative to some other software form, (2) the cost savings incurred by reusing parts of the software in other systems, and (3) the cost savings owing to an extended software lifetime (which delays the introduction of a replacement system). If software restructuring reduces maintenance costs, increases the software's potential for reuse in other

software, and extends the software's lifetime, the internal value of the current software should increase!

This definition provides a common view of software value that will be used in this Tutorial.

There is little reason to believe that the same definition of value is used by all maintenance environments. Software value can be measured in other ways, such as savings in calendar time to implement software changes, increase in maintainer morale, increase in management respect for software maintenance, and so on.

But having *some* definition of software value can materially affect decisions to restructure. Any decision to use a software restructuring approach should try to quantify the added software value, as locally defined, which the approach will provide.

1.5 Keeping Software Restructuring in Perspective

Software restructuring should not be an end in itself. Restructuring should be related to locally defined goals, and achieving goals should be related to perceived software value. If restructuring cannot be justified in terms of higher goals, then these goals should be rethought, or more information collected, before the decision to restructure is made.

For example, if the problem is slow performance of user-requested changes in a software maintenance shop, then maintenance management's higher goal of satisfactory software service is affected. The reason for the slow performance could be hard-to-modify software (in which case software restructuring may be advisable), or unrestrained user requests for change (in which case software restructuring may not be advisable), among other reasons. Further information is needed before one decides to restructure. But if restructuring is selected, it is because of the goal of satisfactory software service and not restructuring for its own sake.

1.6 Keeping Software Structured

Software restructuring should be viewed as part of a more comprehensive solution to poor software structure. Once software is structured, presumably one would like it to stay structured with each software change. Here is where practices that foster good software structure come in—practices like defining and using software standards, giving programmers tools for checking conformance of the software to software standards, performing code reviews, performing software tests with known degree of test coverage, quality assurance, and so on.

Quality assurance and restructuring are more related than one might think. Quality assurance applied from maintenance day one can reduce the need for restructuring later on. If restructuring is required, quality assurance can help keep the software structured.

1.7 The Lack of Quantitative Data on Software Restructuring

A trend in software engineering today is to emphasize getting quantitative data about the effectiveness of a software engineering approach, including software restructuring approaches. Reliable reported data on software restructuring has been sparse. This means many of the observations on software restructuring approaches must be qualitative, not quantitative.

Having good quantitative data is valuable, but until such data becomes widely available it is wise to remember that qualitative observations can still be very useful. (Most day-to-day decisions are based on qualitative information!) The reader will find many valuable ideas in this Tutorial, despite the lack of quantitative data.

2. State of the Art in Software Restructuring Technology

This section briefly outlines the existing technology for software restructuring. A list of software restructuring approaches is presented in section 2.2. How this list was compiled is discussed in section 2.1.

2.1 Criteria for Compiling Software Restructuring Approaches

The list of restructuring approaches to be presented in section 2.2 has been compiled in several ways. Restructuring approaches that clearly change software were immediately included (e.g., Ashcroft and Manna's giant case statement approach, which transforms a program's basic control structure into a case statement). Next to be added were approaches not originally intended for software restructuring, but which could be used for restructuring, nonetheless (e.g., software inspections and reviews). Beyond this, a clear view

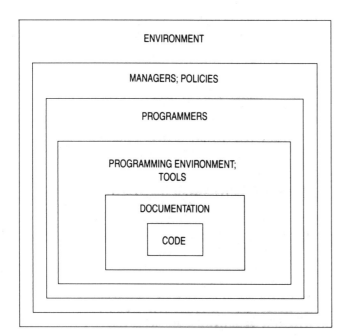

Figure 1: Layers of Factors Which Can Influence Software Structure

of the factors influencing software structure was required. Any approach that influenced these factors could potentially be a software restructuring approach.

I earlier defined structure as "a collection of software attributes that 'make sense' to the perceiver." This implies that software structure is determined by at least two things: the software and the perceiver. Thus anything that can influence the software's state or the perceiver's state might influence software structure.

One view of the factors influencing software structure is given in Figure 1. The clearest influence on software structure comes from the software code itself, at the core of the figure. Next, the in-line software documentation—often the primary documentation programmers depend on (Glass[81])—can have a strong influence on a programmer's perception of structure. Other documentation, when available, up-to-date, easily referenced, clearly written, and so on, can also influence a programmer's perception of structure. Next come the set of available software tools (or programming environment) which can illuminate different views of the software for the programmer. For example, program traces can show dynamic execution behavior, algorithm animation can help programmers understand the dynamic strategy behind an algorithm, global variable cross referencers can help programmers understand the interactions between modules, and pretty printers can make reading code much more appealing.

In the middle layer of Figure 1 is the programmer, the "other side" of software structure. If the programmer either has had a bad day, or is not trained to look for certain aspects of structure, his or her perception of structure will be influenced.

Because programmers' perceptions differ (even in the same programmer at different times), the notion of software structure is not constant, but *dynamic*. In fact, failure to have written notions of structure (such as structural standards) which programmers are aware of, or failure to allow programmers to refresh their notions of structure by viewing software in various ways, can lead to a net *loss* of structure. For example, program patches are insidious structure-reducers because the basis for deciding the intent of the patch typically walks away when the patch's author leaves. In effect, the programmer has promoted in the software his or her structural view without telling others of this view, resulting in a net loss of software structure for others.

At the next higher layer of Figure 1 is the management layer, which can conceivably sensitize a programmer to aspects of software structure. For example, management can emphasize software quality as embodied in a local set of standards. If a programmer's performance review is tied to how well these standards are met, then the programmer's perceptions of software will likely be influenced!

The highest layer of Figure 1 is the environment surrounding the lower levels. This includes physical facilities, degree of influence on software maintenance tasks by computer users, lack of availability of hardware, and so on. All can influence a programmer's attitude, which in turn can influence his or her perception of software structure.

The point of Figure 1 is that by changing the state of items at any of the given levels, "software structure" can be influenced. Thus, approaches that influence any layer(s) of Figure 1 are all candidate software restructuring approaches.

For example, reducing programmer turnover—a problem of the management layer of Figure 1—may be viewed as a structure–preserving technique. Since programmers have invaluable insight into the behavior of software, high turnover of programmers can lead to information loss about the software. High turnover doesn't allow enough time to pass on this information before a person leaves. The result is a progressive net loss in software structure, which is typically manifested by software changes becoming harder to implement. The basic problem of preserving software structure information among programmers may be ameliorated by decreasing programmer turnover.

Drawing a line on what one will allow as a restructuring approach is difficult. We probably won't include programmer psychoanalysis as a software restructuring approach, even though psychoanalysis can influence a programmer's perceptions of software structure! But who knows what ingenious approaches are to come to render software structure more meaningful?

2.2 An Annotated List of Software Restructuring Approaches

The 30-plus restructuring approaches I have compiled are given in Table 1. The approaches have been divided into two categories. The first category contains software restructuring approaches that do not directly involve changes to existing code. These approaches turn on the idea that software structure can be influenced by changing programmer perceptions toward software structure. They have the advantage that bugs are less likely to be introduced as a result of "restructuring."

The second category contains restructuring approaches that normally entail changes to existing code, either directly by hands-on change or indirectly by providing guidance for a change. The second category has been further divided into tools, techniques, and practices. A tool is a restructuring approach for which software has been written to mechanize the approach. A technique is an algorithm, step-by-step procedure, or methodology whose main purpose is software restructuring. A practice is a generally useful activity that may be applied to restructuring software.

Two caveats: Table 1 is not exhaustive—I'm sure readers are aware of yet other ways to restructure software*. Fur-

thermore, the categorizations of Table 1 are not exclusive. Some restructuring approaches could be classed in several categories (e.g., restructuring with preprocessors could be classed under tools as well as practices).

Table 2 gives the level of information being restructured by each restructuring approach. The levels are divided according to the primary target of the restructuring: code (intra-module), module (inter-module), total system (e.g., replacement), design (e.g., flowgraphs), documentation, and information (i.e., provides structural feedback which the programmer may use in various ways).

3. Leverage of a Software Restructuring Approach

When selecting a restructuring approach for practical use, it is important to determine the approach's leverage. By "leverage" I mean the ability of an approach to deliver effective results given the dollars invested.

There are at least four factors that determine the leverage of a restructuring approach:

- The dollars invested to set up the approach
- The staff and facilities needed to support the approach
- The expected return of the approach
- The time-frame for the return

The idea is, if the expected time frame for the return is satisfactory (e.g., does not exceed the expected remaining lifetime of the software), and the expected return (possibly including nonquantifiable benefits such as staff morale) significantly exceeds the return on the way maintenance is currently performed, then consider applying the restructuring approach.

The time frame for the visible, quantifiable return for most restructuring approaches is on the order of months to years. True, the effects of restructuring may appear immediately in the software itself, but the residual effects on maintenance economics can take much longer to appear, and even then must be considered with other factors. The decision to restructure software is much like the decision to undertake software quality assurance: both seem to require patience, perseverance, and measurement before visible rewards can be seen.

Table 2 regrettably does not contain information about each approach's leverage. Perhaps the main reason for this is that so few quantitative records of restructuring activity (or even maintenance activity) have been collected, validated, analyzed, and published. In lieu of "hard" published results, roughly estimating a restructuring approach's leverage still can be helpful in shaping expectations about the approach's return.

4. A Software Restructuring Action Plan

Table 2 is a smorgasbord of restructuring approaches for the consumer. According to the target level of software, a programmer's thinking, or local maintenance goals, candidate restructuring approaches in the table may be selected and applied.

---

*For example, the new COBOL restructuring tool, COBOL Structuring Facility (available in February 1986 from IBM), was not included in this list because there was, at the time of this Tutorial's publication, no paper detailing this tool in the open computer science literature.

The following software restructuring action plan outlines a way to select, apply, and evaluate a restructuring approach. The idea is to start first by discovering the local, real maintenance problems. From these problems, one decides whether restructuring is the right approach at all. If so, then knowledge about the maintenance problems can be used in going to Table 2 to select a set of candidate restructuring approaches. These approaches are then evaluated as to leverage, suitability in the local environment, and so on. Finally, a restructuring approach is used and evaluated.

An Action Plan for
Software Restructuring

1. Talk to maintainers about their perceptions of maintenance problems.

2. Determine current tasks where restructuring software might save staff time, reduce the maintenance budget, or achieve some other significant benefit.

3. Match an appropriate restructuring approach to the most pressing maintenance problems. A restructuring approach should be selected to have most impact on the tasks identified in step 2.

4. Do a feasibility analysis and a technology transfer analysis of the intended restructuring approach. A technology transfer analysis examines the social and psychological issues affecting acceptance and use of the restructing approach in the workplace.

5. Select a restructuring technique, plan its use, and use it.

6. Monitor the restructuring effort, preferably by collecting data and applying measures of structure and of maintenance performance, and evaluate the results.

---

5. Future research issues

Software restructuring as a research topic is in its infancy. The following list gives some interesting topics for future research:

- Restructuring of documentation

  One problem with automated restructuring techniques that modify code is they do not restructure in-line documentation (i.e., rewrite program comments) along with the code. This means that manual labor to restructure documentation is nearly always needed after applying a restructuring approach. Automating the restructuring of documentation is important for making restructuring more cost-effective.

- Linking documentation to code

  This is the general research problem of providing traceability between documentation and code. If the documentation (e.g., software specifications) changes, what code must be changed? If the code is changed, what documentation must be changed?

- Automatic application of standards

  If structure is defined locally with software standards, there usually is much manual labor involved in applying the standards to reveal software structure. In deadline-driven work environments, which software maintenance often becomes, this means software standards application is squelched in favor of meeting deadlines. The process of standards application needs to be heavily automated so even software deadline-driven environments need not suffer structural loss in software.

- System level restructuring (modularization)

  Most techniques in Table 2 involve code-level restructuring. Automatically restructuring systems by modularization is nearly uncharted territory. A Ph.D dissertation by Sobrinho (Sobrinho [84]) has started work in this area.

- Programming interfaces and graphics (e.g., windows, multi-screen workstations, multi-tasking displays)

  Collections of tools, such as MAP mentioned above, allow different views of a program to be displayed one at a time. When a programmer moves from one view to the next, however, he or she is confronted with two problems: (1) retaining the information presented by each view, and (2) maintaining *relationships* between the views. In terms of programmer understanding of software structure, the mental context switching needed as one moves from view to view can interfere with the gradual build-up of understanding about a problem. For example, a serial view of programming—e.g., view through an editor, view of compiler output, view of program output, view of debugger output—may have a high context switching overhead in the programmer's head. This could impair the programmer's ability to integrate the multiple views when solving restructuring problems.

  Allowing programmers to see many software structure dimensions at once (Teitelman [85]), with multiple windows or screens, may be more effective in restructuring than the typical serial

Table 1: Outline of Approaches to Software Restructuring

1. Approaches Not Involving Code Changes

- Buy a package to replace an old system (Canning [84])

    Remember how Columbus solved the stand-the-egg-on-its-end trick by smashing its shell? That's the kind of ingenious solution used here to "restructure" software.

- Upgrade documentation

    Examples of this are adding in-line code comments, making comments more accurate, expanding on cryptic commentary, and so on. Missing or inconsistent documentation seems to be a constant complaint from maintenance programmers.

- Train programmers

    Common examples of this are the training courses in "structured programming" adopted by some companies.

- Hire programmers

    A most direct way to gain fresh insight into software structure. If hiring is the result of turnover, however, there can be a net loss of software structure!

2. Approaches Involving Code Change

2.1 Practices

- Upgrade the programming environment

    Examples of this are adding windows to the programming interface, improving interaction of tools, replacing hard-to-use operating system command languages, and so on.

- Programming standards and style guidelines (e.g., Kernighan [74])

    This idea seems widely accepted, though widely not put into serious practice (Zelkowitz [84]).

- Inspections and walkthroughs (Fagan [76], Freedman [82])

    One of the most effective practices for making software understandable and structure more recognizable.

- Software metrics (e.g., Basili [80], Harrison [82])

    The restructuring idea here is: (1) measure the software with the software metric; (2) from the metric's value, answer the question, "Is the software property measured by the metric satisfactory?"; (3) if not, restructure the software and go to step 1; (4) if so, you're done.

- Restructuring with a preprocessor (Kernighan [76], . . .)

    This approach has the advantages of selectively structuring software (with statements recognized by the preprocessor) while using the rest of the software without change.

- Restructuring code for reusability (Lanergan [84])

    This may be viewed as either salvaging old software for reuse in constructing a system, or restructuring a system to accept reusable code.

- Buy a software package to replace an old system; then extend the package (Canning [84])

    A straightforward approach, provided a suitable, adequately documented package can be found. Getting the package vendor's source code for the package can be a problem. Getting information on how the package works can be a bigger problem.

- Buy a package to replace part of an old system (Canning [84])

    Another straightforward approach, provided a suitable package can be found. Since package vendors tend not to supply the source code for their package, the package must be treated as a black box by the user. Changes must be done through the vendor.

- System structuring principles: information hiding and families of programs (Parnas [72, 79, 84])

    One of several approaches (actually, a set of principles) that deal with modularization of systems. System modularization currently requires much human judgment.

- Data restructuring (Martin [83], Shneiderman [82], . . .)

    Restructuring software tends to connote restructuring its control structure. But possibilities for restructuring data cannot be ignored. One example is putting the relations of a relational data base into third normal form.

2.2 Techniques

- System rejuvenation (Canning [84])

    Defined as "using an existing system as the basis for a new strategic system." This is a methodology that involves cleaning up the existing system, making it more efficient (sometimes restructuring introduces a performance overhead), and putting the rejuvenated system into use.

- Software Improvement Program (Houtz [83])

    This is an ambitious, management-intensive way to both restructure software and upgrade the software engineering practices of a maintenance environment.

- Incremental restructuring (Arnold [85], originated 1983)

    An approach to restructuring software without as much management overhead as the Software Improvement Program. The approach allows "structure" to be defined by users (rather than being built into the restructuring approach); restructuring to be done in small, manageable parts; and a system to have the benefits of restructuring without being totally restructured. The approach is specifically designed to avoid introducing poor structure as a result of maintenance.

- Software renewal (Sneed [84])

    An approach not so much for modifying code as for upgrading system documentation, system specifications, and system tests.

- Logical retrofit with the Warnier methodology (Parikh [84], Warnier [78])

  Advocates using the Warnier structuring methodology when restructuring software. Roughly translated: make your program control structure analogous to the structure of the data the program operates on.

- Baker's graph-theoretic approach (Baker [77])

  The algorithm behind the tool "Struct" for restructuring FORTRAN programs on the UNIX operating system. Go-to's are allowed on a limited basis.

Techniques Based on Structured Programming

By a "structured program" I mean a program that (1) has one entry point, and one exit point and (2) uses the following control structures: sequence, if-then-else, do-until, do-while, and case. The restructuring approaches below typically follow this pattern: (1) transform the program into a flowgraph (an abstraction of control flow roughly similar to a flowchart), (2) restructure the flowgraph according to the approach's procedure, and (3) restructure the program by using the restructured flowgraph as a guide.

- Early goto-less approach (Bohm [66])

  Famous for showing "goto's" are not theoretically necessary to create a computer program. The proof of this contains a way to restructure software.

- Giant case statement approach (Ashcroft [71])

  Another constructive way to remove goto's. The resulting program looks like a giant case statement.

- Refined case statement approach (Linger [79])

  Introduces some procedures and heuristics to make the program resulting from the giant case statement approach easier to read and understand. This approach has some mathematical foundations in the work in Mills [72].

- Boolean flag approach (Yourdon [75])

  A procedure for creating a structured flowgraph by introducing boolean variable(s).

- Duplication of coding approach (Yourdon [75])

  This approach eliminates goto's to shared sections of code by duplicating the shared code and eliminating the sharing. This approach will not work for some looping programs.

- System sandwich approach (Canning [84])

  An ingenious approach for retaining the benefits of code so badly structured it must be treated as a black box and for establishing a base for future evolution. The idea is to sandwich the old system between a new front-end interface (e.g., written in a fourth generation language) and a new back-end data base. The front-end and back-end can directly communicate (e.g., for report generation purposes) and are both linked to the old system. The old system is used just for its outputs.

2.3 Tools

- Structured Retrofit (Lyons [81])

  A tool for restructuring COBOL programs. Marketed by Peat, Marwick, Mitchell & Co., Chicago, Illinois.

- SUPERSTRUCTURE (Morgan [84])

  A tool for restructuring COBOL programs. Marketed by Group Operations, Washington, D.C.

- RECODER (Bush [85])

  A tool for restructuring COBOL programs. Marketed by Language Technology, Salem, Massachusetts.

- Standards checkers and other aids

  These are tools that take a program and automatically report which software standards the program does and does not meet. Based on the reported violations, the code may be modified (restructured) to remove the violations.

- Pretty printing and code formatting

  A way of textually restructuring code by applying spacing between logical subparts, indentation of nested statements, one statement per line, and so on. Normally, this approach does not modify the code's logic.

- Tool collections: MAP (Warren [82]), . . .

  A growing number of tool collections may be used to illuminate aspects of software structure. For example, MAP will display the structure chart for a COBOL system, display a unit interface chart, highlight procedures in the structure chart that contain selected statements, display possible references of modifications to selected variables, and so on. MAP is now available as VIA/INSIGHT from VIASOFT, Phoenix, Arizona.

- Programming environments/workstations (Wasserman [81], Barstow [84], . . .)

  Programming environments offer more comprehensive support for programming needs than do tools collections. For example, the programming environment may allow tools to be easily combined in a control procedure to create new tools. The programming workstation offers increased computing power to the programmer, along with new programming interfaces (e.g., windows).

- Program transformation systems (Partsch [83])

  These systems involve automatic changes to software. The changes are accomplished with rules called transformations. This approach is related to the rule-based systems of artificial intelligence.

- Fourth generation languages (Hessinger [84], . . .)

  Not generally thought of as restructuring tools, fourth generation languages offer significant benefits to the set of applications to which they apply. These benefits include ease of change, usability by end users, and quick development of small systems.

**Table 2. Target Information Levels
for Software Restructuring Approaches**

APPROACH	CODE	MOD.	LEVEL SYS.	DES.	DOC.	INF.
1. Approaches Not Involving Code Changes						
Buy a package to replace an old system (Canning [84])			●			
Upgrade documentation					●	
Train programmers						●
Hire programmers						●
2. Approaches Involving Code Change						
2.1 Practices						
Upgrade the programming environment						●
Programming standards and style guidelines (Kernighan [74], . . .)	●	●		●	●	●
Inspections and walkthroughs (Fagan [76], Freedman [82])	●	●		●	●	●
Software metrics (Basili [80], Harrison [82], . . .)						●
Restructuring with a preprocessor (Kernighan [76], . . .)	●					
Restructuring code for reusability (Lanergan [84])	●	●				
Buy a software package to replace an old system; then extend the package (Canning [84])			●			
Buy a package to replace part of an old system (Canning [84])			●			
System structuring principles: information hiding and families of programs (Parnas [72, 79, 84])		●		●	●	
Data restructuring (Martin [83], Shneiderman [82], . . .)				●		
2.2 Techniques						
System rejuvenation (Canning [84])	●			●	●	
Software Improvement Program (Houtz [83])	●	●		●	●	
Incremental restructuring (Arnold [85], originated 1983)	●	●				
Software renewal (Sneed [84])					●	●
Logical retrofit with the Warnier methodology (Parikh [84], Warnier [78])	●	●		●		
Baker's graph-theoretic approach (Baker [77])	●			●		
Techniques Based on Structured Programming						
Early goto-less approach (Bohm [66])	●			●		
Giant case statement approach (Ashcroft [71])	●			●		
Refined case statement approach (Linger [79])	●			●		
Boolean flag approach (Yourdon [75])	●			●		
Duplication of coding approach (Yourdon [75])	●	●		●		
System sandwich approach (Canning [84])		●	●	●		
2.3 Tools						
Structured Retrofit (Lyons [81])	●			●		
SUPERSTRUCTURE (Morgan [84])	●			●		
RECODER (Bush [75])	●			●		
Standards checkers and other aids	●	●		●	●	●
Pretty printing and code formatting	●					
Tool collections: MAP (Warren [82]), . . .						●
Programming environments/workstations (Wasserman [81], Barstow [84], . . .)						●
Program transformation systems (Partsch [83])	●			●		
Fourth generation languages (Hessinger [84], . . .)	●	●		●		

views of software structure (Shneiderman [85]). With the increasing availability of higher-resolution graphics terminals, multiple windows, multiple screens, and graphics are being used (Reiss [85]) (1) to organize the programmer's understanding of software structure into parallel views maintained by the programming interface and (2) to allow these views to be expressed with images, as well as with text. Such views enhance program structure in several ways: the programmer can display those views which make sense to him/her under the circumstances, the programmer can arrange the views visually to facilitate program understanding and problem solving, and the use of well-designed graphics can increase the information bandwidth about program structure, without overloading the programmer with information.

More psychological and design studies of the effectiveness of interfaces allowing multiple, graphical views of software need to be undertaken.

● Design restructuring

As graphical programming languages evolve, we may be able to interactively restructure graphical programs (e.g., designs). In Rubin [85], programming is reduced to manipulating graphic images. Since code can be automatically generated from the graphic images, code structure is less an issue than image structure. The structure of programs then translates to the visible structure of pictures.

A future trend in programming (and restructuring) may be the drawing, and operation, of pictures! (Child's play?) An entire issue of IEEE *Computer* (IEEE [85]) was recently devoted to this fascinating topic.

● Tools to reveal new aspects of software structure (e.g., algorithm animation)

Graphical displays of static program/system structure are not new (e.g., flowcharts, Nassi-Shneiderman charts, data flow diagrams, and so on). Graphical displays of *dynamic* program structure are new. In Brown [85], graphics are used to create a "dynamic book" for illustrating the dynamic behavior of algorithms. It is unclear at present how effective such illustrations could be in understanding the behavior of poorly structured code, but it appears quite promising for helping programmers understand the dynamic behavior of the algorithms on which programs are based.

● Restructuring economics

An important question to answer is, "When can one expect a return from a restructuring approach relative to the way maintenance is currently done?" Restructuring cost estimation is an important and relatively untouched area of software cost estimation.

● Restructuring criteria

Quantitative criteria can be very helpful in detecting software structure problems and deciding when to restructure. Few examples of quantified criteria appear in the computer science literature.

● Structure-preserving transformations

If the software change process can guarantee that structure is not impaired, then the need for some classes of structure checks is obviated. Automated transformations that preserve structure hold promise here.

● Relationship to software conversion

Software restructuring and software conversion are sister subjects. Software restructuring does not involve porting software, but software restructuring can be an important step in the porting process. Experiences in restructuring software in the early phases of software conversion should be published to detail further applications of software restructuring.

6. Summary

Software restructuring is a tool for meeting maintenance goals and increasing/preserving software structure. Software restructuring is part of a larger solution for maintaining the value of software as the software evolves.

Because software structure depends on programmer perceptions as well as the software state, software structure is dynamic. Steps must be taken to preserve structure in the minds of programmers, otherwise structure will be lost with programmer turnover.

There is a wide variety of restructuring approaches, ranging from approaches that do not modify software at all, but modify programmer perceptions of software, to those approaches that do modify software. The limit to what is a software restructuring approach is a gray area.

There is a lack of quantitative information about software restructuring. What we do know suggests restructuring leverage (the ability of a restructuring approach to "deliver" given the dollars invested) tends to come in the medium to long term (months to years). Even then, the effort to maintain software structure must be diligent, which may translate to higher quality assurance costs per maintenance change. Later, these costs are hoped to be justified through increased software flexibility (faster performance of enhancements), reliability (fewer introduced bugs which each fix), lifetime (through extended usefulness to the enterprise), and reusability (due to the known software structure instilled in the software).

Software restructuring presents a very interesting research area. Besides the need for quantitative studies of restructuring effectiveness, work is needed in areas such as restructuring of documentation to correspond with restructured code, design restructuring, automatic application of software standards, structure-preserving transformations, automatic system modularization, and tools to reveal new aspects of software structure (e.g., program execution animation, graphical programming).

References

Arnold, R.S. *Techniques and Strategies for Restructuring Software*. Seminar notes, May 1985. 205 pp.

Ashcroft, E. and Manna, Z. The translation of 'goto' programs in 'while' programs, in *Proceedings of the 1971 IFIP Congress*. Amsterdam: North-Holland, 1971. pp. 250-260.

Baker, B. An algorithm for structuring flowgraphs. *Journal of the ACM*, Vol. 24, no. 1 (Jan. 1977). pp. 98-120.

Barstow, D.R., Shrobe, H.E., and Sandewall, E. *Interactive Programming Environments*. New York: McGraw-Hill, 1984.

Basili, V. *Tutorial on Models and Metrics for Software Management and Engineering*. Washington, D.C.: IEEE Computer Society, 1980.

Bohm, C. and Jacopini, G. Flow diagrams, Turing machines, and languages with only two formation rules. *Communications of the ACM*, Vol. 9, no. 5 (May 1966). pp. 366-371.

Brown, M.H. and Sedgewick, R. Techniques for algorithm animation, IEEE *Software*, Vol. 2, no. 1 (January 1985). pp. 28-39.

Bush, E. The automatic restructuring of COBOL. *Proceedings of the Conference on Software Maintenance—1985*. Washington, D.C.: IEEE Computer Society, 1985. pp. 35-41.

Canning, R. (ed.) Rejuvenate your old systems. *EDP Analyzer*, Vol. 22, no. 3 (March 1984). pp. 1-16.

Fagan, M. Design and code inspection to reduce errors in program development. *IBM Systems Journal*, Vol. 15, no. 3 (1976). pp. 182-212.

Freedman, D. and Weinberg, G. *Handbook of Walkthroughs, Inspections, and Technical Reviews* (3rd ed.). Boston: Little, Brown, 1982.

Glass, R. L. and Noiseux, R.A. *Software Maintenance Guidebook*. Englewood Cliffs, N.J.: Prentice-Hall, 1981.

Harrison, W., Magel, K., Kluczny, R., and DeKock, A. Applying software complexity metrics to software maintenance. IEEE *Computer*, Vol. 15, no. 9 (Sept. 1982). pp. 65-79.

Hessinger, P.R. Strategies for implementing fourth generation software. *Computerworld* (In Depth section). Vol. XVIII, no. 8 (Feb. 20, 1984). pp. ID/1-ID/11.

Houtz, C. Software Improvement Program (SIP): A treatment for software senility, in *Proceedings of the 19th Computer Performance Evaluation Users Group* (National Bureau of Standards Special Publication 500-104) October 1983. pp. 92-107.

IEEE. Special issue of IEEE *Computer* devoted to visual programming. IEEE *Computer*, Vol. 18, no. 8 (August 1985).

Kernighan, B.W. and Plauger, P.J. *Elements of Programming Style*. New York: McGraw-Hill, 1974.

Kernighan, B.W. and Plauger, P.J. *Software Tools*. Reading, Mass.: Addison-Wesley, 1976.

Lanergan, R.G. and Grasso, C.A. Software Engineering with Reusable Designs and Code. *IEEE Transactions on Software Engineering*, Vol. SE-10, no. 5 (November 1984). pp. 498-501.

Lehman, M.M. Programs, life cycles, and laws of software evolution, *Proceedings of the IEEE*, Vol. 68, no. 9 (Sept. 1980). pp. 1060-1076.

Linger, R.C., Mills, H.D. and Witt, R.J. *Structured Programming: Theory and Practice*. Reading, Mass.: Addison-Wesley, 1979.

Lyons, M.J. Salvaging your software asset (tools based maintenance). *Proceedings of the National Computer Conference 1981*. Arlington, Va.: AFIPS Press, 1981. pp. 337-341.

Martin, J. and McClure, C. *Software Maintenance: The Problem and Its Solution*. Englewood Cliffs, N.J.: Prentice-Hall, 1983.

Mills, H.D. Mathematical foundations for Structured Programming. First written in 1972; reprinted in Mills, H.D., *Software Productivity*. Boston: Little, Brown, and Co., 1983.

Morgan, H.W. Evolution of a software maintenance tool, in *Proceedings of the 2nd National Conference on EDP Software Maintenance*. Silver Spring, Md.: U.S. Professional Development Institute, 1984. pp. 268-278.

Parikh, G. Logical retrofit may save millions of dollars in software maintenance, in *Proceedings of the 2nd National Conference on EDP Software Maintenance*. Silver Spring, Md.: U.S. Professional Development Institute, 1984. pp. 427-429.

Parnas, D.L. On the criteria to be used in decomposing systems into modules. *Communications of the ACM*, Vol. 15, no. 12 (Dec. 1972). pp. 1053-1058.

Parnas, D.L. Designing software for ease of extension and contraction. *IEEE Transactions on Software Engineering*, Vol. SE-5, no. 2 (March 1979). pp. 128-138.

Parnas, D.L., Clements, P.C., and Weiss, D.M. The modular structure of complex systems, in *Proceedings of the 7th International Conference on Software Engineering*. Washington, D.C.: IEEE Computer Society, 1984. pp. 408-417.

Partsch, H. and Steinbruggen, R. Program transformation systems. *Computing Surveys*, Vol. 15, no. 3 (September 1983). pp. 199-236.

Reiss, S.P. PECAN: program development systems that support multiple views, *IEEE Transactions on Software Engineering*, Vol. SE-11, no. 3 (March 1985). pp. 285-302.

Rubin, R.V., Golin, E.J., and Reiss, S.P. Thinkpad: a graphical system for programming by demonstration, *IEEE Software*, Vol. 2, no. 2 (March 1985). pp. 73-79.

Shneiderman, B. and Thomas, G. An architecture for automatic relational database system conversion. *ACM Transactions on Database Systems*, Vol. 7, no. 2 (June 1982). pp. 235-257.

Shneiderman, B., Shafer, P., Simon, R., and Weldon, L. Display strategies for program browsing, in *Proceedings of the Conference on Software Mainte-nance—1985*, Washington, D.C.: IEEE Computer Society, 1985. pp. 136-143.

Sneed, H.M. Software renewal: a case study. *IEEE Software*, Vol. 1, no. 3 (July 1984). pp. 56-63.

Sobrinho, F.G. *Structural Complexity: A Basis for Systematic Software Evolution*, Ph.D dissertation, Dept. of Computer Science and College of Business and Management, University of Maryland, College Park, Md., 1984.

Teitelman, W. A tour through Cedar, *IEEE Transactions on Software Engineering*, Vol. SE-11, no. 3 (March 1985). pp. 285-302.

Warnier, J.-D. *Program Modification*. Boston: Martinus Nijhoff, 1978.

Warren, S. MAP: A tool for understanding software, in *Proceedings of the 6th International Conference on Software Engineering*. Washington, D.C.: IEEE Computer Society, 1982. pp. 28-37.

Wasserman, A.I. *Tutorial: Software Development Environments*. Washington, D.C.: IEEE Computer Society, 1981.

Yourdon, E. *Techniques of Program Structure and Design*. Englewood Cliffs, N.J.: Prentice-Hall, 1975.

Zelkowitz, M.V., Yeh, R.T., Hamlet, R.G., Gannon, J.D., and Basili, V.R. Software engineering practices in the U.S. and Japan. IEEE *Computer*, Vol. 17, no. 6 (June 1984). pp. 57-66.

II. Perspectives on Software Structure

Software restructuring concerns software structure, the attributes of software which "make sense" to the perceiver. What are some specific attributes of software structure? The papers in Part II supply several examples.

The first paper, "Applying Software Complexity Metrics to Software Maintenance," by W. Harrison, K. Magel, R. Kluczny, and A. DeKock, lists 13 software metrics that can be used to measure code level (i.e., intra-module) software structure. The authors point out that, "What is needed is some method of pinpointing the characteristics of a computer program that are difficult to maintain and measuring the degree of their presence (or lack of it)."

The next paper, "Some Stability Measures for Software Maintenance," by S. Yau and J. Collofello, concerns software stability, "the resistance to the amplification of changes in the program." The more stable the program, the more software changes can be confined to one or a few modules. Stability is closely related to ripple effect, the extent of system modification needed to perform a software change. The paper presents a measure of the logical stability of a program.

The next paper, "Good System Structure Features: Their Complexity and Execution Time Cost," by J. Stankovic, concerns the performance impact of good software structure. Software restructuring can cause software performance to degrade, so techniques for regaining software performance while still retaining the benefits of good structure for the programmer are of interest. This paper proposes a technique, called vertical migration, for regaining software performance. The idea is to identify "the control structure and overhead of layered systems for purposes of performance improvement," and then apply automated transformations to perform the improvements. Performance is gained by eliminating unrequired generality present in a layer of a system.

The next paper, "The Dimensions of Healthy Maintenance," by R.S. Arnold and D.A. Parker, discusses the practical application of software metrics to determine problems in software maintenance. This kind of discussion is often omitted when presenting software metrics, yet becomes important when metrics are actually applied in practice. The paper lists some criteria for maintenance adequacy and shows how these criteria may be used both to detect maintenance problems and to find constructive suggestions for improving maintenance. The implication here is that by creating criteria for software restructuring, the approach advocated by this paper can be used to determine where (and if) software should be restructured. The paper's approach has been amplified in Arnold [83].

The final paper, "Human Factors of Software Design and Development" by M. Weiser and B. Shneiderman, surveys the research on the effects of software structure on programmer performance. The paper considers a wide range of issues, from methods for inferring whether software structure impacts programmer performance, to what aspects of programming style positively influence programmers, to how software quality and productivity may be evaluated with software metrics. From a practical viewpoint, the work supplies a rich source of ideas for software structure—information which, for example, can be helpful in deciding one's local definition of software structure standards.

Reference

Arnold, R.S. *On the Generation and Use of Quantitative Criteria for Assessing Software Maintenance Quality.* Ph.D dissertation. Dept. of Computer Science, University of Maryland, College Park, Md. 1983. Available as dissertation number 8402525 from University Microfilms International, 300 N. Zeeb Rd., Ann Arbor, Mich. 48106.

Predicting software complexity can save millions in maintenance costs, but while current measures can be used to some degree, most are not sufficiently sensitive or comprehensive.

Applying Software Complexity Metrics to Program Maintenance

Warren Harrison, Kenneth Magel, Raymond Kluczny, and Arlan DeKock
University of Missouri-Rolla

Over the past several years, computer scientists have devoted a great deal of effort to measuring computer program "complexity," since many large software systems can be used for 10, 15, or even 20 years. A large part of that time involves maintenance activities, which include all changes made to a piece of software after it has been delivered to and accepted by the final user. Consequently, maintenance is most affected by program complexity.

Recent estimates suggest that about 40 to 70 percent of annual software expenditures involve maintenance of existing systems. Clearly, if complexities could somehow be identified, then programmers could adjust maintenance procedures accordingly. What is needed is some method of pinpointing the characteristics of a computer program that are difficult to maintain and measuring the degree of their presence (or lack of it). Such a method could be used in preparing "quality specifications" for programs that are to be written; checking specification compliance of programs after they have been written, but before they are delivered; making proper design trade-offs between development and maintenance costs; and selecting a particular type of software.

Software complexity

The degree to which characteristics that impede software maintenance are present is called software *maintainability* and is driven primarily by *software complexity,* the measure of how difficult the program is to comprehend and work with. Maintenance characteristics that are affected by complexity include software understandability, software modifiability, and software testability.

Various approaches may be taken in measuring complexity characteristics, such as Baird and Noma's[1] approach, in which scales of measurement are divided into the following four types:

(1) *Nominal scales.* The measure classifies the items. For example, programs are grouped into classifications of "not difficult to understand," "moderately difficult to understand," "difficult to understand," and "very difficult to understand."

(2) *Ordinal scales.* The measure actually ranks individual items. For example, we would say not only that program *A,* program *B,* and program C are all "moderately difficult to understand," but also that program *B* was more difficult to understand than program *C,* and program *A* was more difficult to understand than program *B.*

(3) *Interval scales.* The measure not only ranks items in relation to each other but also tells how far apart they are. For example, we would say not only that program *A* was more difficult than program *B* but also that program *A* was 10 "units of difficulty" more difficult to understand than program *B.*

4) *Ratio scales.* The measure not only ranks the items and determines how far apart they are from each other but also determines how far the measures lie from a total lack of the characteristic being measured. This allows multiplication and division to be used on the resulting measures, so we can obtain measures that indicate that program *A* is twice as difficult to understand as program *B.* This property is unique to the ratio scale.

The most flexible type of measurement seems to be the ratio scale, but we would be hard put to find a degree of impeding characteristics that even approaches zero complexity, so this scale is not really the most effective. On the other hand, an ordinal scale would be feasible, and in some cases, even an interval scale could be developed, but a major problem with interval scales is determining the "unit of difficulty" and its meaning.

We believe the ordinal scale to be the best choice for examining complexity metrics, and all measures discussed in this article are in that framework.

Reprinted from *Computer,* Volume 15, Number 9, September 1982, pages 65-79. Copyright © 1982 by The Institute of Electrical and Electronics Engineers, Inc.

Existing complexity measures

Because much of the work on complexity metrics has been done in the last five years, many different methods are being used. Basili[2] has suggested that program size, data structures, data flow, and flow of control can affect maintenance. A number of measures have been developed to evaluate each of these characteristics, and several hybrid measures have been developed to consider more than one simultaneously.

Program size. The most straightforward approach is based on program size, and as Elshoff[3] has pointed out, very large programs incur problems just by virtue of the volume of information that must be absorbed to understand the program. Program size is easy to calculate, is widely applicable, and has definable measures, two of which are lines of code and Halstead's software science.

The most common form of measuring program size is by simply counting the lines of code. Unfortuntely, not everyone agrees on what makes up a line of code, and the question remains whether only executable source statements, executable source statements and data declaration statements, or all statements including comments should be part of the measure.

Halstead's software science[4] is based on a refinement of measuring program size by counting lines of code. It is one of the most widely accepted measures in industry and universities and has been supported by several empirical studies.[5-11]. Halstead's metrics measure the number of unique operators $n1$, the number of unique operands $n2$, the total number of operators $N1$, and the total number of operands $N2$. From these measures Halstead defines the vocabulary of the program as $n = n1 + n2$ and the total length of the program as $N = N1 + N2$. He further computes a predicted program length as $N' = n1 \log2 n1 + n2 \log2 n2$. The calculation of the predicted program length is called length equation and is supported by the empirical results of Halstead,[4] Bohrer,[5] and Elshoff.[6]

Halstead computes program volume as $V = N \log2 n$ and minimal or potential volume as $V* = n* \log2 n*$, where $n*$ is the size of the potential vocabulary. The potential vocabulary is that needed to invoke a "built-in" function (if one exists) to perform the desired task. For example, the potential implementation of a sort procedure might look like call sort (x,n), where x is the array to be sorted and n is the number of elements in the array. The potential vocabulary would include call, sort(. . .), x and n. Therefore, $n*$ is 4.

The program level is subsequently defined as the ratio of potential volume to actual volume and is computed as $L = V*/V$. An approximation of program level is $L' = 2/n1 \times n2/N2$. Halstead found that the approximation has a correlation coefficient of 0.90 to the actual observed value.[4] Clearly, the larger the volume of the existing program relative to the volume of the potential program, the lower the program level.

Halstead uses the volume and program level to calculate the intelligence content of the program, expressed as $I = L' \times V$. He indicates that this relationship correlates best with total programming and debugging time and that intelligence content is a likely candidate for a complexity measure. However, the intelligence content of a program appears to remain invariant under translation from one programming language to another and increases only as the complexity of the problem increases.

Halstead uses the volume and program level to measure the effort required to generate a piece of software by $E = V/L$. Funami and Halstead[7] point out that E has often been used to measure the effort required to comprehend an implementation. For this reason, they suggest that E may be used as a measure of program clarity. The use of Halstead's metrics on a simple bubble sort, adapted from an example used by Fitzsimmons and Love,[12] is shown in Figures 1 and 2 and Tables 1 through 5.

In general, metrics based on measures of program size have been the most successful to date, with experimental evidence indicating that larger programs have greater maintenance costs than smaller ones. However, although program size metrics tend to work well in ranking programs with widely varying sizes, other characteristics such as data structures, data flow, and flow of control become vitally important as the size difference decreases. In other

```
(a)   BEGIN
          DO I = 2 TO N;
              DO J = 1 TO I;
                  IF X(I) < X(J) THEN DO;
                                      SAVE = X(I);
                                      X(I) = X(J);
                                      X(J) = SAVE;
                                  END;
              END;
          END;
      END;



(b)   CALL SORT (X,N)
```

Figure 1. Actual (a) and potential (b) implementations of a bubble sort program.

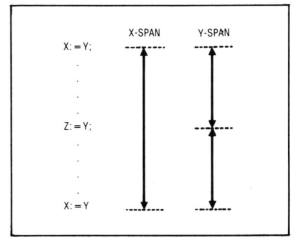

Figure 2. Span between data references.

words, program size metrics can be a very good nominal scale to use in putting programs into one "complexity category," but it may not be able to distinguish between different programs within the same category.

Data structures and data flow. Another factor that influences software complexity is the configuration and use of data within the program. Several methods can be used to measure complexity by the way program data are used, organized, or allocated.

Span between data references. This technique, which is based on the locality of data references within the program, has no supporting empirical studies to demonstrate its correlation with maintenance, but it is intuitively appealing.

A *span* is the number of statements between two references to the same identifier with no intervening references to that identifier. Consequently an identifier has $n-1$ spans for an identifier that occurs n times in the source code (Figure 2).

Elshoff[3] found that of 120 production programs used at General Motors Corporation, over 13 percent had data reference spans of 100 statements or more. Maintenance activities might require a programmer to determine what value a variable has at a particular point, and in more than one case in eight the programmer would have to search through at a level of 100 statements with Elshoff's data.

Segment-global usage pair. This measure, discussed by Basili[2,13] bases program complexity on the use of global data within the program. It is useful for large programs that consist of several modules or segments, but again no empirical studies have been reported.

A segment-global usage pair (p,r) is used to signify the instance of a segment p using the global variable r. That is, r is accessed within p.

The actual usage pair AUP represents the number of times a module actually accesses a global data item. The potential usage pair PUP represents the number of times a module could access a global variable. A potential usage of a variable r by p indicates that the scope of r includes p.

The relative percentage of actual usage RUP is then $RUP = AUP/PUP$. This formula provides a rough measure of the likelihood that an arbitrary segment will reference an arbitrary global variable. The greater the likelihood, the greater the possibility that a given global variable may have its value changed in another segment, without the knowledge of the maintenance programmer.

Such an oversight may increase the chance of error when the software is modified.

For example, assume that we have a program with three global variables, $z1$, $z2$, and $z3$. The program has three subroutines, A, B, and C. If each subroutine has the global variables $z1$, $z2$, and $z3$. The program has three subroutines, A, B, and C. If each subroutine has the global variables $z1$, $z2$ and $z3$ available for its use, then, we have the following nine potential usage pairs:

$(a,z1)$	$(b,z1)$	$(c,z1)$
$(a,z2)$	$(b,z2)$	$(c,z2)$
$(a,z3)$	$(b,z3)$	$(c,z3)$

In this case, $PUP = 9$. Further, suppose subroutine A actually references all three global variables, subroutine B references two, and subroutine C references none. Then, $AUP = 5$, and RUP becomes $RUP = 5/9$.

Table 2.
Operand count for actual implementation.

OPERAND	COUNT
I	5
N	1
J	4
X	6
SAVE	2
$n2 = 5$	$N2 = 18$

Table 3.
Operator count for potential implementation.

OPERATOR	COUNT
CALL	1
SORT(...)	1
$n1^* = 2$	$N1^* = 2$

Table 4.
Operand count for potential implementation.

OPERAND	COUNT
X	1
N	1
$n2^* = 2$	$N2^* = 2$

Table 1.
Operator count for actual implementation.

OPERATOR	COUNT
BEGIN...END	1
;	11
DO...END	3
=	5
<	1
TO	2
IF...THEN	1
( )	6
$n1 = 8$	$N1 = 30$

Table 5.
Software science parameters for bubble sort program.

Unique Operators $N1$	8
Unique Operands $N2$	5
Total Operators $N1$	30
Total Operands $N2$	18
Vocabulary N	13
Observed Length N	48
Calculated Length N'	$8 \log_2 8 + 5 \log_2 5 = 47$
Volume V	$48 \log_2 13 = 192$
Potential Volume V^*	$4 \log_2 4 = 8$
Program Level L	$12/192 = 0.063$
Program Level L'	$2/8 \times 5/18 = 0.069$
Intelligence Content I	$0.069 \times 192 = 13.2$
Effort E	$192/0.069 = 2782$

Chapin's Q *measure.* In this method,[14] data items are viewed differently, depending on how they are used, and data are divided into four categories:

- Role *P* data: input needed to produce a segment's output.
- Role *M* data: data that are changed or created within a segment.
- Role *C* data: data used in a "controlling" role within a segment.

- Role *T* data: data that pass through a segment unchanged.

Since a particular datum can have different roles within different modules or even within the same module, it is counted as having each role.

Chapin observes that each type of data usage contributes different amounts of complexity to the module it is in. He notes that role *C* data contribute most to complexity, since they control which module will be invoked—that is, which course of action will be followed. Role *M* data contribute less than role *C* data but still provide a substantial amount of complexity, since their value is either initially defined or modified. Because role *P* data are often used to modify the value of role *M* data, role *P* data also contribute some complexity. Role *T* data, which have no effect on the module, contribute very little complexity.

An "input-output table" can be used to help classify each datum.[15] This table consists of a list of each input and output datum and its source (destination) for every module or segment in the program. The user computes program complexity *Q* by counting the number of data items used in *C, P,* or *T* roles for input and *M* or *T* roles for output and listing them in the input-output table. For each segment, the user multiplies the count by the appropriate weighting factor suggested by Chapin to account for the differing complexity contributed by each type of data. The weighting factor for role *C* data is 3; for role *M* data, 2; for role *P* data, 1; and for role *T* data, 0.50. These weighted products are then summed for each module, producing an intermediate measure *W'*.

The final measure takes into account the increase in complexity that is due to repetition factor *R*. This *R* value results from data being communicated between iteratively invoked segments and is calculated as follows. First determine which module contains exit tests for iteration that involve more than a single module. For every role *C* datum in these modules whose value comes from outside the loop body, add 2 to the iteration-exit factor *E*, which has an initial value of 0 for each segment. If the *C* role datum is created or modified in a segment other than the segment performing the exit test, but is still within range of the iteration, add 1 to *E*. The repetition factor *R* for each segment is then calculated by $R = (1/3 \times E)^2 + 1$. Note that if the segment does not perform an iteration-exit test, it has an *E* of 0, and hence an *R* of 1.

The index of complexity for each module *Q* is the square root of the sum of the weighted counts for that module *W'* times its repetition factor *R*. That is, $Q = \sqrt{R \times W'}$.

The complexity for the entire program is then computed by calculating the arithmetic mean of the individual segment complexities. The entire process is illustrated in the following example.

We have a program consisting of five segments, whose relationships are shown in Figure 3, and whose input and output are shown in Table 6. The measures for each segment are

- SCAN TEXT $W' = 4$, $R = 1.1111$, $Q = 2.1082$
- GET WORD $W' = 10$, $R = 1.4445$, $Q = 3.8007$

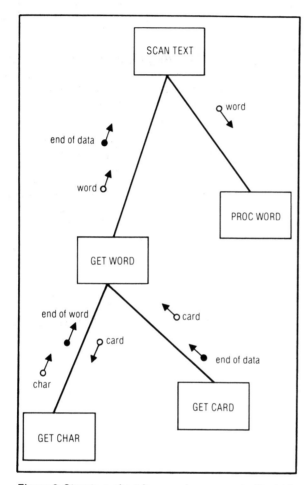

Figure 3. Structure chart for sample program to illustrate Chapin's Q measure of complexity. Table 6 depicts the input-out data classification in the programs.

**Table 6.
Input-output table used in Chapin's Q measure of complexity.**

SEGMENT	INPUT VAR	TYPE	FROM	OUTPUT VAR	TYPE	TO
SCAN TEXT	word	T	GET WORD	word	T	PROC WORD
	end of data	C	GET WORD			
GET WORD	char	P	GET CHAR	word	M	SCAN TEXT
	end of word	C	GET CHAR	end of data	T	SCAN TEXT
	card	T	GET CARD	card	T	GET CHAR
	end of data	CT	GET CARD			
GET CARD	card	CP	GET CARD	card	M	GET WORD
				end of data	T	
GET CHAR	card	P	GET WORD	char	M	GET WORD
				end of char	C	
PROC WORD	word	P	SCAN TEXT	none		

- GET CARD $W' = 8$, $R = 1.0000$, $Q = 2.8240$
- GET CHAR $W' = 3.5$, $R = 1.0000$, $Q = 1.8708$
- PROC WORD $W' = 1$, $R = 1.0000$, $Q = 1.0000$

The total of Q for all segments—that is, the overall program complexity—is 11.6037/5 or 2.3207.

Overall, data structure and flow metrics fail to be very comprehensive because the span between data references indirectly measures program length in some cases, but not consistently enough to qualify as a true hybrid.

Most of these techniques are also not widely applicable. For example, the segment-global usage pair is only useful with software that consists of programs that are segmented and use global data, and Chapin's Q depends on the use of segments that communicate among themselves.

In addition, since the segment-global usage pair and the Chapin's Q depend on data communicated between segments or modules, they clearly fail to be comprehensive even within the area of data complexity. While we can easily see that intermodule or global data can have a detrimental effect on program understandability, other properties of data can have similar effects—for example, the span between data references.

Finally, data structure and flow metrics have not been used in studies of their predictive power for software maintenance.

Program control structures. The majority of the work in software complexity over the past 10 years has dealt with the effects of control flow on program complexity. For example, a 50-line program with 25 IF-THEN-ELSE statements has well over 33 million possible control paths within the 50 statements.[16] Such a configuration can obviously be difficult to comprehend fully.

The complexity of control flow is commonly measured in density of control transfers within the program or in interrelations of control transfers.

Either approach to measuring control flow complexity normally represents a program as a flow graph to expose the control flow topology. The flow graph of a program is simply a directed graph that corresponds to the program's flow of control.

For example, directed graph $G = (V,E)$ consists of a set of nodes V and a set of directed edges E connecting the nodes. In a flow graph, each node represents a "sequential block of code," which is a sequence of instructions that can be entered only at the beginning of the sequence, can be exited only at the end of the sequence, and can contain no transfers of control within the sequence itself. The edges correspond to the flow of control between the various nodes.

In edge (u,v) node u is the initial node, and node v is the terminal node. The number of edges that have a particular node w as the initial node is the *outdegree* of w, and the number of edges that have w as the terminal node is the *indegree* of w.

If an edge exists from some node u to some node v, u is said to immediately precede v, and v is said to immediately succeed u. If a *path* exists from some node u to some node v consisting of one or more edges, u precedes v, and v succeeds u.

Since all the measures discussed in this section incorporate these concepts, we present Figure 4 to illustrate the theory behind program flow control. Note that Node b has an indegree of 1 and an outdegree of 3. Further, node b immediately precedes nodes c, d, and e and immediately succeeds node a. Also, node b precedes, in addition to nodes c, d, and e, nodes g, h, and v.

McCabe's cyclomatic complexity. McCabe[16] has proposed a graph-theoretic complexity measure that is widely accepted, probably because it is easily calculated and is intuitively satisfying. McCabe suggests that cyclomatic complexity is applicable in determining how difficult program testing will be, and empirical studies have been carried out on the effectiveness of this cyclomatic measure with favorable results.[8,9] McCabe's measure is based on the cyclomatic number $V(G)$ of a program's flow graph. For a flow graph with e edges, n nodes, and p connected components (usually 1), the cyclomatic complexity is calculated using $V(G) = e - n + 2 \times p$.

The cyclomatic number may be viewed as the number of linearly independent circuits in a strongly connected graph, meaning that for any two nodes, one is reachable from the other. In other words, the cyclomatic number is the number of basic paths that can be combined to make up any possible circuit on the graph. The formula for calculating the cyclomatic complexity of the weakly connected flow graph in Figure 5 is $V(G) = 17 - 13 + 2 \times 1 = 6$.

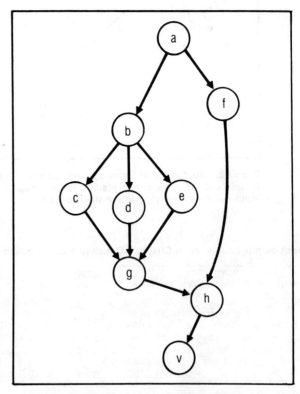

Figure 4. Directed graph illustrating program control flow. Node b is the terminus of only one edge but is the beginning of three edges. It thus has an indegree of 1 and an outdegree of 3.

Further, if we convert the flow graph into a strongly connected graph by adding an edge from the terminal node m to the initial node a (Figure 6), we increase the cyclomatic number by 1. With the new edge, we are adding an additional "implicit" decision—to follow the edge back to node a or to end the path at m. The strongly connected flow graph in Figure 6 contains the following seven independent circuits:

$$a-b-d-a$$
$$a-b-d-h$$
$$a-b-e-h-j$$
$$a-c-g-i-j$$
$$a-c-f-i-j$$
$$j-k-m-a$$
$$j-l-m-a$$

Myers' extension to the cyclomatic number. Myers[17] extends McCabe's theories by noting that predicates with compound conditions are more complex than predicates with a single condition. The following code segments illustrate this point:

IF $x=0$ THEN $s1$ IF $x=0$ and $y=1$ THEN $s1$
   ELSE $s2$ ELSE $s2$

Since both segments involve only a single decision, they can both be illustrated by the same directed graph

(Figure 7), which has a cyclomatic complexity $V(G)$ of 2. However, their predicates differ in complexity.

Myers suggests that by calculating the complexity measure as an interval rather than as a single value, we can get a more accurate complexity measure. In his approach, the interval's lower bound is the number of decision statements plus 1, as in McCabe's $V(G)$, and the upper bound is the number of *individual* conditions plus 1.

In this manner, Myers hoped to construct a complexity measure that would account for both the decision statements themselves and their predicates.

Using Myers' scheme, the first code segment has an associated interval [2,2], and the second segment has [2,3] to allow a finer distinction between programs with similar flow graphs.

Unfortunately, no results comparing Myers' measure to maintenance difficulties have been published, so their applicability is uncertain.

Gilb's logical complexity metric. Gilb[18] defines logical complexity as a measure of how much decision-making logic is in the program. He proposes two measures: *CL,* or absolute logical complexity, which is the number of "binary" decisions in the program's logic and *cl,* or relative logical complexity, which is the ratio of absolute logical complexity to the total number of statements in the program.

Experiments support Gilb's assumption that the degree of decision-making logic in the program can be correlated

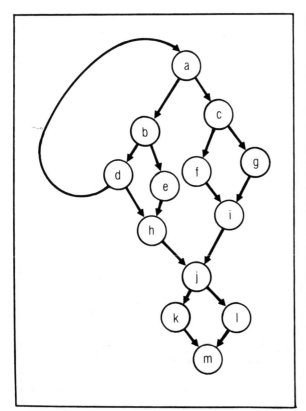

Figure 5. Weakly connected flow graph. In this graph of program flow, not all nodes are reachable from other nodes (m to a, for example). With some adjustment, however, this graph can become strongly connected.

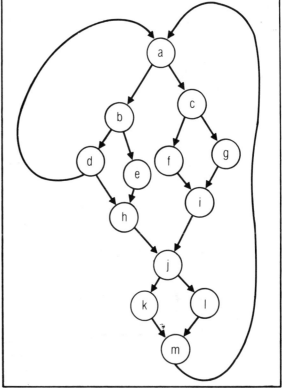

Figure 6. Strongly connected flow graph. The weakly connected program flow graph in Figure 5 has been adjusted by adding an edge from node m to node a. The result is that all nodes are reachable from other nodes.

to characteristics of that program such as error proneness, development cost, and development time. This general notion is suppported by Sime et al.[19,20] who have shown that various forms of conditional constructs that "simplify" control somewhat (IF-THEN-ELSE versus IF-THEN-GO TO) favorably affect programming time and the number of errors. Farr and Zagorski[21] have also found that the degree of decision-making within a program is a significant factor in predicting software costs.

Gilb sees such a measurement as an indirect tool for analyzing and perhaps controlling the program characteristics mentioned above.

The knot count of Woodward, Hennell, and Hedley. Woodward, Hennell, and Hedley[22] suggest a method in which they examine the relations between the physical locations of control transfers rather than simply their numbers. This method can be easily calculated as follows.

Let transfer of control from line a to line b be the ordered pair (a,b), with min (a,b) referring to the first line of the pair (a,b) and max(a,b) referring to the last line. Under these assumptions, a "knot" occurs when $\min(a,b) < \min(p,q) < \max(a,b)$ and $\max(p,q) >$

$\max(a,b)$, or when $\min(a,b) < \max(p,q) < \max(a,b)$ and $\min(p,q) < \min(a,b)$. In other words, a knot occurs when we "jump" out of the scope of the (a,b) transfer (Figure 8).

This technique may be generalized to apply to program flow graphs by letting the ordered pair of line numbers represent an edge of the graph. Hence the pair (a,b) would now refer to the edge with initial node a and terminal node b, rather than a transfer from line a to line b in the program.

Difficulties can arise in obtaining an exact knot count, since the node in a flow graph actually refers to a sequence of instructions that may be entered into only at the beginning and exited from only at the end, with no internal transfers of control. The problem is shown more clearly in Figures 9 and 10. In Figure 9, line c makes up v_3 while line d is v_4. In Figure 10, both lines c and d make up node v_3. Therefore, we can say that if the node includes only one line, a knot is present, but if it contains more than one, a knot is not present.

An interval can be used to get a more precise knot count, with the lower bound being the verifiable number of knots detected and the upper bound the total number of possible knots, assuming every block contains one statement. Neither the interval nor the basic knot count has been applied to the maintenance of real programs, however.

Chen's measure of program complexity. Chen[23] has developed a topological complexity measure that is sen-

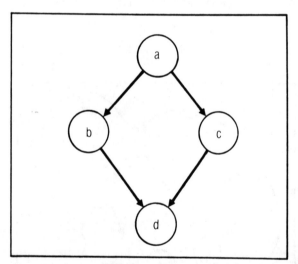

Figure 7. Flow graph of a one-decision code segment.

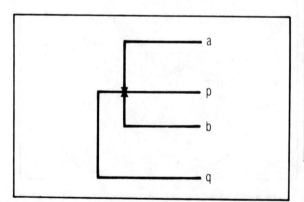

Figure 8. A control flow knot occurs when the transfer from *a* to *b* is interrupted, and some other transfer outside the *a*-to-*b* scope is required.

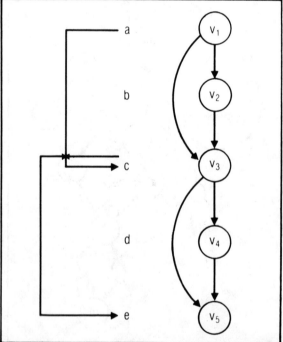

Figure 9. Flow graph with knot. A knot occurs when transfer between two nodes is interrupted. Each node is a sequence of events that has one entrance and one exit with no internal transfers. Therefore, since a one-line-per-code construction requires an internal transfer, a knot results.

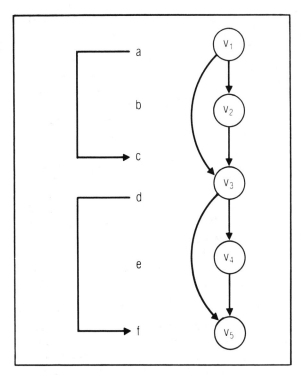

Figure 10. Flow graph without knot. Node v_3 has two lines instead of the one line in Figure 10. Since no internal transfer is needed, no knot occurs.

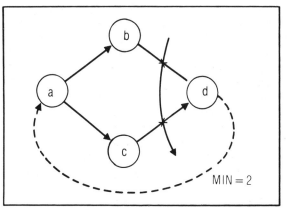

Figure 11. Illustration of maximal intersect number, or *min*. The *min* is derived by first determining the number of regions possible, (edges − nodes) + 2, and then drawing a line so that it enters each region exactly once. The number of times the line intersects the edges is the *min*.

sitive to nested decision structures. His technique uses the maximal intersect number *min* of the program's flow graph.

To compute the *min* the flow graph must be converted (if it is not already) into a strongly connected graph by connecting the terminal and initial nodes with an edge. Such a graph divides the two-dimensional space that it oc-cupies into a finite number of regions. (McCabe showed that the number of regions in a connected, planar graph without bridges, or edges that disturb the weak connectivity of the graph, is equal to the cyclomatic number of that graph by rearranging Euler's theorem from $n-e+r=2$ to $r=e-n+2$.)

The *min,* then, is the number of times a line intersects the edges of the graph when the line is drawn such that it enters every region of the graph exactly one time (Figure 11).

The *min* may be calculated in this manner only for graphs that do not have bridges. If a graph does have a bridge, then the *min* for that graph is calculated by summing the *min*s of the strong components (the maximal subgraphs that do not contain bridges), subtracting twice the number of strong components, and adding 2 (Figure 12).

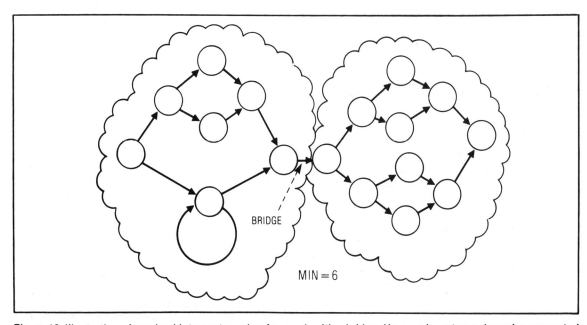

Figure 12. Illustration of maximal intersect number for graph with a bridge. Here we have two subgraphs connected by a bridge. The *min* of the first is 4, as is the *min* of the second. By adding the two *min*s, subtracting twice the number of subgraphs (4), and adding 2, we get a *min* of 6.

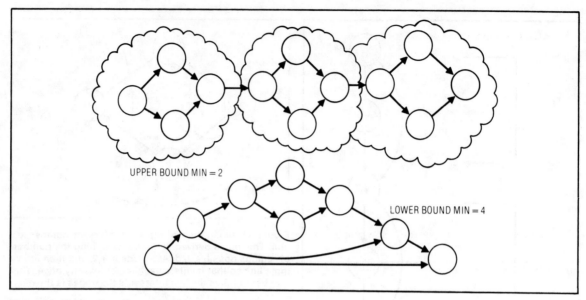

UPPER BOUND MIN = 2

LOWER BOUND MIN = 4

Figure 13. Illustration of upper and lower bounds of maximal intersect number. Note that the upper bound contains nested decisions, while the lower bound decisions are all serial.

In general, the upper bound of a given flow graph's *min* is $n+1$, where the flow graph has n decisions, and the lower bound is 2. The upper bound occurs when the flow of control is arranged so that every decision is nested. The lower bound is obtained when every decision is serial—that is, unnested (Figure 13).

The scope metric. The scope metric,[24],[25] like other metrics that measure control flow complexity, is based on the graph-theoretic representation of a computer program as a flow graph.

Let a computer program be represented as flow graph $G = (V,E)$ with a single initial node and a single terminal node. Then, the set of nodes V can be partitioned into two sets—those with an outdegree of one or less, called *receiving* nodes and those with an outdegree of two or more, called *selection* nodes.

To obtain the scope measure of complexity, we create a subgraph G', consisting of all nodes that immediately succeed a given selection node. That is, the subgraph consists of all nodes that are connected by a single edge from the selection node (including the selection node itself, in a self-loop).

Each of these subgraphs has at least one node in the graph G that is its lower bound. A lower bound is a node that can be reached from every node in the subgraph; that is, it succeeds every node that immediately succeeds the selection node. Most subgraphs will have a number of lower bounds, but the lower bound that precedes every other lower bound of the subgraph is called the *greatest lower bound*.

The number of nodes preceding the greatest lower bound of a selection node's subgraph (excluding the GLB itself) and succeeding the selection node, plus 1, yields the *adjusted complexity* for that selection node. Each receiving node has an adjusted complexity of 1, except for the terminal node, which has an adjusted complexity of 0. The adjusted complexity of each node, both selection and receiving nodes, is summed to get the overall complexity of the flow graph.

The process of computing the scope measure of complexity for the flow graph in Figure 14 is illustrated in Tables 7 and 8.

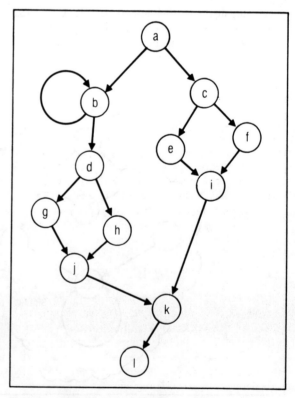

Figure 14. Flow graph used in scope complexity calculations. Subgraphs are explained in Table 7, and scope complexity is computed in Table 8.

Table 7.
Subgraphs within flow graph in Figure 14.

	SELECTION NODE			
	a	*b*	*c*	*d*
SUBGRAPH	*b.c*	*b.d*	*e.f*	*g.h*
COMPLEXITY	10	2	3	3
NODES INCLUDED IN COMPLEXITY	*b.c.d. e.f.g. h.i.j*	*b*	*e.f*	*g.h*

Table 8.
Computation of scope complexity of flow graph in Figure 14.

NODE	COMPLEXITY
a	10
b	2
c	3
d	3
e	1
f	1
g	1
h	1
i	1
j	1
k	1
l	0
TOTAL	25

The scope ratio. The scope number, in essence, is the number of nodes in the flow graph. Obviously, this measure can not always be reliable, since some programs can be trivially rearranged to give flow graphs with different scope measures, as shown in Figure 15. For this reason, the scope ratio was developed.[26]

The scope ratio is calculated by dividing the number of nodes in the flow graph, excluding the terminal node, by the scope number. In this case, as the ratio increases, the complexity decreases, but the scope ratio can be taken as one minus the original ratio. This number is much more satisfactory, since it increases towards one as complexity increases, and decreases to zero as complexity decreases.

If the scope ratio is used to analyze the flow graph in Figure 14, it would yield a value of 1 – (11/25), or 0.56.

The advantage of the scope measure over current forms of control flow metrics is its sensitivity to nested decisions, which is illustrated in the complexity measures of the flow graphs in Figure 16. The results seem to satisfy the rankings we would intuitively assign to these flow graphs.

As with every other measure yet surveyed, the control flow metrics fail to be comprehensive. They do not take into account the contribution of any factor except control flow complexity.

However, control flow metrics do a fairly good job of differentiating between two programs that are otherwise equivalent in other characteristics such as size. A useful approach may be to use control flow metrics to differentiate among programs that have already been placed in the same size categories using size metrics.

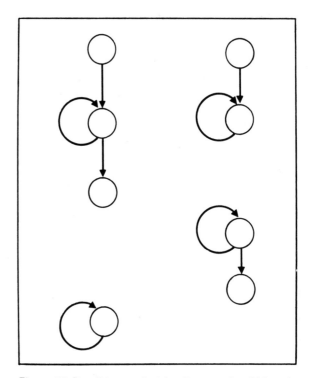

Figure 15. Possible one-decision flow graphs. Although all these graphs depict one decision, the number of nodes involved, and hence the scope measure, is not the same for each.

Hybrid complexity measures. Hybrid complexity measures attempt to remedy one of the shortcomings of the single-factor complexity metrics in use. They consider two or more properties that are thought to contribute to software complexity—program size, program data structures, and program flow of control.

One approach is to borrow part of the measure from an existing metric, such as Hansen's,[27] which combines a measure of control flow and program size. An alternative approach is to develop completely new measures of complexity for the various properties and combine them, as does Oviedo.[28]

Hansen's measure of complexity. Hansen[27] developed a measure that combines the cyclomatic complexity of McCabe and a count of operators similar to Halstead's $n1$.

Hansen's complexity measure consists of a 2-tuple (a,b), where the first value is a count of the number of

- IF, CASE, or other alternate execution constructs and

- iterative DO, DO-WHILE or other repetitive constructs.

The second component of the 2-tuple is a count of operators in the program, which Hansen defines as

- primitive operators such as +, −, *, AND, SUBSTR, etc;
- assignment;
- subroutine or function calls;
- application of subscripts to an array; and
- input and output statements.

23

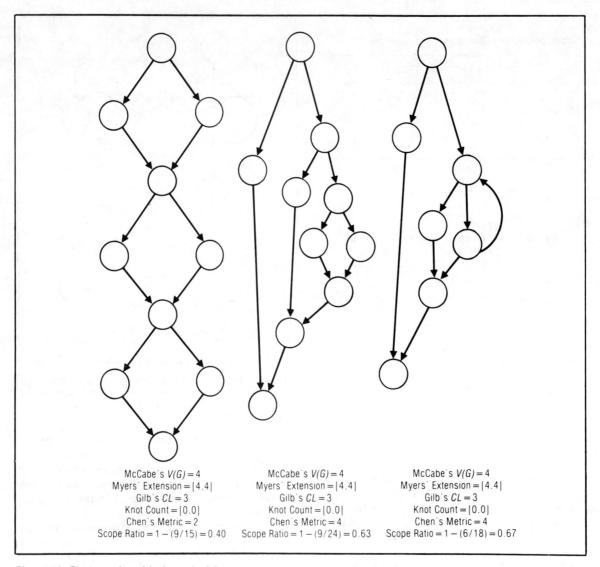

McCabe's $V(G) = 4$	McCabe's $V(G) = 4$	McCabe's $V(G) = 4$
Myers' Extension = |4.4|	Myers' Extension = |4.4|	Myers' Extension = |4.4|
Gilb's $CL = 3$	Gilb's $CL = 3$	Gilb's $CL = 3$
Knot Count = |0.0|	Knot Count = |0.0|	Knot Count = |0.0|
Chen's Metric = 2	Chen's Metric = 4	Chen's Metric = 4
Scope Ratio = $1 - (9/15) = 0.40$	Scope Ratio = $1 - (9/24) = 0.63$	Scope Ratio = $1 - (6/18) = 0.67$

Figure 16. Flow graphs with three decisions.

Hansen suggests that some version of the cyclomatic number is an appropriate measure of control flow complexity, since it is easy to compute and supports the use of an operator count by observing that a program with more operators is bigger; hence "more is going on" within the program. Because each operation must be understood to understand the whole, a bigger program is more complex.

Hansen has demonstrated this technique by applying it to four programs and their revisions, which were published in a popular programming style text by Kernighan and Plauger.[29] In each case, the complexity of the original program's 2-tuple indicated greater complexity than the revised version's 2-tuple, which was written to conform with the text's guidelines on programming style.

Few empirical studies can support Hansen's measure. However, the components of the measure have been independently validated in their original form, which would tend to lend a measure of credibility to this metric.

Oviedo's model of program complexity. Oviedo[28] has developed a method that measures data flow complexity and control flow complexity. First, control flow complex-

ity cf is calculated, and then data flow complexity df is calculated. Total program complexity C is then $C = acf + bdf$, where a and b are appropriate weighting factors. In his preliminary work, Oviedo suggests that the weighting factors be $a = b = 1$ until further experimentation can be done.

The control flow complexity cf is easily calculated once the program is represented as a flow graph—it is simply the number of edges in the graph. The calculation of the data flow complexity is a bit more complicated, however, and requires some preliminary definitions. A *variable definition* occurs when a variable is assigned a value, either through an input statement, an assignment statement, or a function or subroutine call. A *variable reference* occurs when the value of a variable is used, either in an output statement or some sort of expression such as an assignment statement.

In a definition-reference relation, the definition and reference occur in the same node or they occur in different nodes. Allen and Cocke[30] term a variable *locally available* for a block if there is a definition of that variable within the block. A variable is termed *locally exposed* if it is

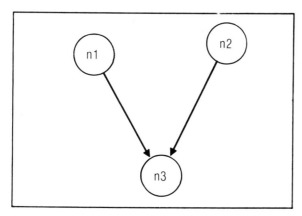

Figure 17. Illustration of locally exposed variables that can reach n3.

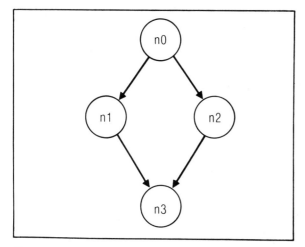

Figure 18. Flow graph of sample program to illustrate Oviedo's complexity model.

referenced in a node and is not preceded in that node by a definition of that variable.

A variable definition in node n_i can reach a block nk if there is a path from n_i to nk such that the variable is not locally available in any node on the path. A variable definition kills all other definitions of the variable when the definition is encountered.

The data flow complexity of node n_i, called df_i, is the number of prior definitions of locally exposed variables in n_i that can reach n_i (Figure 17). Assume that $n1$ of Figure 17 consists of $x: = 1, j: = 2$, and $m: = 5$. Further, let node $n2$ consist of $k: = 1$ and $j: = 3$, and node $n3$ consist of $d: = x + j + k$. Then, the locally exposed variables in node $n3$ are x, j, and k. Note that variables x and k were previously defined one time each and j twice, making df equal to 4.

Data flow complexity for the program is then equal to the sum of the data flow complexity of each node. That is,

$$df = \sum_{i=1}^{|v|} df_i$$

Note that the data flow complexity of the first node $df1$ is always zero. The total program complexity is

$$c = e + \sum_{i=1}^{|v|} df_i$$

For example, let $n0$ be the initial node of a program, and nodes $n1$, $n2$, and $n3$ be defined as above. The flow graph of such a program may appear similar to the flow graph in Figure 18 and the program itself might be

> READ n,x,k
> *If* $n = 1$ THEN
> $x: = 1$
> $j: = 2$
> $m: = 5$
> ELSE
> $k: = 1$
> $j: = 3$
> ENDIF
> $d: = x + j + k$

Notice the addition of the level statement and the IF-THEN-ELSE construct to the previous program. The complexity of node $n0$ that consists of

> READ n,x,k
> IF $n = 1$

is zero, since no prior definitions reach this block. Nodes $n1$ and $n2$ have no locally exposed variables, since they consist only of assignment statements, which use constant values. Node $n3$ has three locally exposed variables, x, j, and k. For each locally exposed variable the following number of definitions reach $n3$:

$$
\begin{array}{cc}
x & 2 \\
j & 2 \\
k & \underline{2} \\
 & 6
\end{array}
$$

Therefore node $n3$ has a data flow complexity of 6, or $df3 = 6$. Then $df = 6$, since $df0 = 0$, $df1 = 0$, $df2 = 0$ and $df3 = 6$. This sample clearly has four edges, so $|e| = 4$. If $a = b = 1$, then $c = 4 + 6 = 10$. Hence, the sample program has an Oviedo complexity of 10.

Integrating software science with the scope measure. To develop a reliable metric that can assign a realistic complexity measure to a given computer program, components must be included that evaluate the other properties contributing to program complexity. A modification to the original scope measure was suggested for this reason,[31] and because it is the most context-sensitive of the program size metrics, software science[4] was selected as part of the modification. As we discussed earlier, software science is used to reflect the complexity contributed by program length and data.

We consider the program as flow graph $G = (V,E)$ and each node has a complexity assigned to it, which is called *raw complexity*.

The raw complexity of node v_i is e_i, the software science measure of effort. The first node $v1$ has raw complexity $e1$, the second node $v2$ has raw complexity $e2$, etc. This measure is calculated in the following manner. The unique operand and operator parameters $n1$ and $n2$ are determined for the entire program—that is, the parameters are *global*. The total use parameters $n1$ and $n2$ for the operator and operand are determined for individual node or block v_i; that is, the parameters are *local*. This results in parameters $n1_i$, $n2_i$, and N_i for the ith node. The computation of total e values E_i is $E_i = (N_i \log 2 \, n)/L'$, where $L' = 2/n1 \times n2/N2$. Note that L' is a global parameter.

The software science e value for each node is used to compute adjusted complexities for the selection nodes. The adjusted complexity for a selection node is the sum of the e values of every node within the "scope" of that selection node, plus the e value of the selection node itself. A node is within the scope of a selection node if it (1) precedes the greatest lower bound of the subgraph consisting of all nodes that immediately succeed the selection node and (2) succeeds the selection node.

Receiving nodes (those with an outdegree of 1) have an adjusted complexity equal to their raw complexity. The complexity of the overall program is the sum of the adjusted compexities of every node in the flow graph.

The hybrid approach to measuring software complexity is clearly the most sensible approach. Software complexity is caused by so many different factors that measuring only one of them cannot help but give unreliable results for a general case.

Since the hybrids presented here are not supported by a great deal of empirical research, their veracity must be evaluated by examining their components.

With Hansen's measure, the component that measures flow of control is similar to Gilb's *CL,* absolute logical complexity. A moderate amount of empirical work supports the utility of measuring the flow of control to determine complexity, and the operator count part of the metric is supported in part by work done to validate Halstead's software science.

However, if Hansen's measure shares some of their support, it must share all of their drawbacks. Gilb's measure lacks context sensitivity, and Halstead's work suffers from a similar problem. However, they are widely applicable to many types of software. Hansen also uses a 2-tuple, which creates problems with two measures such as (5,20) and (3,65), since determining which of the two is more complex is difficult. A single component measure of complexity is much more desirable. Oviedo's model, which measures the number of edges in a flow graph, is similar in principle to McCabe's and Gilb's measures and, like these two, fails to consider the context of each edge. Also, determining an appropriate weighting factor a for control flow complexity may be difficult. The second component, data flow complexity, seems to be intuitively satisfying, but no empirical studies have been reported to support this property's effect on program complexity. The weighting factor b for this component may also be difficult to determine.

The measures just presented represent the metrics being used in larger software-oriented companies and some universities. Some appear quite reliable and valid, but all

**Table 9.
Usefulness of complexity metrics.***

	EMPIRICAL EVIDENCE	CONTEXT SENSITIVE	WIDELY APPLICABLE	COMPREHENSIVE
LINES OF CODE	2	1	3	1
SOFTWARE SCIENCE	3	1	3	2
SPAN BETWEEN DATA REFERENCES	1	1	3	2
SEGMENT-GLOBAL USAGE PAIR	1	2	1	1
CHAPIN'S Q MEASURE	1	2	1	1
CYCLOMATIC NUMBER	3	1	3	1
MYER'S EXTENSION	1	1	3	2
GILB'S CL	2	1	3	1
GILB'S cL	2	1	3	2
KNOT COUNT	1	2	2	1
CHEN'S METRIC	1	2	3	1
HANSEN'S METRIC	1	1	3	2
OVIEDO'S METRIC	1	1	3	2

*$1 =$ poor, $2 =$ fair, and $3 =$ good.

have some problems associated with them. Each metric included can be implemented with a computer program, and while there may be some disagreement on what is included in the calculations (for example, lines of code and Halstead's software science), all can be said to be deterministic.

Table 9, which summarizes the usefulness of each metric, shows that the two qualities most lacking are context sensitivity and comprehensiveness. Most are widely applicable, though of course, they may work better on some types of problems than others. Many are supported by empirical evidence, though many have not been tested. As more work is done in this field, more of these will be subjected to experiments. The initial goal would be to develop measures that can distinguish reliably among the complexity levels of several programs. For example, a progam with five branches will always have the same cyclomatic number, regardless of branch arrangement.

Development of new complexity matrices will probably follow this course over the next several years, as researchers attempt to refine the measures to evaluate the context of use for each property being considered. ∎

Acknowledgment

Work by Harrison and Magel was supported in part by National Science Foundation Grant MCS 8002667.

References

1. J. C. Baird and E. Noma, *Fundamentals of Scaling and Psychophysics,* John Wiley & Sons, New York, 1978, pp. 1-6.

2. V. Basili and A. Turner, "Iterative Enhancement: A Practical Technique for Software Development," *IEEE Trans. Software Eng.,* Vol. SE-1, Dec. 1975, pp. 390-396.

3. J. Elshoff, "An Analysis of Some Commercial PL/1 Programs," *IEEE Trans. Software Eng.,* Vol. SE-2, June 1976, pp. 113-120.

4. M. Halstead, *Elements of Software Science,* Elsevier North-Holland, New York, 1977.

5. R. Bohrer, "Halstead's Criteria and Statistical Algorithms," *Proc. Eighth Ann. Computer Science Statistics Symp.,* Los Angeles, February 1975, pp. 262-266.

6. J. Elshoff, "Measuring Commercial PL/I Programs Using Halstead's Criteria," *ACM SIGPLAN Notices,* May 1976, pp. 38-46. (also GM Research Publication GMR-2012, 1975).

7. Y. Funami and M. Halstead, "A Software Physics Analysis of Akiyama's Debugging Data," *Proc. Symp. Computer Software Eng.,* 1976, pp. 133-138.

8. B. Curtis et al., "Measuring the Psychological Complexity of Software Maintenance Tasks With the Halstead and McCabe Metrics," *IEEE Trans. Software Eng.,* Vol. SE-5, Mar. 1979, pp. 96-104.

9. B. Curtis, S. Sheppard, and P. Milliman, "Third Time Charm: Stronger Prediction of Programmer Performance by Software Complexity Metrics," *Proc. Fourth Int'l Conf. Software Eng.,* 1979, pp. 356-360.

10. A. Feuer and E. Fowlkes, "Some Results from an Empirical Study of Computer Software," *Proc. Fourth Int'l. Conf. Software Eng.,* 1979, pp. 351-355.

11. S. Sheppard, P. Milliman, and B. Curtis, *Experimental Evaluation of On-Line Program Construction,* Tech Report TR-79-388100-6, Arlington, VA, GE Information Systems Programs, 1979.

12. A. Fitzsimmons and T. Love, "A Review and Evaluation of Software Science," *Computing Surveys,* Vol. 10, No. 1, Mar. 1978, pp. 3-18.

13. V. Basili, "Product Metrics," *Tutorial on Models and Metrics for Software Management and Engineering,* IEEE Computer Society Press, 1980, pp. 214-217.

14. N. Chapin, "A Measure of Software Complexity," *Proc. NCC,* 1979, pp. 995-1002.

15. N. Chapin, "Input-Output Tables in Structured Design," *Structured Analysis and Design, Volume 2,* Infotech Int'l., Ltd., Maidenhead, UK, 1978, pp. 43-55.

16. T. McCabe, "A Complexity Measure," *IEEE Trans. Software Eng.,* Vol. SE-2, Dec. 1976, pp. 308-320.

17. G. Myers, "An Extension to the Cyclomatic Measure of Program Complexity," *ACM SIGPLAN Notices,* Oct. 1977, pp. 61-64.

18. T. Gilb, *Software Metrics,* Winthrop Publishers, Cambridge, MA, 1977.

19. M. Sime, T. Green, and D. Guest, "Psychological Evaluation of Two Conditional Constructions Used in Computer Languages," *Int'l J. Man-Machine Studies,* Vol. 5, No. 1, 1973, pp. 105-113.

20. M. Sime, T. Green, and D. Guest, "Scope Marking in Computer Conditionals—a Psychological Evaluation," *Int'l J. Man-Machine Studies,* Vol. 9, No. 1, 1977, pp. 107-118.

21. L. Farr and H. Zagorski, "Quantitative Analysis of Programming Cost Factors: a Progress Report" in "Economics of Automatic Data Processing," *Proc. ICC Symp.,* Frielink, ed., The Netherlands, 1965.

22. M. Woodward, M. Hennell, and D. Hedley, "A Measure of Control Flow Complexity in Program Text," *IEEE Trans. Software Eng.,* Vol. SE-5, Jan. 1979, pp. 45-50.

23. E. Chen, "Program Complexity and Programmer Productivity," *IEEE Trans. Software Eng.,* Vol. SE-4, May 1978, pp. 187-194.

24. W. Harrison and K. Magel, "A Complexity Measure Based on Nesting Level," *ACM SIGPLAN Notices,* Mar. 1981, pp. 63-74.

25. W. Harrison and K. Magel, "A Graph-Theoretic Complexity Measure," *ACM Computer Science Conf.,* St. Louis, Missouri, Feb. 1981.

26. W. Harrison and K. Magel, "A Topological Analysis of Computer Programs With Less Than Three Binary Branches," *ACM SIGPLAN Notices,* Apr. 1981, pp. 51-63.

27. W. Hansen, "Measurement of Program Complexity by the Pair (Cyclomatic Number, Operator Count)," *ACM SIGPLAN Notices,* Mar. 1978, pp. 29-33.

28. E. Oviedo, "Control Flow, Data Flow and Program Complexity," *Proc. COMPSAC 80,* pp. 146-152.

29. B. Kernighan and P. Plauger, *The Elements of Programming Style,* McGraw-Hill, New York, 1974.

30. F. Allen and J. Cocke, "A Program Data Flow Analysis Procedure," *Comm. ACM,* Vol. 19, No. 3, Mar. 1976, pp. 253-261.

31. W. Harrison, "A Hybrid Metric to Measure Software Complexity," MS thesis, University of Missouri-Rolla, 1981.

Warren Harrison is a doctoral student in computer science at the University of Oregon. He has a BS in accounting and information systems from the University of Nevada-Reno and an MS in computer science from the University of Missouri-Rolla. In 1980, he was awarded the Certificate in Data Processing.

Harrison has been a programmer with the Nevada Cooperative Extension Service, a computer scientist with Lawrence Livermore National Laboratory and a member of the technical staff at Bell Laboratories. His research interests include software maintenance, program testing, human factors, and decision support systems.

Kenneth Magel is an associate professor of computer science at the University of Texas at San Antonio. He taught for two years at Wichita State University and then for four years at the University of Missouri-Rolla. His research interests include software metrics, predictive software development tools, and the use of comprehensive models in program optimization.

Magel received a PhD in computer science from Brown University in 1977. He is a member of the IEEE Computer Society and the ACM.

Raymond Kluczny is an associate professor of engineering management at the University of Missouri-Rolla, where he has been since 1979. He received a DBA from Arizona State University in 1979. Kluczny's research interests are management information systems and systems analysis and design. He is a member of the Society for Management Information Systems and the ACM.

Arlan DeKock is professor and chairman of the Computer Science Department at the University of Missouri-Rolla, where he has taught since 1968. Previously, he worked for NASA, was database administrator for the Missouri Department of Social Services, and consulted for numerous private and governmental organizations. His research interests include software engineering, database design, and artificial intelligence. DeKock received his PhD in 1968 in Human Factors Engineering from the University of South Dakota. He is a member of the ACM.

Some Stability Measures for Software Maintenance

STEPHEN S. YAU, FELLOW, IEEE, AND JAMES S. COLLOFELLO, MEMBER, IEEE

Abstract—Software maintenance is the dominant factor contributing to the high cost of software. In this paper, the software maintenance process and the important software quality attributes that affect the maintenance effort are discussed. One of the most important quality attributes of software maintainability is the stability of a program, which indicates the resistance to the potential ripple effect that the program would have when it is modified. Measures for estimating the stability of a program and the modules of which the program is composed are presented, and an algorithm for computing these stability measures is given. An algorithm for normalizing these measures is also given. Applications of these measures during the maintenance phase are discussed along with an example. An indirect validation of these stability measures is also given. Future research efforts involving application of these measures during the design phase, program restructuring based on these measures, and the development of an overall maintainability measure are also discussed.

Index Terms—Algorithms, applications, logical stability, module stability, maintenance process, normalization, potential ripple effect, program stability, software maintenance, software quality attributes, validation.

I. INTRODUCTION

IT IS well known that the cost of large-scale software systems has become unacceptably high [1], [2]. Much of this excessive software cost can be attributed to the lack of meaningful measures of software. In fact, the definition of software quality is very vague. Since some desired attributes of a program can only be acquired at the expense of other attributes, program quality must be environment dependent. Thus, it is impossible to establish a single figure for software quality. Instead, meaningful attributes which contribute to software quality must be identified. Research results in this area have contributed to the definition of several software quality attributes, such as correctness, flexibility, portability, efficiency, reliability, integrity, testability, and maintainability [3]–[6]. These results are encouraging and provide a reasonably strong basis for the definition of the quality of software.

Since software quality is environment dependent, some attributes may be more desirable than others. One attribute which is almost always desirable except in very limited applications is the *maintainability* of the program. Software maintenance is a very broad activity that includes error corrections,

enhancements of capabilities, deletion of obsolete capabilities, and optimization [7]. The cost of these software maintenance activities has been very high, and it has been estimated ranging from 40 percent [1] to 67 percent [2] of the total cost during the life cycle of large-scale software systems. This very high software maintenance cost suggests that the maintainability of a program is a very critical software quality attribute. Measures are needed to evaluate the maintainability of a program at each phase of its development. These measures must be easily calculated and subject to validation. Techniques must also be developed to restructure the software during each phase of its development in order to improve its maintainability.

In this paper, we will first discuss the software maintenance process and the software quality attributes that affect the maintenance effort. Because accommodating the ripple effect of modifications in a program is normally a large portion of the maintenance effort, especially for not well designed programs [7], we will present some measures for estimating the *stability* of a program, which is the quality attribute indicating the resistance to the potential ripple effect which a program would have when it is modified. Algorithms for computing these stability measures and for normalizing them will be given. Applications of these measures during the maintenance phase along with an example are also presented. Future research efforts involving the application of these measures during the design phase, program restructuring based on these measures, and the development of an overall maintainability measure are also discussed.

II. THE MAINTENANCE PROCESS

As previously discussed, software maintenance is a very broad activity. Once a particular maintenance objective is established, the maintenance personnel must first understand what they are to modify. They must then modify the program to satisfy the maintenance objectives. After modification, they must ensure that the modification does not affect other portions of the program. Finally, they must test the program. These activities can be accomplished in the four phases as shown in Fig. 1.

The first phase consists of analyzing the program in order to understand it. Several attributes such as the complexity of the program, the documentation, and the self-descriptiveness of the program contribute to the ease of understanding the program. The *complexity* of the program is a measure of the effort required to understand the program and is usually based on the control or data flow of the program. The *self-descriptiveness* of the program is a measure of how clear the program is, i.e., how easy it is to read, understand, and use [5].

The second phase consists of generating a particular mainte-

Manuscript received April 1, 1980; revised July 25, 1980. This work was supported by the Rome Air Development Center, U.S. Air Force System Command, under Contracts F30602-76-C0397 and F30602-80-C-0139.

S. S. Yau is with the Department of Electrical Engineering and Computer Science, Northwestern University, Evanston, IL 60201.

J. S. Collofello was with the Department of Electrical Engineering and Computer Science, Northwestern University, Evanston, IL 60201. He is now with the Department of Computer Science, Arizona State University, Tempe, AZ 85281.

Reprinted from *IEEE Transactions on Software Engineering*, Volume SE-6, Number 6, November 1980, pages 545-552. Copyright © 1980 by The Institute of Electrical and Electronics Engineers, Inc.

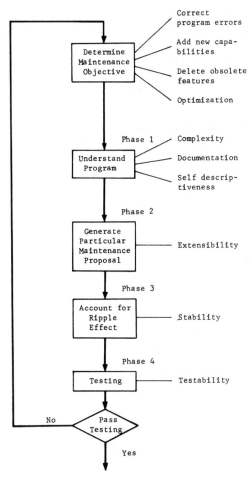

Fig. 1. The software maintenance process.

nance proposal to accomplish the implementation of the maintenance objective. This requires a clear understanding of both the maintenance objective and the program to be modified. However, the ease of generating maintenance proposals for a program is primarily affected by the attribute *extensibility*. The extensibility of the program is a measure of the extent to which the program can support extensions of critical functions [5].

The third phase consists of accounting for all of the ripple effect as a consequence of program modifications. In software, the effect of a modification may not be local to the modification, but may also affect other portions of the program. There is a ripple effect from the location of the modification to the other parts of the programs that are affected by the modification [7]. One aspect of this ripple effect is logical or functional in nature. Another aspect of this ripple effect concerns the performance of the program. Since a large-scale program usually has both functional and performance requirements, it is necessary to understand the potential effect of a program modification from both a logical and a performance point of view [7]. The primary attribute affecting the ripple effect as a consequence of a program modification is the *stability* of the program. Program stability is defined as the resistance to the amplification of changes in the program.

The fourth phase consists of testing the modified program to ensure that the modified program has at least the same reliability level as before. It is important that cost-effective testing techniques be applied during maintenance. The primary factor contributing to the development of these cost-effective techniques is the *testability* of the program. Program testability is defined as a measure of the effort required to adequately test the program according to some well defined testing criterion.

Each of these four phases and their associated software quality attributes are critical to the maintenance process. All of these software quality attributes must be combined to form a maintainability measure. One of the most important quality attributes is the *stability* of the program. This fact can be illustrated by considering a program which is easy to understand, easy to generate modification proposals for, and easy to test. If the stability of the program is poor, however, the impact of any modification on the program is large. Hence, the maintenance cost will be high and the reliability may also suffer due to the introduction of possible new errors because of the extensive changes that have to be made.

Although the potential benefits of a validated program stability measure are great, very little research has been conducted in this area. Previous stability measures have been developed by Soong [3], Haney [6], and Myers [4]. There exist several weaknesses in these measures which have prevented their wide acceptance. Their largest problem has been the inability to validate the measures due to model inputs that are questionable or difficult to obtain. Other weaknesses of these measures include an assumption that all modifications to a module have the same ripple effect, a symmetry assumption that if there exists a nonzero probability of having to change a module i given that module j is changing then there exists a nonzero probability of having to change module j given that module i is changing, and a failure to incorporate a performance component as part of the stability measure.

III. DEVELOPMENT OF LOGICAL STABILITY MEASURES

The *stability* of a program has been defined as the resistance to the potential ripple effect that the program would have when it is modified. Before considering the stability of a program, it is necessary to develop a measure for the stability of a module. The stability of a module can be defined as a measure of the resistance to the potential ripple effect of a modification of the module on other modules in the program. There are two aspects of the stability of a module: the logical aspect and the performance aspect. The *logical stability* of a module is a measure of the resistance to the impact of such a modification on other modules in the program in terms of logical considerations. The *performance stability* of a module is a measure of the resistance to the impact of such a modification on other modules in the program in terms of performance considerations. In this paper, logical stability measures will be developed for a program and the modules of which the program is composed. Performance stability measures are currently under development and the results will be reported in a subsequent paper. Both the logical and the performance stability measures are being developed to overcome the weaknesses of the previous stability measures. In addition, the stability measures are being developed with the following requirements to increase their applicability and acceptance:

1) ability to validate the measures,
2) consistency with current design methodologies,
3) utilization in comparing alternate designs, and
4) diagnostic ability.

It should be noted that the stability measures being described are not in themselves indicators of program maintainability. As previously mentioned, program stability is a significant factor contributing to program maintainability. Although the measures being described estimate program stability, they must be utilized in conjunction with the other attributes affecting program maintainability. For example, a single module program of 20 000 statements will possess an excellent program stability since there cannot be any ripple effect among modules; however, the maintainability of the program will probably be quite poor.

Development of a Module Logical Stability Measure

The logical stability of a module is a measure of the resistance to the expected impact of a modification to the module on other modules in the program in terms of logical considerations. Thus, a computation of the logical stability of a module must be based upon some type of analysis of the maintenance activity which will be performed on the module. However, due to the diverse and almost random nature of software maintenance activities, it is virtually meaningless to attempt to predict when the next maintenance activity will occur and what this activity will consist of. Thus, it is impossible to develop a stability measure based upon probabilities of what the maintenance effort will consist of. Instead, the stability measure must be based upon some subset of maintenance activity for which the impact of the modifications can readily be determined. For this purpose, a primitive subset of the maintenance activity is utilized. This consists of a change to a single variable definition in a module. This primitive subset of maintenance activity is utilized because regardless of the complexity of the maintenance activity, it basically consists of modifications to variables in the modules. A logical stability measure can then be computed based upon the impact of these primitive modifications on the program. This logical stability measure will accurately predict the impact of these primitive modifications on the program and, thus, can be utilized to compute the logical stability of the module with respect to the primitive modifications.

Due to the nature of the logical stability of a module, an analysis of the potential logical ripple effect in the program must be conducted. There are two aspects of the logical ripple effect which must be examined. One aspect concerns intramodule change propagation. This involves the flow of program changes within the module as a consequence of the modification. The other aspect concerns intermodule change propagation. This involves the flow of program changes across module boundaries as a consequence of the modification.

Intramodule change propagation is utilized to identify the set Z_{ki} of interface variables which are affected by logical ripple effect as a consequence of a modification to variable definition i in module k. This requires an identification of which variables constitute the module's interfaces and a characterization of the potential intramodule change propa-

gation among the variables in the module. The variables that constitute the module's interfaces consist of its global variables, its output parameters and its variables utilized as input parameters to called modules. Each utilization of a variable as an input parameter to a called module is regarded as a unique interface variable. Thus, if variable x is utilized as an input parameter in two module invocations, then each occurrence of x is regarded as a unique interface variable. Each occurrence must be regarded as a separate interface variable since the complexity of affecting each occurrence of the variable as well as the probability of affecting each occurrence may differ.

Once an interface variable is affected, the flow of program changes may cross module boundaries and affect other modules. Intermodule change propagation is then utilized to compute the set X_{kj} consisting of the set of modules involved in intermodule change propagation as a consequence of affecting interface variable j of module k. In the worst case logical ripple effect analysis, X_{kj} is calculated by first identifying all the modules for which j is an input parameter or global variable. Then, for each of these modules in X_{kj}, the intramodule change propagation eminating from j is traced to the interface variables within the module. Intermodule change propagation is then utilized to identify other modules affected and these are added to X_{kj}. This continues until the ripple effect terminates or no new modules can be added to X_{kj}. An algorithm for performing this worst case ripple effect has already been developed [7], [8].

The worst case ripple effect tracing can significantly be refined if explicit assumptions exist for each module in the program for its input parameters or global variables. Intermodule change propagation tracing would then examine if a module's assumptions have been violated to determine whether it should become a part of the change propagation. If a module's assumptions have not been violated, then the ripple effect will not affect the module.

There are many possible approaches to refining the worst case ripple effect which would not require a complete set of assumptions made for each interface variable for every module. For example, a significant refinement to the worst case change propagation can result by utilizing the simple approach of examining whether or not a module makes any assumptions about the values of its interface variables. These assumptions can be expressed as program assertions. If it does not make any assumptions about the values of its interface variables, then the module cannot be affected by intermodule change propagation. However, if it does make an assumption about the value of an interface variable, then the worst case is automatically in effect and the module is placed in the change propagation resulting from affecting the interface variable if the interface variable is also in the change propagation as a consequence of some modification.

Both intramodule and intermodule change propagation must be utilized to compute the expected impact of a primitive modification to a module on other modules in the program. A measure is needed to evaluate the magnitude of this logical ripple effect which occurs as a consequence of modifying a variable definition. This measure must be associated with each variable definition in order that the impact of modifying the variable definition during maintenance can be determined. This logical complexity of modification figure will be computed for each variable definition i in every module k and is denoted by LCM_{ki}. There are many possible measures which may be used for LCM_{ki}. All of these measures are dependent upon computation of the modules involved in the intermodule change propagation as a consequence of modifying i. The modules involved in the intermodule change propagation as a consequence of modifying variable definition i of module k can be represented by the set W_{ki} which is constructed as follows:

$$W_{ki} = \bigcup_{j \in Z_{ki}} X_{kj}.$$

The simplest measure for LCM_{ki} would be the number of modules involved in the intermodule change propagation as a consequence of modifying i. This measure provides a crude measure of the amount of effort required to analyze the program to ensure that the modification does not introduce any inconsistency into the program. Other measures which examine not only the number of modules involved in the intermodule change propagation, but also the individual complexity of the modules, provide more realistic measures of the amount of effort required to analyze the program to ensure that inconsistencies are not introduced. One such easily computed measure is McCabe's cyclomatic number [9]. The cyclomatic number $V(G)$ is defined in terms of the number of basic paths in the module. A basic path is defined as a path in the module that when taken in combination can generate all possible paths. Computation of the cyclomatic number is, thus, based on a directed-graph representation of the module. For such a graph G_j, the cyclomatic number can be calculated as the number of branches in G_j minus the number of vertices in G_j plus two. Utilizing the cyclomatic number or any other complexity measure, the complexity of modification of variable definition i of module k can be computed as follows:

$$\text{LCM}_{ki} = \sum_{t \in W_{ki}} C_t$$

where C_t is the complexity of module t.

Since the logical stability of a module is defined as the resistance to the potential logical ripple effect of a modification to a variable definition i on other modules in the program, the probability that a particular variable definition i of a module k will be selected for modification, denoted by $P(ki)$, must be determined. Now, a basic assumption of utilizing primitive types of maintenance activity is that a modification can occur with equal probability at any point in the module. This implies that each occurrence of each variable definition has an equal probability of being affected by the maintenance activity. Thus, for each module we can calculate the number of variable definitions. If the same variable is defined twice within a module, each definition is regarded separately. The probability that a modification to a module will affect a particular variable definition in the module can then be computed as 1/(number of variable definitions in the module).

With the information of LCM_{ki} and $P(ki)$ for each variable definition i of a module k, the potential logical ripple effect

of a primitive type of modification to a module k, denoted by LRE_k, can be computed. The potential logical ripple effect of a module is a measure of the expected impact on the program of a primitive modification to the module. Thus, the potential logical ripple effect can be computed as follows:

$$\text{LRE}_k = \sum_{i \in V_k} [P(ki) \cdot \text{LCM}_{ki}]$$

where V_k is the set of all variable definitions in module k.

A measure for the logical stability of a module k, denoted by LS_k, can then be established as follows:

$$\text{LS}_k = 1/\text{LRE}_k.$$

Development of a Program Logical Stability Measure

A measure for the potential logical ripple effect of a primitive modification to a program, denoted by LREP, can easily be established by considering it as the expected value of LRE_k over all of the modules in the program. Thus, we have

$$\text{LREP} = \sum_{k=1}^{n} [P(k) \cdot \text{LRE}_k]$$

where $P(k)$ is the probability that a modification to module k may occur, and n is the number of modules in the program. A basic assumption of utilizing primitive modifications is that a modification can occur with equal probability to any module and at any point in the module. Utilizing this assumption, the probability that a modification will affect a particular module can be computed as $1/n$, where n is the number of modules in the program. This assumption can be relaxed if additional information regarding the program is available. For example, if the program has only recently been released and it is believed that a significant part of the maintenance activity will involve error correction, then the probabilities that particular modules may be affected by a modification may be altered to reflect the probabilities that errors in these modules may be discovered. This can be accomplished by utilizing some complexity or software science measures [10].

A measure for the logical stability of a program, denoted by LSP, can then be established as follows:

$$\text{LSP} = 1/\text{LREP}.$$

IV. ALGORITHM FOR THE COMPUTATION OF THE LOGICAL STABILITY MEASURES

In this section, an algorithm will be outlined for the computation of these logical stability measures. The following description of this algorithm assumes that there does not exist any prior knowledge which might affect the probabilities of program modification, and McCabe's complexity measure [9] is utilized. The algorithm can easily be modified to allow for prior knowledge concerning the probabilities of program modification or to utilize a different complexity measure. The algorithm consists of the following steps.

Step 1: For each module k, identify the set V_k of all variable definitions in module k. Each occurrence of a variable in a variable definition is uniquely identified in V_k. Thus, if the same variable is defined twice within a module, then V_k

31

contains a unique entry for each definition. The set V_k is created by scanning the source code of module k and adding variables which satisfy any of the following criteria to V_k.

    a) The variable is defined in an assignment statement.
    b) The variable is assigned a value which is read as input.
    c) The variable is an input parameter to module k.
    d) The variable is an output parameter from a called module.
    e) The variable is a global variable.

Step 2: For each module k, identify the set T_k of all interface variables in module k. The set T_k is created by scanning the source code of module k and adding variables which satisfy any of the following criteria to T_k.

    a) The variable is a global variable.
    b) The variable is an input parameter to a called module. Each utilization of a variable as an input parameter to a called module is regarded as a unique interface variable. Thus, if variable x is utilized as an input parameter in two module invocations, then each occurrence of x is regarded as a unique interface variable.
    c) The variable is an output parameter of module k.

Step 3: For each variable definition i in every module k, compute the set Z_{ki} of interface variables in T_k which are affected by a modification to variable definition i of module k by intramodule change propagation [7], [8].

Step 4: For each interface variable j in every module k, compute the set X_{kj} consisting of the modules in intermodule change propagation as a consequence of affecting interface variable j of module k.

Step 5: For each variable definition i in every module k, compute the set W_{ki} consisting of the set of modules involved in intermodule change propagation as a consequence of modifying variable definition i of module k. W_{ki} is formed as follows:

$$W_{ki} = \bigcup_{j \in Z_{ki}} X_{kj}.$$

Step 6: For each variable definition i, in every module k, compute LCM_{ki} as follows:

$$LCM_{ki} = \sum_{t \in W_{ki}} C_t$$

where C_t is the McCabe's complexity measure of module t.

Step 7: For each variable definition i in every module k, compute the probability that a particular variable definition i of module k will be selected for modification, denoted by $P(ki)$, as follows:

$$P(ki) = 1/(\text{the number of elements in } V_k).$$

Step 8: For each module k, compute LRE_k and LS_k as follows:

$$LRE_k = \sum_{i \in V_k} [P(ki) \cdot LCM_{ki}]$$

$$LS_k = 1/LRE_k.$$

Step 9: Compute LREP and LSP as follows:

$$LREP = \sum_{k=1}^{n} [P(k) \cdot LRE_k]$$

where $P(k) = 1/n$, and n is the number of modules in the program. Then

$$LSP = 1/LREP.$$

V. Applications of the Logical Stability Measures

The logical stability measures presented in this paper can be utilized for comparing the stability of alternate versions of a module or a program. The logical stability measures can also be normalized to provide an indication of the amount of effort which will be needed during the maintenance phase to accommodate for inconsistency created by logical ripple effect as a consequence of a modification. Based upon these figures, decisions can be made regarding the logical stability of a program and the modules of which the program is composed. This information can also help maintenance personnel select a particular maintenance proposal among alternatives. For example, if it is determined that a particular maintenance proposal affects modules which have poor stability, then alternative modifications which do not affect these modules should be considered. Modules whose logical stability is too low may also be selected for restructuring in order to improve their logical stability.

The logical stability measures can be normalized by first modifying the computation of the module logical ripple effect measure to include the complexity of the module undergoing maintenance. Let LRE_k^+ denote this new logical ripple effect measure for module k which is calculated as follows:

$$LRE_k^+ = C_k + \sum_{i \in V_k} [P(ki) \cdot LCM_{ki}]$$

where C_k is the complexity of module k. This enables LRE_k^+ to become an expected value for the complexity of a primitive modification to module k. Let C_p be the total complexity of the program which is equal to the sum of all the module complexities in the program. Note that $LRE_k^+ \leqslant C_p$ since the ripple effect is bounded by the number of modules in the program. The normalized logical ripple effect measure for module k, denoted as LRE_k^*, can then be calculated as follows:

$$LRE_k^* = LRE_k^+/C_p.$$

The normalized logical stability measure for module k, denoted as LS_k^*, can then be calculated as follows:

$$LS_k^* = 1 - LRE_k^*.$$

The normalized logical stability measure has a range of 0 to 1 with 1 the optimal logical stability. This normalized logical stability can be utilized qualitatively or it can be correlated with collected data to provide a quantitative measure of stability.

The normalized logical stability measure for the program, denoted as LSP*, can be computed by first calculating the normalized logical ripple effect measure for the program, denoted as LREP*, as follows:

$$LREP^* = \sum_{k=1}^{n} [P(k) \cdot LRE_k^*].$$

The normalized logical stability measure for the program can then be calculated as follows:

$$LSP^* = 1 - LREP^*.$$

LSP^* has the same range and interpretation as LS_k^*.

VI. EXAMPLE

In this section the logical stability measures for the program in Fig. 2 will be calculated according to the previously described algorithm as follows:

$$LRE_{MAIN} = 4, \quad LRE_{RROOTS} = 2.9, \quad LRE_{IROOTS} = 2.7.$$

The logical stability of each of the modules is given by

$$LS_{MAIN} = 0.25, \quad LS_{RROOTS} = 0.34, \quad LS_{IROOTS} = 0.37.$$

The potential logical ripple effect of the program is

$$LREP = 3.2$$

and hence the logical stability of the program is given by

$$LSP = 0.31.$$

The normalized logical stability measures for each of the modules and the program are given as follows:

$$LS_{MAIN}^* = 0$$

$$LS_{RROOTS}^* = 0.02$$

$$LS_{IROOTS}^* = 0.06$$

$$LSP^* = 0.0267.$$

These measures indicate that the stability of the program in Fig. 2 is extremely poor. An examination of the program provides intuitive support of these measures since the program utilizes common variables in every module as well as shared information in the form of passed parameters. Thus, the change propagation potential is very high in the program.

VII. VALIDATION OF STABILITY MEASURES

As previously mentioned, an important requirement of the stability measures necessary to increase their applicability and acceptance is the capability of validating them. The previous stability measures [3], [4], [6] failed to satisfy this requirement due to calculations involving subjective or difficult to obtain inputs about the program being measured. The stability measures presented in this paper do not suffer from these limitations since they are produced from algorithms which calculate intermodule and intramodule change propagation properties of the program being measured. Thus, these measures easily lend themselves to validation studies.

The stability measures presented in this paper can be validated either directly through experimentation or indirectly through a discussion of how they are influenced by various established attributes of a program which affect its stability during maintenance. The direct approach to validation requires a large database of maintenance information for a significant number of various types of programs in different languages which have undergone a significant number of modifications of a wide variety. One experimental approach would be to examine sets of programs developed to identical

```
C MODULE MAIN
C SOLUTION OF THE QUADRATIC EQUATION
C A*X*X+B*X+C = 0
      COMMON HR1,HR2,HI
      READ 100 (A,B,C)
100 FORMAT (3F10.4)
      H1 = -B/(2.*A)
      HR = H1*H1
      DISC = HR - C/A
      CSID = H1*H1 - C/A
      CALL RROOTS (CSID,DISC,H1)
      WRITE 100 HR1,HR2,HI
      END


C MODULE RROOTS
      SUBROUTINE RROOTS (CSID,DISC,H1)
      COMMON HR1,HR2,HI
      IF (DISC.LT.0) GOTO 10
      H2 = SQRT (DISC)
      HR1 = H1 + H2
      HR2 = H1 - H2
      HI = 0.
10 CONTINUE
      CALL IROOTS (CSID,DISC,H1)
      RETURN


C MODULE IROOTS
      SUBROUTINE IROOTS (CSID,DISC,H1)
      COMMON HR1,HR2,HI
      IF (CSID.GE.0) GOTO 10
      H2 = SQRT(-DISC)
      HR1 = H1
      HR2 = H1
      HI = H2
10 CONTINUE
      RETURN
```

Fig. 2. An example program for computing the stability measures.

specifications but differing in design or coding. Logical stability measures for each version of the program could then be calculated to determine which possesses the best stability. A set of identical modifications to the specifications of each program could then be performed. For each modification to each program, a logical complexity of modification, LCM, could then be calculated based upon the difficulty of implementing the particular modification for the program. One particular method for calculating an LCM has previously been described [7], [8]. After a significant number of identical specification modifications have been implemented on all versions of the program, an average logical complexity of modification, ALCM, could be computed for each version of the program. This ALCM reflects the stability of the program and, thus, the ALCM can be utilized as a variable in the experiment. After a significant number of sets of programs have undergone their sets of modifications, experimental conclusions based upon a statistical analysis of the ALCM figures and the stability measures could be formulated.

This direct approach to validation of the stability measures will be difficult due to the number of programs and modifications necessary to produce significant statistical results. Thus, this direct approach to validation will be performed utilizing the maintenance data base which will be created in conjunction with the validation of our program maintainability measure which is currently under investigation.

The stability measures presented here can also be indirectly validated by showing how the measures are affected by some attributes of the program which affect its stability during maintenance. One program attribute which affects maintainability is the use of global variables. The channeling of communication via parameter-passing rather than global variables is characteristic of more maintainable programs [11]. Thus,

33

an indirect validation of the stability measures must show that the stability of programs utilizing parameter passing is generally better than that of programs utilizing global variables. This can be easily shown since the calculation of LS_i is based upon the LCM of each interface variable in module i. Since global variables are regarded as interface variables and since the LCM of an interface variable is equal to the sum of the complexity of the modules affected by modification of the interface variable, LS_i will be small for modules sharing the global variable. Thus, the logical stability of the program will also be small. On the other hand, if communication is via parameter passing instead of global variables, the LCM of the parameters will generally be small, and hence LS_i and LSP will generally be improved. Thus, the stability measures indicate that the stability of programs utilizing parameter passing is generally better than that of programs utilizing global variables.

The stability of a program during maintenance is also affected by the utilization of data abstractions. Data abstractions hide information about data which may undergo modification from the program modules which manipulate it. Thus, data abstraction utilization is characteristic of more maintainable programs. An indirect validation of the stability measures must, therefore, show that the stability of programs utilizing data abstractions is generally better than that of programs whose modules directly manipulate data structures. This can easily be shown by examining the stability measures of a program that utilizes data abstractions and comparing those measures to that of an equivalent program in which the modules directly access the data structure, i.e., data abstractions are not utilized. The modules which utilize a data abstraction to access a data structure will have fewer assumptions about their interface variables and hence have higher stability than that of the modules directly accessing the data structure and hence having many assumptions about it. For example, consider a data structure consisting of records where each record has an employee number and a department number. Assume that module INIT initializes the data structure and orders the records by the employee number. Also, assume modules X, Y, and Z must access the data structure to obtain the department for a given employee number. In this design, if module INIT is modified so that the records in the data structure are ordered by the department instead of the employee number, then modules X, Y, and Z must also be modified. This potential modification is reflected in the calculation of LS_{INIT} and, consequently, LSP. If, however, modules X, Y, and Z access the data structure through a data abstraction, then the same modification to module INIT will affect the data abstraction algorithm, but not modules X, Y, and Z. Consequently, LS_{INIT} and, consequently, LSP will be larger in the program which utilizes the data abstraction than the measures for the program which does not. Thus, the stability measures proposed in this paper indicate that the stability of programs utilizing data abstractions is generally better than that of programs which do not.

Another attribute affecting program stability during maintenance is a program control and data structure in which the scope of effect of a module lies within the scope of control of the module. This implies that the only part of a program affected by a change to a module, i.e., its scope of effect, is a subset of the modules which are directly or indirectly invoked by the modified module, i.e., its scope of control [12]. An indirect validation of the stability measures must, therefore, show that the stability of programs possessing this type of control and data structure are better than that of programs which do not possess this attribute. Now a program which exhibits this scope of effect/scope of control property has a logical stability which is calculated from the logical stability of its modules, each of which is bounded above by the sum of the complexity of the modules which lie within its scope of control. If the scope of effect of a modification to a module does not lie within the scope of control of the module, the logical stability of the module is only bounded above by the complexity of the entire program. Thus, the stability measures indicate that the stability of programs possessing the scope of effect/scope of control attribute are generally better than that of programs which do not possess this attribute.

Another attribute affecting program stability during maintenance is the complexity of the program. Program complexity directly affects the understandability of the program and, consequently, its maintainability. Thus, an indirect validation of the stability measures must, therefore, show that the stability of programs with less complexity is generally better than that of programs with more complexity. This is readily apparent from the calculation of the logical complexity of modification of an interface variable. Thus, complexity is clearly reflected in the calculation of the stability measures.

The stability measures presented here can, thus, be indirectly validated since they incorporate and reflect some aspects of program design generally recognized as contributing to the development of program stability during maintenance.

VIII. CONCLUSION AND FUTURE RESEARCH

In this paper, measures for estimating the logical stability of a program and the modules of which the program is composed have been presented. Algorithms for computing these stability measures and for normalizing them have also been given. Applications and interpretations of these stability measures as well as an indirect validation of the measures have been presented.

Much research remains to be done in this area. One area of future research involves the application of the logical stability measures to the design phase of the software life cycle. An analysis of the control flow and the data flow of the design of the program should provide sufficient information for calculation of a logical stability measure during the design phase.

Another area of future research involves the development of a performance stability measure. Since a program modification may result in both a logical and a performance ripple effect, a measure for the performance stability of a program and the modules of which the program is composed is also necessary [7], [8].

Much research also remains to be done in the identification of the other software quality factors contributing to maintainability. Suitable measures for these software quality factors must also be developed. These measures must then be integrated with the stability measures to produce a maintainability measure. This maintainability measure must be calculatable at each phase of the software life cycle and must be validated.

Another area of future research involves the development of automated restructuring techniques to improve both the stability of a program and the modules of which the program is composed. These restructuring techniques should be applicable at each phase of the software development. Restructuring techniques must also be developed to improve the other quality factors contributing to maintainability. These restructuring techniques must automatically improve the maintainability of the program at each phase of its development. The net results of this approach should be a significant reduction of the maintenance costs of software programs and, consequently, a substantial reduction in their life cycle costs. Program reliability should also be improved because fewer errors may be injected into the program during program changes due to its improved maintainability.

REFERENCES

[1] B. W. Boehm, "Software and its impact: A quantitative assessment," *Datamation*, pp. 48–59, May 1973.
[2] M. V. Zelkowitz, "Perspectives on software engineering," *ACM Comput. Surveys*, vol. 10, pp. 197–216, June 1978.
[3] N. L. Soong, "A program stability measure," in *Proc. 1977 Annu. ACM Conf.*, pp. 163–173.
[4] G. J. Myers, *Reliable Software through Composite Design*. Petrocelli/Charter, 1979, pp. 137–149.
[5] J. A. McCall, P. K. Richards, and G. F. Walters, *Factors in Software Quality, Volume III: Preliminary Handbook on Software Quality for an Acquisition Manager*, NTIS AD-A049 055, Nov. 1977, pp. 2-1–3-7.
[6] F. M. Haney, "Module connection analysis," in *Proc. AFIPS 1972 Fall Joint Comput. Conf.*, vol. 41, part I, pp. 173–179.
[7] S. S. Yau, J. S. Collofello, and T. M. MacGregor, "Ripple effect analysis of software maintenance," in *Proc. COMPSAC 78*, pp. 60–65.
[8] S. S. Yau, "Self-metric software–Summary of technical progress," Rep. NTIS AD-A086-290, Apr. 1980.
[9] T. J. McCabe, "A complexity measure," *IEEE Trans. Software Eng.*, vol. SE-2, pp. 308–320, Dec. 1976.
[10] M. H. Halstead, *Elements of Software Science*. New York: Elsevier North-Holland, 1977, pp. 84–91.
[11] L. A. Belady and M. M. Lehman, "The characteristics of large systems," in *Research Directions in Software Technology*, P. Wegner, Ed. Cambridge, MA: M.I.T. Press, 1979, pp. 106–139.
[12] E. Yourdon and L. Constantine, *Structured Design*. Yourdon, 1976.

Stephen S. Yau (S'60–M'61–SM'68–F'73), for a photograph and biography, see p. 434 of the September 1980 issue of this TRANSACTIONS.

James S. Collofello (S'78–M'79) received the B.S. and M.S. degrees in mathematics/computer science from Northern Illinois University, Dekalb, in 1976 and 1977, respectively, and the Ph.D. degree in computer science from Northwestern University, Evanston, IL, in 1978.

After graduating, he was a visiting Assistant Professor in the Department of Electrical Engineering and Computer Science, Northwestern University. He joined the faculty of the Department of Computer Science, Arizona State University, Tempe, in August 1979 and is currently an Assistant Professor there. He is interested in the reliability and maintainability of computing systems and the development, validation, and application of software quality metrics.

Dr. Collofello is a member of the Association for Computing Machinery and Sigma Xi.

Good System Structure Features: Their Complexity and Execution Time Cost

JOHN A. STANKOVIC, MEMBER, IEEE

Abstract—This paper describes a multistep technique that can be applied to improve system structure and to improve performance when necessary. The technique begins with the analysis of system structure via the structured design guidelines of coupling and cohesion. Next, manual system structure improvement transformations are applied. The effect of the transformations on execution time is then determined. Finally, vertical migration is used on the restructured system to improve its performance. Using the results of this paper, system programmers can identify specific cases where both good system structure and good performance are attainable, and others where tradeoffs must be made. The technique is most applicable during the maintenance phase of the software life cycle.

Index Terms—Execution time performance, hierarchical model, large systems, maintenance, software complexity, software methodology, structured design, transformations, vertical migration.

I. INTRODUCTION

THE overall cost of complex software systems makes it imperative that "good system structure" be used in their development and implementation. Yet, the effect of good system structure on execution time performance cannot be ignored. Certainly there will be instances when a system will have a "good" structure and still meet performance requirements. In other cases, compiler optimizations, cache memories, faster CPU's, etc., may be needed to permit a well-structured system to perform well. In yet other cases, the complexity of ill-structured systems might obscure some gross inefficiencies. With good system structure such inefficiencies might be easily identified and eliminated. Hence, the well-structured system may perform better than the ill-structured system, designed purportedly for efficiency. All these cases aside, what about those instances when good structure conflicts with performance requirements? Then precise understanding of how the structure of a system affects its performance is needed to help system designers and system programmers make reasonable tradeoffs between good structure and acceptable performance. However, the subjective nature of good system structure makes it difficult to decide what tradeoffs are appropriate.

In this paper two existing methodologies are combined and extended so system programmers can determine the precise execution costs of "good" system structure. The technique begins by analyzing system structure via the structured design guidelines of coupling and cohesion. Structured design [23] is a methodology for constructing comprehensive, large software systems. Next, manual system structure improvement transformations are applied, and the impact of the transformations on execution time is determined. Finally, performance is improved by vertical migration [25]-[27], a performance improvement methodology for migrating primitives from software to either lower levels of software or to firmware. Experimental results using the techniques are described.

In Section II a multilevel performance model is developed to illustrate vertical migration (VM) and the performance improvements attainable by VM. This model is used later in the paper to describe the performance cost of system structure features. In Section III the VM model is extended to include the system structure issues of structured design, and a set of manual transformations to improve system structure is developed. The effect of these transformations on execution time performance is described in Section IV. In Section V we show how vertical migration can reduce the performance impact of these transformations. Section VI summarizes the paper and suggests that the results of this work be used during software maintenance to reduce the complexity of system structure while still meeting execution time performance constraints.

II. VERTICAL MIGRATION

Vertical migration[1] is a systematic, partially automated method for improving the performance of a dedicated application or class of applications in a multilevel firmware-software hierarchical system by reducing CPU overhead (Fig. 1). Each level in Fig. 1 has an associated execution time overhead. The execution time overhead of a level is lowest for the hardware and increases for each level as you proceed up the hierarchy from the hardware to the application program level. This is because the higher levels typically make use of the lower levels, incurring the overhead of the lower levels in addition to their own overhead. The method for reducing overhead involves reimplementing either entire functions or paths through them which are CPU intensive on lower levels, for example, reimplementing an OS-level 1 function as an OS-

Manuscript received January 5, 1982. This work was performed in partial fulfillment of the Ph.D. degree from the Department of Computer Science, Brown University, Providence, RI, and was supported in part by the National Science Foundation under Grant MCS-76-04002, the Office of Naval Research under Contract N14-75-C-0427, and Brown University.

The author is with the Department of Electrical and Computer Engineering, University of Massachusetts, Amherst, MA 01003.

[1] The term vertical migration denotes migrations between levels on a single processor, in contrast to horizontal migration, which is the optimization of program performance by distributing modules between two or more independent processors, considered on the same level [21].

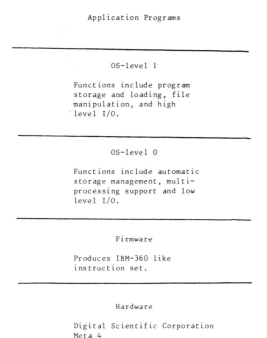

Application Programs

OS-level 1

Functions include program storage and loading, file manipulation, and high level I/O.

OS-level 0

Functions include automatic storage management, multi-processing support and low level I/O.

Firmware

Produces IBM-360 like instruction set.

Hardware

Digital Scientific Corporation Meta 4

Fig. 1. The Brown University Graphics System. A typical multilevel firmware–software hierarchical system.

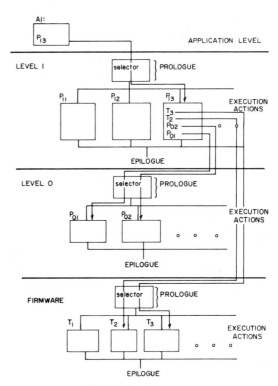

Fig. 2. The VM model.

level 0 function, or reimplementing an OS-level 2 function in the firmware. Exactly what overhead consists of is described as part of the model below.

One purpose of this research is to analyze the performance impact of good system structure. Another is to improve the performance of the system whenever good system structure impacts performance negatively. Vertical migration (VM) is a good candidate to use in trying to attain these goals because 1) it has been previously shown [27] that it offers order-of-magnitude performance improvement for individual modules and as much as 50 percent improvement for application programs, 2) it can be used in conjunction with other performance improvement techniques, and 3) it improves performance without destroying good system structure. It is not the intent of this paper to fully describe VM. In this section of the paper the model for vertical migration (Fig. 2) is briefly described, and serves as a basis for the remaining sections of the paper.

The VM model is a multilevel interpretive model based on both the "USES" relation[2] [15] and the mapping/execution model[3] [6]. The utility of the VM model consists of identifying the control structure and overhead of layered systems for purposes of performance improvement.

In the VM model the invocation and execution of a function that exists at a particular level in a multilevel interpreter system consists of two components: *mapping actions* and *execution actions*. Mapping actions are those actions performed to map flow of control and data parameters from the caller level

to the level of the invoked function and back. Execution actions refer to those steps that perform the semantic operations for the invoked function.

The mapping actions may be viewed as *overhead* in that they implement the actual interlevel call mechanism as well as the processing conventions common to each level. For software level to firmware level calls, these mapping actions include instruction fetch and decode, operand address computation and fetch, etc. For interlevel software calls the mapping actions will likely include the use of an interrupt mechanism (i.e., supervisor call (SVC) on 360's or EMT on PDP/11's) with the associated common processing of context saving, manipulation, and restoring. At each level, the common processing constituting the mapping actions for invoking and returning from the execution actions is defined as mapping *prologue* and *epilogue*. Then the *selector* is defined as that part of the mapping action prologue that determines if the function exists at this level.

Fig. 2[4] is a high-level symbolic model of three software levels and a firmware level with the processing at each level partitioned into mapping actions and execution actions. The mapping actions of each level are shown as common prologues and epilogues. The execution actions for each function on the firmware level are labeled T_1 (target instruction 1), T_2, $T_3, \cdots$; for level 0, P_{01} (function at level 0), $P_{02}, \cdots$; P_{11} (function at level 1), $P_{12}, P_{13}, \cdots$; and finally for the applications level, A_1 (application module 1), etc.

When P_{13}, a function at level 1, is invoked at the application level it is executed by going through the level 1 prologue, the four execution actions of P_{13}, i.e., the calls to functions

---

[2] The "USES" relation (Pi, Pj) is defined as: Pi calls (invokes) Pj and Pi is considered incorrect if Pj does not function properly. The "USES" relation implies a "USES" hierarchy.

[3] While Fuller's mapping/execution model deals directly with the task of emulation, he does suggest its applicability to multiple levels of machines, which is how we make use of his concepts.

[4] This figure and the following example are similar to those in [27].

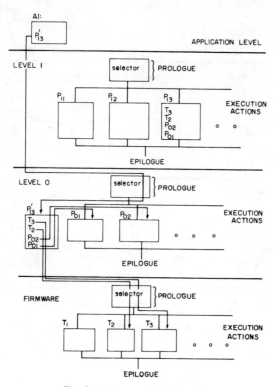

Fig. 3. An example of migration.

T_3, T_2, P_{02}, P_{01} of which it is comprised, and the epilogue. For each of the execution actions T_3 and T_2 the firmware prologue (and epilogue) must be executed, and similarly for each of the execution actions $P_{02}P_{01}$ the level 0 prologue (and epilogue) must be executed. The logical flow of control to these four prologues is shown in Fig. 2; flow of control returns to P_{13} after the respective epilogues have been executed.

In the vertical migration methodology, performance is improved by migrating specific functions, i.e., their execution actions, to a lower level. For example, P_{13} is migrated down to level 0 by reimplementing P_{13}, and is labeled P_{13}' in Fig. 3. When implementing P_{13}', functions above level 0 cannot be employed in order to preserve the hierarchy. The performance improvement realized is due to two distinct savings. First, migrating a complete function allows a lower level mapping action to be substituted for a higher level mapping action, i.e., in place of A_1 invoking the level 1 prologue/epilogue for P_{13}, it invokes the level 0 prologue/epilogue for P_{13}'. Remember that the mapping action execution costs increase with increasing level number as described above. As an example, for the Brown University Graphics System (BUGS), on which the experiments associated with this paper was performed, the level 1 mapping action is 1500 μs, while the level 0 mapping action is 100 μs (see Fig. 4). Consequently, 1400 μs are saved per invocation of P_{13}'.

The second saving arises when interlevel calls that were part of the migrated execution action become simple, intralevel calls (i.e., calls to P_{02} and P_{01}). Intralevel calls transfer control within a level without invoking the mapping actions of that level (Fig. 3). The mapping actions for the P_{02} and P_{01} interlevel calls are therefore saved (in this case two passes through the level 0 prologue/epilogue at 100 μs each). The

---

OS-level 1 overhead (1500 microsecs)

includes determination if the function is supported at this level, saving of registers, checking of masks for I/O interrupts, and setting up the proper environment. This overhead processing is performed by combinations of target instructions and OS-level 0 functions.

OS-level 0 overhead (100 microsecs)

includes determination if the function is supported on this level, context saving and restoring to support multiprogramming, and allocation of automatic storage. This overhead processing is performed by combinations of target instructions which are interpreted by the firmware level thereby also incurring the firmware level overhead.

Firmware Overhead (3 microsecs)

includes instruction fetch and decode, operand address calculation and fetch, and determining whether the function is supported in firmware.

Fig. 4. BUGS overhead.

extent of the performance improvement is therefore dependent on the relative cost of the various mapping actions and the number of mapping actions that are saved. This cost can be calculated automatically by using runtime statistics of how often each routine is invoked and prior calculations of mapping action overhead for each level.

As an example, consider a level 0 function migrated to the firmware level. The first type of saving results from the substitution of a firmware mapping action for a level 0 mapping action (approximately 3 μs versus 100 μs on BUGS). The second saving is due to the replacement of the sequence of target instructions that comprised the level 0 function's execution action by the functionally equivalent sequence of microinstructions of the firmware level execution action. Logically speaking, the interlevel mapping action (including target instruction fetch) of each target instruction is deleted when we replace the level 0 execution action with the equivalent firmware level execution action (a savings of 3 μs per target instruction for BUGS).

Note that all computer systems exhibit the behavior described by the VM model for at least two levels (software and hardware). Most systems have at least several additional levels—firmware and/or one or more operating system levels. The model then is widely applicable to systems in use today. Although the model is widely applicable, in practice, few programmers have access to the operating system or firmware. Therefore, our techniques are meant for systems programmers who do have the proper access. Any programmer, though, can make use of the structure improvement transformations to be described in the next section.

III. SYSTEM STRUCTURE: ITS COMPLEXITY

The VM model as just described deals exclusively with performance issues. There is no concern for the complexity of the mapping or execution actions, or for the types and numbers of interconnections between modules (except that modules be interconnected in a hierarchical fashion). Good structure requirements are now imposed on the model by requiring adherence to the structured design guidelines [23]. Based on the structured design methodology this section describes the method for identifying and quantifying system structure complexity and the transformations needed to decrease software complexity. The execution time cost of the structure resulting from the transformations is treated in Section IV. First, a few basic definitions are presented, followed by descriptions of coupling and cohesion. The section then ends with a description of the manual structure transformations.

A *system* is a set of modules performing a (set of) task(s). A *system structure*[5] is the set of modules themselves and their interrelationships. A module is a callable collection of executable statements that can exist on any software level.[6] Modules have two aspects, functionality and internal logic. A module's function defines what it does, and this property is a relevant part of the system structure. A module's internal logic describes how it performs its function, and is not relevant to system structure. As an example, the function of a square-root module is to compute the square root of a number. The internal logic may use a table or compute a logarithm but the logic it uses does not affect the functionality.

In this research, primary interest is in the complexity of functions of modules and of their interrelationships, not in the complexity of their internal logic. Internal complexity can be controlled by using structured programming techniques [2], [4]. We have focused on complexity at the higher level of system structure. A basic assumption of this research is that good system structure implies low system complexity and high understandability, while poor system structure implies high system complexity and poor understandability. One goal of this research was to reduce the complexity of a system by producing good system structure.

We believe that it is valid to make this assumption because it is widely accepted that understandable, good system structure has the following properties: 1) it is *partitioned* into components (modules) with identifiable and simple boundaries, 2) there is a high *independence* among components (modules) of the system, and 3) the relationships between components (modules) form a *hierarchy*[7] [1], [5], [14], [16], [20], [28]. However, this description is not detailed enough for our needs. We therefore make use of the *coupling* and *cohesion* parameters of the structured design methodology. The goal for system structure design is to reduce system complexity by designing systems with the weakest possible coupling among modules, and the highest possible cohesiveness within a module.

Coupling

Coupling occurs between pairs of modules that are directly interconnected in some way. The interconnection may be explicit or implicit. Explicit coupling exists if and only if module "*A*" *directly* calls module "*B*." If "*A*" calls "*B*," which calls "*C*," "*A*" is not considered coupled to "*C*." This

is because "*A*" is defined and understood in terms of its sub-components, which do not include "*C*." On the other hand, implicit coupling arises when modules "*A*" and "*D*" both reference the same data structure. In this case "*A*" and "*D*" are directly but implicitly coupled.

Each interconnection between a module and a module to which it is coupled is quantifiable by the degree of coupling. For example, passing data by a global variable is a high degree of coupling because any changes to the representation of the data will cause all modules using that data to be altered. Passing data via a parameter is a low degree of coupling because the assumptions made about the data are explicit and visible in the interface. The higher the degree of coupling, the more dependent modules are on one another, and a seemingly innocent change in one module can easily cause the other module to malfunction.

Coupling is quantified using the scale from zero to one given below. These numbers were based on the scores assigned to these properties in the structured design stability model [12]. The numbers are meant only to roughly represent the relative strengths of the different types of coupling.

The quantification of system structure serves several purposes: 1) it highlights the fact that some form of a system structure analysis should be performed, 2) it is a means for facilitating discussion about a set of properties while performing and describing experiments (e.g., a coupling of 0.6 assigned to a module in an experiment indicates external coupling and all its inherent properties), 3) it serves to identify relationships between these properties for purposes of improving system structure and performing an execution time analysis (e.g., data and stamp coupling are the best forms of coupling and all other forms should be transformed to them), 4) it acts as a framework on which to continually refine the properties and the measures themselves, and 5) based on further experience, it may evolve into a predictive measure for performance, maintainability, or reliability. Use of the quantification measure for 5) would require large empirical studies which are beyond the scope of the resources available to us and are not addressed in this research. It is important to note that this research only requires the identification of desirable and undesirable types of coupling and not their quantification. However, the quantification listed below is used primarily for reason 2) above. Data and stamp coupling are identified as the desirable types of coupling and all others are identified as undesirable. Therefore, the subjective assignment of scores to each type of coupling serves only the purposes listed above and no greater significance should or can be made. The higher the number on this scale, the more complex is the coupling. The coupling quantification used, whose terms are explained below, is as follows:

Score	Type
0.2	data coupling
0.35	stamp coupling
0.5	control coupling
0.6	external coupling
0.7	common coupling
0.95	content coupling

---

[5] The following definitions are an adaptation of definitions presented in [12].

[6] Target instructions are not considered modules and are not subjected to system structure analysis.

[7] Partitioning, independence, and hierarchy are related but independent properties. It is possible, for example, to have a strictly hierarchical system and still have poor structure by violating the partitioning or independence properties.

Briefly, two modules are *content coupled*[8] if one module makes a direct reference to the contents of the other module, e.g., by branching into the middle of another module, or if an assembly language module references a word at some numerical displacement within another module. This type of poor coupling is prevented by most higher level languages. Two modules that are content coupled are extremely dependent and result in poor modifiability. Any change to one module will probably affect the other. This is the worst form of coupling and should be avoided.

A group of modules are *common coupled* if they reference (read/write) a shared global heterogeneous data item (e.g., a Fortran COMMON environment). Two modules are *external coupled* if they both reference the same externally declared data symbol, where the symbol is an homogeneous data item (e.g., a simple variable or array). Common and external coupling induce poor understandability, modifiability, and reliability for many reasons; among these are that the global data inhibits program readability, introduces side effects, and creates dependencies among all modules using the global data since each of these modules must be aware of the representation of that global data. In general, heterogeneous data items (e.g., PL/I structures) are more difficult to understand than homogeneous data items; hence, common coupling is rated more complex than external coupling.

Two modules are *control coupled* if one module passes elements of control (e.g., control flags, module names, and labels) to the other module. Two modules that are control coupled are dependent on each other because they know something about the internal logic of each other. This dependency induces poor modifiability. However, passing a flag between two modules only creates a dependence between two modules. External and common coupling potentially affect many modules; hence, control coupling is not rated as poorly as external and common coupling.

Two modules are *stamp coupled* if they reference the same heterogeneous data structure, providing that this data structure is not global. This implies that the heterogeneous data structure is passed as a parameter.

Finally, two modules are *data coupled* if one calls the other and they are not content, common, external, control, or stamp coupled and all input and output to and from the called module are passed as homogeneous arguments. Stamp and data coupling are the best forms of coupling; programs that adhere to these forms are typically easier to understand and modify because all interconnections are explicit and inputs and outputs should be clearly identified. The module may be viewed primarily as an independent entity and, therefore, more easily understood.

Each of these coupling parameters except control coupling is objective and, hence, can be calculated automatically. The subjective nature of control coupling arises from a) the open-endedness of the definition, and b) the determination of whether a parameter is a flag or not. To make control coupling as objective as possible, the open-endedness of Myers' defini-

tion of control coupling is redefined in a precise manner. Two modules are control coupled if one module passes flags, module names, or labels to the other module. The determination of whether a parameter is a module name or label is objective. Parameters that act as flags are often easy to distinguish but in a few cases are subject to personal interpretation. Structured design suggests the following guideline in this case: the classification of control versus data is dependent upon how the sending module "A" perceives them and not on how the receiving module "B" perceives them. If "A" tells "B" what to do, then "A" and "B" are not independent and are control coupled.

In practice the identification of control coupling has not been a problem. For example, let module "A" call module "B" and pass parameter C where C is the salary of an employee. In this case module "B" is free to interpret C, i.e., "B" might perform a) if $C < 10\,000$ and b) if not. Furthermore, a change in specification, e.g., to perform c) if salary $> 20\,000$ could only require a change to "B." Hence, "A" and "B" are independent and are data coupled. On the other hand, if "A" were to interpret the salary and pass "B" a 1 for $C < 10\,000$ and a 2 for $C \geqslant 10\,000$, then "A" and "B" are control coupled. "A" is aware of the internal logic of "B," and a change in the specification as just described would require changes to both "A" and "B," making them dependent on each other.

We define the degree of coupling (DC) of module "A" to be the sum of the scores of each interconnection of module "A" to other modules (but one score per pair of interconnected modules, as detailed below). Hence, the DC of a module is dependent on the number of connections to different modules a module possesses. However, each of the interconnections may have several different degrees of coupling. As a score for each interconnection the worst degree of coupling that the interconnection possesses is chosen. For example, modules "A" and "B" may be explicitly connected by sharing five external variables (external coupling), each with a score of (0.6), and implicitly connected by common coupling (0.7) due to one shared global data structure. The score for the interconnection between "A" and "B" is 0.7. Note, that the score given to an individual connection is not weighted; this implies that sharing "one" global data structure between two modules is worse than sharing any number of external variables, or that sharing "n" external variables is no worse than sharing more than "n" external variables. Since this work is primarily concerned with identifying the poorest form of coupling, removing it, and repeating the cycle until the goal of minimal coupling is met, this assumption is acceptable. If an attempt was made to extend the measure to become predictive, then other assumptions are needed, such as: few external variables are shared because of other design guidelines (e.g., functional cohesion), and hence the weighting of individual connections is a second-order effect. On the other hand, a different weighting scheme would have to be investigated if many external variables were shared.

When measuring a module "A," interconnections from other modules to "A" are not scored because of the assumption that the system contains a hierarchical structure in which the complexity of a module is independent of the number of users of that module.

[8] For a more detailed description of the coupling parameters see [11]–[13], [23].

Cohesiveness

Cohesiveness is a measure of the relationships among the elements within a single module. Here, as in the coupling case, the quantification serves only a limited purpose. The importance of using the scale is that the desirable (functional and informational) and undesirable (all others) forms of cohesion are identified. The cohesiveness quantification is as follows:

Score	Type
0.2	functional
0.2	informational
0.6	sequential
0.7	temporal
0.8	logical
0.95	coincidental

Briefly, *functional cohesiveness* means that all of the elements of a module are related to the performance of a single function. This is the most understandable form of cohesiveness.

A module with *informational cohesiveness* performs multiple functions where the functions, represented by entry points in the module, deal with a shared local data structure. Informational cohesiveness is an important form of data abstraction;[9] for example, CLU clusters [10] may possess informational cohesiveness if each operation on the cluster is functional. Functional and informational cohesiveness induce understandability, modifiability, and reliability in systems because the relationships of the statements in the module are strongly related to one task. Therefore, they are most desirable.

Modules with *sequential cohesiveness* perform multiple functions and the output data from one element are the input for the next element. Because of the multiple functions, because of not being based on a data abstraction, and because of the existence of intertwined code that these modules usually possess, sequential modules are more complicated than necessary and, hence, more difficult to modify or extend.

Modules with *logical cohesiveness* perform multiple functions in which there is some logical relationship between the elements of the module (e.g., a module which performs all the input and output for a program).

Modules exhibiting *temporal cohesiveness* also perform multiple functions which are logically bound, but additionally these multiple functions are related in time. Therefore, the multiple functions are grouped together with more reason than those in modules with logical cohesiveness. An example of a module with temporal cohesion might be a set of functions grouped into an initialization module. An example of a module with logical cohesion is a module that contains one entry point and the multiple functions of "create" and "update" for a particular global data structure. In addition, the global data may be accessed by other modules, such as a "deletion" module. This induces more interconnections into the system than necessary. Furthermore, both temporal and logical modules contain a single interface for multiple functions. Hence, the interface and the interconnections are more

complicated than they need be and, thus, are more difficult to understand. For example, if a module is performing too many functions, its functionality can be obscured by the tests to distinguish among the different functions.

Finally, *coincidental cohesiveness* implies that no meaningful relationship exists among the elements of a module. Coincidental modules are not independent because the elements are not related to one another, but are related to elements within other modules. Furthermore, their interfaces are usually large, inducing additional complexity. These facts degrade program maintainability and extensibility. The multiple functions of a coincidental module have the least reason for being combined in one module; hence, this is the worst form of cohesion. Note that cohesiveness, unlike coupling, is largely subjective and that each module has a single measure of cohesiveness (Co).

Overall, the measure for the complexity of a module is the ordered pair (the degree of coupling, the measure of cohesiveness), represented as (DC, Co). This describes a module's complexity in terms of system structure properties.

Transformations

Given a particular module, it is possible to measure its "system structure" properties with our quantification scheme. Also proposed are the "desired goals" of data and stamp coupling, and functional and information cohesion. Given these goals, manual transformations can be used to improve system structure. Fortunately, once the coupling and cohesion framework is established, many of the transformations required to improve structure become obvious. On the other hand, the analysis required to determine the system structure properties of a module is the more difficult task because the properties may be obscured by poor internal logic.

Consider a *class of transformations* to be the set of all transformations that map a given point in the coupling or cohesion scale to another point on the respective scale, for example, all transformations that map coincidental cohesion to functional cohesion form a class of transformations. In general, there may be many transformations in each class. On the other hand, the number of classes is limited as is shown next.

Let n equal the number of types of coupling (or cohesion). There are $(n-1)$ classes of transformations needed to map from each point to all lower points with the exception of the lowest. The total number of classes of transformations $T(n)$ is then

$$T(n) = \sum_1^n (k-1) = n(n-1)/2.$$

Since there are six points on each of the coupling and cohesion scales, there might be as many as $T(6) = 15$ classes of transformations for each scale. In deriving this total, the transformations that degrade structure are not taken into account, e.g., mappings from data to external coupling. This type of inverse transformation is highly discouraged; nevertheless it may result in significant performance gains in some cases. For example, in a performance bound application, a transformation to global data in selected locations may gain

---

[9] A data abstraction is a group of related operations that act upon a particular class of objects, with the constraint that the behavior of the objects can be observed only by applications of the operations [10].

significant performance but at the same time degrade structure. This can be an acceptable tradeoff in some cases, especially if it can be accomplished automatically.

Classes of Coupling Transformations

After analyzing the 15 possible classes of coupling transformations, only the four listed below are desirable. The other classes of transformations often produce counter productive results. For example, while the common → external transformation is theoretically possible (by splitting heterogeneous (common) data structures into multiple homogeneous (external) ones) it is not desirable because 1) the transformation increases the number of interconnections unnecessarily, 2) an equally simple common → stamp transformation exists that produces an even greater benefit, an 3) the heterogeneous data structure may already be a good, understandable data abstraction. Similar arguments eliminate from consideration the other classes of coupling transformations not investigated here. It is also true that eliminating content coupling does not necessarily produce a data or stamp coupling. There may still exist external, common, or control coupling which must be subsequently eliminated by one of the other transformations. Hence, the transformations for eliminating content coupling can be described as content → noncontent. Thus, the following transformations are treated:

external → data
common → stamp
control → data/stamp
content → noncontent

For each of these four classes of transformation a collection of specific transformations has been developed and it has been shown that each of the above nongoal states is *always* transformable into a goal state. As an example, the external → data transformation is now described.

external → data

This is essentially a transformation from homogeneous global data to local data. This transformation is always possible since any program with global data can be transformed into an equivalent program with no global data. To make the global data item nonglobal, create a new module and hide the data as local data within the module. Find all previous references and alterations on this global data and make these the functions of the new module. Remove these operations from the other modules and replace the operations with calls to the new module.

Classes of Cohesion Transformations

Whether the goal of the cohesion transformations is functional or informational, cohesion is dependent on the particular abstractions encompassed by the original module under analysis. For example, a coincidental module may encompass several action and/or data behavior abstractions at the same time. Therefore, a transformation of this coincidental module may result in several functional and several informational modules. This situation is indicated by depicting the transformations as coincidental → *n* informational/functional. Only four classes of cohesion transformations are required in practice rather than the possible 15 for $T(6)$. This is because each of the coincidental, logical, temporal, and sequential types of cohesion has multiple functions, and can just as easily be transformed to one of the goal states as to a nongoal state. The four classes of cohesion transformations are

coincidental → *n* informational/functional
logical → *n* informational/functional
temporal → *n* informational/functional
sequential → *n* informational/functional

For the cohesion case, cogent arguments proving that each of the nongoal states is always transformable into the goal state do not seem possible because of the subjective nature of cohesion and the unbounded variety of coincidental, sequential, temporal, and logical modules that exist. However, a grab bag of these transformations that typify the types of transformations possible was developed. As an example of one of these cohesion transformations the logical → *n* informational/functional transformation is now described.

logical → n informational/functional

Fig. 5(a) shows a logical module Y containing multiple functions: edit master, update record, add record, and delete record. Also shown are several branch instructions that cause the code to be intertwined. Applying the logical → *n* informational/functional transformation entails creating separate functional entities for edit master, update record, add record, and delete record. These are then grouped in one informational module with no intertwined code. A representation of the informational module is also shown in Fig. 5(b). Here master, update, add, and delete are each separate syntactic entities and are also functional. Branch instructions are replaced by calls which make the functions less dependent. These functions are then grouped to operate on the data abstraction "record" creating an informational module.

In general, all of the cohesion transformations are similar, except the relationship between elements within the module is either nonexistent, logical, time, or ordered.

In summary, each of the eight classes of transformations (four for coupling and four for cohesion) is eliminating system properties that induce poor system structure and is replacing them with properties that induce good system structure. However, these transformations are applied only to systems meeting the initial assumptions (a hierarchy and structured programming for internal logic). There is no attempt to transform arbitrary structures, nor are the transformations automatic.[10] Engineering judgment must be used in applying the transformations.

---

[10] There exist techniques to transform the internal logic of arbitrary programs into 1-in, 1-out structured programming constructs. However, for internal logic these transforms often do not improve understandability, modifiability, and reliability. These transformations replace complex branching by setting and subsequent testing of control flags, which is not conducive to understandability, modifiability, and reliability. Hence, the problem is that these internal logic transforms operate on arbitrary programs and do not replace poor internal logic with good internal logic.

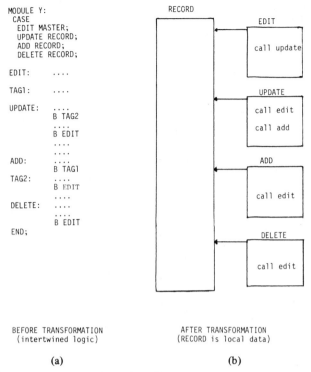

```
MODULE Y:                        RECORD
    CASE                                          EDIT
        EDIT MASTER;
        UPDATE RECORD;                        call update
        ADD RECORD;
        DELETE RECORD;

    EDIT:    ....                                UPDATE

    TAG1:    ....                               call edit
                                                call add
    UPDATE:  ....
             B TAG2
             B EDIT
             ....                                  ADD
             ....
    ADD:     ....
             B TAG1                             call edit
    TAG2:    ....
             B EDIT
             ....
    DELETE:  ....                               DELETE
             ....
             B EDIT
    END;                                        call edit
```

BEFORE TRANSFORMATION   AFTER TRANSFORMATION
(intertwined logic)   (RECORD is local data)

(a)   (b)

Fig. 5. Logical → n informational/functional transformation example.

IV. System Structure: Its Execution Cost

There are systems and situations in which each of the eight classes of transformations given in Section III causes a performance loss. It is also true that even if a structure improvement transformation has a small effect on the application program (say <5 percent), this may be an intolerable performance loss. Three general observations apply.

1) *Greatest Peformance Loss:* External → data and common → stamp coupling transformations have potential for large performance loss.

2) *Performance Improvement:* All cohesion transformations may *improve* performance by eliminating generality found in the execution actions.

3) *Negligible Performance Impact:* Content → noncontent and control → data/stamp transformations typically have negligible impact on performance.

Using the VM model, we now analyze the first observation and, as an example, describe an experiment on BUGS. Due to space limitations the second and third observations are only briefly discussed.

Greatest Performance Loss

One method of implementing the external → data and common → stamp coupling transformations is by creating an access module that encapsulates the external or common data. All modules using that data must now call the access module. The execution cost to an application program of such a transformation is the sum of the costs of the calls to the access module plus the sum of all additional processing that must be performed once accessed. Both of these factors can vary widely within a system and can have a great negative impact on performance.

In a system with multiple levels, as described by the VM model, two types of calls exist, inter- and intralevel calls. An interlevel call is a call that results in the execution of the mapping actions of a level. An intralevel call transfers control between two modules on the same level without executing that level's mapping actions. Interlevel calls are costly, and the cost varies depending on the level. As an example, on BUGS, invoking a firmware module requires 3 μs, a level zero module 100 μs, and a level one module 1500 μs. This is an order-of-magnitude difference for each successive level. If the new access module is placed on a level where most of the invocations require interlevel calls, the cost is significant for high-use modules. Placing the new access module on the same level as where there is a high frequency of invocation and then using a cheaper intralevel call will save execution time.

While intralevel calls are usually cheaper than interlevel calls, their cost can also be significant. Each level may have a number of intralevel calls available, each with its own cost. Furthermore, a particular intralevel call may be available at more than one level, e.g., a simple BAL assembly language subroutine transfer instruction is available to level 0, on BUGS. It is also available to all higher levels and can serve as an intralevel call in any of these levels. At high levels one usually finds more environmental setup associated with an intralevel call (e.g., a PL/I call) and, hence, greater cost.

The significant cost factors that contribute to performance loss for the external → data and common → stamp coupling transformations in a multilevel environment are:

1) the costs of each of the different intralevel calls,

2) the cost of interlevel calls,

3) the frequency of use of each new call to the access module,

4) the total amount of processing done by the access module to retrieve the data that were previously accessed directly, and

5) the number of modules affected by the coupling transformation, i.e., the number of modules previously coupled due to global data.

In general, all these cost factors degrade performance, each to a different extent for different application programs, levels, and systems. The greater each of these factors, the greater is the performance loss.

The use of the structure complexity analysis, the structure improvement transformations, and the above performance factors is now described in the context of an experiment run on BUGS. In the experiment, a module called RETRIEVE was quantified as (DC, Co) = (8.7, 0.2). RETRIEVE is a BUGS OS-level 1 module that retrieves records from disk (see the Appendix). Prior to the structure improvement transformations, RETRIEVE was coupled to 13 modules, four with complexity 0.6 (external coupling) and nine with complexity 0.7 (common coupling), to produce a coupling complexity for RETRIEVE of 8.7. The cohesion of RETRIEVE was functional, i.e., 0.2. Applying the external → data and common → stamp transformations reduced the complexity of RETRIEVE to (2.6, 0.2). Since global data were involved in the transformations, all modules accessing those data (and, hence, connected to RETRIEVE) also had their coupling complexity improved. In total, the system coupling complexity was reduced by a score of 28. In the subsystem of 13 modules and six global data items under consideration, there were 104 interconnections before the transformations. After the transformations there were 19 modules (six new modules to encapsulate the global data) and only 32 interconnections. The purpose of this experiment was to analyze the cost of the new access modules. Hence, no attempt was made to reduce the number of modules by creating informational modules (possibly further reducing the number of interconnections) as was done in another case study described in [22]. In this experiment, by removing all the implicit interconnections through the transformations, seven modules (GETAREA, RELEASE, FREEKEYZ, SETKEY, RGETSPACE, LOGIN, and EMERGENCY) were no longer interconnected to RETRIEVE (see the Appendix).

Next, the five cost factors listed above must be investigated. The first factor is the cost of intralevel calls. In this experiment one common and four external data couplings were transformed and subsequently required intralevel calls from RETRIEVE. We implemented the intralevel calls and subsequent processing with the minimum cost (18 μs for BUGS). Prior to the transformations only 3.9 μs were required to perform the same calling function; hence, there was a 4.6 times increase in execution overhead per call. Running an application program that makes a copy of a large disk file, there were a total of 1820 intralevel calls from RETRIEVE to the five newly created access routines. Furthermore, because of the number of modules affected by the coupling transformation (the fifth cost factor) seven other modules[11] [GETAREA (92), RELEASE (92), PREFIX (553), SETKEY (92), MAKEPTR (1465), RGETSPACE (144), LOGIN (1)] were also altered to include intralevel calls to the new access routines. In total, the intralevel calls required by the transformation cost RETRIEVE a 27 percent performance degradation and the application program a 3.5 percent loss in execution speed. Note, however, that in general the potential for performance loss increases as any of the five significant factors (except the second) grows larger.

Next, a similar analysis is performed for the interlevel calls required in the structure transformation. In this experiment only one common data coupling needed to be transformed, with the newly created access module being implemented in level 0, and subsequently requiring interlevel calls. One invocation of this interlevel call cost 134 μs,[12] an increase of 34.4 times over the previous cost of 3.9 μs. There were 364 interlevel calls from RETRIEVE to this new access module. Furthermore, the interconnections caused by this common data caused four other level 1 modules to be altered to now access the newly created module via interlevel calls [EMERGENCY (554), GETAREA (92), RELEASE (92), PREFIX (553)]. One level 0 module [SETBASE (456)] was altered to access

the new module as an intralevel call. The total performance degradation of the application program due to interlevel calls was 4 percent. Once again the potential for increased performance loss grows as any of the five significant factors grows.

Since the intra- and interlevel calls are totally independent, the performance losses can be added and we obtain a 7.5 percent total performance loss for the application program in this experiment. After identifying five significant cost factors for implementing external → data and common → stamp transforms and illustrating their overall effect on performance with this experiment, it seems that such transforms are too costly unless the frequency of calls to the new access modules is low. In the next section another method is introduced to deal with the high costs of these transforms when the frequency of calls is high.

Another observation drawn from this experiment is that if an external or common data item interconnects a large number of modules (say >25) the performance impact may be so great that even with a low frequency of calls a structure transformation may not be feasible. That is, the current design was so totally based on this data item being global that trying to localize the data item would have widespread and unacceptable impact on performance. If the performance improvement techniques of the next section cannot be applied, then this global data item must be flagged as being an exception and the complexity it imposes must be tolerated.

Therefore, the goal of the guidelines to implementing external → data and common → stamp coupling transformations is to minimize each of the five cost factors, if possible. For example, implement the cheapest intralevel call possible, place data and its access routine on the lowest level possible to minimize interlevel costs, and limit the frequency of calls by accessing larger amounts of information with fewer accesses.

Performance Improvement

The major technique of improving performance by vertical migration is the elimination of the unrequired generality provided by a level in the system. That is, the mapping actions of the level are avoided. Complexity analysis (defined in this paper as deciding the coupling and cohesion properties of modules) aids in the identification of a second type of generality that may be avoided in some instances, i.e., execution action generality.

All classes of cohesion transformations have the potential for identifying unnecessary execution action generality. As a simple example, assume that a coincidental module A is composed of n distinct functions $A(1) A(2) \cdots A(n)$. Since these functions are grouped together in one module, the execution actions of A must decide between each of these functions. Applying the coincidental → n informational/functional cohesion transformation creates $A(1), A(2), \cdots, A(n)$ as separate functional modules. The execution actions needed to decide among the $A(i)$'s have been eliminated. We refer to this as the elimination of execution action generality. In general, cohesion transformations can provide more significant elimination of execution action generality than presented in this example.

---

[11] The frequency of the intralevel calls from these modules is in parentheses following the module name.

[12] Recall that this cost increases by an order of magnitude for successively higher levels, so this factor becomes more and more significant the higher the level of the module called by the interlevel call.

Continuing with this example, note that module A must exist at the highest level required by any of its $A(i)$ functions. Assume that $A(1)$ must exist at level 4 while all other $A(i)$'s require only level 2. In this case module A exists at level 4. Any program invoking A then pays the execution costs of the mapping actions of level 4, even if this program only wants to make use of, say, $A(2)$. After the above coincidental $\to n$ informational/functional cohesion transformations each $A(i)$ could be placed at its most efficient level. A program invoking $A(2)$ pays the execution costs of the mapping actions of level 2, not level 4, thereby improving performance further. In general, though, an application program may need to use more than one of the $A(i)$'s on a given invocation of A. While this is not expected for a coincidental module, it is expected for other types of modules, e.g., a sequential module. Before the transformation, when more than one of the $A(i)$'s is required on a given invocation, only one mapping action cost is incurred. After the transformation, there is one mapping action cost (although some or all of the costs may be smaller than the original mapping action cost) for each $A(i)$ invoked. Therefore, the final performance effect on an application program depends on the savings incurred by eliminating execution action generality and the net difference between mapping action costs.

Negligible Performance Impact

There are two classes of transformations that typically have a negligible performance impact. They are the content $\to$ noncontent and control $\to$ data/stamp coupling transformations. The content $\to$ noncontent transformation can be implemented by repeating code. As an example, in Fig. 6(a) FREEMEM and GETMEM are content coupled because GETMEM branches into the middle of FREEMEM. Implementing the content $\to$ noncontent transformation by repeating code results in Fig. 6(b). In this example a branch immediate instruction (BI) in GETMEM is replaced by repeating two instructions (NBI and BR). This is actually an execution time savings of one branch instruction per invocation at a memory cost of one additional memory location. Note that the same performance analysis applies regardless of how many locations are saved.

If a large amount of code needs to be duplicated in implementing the content $\to$ noncontent transformation and it has functional cohesion, an alternate transformation is to make the common code a module. This new module is now called from the module that previously branched to it and from the module originally containing the code. Any other modules branching directly to this common code should also be transformed to access the newly created module. Depending on the level of the new module, each call may be either an intra- or an interlevel call. In general, the overall cost is dependent on the cost of the new calls and the number of times each is invoked. Although these factors are sufficient to produce significant performance loss in some cases, only a small number of locations from which the new module is called is expected. This is based on the observation that systems in practice do not have a large degree of content coupling. How-

```
/* In the example GETMEM/FREEMEM are content coupled */

GETMEM:    .....
           .....
           .....
           .....

           BI MEMOUT *unconditional branch instruction
FREEMEM:   .....
           .....
           .....

MEMOUT:    NBI FMLSEMA+1,255-1
           BR R14
                        (a)

/* Apply the content -> non-content coupling transformation */

GETMEM:    .....            FREEMEM:   .....
           .....                       .....
           .....
           .....                       NBI FMLSEMA+1,255-1
                                       BR R14
           NBI FMLSEMA+1,255-1
           BR R14
                        (b)
```

Fig. 6. (a) Content coupling. (b) Noncontent coupling.

ever, if there are many modules affected or the frequency factor is high, then this type of transformation can produce a large performance loss. If this is found to be true, it is a simple matter to perform the content $\to$ noncontent transformation by repeating code as described in the previous paragraph. This results in no execution time performance loss but, in practice, is only feasible if the space penalty can be tolerated. Assuming space is not a problem, we note that the content $\to$ noncontent transformation usually has negligible execution cost.

In the implementation of the control $\to$ data/stamp transformations the data necessary to determine the current setting of the control flag are transmitted in lieu of the flag. In many cases there is no cost difference in transmitting the data or the flag. For example, in some cases the module setting the flag would no longer have to process the data to determine the flag setting, but can leave that processing to the called module. Consequently, there is a rearrangement of processing costs but no net change. If the original module setting the flag also was required to process the data, then the cost of the transformation is the cost of repeating this processing in the called module. Typically there is not great cost involved in repeating the processing of data to determine a condition. Therefore, this transformation cost is usually negligible.

In summary, using the VM model with complexity concerns added, a systems programmer can determine the precise execution cost of a structure improvement transformation for a given application program. If the cost is negligible, the transformation should be implemented since we gain the benefits of good structure. In some cases performance improvement may result from the cohesion transformations. Here, both improved structure and improved performance are obtained. Finally, if there is a significant cost to the transformations, then a design decision is made as to whether the improved structure is worth the cost. If so, the transformations are implemented. Another technique is to implement a subset of the improvements up to some acceptable performance loss. If not, the vertical migration transformations are attempted to reclaim the performance loss due to the structure improvement transformations.

V. Structure Improvement and Performance Enhancement

The technique proposed in this paper is to first apply the structure improvement transformations, then determine their performance impact. Finally, the VM performance improvement transformations might be applied if needed. If the performance transformations are applied then the results of combining structure and performance transformations can be described in three broad categories. The first and most interesting category, described in this section, includes means for reclaiming the performance loss due to those structure improvement transformations that have significant costs (the external → data and common → stamp transformations). When either performance improvement or negligible cost results from the structure transformations, then both good system structure and good performance are attainable. This is the second category. The third category is the increased potential of performance improvement due to structure transformations. The second and third categories are not described in this paper (see [22]).

Reclaiming Performance Loss

The need for reclaiming performance loss due to structure transformations arises mainly for the external → data and common → stamp coupling transformations. By applying vertical migration in these instances, either some of the loss, or all of the loss may be recovered, and even a performance improvement may be obtained.

Consider the five significant cost factors which are responsible for this performance loss (repeated here for clarity):

1) intralevel call costs,
2) interlevel call costs,
3) frequency of use of each new call to the access module,
4) the total amount of processing done by the access module to retrieve the data that were previously accessed directly, and
5) the number of modules affected by the coupling transformations.

By reducing any of these factors some of the performance loss can be reclaimed. However, vertical migration can only help with reducing the cost of intra- and interlevel calls. The other three factors are not impacted by vertical migration.

First, let us consider intralevel calls. When implementing structure improvement transformations, several new modules may be created. Each of these modules must be placed in its right level and may be required to make intralevel calls. It is suggested that the cheapest available intralevel call that performs the necessary function be used. For example, modules on a given level might be permitted to make one of the following two intralevels calls, a BAL or a CALL. Let BAL simply be a branch and link instruction which transfers control from one module to another, saving no environment. Let the CALL statement transfer control and save environment information. If the new module can operate correctly using the BAL statement, then implement the intralevel call with the BAL statement. Furthermore, this new module may not have had access to the BAL instruction prior to the structure transformation because it may have been on a higher level where only the CALL statement was available.

The second significant cost factor is the new interlevel calls required by the structure transformations. But migration of a module invoked by the new interlevel call automatically reduces the cost of the new interlevel call by replacing it with a cheaper invocation mechanism. For example, the module(s) originally under consideration may be on level 3. The structure transformations may require that they remain on level 3 but a new module may be created on level 2 with a subsequent interlevel call from level 3 to level 2. Migrating this new module to level 1 replaces the level 2 interlevel call with a cheaper level 1 interlevel call. Furthermore, each call in the transformed set of modules should be reevaluated to determine which interlevel calls can be transformed to intralevel calls and which intralevel calls can be transformed to cheaper intralevel calls. Reducing the costs of intra- and interlevel calls may reduce to an acceptable level the amount of performance loss due to the structure improvement transformations.

Although the reduction of the cost of individual new calls is made possible by vertical migration, the real significant savings of vertical migration is due to the elimination of mapping actions. Hence, whether or not the cost of the structure transformations is reduced, fully recovered, or even surpassed is based primarily on the values of the parameters in the following formula. Let $C(TVM)$ be the cost (savings) of applying vertical migration to the modules affected by the structure transformations. Then,

$$C(TVM) = C(T) - C(R) - S(VM)$$

where $C(T)$ is the cost (savings) of the structure transformations, $C(R)$ is the reduction of costs due to replacing new calls required by the transformations with cheaper ones made available because of vertical migration, and $S(VM)$ is the total savings of mapping actions accrued by vertical migration. If $C(TVM)$ is negative (a savings) we have improved structure and improved performance. This condition often exists in high-use modules because the savings of mapping actions dominate.

For example, in the RETRIEVE experiment the cost of RETRIEVE was 1.302, and the cost of the migrated version of RETRIEVE was 0.235 s. This is an 82 percent improvement in the RETRIEVE primitive. Furthermore, there was a 30 percent improvement in the application program. It was also determined that the cost in execution time of employing the structure improvement transformations was 7.5 percent. Finally, in performing vertical migration on the subsystem of modules created by the structure improvement transformations, there was no savings due to cheaper calls, but the mapping action savings was still 30 percent, dominating the 7.5 percent cost of the structure transformations. The result is then improved structure by virtue of the transformations and improved performance of 22.5 percent by virtue of vertical migration. In this experiment the cost factors of the structure improvement transformations were dominated by the savings factors of vertical migration (difference in mapping actions times frequency). As long as the difference in mapping actions of adjacent layers are an order of magnitude, the savings due to vertical migration will dominate the structure transformation costs for high-use functions in most cases. Significantly, we can still attain good structure and good performance since the highest costs of the transformations would be for high-use functions (assuming vertical migration were not performed), and we can now reclaim those costs by vertical migration.

Another technique used to reclaim performance loss is *not* to restrict vertical migration to those modules that caused the performance loss. Depending on the requirements, vertical migration is applied until acceptable performance is reached, until the loss is reclaimed, or until all of the high-use modules that can be migrated are migrated.

Performance loss also occurs in cohesion transformations when new calls are added and no excess action generality is eliminated. In this case the same reduction techniques for the new intra- and interlevel calls as just described are applied and the same cost equation is applicable.

In summary, the implication of applying vertical migration transformations in conjunction with structure improvement transformations is that structure and performance can be improved simultaneously. This is true *when* vertical migration improvements dominate (for single modules or for the system as a whole), or when the costs of structure improvement transformations are negligible or improve performance. Using the factors identified, it is also possible to determine the *amount* of the improvements. Furthermore, the opposite situation can be identified, i.e., *when* and by *how much* we do not improve performance. Improved performance will not occur if $C(T)$, the effect of structure transformations, is greater than $S(\text{VM}) + C(R)$, where $S(\text{VM})$ is the gain from vertical migration by eliminating mapping actions, and $C(R)$ is the reduction in costs of calls.

VI. Conclusion

Within the emerging discipline of software engineering the following software development life cycle has been identified: 1) requirements analysis, 2) specification, 3) design, 4) coding, 5) testing, and 6) operation and maintenance [29]. The results presented in this paper have primary significance for the operation and maintenance phase of the software development life cycle. We believe "what is fundamental to achievement of better software management and minimal life-cycle costs, is the recognition that complexity grows *unless* and until effort is invested in restructuring" [1]. Therefore, continual structural complexity analysis (as defined in this paper) and structure improvement transformations applied by system programmers should maintain good system structure and extend the useful lifetime of a system. Furthermore, since we are able to identify execution-time costs related to specific transformations, this gives system programmers the luxury of having precise design tradeoffs at hand, e.g., module A with complexity x at execution cost y, or module A' with complexity x' at execution cost y'. In other words, the structural complexity analysis, the transformations, and the ability to determine their execution costs should act as a methodology for system software maintenance.

Another implication of these results is that additional programming features and/or structure improvement transformations which affect coupling and cohesion can easily be added to the quantification scheme and analyzed. In other words, the framework for this type of analysis has been established, and at present we are working with all the known categories. Furthermore, by investigating the relationship between system structure and performance, we found, surprisingly perhaps, that several classes of transformations required no execution time performance loss while others could actually improve performance. In this research there was no attempt to integrate other "costs" into the analysis (e.g., programmer time).

In summary, the structure and performance improvement transformations can be considered prescriptive guidelines on how to maintain and improve a system. The technique developed gives system programmers the ability to determine execution time costs and to identify precise design tradeoffs. The result is a more scientific and quantitative understanding of system structure, its costs, and means for improving it.

Appendix

The experiments described in this paper deal with a set of system programs that implement sophisticated file management, automatic storage, and virtual memory functions. Only those modules supporting these functions that were mentioned in the paper are described below. As part of the file management function records and areas (a collection of records) can be retrieved or stored by keys. Note that all the experiments were performed on a currently running and real operating system of which the modules described below are a part.

Module Name	Function
Emergency	initialization of data structures to support file management, automatic storage and virtual memory functions
Freekeyz	files may have several levels of indexing; this function clears a bit mask used to identify the indexing levels
Freemem	frees "m" memory locations in core
Getarea	allocates a new area for a file and connects it to the file
Getmem	gets "n" memory locations in core
Login	identifies how a file is to be managed; opens files
Makeptr	creates a pointer to a new area
Prefix	parses requests for file management and keyword requests
Release	an area is returned to disk and/or deleted
Retrieve	retrieves a record or area of a file from disk; can be based on keys
Rgetspace	recovers space from a deleted area of a file
Setbase	sets up and maintains the mapping of file records and areas to memory
Setkey	assigns a keyword to a record or area of a file

Acknowledgment

I would like to thank D. Bulterman, J. Stockenberg, and A. van Dam for many stimulating technical discussions concerning the vertical migration methodology. I would also like to thank L. Clarke for her comments on an early draft of this paper. Finally, comments and suggestions by J. Goodenough and several anonymous reviewers greatly improved the paper.

REFERENCES

[1] L. A. Belady and M. M. Lehman, "The characteristics of large systems," in *Research Directions in Software Technology*. Cambridge, MA: M.I.T. Press, 1979.

[2] W. Boehm, "Overview of structured programming: A quantitative assessment," *IEEE Comput. Mag.*, vol. 8, pp. 38–40, June 1975.

[3] —, "Software engineering: R & D trends and defense needs," in *Research Directions in Software Technology*. Cambridge, MA: M.I.T. Press, 1979.

[4] N. Chapin and S. P. Denniston, "Characteristics of a structured program," *ACM SIGPLAN Notices*, vol. 13, pp. 36–45, May 1978.

[5] E. W. Dijkstra, "The structure of 'THE' multiprogramming system," *Commun. Ass. Comput. Mach.*, vol. 11, pp. 341–346, May 1968.

[6] S. H. Fuller, V. R. Lesser, C. G. Bell, and C. H. Kaman, "The effects of emerging technology and emulation requirements on microprogramming," *IEEE Trans. Comput.*, vol. C-25, Oct. 1976.

[7] R. W. Hartenstein, "Increasing hardware complexity—A challenge to computer architecture education," in *Proc. 1st Annu. Symp. Comput. Architecture*, Dec. 1973.

[8] B. H. Liskov, "The design of the Venus operating system," *Commun. Ass. Comput. Mach.*, vol. 15, pp. 144–149, Mar. 1972.

[9] —, "A design methodology for reliable software systems," in *Proc. Fall Joint Comput. Conf.*, AFIPS, 1972, pp. 191–199.

[10] B. H. Liskov, A. Snyder, R. Atkinson, and C. Schaffert, "Abstraction mechanisms in CLU," *Commun. Ass. Comput. Mach.*, vol. 20, pp. 564–576, Aug. 1977.

[11] G. J. Myers, *Reliable Software Through Composite Design*. London, England: Mason/Charter, 1975.

[12] —, *Software Reliability and Practices*. New York: Wiley, 1976.

[13] —, *Composite Structured Design*. New York: Van Nostrand Reinhold, 1978.

[14] D. L. Parnas, "A technique for software module specification with examples," *Commun. Ass. Comput. Mach.*, vol. 15, May 1972.

[15] —, "On the criteria to be used in decomposing systems into modules," *Commun. Ass. Comput. Mach.*, vol. 15, pp. 1053–1058, Dec. 1972.

[16] —, "On a 'BUZZWORD': Hierarchical structure," in *Proc. IFIP Cong. 74*, Stockholm, Sweden, 1974.

[17] D. L. Parnas and D. P. Siewiorek, "Use of transparency in the design of hierarchically structured systems," *Commun. Ass. Comput. Mach.*, vol. 18, pp. 401–408, July 1975.

[18] D. L. Parnas, "On the design and development of program families," *IEEE Trans. Software Eng.*, vol. SE-2, pp. 1–9, Mar. 1976.

[19] —, "Designing software for ease of extension and contraction," in *Proc. 3rd Int. Conf. Software Eng.*, May 10–12, 1978, pp. 1264–1277.

[20] H. A. Simon, *The Sciences of the Artificial*. Cambridge, MA: M.I.T. Press, 1969.

[21] G. M. Stabler, "A system for interconnected processing," Ph.D. dissertation, Brown Univ., Providence, RI, 1974.

[22] J. A. Stankovic, "Structured systems and their performance improvement through vertical migration," Ph.D. dissertation, Brown Univ., Providence, RI, 1979.

[23] W. P. Stevens, G. J. Myers, and L. L. Constantine, "Structured design," *IBM Syst. J.*, vol. 13, pp. 115–139, 1974.

[24] J. E. Stockenberg, P. C. Anagnostopoulos, R. E. Johnson, R. G. Munck, G. M. Stabler, and A. van Dam, "Operating system design consideration for microprogrammed mini-computer satellite systems," in *Proc. Nat. Comput. Conf. Expo.*, June 1973.

[25] J. E. Stockenberg and A. van Dam, "STRUCT programming analysis system," *IEEE Trans. Software Eng.*, vol. SE-1, Dec. 1975.

[26] J. E. Stockenberg, "Optimization through migration of functions in a layered firmware–software system," Ph.D. dissertation, Brown Univ., Providence, RI, 1977.

[27] J. E. Stockenberg and A. van Dam, "Vertical migration for performance enhancement in layered hardware–firmware–software systems," *IEEE Comput. Mag.*, vol. 11, May 1978.

[28] R. W. Witty, "The design and construction of hierarchically structured software," Atlas Computing Div., Rutherford Lab., England, 1978.

[29] M. Zelkowitz, "Perspectives on software engineering," *ACM Comput. Surveys*, vol. 10, pp. 197–216, June 1978.

John A. Stankovic (S'77-M'79) received the Sc.B. degree in electrical engineering in 1970 and the Sc.M. and Ph.D. degrees in computer science in 1976 and 1979, respectively, all from Brown University, Providence, RI.

Currently, he is an Assistant Professor of Electrical and Computer Engineering at the University of Massachusetts, Amherst. He is currently doing research in the decentralized control of distributed systems. His other research interests include software engineering and operating systems.

Dr. Stankovic was Co-Editor of a Special Issue on Distributed Processing of IEEE COMPUTER MAGAZINE and now serves as Vice Chairman for the IEEE Technical Committee on Distributed Operating Systems. He is a member of the Association for Computing Machinery and Sigma Xi.

The Dimensions of Healthy Maintenance*

Robert S. Arnold

Computer Science Department
University of Maryland
College Park, Md. 20742

Donald A. Parker

NASA/Goddard Space Flight Center
Systems Engineering Branch
Code 821
Greenbelt, Md. 20771

ABSTRACT

What characterizes "healthy" or "satisfactory" software maintenance? How can we know it when we see it? This paper gives initial answers to these questions. We first argue the need for objectively measurable maintenance performance criteria in judging the "adequacy" of maintenance and present a set of criteria for judging maintenance performance in a particular software environment. We then subject the criteria to a practical test by applying them in this environment. We show how applying the criteria enables an informed overall maintenance performance appraisal, locates general maintenance problems, stimulates suggestions for improving maintenance on individual projects, allows these projects' maintenance to be compared and the projects ordered for improvement, and assesses the potential effectiveness of the suggestions in new project maintenance. We also sketch how criteria application can be generalized to software development monitoring and design methodology evaluation.

Introduction

Software maintenance is costly [17] and certainly needs improvement. To meet this challenge, research has been performed on the phenomenology of maintenance. A rationale behind this is that by better understanding the existing nature of the maintenance problem, we as researchers and practitioners will be better able to ameliorate it. The maintenance phenomenology research has been very useful in understanding maintenance, but has generally not given highly environment-specific suggestions for improving maintenance (exceptions are [12,14]). In this paper we will show how establishing criteria for judging maintenance quality can lead to environment-specific suggestions for its improvement. These suggestions will take the form of (1) locating potential maintenance and development problems from existing software maintenance data, and (2) suggesting improvements using the available software development and maintenance technology.

What is software maintenance?

Software maintenance is that collection of activities that relates to correcting, adapting, or perfecting software in production use. "Software" includes not only program code, but also the designs and documentation concerning the program code. "Correcting" software means removing functional errors (or, changing software to conform to a pre-established specification). "Adapting" software means installing enhancements. "Perfecting" software means improving processing efficiency or performance, or restructuring the software to improve changeability. Finally, "in production use" means the software has been formally accepted and put into use by its users. [1]

* The views in this paper are the authors' only, and not necessarily those of NASA or the U.S. Government. This research was supported in part by U.S. Air Force grant F49620-80C001-P1 and National Science Foundation grant MCS-79-23662.

Several empirical maintenance phenomenology studies have been performed. Belady and Lehman [4,5] did pioneering work on modelling the maintenance of OS/360, and in forming "laws" governing the evolution of large software systems. Lehman [12] further showed how such knowledge can be applied in practice. Yuen [21] tried to statistically validate Belady and Lehman's "laws" governing large system growth, but with generally negative results. Lientz, Swanson, and Tompkins [13,14,15] surveyed managers' perceptions of their data processing departments' maintenance activity. Another important study [10] examined software maintenance problems within the U.S. Federal Government.

It is important to know the nature of a problem before attempting to solve it. And the above studies do give valuable information about the software maintenance problem. However, obtaining information about maintenance (task A) and translating this knowledge into environment-specific improvements (task B) for maintenance are quite different tasks.

We know of no systematic way to handle task B for software maintenance. Boehm and others [6], Basili [3], and McCall and others [16,19] all gave useful approaches for using metrics for software development quality assurance, but gave relatively little attention to applying their ideas during software maintenance. There is reason to believe that maintenance needs special quality treatment, since, as argued by Hamlet [9], maintenance activity does not necessarily follow a "mini-development" cycle.

One reason task B has been neglected is that few people have formed clear goals for what is or is not "adequate" or "good" maintenance. By "adequate maintenance" we mean minimally acceptable maintenance activity to the software enterprise. Maintenance has unfortunately been largely a goal-less activity. That is, standards for the collective maintenance performance of changes are usually lacking in a given maintenance organization. This is typified by the difficulty many software managers have in giving pre-established, objectively measurable criteria for determining whether their organization's performance of maintenance is "adequate."

We believe that having objectively measurable maintenance performance criteria is important for two reasons. First, a performance baseline is established against which maintenance performance can be objectively gauged. This adds formality and visibility to the judgment process and lessens dependence on a manager's informal feelings about maintenance. Second, the criteria, when used across projects, can be used to compare maintenance performance on different projects.

Criteria, i.e., testable conditions with judgments attached to their outcomes, are fundamental to our basic research goal: to create an easily-applied, metrics-based methodology for software maintenance goal statement and pursuit. This goal grew out of our general concern that large software maintenance efforts needed more direction using software metrics. This paper presents a study preparatory to defining such a methodology. (The methodology will be defined in [2].)

Our paper's thesis is: by introducing and applying criteria for judging software metrics' values on software maintenance data, a number of practical maintenance results happen. Specifically, in this paper we give some objectively measurable criteria for assessing collective maintenance performance for a particular maintenance environment, defend the criteria, and apply the criteria to that environment. We do not offer universal criteria for judging maintenance, but instead illustrate the usefulness in establishing criteria in a particular environment. We show how applying the criteria enables an informed overall maintenance performance appraisal, locates general maintenance problems, stimulates suggestions for improving maintenance on individual projects, allows these projects' maintenance to be compared and the projects ordered for improvement, and assesses the potential effectiveness of the suggestions in new project maintenance.

We believe the criteria presented offer a useful starting point in establishing similar criteria in other environments. Accordingly, this paper is for (1) software metrics developers interested in actually using their results in practice, and (2) software maintenance managers interested in applying software metrics in their maintenance environments.

Our work here is an extension for maintenance of the work by McCall [16] and Walters [19] on using metrics for software development quality assessment and management. We shall compare our work with theirs in the final section of this paper.

1. Establishing the Criteria

1.1. Criteria First, Data Second?

Objectively testable, empirical criteria depend on having reliable data about software maintenance. The data is analyzed to determine whether the criteria are met. Thus it seems generating criteria must precede defining the required data and gathering it.

But what if maintenance data was collected independent of the criteria for judging it? Must we disregard this data because it may not be suitable for testing ideal criteria? Rather than ignore a possibly substantial collection of maintenance data, we prefer instead to change our criteria so they can be tested on the available data. If the criteria then become too weak, this is still the best we can do until newer data becomes available for testing stronger criteria. (Weiss [20] gave an approach for empirically answering questions about software development using change data, the same kind of data potentially available during software maintenance. He insisted on specifying study goals before change data collection, however.)

In the analyses below, we in fact formed criteria after maintenance data was collected and after the actual maintenance was performed. (Often experience with maintenance suggests criteria to apply.) The study of this paper therefore uses the quantitative behavior of past project maintenance to surmise and refine the kind of outputs to be expected when criteria are applied on future project maintenance.

1.2. Criteria Derivation

1.2.1. Level of Available Data

The data available to us was software maintenance change data for 40 satellite telemetry processing projects during the period 1973-1981 at NASA/Goddard Space Flight Center (NASA/GSFC) in Greenbelt, Maryland. Initial analysis in mid-1981 showed the original data base was unsuited for rigorous maintenance research. (For example, many inconsistencies in filling data fields were uncovered.) The data base was then carefully validated and enhanced, using written validation standards, archived hard-copy maintenance change records, and the experience of people who performed the maintenance.

After validation and enhancement, we had the following information for each change:

index number -

> the number assigned for uniquely identifying the change

associated project -

> the name of the project to which the change is related

priority -

> the urgency with which the change should be resolved

change type -

> the nature of the change solution (e.g., enhancement, restructuring, fix)

subject area -

> the object of the solution (e.g., project software, operating system software, hardware)

phase -

> whether the change was part of development or maintenance

disposition -

> how the change was resolved (e.g., successfully completed, never completed, still open)

effort -

> the estimated person-days (pd; 8 hrs/pd) taken by maintainer(s) to perform--to understand, design, implement, and unit test--the change, assuming normal availability of computer resources and continuous work on the change from start to finish. Effort scale: A (1-2 pd), B (3-5 pd), C (6-10 pd), D (11-15 pd); E (more than 15 pd); M (some work performed, but not possible to reliably estimate).

date started -

> date when the change was started by the maintainer, or when the change was received by the maintenance organization

date closed -

> date when the change was agreed closed by maintenance administration

Detailed information about specific lines of code and modules changed was unfortunately not available.

In late 1981, we generated static distributions of the data. These static distributions gave both the frequency of and effort required for the different types of software maintenance changes in the data base. (We plan to extend our work using dynamic distributions, i.e., those giving the occurrence of changes through time, in 1982.)

Our change effort data and derived static distributions measure a combination of the maintenance process and the products being maintained. The factors affecting maintenance are technical (programming-oriented), psychological, sociological, economic, and political. We have little data on each of these areas individually, but much on their combined software maintenance impact for our environment.

1.2.2. Assumptions

The assumptions we made before defining our criteria can be divided into definitions and environment assumptions.

Definitions

enhancement - The change solution involved changing the software in such a way that the software specifications, had they existed, should also be changed. Enhancements also include general changes for improvement where no specifications were expected to exist (e.g., fine tuning the system interface), or changes which simply add specifications.

fix - The change solution involved changing the software to conform to the software specifications, had they existed. Here a software change does not also mean a specifications change (as it normally does with enhancements). However, if the specifications were faulty and the software code change is to conform to corrected specifications (as far as can be determined), the change is also considered a fix. Errors of omission are also included under fixes.

restructuring - The change solution was a software change for performance improvement (e.g., enlarging a compiler's capacity to compile larger programs, improving code efficiency, reformatting a disk, rewriting suspect code, rearranging code, and improving code to conserve output

paper usage), robustness (i.e., to relieve error-proneness of human action; to aid reliability with different kinds of data), system conversion, or system compatibility. This type also includes changes solely involving removal of faulty code or unneeded functionality.

These definitions are refinements of the adaptive, corrective, and perfective maintenance definitions, respectively, given by Swanson [18].

Environment Assumptions

Resources devoted to maintenance. The number of full-time maintainers is not less than 30% of the available full-time programmers. Maintenance is a non-trivial problem for the environment.

Occurrence of changes. Management will equally consider all suggested changes. If, for example, management has decided to freeze all enhancements, then our criteria do not apply.

Packaging of changes. "Small" changes are consistently reported as "small" changes, rather than collected and packaged together under one "large" change. We do allow changes to be collected and performed in a batch, but we do not allow these normally individual changes to artificially lose their identity under one big change. (In this case the overhead in handling individual changes could vary significantly, ruining comparability of changes.)

Handling of enhancements, restructurings, and fixes. When a fix occurs, work on some enhancements and restructurings (e/r's) is probably delayed while the fix is performed. A fix is non-productive in the sense that it is anti-regressive rather than progressive system growth [11].

Work on e/r's promotes positive system growth and is more desirable, though perhaps less necessary, than work on fixes. E/r work is therefore preferred maintenance over fixes, and fixes will be regarded as disruptive.

Imperfect development and maintenance. Building and maintaining software is an imperfect process [4]. The occurrence of fixes is inevitable.

1.2.3. Criteria for Judging Adequacy of Maintenance Performance from Static Change Frequency and Effort Distributions

We can now state criteria for objectively measuring the adequacy of maintenance performance for our maintenance environment. These criteria are based on our deductions, explained below, from the above data, definitions, and assumptions, and on our perception of a healthy maintenance environment. One of us (DAP) has helped manage the maintenance of all the projects to which we apply the criteria, and so has advantageous experience on which to base these criteria. The other of us (RSA) has studied the projects' maintenance data as an outsider and has acted to keep the criteria rigorous and testable. (Boehm [7] has surveyed other techniques, such as the Delphi method, from which quantitative criteria can be generated from qualitative perceptions.)

The criteria are our first approximation to "adequate maintenance" and are subject to revision as our experience increases and maintenance objectives change. Nevertheless, we believe the given criteria provide a good basis for evolving a precise, testable characterization of "adequate maintenance." As mentioned earlier, we do not offer universal criteria for judging maintenance, but instead illustrate the usefulness in establishing criteria in a particular environment.

Each criterion is represented informally and formally, followed by a short qualitative justification. The informal criterion loosely describes the intent of the criterion. The formal criterion describes the criterion in a testable and reproducible way. We have found it helpful to think of criteria rather loosely when creating or discussing them, but to use precise criteria when actually applying them.

The differences between informal and formal criteria can be confusing when we later speak of "satisfying" or "meeting" a criterion for maintenance adequacy. To resolve this potential confusion, when we speak of a "satisfied" or "met" criterion, we mean the applied (formal) criterion result supported maintenance adequacy.

In the following criteria, bear in mind the given percentages represent our goals, and these will vary from environment to environment. So, more important than the percentages themselves is the reasoning behind the percentages.

C1. Desired effort distribution

a. Informal (I): Work on e/r's should consume 85% or more of the total programmer effort (in person-days) devoted to maintenance.

Formal (F): If a1 < 85%, then maintenance is not adequate. a1 = m / n, where

m = sum of effort field values over all data base entries for successfully completed software maintenance (scsm) e/r's

n = sum of effort field values over all data base entries for scsm e/r's and fixes

Note: A change is "successfully completed" if the change was actually started by a maintenance programmer and was eventually incorporated into the production system. A change is "closed-out" if the change was terminated and never incorporated into the production system.

This conforms to our belief that most work in a healthy maintenance environment should be expended on e/r's.

b. I: Work on fixes should consume 15% or less of the total programmer effort devoted to maintenance.

F: If a2 > 15%, then maintenance is not adequate. a2 = 1 - a1.

Asserting that no time should be spent on fixes is unrealistic, since we believe fixes will always occur. However, we believe 15% effort is enough to perform fixes without being excessive.

C2. Desired frequency distribution

a. I: The number of e/r change reports approved for action should be 65% or more of all software change reports approved for action.

F: If b1 <= 65%, then maintenance is not adequate. b1 = j / k, where

j = count of all data base entries for software maintenance e/r's which were actually initiated (i.e., not initially rejected or deferred by management)

k = count of all data base entries for software maintenance e/r's and fixes which were actually initiated

b. I: The number of fix change reports approved for action should be 35% or less of all software change reports approved for action.

F: If b2 > 35%, then maintenance is not adequate. b2 = 1 - b1.

Each change report requires overhead in understanding, reviewing, and tracking. We prefer this overhead be incurred for e/r's than for fixes. We have less stringent percentage bounds here than for effort distributions because overhead effort is not regarded as critical a resource as maintenance change effort.

C3. Completion rates

a. I: The e/r completion rate should be 80% or more.

F: If c1 < 80%, then maintenance is not adequate. c1 = r / (r + s), where

r = count of all scsm e/r data base entries

s = count of all closed-out, software maintenance e/r data base entries

b. I: The completion rate for fixes should be 90% or more.

F: If c1 < 90%, then maintenance is not adequate. c1 = p / (p + q), where

p = count of all scsm fix data base entries

q = count of all closed-out, software maintenance fix data base entries

The impact of an incompleted enhancement is normally not regarded as severe as the impact of an incompleted fix. Completion rates are not 100% to allow for changes terminated upon being found inadvisable after their start.

C4. Effort per change

a. I: 70% or more of the successfully completed e/r change reports should take one person-week or less.

F: If d1 < 70%, then maintenance is not adequate. d1 = u / v, where

u = count of all scsm, e/r data base entries which have a change effort of one person-week or less

v = count of all scsm e/r data base entries, regardless of effort

b. I: 80% or more of the successfully completed fix change reports should take one person-week or less.

F: If d2 < 80%, then maintenance is not adequate. d2 = x / y, where

x = count of all scsm fix data base entries which have a change effort of one person-week or less

y = count of all scsm fix data base entries, regardless of effort

"Long" fixes (more than one person-week) are regarded as especially disruptive. If a fix must occur, we prefer it to be short.

Long e/r's, on the other hand, are more tolerable since we've found people are more patient if a new benefit is forthcoming. However, many long enhancements can in a sense be disruptive of the short enhancements by excessively delaying their implementation. We therefore also desire to limit the number of long enhancements.

1.2.4. Double-Checking the Criteria

Our criteria were subjectively derived by two people for a particular maintenance environment, so we wanted to see how other NASA/GSFC maintenance managers viewed the criteria. We therefore undertook a short opinion-gathering survey of 16 software managers at NASA/GSFC.

Author DAP made the initial participant selection, based on his acquaintance with NASA/GSFC software maintenance managers. The participants themselves then suggested other maintenance managers to survey. Author RSA then administered the survey individually to each participant, giving each participant the above set of informal criteria, with blanks in place of the actual percentages. The participants were then requested to fill the blanks, if possible, based on their perceptions of "adequate maintenance." (Answers were never "forced" from participants.) Author RSA was present to answer questions, reduce misunderstandings, and record comments about the criteria.

The raw survey results are given in table 1-1.

Our goal here was to determine the extent that other NASA/GSFC software maintenance managers agreed or disagreed with the percentages in our criteria. The following analysis is based on the ten

```
----------------------------------------------------------------
                           Criteria

 person              C1          C2          C3          C4

 Arnold/     a.      85%         65%         80%         70%
 Parker (1)  b.      15%         35%         90%         80%

 Mgr A       a.      40          40          75          (2)
             b.      60          60          50          60

 Mgr B       a.      67          67          90          (2)
             b.      33          33          90-95       (2)

 Mgr D       a. 85 +-10      85 +-10         95          25
             b. 15 +-10      15 +-10         99          50

 Mgr E       a. 80           85-90           75          45-50
             b. 20           15-10           90          85

 Mgr F       a. 75 +-10      25 +-10       90 +-10     75 +-10
             b. 25 +-10      75 +-10       90 +-10     90 +-10

 Mgr G       a. 67             67            90          (2)
             b. 33             33            95          (2)

 Mgr J       a. 70             (3)           85          (3)
             b. 30             (3)           85          (3)

 Mgr K       a. 90 +-25      70 +-25      80 +-25      20 +-25
             b. 10 +-25      30 +-25      95 +-25   70-75 +-25

 Mgr L (4)   a. [30,70]      [80,5-10]       80          (3)
             b. [70,30]      [20,95-90]      95          90

 Mgrs M/N    a. 90            50             95          20
   (5)       b. 10            50             95          80

 Mgrs C,P       (6)

 Mgrs H,I,O  (7)
```

(1) From this paper.

(2) Gave another criterion instead.

(3) Could not relate to the criterion for his maintenance environment.

(4) Mgr L gave criteria which varied in the time they were to be applied. [c,b] means "c is applicable during the first 6 months of maintenance" and "b is applicable after the first 6 months of maintenance until system retirement."

(5) Two managers together answered the survey.

(6) Manage software maintenance at NASA/GSFC, but could not relate to the criteria for their environments.

(7) Not involved with managing software maintenance at NASA/GSFC; could not relate to criteria.

Table 1-1. Raw percentages obtained from opinion survey.

----

sets of criteria for which assessments were made.

Table 1-2 gives the number of exact agreements/disagreements between our criteria percentages and the participants' percentages. As can be seen, exact agreement was negligible.

Table 1-3 gives the number of relationship agreements/disagreements between our criteria percentages and the participants' percentages. A participant's percentages showed relationship agreement with our percentages if the relationship between his/her "a" and "b" criterion percentages was the same as on our percentages. For example, manager F had relationship agreement on criterion C1, since 75% > 25% (mgr F) preserves the relationship 85% > 15% (Arnold/Parker). Table 1-3 shows our criteria were usually preserved, though C3 showed weakest agreement. C4—especially C4a—was controversial.

Table 1-4 gives the ranges and averages of participants' criteria percentages. Where a range of values was given in answer to a criterion, the average of the range was used in figuring the overall average. Also, manager L's "later" period answers were used. From table 1-4 we conclude that the maintenance managers generally expected

-   more effort on e/r's than on fixes. (Column C1)

-   slightly lower occurrence of fixes than of e/r's. (Col. C2)

-   both e/r's and fixes to be completed, though fixes slightly more so than e/r's. (Col. C3)

-   fixes to be short more often than e/r's. (Col. C4)

Thus the averages tend to confirm the relationships in our criteria.

Finally, in table 1-5 we give the Arnold/Parker (A/P) and participants' average (avg) criteria percentages and their difference (A/P - avg). Since the largest absolute percentage difference is 12% or less for all criteria except C4a, we find our percentages reasonably supported by the managers' percentages. Criterion C4a might be revised, however.

1.3. Criteria Set Completeness and Inference

The concept, "adequate maintenance performance," is complex and fuzzy. It is unlikely we can define enough criteria to capture its full meaning. To describe the concept of "adequate maintenance performance" in a testable way, we therefore content ourselves above with defining a subset $S = \{C1, C2, C3, C4\}$ of an ideal set I of defining criteria. Satisfying each of the criteria in S is, in our view and for our environment, necessary for "adequate maintenance performance," but not sufficient in an ideal sense. (We say nothing about the necessary criteria in set I - S.) That is, if any criteria in S are not satisfied, then "adequate" or "satisfactory" maintenance performance is not achieved. However, if all criteria in S are satisfied, then "satisfactory" maintenance performance has been achieved, to the extent that we have described the concept. It is possible that other criteria from I - S (which is not totally known in practice) may not be satisfied.

The set S is not static, but evolving. Criteria may always be added, changed, or deleted, to conform to

-   new views of the concept, "adequate maintenance performance"

-   new or changed data or metrics

-   changed economic concerns of the software enterprise

-   changes in the maintenance environment

Even though our criteria only partially embody the ideal concept of "adequate maintenance performance," we nevertheless can usefully apply them to maintenance. Actually applying the criteria is straightforward: collect validated maintenance data, compute the actual values for metrics required by the criteria, and compare these values with the criteria. According to the results of the comparison, we make the following assertions concerning maintenance:

Under the above definitions and assumptions, in our software environment,

(1) if no criteria are satisfied, then maintenance performance is not adequate.

(2) if all criteria are satisfied, then maintenance performance is adequate (to the extent that our criteria sufficiently embody the concept "adequate maintenance performance").

(3) if some criteria are satisfied and other(s) not, then maintenance performance is not ade-

```
-----------------------------------------------------------------------
                          Criteria

           C1        C2      C3a      C3b      C4a      C4b

no. a/d    1/9       0/9     1/9      3/7      1/4      1/6


   Table 1-2. Exact agreement/disagreement (a/d) between participants'
              and Arnold/Parker's criteria percentages.

-----------------------------------------------------------------------
```

```
-----------------------------------------------------------------------
                          Criteria

           C1         C2              C3              C4

no. a/d    9*/1       7*/3            6/4             5/0
                                                      (also, 5 incomplete
                                                       in C4)

* based on later maintenance period in Mgr L's answers

   Table 1-3. Relationship agreement/disagreement (a/d) between
              participants' and Arnold/Parker's percentages.

-----------------------------------------------------------------------
```

```
-----------------------------------------------------------------------

                          Criteria

           C1           C2           C3           C4

        range avg    range avg    range avg    range avg

a.      [40,90] 73   [5,90] 55    [75,95] 86   [20,75] 38

b.      [60,10] 27   [95,10] 45   [50,95] 89   [50,90] 75


   Table 1-4. Ranges and averages on participants' answers.

-----------------------------------------------------------------------
```

```
-----------------------------------------------------------------------

                          Criteria

            C1            C2            C3            C4

         A/P   avg     A/P   avg    A/P   avg     A/P   avg

a.        85    73      65    55     80    86      70    38

difference  +12          +10          -6          +32

b.        15    27      35    45     90    89      80    75

difference  -12          -10          +1           +5

Table 1-5. Differences between Arnold/Parker's (A/P) and
           participants' average (avg.) criteria percentages.

-----------------------------------------------------------------------
```

quate to the degree that the criteria are not satisfied.

How assertion (3) is interpreted depends on how we weight not achieving a given criterion. If some criteria in S can be characterized as "more critical to satisfy" in a practical sense, we would prefer these "more critical" criteria be satisfied before the others.

This multi-dimensional judgment process can be formalized, for example, by determining a linear "figure of merit" [7]

$$J = \sum_{C(i)\ in\ S} [w(i) * D(C(i))]$$

where

SUM = summation

S = original set of independent criteria we have defined

= {C1,C2,C3a,C3b,C4a,C4b}

C(i) = criterion i in S

w(i) = a numerical weight associated with not achieving criterion C(i)

$$D(C(i)) = \begin{cases} 0, & \text{if } C(i) \text{ is met } * \\ 1, & \text{if } C(i) \text{ is not met } * \end{cases}$$

* Depends on actual metrics' values, as well as the criterion.

The lower the value of J, the less inadequately maintenance is being achieved. J = 0 corresponds to assertion (2), adequate maintenance. Here, the "more critical" criteria would have relatively higher weights. Measure J can be easily generalized by making the weights dynamic functions of time and other factors, such as manpower, computing resources, budget, deadlines, etc.

2. Applying the Criteria

Criteria application can occur any time during maintenance by utilizing the available maintenance data. It can therefore be used to continuously monitor the "health" of maintenance, as well as give a final project maintenance appraisal.

We now apply the criteria to the satellite telemetry projects' software maintenance data. The data we analyze is from 10 projects having sufficient

software maintenance change reports (60 or more) for statistical analysis. This data accounts for 83% of the data base. Some of these projects have already ended, but for our analysis we shall assume all are still alive.

The projects analyzed had the following general characteristics:

purpose -

scientific research and development; for satellite telemetry processing, or data collection and reduction.

production orientation -

goal was to perform assigned task; commercial profit-making or marketing of the software were not relevant

lifetime -

usually used one time (for one satellite), then archived in a library. Code for one project could be partly reused in another project.

run-time environment -

run on top of a standard vendor operating system

programming language -

written in assembly language and/or FORTRAN

Table 2-1 gives descriptions of the projects.

In table 2-2 we give the initial distribution of e/r's, fixes, and "other" change reports for maintenance data from the validated data base. The ordered pairs at table bottom give means and standard deviations, respectively, for the columns. All columns are self-explanatory except the "other" column. This column accounts for defective and/or non-software change reports such as changes for which we could find no archived change reports, changes we could not reliably classify, hardware changes, human operating procedure changes, and problems with faulty data. For comparison, we also give in table 2 an analogous change type distribution (means only) given by Lientz and others [13].

Comparing the distributions, we see the typical commercial maintenance environment studied in [13] has roughly twice as many enhancements, half as many fixes, and a sixth as many "other" changes. How managers arrived at their estimates in the Lientz study is not

---

project	description
A	a real time telemetry collection/editing/accounting system
B,D,E,G,H,I	real time and batch telemetry processing systems designed for particular spacecrafts
C	a hybrid operating system having a NASA-built part and a standard vendor operating system. "Project code" or "project documentation" for this project will refer to the NASA-built part.
F	a data capture system for recording, sorting, and transmitting data messages
J	a telemetry data accounting system

Table 2-1. Projects studied.

---

proj.	tot. rpts	fractions of total reports		
		e/r's	fixes	other
Proj A	618	0.33	0.29	0.37
Proj B	270	0.21	0.47	0.31
Proj C	170	0.44	0.28	0.29
Proj D	165	0.52	0.38	0.10
Proj E	164	0.48	0.41	0.10
Proj F	154	0.24	0.28	0.48
Proj G	117	0.49	0.45	0.06
Proj H	79	0.57	0.39	0.04
Proj I	65	0.25	0.29	0.46
Proj J	63	0.25	0.37	0.38
TOTAL	1865	(.38,.14)	(.36,.07)	(.26,.17)
Lientz and others (1978) [13]		.79	.17	.04

Table 2-2. Validated data base maintenance change report distribution.

---

clear, but even if we allow up to 20% error in their estimates, our comparison suggests the NASA/GSFC telemetry processing maintenance environment and Lientz commmercial-software maintenance environment are substantially different. This is further reason to expect our criteria will vary from environment to environment.

Although not shown in table 2-2, validation of our data base has been crucial in getting reliable data and results. In the original unvalidated data base, for example, the e/r, fixes, and "other" categories were 23%, 75%, and 2%, respectively. Validation revealed the e/r, fixes, and "other" categories to actually be 38%, 36%, and 26%, respectively. Because reliable maintenance data is difficult to get, researchers and managers may be tempted to perform criteria application on preliminary, unvalidated data. Our work suggests this is very risky.

Another validation result was that we estimate less than 2% of all change reports for the selected projects concerned correcting faulty changes (error regressions). The occurrence of faulty changes was relatively rare.

Criteria C1-C4 concern only software maintenance enhancements, restructurings, and fixes. The following analyses will therefore only consider this body of changes for the 10 selected projects. Changes in the "other" category will not be considered.

Table 2-3 compares statistics of the actual data with the criteria. The starred numbers indicate where the criteria were not met.

Based upon our criteria for "adequate maintenance," with table 2-3 we can appraise the overall state of maintenance for our environment: Criterion C1 not being satisfied implies too much effort is spent on fixes. (We could also say not enough effort is spent on e/r's, but we choose here to emphasize fixes.) Criterion C2 not being satisfied implies fixes are occurring too frequently. Criterion C3b not being satisfied for fixes implies fixes aren't being successfully completed enough. However, this may be a minor problem since fixes fail the criterion by only 4%. Criterion C3a being satisfied for e/r's implies the completion rate for e/r's is satisfactory. Finally, criterion C4 being satisfied implies the actually occurring changes are generally "easy" enough.

As indicated earlier in the definition of judgment function J, our ultimate maintenance appraisal is influenced by how heavily we weight not satisfying the individual criteria. We feel C1 and C2 are at least equally as important as C3 and C4, so let $w(i) = 1$, for all i, in J. Since from table 2-3, C1,C2, and C3b are not satisfied, and C3a, C4a, C4b are satisfied, we have

$$J = 1 \times 1 + 1 \times 1 + 1 \times 1$$
$$+ 1 \times 0 + 1 \times 0 + 1 \times 0$$
$$= 3$$

Since $J > 0$, we therefore assess the maintenance environment as needing improvement, especially in reducing the effort devoted to and the occurrence of fixes.

By itself, the table 2-3 data gives no clue to how individual projects contributed to C1 and C2 not being achieved. Often localizing potential sources of problems can trigger concrete hypotheses concerning specific maintenance problem causes. So in table 2-4 we have expanded rows C1 and C2 of table 2-3 into data for individual projects, and have added a column which gives candidate major reasons, from our experience with the projects' maintenance and development, why each project failed both criteria.

After considering the problems in table 2-4, we arrived at the following suggestions for improving maintenance (i.e., reducing fixes) project by project. The discussions are our perceptions based on experience with maintaining the projects and with the currently known software development and maintenance technology. Next to each project discussion is an ordered pair of percentages which give the difference between the actual fix values and the criteria values for C1b and C2b, respectively. These differences give a measure of the degree of achievement of the criteria. (The lower the percentages, the better.)

Project A (23%, 12%). This was a new system implementing new concepts, so extra development and maintenance problems might have been expected. Still, prototyping the system might have been useful in reducing bugs. Also, the system assumed an overly knowledgeable computer operator and defined a complicated operator/system interface, perhaps making later e/r's more frequent. To lessen interface problems, the operators should have been more involved at the design phase, and whenever interface changes were planned. An operator interface design/change review group might have been useful.

Project B (44%, 34%). This system had a very complicated operating system/application system interface, and a short development schedule. The complicated interface perhaps reflected uncertainty by designers and maintainers alike, leading to design changes and implementation errors. In retrospect, we feel the early delivery date should have been relaxed (if possible), more time spent in designing the interface, and more specific documentation written to help maintainers.

Project C (6%, 4%). This system performed complicated analog/digital conversion. The system (built 1964) had many changes before its maintenance began being recorded in our data base. The changes probably made the system harder to change. We feel the maintainers should have documented their changes more carefully and kept the system documentation up-to-date.

Project D (28%, 7%). This system required a change to a basic design assumption, apparent only after the spacecraft was in orbit. The resulting errors required the spacecraft/ground time correction algorithm be rewritten. We can handle the case of a basic assumption going bad in two ways: take special steps to ensure the assumption stays correct, and build flexibility into code for basic assumptions found by experience to be changeable.

Criteria	Actual		e/r	Crit. e/r	Actual Fixes	Crit. Fixes
	Enh	Rstr				
C1. Effort fraction(1)	.51	.05	.56*	>=.85	.44*	<=.15
C2. Frequency (2)	.45	.06	.51*	>=.65	.49*	<=.35
C3. Completion Rate	.89	.92	.89	>=.80	.86*	>=.90
C4. Fraction changes one person-week or less (3)	.78	.95	.80	>=.70	.85	>=.80

(1) Based on only those e/r's and fixes for which we could reliably assign an effort an effort of A,B,C,D, or E. These entries comprised 93% and 88% of the successfully completed software maintenance e/r's and fixes, respectively.

(2) "Actual" numbers in the row are normalized to exclude "other" category software changes.

(3) Based only on those changes for which we could reliably assign an effort of A,B,C,D, or E.

* Fails to meet corresponding criterion bounds

Table 2-3. Comparison of criteria with actual statistics over all projects.

Project E (45%, 11%). This system had complicated real time assembly language programs. The complexity was due to the task, but we feel assembly language made implementing the task harder. Recoding troublesome routines in a high level language might have helped, along with code reviews and better unit testing.

Project F (23%, 19%). Like project A, this system had another inadequately designed operator/system interface. The system proved too complicated to use and had to be changed as operators complained. Besides an operator interface design/change review group, design testing with a user/system interface simulator might have uncovered the interface flaws earlier.

Project G (31%, 13%). This system was a stopgap interim system to operate until a new system became available. As a result, the project G design was implemented quickly. This led to more errors later when the system's lifetime extended longer than expected. Under the necessary tight deadlines, we feel only proven people should have been used for system development, along with quickly creating a smaller, more robust system with less functionality.

Project H (13%, 6%). This system, like system C, performed complicated analog/digital signal conversion. Documentation on system H was inadequate, making change difficult. We feel the system documentation should have been carefully reviewed before releasing the system.

Project I (33%, 19%). System I contained a design oversight concerning the noisiness of the data: The data turned out to be noisier than expected, requiring changes to the system. A design review by people especially experienced in the application (if such people are available) might have caught the error. The suggestions for project D are also relevant here.

Project J (49%, 25%). The implementing team misunderstood the intentions for the system design. The system had to be changed as the design misunderstandings were uncovered. We feel the implementing team should have made their design more visible and should been more responsive to ensure the original design was sufficient.

If we rank these project suggestions by the sum of their percentage differences (add the ordered pairs of percentages given above), where a higher "urgency"

	Effort Dist.*		Frequency Dist.*		
crit.->	C1:(>=.85)	(<=.15)	C2:(>=.65)	(<=.35)	
proj.	Act. E/R	Act. Fixes	Act. E/R	Act. Fixes	Major Reasons for Failing the Criteria
Proj A	.62	.38	.53	.47	Inadequately designed operator/system interface
Proj B	.41	.59	.31	.69	Overly complicated, error-prone, system/ system interface
Proj C	.79	.21	.61	.39	Problems with analog/ digital (a/d) conversion
Proj D	.57	.43	.58	.42	Time correcting algo- rithm based on assumption which later proved incorrect
Proj E	.40	.60	.54	.46	Very complicated real- time assembly language software; much fine-tuning needed
Proj F	.62	.38	.46	.54	Inadequately designed operator/system interface
Proj G	.54	.46	.52	.48	A stopgap with a very short delivery time; less time for design and testing
Proj H	.72	.28	.59	.41	Inadequate initial documentation, plus assembly language, made change difficult
Proj I	.52	.48	.46	.54	Design bug in decoding telemetry signals
Proj J	.36	.64	.40	.60	Inadequate specifica- tions; inadequate communications with implementing team

* none of the criteria in these columns are satisfied

Table 2-4. Criteria C1, C2 applied to projects, with candidate major
    reasons why each project failed these criteria.

sum implies increased need to adopt the given suggestions (or a worse project maintenance performance), we can order the suggestions by decreasing urgency. This is done in table 2-5.

The table 2-5 information can be used in two ways to improve software mainte- nance. First, it indicates which projects have the worst and best maintenance per- formance. This helps in deciding on which projects to improve maintenance first. Second, table 2-5 indicates potential benefits for our suggestions. That is, we conjecture that following those sugges- tions with higher urgency scores will, for

our environment, potentially aid mainte- nance more than following those with lower scores. Stating this differently, not fol- lowing those suggestions with lower scores will be potentially less damaging than not following those with higher scores. (For this analysis we ignore possible outside factors--e.g., budget, deadlines, resources, or political situation--which can influence a suggestion's selection.)

Note that most of the table 2-5 suggestions concern improving software development. Thus a result of our criteria-based maintenance study is that improved development, more than improved

---

Project	Urgency	Suggestion
Proj B	78	Relax tight production deadlines; allow more time for development
Proj J	74	Ensure good understanding between implementing team and users
Proj E	56	If possible, avoid programming a complex task in assembly language; use a high level language instead
Proj I	52	Design review by experienced application personnel to inspect the design for oversights
Proj G	44	Use rapid prototyping and proven people when developing an interim stopgap system
Proj F	42	Allow users (operators) to actively take part in the design of a user/system interface; use a user/system interface simulator
Proj A	35	Create a user (operator) group to review a proposed user/system interface design/change
Proj D	35	Take special care to ensure basic design assumptions stay correct; build flexibility into code for assumptions which might change
Proj H	19	Carefully review system documentation before releasing the system
Proj C	10	Maintainers should design changes more carefully, and keep associated documentation up-to-date

Table 2-5. Maintenance improvement suggestions, in order of decreasing urgency. Dual interpretation: ranking of project maintenance performance from worst to best.

---

maintenance, will aid maintenance in our environment. From this conclusion our criteria have a dual purpose: as indirect development adequacy indicators as well as direct maintenance adequacy indicators.

We summarize here the major results of criteria application. First, we made an overall maintenance performance appraisal for our environment (not adequate; needs improvement), and indicated its general maintenance problems (fixes occur too often; too much effort expended on them). Next we found which projects contributed to these problems (all did). This stimulated suggestions for maintenance improvement, both during maintenance and during development. We then were able to rate project maintenance performance from worst to best, helping us decide which project's maintenance to improve first (Proj B). We also rated the potential effectiveness of our suggestions, allowing us to order the application of suggestions when improving maintenance for a new project. Finally, we noted from our suggestions that improving software development would likely most

help software maintenance for our environment.

3. Conclusion

3.1. A Simplified View of Criteria Application

As presented above, criteria application (CA) is a technique to improve maintenance performance. But CA also has an important more general purpose: to bridge the gap between software metrics on some software object and determining actions to improve the object. Figure 3-1 illustrates this gap.

Software metrics by themselves are informative, not interpretive. They describe certain properties of an object without providing means for using this information to improve the object. Calibrating the metric—interpreting the scale of a metric's values—is only a start towards the desired actions.

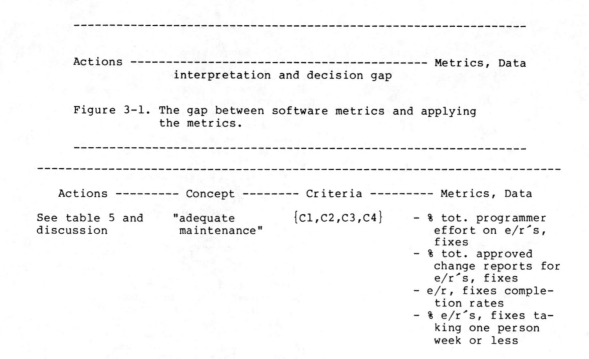

```
        --------------------------------------------------------------

   Actions ----------------------------------------- Metrics, Data
                    interpretation and decision gap


      Figure 3-1. The gap between software metrics and applying
                  the metrics.

            --------------------------------------------------------

--------------------------------------------------------------------------

     Actions --------- Concept -------- Criteria --------- Metrics, Data

   See table 5 and      "adequate       {C1,C2,C3,C4}    - % tot. programmer
   discussion            maintenance"                       effort on e/r´s,
                                                            fixes
                                                         - % tot. approved
                                                            change reports for
                                                            e/r´s, fixes
                                                         - e/r, fixes comple-
                                                            tion rates
                                                         - % e/r´s, fixes ta-
                                                            king one person
                                                            week or less
```

Figure 3-2. How CA fills the metrics-actions gap.

CA seeks to fill the metrics-actions gap, or at least break it into more tractable subparts. This is illustrated in figure 3-2.

Briefly, in CA a concept of concern ("adequate maintenance") is identified. A set of criteria is then designed which characterizes this concept. (Designing these criteria is often the hardest part of CA.) The criteria should contain metrics derivable from the available data. The criteria are then applied to metrics on the actual data. If all criteria are satisfied, no actions may be necessary to achieve the concept. If some are not satisfied, then actions are necessary to determine the problems responsible. If the problems are unique, tailored solutions must be found. If the problems are common, pre-planned solutions using the available maintenance technology may be applied.

3.2. Relation to Previous Work

McCall and Walters [16,19] did important earlier work in filling the metrics-actions gap (during software development). McCall described a "factors--criteria--metrics" hierarchy to relate software quality factors (e.g., correctness, reliability, maintainability, flexibility) with specific software metrics. McCall's "factors" correspond to our "concepts." However, McCall's "criteria" appear themselves to be refined factors, not testable conditions as in our work. McCall also mentioned the need for a judgment function (cf. J in section 1.3) to help rate a given factor. However, his judgment function was only a function of metrics' values, not of metrics' values and associated criteria values as in $D(C(i))$ of section 1.3.

Walters [19] clearly described the idea of applying desired "performance ratings" to overall judgment ratings obtained for a "factor" or "concept." In this paper, we have gone further by describing desired performance ratings (i.e., criteria) on specific software metrics' values, not just for the overall judgment metric. We then combine the quantitative results of these low level criteria comparisons to both (1) get an overall assessment of a concept's achievement and (2) stimulate and direct specific work to achieve the concept.

3.3. Future Applications and Work

With our simplified view of CA, we can apply CA whenever we have the problem of determining what to do next when given a software metric's values. This problem occurs, for example, in development monitoring and design methodology evaluation. In development monitoring we may be interested in "adequate productivity." We then create characterizing criteria and apply them periodically to assess the state of development productivity. In design methodology evaluation, we may be interested in "adequate design flexibility" and "adequate design reliability" for designs produced under different design methodologies. We then develop criteria for each of the concepts, apply the criteria on the designs produced using the methodologies, then conclude concerning the methodologies.

A further application of CA is in developing maintenance specifications, prior to software development. Previously-refined maintenance criteria may be used for specifying development quality, as determined during software maintenance. When the previously specified maintenance criteria are failed, and these failures are found to be development-originated, then the original developers (and not necessarily the current maintainers) may be responsible for necessary improvements.

CA for maintenance can be extended. In the future we will develop criteria for other maintenance concepts (e.g., maintenance stability) and examine when and how to change criteria.

Acknowledgements

The authors would like to acknowledge the contribution to this work of Dr. Raymond Yeh, who, had he not been on the executive committee of this conference, would have been listed as a coauthor. He asked his name be removed from the paper to avoid any conflict of interest. We also thank Warren Miller, for his technical assistance with the maintenance data base, the criteria survey participants, and Frank McGarry and the referees, for their valuable comments on earlier drafts of this paper.

References

1. Arnold, R.S. "A Metrics-Based Approach to Software Maintenance Monitoring." unpublished Ph.D dissertation proposal, Computer Science Department, University of Maryland, College Park, Md. 13 March 1981.

2. Arnold, R.S. On the Generation and Use of Quantitative Criteria for Assessing Software Maintenance Quality. (tentative title) Ph.D Dissertation, Computer Science Department, The University of Maryland, College Park, Md. To appear, Fall 1982.

3. Basili, V.R. Data collection, validation, and analysis. In Basili,V.R. (ed.), Tutorial on Models and Metrics for Software Management and Engineering. IEEE cat. no. EHO-167-7. IEEE, 1980.

4. Belady,L.A. and Lehman,M.M. A model of large program development. IBM Systems Journal, V.15, n.3, (1976). pp. 225-252.

5. Belady,L.A. and Lehman,M.M. Characteristics of large systems. In Wegner,P. (ed.) Research Directions in Software Technology. Cambridge, MA: MIT Press, 1979.

6. Boehm,B.W., Brown,J.R., Kaspar,H., Lipow,M., MacLeod,G.J., and Merritt,M.J. Characteristics of Software Quality. New York: North-Holland, 1978.

7. Boehm,B.W. Software Engineering Economics. Englewood Cliffs, NJ: Prentice-Hall, 1981.

8. Cooper, J.D. and Fisher, M.J. (eds.) Software Quality Management. New York: Petrocelli, 1978.

9. Hamlet, R. Program maintenance: a modest theory. Proc. 15th Hawaii Conf. on System Sciences. January, 1982.

10. General Accounting Office (GAO). "Federal Agencies' Maintenance of Computer Programs: Expensive and Undermanaged." Report AFMD-81-25. February 26, 1981.

11. Lehman,M.M. "Programs, Cities, Students - Limits to Growth?" Inaugural Lecture, 14 May 1974. Published in Imperial College (London, England) of Science and Technology Inaugural Lecture Series, V. 9, 1970-1974.

12. Lehman,M.M. Programs, life cycles, and laws of software evolution. Proc. of the IEEE, V. 68, n. 9, (Sept. 1980).

13. Lientz,B.P., Swanson, E.B., and Tompkins, G.E. Characteristics of application software maintenance. CACM, V. 21, n. 6 (June 1978).

14. Lientz,B.P. and Swanson,E.B. Software Maintenance Management. Reading, Mass.: Addison-Wesley 1980.

15. Lientz,B.P. and Swanson, E.B. Problems in application software maintenance. CACM, V. 24, n. 11 (Nov. 1981).

16. McCall, J.A. An introduction to software quality metrics. In [8].

17. Morrissey,J.H. and Wu,L.S.-Y. Software engineering... an economic perspective. Proc. 4th Int. Conf. on Software Engineering, Sept. 1979.

18. Swanson, E.B. The dimensions of maintenance. Proc. 2nd Int. Conf. on Software Engineering. Oct. 1976.

19. Walters, G.F. An application of metrics to a software quality management (QM) program. In [8].

20. Weiss, D.M. Evaluating Software Development By Analysis of Change Data. Ph.D dissertation. Computer Science Department, The University of Maryland, College Park, Md. November, 1981.

21. Yuen, C.K.S. Chong Hok. A Phenomenology of Program Maintenance and Evolution. Ph.D dissertation, Dep. Computing, Imperial College of Science and Technology, University of London, London, England. 1981.

Section 10.6: Human Factors of Software Design and Development

Mark Weiser
Ben Shneiderman

Computer Science Department
University of Maryland
College Park, MD 20742

Table of Contents

Human factors of software design and development is a subset of the science of "Software Psychology", the study of human performance in using computer and information systems. We focus in this paper on human factors issues of the *process* of software design and development, and do not discuss the human factors of the software product itself as seen by its end-users. Some aspects of human factors of the software product are covered instead in section 10.7 of this handbook. Other reviews of software psychology were done by Curtis [Curtis 84], Sheil [Sheil 81], Moher and Schneider [Moher & Schneider 81], and Shneiderman [Shneiderman 80].

The human factor is pervasive in software creation. Unlike cars which are stamped out in factories by the millions, software is individually hand-crafted. The cost of a software product is mostly related to the intellectual effort of researchers, designers, implementors, and maintainers, with very little manufacturing cost.

Of all the steps in creating software, the one called programming is the best understood. Other steps-specification, design, testing, debugging and maintenance, etc., are less well understood. This paper contains much information about the programming step, and less about the other steps. They are not less important, just less studied.

Applying human factors techniques to software development in large part means measuring what is happening. We do not have good grasp on all the relevant human factors which contribute to successful software development. Some of the factors which are known are described below, but there is no guarantee that these are more important than other factors which have not been studied. Also lacking are strong predictive or even explanatory theories, although there are useful fragments and promising attempts (see section 10.6.4 below).

All the steps of software creation require a high level of knowledge of the problem domain and computer-related concepts and a high level of skill in problem solving. Software creation is highly innovative and therefore unpredictable. Because of these factors there is extreme variability in individual performance. One person may take 10 or 20 weeks to accomplish what someone else does in one week [Curtis 81]. Because of this high variability, within subjects (repeated measures) experimental designs are preferred.

The impact of experience and knowledge is difficult to assess. Months of programming experience have not been shown to correlate well with performance measures. Stonger correlations occur with diversity of skills. (See section 10.6.6, below.)

10.6.1. Methodology

When analyzing the human factors of the programming process, the key problem is gathering reliable information about what the programmers are doing. Several methods are outlined below.

10.6.1.1. Introspection and Protocol Analysis

The simplest form of gathering information about the programming process is *introspection*, in which the experimenters or the subjects simply reflect on how they write, study, and debug programs or how they use the software product. Unfortunately, introspection is done differently by each individual, and the conclusions that one person reaches may not be shared by others. Folklore about the diverse idiosyncrasies of programmers should be enough to convince most people that introspection may not produce results which would be applicable to a wide range of users. On the other hand, introspection is the way that most new ideas are discovered—by an individual working alone in his or her office and thinking quietly. Introspective judgments based on experience in using, designing, and teaching systems play an essential role in generating novel ideas.

Introspection experiments might be conducted by asking a group of subjects to evaluate their use of indentation, commenting techniques, mnemonic variable names, flowcharts, modularity, or debugging tools. Such forced thinking may compel subjects to understand their usage patterns for long or short variable names, for subscripts or statement labels, and for module or system names. As soon as one person makes his or her style explicit, it becomes possible to verify the utility of that rule and teach it to others. If the rule is widely accepted, old-timers will claim that they have been following it implicitly for decades, but, without an explicit rule, discussion is uncommon and teaching difficult.

A variant of introspection is *protocol analysis* in which the experimenter or the subject keeps a written or taped record of his or her perceived thought processes. This permanent record or transcript can be reviewed at leisure and analyzed for frequency counts of certain words, first or last occurrence of a word or behavior, or clusters of behavioral patterns. Lewis [Lewis 82] discusses how to use this method, calling it "thinking aloud".

Standish [Standish 73] produced some interesting protocols of his work on a few popular problems, such as the eight queens problem, with summary observations and hypothesis. Brooks [Brooks 77] has performed extensive protocol analyses of program composition tasks using computer string processing facilities to help develop a model of the cognitive processes in program development. Adelson and Soloway [Adelson & Soloway 84] used protocol analysis to follow the design process with expert and novice programmers. Grantham and Shneiderman [Grantham & Shneiderman 84] used thinking aloud to study the cognitive processes in programming.

Introspection is worthwhile when the subject is a capable and sensitive programmer since important insights may be obtained. But, there is no guarantee that other programmers will behave in the same manner or even that the subject will repeat the same process tomorrow. Analyzing protocols for substantial numbers of individuals is difficult, time-consuming, and expensive.

Table 1. Introspective Methods

Video or audio tape recording.
Thinking aloud, with or without recording.
'Pencil movement' studies.
Keystroke recording.
Command recording.

10.6.1.2. Case Studies and Field Studies

Case or field studies involve careful study of programming practices or computer usage at one or more sites. This approach has been used to compare management techniques, programming languages, and error patterns and is effective in discovering how people actually use computer systems. Many researchers performing case or field studies collect voluminous amounts of data in the hope that "something interesting" will emerge. Worthwhile insights may be gained but the lack of experimental controls means that there is no guarantee that results are replicible or generalizable. The same study conducted at a different time, by a different researcher, or at a different site may not give the same results. In spite of these problems, case and field studies are popular since they provide worthwhile data to compare performance against and can reveal unexpected usage patterns.

Knuth's famous "Empirical Study of FORTRAN Programs" [Knuth 72] showed heavy use of the simplest forms of FORTRAN statements. Eight-six percent of the assignment statements involved no more than one arithmetic operator, 95 percent of DO loops used the default increment of 1, and 87 percent of the variables had no more than one subscript. Similar studies were done for PL/I [Elshoff 76a] and APL [Saal & Weiss 77]. These studies were conducted by capturing samples of programs from program libraries. A similar set of studies using programs submitted for execution during normal production focus on errors that programmers make during program development [Youngs 74] [Boies & Gould 74] [Gould 75] [Gannon 75]. Studies of terminal usage provide data about use of interactive systems [Boies 74] and programming productivity [Thadhani 84].

One of the most famous field studies was the IBM/New York Times Information Bank Project in which new programming technologies such as chief programmer team and structured coding were tested [Baker 72]. This study showed dramatic improvements in productivity with reduced error rates when the new techniques were used, but it has been criticized for lack of experimental controls and exaggerated reporting. The project's high visibility and the dedicated work of expert programmers may have been as important as the new techniques. A field study by IBM in England [Lambert 84] found improved productivity when a team had shorter response time and individual terminals. A recent study at the University of Maryland showed that programmers do quite well without running their programs at all [Selby & Basili 84].

Even if no initial hypothesis is advanced and no new technique is being "tested", data collecting case or field studies are useful in developing an image of actual computer usage and programmer performance. Often the statistical analysis, coupled with informal interviews of participants and experimenters, can suggest insights which are immediately useful or provide the basis for a controlled experiment.

10.6.1.3. Controlled Experimentation

Controlled experimentation is the fundamental paradigm of scientific research. By limiting the number of independent variables, controlling for external bias, carefully measuring dependent variables and performing statistical tests, it is possible to verify hypotheses within stated confidence levels. Controlled experimentation depends on a reductionist approach which limits the scope of the experiment, but yields a clear convincing result. Critics complain that controlled experimentation concentrates on minor issues, but supporters argue that each small result is like a tile in a mosaic: a small fragment with clearly discernible color and shape which contributes to the overall image of programming behavior. We summarize the shape of many of the software design and development tiles in this section.

10.6.1.4. Experimental Design

It is not our intent to include a summary of experimental design in this subsection. The interested reader can consult one of the many good textbooks on the subject [Kirk 68] [Runyon & Haber 84]. However, some aspects of experimental design for programming are specific to programming, in particular the choice of dependent and independent variables. The choice of dependent variables depends heavily upon what is being studied, and in fact this entire paper could be considered as a long treatment of dependent variables for programming studies.

Independent variables are less governed by the topic of study and more by issues of expediency and relevence. The table below summarizes the major types of independent variables that have been used in programming studies. Of these, error counts are the most realistic, but also the most difficult to perform. Timing measurements are easier to gather but slightly more suspect because they result from a blending of times for many different tasks. Both error rate and time have immediate on-the-job consequences.

Realistic performance tasks, such as modifying or simulating a program, are suitable for a controlled environment but are also close to tasks a professional programmer might actually perform. They thus form the most widely used group of dependent measures.

Slightly more removed from professional practice are the unrealistic performance tasks. These are easy to control and measure but don't obviously relate to any actually programmer activity. Memorization is probably the best measure here, since it has been shown to correlate with programming performance as well as performance in a number of other skilled tasks such as chess and physics.

Program product based measures are the most suspect for independent measures, in part because it is not clear what if anything these measures have to do with anything. A small object code size is important for a program on a limited memory computer, but it says nothing about that program's quality. Code metrics are even worse, so much so that they are themselves a primary dependent variable for a number of experiments (see section 10.6.5). Automatic measures of programs have great future potential but are not yet to be relied upon.

Table 2. Some Independent Variables for Programming Language Experiments

Type of Measurement (see text)	Specific Measure
error counts	compile-time errors run-time errors design errors number of runs
more realistic	comprehension tests program modification hand simulation
less realistic	memorization cloze quality judgement exam scores
times	time to debug time to program time to compile
code metrics	source code size object code size metrics (see section 10.6.5)

10.6.1.5. Experimental Ethics

Experiment designers should make every effort to protect the integrity of experimental subjects. Since programming experiments rarely place subjects at physical risk, the more serious problems of medical experimentation are avoided. Emotional threats such as heightened anxiety, increased fear of failure, or decreased confidence; and personal threats such as the misuse of experimental data or invasion of privacy must be carefully reviewed and minimized. Experimental results should not influence a student's course grade or a professional's career and participation should be voluntary. Subject names or other identifying information should not be collected, unless absolutely necessary. Anonymous forms protect the subjects from invasion of privacy and protect experimenters from accusations that privacy has been invaded. Subjects should be informed that they are participating in an experiment and give their informed consent.

In the following sections we review in brief experimental results in software design and development. Generally, only statistically significant results and results which form a pattern of failure to find significance are reported. While this means some well known studies are not represented, it permits the human factors practitioner to better rely on our tables. Many of the original papers referenced below have been collected by Curtis [Curtis 82].

10.6.2. Programming Style

Programming style describes non-algorithmic variations among programmers in the use of a programming language. Style affects comments, variable names, indenting, choice of modules, all of which have little or no bearing on the algorithm being computed, but which may have a very great bearing on how that program is understood by its current and future programmers. Of these four stylistic features 'choice of module' is the one least studied, perhaps because of the difficulty of studying the very large software projects for which modularity is predicted to make a difference. This is in area of high current interest however, and some studies in progress may soon remedy the lack of concrete results [Parnas 81].

10.6.2.1. Commenting

A comment in a program is a section of text which is ignored by the programming language. Comments may be just a few words or many pages (see Figure 1). They are usually in a natural language (e.g. English) but may include diagrams or pseudo-code. Commenting facilities exist in all programming languages, but there is controversy over their benefits and much discussion about the best kind of comments. Most introductory programming texts encourage students to comment (comments "serve a valuable documentary purpose," [Cress et al. 70]). But some critics claim that they obscure the code, interfere with debugging by misleading the programmer, and are dangerous if not updated when the program is changed. In an early book Weinberg wrote "the population of programmers seems hopelessly split on the desirability of using comments in programs. Some see them as a distraction which is likely to draw attention and energy from more fruitful documentation efforts. Others, equally skilled and conscientious, advocate the liberal use of comments, sometimes to the extent of explaining every statement in the program." [Weinberg 71] For further infor-

mation about commenting techniques see Handbook section 10.8.

The experimental results for comments are mixed, but it is low level comments which fare the worse. In practice comments will be more useful for large programs than for small, and even then are likely to be helpful only if applied to large segments of code (no smaller than a subroutine or module), and harmful otherwise.

Table 3. Comments.

Result	Reference
On a hand interpretation task, no comments were better than comments, and comments were better than incorrect comments.	Okimoto 70
On a hand interpretation task, comments aided speed of completion at the expense of errors.	Weissman 74
On recall and modification tasks, a single explanatory (high-level) comment per routine was better than many detailed (low-level) comments.	Shneiderman 77
Comments were of limited help for short programs.	Sheppard et al 79a

10.6.2.2. Variable Names

Except for length limitations, choice of variable name is usually unrestricted by any rules of a specific programming language. For the human reader, poorly chosen names can obscure or even disguise the meaning of a program. There is no excuse for names such as 'X' or 'I', when 'MAX' and 'NEXT' convey so much more, in a program whose useful life is more than a few days.

Meaningful mnemonic names can help the reader grasp the semantic structure and therefore aid comprehension and retention. As for comments, mnemonic names are more useful for larger, more difficult programs, but are of little importance for short programs.

A   X : = 1827 ;/* Comment: LVB RIP */

B   /*
       FACTOR finds the prime factors of NUM and returns them in array FACT.
       When FACTOR is called, N should contain the maximum length of FACT.
       On return, N is set to the number of factors found or 0 in case of error.
       */
       SUBROUTINE FACTOR (NUM , FACT , N)
       . . .

Figure 1. Examples of Comments. A is a short comment in poor style. B is a longer comment in better style.

Table 4. Variable Names.

Result	Reference
Programmers feel they understand programs using mnemonic names better, although comprehension tests don't bear them out.	Weissman 74
On a comprehension task, non-mnemonic names were better than mnemonic names when all names were defined.	Newsted 75
On a comprehension task, mnemonic names helped more on hard programs than on easy programs.	Newsted 75
Mnemonic variable names were of little help for short programs.	Sheppard et al 79a
On a comprehension task for uncommented programs, mnemonic names were better than nonmnemonic.	Shneiderman 80 p. 70

10.6.2.3. Indentation.

Blank space (or 'blanks') in a program text is usually not significant for the algorithm being computed, leaving the programmer free to use blanks for stylistic purpose. The horizontal positioning of lines of code is called *indentation*. (Vertical layout has received little attention, except for some weak results regarding the difficulty of reading program functions printed on more than one sheet of paper [Weissman 74]. This result has led to the widely used, but not strongly justified, rule-of-thumb limiting functions to no more than 60 lines of code-one printed page).

Indenting has often been advocated as a means of illustrating the control dependencies of a program. However there are as many experimental results against it as in favor of it. Indentation may be bad because it can interfere with rapid scanning up and down a listing, lead to additional line breaks, and emphasize the syntactic structure while clouding the high-level semantic structure (see figure 2).

```
A     if b > max
      then b : = max
      else if c > max
      then c : = max
      else a : = max

B     if b > max
      then b : =
      max
      else if c > max
      then c : =
      max
      else a : =
      max
```

Figure 2. Examples of Indenting. A is an unindented program. B is an indented program, showing the broken line (exaggerated) that can hinder program reading.

Indentation is sometimes called 'prettyprinting', and there are many different styles. Most prettyprinting articles have appeared in Sigplan Notices, the newsletter of the Special Interest Group on Programming Languages of the Association for Computing Machinery. No consensus has yet emerged on which styles are better.

Table 5. Indentation

Result	Reference
Indentation had no significant effect in a hand simulation task.	Weissman 74
In a hand simulation task, comments and indenting together are worse than either alone.	Weissman 74
Indentation had no significant effect in a modification task.	Shneiderman & McKay 76
Indentation had no significant effect in a comprehension task.	Love 77
Reconstruction of FORTRAN programs was not aided by indentation.	Norcio & Kerst 78
Filling in missing lines of a program was facilitated by the presence of indentation.	Norcio 82
Indenting, any style, can aid program comprehension. 2-4 spaces were better than 0 or 6 spaces.	Miara et al 83

10.6.3. Programming Language Features and Tools

10.6.3.1. Conditional Statements

Programming language features are what distinguishes one language from another. Of the many ways in which languages differ only a few have been studied, primarily those having to do with flow-of-control. A great many studies have compared 'structured' control features, such as WHILE-DO and IF-THEN-ELSE, with the once ubiquitous GOTO statement Apparently, the GOTO is to be avoided (but see the results of Smith and Dunsmore [Smith & Dunsmore 82]), and structured constructs are good.

Sime [Sime et al 77] and Embley [Embley 78] each studied a novel feature which no real programming language has yet incorporated but which proved better than the standard features. Apparently there is room for improvement in most programming languages.

Gannon's unique study [Gannon 77] demonstrates that typed languages (such as Pascal, Ada, Mesa, and Modula-2) are better than untyped languages (such as Lisp and FORTRAN) for at least some tasks. Most new languages designed since Gannon's paper have been typed, with the notable exception of Forth.

Table 6. Structured vs. Unstructured Constructs.

Result	Reference
On a program correctness measure, GOTO's after IF's were worse than IF-THEN-ELSE.	Sime et al 73
Students preferred using structured constructs.	Weissman 74
Programmers untrained in structured concepts take more computer runs to code with GOTO's.	Lucas & Kaplan 76
Avoiding GOTO's decreased programming time, compile time, and object code size.	
Structured FORTRAN programs were easier to remember than unstructured programs.	
On program memorization and modification tasks performed by professional programmers, structured FORTRAN code was better than unstructured.	
IF-THEN is better than GOTO for comprehension by novices of FORTRAN.	Smith & Dunsmore 82
GOTO is better than IF-THEN/WHILE-DO for comprehension by novices of FORTRAN.	
A study of BEGIN-END vs. IF-ENDIF styles of scope delimiters suggests that IF-ENDIF is better.	Sykes et al 83

Table 7. Other Control Constructs.

Result	Reference
On a comprehension task, FORTRAN arithmetic-IFs were harder for novice programmers than logical-IFs, but not for intermediate programmers.	Shneiderman 76
On a program correctness measure, IF-condition-THEN-ELSE-not-condition was better than normal IF-condition-THEN-ELSE.	Sime et al 77
On comprehension and self-evaluation measures, combined CASE and ITERATION construct did better than either IF-THEN-ELSE or CASE.	Embley 78

10.6.3.2. Flowcharts

The use of detailed and system flowcharts has been popular since the earliest days of programming. In recent years, critics have reflected the increasing anger that many programmers have when they are required to produce detailed flowcharts. Brooks [Brooks 75] called flowcharts "a curse." Ledgard and Chmura [Ledgard & Chmura 76], using more moderate language, argue that "program flowcharts can easily suppress much useful information in favor of highlighting sequential control flow, something which distracts the programmer from the important functional relationship in the overall design." Advocates of flowcharting, such as Marilyn Bohl in her 1971 book *Flowcharting Techniques*, claim that the flowchart is "an essential tool in problem solving".

If the flow charts are much longer than the program then they may be more difficult to study and distract attention. Compact higher level flowcharts can reveal relationships among program modules that are difficult to recognize from studying the code. For further information about flowcharts see Handbook section 10.8.

The practitioner should consider high-level language (PDL) descriptions of algorithms instead of flowcharts, and in any case low-level flowcharts should be avoided. Documentation of program algorithms should be supplemented by complementary documentation, such as descriptions of data structures.

Table 8. Flowcharts.

Result	Reference
Prose procedures are easier to remember than flowcharts.	Wright & Reid 73
Fewer errors were made following a flowchart than following a written (English) procedure.	Kammann 75 Wright & Reid 73
On a set of diverse tasks (composition, comprehension, debugging, and modification), flowcharts failed to be significantly useful.	Shneiderman et al 77
Flowcharts are useful for tracing program control flow, but do not help identify faults in the program.	Brooke & Duncan 80a Brooke & Duncan 80b
Data structure documentation was better than either flowchart or PDL documentation for program comprehension.	Shneiderman 82
Programmers wrote higher quality PDL (program design language) designs than flowchart designs.	Ramsey et al 83
PDLs were no better and no worse than flowcharts for comprehension or subsequent coding.	

Table 9. Types of Bugs in Student Programs

Percent bugs found in student programs [Moulton & Muller 67]								
Ok 31%	Execution 33%			Compile 36%				
	I/O 21%	Declaration 10%	Arithmetic 2%	Assignment 9%	Format 8%	Identifiers 5%	DO 3%	Other 11%

10.6.3.3. Debugging

Debugging is the process of finding and correcting errors in programs. Studies of debugging have looked at types of bugs, methods of debugging and programming language constructs which influence debugging.

The debugging results present no clear picture to the

Table 10. Types of Bugs in Professional Programs

Percent of runs with compilation bugs found in professional programs [Boies & Gould 74]	
PL/I	17%
FORTRAN	16%
Assembler	12%

Table 11. Debugging Results

Result	Reference
Experienced and novice programmers had error types in approximately the same percentage.	Youngs 74
Novices and professionals have the same number of bugs on their first run, but professionals eliminate bugs faster.	
Experienced programmers did not use an interactive debugging tool.	Gould 75
Telling programmers the line number of bug reduced median time from 6.5 to 3 minutes.	
Bugs in assignment statements were harder to identify than iteration or array bugs.	
Graduate student programmers using a statically-typed language made fewer errors than those using a typeless language.	Gannon 77
Programmers made more errors using a typeless language even if they had already solved the same problem in a statically typed language.	
When debugging, programmers focus on coherent program subsets called "slices".	Weiser 82

practitioner. It appears that debugging aids are not used, but that does not mean their use would not be beneficial. Perhaps the strongest results are those showing the influence of language features on bugs. To have the fewest errors use a strongly typed language without arrays.

10.6.4. Cognition in Program Design

What goes on in programmers' minds when they are programming? What makes the difference between an experienced programmer and a beginning programmer? Answering these questions is important to understanding human factors of programming, but work is just beginning. Some examples are the work of Weiser [Shertz & Weiser 81] and Soloway et al [Soloway et al 83b] [Soloway et al 83a] [Ehrlich & Soloway 84]. This research studies the "tacit plan knowledge" that programmers have of programs. Plan knowledge enables programmers to quickly make sense of programs they have never seen before by categorizing programs into a relatively few different types. This new area of research has great potential payoff in terms of educating new programmers, testing for programming knowledge, and developing better automatic aids to programming. (For instance, see Rogers [Rogers 84].)

10.6.4.1. Cognitive Models

Individual experiments can provide guidance on specific issues in programming language design, programming style, or design strategies, and at the same time contribute to the development of a theory of programmer behavior. Each experimental result is small but clear in its implications. Collections of experiments and replications of results will lead to deeper theories about programming.

Useful theories not only explain previous results, but also suggest predictions in novel situations. Unfortunately, there are few theories about how programmers do their work. Brooks [Brooks 77] attempted to model programmer behavior by designing a computer program. Anderson [Anderson 83] designed a computer program which modelled the learning process for LISP. Shneiderman and Mayer [Shneiderman & Mayer 79] proposed a cognitive model of programming knowledge and processes. We expand below on the Shneiderman and Mayer model (also called the 'syntactic/semantic model'), distinguishing two kinds of semantic knowledge.

A successful model of programmer behavior should help analyze performance during multiple stages of the programming process:

— design of a new program
— composition of a program based on an explicit design
— comprehension of a program
— debugging of a given program
— modification of a given program to accommodate new demands
— earning new programming techniques
— novice learning of programming.

A successful model should describe both the knowledge structures and the cognitive processes that people use. Knowledge structures are stored in human long-term memory that can be studied by asking subjects to describe their knowledge, by observing programmers doing work, or by arranging specific tasks which reveal the knowledge structure. Cognitive processes involve short-term memory as people study programs and also working memory when they problem-solve to design, compose, debug, or modify programs. Long-term knowledge influences the way inputs from perception are organized and facilitates problem-solving in working memory (Figure 3).

10.6.4.2. Knowledge Structures in Long-term Memory

In the syntactic/semantic model, long-term knowledge is of three types:

- Semantic knowledge of application domain: This is the programmer's knowledge of payroll practices, orbital mechanics, liver disease treatment, or chess strategies. It may take a lifetime to acquire this knowledge and it is independent of the computer implementation.

Semantic knowledge of the application domain is level structured (Figure 4). In chess there are low-level details about how each chess piece moves, middle-level plans about developing an attack or defense, and high-level strategies about controlling the center of the board or pursuing the end-game. Novices learn the low-level details and then spend a life-time acquiring more and more experience with patterns of attack or strategies for dominating play. A similar decomposition could be made about orbital mechanics or other application domains. Hierarchical and level structured patterns are a vital approach for the human organization of complex knowledge. Experts have a clear sense of when they are pursuing details and when they are debating high-level plans; novices sometimes pursue details and forget high-level plans.

- Semantic knowledge of programming concepts: This is the programmer's knowledge of programming practices, algorithms, file structures, data structures, programming language features, operating systems, text editors, or disk libraries. This knowledge may also take a long time to acquire and it is independent of the application domain of a particular program.

Semantic knowledge is also language independent, that

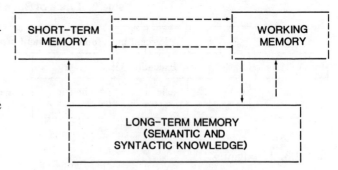

Figure 3. Components of memory in problem solving.

is, a programming concept such as finding the largest element of an array may be learned in one programming language but the concept is easily applied in another programming language.

Semantic knowledge is acquired through "meaningful learning" which connects the concept to the programmer's large base of knowledge. Analogies, specific examples, or general theories can be used to convey semantic knowledge. Once acquired, semantic knowledge is relatively stable in long-term memory.

Semantic knowledge of programming concepts is level-structured, ranging from low-level semantic items to high-level concepts. Low-level items may be the effect of an assignment statement, a conditional, or a multiplication operator. These items are clustered into knowledge about patterns of use, such as three assignment statements to form a swap operation, or nested conditionals, or arithmetic expressions. These mid-level patterns are woven together to form higher level program plans or templates such as performing a sort, implementing a decision table, or carrying out numerical integration.

- Syntactic knowledge: These are the details about how to express a semantic knowledge concept in a programming language. The syntax of similar concepts may be very different across different programming languages. The strings of characters are often arbitrary and therefore difficult to maintain in memory without frequent rehearsal. For example, SQR is the square root function in BASIC, but it squares a number in PASCAL, and SQRT is the square root function in FORTRAN. WRITE, PUT, PRINT, and OUTPUT are the keywords for printing a string or variables in different programming languages. Special characters, such as the assignment operator, may vary from an equals sign, to a colon and an equals sign, to a back arrow. Syntax for looping strategies also varies widely across programming languages.

Syntactic knowledge is language dependent, is arbitrary, must be rote memorized, and is subject to forgetting unless frequently rehearsed. Programmers who stay away from a programming language for a few months may have difficulty recalling the syntax for composing programs, but when they read a program the syntax provides the cues for the semantics of the language. By imitating the syntax of a given program the programmer's memory is refreshed.

The boundaries between semantic knowledge of the application domain, semantic knowledge of computer programming concepts, and syntactic knowledge are not always as sharp as in Figure 4, but this separation can be useful. The syntactic/semantic model suggests that when teaching programming, novices can be best motivated by examples from the application domain, that the algorithms should then be described with computer programming concepts, and that the syntactic details should be presented last. By using examples from familiar application domains, the students can more quickly associate the programming concepts, than if nonsense programs are used as examples.

For programmers who are learning a new programming language, there is no need to teach the computer concepts again, assuming that the languages have similar semantic structures. A simple translation of the syntax is all that is necessary to show the linkage between the known and the novel language. Of course, where there are semantic differences extra care must be taken to highlight these differences.

For programmers learning a new application domain, there may be a substantial investment necessary before they become productive. Expert programmers recognize that they are novices in new application domains and take the time to learn the low-level details and the high-level goals before beginning to write programs.

10.6.4.3. Cognitive Processes in the Syntactic/Semantic Model

Comprehending a given program is a major intellectual effort which requires all three types of long-term knowledge. First, the programmer must recognize the syntax and separate the comments from the program, isolate the names of procedures and variables, and discriminate among statement types. Then the low-level semantic structure of the program is organized by recognizing the function of individual statements, module boundaries in the code, and distinctions between procedural and declarative information. Next higher level computer programming concepts are spotted such as initializations of arrays, familiar algorithms, output formats, and error conditions. Finally, the reader of a program grasps the relationship between a line of code and some intention in the application domain: finding the shortest route for a milk delivery truck, computing the payroll, or determining the preferred dosage for a patient.

Again, this model is an idealization of reality. Sometimes knowledge of the application domain will guide the insecure programmer in searching for the line of code which determines whether the delivery route is optimal. A person who is knowledgeable in an application domain might learn something about programming by studying programs in his/her domain. Similarly, programmers can learn about an application domain by reading relevant programs. Programs are a means of communication and education.

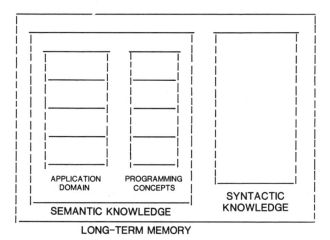

Figure 4. Long-term knowledge in the syntactic/semantic model.

In summary, readers of programs rapidly associate syntactic details with low-level semantics, organize this knowledge into higher level units and further convert this knowledge into compact language independent concepts in the application domain. After reading a three hundred line program, a knowledgeable programmer can convey its contents briefly, e.g., "This program does Dijkstra's spanning tree algorithm for the Northeastern pipeline system." Another programmer, familiar with the application domain and the programming concepts, could take this brief description and reconstruct a semantically equivalent program.

The capacity of expert programmers to encode a program into some internal semantic structure was demonstrated in a program memorization and reconstruction task [Shneiderman 80]. After two minutes of study, expert programmers were able to reconstruct the 20-line program successfully, although they made orderly syntactic errors. They would replace the FORTRAN statement numbers consistently, alter variable names consistently, or change the order of execution when it did not effect the semantics of the program.

The presence of a language independent representation of programs was demonstrated in a recent informal experiment. Advanced undergraduates were given a 22-line Pascal program to study for two minutes. Then half the students were asked to reconstruct the program from memory. The other half of the students were asked to rewrite the program in any other programming language in which they were fluent. Both groups succeeded in reconstructing the program successfully. Participants could easily describe the program's semantics without using the syntax or keywords of any programming language.

This informal experiment and others contribute to the clarification of this model, but much work remains to be done to formulate a predictive model.

During program composition expert programmers begin with the problem domain and can construct a top-down, level-structured design for the program. They can then iteratively refine the programming concepts and finally produce the syntactic details for a specific language. Novices tend to emphasize syntactic details and have erratic patterns of moving from problem domain to programming concepts and from high-level to low-level details [Adelson & Soloway 84].

10.6.5. Software Quality Evaluation

Software quality measurement is an infant discipline. As this speciality matures, the ability to measure will develop, but in its youthful phase, there are conflicting opinions as to what and how software characteristics should be measured. With time, reliable and useful standard measuring concepts will emerge.

Boehm, Brown and Lipow [1977] identify key issues such as the definition of criteria for software quality which are measurable, nonoverlapping, and evaluated automatically. They conclude that an automated tool for software quality evaluation should not merely produce a variety of metrics but should identify where and how a product is deficient. This is an ambitious goal since we do not even agree on which metrics are useful or on satisfactory values for metrics. The simple quantitative formulas for quality have counterexamples in which programs having high ratings are of low quality. Software design methodology is evolving so rapidly that it is difficult to establish useful metrics and to "write metrics in stone" could reinforce practices which might later prove to be undesirable.

Through the years a great many metrics have been proposed. (Harrison [Harrison 84] offers a guide to further reading.) Most metrics we report on below have been subjected to experimental verification.

10.6.5.1. "Software Science" Metrics

The software science metrics [Halstead 77] are defined below. The efficacy of the software science metrics are in dispute: some relevant papers are Gordon & Halstead 76, Fitzsimmons & Love 78, Elshoff 76b, Elshoff 78, Curtis 80, Love & Bowman 76. A recent critical review is by Shen [Shen et al 83].

Table 12. Some Software Science Equations.

n_1 = number of unique operands.
n_2 = number of unique operators.
n = vocabulary = $n_1 + n_2$.
N_1 = total number of operands.
N_2 = total number of operators.
N = implementation length = $N + N_2$.
n_1^* = minimum number of unique operands.
n_2^* = minimum number of unique operators.
Volume: $V = N \log_2 n$.
Potential Volume: $V^* = (2 + n_2^*)(\log_2(2 + n_2^*))$.
Program Level: $L = V^*/V$.
Programing Effort: $E = V/L$.

It appears that simply counting lines of code is as good as computing complicated metrics for predicting programmer effort and number of errors.

10.6.5.2. Productivity Metrics

Measuring productivity in programming is an extremely elusive goal because of the difficulties of measuring program quality. Most productivity results below use a measure such as lines-of-code per programmer per month, and ignore the difference between low quality and high quality lines of code. it is even unknown whether high quality and lines-of-code rate are related. Section 10.6.6 has more suggestions and results for managing and measuring quality.

Perhaps the most important productive result is Weinberg and Schulman's, which states that programmers will be productive on whatever dimension they are told is important. Careful instructions to programmers are essential.

Table 13. Some Productivity Results

Results	Reference
Programming teams, when given different objectives (minimum core, output clarity, program clarity, minimum source statements, minimum hours), beat all other teams on their selected objective.	Weinberg & Schulman 74
$R = L/(ST)$ where: R is lines of souce code per person-month, L is lines of code in finished product, S is staffing level, T is scheduled calendar time in months.	Zak 77
A least squares to fit to productivity data on 60 projects produced the equation: Person-months = 5.2* thousands-of-delivered-source-lines.	Walston & Felix 77
Productivity is highest when source code is NOT reused.	Walston & Felix 77
Productivity decreases when development is spread over more than one location.	Walston & Felix 77
Programmer productivity can be predicted by 9 program characteristics and 5 programmer characteristics.	Chrysler 78
Disciplined programming teams worked faster with fewer errors than undisciplined teams or individuals.	Basili & Reiter 79
For student programmers, a log-normal random variable provides a good model of cpu and number-of-runs resource measures during programming.	McNicholl & Magel 84

10.6.5.3. Complexity Metrics

Program complexity can be logical, structural or psychological. Logical complexity involves program characteristics which make proofs of correctness difficult, long, or not possible. For example, an increase in the complexity of expressing a program's function in first order logic will increase its logical complexity. Structural complexity is determined by the organization of the program, such as the number of distinct program paths. Psychological complexity (better called "comprehensibility") refers to characteristics which make it difficult for humans to understand software. Psychological complexity can be influenced by both logical and structural complexity, and also by other things such as quality of commenting or external documentation.

Structural complexity is the easiest to measure but the least interesting by itself. Therefore most studies attempt to relate structural complexity metrics (usually just called 'program metrics') to some other measure of psychological complexity such as time to debug or time to understand.

The most comprehensive empirical study of program metrics was done by Basili and Reiter [Basili & Reiter 79], who compared more than 100 metrics across different programming methods. Sheppard, Bort, and Love [Sheppard et al 78] showed program comprehension was correlated with program length, McCabe's metric [McCabe 76], and program structuring, but not with Halstead's effort metric E. Dunsmore and Gannon [Dunsmore & Gannon 79] showed that metrics based on number of data references and number of live variables could predict programming and maintenance effort.

10.6.6. Programming Management

The first two decades of programming history produced the image of the introverted, isolated programmer surrounded by stacks of output. Fortunately this image is becoming only a wild caricature of reality. The lonely days of the programming frontier are giving way to community, interdependency and stability.

Personality studies of programmers [Couger & Zawacki 78] still show their social need for interaction is significantly lower than for many other professionals. Some other important results for managing programmers are summarized below.

10.6.7. Conclusion

Researchers in software design and development have a golden opportunity to improve programmer's productivity and quality, as well as to gain fundamental insights into human cognition. We see opportunities to refine contemporary programming languages, coding style guidelines, design strategies, quality and productivity measures, management techniques, and software tools. Human factors are crucial to better software design and development, and objective experimentation and measurement are crucial to better human factors.

Table 14. Some Results for Management

Results	Reference
Professional programmers vary in performance by 20:1 or more.	Sackman et al 68 Curtis 81
"Egoless programming" is a state of mind in which programmers separate themselves from their products, thus aiding team effort.	Weinberg 71
"Chief programmer teams" surround a superior programmer with many assistants, but crucial coding is carried out by the chief programmer.	Baker 72
Program inspections can save one programming month per 1000 noncomment source statements.	Fagan 74
Programmers rating other programmers tend to agree among themselves on program quality.	Anderson & Shneiderman 77
Three person teams doing debugging were only modestly more effective than individuals, but consumed much more time.	Myers 78
Student programmers required to meet with colleagues during class time and make written critiques of each others work did better on the final exam than students who had no group debugging experience.	Lemos 79
For less experienced programmer, diversity of experience counts for more than number of years experience.	Sheppard et al 79a
Type of programming task can determine the proper choice among Chief Programmer or Egoless programming methods.	Mantei 81

REFERENCES

[Adelson & Soloway 84] Adelson, Beth and Soloway, Elliot. Designing software: novice/expert differences. *Proceedings of the First USA/Japan on Human/Computer Interfaces*, 1984.

[Anderson 83] Anderson, John R. learning to Program. *Proceedings of the 8th International Conference on Artificial Intelligence*, pp. 57-62, August 1983.

[Anderson & Shneiderman 77] Anderson, N. and Shneiderman, B. Use of peer ratings in evaluating computer program quality. *Proceedings of the 15th Annual Conference of the ACM Special Interest Group on Computer Personnel Research*, 1977.

[Baker 72]   Baker, F.T. System quality through structured programming. *Proceedings of the Fall Joint Computer Conference*, Montvale, New Jersey, pp. 339-343, AFIPS Press, 1972.

[Basili & Reiter 79]   Basili, V.R. and Reiter, R.W. An Investigation of human factors in software development. *Computer* 12, 12, pp. 21-38, December 1979.

[Boehm et al 77]   Boehm, B.W., Brown, J.R., and Lipow, M. Quantative evaluation of software quality. *Software Phenomenology Working Papers of the Software Lifecycle Management Workshop*, pp. 81-94, August 1977.

[Bohl 71]   Bohl, M. *Flowcharting Techniques*. Science Research Associates, Chicago, 1971.

[Boies & Gould 74]   Boies, S.J. and Gould, J.D. Syntactic errors in computer programming. *Human Factors* 16, pp. 253-257, 1974.

[Boies 74]   Boies, S.J. User behavior on an interactive computer system. *IBM Systems Journal* 13, 1, pp. 1-18, 1974.

[Brooke & Duncan 80a]   Brooke, J.B. and Duncan, K. D. Experimental studies of flowchart use at different stages of program debugging. *Ergonomics* 23, 11, pp. 1057-1091, 1980.

[Brooke & Duncan 80b]   Brooke, J.B. and Duncan, K. D. An experimental study of flowcharts as an aid to identification of procedural faults. *Ergonomics* 23, 4, pp. 387-399, 1980.

[Brooks 75]   Brooks, Frederick P. Jr. *The Mythical Man-Month*. Addison-Wesley, 1975.

[Brooks 77]   Brooks, R. Towards a theory of the cognitive processes in computer programming. *International Journal of Man-Machine Studies* 9, pp. 737-751, 1977.

[Chrysler 78]   Chrysler, Earl. Some basic determinants of computer programming productivity. *Communications of the ACM* 21, 6, pp. 472-483, June 1978.

[Couger & Zawacki 78]   Couger, J.D. and Zawacki, R. A. What motivates DP professionals. *Datamation* 24, 9, pp. 116-123, September 1978.

[Cress et al. 70]   Cress, P., Dirksen, P., and Graham, J.W. *FORTRAN IV with WATFOR and WATFIV*. Prentice-Hall, Inc., Englewood Cliffs, New Jersey, 1970.

[Curtis 82]   Curtis, Bill. *Human Factors in Software Development*. IEEE Computer Society, Washington, D.C., 1981. (Revised 1986)

[Curtis 80]   Curtis, Bill. Measurement and experimentation in software engineering. *Proceedings of the IEEE* 68, 9, pp. 1144-1157, September 1980.

[Curtis 81]   Curtis, Bill. Substantiating programmer variability. *Proceedings of the IEEE* 69, 7, p. 533, July 1981.

[Curtis 84]   Curtis, Bill. Fifteen years of psychology in software engineering: individual differences and cognitive science. *Proceedings of the 7th International Conference on Software Engineering*, Orlando, Florida, pp. 97-106, April, 1984.

[Dunsmore & Gannon 79]   Dunsmore, H. E. and Gannon, J.D. Data referencing: an empirical investigation. *IEEE Computer* 12, pp. 50-59, December 1979.

[Ehrlich & Soloway 84]   Ehrlich, Kate and Soloway, Elliot. An Empirical Investigation of the Tacit Plan Knowledge in Programming. pp. 113-134 in *Human Factors in Computer Systems*, ed. Michael L. Schneider, Ablex Publishing, Norwood, New Jersey 07648, 1984.

[Elshoff 76a]   Elshoff, James L. An analysis of some commercial PL/1 programs. *IEEE Transactions on Software Engineering* SE-2, pp. 113-121, 1976.

[Elshoff 76b]   Elshoff, James L. Measuring commercial PL/I programs using Halstead's criteria. *ACM SIGPLAN Notices* 7, 5, pp. 38-46, May 1976.

[Elshoff 78]   Elshoff, James L. An investigation into the effects of the counting method used on software science measurements. *ACM SIGPLAN Notices* 13, 2, pp. 30-45, February 1978.

[Embley 78]   Embley, D.W. Empirical and formal language design applied to a unified control structure. *International Journal of Man-Machine Studies* 10, pp. 197-216, 1978.

[Fagan 74]   Fagan, M. Design and code inspections, and process control in the development of programs. IBM Technical Report 21.572, December 1974.

[Fitzsimmons & Love 78]   Fitzsimmons, Ann and Love, Tom. A review and evaluation of software metrics. *Computing Surveys* 10, 1, pp. 3-18, March 1978.

[Gannon 75]   Gannon, John D. *Language Design to Enhance Programming Reliability*. University of Toronto, January 1975. Ph.D. Thesis

[Gannon 77]   Gannon, John D. An experimental evaluation of data type conventions. *Communications of the ACM* 20, 8, pp. 584-595, August 1977.

[Gordon & Halstead 76]   Gordon, R.D. and Halstead, M. H. An experiment comparing FORTRAN programming times with the software physics hypothesis. *Proceedings of the National Computer Conference* 45, Montvale, New Jersey, pp. 935-937, AFIPS Press, 1976.

[Gould 75]   Gould, J.D. Some psychological evidence on how people debug computer programs. *International J. of Man-Machine Studies* 7, pp. 151-182, 1975.

[Grantham & Shneiderman 84]   Grantham, Charles and Shneiderman, Ben. Programmer Behavior and Cognitive Activity: An Observational Study. *Proceedings ACM*

Washington DC Chapter Annual Technical Symposium, June 1984.

[Halstead 77]   Halstead, M. *Elements of Software Science*. Elsevier Computer Science Library, 1977.

[Harrison 84]   Harrison, W. Softare complexity metrics: a bibliography and category index. *ACM SIGPLAN Notices* **19**, 2, pp. 17-27, February 1984.

[Selby & Basili 84]   Jr., R.W. Selby and Basili, V.R. CLEANROOM Software Development: An Empirical Evaluation. Tech. Rep. TR-1415,, Dept. Com. Sci., Univ. Maryland, College Park, MD, July 1984. submitted to the *Communications of the ACM*.

[Kammann 75]   Kammann, R. The comprehensibility of printed instructions and flowchart alternative. *Human Factors* **17**, pp. 183-191, 1975.

[Kirk 68]   Kirk, R.E. *Experimental Design: Procedures for the Behavioral Sciences*. Brooks-Cole, Monterey, CA, 1968.

[Knuth 72]   Knuth, D.E. An empirical study of FORTRAN programs. *Software-Practice and Experience* 1, pp. 105-133, 1972.

[Lambert 84]   Lambert, G.N. A comparative study of system response time on program developer productivity. *IBM Systems Journal* **23**, 1, pp. 36-43, 1984.

[Ledgard & Chmura 76]   Ledgard, H. and Chmura, L. *COBOL with Style*. Hayden, Rochelle Park, New Jersey, 1976.

[Lemos 79]   Lemos, Ronald S. An implementation of structured walk-throughs in teaching COBOL programming. *Communications of the ACM* **22**, 6, pp. 335-340, June 1979.

[Lewis 82]   Lewis, Clayton. Using the "Thinkingaloud" Method in Cognitive Interface Design. RC 9265, IBM Yorktown Heights, February 1982.

[Love & Bowman 76]   Love, Tom and Bowman, Ann B. An independent test of the theory of software physics. *ACM SIGPLAN Notices* **7**, 10, pp. 42-49, November 1976.

[Love 77]   Love, Tom. Relating individual differences in computer programming performance to human information processing abilities. Ph.D. Dissertation, University of Washington, 1977.

[Lucas & Kaplan 76]   Lucas, H.C. and Kaplan, R.B. A structured programming experiment. *The Computer Journal* **19**, 2, pp. 136-138, 1976.

[Mantei 81]   Mantei, Marilyn. The effect of programming team structures on programming tasks. *Communications of the ACM* **24**, 3, pp. 106-113, March 1981.

[McCabe 76]   McCabe, T.J. A complexity measure. *IEEE Transactions on Software Engineering* **SE-2**, 4, pp. 308-320, December 1976.

[McNicholl & Magel 84]   McNicholl, Daniel G. and Magel, Kenneth. Stochastic modeling of individual resource consumption during the programming phase of software development. pp. 79-112 in *Human Factors in Computer Systems*, ed. Michael L. Schneider, Ablex Publishing, Norwood, New Jersey 07648, 1984.

[Miara et al 83]   Miara, Richard J., Musselman, Joyce A., Navarro, Juan A., and Shneiderman, Ben. Program Indentation and Comprehensibility. *Communications of the ACM* **26**, 11, pp. 861-867, November 1983.

[Moher & Schneider 81]   Moher, T. and Schneider, G. M. Methods for improving controlled experimentation in software engineering. *Proceedings of the Fifth International Conference on Software Engineering*, pp. 224-233, 1981.

[Moulton & Muller 67]   Moulton, P.G. and Muller, M. E. DITRAN-a compiler emphasizing diagnostics. *Communications of the ACM* **10**, pp. 45-52, 1967.

[Myers 78]   Myers, G.J. A controlled experiment in program testing and code walkthroughs/inspections. *Communications of the ACM* **21**, 9, pp. 760-768, September 1978.

[Newsted 75]   Newsted, P.R. Grade and ability prediction in an introductory programming course. *ACM SIGCSE Bulletin* **7**, 2, pp. 87-91, June 1975.

[Norcio & Kerst 78]   Norcio, A.F. and Kerst, S.M. *Human memory organization for computer programs*. Catholic University of America, Washington, D.C., 1978. unpublished ms.

[Norcio 82]   Norcio, A.F. Indentation, documentation and programmer comprehension. *Proceedings of Human Factors in Computer Systems*, pp. 118-120, ACM Washing, DC Chapter, 1982.

[Okimoto 70]   Okimoto, G.H. The effectiveness of comments: A pilot study. IBM SDD Technical Report TR 01.1347, July 27, 1970.

[Parnas 81]   Parnas, Kathryn Heninger Britton, R. Alan Parker, David L. A Procedure for Designing Abstract Interfaces for Device Interface Modules. *Proceedings of the Fifth International Conference on Software Engineering*, pp. 195-204, IEEE, 1981.

[Ramsey et al 83]   Ramsey, H. Rudy, Atwood, Michael E., and Van Doren, James R. Flowcharts versus program design languages: an experimental comparison. *Communications of the ACM* **26**, 6, pp. 445-449, June 1983.

[Rogers 84]   Rogers, Jean B.. Inferring cognitive focus from students' programs. *Proceedings of the Computer Science Education Conference*, 1984.

[Runyon & Haber 84]   Runyon, Richard P. and Haber, Audrey. Fundamentals of *Behavioral Statistics, Fifth Edition*. Addison-Wesley Publishing Co., Reading, MA, 1984.

[Saal & Weiss 77]   Saal, H.J. and Weiss, Z. An empirical study of APL programs. *Computer Langauges* **2**, 3, pp. 47-60, 1977.

[Sackman et al 68]   Sackman, H., Erickson, W.J., and Grant, E.E. Exploratory experimental studies comparing online and offline programming performance. *Communications of the ACM* **11**, 1, pp. 3-11, January 1968.

[Sheil 81]   Sheil, B.A. The psychological study of programming. *Computing Surveys* **13**, pp. 101120, March 1981.

[Shen et al 83]   Shen, V.Y., Conte, S.D., and Dunsmore, H.E. Software Science Revisited: A Critical Analysis of the Theory and Its Empirical Support. *IEEE Transactions on Software Engineering* **SE-9**, 2, pp. 155-165, March 1983.

[Sheppard et al 78]   Sheppard, S.B., Borst, M.A., and Love, L.T. Predicting software comprehensibility. Technical report TR 77-388100-1, General Electric Information Systems Programs, Arlington, Va, February 1978.

[Sheppard et al 79a]   Sheppard, Sylvia B., Curtis, Bill, Milliman, Phil, and Love, Tom. Modern coding practices and programmer performance. *IEEE Computer*, pp. 41-49, December 1979.

[Sheppard et al 79b]   Sheppard, Sylvia B., Milliman, Phil, and Curtis, Bill. *Experimental Evaluation of On-Line Program Construction*. General Electric Information Systems Programs, Arlington Va., December 1979. TR-&(-388100-6

[Shertz & Weiser 81]   Shertz, Joan and Weiser, Mark. Programming problem representation in novice and expert programmers. *International Journal of Man-Machine Studies*, Dec 1983.

[Shneiderman 82]   Shneiderman, Ben. Control flow and data structure documentation: two experiments. *Communications of the ACM* **25**, 1, pp. 55-63, January 1982.

[Shneiderman 76]   Shneiderman, B. Exploratory experiments in programmer behavior. *International J. of Computer and Information Sciences* **5**, 2, pp. 123-143, 1976.

[Shneiderman & McKay 76]   Shneiderman, B. and McKay, D. Experimental investigations of computer program debugging and modification. *Proceedings of the 6th International Congress of the International Ergonomics Association*, July 1976.

[Shneiderman 77]   Shneiderman, B. Measuring computer program quality and comprehension. *International Journal of Man-Machine Studies* **9**, 1977.

[Shneiderman et al 77]   Shneiderman, B., Mayer, R., McKay, D., and Heller, P. Experimental investigations of the utility of detailed flowcharts in programming. *Communications of the ACM* **20**, pp. 373-381, 1977.

[Shneiderman & Mayer 79]   Shneiderman, B. and Mayer, R. Syntactic/semantic interactions in programmer behavior: a model and experimental results. *International J. of Computer and Information Sciences* **7**, pp. 219-239, 1979.

[Shneiderman 80]   Shneiderman, B. *Software Psychology: Human Factors in Computer and Information Systems*. Winthrop, 1980.

[Sime et al 73]   Sime, M.E., Green, T.R.G., and Guest, D. J. Scope marking in computer conditionals -a psychological evaluation. *International J. of Man-Machine Studies* **5**, pp. 105-113, 1973.

[Sime et al 77]   Sime, M.E., Green, T.R.G., and Guest, D.H. Scope marking in computer conditionals-a psychological evaluation. *International Journal of Man-Machine Studies* **9**, pp. 107-118, 1977.

[Smith & Dunsmore 82]   Smith, C.H. and Dunsmore, H.E. On the relative comprehensibility of various control structures by novice Fortran programmers. *International Journal of Man-Machine Studies* **17**, pp. 165-171, 1982.

[Soloway et al 83a]   Soloway, Elliot, Ehrlich, Kate, Bonar, Jeffrey, and Greenspan, J. What do novices know about programming?. in *Directions in Human-Computer Interactions*, ed. A. Badre, Ablex Publishing, 1983.

[Soloway et al 83b]   Soloway, Elliot, Bonar, Jeffrey, and Ehrlich, Kate. Cognitive strategies and looping constructs: an empirical study. *Communications of the ACM* **26**, 11, pp. 853-860, November 1983.

[Standish 73]   Standish, Thomas A. Observations and hypotheses about program synthesis mechanisms. Automatic Programming Memo 9, Report No. 2780, Bolt Beranek and Newman, Cambridge, MA, Dec 19, 1973.

[Sykes et al 83]   Sykes, Floyd, Tillman, Raymond T., and Shneiderman, Ben. The effect of scope delimiters on program comprehension. *Software-Practice and Experience* **13**, pp. 817-824, 1983.

[Thadhani 84]   Thadhani, A.J. Factors affecting programmer productivity during application development. *IBM Systems Journal* **23**, 1, pp. 1935, 1984.

[Walston & Felix 77]   Walston, C.E. and Felix, C.P. A method of programming measurement and estimation. *IBM Systems Journal* **16**, 1, pp. 54-73, 1977.

[Weinberg 71]   Weinberg, G.M.. *The psychology of computer programming*. Van Nostrand Company, New York, N.Y., 1971.

[Weinberg & Schulman 74]   Weinberg, G.M. and Schulman, E. L.. Goals and performance in computing programming. *Human Factors* **16**, 1, pp. 70-77, 1974.

[Weiser 82]   Weiser, Mark. Programmers use slices when debugging. *Communications of the ACM* **25**, 7, pp. 446-452, July, 1982.

[Weissman 74]   Weissman, L. A methodology for studying the psychological complexity of computer programs. Ph.D. Thesis, University of Toronto, 1974.

[Wright & Reid 73]   Wright, P. and Reid, F. Written information: Some alternatives to prose for expressing the outcomes of complex contingencies. *Journ*... *Psychology* **57**, pp. 160-166, 1973.

[Youngs 74]   Youngs, E.A. Human errors in... ming. *International Journal of Man-Machine S*... pp. 361-376, 1974.

[Zak 77]   Zak, D. Initial experiences in programmin... ductivity realized using implementation language. *annual Conference Principles of Software Developm*... pp. 191-219, Control Data Corporation, November 197...

of Applied

program-

udies **6**,

g pro-

Fifth

ent',

7.

III. Origins/Effects of Poor Software Structure

How does poor structure creep into code in the first place? The papers of Part III supply some answers.

The first paper, "A Guided Tour of Program Design Methodologies" by G.D. Bergland, is an informative discussion of software structure, software development methodologies, and software change. The author believes that "the quality of the program structure resulting from a design methodology is the single most important determinant of the life-cycle costs for the resulting software system." Through plausible examples on similar software developed with different design methodologies, the author shows how poor structure may very easily be introduced. Seeing such examples gives clues to how poor structure may be prevented.

The next paper, "Why Does Software Die?" by P.J. Brown, gives several events that can ruin software structure. These include changes in the model of the outside world on which the software is based, changes to hardware, and software requirements changes. The author surveys several approaches for making software structure more resilient for changes.

The next paper, "Observations on the Evolution of a Software System" by E. Allman and M. Stonebraker, describes a real-life experience in building and restructuring a data base management system. Because the system originated in a university environment with few development and maintenance standards, the system rapidly reached a stage where new maintainers (students) found it difficult to maintain. What followed was a period of engineering which eventually made the system more understandable and maintenance more controllable. Some valuable insights into what to do correctly the next time, from people who've "been there," forms a valuable conclusion to the paper.

The next paper provides a sadly amusing, if all too common, example of code-improving "tricks" that eventually lead to outrageous devaluing of a valuable software asset. In "Software Malpractice—A Distasteful Experience," M.J. Spier shows how an anonymous programmer's optimization, complete with bug, led to compiler errors which were extremely difficult to analyze. Ultimately this led to the compiler being used despite known, unsolved bugs. The compiler had become just too widely used for a new (or restructured) compiler to be commissioned. Sometimes the act of unravelling poor structure can uncover bugs which themselves may be too "politically sensitive" to reveal and fix!

The final paper, "Kill That Code!" by G. Weinberg, suggests that very small changes are much more prone to error than larger changes. Why? People may take very small changes less seriously and therefore not think them through or test them as carefully as more "substantial" changes. The paper is a sobering reminder of the fragility of even the slightest change to software.

Reprinted from *Computer*, Volume 14, Number 10, October 1981, pages 18-37. Copyright © 1981 by The Institute of Electrical and Electronics Engineers, Inc.

After describing, applying, comparing, and evaluating four major methodologies, this guided tour concludes with an interim procedure for use until the "right" method appears.

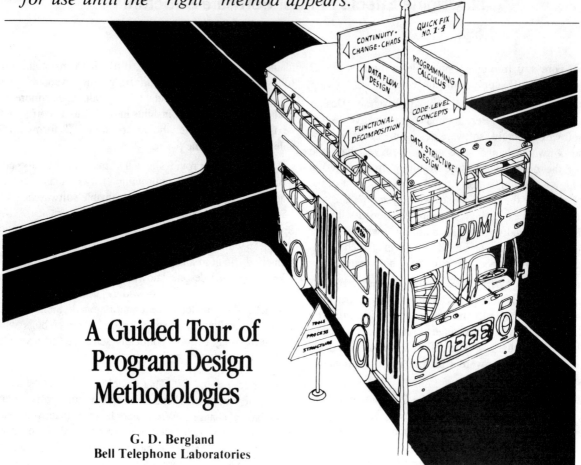

A Guided Tour of Program Design Methodologies

G. D. Bergland
Bell Telephone Laboratories

Much as a building architect specifies the structure and construction of a building (see Figure 1), the software architect must specify the structure and construction of a program. This guided tour examines some of the concepts, techniques, and methodologies that can aid in this task.

During this guided tour, the software problem and the attempts at its solution are briefly described. Software engineering techniques are classified into three groups: those that primarily impact the program structure, the development process, and the development support tools. Structural analysis concepts are described that have their major impact at the code level, the module level, and the system level. Then, four of the major program design methodologies that have been reported in the literature are developed and compared. Functional decomposition, data flow design, data structure design, and programming calculus are described, characterized, and applied to a specific example.

While no one design methodology can be shown to be "correct" for all types of problems, these four methodologies can cover a variety of applications. Finally, an interim approach for large software design problems is suggested that may be useful until an accepted "correct" methodology comes along.

Motivation. The major motivation for looking at program design methodologies is the desire to reduce the cost of producing and maintaining software. Developing programs that are reliable enough to support nonstop computer systems can sometimes be a secondary motivation, but these applications seem to be in the minority.

Figure 1. A good design implies a good structure.

A host of claims in technical journals, conference proceedings, and short-course advertisements herald the virtues of new design methodologies—claims such as 1.9 to 1 increase in productivity, 39 percent savings in programming costs, 80 percent reduction in bugs, etc. Their inconsistencies suggest that without a good set of metrics, you can prove anything you want. Alternatively, software development is so inefficient that almost anything can improve it.

If one were to take these claims at face value, it would seem that at least some of the problems of producing inexpensive, reliable software have been solved. Unfortunately, the benefits of structured programming, software engineering techniques, or whatever have remained either nebulous or illusive to many people. Even though structured programming has been with us for more than a decade, we are still far from having all the answers or, for that matter, even all of the questions. While it is clear that progress has been made, there is still much to be done.

Historical perspective. During the 1950's, programming was in its golden age. The approach was to take a small group of highly qualified people and solve a problem by writing largely undocumented code maintained by the people who wrote it. The result was inflexible and inextensible code, but it was adequate to the demands of the time. Buxton[1] called this "cottage industry" programming.

The software crisis hit in the 1960's. The problems got two orders of magnitude harder, and we were introduced to the problems of having many people work on large programs that were continually changing. This was the beginning of "heavy industry" programming.[1]

The structured programming of the 1970's was primarily an attempt to address the problems of heavy industry programming. This quest for a better way was started in response to rapidly rising costs[2]—more than one percent of the gross national product was being spent on software in the US—and the feeling that change was technically feasible. Thus started a variety of approaches that are collectively known as structured programming.

Techniques hierarchy. Software engineering has been defined by Parnas as multiperson construction of multiversion programs.[3] As such, there is much emphasis on the development process, its attendant support tools, and the basic structure of a program. Many of the concepts which people tend to apply first—like teams, design reviews, and program librarians—primarily involve changing the development process. Vyssotsky characterized these techniques as dealing with programmer "crowd control."[4] While they can be implemented relatively quickly, their major benefits can only be realized in the context of a well-structured program. Those techniques dealing with program structure form the foundation on which the other techniques should be applied[5] (see Figure 2). Admittedly, the support tools and the development process strongly influence the structure of the program; however, the tools should be adapted to support the desired structure, not vice versa.

While there are many design methodologies around, only a few of them have been extensively tested. Four methodologies used or discussed more than most are

- functional decomposition,
- data flow design,
- data structure design, and
- programming calculus.

I believe that the quality of the program structure resulting from a design methodology is the single most important determinant of the life-cycle costs for the resulting software system. Thus, before discussing the methodologies in detail, it seems worthwhile to discuss some of the concepts that play a role in evaluating the structure of a program.

Structural analysis concepts

While most structural analysis concepts apply at more than one level of a software system, it is convenient in this discussion to separate them into three categories. Concepts are discussed that have their major impact at the code level, the module level, and the software system level.

Code-level concepts. Concepts having their major impact at this level include abstraction, communication, clarity, and control flow constructs.

Abstraction. Abstraction is defined as the consideration of a quality apart from a particular instance. In programming, the application of abstraction ranks as one of the most important advances that has occurred in the last 20 years. It is the basis for high-level languages, virtual machines, virtual I/O devices, data abstractions, plus both top-down and bottom-up design.

The whole concept of bottom-up design consists of building up layers of abstract machines that get more and more powerful until only one instruction is needed to solve the problem. While people usually stop far short of defining that one superpowerful instruction, they do significantly enhance the environment in which they have to program. Device drivers, operating system primitives, I/O routines, and user-defined macros are built on the concept of abstraction. All of them raise the level at which the programmer thinks and programs.

Often, the objective is to abstract many of the complicated interactions that can occur when many users or user programs are sharing the same machine. In other in-

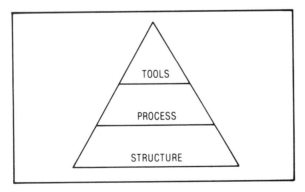

Figure 2. Software engineering techniques hierarchy.

stances, a virtual machine is created to hide the idiosyncrasies of a particular machine from the user so that the resulting program will be more portable.

When the modular programming era began in the 1960's, many people hoped that hundreds of reusable building-block programs could be abstracted and added to their programming libraries so that they could finally begin to "build on the work of others." Unfortunately, as Weinberg noted, "Program libraries are unique; everyone wants to put something in but no one wants to take anything out."[6]

Communication. A program communicates with both people and machines. The effect of comments can be profound. A ten-year-old program I've seen that has the comment "subtle" in it is still left alone at all costs. Although the person who wrote the program is long gone, he has left a legacy of problems that will last as long as the program.

Another program contained the comment, "They made me do it!" This comment was undoubtedly an apology for corrupting the structure of the program to provide an expedient fix to a pressing problem. Clearly, the program is a little harder to understand and modify now. This type of change is not unusual. It's the apology that's unusual.

In the long run, changes tend to obscure the structure of a program, thus making the processes of error correction and feature addition difficult and dangerous. A well-written and well-maintained program is meant to communicate its structure to the programmer as well as to give instructions to the machine. I believe that the life-cycle cost of operating a program usually depends far more on how well it communicates with people than on how fast it initially runs.

Clarity. It has been said that a person who writes English clearly can write a program clearly. In studying English, we are taught first to read and then to write. This seems to work well. In programming, however, we are usually taught only to write. I think we miss something by not learning to read programs first. At one time it was even considered fashionable to write unreadable programs. It got so bad that one language, famous for its "one-liners," was dubbed a "write-only" language.

The structure* of an article, paper, or book is very important in clearly communicating ideas. The structure of a program is equally important in communicating both the algorithm and the context of a problem solution. This structure should be apparent when one reads a program.

Clarity of program structure was obviously not the primary concern of the person who wrote the program represented in Figure 3. This program has been running for more than 10 years. Fortunately, few changes or feature enhancements have been required. In an attempt to understand how the program worked, this diagram was drawn by the last person who had to change it.

The "structuredness" of this program—and, for that matter, of any program—is not well-defined. There is still

*An adequate but not inspired definition of "structure" is "the arrangement or interrelation of parts as dominated by the general character of the whole."

no generally accepted metric for characterizing the merit of a program structure. The unavailability of such a metric results in some strange phenomena. For example, do you know someone who writes complicated and unintelligible code, who spends long hours and late nights on it, finally getting it "done" just before the deadline—all the while letting everyone know how difficult his task is and what a hero he is for having gotten it done just in time?

In contrast, consider the neat, well-organized programmer who takes care to plan ahead, do a proper design, document her work, and get done well ahead of the deadline, with no one even aware that she was involved. How often have you thought "Boy, John has certainly earned his wings with that difficult program, while Jane hasn't had a chance to prove herself."

In the best of all worlds, the criterion of clarity could be applied quantitively. Lacking that, we'll have to stick with peer pressure applied in design reviews and code walkthroughs to ensure the clarity of the final product.

Control flow constructs. The concept of limiting the number and type of control flow constructs, to more clearly express algorithms, is now pretty generally accepted. The notation recommended by Michael Jackson[7] is shown in Figure 4.

The *sequence* and *selection* constructs shown in this figure can be generalized in the obvious way to a sequence or selection of N items for arbitrary N. The *iteration* stands for "zero or more" program executions. The advantage of

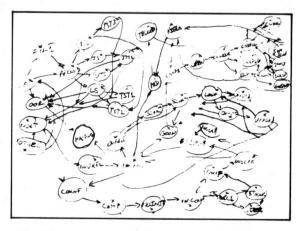

Figure 3. A clearly presented program structure?

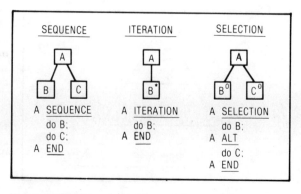

Figure 4. The three basic control flow constructs.

these constructs is that they tend to provide a map of the program structure rather than an itinerary of tasks.

The transformation of a program that uses these graphical constructs to structure text (also shown in Figure 4) is remarkably straightforward, as is the later transformation to a specific programming language.

Module-level concepts. Cohesion, coupling, complexity, correctness, and correspondence are concepts with major impact at the module level.

Cohesion. Cohesion is the "glue" that holds a module together. It can also be thought of as the type of association among the component elements of a module. Generally, one wants the highest level of cohesion possible. While no quantitative measure of cohesion exists, a qualitative set of levels for cohesion has been suggested by Constantine[8] and modified by Myers.[9] The levels proposed by Constantine are shown in Figure 5.

Coincidental cohesion is Constantine's lowest level of cohesion. Here, the component parts of a module are there only by coincidence. No significant relationship exists among them.

Logical cohesion is present when a module performs one of a set of logically related functions. An example would be a module composed of 10 different types of print routines. The routines do not work together or pass work to each other but logically perform the same function of printing.

Temporal cohesion is present when a module performs a set of functions related in time. An initialization module performs a set of operations at the beginning of a program. The only connection between these operations is that they are all performed at essentially the same time.

Procedural cohesion occurs when a module consists of functions related to the procedural processes in a program. Functions that can be well represented together on a flowchart are often grouped together in a module with procedural strength. Conversely, when a program is designed by using a flowchart, the resulting module often has procedural cohesion.

Communicational cohesion results when functions that operate on common data are grouped together. A data abstraction, or data cluster,[10] is a good example of a module with communicational cohesion.

Sequential cohesion often results when a module represents a portion of a data flow diagram. Typically, the modules so formed accept data from one module, modify or transform it, and then pass it on to another module.

Functional cohesion results when every function within the module contributes directly to performing one single function. The module often transforms a single input into a single output. An example often cited is square root. This is the highest level of cohesion in the hierarchy. As such, it is desirable whenever it can be achieved.

A program of any reasonable size will usually contain modules of several different levels of cohesion. Many modules simultaneously exhibit characteristics of a multiplicity of levels. Where possible, functional, sequential, and communicational strength modules should be given preference over modules with lower levels of cohesion. On a scale of 0 to 10, Yourdon[8] rates coincidental, logical, and temporal cohesion as 0, 1, and 3, respectively. Procedural cohesion would score 5. Communicational, sequential, and functional cohesion would score 7, 9, and 10, respectively.

While levels of cohesion can be useful guides in evaluating the structure of a program, they don't provide a clear-cut method for attaining high levels of cohesion. Furthermore, levels of cohesion do not allow us to say that program A is right and program B is wrong. They do, however, represent a definite step forward. Before levels of cohesion were introduced, there was no recognized basis for comparison. Now, at least one can say that structure A is probably better than structure B.

Coupling. Coupling is a measure of the strength of interconnection (i.e., the communication bandwidth) between modules. In Figure 6, two program structures are represented that would result in significantly different degrees of coupling.

High coupling among program modules results when a problem is partitioned in an arbitrary way such as cutting off sections of a flowchart. This method of chopping up a large program often complicates the total job because of the resultant tight coupling between the pieces. This latter type of partitioning leads to "mosaic" modularity.[11]

The other extreme in structuring a program is to consider only pure tree structures. These structures give rise to the concept of hierarchical modularity and provide many advantages for abstraction, testing, and later mod-

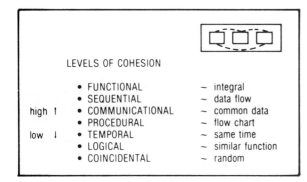

Figure 5. Levels of cohesion.

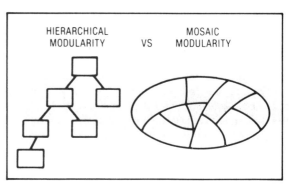

Figure 6. Partitioning method affects level of coupling.

ification. Jackson would accuse you of "arboricide" (the killing of trees) whenever you deviate from a pure hierarchical tree structure. Brooks has said, 'I am persuaded that top-down design (incorporating hierarchy, modularity, and stepwise refinement) is the most important new programming formalization of the decade."[12] And Dijkstra has said that "the sooner we learn to limit ourselves to hierarchical program constructs the faster we will progress."[13]

Modular programs can be characterized as

- implementing a single independent function,
- performing a single logical task,
- having a single entry and exit point,
- being separately testable, and
- being entirely constructed of modules.

When these rules are followed, a set of nested modules result that can be connected in a hierarchy to form large programs. In an attitude survey,[14] users perceived that modular programs were easier to maintain and change, easier to test, and more reliable. The major perceived disadvantage was the feeling that the final program was less efficient than it could have been.

When modularity is used without hierarchy, one can only implement independent functions that can be executed in sequence, which corresponds to drawing circles around portions of a flowchart. Although this approach tends to work on small programs, it can seldom be applied to complex programs without seriously compromising module independence, connectivity, and testability. Only when the concepts of modular programming are combined with the concepts of hierarchical program structure can one implement arbitrarily complex functions and still maintain module integrity.

Modularity can be applied without hierarchy in cases that lend themselves naturally to the efficient use of a very high level language. Very high level language statements are examples of functions that can be implemented relatively independent of each other but still be strung together sequentially in a useful form. Unfortunately for most applications, the design of a convenient and efficient very high level language is difficult.

Hierarchical modularity forms an extremely attractive foundation for most of the other software engineering techniques. While some of these techniques can be used without having a hierarchical program structure, the primary benefit can only be gained when the techniques are used as a unit and build on each other. Specifically, a hierarchical modular program structure enhances top-down development, programming teams, modular programming, design walkthroughs, and other techniques that deal with improving the development process.

Complexity. The control of program complexity is the underlying objective of most of the software engineering techniques. The concept of "divide and conquer" is important as an answer to complexity, provided it is done correctly. When a program can be divided into two independent parts, complexity is reduced dramatically, as shown in Figure 7.

Consider program A, where you have access to only the input and the output.[9] A noble goal would be to com-

pletely test this program by executing each unique path. In the example shown, there are approximately 250 billion unique paths through this module. If you were capable of performing one test each millisecond, it would take you eight years to completely test all of the unique paths. If, however, you had knowledge of what was inside the program and recognized that it could be partitioned into two independent modules B and C, which have low connectivity and coupling, your testing job could be reduced. To test both of these modules separately requires that you only test the one million unique paths through each module. At one millisecond per test, these tests would take a total of only 17 minutes.

In this particular example, from a testing viewpoint, it is clearly worth trying to partition the problem so that small, independently testable modules can be dealt with instead of just the input and output of a large program. Unfortunately, partitioning most programs into independently testable modules requires much more work than simply drawing small circles around portions of the flowchart.

It should also be clear from this example that the testing problem is best solved during the design stage. It is impossible to exhaustively test any program of significant size. Testing is experimental evidence.[7] It does not verify correctness. It simply raises your confidence.

Correctness. A "correct" program is one that accurately implements the specification. A "correct" program often has limited value since the specifications are in error. Again, correctness cannot be verified by testing. Searching for errors is like searching for mermaids. Just because you haven't seen one doesn't mean they don't exist.

It is also unfortunate that, for most problems, mathematical proofs of correctness are as difficult to produce as a correct program. Some people can write and prove their program simultaneously. For most of us, however, day-to-day proving of programs is still a long way off.

The most promising approach for the near future may lie in finding a constructive proof of correctness. We will really have something if a design methodology can be

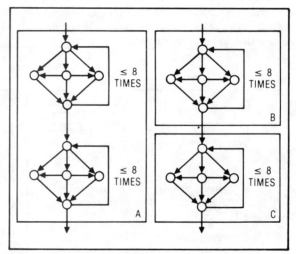

Figure 7. Control of complexity.

found that leads one through the design process step-by-step and guarantees the correctness of the final program if each of the steps has been done correctly. While I don't remember that 321 × 25 is 8025, I do remember that 5 × 1 = 5, and 5 × 2 = 10, and 5 × 3 = 15, etc. Knowing these values and the steps of multiplication, I can rest assured that 8025 is indeed the correct answer. If only a program design process existed that was as foolproof and easy to apply.

Without such a process, we must live with a limitless capacity for producing error. Weinberg once pointed out that errors can be produced in arbitrarily large numbers for an arbitrarily low cost.

Correspondence. In Jackson's view, perhaps the most critical factor in determining the life-cycle cost of a program is the degree to which it faithfully models the problem environment[7]—that is, the degree to which the program model corresponds to the real world. All too often, a small local change in the problem environment results in a large diffuse change in the program.

The world is always bigger than the program specification says it is, but a specification can always be extended if it corresponds to reality. Since users tend to be gradualists, the changes in a realistic problem model will tend to be gradual. If the program structure is formed around the static instead of the dynamic properties of the problem, it should prove to be more resilient to changes.

While a program's model of the world cannot be complete, it must at least be useful and true. If these criteria are met, many maintenance and feature enhancement problems will be avoided in the future.

System-level concepts. Concepts of major impact at this level include consistency, connectivity, continuity, change, chaos, optimization and packaging.

Consistency. An important objective of a good design methodology is that it should produce a consistent program structure independent of whoever is applying it. Three different programs—created by using the same design methodology to model the same problem environment—should have the same basic structure. Unless consistent designs can be achieved, there can never be a true right or wrong structure for a given problem solution.

One problem with most design methodologies is that

there is no one consistently obtainable solution. Instead, designers seem to pull unique solutions out of the air. Consequently, there is never discussion of a solution being right or wrong—only discussion of my style versus your style.

Connectivity. The harmful effects of high connectivity on system modifiability can best be illustrated by using an analogy.[15]

Consider a system composed of 100 light bulbs. Each light in the system can either be on or off. Connections are made between the light bulbs so that if the light is on, it has a 50 percent chance of going off in the next second. If the light bulb is off, it has a 50 percent chance of going on in the next second—provided one of the lights to which it is connected in on. If none of the lights connected to it is on, the light stays off. Sooner or later, this system of light bulbs will reach an equilibrium state in which all of the lights go off and stay off.

The average length of time required for this system to reach equilibrium is solely a function of the interconnection pattern of the lights. In the most trivial interconnection pattern, all of the lights operate independently. None of them is connected to any of its neighbors. Here, the average time for the system to reach equilibrium is approximately the time required for any given light to go off—about two seconds. Thus, the system can be expected to reach equilibrium in a matter of seconds.

At the other extreme, consider the case when each light in the array is fully connected to all other lights in the array—that is, assume that there is a connectivity matrix for the lights similar to the program connectivity matrix shown on the left side of Figure 8, where N is equal to 100. The array on the left side of the figure then describes the connectivity matrix of the lights and shows that every light is connected to every other light. In this case, the length of time required for the system to reach equilibrium is 10^{22} years. This is a very long time when you consider that the current age of the universe is only 10^{10} years.

Now, consider one final interconnection pattern in which the set of 100 lights is partitioned into 10 sets of 10 lights each, with no connections between the sets, but with full interconnection within each set. In this case, the time required for the system of lights to reach equilibrium is about 17 minutes. This example dramatically shows the effect of connectivity. In terms of the concepts presented earlier, this example corresponds to high cohesion within each module and low coupling between modules.

Much as proper physical partitioning can dramatically reduce the time required for the system of lights to reach equilibrium, proper functional partitioning can dramati-

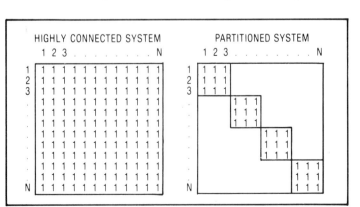

Figure 8. Low connectivity implies low maintenance costs.

LAW OF CONTINUING CHANGE: A SYSTEM THAT IS USED UNDERGOES CONTINUING CHANGE UNTIL IT IS JUDGED MORE COST-EFFECTIVE TO FREEZE AND RECREATE IT.

LAW OF INCREASING UNSTRUCTUREDNESS: THE ENTROPY (DISORDER) OF A SYSTEM INCREASES WITH TIME UNLESS SPECIFIC WORK IS EXECUTED TO MAINTAIN OR REDUCE IT.

Figure 9. Continuity/change/chaos.

COMPUTER

cally reduce the time required for a program that is being debugged to reach stability.

Continuity/change/chaos. As noted by Belady and Lehman,[16] a large program often seems to live a life of its own, independent of the noble intentions of those trying to control it. Two important observations are summarized in the Law of Continuing Change and the Law of Increasing Unstructuredness shown in Figure 9.

These laws dramatize the key role played by the program structure during the life cycle of software systems. The natural order of things is to produce disorder. If the program structure is unclear from the beginning, things will only get worse later. These two laws coupled with a poor program structure have produced many of the maintenance-cost horror stories.

Optimization and packaging. All too often, people confuse packaging and design. Design is the process of partitioning a problem and its solution into significant pieces. Optimization and packaging consist of clustering pieces of a problem solution into computer load modules that run within system space and time requirements without unduly compromising the integrity of the original design.[8]

At least three different types of modules must be considered in programming—functional modules, data modules, and physical modules. Packaging is concerned with placing functional modules and data modules into physical modules. In packaging a program, several of these pieces of the program may be put together as one load module or may even be written together as one program.

It is in the packaging phase of a design that optimization should be considered for the first time. This phase is done at the end, and great care should be taken to preserve the program structure that you have worked so hard to create. In Jackson's words, "It is easy to make a program that is right, faster. It is difficult to make a program that is fast, right." Once an optimization has been cast in code, it's like concrete. It is very difficult to undo.

Functional decomposition

Functional decomposition is simply the divide-and-conquer technique applied to programming, as shown in Figure 10. Various forms of functional decomposition have been popularized by a host of people including Dijkstra, Wirth, Parnas, Liskov, Mills, and Baker.[17-22]

By viewing the stepwise decomposition of the problem and the simultaneous development and refinement of the program as a gradual progression to levels of greater and greater detail, we can characterize functional decomposition as a *top-down* approach to problem-solving. Conversely, we can form and layer groups of instruction sequences together into "action clusters," starting at the atomic machine instruction level and working our way up to the complete solution. This approach leads to a *bottom-up* method.[21]

Often, the preferred strategy is to shift back and forth between top-down functional decomposition and the bottom-up definition of a virtual machine environment.

Design strategy. The design process can be divided into the following steps:[19]

(1) Clearly state the intended function.
(2) Divide, connect, and check the intended function by reexpressing it as an equivalent structure of properly connected subfunctions, each solving part of the problem.
(3) Divide, connect, and check each subfunction far enough to feel comfortable.

In following this procedure, the key to successful program design is rewriting followed by more rewriting. Every effort should be made at each step to conceive and evaluate alternate designs.

A useful mind set is to pretend that you are programming on a machine that has a language powerful enough to solve your problem in only a handful of commands. In your level 1 decomposition, you simply write down that handful of commands and you have a complete program. In your level 2 decomposition, you try to refine each of your level 1 instructions into a set of less powerful instructions. By continuing to successively refine each instruction, one level at a time, you eventually get to a program that can be executed on your own real computer. In carrying out this process, you will have decomposed the problem into its constituent functions by "stepwise refinement."

There are several problems involved in applying this technique. First, the method specifies that a functional decomposition be performed, but it does not say what you are decomposing with respect to. One can decompose with respect to time order, data flow, logical groupings, access to a common resource, control flow, or some other criterion. If you decompose with respect to time, you get modules like initialize, process, and terminate, and you have a structure with temporal cohesion. If you cluster functions that access a shared data base, you have made a start toward defining abstract data types and will get communicational cohesion. If you decompose using a data flow chart, you may end up with sequential cohesion. If you decompose around a flowchart, you will often end up with logical cohesion. The choice of "what to decompose with respect to" has a major effect on the "goodness" of the resulting program and is therefore the subject of much controversy.

The major advantage of functional decomposition is its general applicability. It has also been used by more people longer than any of the other methods discussed. The dis-

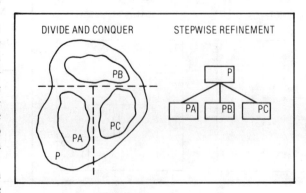

Figure 10. Functional decomposition.

advantages are its unpredictability and variability. The chance of two programmers independently solving a given problem in the same way are practically nil. Thus, each new person exposed to a program starts by saying, "This isn't the way I would have done it, but. . ." To some extent, this problem can be reduced by using functional decomposition in combination with some other technique that determines what each function should be composed with respect to.

McDonald's example. The McDonald's functional decomposition solution, presented below, is patterned (with permission) after a story called "Getting it Wrong" that has been related by Michael Jackson on numerous occasions in his short courses and seminars. The McDonald's frozen-food warehouse problem is, of course, entirely fictitious.

Problem specification. McDonald's frozen-food warehouse receives and distributes food items. Each shipment received or distributed is recorded on a punched card that contains the name of the item, the type of shipment (R for received, D for distributed), and the quantity of each item

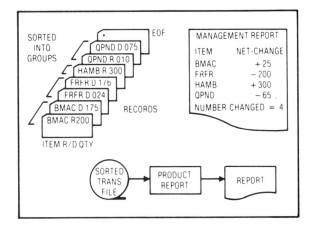

affected. These transaction cards are sorted by another program and appear grouped in alphabetical order by item name. A management report, showing the net change in inventory of each item, is produced once a week. The input file and output report formats are shown in Figure 11.

Design phase. The hero who originally designed this program is named Ivan. Ivan is a very "with it" fellow. He swore off GO TOs years ago. His code is structured like the Eiffel Tower. He can whip out a neatly indented structured program in nothing flat. In doing his design, Ivan was careful to do the five-level, hierarchical, functional decomposition shown in Figure 12.

In this figure, PRODUCE REPORT is shown to be a sequence of PRODUCE HEADING followed by PRODUCE BODY followed by PRODUCE SUMMARY. PRODUCE BODY is shown to be an iteration of PRODUCE CARD that is a selection between PROCESS FIRST CARD IN GROUP and PROCESS SUBSEQUENT CARD IN GROUP.

Clearly, recognizing the first card of each item group is important. Once this card is found, everything else falls into place.

At this point, it may be worth examining the structure of Ivan's program. The obvious question is, "Is this a good decomposition?" The obvious reply is, "Good with respect to what?"

If we apply the concept of cohesion to this structure, it might seem that the level 1 PRODUCE REPORT module has temporal cohesion since the PRODUCE HEADING module is something like an initialization module and the PRODUCE SUMMARY module is something like a terminate module. On the other hand, one could argue that the heading, body, and summary are such integral parts of the report that this is really functional cohesion.

Likewise, the PROCESS CARD module seems to have been partitioned along temporal lines as well. On the other hand, PROCESS CARD seems to be an integral part of the PRODUCE BODY module, so maybe PRODUCE BODY is also functionally cohesive.

As you can tell by the preceding examination, while levels of cohesion may constitute an improvement over having no basis for comparison, they are still difficult to apply consistently. In cases where more than one type of cohesion seem to be present, the rule[8] is to assume that it is really the higher of the two levels.

Ivan wrote the level 1, 2, and 3 programs shown in Figure 13. The level 4 decomposition shown in Figure 14 started to look like a finished product. The level 5 decomposition shown in Figure 15 was the finished product.

In his normal thorough manner, Ivan volume-tested his program and turned it over to the user. It was perfect except for one small glitch. You see, the systems programmers were still playing with the compiler and obviously hadn't fixed all the errors. As a result, the program worked fine, but some garbage appeared on the first line of the output immediately after the headings. It was believed, of course, that this would disappear as soon as they fixed that %&"**?> compiler.

Friendly user phase. Now, Ronald McUser is a friendly sort of person. Since he was in a hurry to use the program,

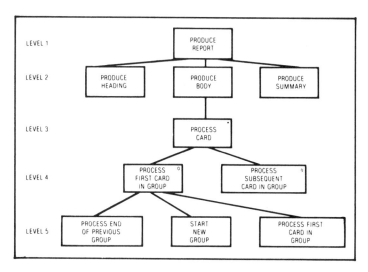

Figure 12. A five-level functional decomposition.

he did not complain about the small glitch that would, of course, disappear very soon. Ronald's boss, Big Mac, however, failed to see the humor of it all. The compiler had been fixed for three months now, and the management report that went to the board of directors still had that garbage in it.

Finally, one day, Ronald could stand it no longer. The program *had* to be fixed. When Ronald arrived, Ivan was in his cubicle, listening to an audio cassette of Dijkstra's Turing lecture. He, of course, didn't learn anything; that's the way he had always done his designs. Ronald showed Ivan a printout.

After a few MMMs and AAAHHHHs and AAAHHHAAAs, he saw the problem. This first time through the program, there was no previous group. Thus, the output was just random data. The solution to any first-time-through problem is, of course, obvious. Add a first-time switch (see Figure 16).

Maintenance phase. Six months later, our hero was in McDonald's "think room" when Ronald McUser came in and said, "I put 80 transactions in last week and nothing came out!" Our hero looked at the printout and saw that, indeed, only the heading had come out.

Ivan knew immediately what the problem was. It must be a hardware problem. After all, his program had been running nearly a year now with only one small complaint.

Ivan spent most of the night running hardware diagnostics until Steve Saintly, a keypunch operator, wandered by and said, "That nationwide special on Big Macs last week was all we handled. Everything else had to wait."

A little later, Sally Saintly came by and said, "Isn't it about time you included those new Zebra sodas in the management report?"

By this time, Ivan was very discouraged with his diagnostics, so he followed last week's inputs through the code. "Horrors! There was only one item group processed last week—Big Macs!"

As Ivan soon discovered, the last item group was never processed. Since only one item group was processed all week, nothing was output. Up until this time, only Zebra sodas had been skipped. Since they were not a big winner, it seems that no one had even cared that they had been left off. In fact, everyone assumed they were being left off on purpose. Ivan's solution is shown in Figure 17.

```
P: PRODUCE HEADING;

    READSTF;
    DO WHILE (NOT EOF—STF);
       IF FIRST CARD IN GROUP THEN
          DO;
                  PROCESS END OF PREVIOUS GROUP;

                  PROCESS START OF NEW GROUP;
                  PROCESS CARD;

          END;
       ELSE DO; PROCESS CARD;
          END;
       READ STF;
    END;

    PRODUCE SUMMARY;
    STOP;
```

Figure 15. The final functional decomposition.

```
LEVEL 1     P: PRODUCE REPORT;
               STOP;

LEVEL 2     P: PRODUCE HEADING;
               PRODUCE BODY;
               PRODUCE SUMMARY;
               STOP;

LEVEL 3     P: PRODUCE HEADING;
               READ STF;
               DO WHILE (NOT EOF-STF);
                  PROCESS CARD;
                  READ STF;
               END;
               PRODUCE SUMMARY;
               STOP;
```

Figure 13. Steps in functional decomposition.

```
P: PRODUCE HEADING;

    READ STF;
    DO WHILE (NOT EOF—STF);
       IF FIRST CARD IN GROUP THEN
          PROCESS FIRST CARD IN GROUP;
          ELSE PROCESS SUBSEQUENT CARD IN GROUP;
       READ STF;
    END;

    PRODUCE SUMMARY;
    STOP;
```

Figure 14. Level 4 functional decomposition.

```
P: PRODUCE HEADING;
   SW1: = 0;
      READSTF;
      DO WHILE (NOT EOF—STF);
         IF FIRST CARD IN GROUP THEN
            DO; IF SW1 = 1 THEN
               DO; PROCESS END OF PREVIOUS GROUP;
               END; SW1; = 1;
                  PROCESS START OF NEW GROUP;
                  PROCESS CARD;

         END;
         ELSE DO; PROCESS CARD;
            END;
         READ STF;
      END;

   PRODUCE SUMMARY;
   STOP;
```

Figure 16. Quick fix no. 1.

Meanwhile, Sally Saintly asked, "Why didn't you see that during all the volume-testing you did? You tied up the machine for most of a day."

The answer again is obvious. In volume-testing, you put in thousands of inputs but don't look at the output.

Passing the baton. Six months later, Ivan was feeling pretty pleased with himself. He had just turned the program over to a new hire. There would still be some training, but everything should go well. After all, hadn't the program run for nearly a year and a half with only a couple of small problems? Suddenly, Ronald burst in, "I thought you fixed this first-line problem. Here it is again."

Ivan knew immediately what the problem was. The new program librarian they had forced him to use had put in an old version of the program without his first patch.

```
P: PRODUCE HEADING;
   SW1: = 0;
      READSTF;
      DO WHILE (NOT EOF—STF);
         IF FIRST CARD IN GROUP THEN
            DO; IF SW1 = 1 THEN
                  DO; PROCESS END OF PREVIOUS GROUP;
                  END; SW1: = 1;
                        PROCESS START OF NEW GROUP;
                        PROCESS CARD;

            END;
         ELSE DO; PROCESS CARD;
               END;
         READ STF;
      END;
                  PROCESS END OF LAST GROUP;

   PRODUCE SUMMARY;
   STOP;
```

Figure 17. Quick fix no. 2.

After many heated comments plus a core dump, Ivan was still baffled. Finally, in desperation, he sat down to look at the input data and found out there wasn't any. Last week, a trucker's strike had shut down the warehouse. Nothing came in; nothing went out. They ran the program anyway. Good grief, who would have thought that they would run the program with no inputs!

The problem, as it turns out, was that the new PROCESS END OF LAST GROUP module needed protection just like the PROCESS END OF PREVIOUS GROUP module had before. Since that first-time switch had worked so nicely earlier, it was clearly the solution to apply again (see Figure 18).

We all know that Ivan's troubles are over now. Or are they? Two months later, Sally Saintly came in and said, "Where are the Zippo sandwiches? They were in for two months, but now they've suddenly disappeared from the report."

After complaining that the new hire was supposed to be maintaining that program now, Ivan looked at the input data and noticed that only one order per item had been issued during the whole run.

"What happened?" he exclaimed.

It seems that a new manager, Mary Starr, had started a new policy to try to get things better organized. She had asked each of the stores to place only one order a day instead of placing orders at random. She had also said that it would be nice if they could schedule things so that the warehouse had to be concerned only with receiving one particular item on one day and with distributing that item the next day. In addition, she wanted the management report program run once a day from now on. The effect on Ivan's program was that Zippo sandwiches was dropped.

Instead of moving the set for SW2, the safest thing to do—according to the principles of defensive programming—is to add an extra set. Since you don't know what you're doing, you never touch a previous fix—just add a new one (see Figure 19).

Now we can all rest assured that Ivan's program works, right?

```
P: PRODUCE HEADING;
   SW1: = 0;  SW2: = 0;
      READSTF;
      DO WHILE (NOT EOF—STF);
         IF FIRST CARD IN GROUP THEN
            DO; IF SW1 = 1 THEN
                  DO; PROCESS END OF PREVIOUS GROUP;
                  END; SW1: = 1;
                        PROCESS START OF NEW GROUP;
                        PROCESS CARD;

            END;
         ELSE DO; PROCESS CARD;  SW2: = 1;
               END;
         READ STF;
      END; IF SW2 = 1 THEN
            DO; PROCESS END OF LAST GROUP;
            END;
   PRODUCE SUMMARY;
   STOP;
```

Figure 18. Quick fix no. 3

```
P: PRODUCE HEADING;
   SW1: = 0;  SW2: = 0;
      READSTF;
      DO WHILE (NOT EOF—STF);
         IF FIRST CARD IN GROUP THEN
            DO; IF SW1 = 1 THEN
                  DO;  PROCESS END OF PREVIOUS GROUP;
                  END; SW1: = 1;
                        PROCESS START OF NEW GROUP;
                        PROCESS CARD;
                        SW2: = 1;

            END;
         ELSE DO; PROCESS CARD;  SW2: = 1;
               END;
         READ STF;
      END; IF SW2 = 1 THEN
            DO; PROCESS END OF LAST GROUP;
            END;
   PRODUCE SUMMARY;
   STOP;
```

Figure 19. Quick fix no. 4.

The effect of all of these changes on the program structure is shown in Figure 20.

What was Ivan's major sin? Simply that the program structure didn't correspond to the problem structure. In the original data, there existed something called an item group. There is no single component in Ivan's program structure that corresponds to an item group. Thus, the actions that should be performed once per group, before a group, or after a group have no natural home. They are spread all over the program, and we have to rely on first-time switches and the like to control them. Instead of components that start a new group, process a group, or process the end of a group, we have a mess.

In Jackson's words, when this correspondence is not present, the program is not poor, suboptimal, inefficient, or tricky. It's *wrong*. The problems we have seen are, in reality, nothing but self-inflicted wounds stemming from an incorrect program structure.

Data flow design

The data flow design method first proposed by Larry Constantine[8] has been advocated and extended by Ed Yourdon[8] and Glen Myers.[9] It has been called by several different names, including "transform-centered design" and "composite design." In its simplest form, it is nothing more than functional decomposition with respect to data flow. Each block of the structure chart is obtained by successive application of the engineering definition of a black box that transforms an input data stream into an output data stream. When these transforms are linked together appropriately, the computational process can be modeled and implemented much like an assembly line that merges streams of input parts and outputs streams of final products.[8,9]

Design strategy. The first step in using the data flow design method is to draw a data flow graph (see Figure 21). This graph is a model of the problem environment that is transformed into the program structure. An example of its use will be given later.

While the modules in functional decomposition often tend to be attached by a "uses" relationship, the bubbles in a data flow graph could be labeled "becomes." That is, data input A "becomes" data output B. Data B becomes C, C becomes D, etc. The only shortcoming of this decomposition is that it tends to produce a network of programs—not a hierarchy of programs. Yourdon and Constantine solve this problem by simply picking the data flow graph up in the middle and letting the input and output data streams "hang down" from the middle. At each level, a module in one of the input or output data streams can be factored into a "get" module, a "transform" module, and a "put" module. By appropriate linking, a hierarchy is formed. Thus, once the data flow graph is drawn, the hierarchical program structure chart can be derived in a relatively mechanical way.

Given the data flow graph of Figure 21, the modules of the structure chart are defined as GET A, GET B, and GET C. Also defined are the modules that transform A into B, B into C, C into D, and so on. The output module

is illustrated by the PUT D module. The GET modules are called "afferent modules" and the PUT modules are called "efferent modules."[8] The TRANSFORM C TO D module is known as the "central transform."

The data flow design method can be broken into the following four basic steps:

(1) Model the program as a data flow graph.
(2) Identify afferent, efferent, and central transform elements.
(3) Factor the afferent, efferent, and central transform branches to form a hierarchical program structure.
(4) Refine and optimize.

This procedure is represented schematically in Figure 22.

Note that while the connections between modules in the data flow graph context were motivated by a "becomes" or "consumes/produces" relationship, the factoring procedure leads to modules that are connected by a "calls/is called by" relationship. Thus, the hierarchy formed is really being artificially imposed by the scheduling and has little to do with modeling the problem in

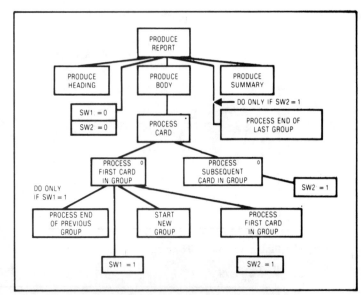

Figure 20. Functional decomposition with quick fixes.

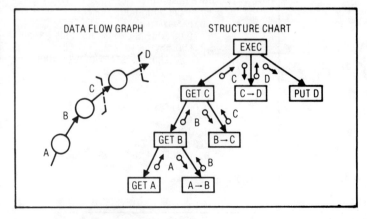

Figure 21. Data flow design method.

94

hierarchical fashion. This contrasts with both the "uses" relationship of decomposition with respect to function and the "is composed of" relationship that motivates a data structure design.

Also note that a lot of data passes between modules in the structure in assembly-line fashion. This results in sequential cohesion. By Constantine's measure of goodness, the data flow design method produces a very good program structure.

The act of concentrating the I/O functions in the afferent and efferent "ears" of the program structure may or may not produce a structure that models the problem environment accurately. This partitioning often seems artificial to me and would seem to violate the principle of correspondence.

The central transform is located between the data flow graph's most abstract input and most abstract output.

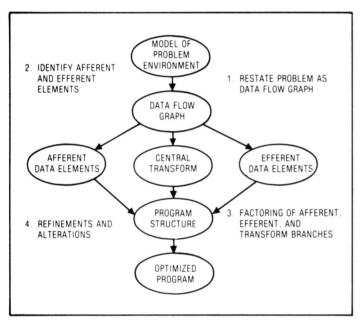

Figure 22. Data flow design procedure.

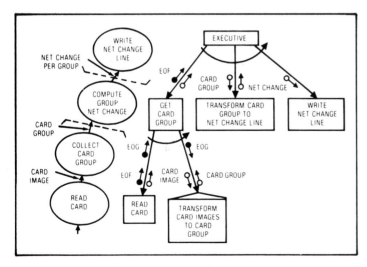

Figure 23. Data flow design structure.

While the graph shows it as simply transforming Cs into Ds, it often requires a sophisticated functional decomposition in its own right. That is, except for the "ears" which come from the data flow graph, one is forced right back to the art of functional decomposition.

McDonald's example. The heroine who designed the next program was Ivan's sister, Ivy. Ivy is a child of the late 1960's. When modular programming came in, she jumped right on the bandwagon. Her modules had only one entrance and one exit. She passed all her parameters in each call statement. Each of her modules performed only a single logical task, was independent, and could be separately tested. She read daily from the gospel according to Harlan Mills[19] and remembered nearly every error that she had ever made. She well remembers the day she designed this program.

Model problem. The data flow graph for the McDonald's example is shown on the left side of Figure 23. The data items being passed between bubbles are labeled, and the modules are named with an action verb and an object. Note that one or more *card images* "become" a *card group* after being processed by the COLLECT CARD GROUP function.

Afferent, efferent, and central transform elements. The most abstract input in the data flow graph is a *card group*. The most abstract output is the *net change* resulting from processing each card group. Thus, the COMPUTE GROUP NET CHANGE module is the central transform, the WRITE NET CHANGE LINE module is the efferent (or output) element, and the READ CARD and COLLECT CARD GROUP modules are the afferent (or input) elements.

Factor branches. Note that the concept of a card group emerges naturally out of the data flow diagram and leads to a reasonably straightforward program structure (see Figure 23). The TRANSFORM CARD IMAGES TO CARD GROUP module is shown with a roof that denotes lexical inclusion. That is, while TRANSFORM CARD IMAGES TO CARD GROUP is a functional module, it is not necessarily a physical module. In this example, it will be packaged together with the GET CARD GROUP module.

The curved arrows in Figure 23 denote iteration. That is, the GET CARD GROUP module calls its two subtending modules once per card image. The EXECUTIVE module calls its three subtending modules once per card group. Note that the READ CARD module is assumed to pass an "end of file" flag up the chain when it is detected. (The passing of control information is denoted by the small arrows with solid tails, while the passing of data is shown by the small arrows with open tails.) Ivy's program listing is shown in Figure 24.

Only three of the six modules are shown. The TRANSFORM CARD IMAGES TO CARD GROUP module was lexically included in the GET CARD GROUP module. The other two modules are not necessary for this particular discussion. Note that the READ CARD module leaves much to be desired.

Program testing. Ivy has learned to make good use of a program librarian. She wrote the program, gave the coding sheets to the librarian, and went back to her reading. The program librarian faithfully executed his duties and brought back a printout that said "CRITEM undefined."

Ivy had forgotten to make sure that all of her variables were initialized. Oh well, this should be easy. How about setting CRITEM: = XXXX at the beginning of the GET CARD GROUP module? That would be before CRITEM was used the first time, and when it has a symmetry with the way EOG (end of group) is initialized.

Unfortunately, something just didn't seem right about it. GET CARD GROUP is executed many times during the program, and CRITEM only needs to be initialized once.

Ivy decided to initialize CRITEM at the beginning, instead. While that means passing it as a parameter up two levels, it certainly sounded better than a bunch of first-time switches.

On the next run, Ivy's efforts were rewarded with some output—nothing fancy, but still some output.

"What happened to the heading?" exclaimed Ivy. "That data link must be dropping bits again."

"Where did you write out the heading?" asked the program librarian. Enter quick fix number 2, shown in Figure 25.

"Wait, what about that garbage in the front?"

The problem, of course, is that the program has no way of knowing when it's through with a group until it's already started processing the next group. Thus, the first card of a new group serves as a key to tell the rest of the program to send on the previous group. It can't do this, however, without distorting the structure.

"I think it's time to call out my secret weapon," said Ivy, "my UNREAD command." Enter quick fix number 3, shown in Figure 26.

Field debugging. This fix apparently worked fine for about two months. It was not exactly speedy, but it did work. Then, all of a sudden, a visit from on high. Big Mac himself came down and said, "Our people in Provo, Utah, have been trying to bring up your program, and it just doesn't work."

It turns out that in Provo they never found it necessary to buy a tape reader. Ivy's UNREAD operation didn't work on cards. That meant that Ivy had to find another way of UNREADing.

In this data flow design, the equivalent of an UNREAD is, at best, messy. It corrupts the structure badly, no matter how it's done. Modules end up storing internal states or values, and first-time switches abound.

In Ivy's case, she chose to read ahead by one, passing state information by SW1 and storing the NEW CARD value within module READ CARD. Other solutions are possible, of course, but it isn't clear that they are a whole lot better (see Figure 27). The effect of these changes on the program structure is shown dramatically in Figure 28.

Ivy has committed arboricide, to use Jackson's words. What was a nice clean tree structure now has two programs calling the same READ CARD module. I think

```
EXECUTIVE:  EOF: = FALSE;

    DO WHILE(EOF = FALSE);
       GET__CARD__GROUP(CG,EOF              );
       TRANSFORM__CG__TO__NC__LINE(CG,NC);
       WRITE__NC__LINE (NC,EOF);
    END;                      STOP;

GET__CARD__GROUP(CG,EOF              ): EOG: = FALSE; I: = 0;
    DO WHILE (EOG = FALSE); I: = I + 1;
       READ__CARD(CI,EOG,EOF              );CG(I) = CI;
    END;             RETURN;

READ__CARD(CI,EOG,EOF              ):
    NEW__CARD: = READ STF;
       IF NEW__CARD__ITEM ≠ CRITEM THEN
          DO; EOG: = TRUE; CRITEM = NEW__CARD__ITEM;
                        END;
       ELSE     CI: = NEW CARD;
       IF CI = EOF__STF THEN EOF: = TRUE; RETURN;
```

Figure 24. Data flow design program.

```
EXECUTIVE:   EOF: = FALSE;
    CRITEM: = XXXX;
    DO WHILE(EOF = FALSE);
       GET__CARD__GROUP(CG,EOF,CRITEM     );
       TRANSFORM__CG__TO__NC__LINE(CG,NC);
       WRITE__NC__LINE (NC,EOF);
    END;                      STOP;

GET__CARD__GROUP(CG,EOF,CRITEM     ): EOG: = FALSE; I: = 0;
    DO WHILE (EOG = FALSE); I: = I + 1;
       READ__CARD (CI,EOG,EOF,CRITEM     );CG(I) = CI;
    END;             RETURN;
READ__CARD(CI,EOG,EOF,CRITEM     ):
    NEW__CARD: = READ STF;
       IF NEW__CARD__ITEM ≠ CRITEM THEN
          DO; EOG: = TRUE; CRITEM: = NEW__CARD__ITEM;
                        END;
       ELSE    CI: = NEW__CARD;
       IF CI = EOF__STF THEN EOF: = TRUE; RETURN;
```

Figure 25. Quick fix no. 1.

```
EXECUTIVE:   EOF: = FALSE: WRITE HEADING;
    CRITEM: = XXXX:
    DO WHILE(EOF = FALSE):
       GET__CARD__GROUP(CG,EOF,CRITEM     ):
       TRANSFORM__CG__TO__NC__LINE(CG,NC):
       WRITE__NC__LINE (NC,EOF):
    END:                      STOP:

GET__CARD__GROUP(CG,EOF,CRITEM     ): EOG: = FALSE: I: = 0:
    DO WHILE (EOG = FALSE): I: = I + 1:
       READ__CARD (CI,EOG,EOF,CRITEM     ): CG(I) = CI:
    END:             RETURN:

READ__CARD(CI,EOG,EOF,CRITEM     ):
    NEW__CARD: = READ STF:
       IF NEW__CARD__ITEM ≠ CRITEM THEN
          DO: EOG: = TRUE: CRITEM: = NEW__CARD__ITEM:
          UNREAD STF: END:
       ELSE    CI: = NEW__CARD:
       IF CI = EOF__STF THEN EOF: = TRUE: RETURN:
```

Figure 26. Quick fixes no. 2 and no. 3.

```
EXECUTIVE:   EOF: = FALSE;WRITE HEADING; SW1: = FALSE;
    CRITEM: = XXXX;       READ__CARD(CI,EOG,EOF,CRITEM,SW1);
    DO WHILE(EOF = FALSE);
        GET__CARD__GROUP(CG,EOF,CRITEM,SW1);
        TRANSFORM__CG__TO__NC__LINE(CG,NC);
        WRITE__NC__LINE(NC,EOF);
    END;                  STOP;

GET__CARD__GROUP(CG,EOF CRITEM,SW1): EOG: = FALSE; I: = 0;
    DO WHILE (EOG = FALSE), I: = I + 1;
    READ__CARD (CI,EOG,EOF,CRITEM,SW1);CG(I) = CI;
    END; SW1: = TRUE; RETURN;

READ__CARD(CI,EOG,EOF,CRITEM,SW1):IF SW1 = FALSE THEN
    NEW__CARD: = READ STF;
        IF NEW__CARD__ITEM ≠ CRITEM THEN
            DO; EOG: = TRUE; CRITEM = NEW__CARD__ITEM;
            SW1: = TRUE;                END;
        ELSE DO; CI: = NEW__CARD;SW1: = FALSE; END;
        IF CI = EOF__STF THEN EOF: = TRUE; RETURN;
```

Figure 27. Quick fix no. 4.

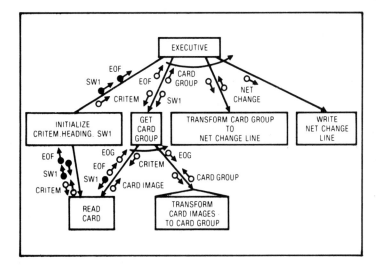

Figure 28. Data flow design with fixes.

```
EXECUTIVE: EOF: = FALSE; WRITE HEADING; SW1: = FALSE;
    CRITEM: = XXXX; CI: = READ STF;
    DO WHILE (CI NOT EOF – STF);
        EOG: = FALSE I: = 0;
        DO WHILE (EOG=FALSE); I: = I + 1;
            IF SW1 = FALSE THEN NEW__CARD: = READ STF;
            IF NEW__CARD__ITEM ≠ CRITEM THEN
                DO; EOG: = TRUE; CRITEM: = NEW__CARD__ITEM;
                SW1: = TRUE;
                END;
            ELSE DO; CI: = NEW__CARD SW1: = FALSE;
                END;
                CG(I): = CI;
        END;
        SW1: = TRUE;
        TRANSFORM__CG__TO__NC__LINE (CG,NC);
        WRITE__NC__LINE (NC,EOF);
    END;
    STOP;
```

Figure 29. Data flow design packaged in one module.

read and write operations should be thought of as general-purpose routines callable from anywhere within the program structure. To hope to constrain them to the "ears" of a structure chart seems, at best, unwise.

Optimization. In this program, things look much better if we simply package the whole thing as one module, as shown in Figure 29.

The point, however, is that the problems Ivy had were representative of larger problems that could appear in larger programs each time the data flow design method is applied.

Data structure design

Slightly different forms of the data structure design method were developed concurrently by Michael Jackson[7] in England and J. D. Warnier[23] in France. In this discussion, Jackson's formulation and notation are used.

The basic premise is that a program views the world through its data structures and that, therefore, a correct model of the data structures can be transformed into a program that incorporates a correct model of the world. The importance of this view, stated earlier as the principle of correspondence, is emphasized by Michael Jackson's words that "a program that doesn't directly correspond to the problem environment is not poor, is not bad, but is wrong!"

When the program structure is derived from the data structure, the relationship between different levels of each resulting hierarchy tends to be a "is composed of" relationship. For example, an output report is composed of a header followed by a report body followed by a report summary. This is generally a static relationship that does not change during the execution of the program, thus forming a firm base for modeling the problem.

Since a data-structure specification usually lends itself well to being viewed as correct or incorrect, the program structure based on a data-structure specification can often be viewed as being correct or incorrect. Jackson[7] purports that two people solving the same problem should come up with program structures that are essentially the same. Thus, this method satisfies the principle of consistency to a large degree.

Design strategy. The programming process can be partitioned into the following steps:

(1) Form a system network diagram that models the problem environment.
(2) Define and verify the data-stream structures.
(3) Derive and verify the program structures.
(4) Derive and allocate the elementary operations.
(5) Write the structure text and program text.

These steps can usually be performed and verified independently, separating concerns by partitioning both the design process and the problem solution. For large problems, the objective is a network of hierarchies, each representing a simple program. Jackson's premise is that although simple programs are difficult to write, complex programs are impossible. The trick, then, is to partition complex problems into simple programs.

These simple programs, individually implemented as true hierarchical modular structures, are connected in a data-flow network. This network can be placed into a "calls" or "is called by" hierarchy by a scheduling procedure called "program inversion"[7] that is performed as a separate step after the structure of the program has been defined.

The system network diagram for a simple program is represented schematically in the upper left corner of Figure 30 and is explained further in the example. In its simplest form, it represents a network of functions that consume, transform, and produce sequential files. Below this network diagram, the data structure of each file is shown to be represented by data structure diagrams. The notation used is similar to that shown in Figure 4.

If the data structures correspond well, a program structure diagram can be drawn that encompasses both data structures. When a diagram cannot encompass both data structures, a *structure clash*[7] exists.

Since the program structure models the data structures, and since most operations are performed on data elements, one can list and allocate executable operations to each component of the program structure. These elementary operations are denoted by the small squares in the structure diagram and are shown in a list in the lower left corner of Figure 30.

The basic data structure design procedure can also be represented schematically, as shown in Figure 31. The arrows represent the flow of work and the results required in following the basic design procedure. Note that the final program structure is formed by first finding data structure correspondences and then by adding in the executable operations also derived from the data structures. The problem model is usually documented by a system network diagram, the data structures and program structure by structure diagrams, and the program text by structure text. Examples of each of these are given below in the McDonald's example.

The major problem with Jackson's data structure design methodology is that, in Jackson's words, "it is being developed from the bottom up." That is, although it is clear at this point how to apply it to small problems, the "correct" method for extending it to large system problems is still being developed.

McDonald's example. Ida is a data structure designer from way back. She went to London to study the Jackson design method. She learned French just so she could read Warnier's six paperbacks. (She says they lose a lot in translation.) With the McDonald's problem, she is certain that a data structure design is the only way to go—after all, it fits into Jackson's "stores movement" problem solution format.[7]

Model step. The system network diagram for the McDonald problem was given at the bottom of Figure 11.

Data step. The second design step was to construct and verify the input and output data structures for each file shown in the system network diagram. The three basic program constructs of sequence, iteration, and selection—shown in Figure 4—apply equally well to describing the structure of a data file (see Figure 32). Note that the SORTED TRANSACTION FILE is an iteration of ITEM GROUP, which is an iteration of TRANSACTION RECORD, which—in turn—is a selection of a RECEIVED RECORD or a DISTRIBUTED RECORD. The output report is a sequence of the REPORT HEADING followed by the REPORT BODY followed by the REPORT SUMMARY. The REPORT BODY is an iteration of REPORT LINE. (Note that REPORT BODY is an iteration of REPORT LINE—not REPORT LINES. Plural names in data component boxes often indicate an error in naming.)

After the input and output data structures were diagrammed, one-to-one correspondences were shown by arrows. For example, one SORTED TRANSACTION FILE is consumed in producing one REPORT, and one ITEM GROUP is consumed in producing one REPORT LINE.

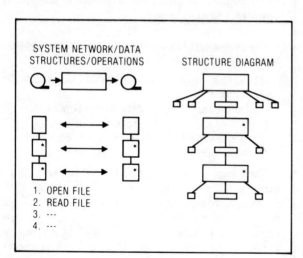

Figure 30. Data structure design method.

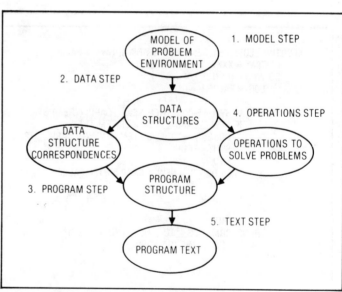

Figure 31. Basic data structure design procedure.

Program step. From these data structures, a program structure was constructed encompassing all of the parts in each data structure. Where there were one-to-one correspondences, the modules took the form of CONSUME. . . TO PRODUCE. . . .Where there were modules corresponding to only the input data structure, the form was CONSUME. . . .Where there were modules corresponding to only the output data structure, the form was PRODUCE. . . .All of these are shown in Figure 32.

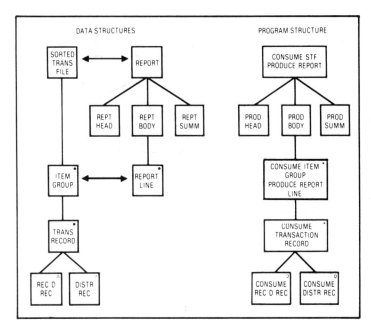

Figure 32. Data and program structures.

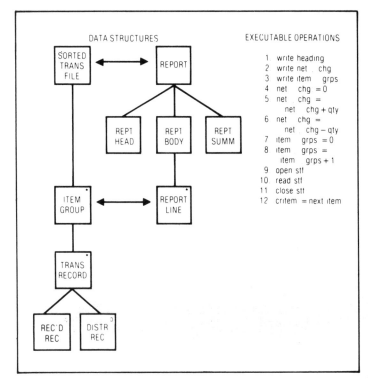

Figure 33. Listing executable operations.

In finding the producer-consumer correspondences, the question is always, ''Does one instance of this result in one instance of that?'' This question should be asked again during the verification procedure, which consists of showing that both the input and output data structures are subtrees of the program structure.

Operations step. The input, output, and computational operations are identified by working back from the output data structure to the input data structure (see Figure 33). If necessary, the equivalent of a data flow diagram can be drawn with nodes to represent intermediate variables.

The operations must be sufficiently rich to guarantee that each output can be produced and each input can be consumed. Computational operations must also be specified that will implement the algorithms which link the two. One other type of operation is usually required for completeness. In our example, this is shown as operation 12. This operation provides the key that will be used in determining item group boundaries, and it is usually called a ''structure-derived operation.''

While it is desirable to have a complete list of operations from the start, it is not required, since missing operations will become apparent later in the process.

The last part of the operations step involves allocating all of these executable operations to the program structure (see Figure 34). In each case, the questions to ask are ''How often should this operation be executed?'' and ''Should this operation occur before or after. . .?'' For this example, the answer to the first question could be once per report, once per sorted transaction file, once per heading, once per summary, once per item group, once per report line, once per transaction record, once per item received record, or once per item distributed record. Clearly, you open the sorted transaction file, or STF, before you read it, you close the STF before you stop, etc. Using the read-ahead rule,[7] you read one card ahead and then read to replace (see operation 10).

At the end of this step, one should verify that all outputs are produced, all intermediate results are produced, and all inputs are consumed.

Text step. Although the structure of the program is now secure, Jackson recommends one final step before coding. That fifth step is to translate the structure diagram into structure text, as shown in Figure 35. This is done using the three basic program constructs shown in Figure 4.

Structure text is straightforward and easy to understand as long as your program labels are short and descriptive. With long program labels, it can become a mess. In Figure 35, the letters C and P are sometimes used as abbreviations for CONSUME and PRODUCE.

Ida's final program was produced by translating the structure text of Figure 35 into the target programming language of Figure 36. The major disadvantage of this method is that the number of distinct steps and procedures involved imply that both the data structure diagram and the structure text should be kept as permanent parts of the documentation. This seems unlikely unless an automated structure chart drawer is available that will store the structure chart with the program in a convenient form so that it can be updated when the program is changed. At this point, available machine aids are far from adequate. Another disadvantage is that for certain classes of problems, the data structure diagrams and the resulting program structures can get unduly cumbersome.

A programming calculus

While a "proof of correctness" is disappointingly difficult to develop after a program has been written, the constructive proof-of-correctness discipline taught by Dijkstra[20] and Gries[24] is relatively encouraging. Dijkstra's design discipline can be methodically applied to obtain a modest-sized "elegant" program with a "deep logical beauty." Using this method, the program and the proof are constructed hand-in-hand.

Design strategy. The initial design task consists of formally specifying the required result as an assertion stated in the predicate calculus. Given this desired postcondition, one must derive and verify the appropriate preconditions while working back through the program being constructed. The program and even individual statements play a dual role in that they must be viewed in both an operational way and as predicate transformers. The method is a top-down method to the extent that both the resulting program and the predicates can be formed in stages by a sequence of stepwise refinements.

Definitions. The programming language is used as a set of statements that perform predicate transformations of the form[20,24,25]

$$\{Q\} S \{R\} \qquad (1)$$

In this expression, Q represents a precondition that is true before execution of statement S. R represents a postcondition that is true after the execution of statement S. In simple terms, the formula means that the execution of statement S beginning in a state satisfying Q will terminate in a state satisfying R, but Q need not describe the largest set of such states. When Q does describe the largest set of such states, it is called the weakest (least restrictive) precondition.

When Q is the weakest precondition, this is expressed in the form

$$Q = wp(S, R) \qquad (2)$$

When S is an *assignment* statement, it takes the form

$$x := e \qquad (3)$$

where e is an expression. Its definition as a predicate transformer is given by

$$wp("x := e", R) \equiv R_e^x \qquad (4)$$

The term R_e^x is used to denote the textual substitution of expression e for each free occurrence of x within expression R.

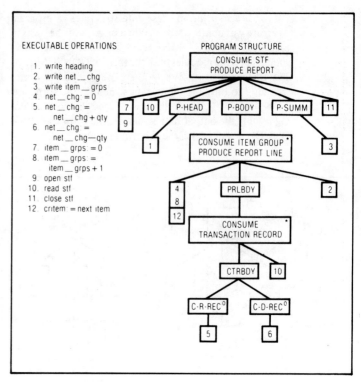

Figure 34. Allocating executable operations.

When s is a *Selection* statement, it takes the form

$$
\begin{aligned}
\text{IF} \equiv \ &\textbf{if} \ \ B_1 \rightarrow S_1 \\
&[]\ \ \ B_2 \rightarrow S_2 \\
&\quad \cdots \\
&[]\ \ \ B_n \rightarrow S_n \\
&\textbf{fi}
\end{aligned} \qquad (5)
$$

```
P seq
    item__grps: = 0;
    open stf; read stf;
    write heading;
    P-BODY itr until (eof-stf)
        C-ITEM-GRP-P-REPT-LINE seq
            net__chg: = 0;
            item__grps: = item__grps + 1;
            critem: = next item;
            PRLBDY itr while (next item = critem)
                C-TRANS-REC seq
                    CTRBDY sel (code − R)
                        net__chg: = net__chg + qty;
                    CTRBDY alt (code − D)
                        net__chg: = net__chg − qty;
                    CTRBDY end
                    read stf;
                C-TRANS-REC end
            PRLBDY end
            write net__chg;
        C-ITEM-GRP-P-REPT-LINE end
    P-BODY end
    write item__grps; close stf;
P end
```

Figure 35. Structure text.

This is valid where $n > 0$, the B_i are boolean expressions called guards, and the S_i are statements. The vertical bar "$[]$" serves to separate otherwise unordered alternatives. To execute IF, at least one of the guards B_i must be true. To execute it, choose one guard that is true (nondeterministically) and execute the corresponding statement. The expression $B_1 \rightarrow S_1$ may be read as "When guard B_1 is true, statement S_1 may be executed." The definition of IF as a predicate transformer is given by

$$wp(\text{IF}, R) \equiv \text{BB and } (\text{A } i : 1 \le i \le n : B_i => wp(S_i, R)) \quad (6)$$

where $\text{BB} \equiv B_1 \text{ or } B_2 \text{ or } \ldots \text{ or } B_n$. Thus, we must prove that executing any S_i when B_i and Q are true establishes R. In practice, given R and S_i, we derive B_i using the weakest precondition.

The *iteration* statement takes the form

$$
\begin{aligned}
\text{DO} \quad \equiv \quad &\textbf{do } B_1 \rightarrow S_1 \\
&[] \quad B_2 \rightarrow S_2 \\
&\quad \ldots \\
&[] \quad B_n \rightarrow S_n \\
&\textbf{od}
\end{aligned}
\quad (7)
$$

Iteration continues as long as at least one of the guards $B_1, \ldots, B_n$ is true. From the set of statements with true guards, one is selected (nondeterministically) for execution. The definition of DO as a predicate transformer is given by

$$wp(\text{DO}, R) \equiv (\text{E } k : k \ge 0 : H_k(R)) \quad (8)$$

where $H_k(R)$ for $k \ge 0$ is the weakest precondition such that execution of DO will terminate after, at most, k "iterations" and in a state satisfying R. In developing a program that contains a loop structure, this is found by completing the following steps:

1. Write a formal specification of the desired result R.
2. Determine an invariant P.

```
PB:      item__grps: = 0;
         open stf;
         read stf;
         write heading;
PBB:     do while (not eof—stf);
         net__chg: = 0;
         item__grps: = item__grps + 1;
         critem: = next item;
PRLBB:   do while (next item = critem);
CTRBB:   if (code = R) then
             net__chg: = net__chg + qty;
         else if (code = D) then
CTRBE:       net__chg: = net__chg — qty;
         read stf;
PRLBE:   end;
         write net__chg;
PBE:     end;
         write summary;
PE:      close stf;
```

Figure 36. Final data structure design program.

3. Derive a loop body such that:
   a. $Q => P$ (i.e., P is initially true).
   b. $\text{A } i : \{ P \text{ and } B_i \} S_i \{ P \}$
      (i.e., P remains invariantly true).
   c. $(P \text{ and not } \text{BB}) => R$
      (i.e., upon termination R is true).
   d. Show the loop terminates:
      (1) $(P \text{ and } \text{BB}) => t > 0$
          (i.e., before termination, t is positive).
      (2) $\text{A } i : \{ P \text{ and } B_i \} \tau := t; S_i \{ t \le \tau - 1 \}$
          (i.e., t decreases with each iteration).

In step 3d, t is a termination function chosen to be positive during the execution of the iteration and zero upon completion; τ is a fresh integer variable.

McDonald's example. The problem is initially simplified by eliminating the R/D field of each transaction and considering the quantity field $q(j)$ as positive for items received and negative for items dispersed. The R/D field is reintroduced later when the final pseudocode is written so that the resulting program can be readily compared with previous designs.

Problem specification. Note that the STF is an iteration of item group, which is an iteration of transaction, which—in turn—is a sequence of the item field $f(j)$ and the quantity field $q(j)$ for $1 \le j < m$ and $f(m) = EOF$.

Since the transaction file has been sorted, an item group $g(j, k)$ can be defined as

$$
\begin{aligned}
g(j, k) \equiv & f(j) \ne f(j - 1) \text{ and } f(j) = f(k) \quad (9) \\
& \text{and } f(k) \ne f(k + 1)
\end{aligned}
$$

Similarly, a partial item group $\hat{g}(j, k)$ can be defined as

$$
\begin{aligned}
\hat{g}(j, k) \equiv & f(j) \ne f(j - 1) \text{ and } f(j) = f(k) \quad (10) \\
& \text{and } f(k) = f(k + 1)
\end{aligned}
$$

The number of complete groups over the range 1 through k can be defined as

$$n(1, k) \equiv (\text{N } p : 1 \le p \le k : f(p) \ne f(p + 1)) \quad (11)$$

where $\text{N } p$ is the number of distinct values of p over the range $1 \le p \le k$ for which $f(p) \ne f(p + 1)$.

Formal specification of R. Step 1 in the design procedure is to develop, in a top-down fashion, a formal specification of the desired result R. A first attempt could look something like this:

R : The total number of item groups i is calculated. The net change in inventory c is calculated for each item group.

More formally:

$$R : (\text{A } j, k : 1 \le j \le k < m \text{ and } g(j, k) \quad (12)$$

$$: i = n(1, k) \text{ and } c(i) = \sum_{r=j}^{k} q(r))$$

This whole expression may be read "If R is true, the following holds: For all j and k such that $1 \le j \le k < m$ and the transactions between j and k inclusive form a group, it is true that i is set equal to the number of complete groups over the interval 1 through k and $c(i)$ is formed as the sum of the quantity fields within each complete group." This notation is consistent with that used by Dijkstra and Gries.[25] Note that the result assertion specifies *what* is to be derived—not *how* it is to be derived.

When we examine (12), the requirement for counting the number of complete groups and the summation required for computing $c(i)$ suggest that at least one loop structure is required in the program. Thus, our next step is to determine an invariant P.

Determine an invariant P. When step 2 is performed, the result assertion (12) is weakened to form an invariant P. In this example, R may be weakened by introducing a variable $\hat{m}$, where $1 \le \hat{m} \le m$, such that

$$P : (1 \le \hat{m} \le m)$$

$$\text{and } (\mathbf{A}\, j,k : 1 \le j \le k < \hat{m} \text{ and } g(j,k)$$

$$: i = n(1,k) \text{ and } c(i) = \sum_{r=j}^{k} q(r))$$

$$\text{and } (\mathbf{A}\, j,k : 1 \le j \le k < \hat{m} \text{ and } \hat{g}(j,k) \text{ and } k = \hat{m} - 1$$

$$: \hat{c} = \sum_{r=j}^{k} q(r)) \tag{13}$$

This invariant states that "If P is true, the following holds: For all the complete item groups, i is set to the group number and $c(i)$ is set to the sum of the q fields within each group. For the last partial item group, $\hat{c}$ is set to the sum of the q fields."

Derive the program. Step 3d(1) requires that a termination function t be chosen that is greater than zero while any of the guards B_i are still true and that decreases with every execution of S_i. For our example, a termination function that can readily be made to satisfy these conditions is

$$t = m - \hat{m} \tag{14}$$

This function will equal zero on termination if the guard B_1 is set to terminate the iteration when $\hat{m} = m$.

With this in mind, the basic program form becomes

```
"define Q to establish P";
{P}
do m̂ ≠ m →
    "decrease t while maintaining P"          (15)
od
{R}
```

A statement that would decrement t is

$$\hat{m} := \hat{m} + 1 \tag{16}$$

As noted in step 3a, we must next show that P is initially true. In other words, the initial state $\{Q\}$ must be so defined that Q implies P. That is

$$Q => P \tag{17}$$

Note that if the program starts with the statement

$$\hat{m}, i, \ \hat{c} := 1,0,0 \tag{18}$$

then P holds.

To satisfy step 3b, we must show that P remains true after statement (16) is executed. One way of meeting this requirement is to introduce further guards B_i by embedding an IF selection statement within the loop construct. The IF statement format is shown in (5). The program is now in the form

```
m̂, i, ĉ := 1,0,0;
{P}
do m̂ ≠ m →
    if
        "statements that reestablish P"       (19)
    fi;
    m̂ := m̂ + 1
{P}
od
{R}
```

The guards of the IF statement must be chosen such that P remains true after statement (16) is executed. In general, guards B_i must be chosen so that

$$P \text{ and } B_i => wp(S_i, P) \tag{20}$$

In our example, we must find

$$wp\,(``\hat{m} := \hat{m} + 1", P)$$

$$= (1 \le \hat{m} + 1 \le m)$$

$$\text{and } (\mathbf{A}\, j,k : 1 \le j < k < \hat{m} + 1 \text{ and } g(j,k)$$

$$: i = n(1,k) \text{ and } c(i) = \sum_{r=j}^{k} q(r)) \tag{21}$$

$$\text{and } (\mathbf{A}\, j,k : 1 \le j \le k < \hat{m} + 1 \text{ and } \hat{g}(j,k)$$
$$\text{and } k = \hat{m}$$

$$: \hat{c} = \sum_{r=j}^{k} q(r))$$

Consequently, we must choose guards for the IF that ensure that all three of the terms of (21) are satisfied when (16) is executed. The first term

$$1 \le \hat{m} + 1 \le m \tag{22}$$

can be established directly from P and the iteration guard ($\hat{m} \ne m$). The second term of (21)

$$\mathbf{A}\, j,k : 1 \le j \le k < \hat{m} + 1 \text{ and } g(j,k) \tag{23}$$

$$: i = n(1,k) \text{ and } c(i) = \sum_{r=j}^{k} q(r)$$

can be established if P is true and if

$$f(\hat{m}) \neq f(\hat{m}+1) \to i := i+1; c(i): = \hat{c} = q(\hat{m}); \; = \hat{c}: = 0 \tag{24}$$

where initially

$$\hat{c} = \sum_{r=j}^{\hat{m}-1} q(r) \tag{25}$$

It can also be shown that the third term of (21)

$$\cdot \; \mathbf{A} \, j,k: 1 \leq j \leq k < \hat{m}+1 \text{ and } \hat{g}(j,k) \text{ and } k = \hat{m} \tag{26}$$

$$: \hat{c} = \sum_{r=j}^{k} q(r)$$

is true if P is true and if

$$f(\hat{m}) = f(\hat{m}+1) \to \hat{c}: = \hat{c} + q(\hat{m}) \tag{27}$$

With these observations, our final program becomes

$\hat{m}, i, \hat{c}: = 1,0,0;$
$\{P\}$
do $\hat{m} \neq m \to$
    if $f(\hat{m}) = f(\hat{m}+1) \to \hat{c}: = \hat{c} + q(\hat{m})$ (28)
    $[\!] \, f(\hat{m}) \neq f(\hat{m}+1) \to i: = i+1; c(i): = \hat{c} + q(\hat{m}); \hat{c}: = 0$
    fi;
    $\hat{m}: = \hat{m}+1 \; \{P\}^{\cdot}$
od
$\{R\}$

Show the loop terminates. During the design procedure, we have verified the truth of the first three conditions stated earlier in step 3 regarding the invariant P. Step 3d can be satisfied by showing that t remains positive while at least one guard is true and that each iteration decreases t. These final termination conditions should be verified by the reader.

Pseudocode. A pseudocode version of the final program is shown in Figure 37. Note that the meanings of code R, code D, and EOF have been restored. In this figure, i becomes *item_grps*, $\hat{c}$ becomes *net_chg*, $\hat{m}$ corresponds to *curr_rec*, and $f(\hat{m})$ corresponds to *curr_item*.

Conclusion

Comparison. While there is something to be learned from examining the pseudocode resulting from the four solutions to the McDonald's problem, more significant points can be made by comparing the differences in program structure.

Functional decomposition solution. A skeleton structure diagram for the functional decomposition solution is shown in Figure 38. Note that the basic operation was assumed to be PROCESS CARD and that this design treats the first card as different from the subsequent cards quite early. This results in a structure that favors the addition of changes that can be keyed to the beginning of a group. Changes that must be keyed to the end of a group are added with more difficulty.

Data flow design solution. The data flow design solution had the basic structure shown in Figure 39. Note that in this case there is a difference between a lead card and the last card in a group. That is the last card in a group gets treated in a special way—not the first card. For later modification, this means that operations added to the end of a group will be favored while operations added to the beginning of a group will not fit in as naturally.

Even through the concept of group is well localized on the diagram, the data flow nature of the processing forces one to do some of the group operations at the PROCESS CARD level. In this case, an end-of-group control signal must be inserted at the PROCESS CARD level so that other end-of-group processing functions can be activated within the PROCESS GROUP function.

The resulting program has sequential cohesion. Both data and control are passed up the structure diagram. Generating the end-of-group indication still causes a few minor problems, but in this particular example keying on the last card in a group turns out to be a better choice than keying on the first card in a group.

Data structure design solution. The data structure design solution is shown in Figure 40. In this solution, all of the cards are processed by the same PROCESS CARD function. The keying of groups is done automatically

```
item_grps: = 0;
net_chg: = 0;
open stf;
curr_rec: = read stf;
write heading;
do curr_rec ≠ EOF
   next_rec: = read stf;
   if curr_item = next_item →
      if code = R → net_chg: = net_chg + qty;
      [] code = D → net_chg: = net_chg − qty;
      fi
   [] curr_item ≠ next_item →
      item_grps: = item_grps + 1;
      if code = R → net_chg: = net_chg + qty;
      [] code = D → net_chg: = net_chg − qty;
      fi
      write net_chg;
      net_chg: = 0;
   fi
   curr_rec: = next_rec;
od
write item_grps;
close stf;
```

Figure 37. Programming calculus McDonald's solution.

within the control structure through use of the read-ahead rule. Thus, no cards are treated with special functions, and everything looks clean. This solution can handle further additions that require special action at the beginning or at the end of a group with relative ease.

Programming calculus solution. The programming calculus solution structure diagram is shown in Figure 41. Note that this solution treats the last card as special, favoring extensions that occur at the end of a group. Since most of the McDonald's problem group functions are end-of-group functions, the resulting solution looks quite clean. In the long run, this solution could cause problems when new beginning-of-group operations are added.

Of these four solutions, the one that seems to model the problem best is the data structure design solution shown in Figure 40. A proper choice of loop invariants using the predicate calculus may have led to the same structure, but the choice that was made didn't. Likewise, a proper application of functional decomposition also could have led to the same structure. Even the data flow design method does not completely rule out this preferred solution.

It might be argued that all four design methodologies were capable of yielding any of the other solutions. My view is that it would take a designer with unusual insight to reliably proceed toward the preferred solution using any of these techniques. I do feel, however, that for the class of problems represented by the McDonald's example, people are more likely to derive the preferred solution

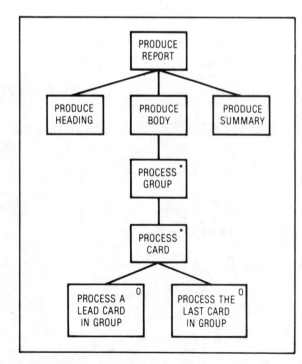

Figure 38. Functional decomposition structure diagram.

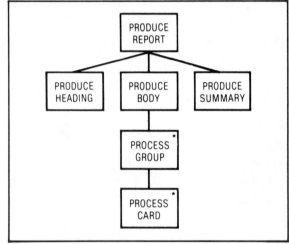

Figure 40. Data structure structure diagram.

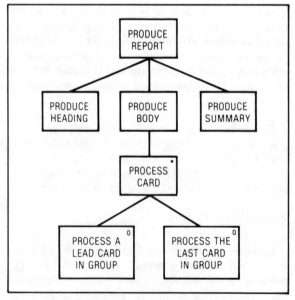

Figure 39. Data flow structure diagram.

Figure 41. Programming calculus structure diagram.

by using data structure design than by using any of the other methods. For a different class of problems, of course, the results could be different.

Critique. Since functional decomposition has been around for more than a decade, there have been many well-documented success stories and even a few well-documented failures.

One success story was summarized by its designers, using the diagrams in Figure 42. Perceived project visibility was dramatically improved by the application of functional decomposition together with other techniques. They also felt that project staffing could be reduced over that normally required. In this particular project, there was a lot of personnel turnover but this was taken in stride, partly owing to the beneficial effects of the new techniques.

It seems that functional decomposition can lead to a "good" hierarchical program structure if carefully applied. If not used carefully, however, it can lead toward logical cohesion and, occasionally, toward telescoping—that is, toward defining smaller and smaller modules that are not independent but have strong coupling with each other. Applying functional decomposition to obtain mathematical functions (e.g., square root) is relatively straightforward.

For any given problem, the number of potential decompositions can be large. This makes applying the technique much more of an art than a science. I know that Dijkstra can do beautiful functional decompositions.

In Johnson's[11] words, functional decomposition seems to be a triumph of individual intellect over lack of an orderly strategy. The question "Decomposition with respect to what?" is always a point to ponder. The measures of "goodness" are difficult to apply consistently. Finally, this method requires that the intellectual tasks of problem modeling and program construction be addressed simultaneously. Ideally, these two tasks would be separated.

Because the concept of data flow design came later than pure functional decomposition, it has not been used as extensively. Apparently, several projects within IBM have used the "composite design" version of data flow design with varying degrees of success. I have personally seen a number of success stories that praise data flow design.

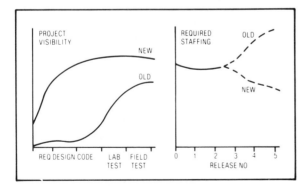

Figure 42. Experience with functional decomposition as used with hierarchical structure, stepwise refinement, high-level language, teams, walkthroughs, cause/effect charts, etc.

The concepts of coupling and cohesion, which accompanied the introduction of the data flow design method,[8] have been thought-provoking and, on some occasions, revealing. They have given people a language to express previously unverbalized thoughts.

The data flow design method can be used to produce a hierarchical program structure with all of its intrinsic advantages. The tendency is strongly toward modules with sequential cohesion at the system level, although anything can happen within the central transform. The data flow chart, which forms the basis for decomposing with respect to data flow, is a useful contribution and may be the best approach currently available at the system design level. It's not clear that the later step of putting things into a "calls" hierarchy using "transform centered design"[8] is as useful. It seems to produce a structure with a lot of data passing and adds artificial "afferent" (input) and "efferent" (output) ears to the structure chart, while reverting back to standard functional decomposition for the "central transform" which is the heart of the problem. It isn't clear that anything is gained over simply using functional decomposition from the start.

In summary, the concepts of cohesion and coupling represent a real step forward from straight functional decomposition. A qualitative measure of goodness is not as good as a quantitative measure, but it is a start. Furthermore, the data flow chart separates the modeling of the problem from detailing the structure of the program. The hard part becomes deriving the correct data flow chart (or "bubble chart"), which is still an art for large systems.

Neither the Jackson nor the Warnier methodologies for data structure design were widely used in this country until quite recently. They have, however, been used for a number of years in Europe. Jackson's method seems closer to a true methodology than the other design methodologies currently available. It is repeatable, teachable, and reliable in many applications. It usually results in a program structure that faithfully models the problem.

The data structure design method results in a hierarchical program structure, if the data structure is hierarchical. It produces multiple, independent hierarchies, if they are present in the problem environment. It is difficult to determine the level of cohesion of the modules within the resulting program structure. Sometimes it tends to be functional, in other cases communicational. By modeling the data structures and therefore the problem environment first, the problem modeling task is done before the program construction task.

While there is still no clear methodology for large systems and deriving the "correct" data structures can be difficult, it still seems that this method is a big step forward. Being able to ask whether a structure is right or wrong is somehow much more satisfying than trying to decide if it is good, better, or best.

Both Jackson's and Warnier's data structure design methods were first applied in business data processing. At this point, they have also been applied to a number of on-line problems, although they are still unproven for large real-time applications.

The number of people who use the programming calculus method regularly and proficiently is extremely small. The primary disadvantage is that a relatively high degree of logical and mathematical maturity is required to produce even "simple" programs. The mathematical proofs involved are usually several times longer than the program derived.

A second and perhaps less important disadvantage is that this method admits the existence of multiple solutions to the same problem. Different choices of an invariant assertion can lead to different program structures. The resulting programs do not necessarily portray accurate and consistent models of the problem's environment or its solution. That is, a "correct" program may still have the "wrong" structure.

In spite of these problems, Dijkstra's programming calculus design discipline is an encouraging step forward on the road to developing correct programs. It is a method that you should be aware of, for it holds promise for the future.

Summary. As shown in Figure 43, many claims have been made about the different strategies for designing software. For functional decomposition, the proponents have largely said, "D is good design, believe me." For data flow design methods, people have said, "Program C is better than program D. Let me tell you why." For data structure design methods, the claim is that "B is right; C and D are wrong. A program that works isn't necessarily right." In the programming calculus, the contention is that "Program A is probably correct. B, C, and D are unproven."

In my view, there is still much room for innovation in the area of program design methodologies. The current state of the art was represented schematically by Johnson[11] in the form of Figure 44. Functional decomposition has been described as the ideal methodology for people who already know the answer. The other three methodologies seem less reliant on knowing the answer before you start.

All of the methodologies rely on some magic. For functional decomposition, the magic gets applied very close to the end product. In the other three methodologies, at least some of the magic gets applied at the problem-model level. Clearly, we need to get a much better handle on the magic part of all four of the methodologies.

Prognosis. Many different design methodologies are available. Although the first three methodologies discussed in this article have been used extensively and to a large measure successfully, there is still much to be done.

Desired results. The results I would like to see from the work yet to come are

- a complete methodology for partitioning "big" problems,
- better documentation for both the shortcomings and attributes of existing methodologies,
- guidelines for combining methods when appropriate,
- a generally accepted metric for quantifying program complexity (or entropy),
- help for the four out of five programmers who are maintaining and enhancing old programs, and
- more published examples of real-time applications.

Hopes for the future. Some possible requirements on a "complete" methodology could include the following:

- It must include a rational procedure for partitioning and modeling the problem.
- It should result in consistent designs when applied by different people.
- It must systematically scale upward to large problems while interacting consistently with a model of the real world.
- It must partition the design process as well as the problem solution.
- The correctness of individual design steps must guarantee the correctness of the final combination.
- It should minimize the innovation required during the design process. The innovation should occur in the algorithm specification phase.

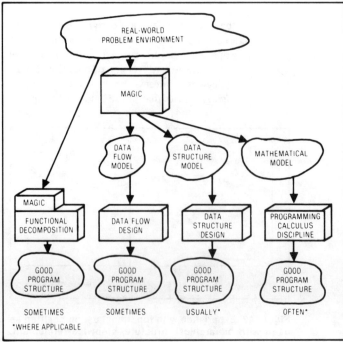

Figure 44. Current state of the art.

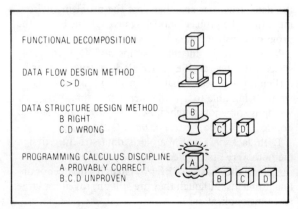

Figure 43. Summary of program design methodology claims.

An interim procedure. Until we know the "right" method for designing the structure of a large program, I would propose the following interim procedure:

- Define the high-level language and operating system macros bottom-up, using the principle of abstraction to hide the peculiarities of the hardware and to create a desirable virtual machine environment.
- Map the system flow diagram into your virtual machine environment.
- Work through the inversion[7] process or construct a data flow model of the "big" problem.
- Construct data structure diagrams that correspond to each data flow path.
- Cluster and combine bubbles that can be treated by one of Jackson's "simple" programs.
- Use the Jackson data structure design method to combine simple programs and reduce the number of intermediate files.
- Implement each cluster as concurrent, asynchronous processes if you are operating under a suitable programming environment—for example, Simula or Unix.[26]*
- If a decent operating system is not available, construct some scheduling kludge.

While these interim suggestions do not fit together well enough to call them a method, they may form a reasonable approach to follow until a true methodology for large problems is found. ∎

*Unix is a trademark of Bell Laboratories.

Acknowledgments

Much of the material presented here was developed and discussed over the last several years with R. D. Gordon and J. W. Johnson. The functional decomposition and data structure design solutions to the McDonald's problem are extensions of work described by Michael Jackson. The programming calculus solution to the McDonald's problem was developed after discussions with F. Schneider, G. Levin, and R. D. Gordon. Their inputs and support are gratefully acknowledged.

Several excellent suggestions from R. R. Conners, B. Dwyer, M. R. Gornick, R. C. Hansen, W. R. Nehrlich, and D. Sharma were incorporated in the final draft of this article.

References

1. J. N. Buxton, "Software Engineering," *Programming Methodology,* ed. D. Gries, Springer-Verlag, New York, 1978, pp. 23-28.

2. B. W. Boehm, "Software Engineering," *IEEE Trans. Computers,* Dec. 1976, Vol. C-25, No. 12.

3. D. L. Parnas, "Software Engineering or Methods for the Multi-Person Construction of Multi-Version Programs," *Programming Methodology,* Lecture Notes in Computer Science, No. 23, Springer-Verlag, New York, 1975, pp. 225-235.

4. V. A. Vyssotsky, "Software Engineering," keynote speech delivered at COMPSAC 79, Nov. 6-8, 1979, Chicago, Ill.

5. G. D. Bergland and R. D. Gordon, *Tutorial: Software Design Strategies,* IEEE Computer Society Press, Silver Spring, Md., 1979, pp. 1-14.

6. G. M. Weinberg, *The Psychology of Computer Programming,* Van Nostrand Reinhold, New York, 1971.

7. M. A. Jackson, *Principles of Program Design,* Academic Press, New York, 1975.

8. E. Yourdon and L. L. Constantine, *Structured Design,* Yourdon Press, New York, 1975.

9. G. J. Myers, *Reliable Software Through Composite Design,* Petrocelli/Charter, New York, 1975.

10. B. Liskov and S. Zilles, "Programming with Abstract Data Types," *SIGPLAN Notices,* Vol. 9, No. 4, Apr. 1974, pp. 50-59.

11. J. W. Johnson, "Software Design Techniques," *Proc. Nat'l Electronics Conf.,* Chicago, Ill., Oct. 12, 1977.

12. F. P. Brooks, Jr., *The Mythical Man-Month,* Addison-Wesley Pub. Co. Reading, Mass., 1975.

13. E. W. Dijkstra, "The Humble Programmer," *Comm. ACM,* Vol. 15, No. 10, Oct. 1972, pp. 859-866.

14. *Implications of Using Modular Programming,* Central Computer Agency, Her Majesty's Stationery Office, London, 1973.

15. C. Alexander, *Notes on Synthesis of Form,* Harvard University Press, Cambridge, Mass., 1964.

16. L. A. Belady and M. M. Lehman, "Characteristics of Large Systems," *Proc. Research Directions in Software Technology,* Brown University, Oct. 1977.

17. F. T. Baker, "Structured Programming in a Production Programming Environment," *IEEE Trans. Software Eng.,* June 1975, Vol. SE-1, No. 2, pp. 241-252.

18. D. L. Parnas, "On the Criteria to be Used in Decomposing Systems into Modules," *Comm. ACM,* Vol. 15, No. 12, Dec. 1972, pp. 1053-1058.

19. R. C. Linger, H. D. Mills, and B. I. Witt, *Structured Programming Theory and Practice,* Addison-Wesley, Reading, Mass., 1979.

20. E. W. Dijkstra, *A Discipline of Programming,* Prentice-Hall, Englewood Cliffs, N.J., 1976.

21. N. Wirth, *Systematic Programming,* Prentice-Hall, Englewood Cliffs, N.J., 1973.

22. B. H. Liskov, "A Design Methodology for Reliable Software Systems," *AFIPS Conf. Proc.,* Vol. 41, FJCC 72, 1972, pp. 191-199.

23. J. D. Warnier, *Logical Construction of Programs,* Van Nostrand Reinhold Co., New York, 1974.

24. D. Gries, "An Illustration of Current Ideas on the Derivation of Correctness Proofs and Correct Programs," *IEEE Trans. Software Eng.,* Vol. SE-2, No. 4, Dec. 1976, pp. 238-244.

25. E. W. Dijkstra and D. Gries, "Introduction to Programming Methodology," Ninth Institute in Computer Science, University of California, Santa Cruz, Aug. 1979.

26. D. M. Ritchie and K. Thompson, "The UNIX Time-Sharing System," *Bell System Technical J.,* Vol. 57, No. 6, Part 2, July-Aug. 1978, pp. 1905-1929.

Glenn D. Bergland is head of Bell Telephone Laboratories' Digital Systems Research Department in Murray Hill, New Jersey. In 1966, when he joined Bell Telephone Laboratories in Whippany, New Jersey, he conducted research in highly parallel computer architectures. In 1972, he became head of the Advanced Switching Architecture Department in Naperville, Illinois. Later, he became head of the Software Systems Department, which was involved in feature development for the No. 1 electronic switching system. Currently, his major research areas are software design methodologies, digital telecommunications services, personal computing, and nonstop computer systems.

Bergland received the BS, MS, and PhD in electrical engineering from Iowa State University in 1962, 1964, and 1966. He is a member of the IEEE and ACM.

WHY DOES SOFTWARE DIE?

P.J. Brown

Computing Laboratory
The University
Canterbury, United Kingdom

Complexity is the prime contributor to the premature death of software. How can we effectively fight complexity, whilst increasing flexibility and portability? Causes of short-lived software are first reviewed. The paper examines the preventive measures involved in building flexible software structures for the design of long-lived programs and for reducing the high cost of keeping systems alive.

CAUSES OF DEATH

In order to understand how to make software live longer, it is fruitful to examine why software dies. Death of established software comes from one of two causes:

1. Failure to adapt to change.

2. Murder: the software is overthrown by another, stronger, piece of software which does the same task.

The relative danger of these two depends on the nature of the product. If the software is designed to meet one special need, then competition may be non-existent. The chance of murder is therefore negligible, but if, as a result of change, the software no longer satisfies its one purpose, it will immediately wither away. General-purpose software, on the other hand, is in a more competitive market, and there is a greater likelihood of murder; murder is all the more probable if the software is weakened because it has not responded to change.

Infant mortality

A frighteningly large proportion of software projects die between conception and maturity in the sense that no established final product results. The good practices needed to ensure that established software will have a long and prosperous life are just as important in avoiding death in infancy. Infant software faces all the dangers of adult software (plus a lot more besides).

Death due to change

The changes that can kill software can arise in several possible areas. There may be changes in the operational environment, which involves hardware, software and standards. The model of the outside world on which the software is based may change; a payroll program, for example, can be ruined by a radical change in tax laws. There may be changes in user attitudes and in the way they wish to communicate with software. There may be, indeed there will be, changes made to correct bugs in the software. Finally, there will be changes as a result of user requests for new facilities.

On top of all of these there may be cataclysmic changes caused by such events as natural disasters, wars, riots, bankruptcies or by highly-paid outside experts reorganizing the software. No amount of planning in the design of software will help avoid such happenings, so we shall exclude them from our consideration. Instead we shall consider in detail some of the changes for which preventive medicine may be possible.

Hardware changes

Much software is killed in the prime of life by a change of hardware. Typically the casualty is tied to one machine by virtue of being encoded in assembly language or a non-standard high-level language; the original machine is replaced by another, different, one and death is instantaneous. Even software that was supposedly based on a standard high-level language, such as COBOL, is not immune.

There has been so much slaughter of good software by hardware changes that more recently the pace of change in machine order codes has been slowed. New hardware is now much more frequently designed to be compatible with the old, though not as compatible as the salesmen would have us believe. The problem of hardware change remains a serious one.

Hardware differences are also important when software is so successful on one range of machines that it is decided to implement it on several other machines as well. If software is available on many machines it has an added strength and vitality that should help see it through to old age.

This gives further impetus to the desire to design software to be portable from machine to machine, so we shall discuss the subject of portability in some detail later.

Hardware changes less drastic than a machine replacement can still kill software. A new periph-

First published in the *Pergamon Infotech State of the Art Report* 'Life Cycle Management,' Pergamon Infotech Ltd., 1980.

eral device attached to an existing machine can have dramatic consequences. In the past, we have seen examples of this where a disk has been added to what was previously a machine based on magnetic tape. Changes of a similar magnitude are likely during the lifetime of any successful software. Failure to respond to such changes will not cause immediate death, but a gradual loss of friends among users, perhaps ending in eventual murder.

Software changes

All software systems have others that they depend on. Thus, an application program may depend on an operating system, a compiler, and probably on other supporting aids such as editors and documentation systems.

Even the operating system, which has nothing between it and the underlying hardware, still depends on its compilers, its utilities and its application programs, as without these it is useless.

For most of us, the biggest and most burdensome dependence is on the manufacturer's systems software. Unlike changes of hardware, which are infrequent but earth-shattering events, changes of software are frequent and often apparently minor. However, if you have an applications program and leave it alone for a year, you can almost guarantee problems: when you come to run it again it will fail because of some subtle 'small' change in the systems software. If you leave it for, say, three years, you can equally guarantee that not only will the software fail, but it will be almost impossible to trace all the minor systems software changes that have caused it to fail. Your software has died of neglect.

Thus, catering for software changes is a matter of constant vigilance and attention to detail. If you have not been careful, a small change in the systems software might completely invalidate the principles on which your software is based. In addition, every few years the vendor may issue a complete rewrite of his systems software, an event almost as far-reaching as a hardware change.

Our discussion of portability will consider software changes as well as hardware ones. In addition we shall discuss the subject of interfaces, which also has a bearing on software changes.

Changes in requirements

Consider a suite of programs that is used to aid document preparation. The following examples illustrate requirements changes that may occur during the program's lifetime:

1. **Change of parameter.** The standard page width is changed.

2. **Additional feature.** The program is required to work on texts in a foreign language, which uses a different character set and allows accents to be attached to each character.

3. **Change of algorithm.** The program is required to improve its algorithm for determining spacing and hyphenation.

4. **Change of user interface.** Users wish to communicate with the program interactively, whereas the software works in batch mode.

5. **Consolidation.** The software is to be combined with another software suite, which makes spelling checks and cross-reference listings, and has been written using different conventions.

To the software writer, the striking facet of such changes in requirements is that they represent bullets that may strike randomly at each and every aspect of his software. The parts of the software that are susceptible to hardware or software changes can, with care, be predicted in advance, and preventive action can be taken in the appropriate cases. Any attempt to lessen the effects of future requirements changes cannot be localized but must permeate the entire structure of the software.

Changes caused by errors

All software that is in practical use contains errors. Like changes of requirements, errors strike randomly at all parts of software, but fortunately the software writers have more control over errors than over requirements changes. We shall discuss control of errors later.

Errors are a deadly and merciless killer of software. Death can come in two ways. Firstly, if software is riddled with errors, users will abandon it, and it will thus die of neglect; this is a big cause of infant software mortality. Secondly, software may be killed by poverty, because the effort of correcting errors has become so expensive that it uses up all the maintenance budget. A particular danger is the **error explosion**.

It is well known that in correcting one error there is a relatively high chance of introducing a further error. Typically, correcting one error introduces 0.5 further errors, so the error correction process eventually converges. On some projects, however, correcting one error introduces 1.5 further errors. The result is a long and increasingly painful illness with inevitable death after a year or so.

Summary

If we are going to produce long-life software which will withstand all the changes we have outlined, we must make it good and keep it good. In order to keep software good we must protect it from the sudden fatal diseases that may strike it down in the prime of life, and from the steadily debilitating diseases which will increasingly affect it in its later years. But our aim is not just to keep our software alive, but to make it increasingly strong and vigorous - to make it a murderer rather than a victim. Our aim is also to keep our costs down; if it is too expensive to keep the patient alive, the management will have no scruples about euthanasia.

SIMPLE SOLUTIONS

For every difficult problem in life there are a hundred people, some sincere, others not, offering simple solutions. Thus we hear propounded simple ways to solve a nation's economic problems or the social problems of the inner cities, and as individuals we are offered simple ways to make a killing on the stock exchange, to impress our friends and neighbours, to win at gambling, or to maintain perfect health.

It is tempting to dismiss the lot as worthless, but many of them do actually contain some sound sense, even if the effects are somewhat oversold. People who have inflicted problems on themselves through some gross and simple mistake may indeed find the simple solution invaluable. To take a concrete example, assume a simple remedy for ill-health is based on following some prescribed diet. If your diet previously consisted only of deep-frozen suet pudding with chemical beer, then following the diet may have dramatic beneficial effects. If, on the other hand, your diet is already a sensible one and your problems of ill-health are deep-seated, then the new diet will not help at all.

So it is with the simple remedies for bad software. If your methods were previously hopelessly bad, a simple remedy may be a godsend to you; if you already run a decent outfit and your problems are the deep-seated ones found in any complex software, do not expect too much.

We shall examine a few of these simple remedies, in case they do help.

Simple remedy 1--the analogy

A popular line of argument goes like this. Some home-spun analogy is drawn between software production/maintenance and some other well understood sphere. It is shown that problems in the second sphere were solved at some time by a particular method. Therefore, runs the argument, all the problems of software can be solved in a similar way. 'Producing software is like riding a bicycle,' you may be told. 'If you go at a reasonable speed you won't fall off, but if you go slowly you will lose your balance.' Having heard this you are convinced that going at a reasonable speed will solve all your software problems, and when you get back to work all those nasty and complicated difficulties will be swept away by your speedy new broom.

Analogies are not valueless. An analogy between writing software and riding bicycles, building bridges or whatever, may enable us to see ourselves more clearly, and possibly to see where current trends are leading. But there is always

some fundamental mismatch between the analogy and the real thing. Some factor will differ by an order of magnitude: it may be the cost of reproduction (which for software is tiny), the complexity, the pace of change, or simply the nature of the human beings who build and use the software.

Simple remedy 2--the general solution

Software design has been riddled with attempts to build general tools which cover the function of a host of special tools. Periodically there have been designs for general languages that cover all applications, general compilers that compile all languages for all machines, general interfaces (such as UNCOL), and general operating systems which cover commercial batch processing, airline reservation systems and educational BASIC. In the early 'seventies there was a big movement into 'extensible languages,' which were programming languages that could be moulded to meet any given need.

The success rate for all these projects has been low. This is because in any discipline there is a point beyond which generality is infeasible because of the overall complexity and conflicting requirements. Thus for transportation there are cars that are general enough to cover both city traffic and the fast open road, but there are not cars that can also fly and travel by sea. In software we are beginning to get a feel for where the sensible limits of generality lie, and to be very wary of new super-general projects. (Readers can judge for themselves whether our reference to transport is a good example or the epitome of the mistaken analogy we have previously chided.)

A movement which may well be a current example of over-generalization is the attempt to provide general software components. Granted, you can build general packages and general subroutines to do some well defined common tasks (particularly mathematical functions, sorting algorithms and the like), but is it sensible to think of building a large piece of software out of a host of prefabricated components?

Simple remedy 3--the new methodology

At any conference one finds a persuasive speaker extolling the merits of some new methodology that will solve all the problems of software production and maintenance. To many of these experts a pertinent question is: 'Why, instead of spending your time talking about your methodology, do you not set up a company which will use the methodology to produce software ten times cheaper than anyone else, and thus make a real killing?'

PREVENTIVE MEDICINE

Having said that simple remedies do not provide a complete answer to the problem of software production and maintenance, it is now time to examine more elaborate methods, which involve a good deal of work, but which provide an eventual payoff. Before going into details we shall examine a fundamental law that affects all software maintenance work.

Large and small programs

If we have two pieces of software, x and y, where y is similar to x except that each component is twice as large, then y will be four times as expensive to produce and maintain. We call this the square law. The square law comes about largely because communication problems multiply extremely rapidly as software gets bigger. These problems come, at one level, with the way pieces of software communicate with one another, and, at another level with the way that humans who write and maintain the software intercommunicate. Also of prime importance is the capacity of the human mind; some programs are just too complicated for humans to comprehend, and are therefore unmaintainable.

The key to successful maintenance of large software--and it is large software that interests us, because small software is easy--is to cheat the square law. The basic technique is to split a large program up so that it appears as two small programs. If these two programs were each half the size of the original, and were totally independent of one another, then, given the square law, the pair of them would be twice as easy to maintain as the original. If we could keep halving our maintenance costs in this simple way, life would indeed be perfect (except perhaps for those two-thirds of the world's programmers who would be made redundant as a result). In practice, however, it is simply not possible to chop programs into two independent halves. In fact, if an unskilled butcher does the chopping--and there are lots of such people about--the two halves will have elaborate interdependence and communication requirements. The result will be that the two halves will actually be more complicated than the original, and therefore more expensive to maintain.

The aim must be to find a way of splitting programs up which, while inevitably short of perfection, avoids butchery; the goal is to split a program up into two (or more) parts with controlled and simple interdependence so that the sum of the parts is perhaps 30% easier to maintain than the original whole. This splitting should continue until the parts, or modules as they are often called, are reduced to an easily managed size, at which point splitting is of no further advantage. It is this goal that the huge volume of literature on 'structured programming' is seeking to achieve.

Interfaces

The more a large program is split up, the more interfaces are needed between the constituent modules. Those experienced in software production and maintenance will often tell you that the design of interfaces is what software is all about.

Clearly in any large software system, where modules will continually be added, replaced or deleted during the maintenance period, some all-pervading and systematic design of interfaces is vital. This standard interface must be general enough to cover all capabilities, and must be simple to understand, simple to use and, above all, simple to enforce. It is important to realise that a fixed interface will not always provide the best means of communication between any two particular modules; instead it should provide one standard way. Programmers will be tempted to extend or vary the interface in those cases where it turns out to be a bit clumsy, but such temptation should be resisted at all costs.

A good deal of work in programming language design is now concerned with making interfaces clean and explicit. An important part of this is the import and export of variables (and other entities). A variable that is exported is one that 'belongs' to a given module but is used by other modules, which import it. A good example of these ideas, and one which may have a huge impact on the software community, whether we like it or not, is the ADA language (004).

Structuring

A lot has been written about structuring software and indeed a whole Infotech report (003) is devoted to it.

There are many available structuring methods, but they are fundamentally quite similar and all aim to meet the following goals:

o To aid both the production of software and its maintenance

o To cover both the way the software is coded and the way it is documented

o To encompass some of the ideas in the classic book 'Structured Programming' (002).

We shall not try to describe here what has already been presented in detail many times, but will simply reiterate that the most important thing is to have some sensible methodology--the particular one selected is less important--and that this methodology should pervade all aspects of design and be reflected in the documentation. The key to producing an easily-maintained product is to make it a good product in the first place.

Information hiding

A concept that has a bearing on structure and division into modules is information hiding. The concept was introduced by Parnas (006) and is of special relevance to program maintenance. The idea of information hiding is that modules should be chosen so that the effects of each design decision are confined to a single module. To take our earlier example of the documentation program, the way that text is stored should only be known by one module. Similarly, if a particular sorting algorithm is used to produce indexes, concordances, etc., then the implications of this should also be confined to a single module. The advantage is, of course, that if the method of text storage and/or the sorting algorithm needs to be changed, then the effects are confined to single modules and do not, as often happens, subtly permeate the entire software design.

Program families

Another area with which the name of Parnas is associated is program families (007,008). A set of programs is a family if 'they have so much in common that it pays to study their common aspects before looking at the aspects which differentiate them.' Some examples of families are:

1. A set of similar programs that run on different machines.

2. A set of programs that perform identical tasks but have differing ways of entering data.

3. A set of programs that are issued in various cut-down versions to work, say, in small storage or with minimal run time overhead.

Many of us have found that if we are responsible for such families the maintenance task soon gets out of hand. Moreover, market conditions often dictate the creation of program families even if this was not the original design intention. (There is a similar situation with hardware families.)

Parnas advocates that a software family be designed from the very start to be a minimal usable kernel together with various extensions to build other family members. This not only helps when a family is the original design intention, but also when changes during the maintenance of a program cause the ad hoc creation of family members. Parnas gives a detailed example in (008), and this is an excellent starting point for those wishing to pursue the ideas in depth.

Parameterisation

Some provision for change can be allowed for in the way programs are encoded. In particular, constants (for example the size of a built-in array) should not be embedded deeply in the code, but should be assigned as parameters at the start. Most high-level languages allow for this by providing such facilities as 'manifest constants,' 'constant declarations,' or 'macros.' (Macros, if available, allow even more flexibility than just substituting values for constants.) Some software writers claim that programs should contain no explicit constants other than 0 or 1, as anything else is likely to need changing.

It is also vital, when encoding a program, to ensure that the formats of tables and the way they are accessed can easily be changed. It is absolutely certain that such formats will need changing during the life of successful software, and programs should be designed so that changes in the ordering or size of fields can be done by changing only the relevant data declarations. Otherwise a typical result would be a program that becomes

useless if, say, interest rates unexpectedly climb into double figures; such programs are a lasting rebuke to their writers.

Freezing

During the life-cycle of any software project there are times when the forces of change are so burdensome and so destructive to progress that the management freezes some or all of the software components. In determining whether to freeze, it is important to analyze the nature of the requests for change. This may indicate that the software is fundamentally wrongly designed, and is not satisfying its design goals; if so, freezing the rubbish may be a short-term palliative but in the long term will be useless. Instead a redesign is needed, painful as that may be. It is quite common for the bulk of requests for improvements in software to be concentrated in one module of it, and this is a strong indication that the particular module is a weak point and needs redesigning.

On the other hand an analysis of requests for change may show that they are all for extra bells and whistles--or for special facilities to combine frequently used sets of operations. If so, the software is in a healthy state and can be frozen if circumstances dictate. Indeed the designers should be much more worried if there are no requests for change.

Standards

Standards play a large part in making programs easy to maintain and to disseminate. There is a spectrum of standards starting at individual standards, and going through company and national standards to international standards. Standards can never be perfect. Among their defects are the following:

1. Standards change; typically international standards for programming languages change every six years.

2. Standards take a long time to become effective, and by then they may be obsolete. Users may then be forced to deviate from a standard because they need some new facility.

3. Some standards are too lax (e.g.; in the precision and accuracy of arithmetic) whereas others are too restrictive (e.g., they may drive away advocates of 'GOTO-less programming').

4. Standards sometimes do not gain acceptance, with the result that the 'standard' site is actually the odd one out.

As one proceeds across the spectrum towards international standards these defects get worse, but on the other hand the standard itself is potentially more valuable.

In spite of all the problems, standards, albeit defective, are better than no standards at all.

Portability

Software is portable if it can easily be moved from one environment to another. The change of environment may be a change of hardware or a change of systems software.

The easiest way to make software portable is to encode it in a standard high-level language. This is especially good if the language has a portable compiler. Programming languages such as PASCAL and BCPL, which (as yet) have no international standard, have achieved great success because they have portable compilers. If software written in, for example, BCPL needs to be moved to a new machine, then if that machine lacks a BCPL compiler, it is not a major job to port the compiler across, thus making the software written in BCPL portable. Another advantage of portable compilers is that it is much easier to exchange software from one compiler to another. This is not true for languages without portable compilers, as anyone who has moved a 'standard' COBOL program from one machine to another will know.

Because of the defects of standards it may not be possible to encode all one's software in existing portable high-level languages. To solve this problem, organizations often design their own language extensions and write a preprocessor to map these extensions into the standard language. The benefits of portability given by the standard are not lost but great flexibility is gained. Examples of this are RATFOR (005), which is designed to surmount the lack of structuring in FORTRAN IV, and GENTRAN (010), which is concerned with the portability of civil engineering software.

Systems software, particularly operating systems and compilers, present special problems in portability. For a discussion of these, and for a fuller discussion of other aspects of portability, see (001).

Like all the other measures to ease maintenance problems, portability costs time and money in the program production stages. It is no use simply issuing an edict that certain standards must be followed, and then expecting that there will be no problems when attempts are made to port the software in future years. Portability must be checked and verified at each stage of software production. To help this there exist verifiers such as PFORT (009), which help check whether a given program adheres to language standards. These verifiers are not, and cannot be, perfect, and there is no substitute for practical testing of portability at an early stage by actually moving the software, or certain modules of it, to a different environment. This is sure to reveal a host of nasty little problems which can then be cured before the software is developed further.

Documentation

It is imperative that the documentation of software have the same structure, the same standards and the same flexibility as the programming. Unfortunately this rarely happens in practice. This is often because too much emphasis is placed on the size of documentation and too little on quality and interrelationships between the parts. Documentation standards, which may, for example, specify a fixed form for the documentation of each subroutine, may aid comprehensiveness, but cannot help readability.

The most common error in documentation is to provide masses of detail, which could equally well be found from the program listing, but little on overall organization, on the reasons for design decisions, on how things can be changed, and on relationships between parts. Rarely does the author of the documentation put himself in the reader's position of trying to proceed in easy stages from total ignorance to a complete grasp of a complicated piece of software. A way to help remedy this defect is to subject documentation to a thorough scrutiny by ignorant readers at an early stage. This costs time and effort but helps ensure that gross inadequacies of documentation are found before the author leaves the company at some future date.

Obtaining good documentation is often a question of changing the attitude of those who produce it. Doing a good job is an interesting and challenging task, just like writing a good program. It is the producing of voluminous bad documentation that is a dull task.

Errors

When software has been encoded it is inevitable that it will contain semantic errors (i.e., errors that cause the software to do the wrong thing when it is run). These semantic errors may arise from programming slips or from design errors. Good design and perhaps verification methods can lessen but not eliminate such errors.

The best single action that can be taken to increase software's life is to eliminate these errors before the software is issued. This is done by writing a good suite of test programs. Consider the possible history of a single semantic error. One possible history is for the bug to be found during the production stage of the software. Another possible history is for the bug to be found two years later by a user in the field. This second case brings about the following sequence of events:

1. The user finds the bug. For each such bug the reputation of the software and its supplier drops a little.

2. The user reports the bug.

3. The supplier recreates the bug at his own

site. This is often difficult and expensive to do, because of communication problems, hardware differences, version numbers, etc.

4. The supplier tries to localize the part of the software that caused the bug. Sometimes this is easy, sometimes (e.g., because of a subtle corruption of storage) it is difficult.

5. The maintenance personnel dig out listings and documentation of the appropriate version of the offending module, and try to comprehend what is going on.

6. The bug is found and remedied.

7. A test program is written to show that the correction works.

8. The bug is also corrected in subsequent versions of the software, particularly in the next one to be issued.

9. The corrected software is issued to users, either immediately or at the next scheduled release date, depending on urgency.

On the other hand if the same bug had been detected at the production stage, soon after it had been made, then:

1. The offending piece of code should be easy to detect. It is quite likely to be the part most recently added to the system.

2. The workings of the offending code are still in the designer's/programmer's mind.

As a result the only actions needed are 6 and 7 above. Hence it is likely that the expense of correcting the bug is ten times less than correcting the same bug found later in the field.

Testing

Testing is a topic that has been the subject of entire conferences. We shall confine ourselves to a few points that we feel passionately about.

1. It is imperative to have a comprehensive test suite that is used not only at the first release of software but at every subsequent release too.

2. The only people who can write decent tests are the original designers/programmers, since they know the workings of the software and its weak points. If their testing work is supplemented by a separate Quality Assurance department, so much the better, but this is only a supplement.

3. It is tragically false economy if software is released without proper testing in order to meet a deadline. What it means is that maintenance will be many times more expensive and future deadlines will be even harder to meet.

4. It is vital that those who write the software actually use it. Incredibly, many software writers make no serious attempt to use their product. The result is a hopeless user interface, and a host of requests for changes when the software goes into the field.

5. All software should contain decent debugging aids, so that those responsible for correcting errors can find out what is going on. It is particularly important to be able to print out internal tables in a comprehensible manner. If the only debugging aid is a hexadecimal dump, bugs will cost much more to correct.

We believe that attention to these five points at the software design stage could have dramatically reduced the maintenance costs of a lot of current software, and would have greatly increased life expectancy.

CONCLUSIONS

In order to make software have a long and healthy life, it is necessary to put a lot of extra effort into the initial product. Software that works may be expensive to produce, but software that works and stays working costs more still. The extra effort goes into building a structure that allows for change, in producing readable documentation, in making the software portable and above all in keeping bugs down so that they do not make a big hole in the maintenance budget.

REFERENCES

001 Brown, P.J. (editor), Software Portability, Cambridge University Press (1977)

002 Dahl, O.-J., Dijkstra, E.W., and Hoare, C.A.R. Structured Programming, Academic Press, London (1972)

003 Hosier, J. (editor), Structured Analysis and Design, Infotech State of the Art Report, Infotech Ltd., Maidenhead, Berks (1978)

004 Ichbiah, J.D. et al., "Preliminary ADA Reference Manual," SIGPLAN Notices, Volume 14, Number 6 (1979)

005 Kernighan, B.W. and Plauger, P.J., Software Tools, Addison-Wesley, Reading, MA (1976)

006 Parnas, D.L., "On the criteria to be used for decomposing systems into modules," Communications of the ACM, Volume 15, Number 12, pages 1053-1058 (1972)

007 Parnas, D.L., "On the Design and Development of Program Families", IEEE Transactions on Software Engineering, Volume 2, Number 1, pages 1-9 (1976)

008 Parnas, D.L., "Designing Software for Ease of Extension and Contraction," Proceedings of the 3rd International Conference on Software Engineering, Atlanta, GA, pages 264-277 (1978)

009 Ryder, B.G., "The PFORT Vertifier," Software--Practice and Experience, Volume 4, Number 4, pages 359-378 (1974)

010 Shearing, B.M. and Alcock, D.G., "Gentran," Proceedings Colloque International sur les Systems Integres on Genie Civil, Liege (1972)

A 75,000-line program that evolved over several years into a functional prototype has reached a level of complexity that taxes the university environment to its limit.

Observations on the Evolution of a Software System

Eric Allman and Michael Stonebraker, University of California, Berkeley

Reprinted from *Computer*, Volume 15, Number 6, June 1982, pages 27-32. Copyright © 1982 by The Institute of Electrical and Electronics Engineers, Inc.

The Ingres data base system[1,2] encompasses about 75,000 lines of code in the programming language "C"[3] and runs on top of the Unix operating system. Over the past six years, Ingres has evolved into a functionally complete and usable prototype. Development required 25 to 30 programmer-years by a total of 19 people, and the system is now in use at over 125 sites around the world.

In this article we will attempt to answer a question that we are often asked: "How did you manage to get a large software system to work in a university environment?" A chronology of the project and the major technical mistakes have been reported elsewhere,[2] so we will concentrate on the software engineering process and what we have learned about it. Although our experience is in a research environment, we believe that many of these lessons can be applied to most software development efforts.

Chronology

The Ingres experience can be divided into three periods that can be examined individually.

Initial design and implementation (1974-1976). The initial goal was to build a functional relational data base system. During this period we wrote about 60,000 lines of code. The attitude of the design team was to "make the system work" regardless of the methods used.

The project developed out of a graduate seminar; hence, the initial programmers were all graduate students. They were organized as a chief programmer team of four programmers plus a lead programmer. The project directors, Michael Stonebraker and Eugene Wong, acted largely as "creative consultants." Their role was to define the major structure of the system and determine general strategy. Although they were the final arbitrators on technical matters, most problems were handled by the chief programmer.

The role of the chief programmer was first to write code and second to arbitrate conflicts and supervise global design. Since the PDP-11 computer on which implementation began had a 64K-byte address space limitation, Ingres clearly had to run as several Unix processes. The division of the implementation effort among the programmers followed process boundaries. Hence, for the most part, each programmer could code in his own Unix process and have an address space to himself. Minimal cooperation was necessary once the function of each process was finalized and its interface defined. Each programmer could implement the functions in his process any way he wished. Initially, there was no attempt to share subroutines, and even the routines for interprocess communication were customized for each process. Moreover, there was no utilization of software engineering practices such as structured walk-throughs or reading the code produced by others.

The absence of organizational structure directly reflected the multiprocess environment in which no shared code for Ingres existed. This absence of structure below the process level contributed to many later problems.

Making it work (1976-1978). Once an initial prototype was working, we were eager to have people outside the university use it. By mid-1977 there were about ten users, and the sites were all bold, innovative, and sophisticated. The feedback from these initial users was extremely helpful. In addition to receiving useful information about what "real" people wanted to do, we also gained considerable exposure. Many of the comments concerned the awkwardness of the user interface and the absence of helpful error messages.

Much effort went into making improvements to the system during this time. For example, error returns from system calls had not been consistently checked in the initial version. When the disk became full and no new blocks were available for expansion, the data base would be irrevocably corrupted. We spent considerable time fortifying the system against these kinds of events. We also added crash recovery, concurrency control, additional access methods and did substantial algorithm modification to improve performance.

When implementing a major system, it would seem wise to plan to build a prototype that will be tested and thrown away.

The project continued to be organized as a chief programmer team of three to five people. As the initial collection of programmers left, we replaced them with undergraduates exclusively. The idea was to obtain two to three years of continuous employment in order to justify the long training period (typically one academic quarter). Also, while graduate students were intrigued with the problem of building a data base system from scratch, they found the extension of an existing system less appealing.

During this period the number of installations climbed steadily, and the chief programmer spent more and more time providing user support, usually by telephone. While early feedback was very useful in isolating poorly designed features and uncovering bugs, later interactions focused on misinterpretations concerning the setup instructions, the reference manual, or Unix. The feedback from these later users was of less value. As we gained a reputation, the new users we attracted were frequently less sophisticated and were starting to demand a turnkey system. We began to act less like a research group and more like a software house.

Back to research (1978-). In 1978 it became clear that the Ingres project was soon to accomplish the goals set in 1974. To maintain a climate of intellectual inquiry, the project expanded its goals to include the following:

(1) Build a distributed data base management system. This necessitated extensive data base code to provide consistency control in a distributed environment as well as distributed query processing.

(2) Integrate Arpanet services. These are required to achieve the goal listed above.

(3) Develop operating system extensions to support local networking.[4] These are also required for goal number 1.

(4) Build a data base machine. Given the design philosophy of Muffin,[5] this was a natural outgrowth of distributed data bases. However, it required a local network and a small real-time operating system. No candidate for either was available at the time we began.

(5) Build a new data base programming language, Rigel.[6] This project was undertaken by Lawrence Rowe.

As a result of these decisions, we found ourselves doing development in the areas of language processing, networking, and operating systems. This has created a large increase in the complexity of the Ingres project.

As before, we continue to have a chief programmer and a staff of three to five programmers, augmented by other individuals or groups. The chief programmer team continues to maintain and extend the core of the Ingres system, while networking and language work are carried out by other autonomous groups. This allows the necessary specialization, although it has increased the number of conflicting factions. For example, networking code requires operating system modifications that often interfere with the data base effort. Moreover, Rowe and Stonebraker, who now share the task of general technical direction, occasionally operate at cross purposes. Frequently, there is no clear resolution of the situation; hence, setting priorities and goals has become exceedingly difficult.

Lessons and observations

Setting goals. Our policy has always been to set long-term goals that are nearly unattainable. This policy has led to great intellectual expansion for the participants and appears to help in the recruitment of talented people, which the success of the project ultimately depends on. Nevertheless, it seems crucial to choose achievable short-term targets. This avoids the morale problems related to tasks that appear to go on forever. The decomposition of long-term goals into manageable short-term tasks continues to be the main job of the project directors.

Short-term goals were often set with the full knowledge that the longer-term problem was not fully understood or that a crucial variable (such as crash recovery) was deliberately being ignored. Consequently, many steps were taken that were ultimately wrong, and they were retraced later when the issues were better understood. The alternative is to refrain from development until the problem is well understood. We found that taking any step often helped us find the correct course of action. Also, moving in *some* direction usually resulted in higher project morale than a period of inactivity. In short, it appears more useful to "do something now even if it is ultimately incorrect" than to only attempt things when success is assured.

As a consequence of this philosophy, we take a relaxed view toward discarding code. Throughout the Ingres project, we have repeatedly done complete rewrites of large portions of the system. Whenever the code became top-heavy with patches, or when we learned that it should have been structured differently, we simply "bit the bullet" and rewrote it. Our philosophy has always been that "it is never too late to throw everything away." Although this has proved expensive at times, it usually served us well by eliminating unwieldy pieces of code. However, as the system grew, larger and larger pieces of code came under the scalpel. There came a point at which rewriting bulky and uninteresting pieces of code became impossible because the rewrite was so tedious that it would incur an intolerable morale cost.

When implementing a major system, it would seem wise to plan to build a prototype that will be tested and thrown away. This was the strategy followed by the System R design team.[7] Only well-understood problems can be properly implemented the first time.

System decomposition. Advantageous system decompositions and well-defined interfaces enhance understandability of the entire system and simplify system construction. Moreover, we found it desirable for each programmer to have a major module to himself so that he can feel like a substantial contributor. Only good system decompositions allow this without having people interfering with each other.

Top-down design is usually suggested as the correct mechanism to achieve this goal. However, we have had frequent difficulty following this seemingly sound advice. Several examples have been presented elsewhere.[2]

Top-down design assumes that the problem is completely understood and that there are no external constraints to contend with. Since we were bound by the maximum size of a PDP-11 address space, we frequently found that a process was not large enough to contain the code for planned functions. When this happened, we were forced to restructure the code. Also, we found that in several areas of the system a clean top-down design incurred an intolerable performance penalty.[2]

Although we had the freedom to begin with a top-down design, thereafter we were restricted to making feasible changes to a running system. In a sense, there is a collection of "next states" to which the software can evolve in the next iteration. Such states are highly constrained by previous (perhaps incorrect) decisions.

For example, in 1977 we added crash recovery to a working system. This entailed identifying all failure patterns and leaving enough "footprints" in the data base so that a recovery utility could correctly clean up after the failure was repaired. This code involves myriad low-level changes to dozens of routines. Restructuring all the low-level routines in order to cleanly add recovery was not even considered because it would have necessitated a large rewrite that was not considered feasible. Rather, crash recovery was inserted incrementally in an ad hoc way.

As the above example illustrates, we were constantly pulled between two points of view: restructuring and rewriting to achieve a clean design in the next iteration, or seeking an ad hoc solution because the cost of the first alternative might be too high.

In summary, top-down design seems to have been effective when requirements were well understood. However, much of the Ingres code evolved as requirements were identified during or following initial implementation. In retrospect, the intuition of the system designers seems to have been the most reliable design technique.

When the Ingres system was initially designed, we expected a multiprocess organization to be highly advantageous. It offered the possibility of parallelism, forced a clean decomposition of function at the top level, and gave each programmer an isolated environment. Unfortunately, we found that multiple processes were fundamentally undesirable. Not only are they hard to reset when errors occur, but they are also inflexible when the top-level control structure inevitably changes. Lastly, repetition of functions is often required. For example, all processes must individually open the files in which system catalog information is kept.

Although Ingres is forced to use multiple processes because of the address space limitations on a PDP-11, these processes are perfectly synchronized; each waits for a successful return from its neighbor before it accepts new work. The 32-bit address space available on VAX computers allowed us to collapse all processes together.

Clean code. By and large, we made continuous and demonstrable progress during the initial stages of the project. We chose to ignore hard problems and write "dirty code." But as the Ingres system grew larger, it became impractical to write badly structured code, since this had a tendency to complicate future debugging and maintenance.

Coding standards should be drawn up by a single person to ensure unity of design; however, input should be solicited from all programmers.

Many programmers lean toward twisted, tricky solutions to problems. Although this may improve efficiency in the short run, we found complex code undesirable. Inevitably, it was hard to debug and maintain. When the original designer of a module departed, leaving it in the hands of a new person, maintenance costs escalated. If "tricks" are truly necessary to meet performance requirements, they should be elevated to the status of carefully documented techniques.

The transition from dirty code to clean code was a painful one. Perhaps we should have started writing clean code from the beginning. However, this would have increased the time required to produce an initial prototype, and a working prototype was essential to establish a reputation. Moreover, at the time, we were unaware of the ultimate pitfalls of dirty code. As a result, we believe that a phase of dirty code was a necessary stage in our evolution, as were the growth pains of cleaning it up.

Coding standards. When a module changes hands, the recipient frequently alters the program to suit his particular style. A certain amount of this is desirable because the new programmer may notice an easier way to do something and make appropriate changes. However, we found that an inordinate amount of time was spent adjusting Ingres code to the personal style of each programmer (e.g., changing the way programs were laid out on line-printer output). In an attempt to restrict this extra editing, we instituted a set of coding standards.

The initial reaction was exceedingly negative. Programmers used to having an address space of their own felt an encroachment on their personal freedom. In spite of this reaction, we enforced standards that in the end became surprisingly popular. Basically, our programmers had to recognize the importance of making code easier to transfer to new people, and that coding standards were a low price to pay for this advantage. The results met our goal; random changing of program style has all but disappeared, and readability of the system has increased.

When the Ingres project began building a distributed data base system, we left a period of "bulletproofing" the system and entered one of less structured experimentation. At this time, there was a proposal to drop the coding standards. Popular opinion, however, called for them to remain, although ironclad enforcement has disappeared.

Coding standards should be drawn up by a single person to ensure unity of design; however, input should be solicited from all programmers. Once legislated, the standards should be rigidly adhered to.

Documentation. The Ingres source code is well documented and a creditable reference manual exists. However, no documentation for major internal interfaces has ever been written, nor has a guide for new people ever been devised. As a result, there is a long learning curve for new Ingres programmers. In addition, considerable interaction with other project members is required during the training period, and it is almost impossible to make use of transient help. Currently, this is considered a major weakness.

A university is not a software house, and there is little incentive to produce documentation. We probably could have benefited from imposing documentation requirements on the entire staff from the beginning, but the cost of producing substantial internal documentation today is very high.

Proposals have been made for internal documentation in the form of comment blocks preceding programs and procedures. These would include fields such as *name, function, algorithm, parameters, returns, globals, calls, called by,* and *history.* We attempted to use this style of comment block in new Ingres code for two years. The results were mixed. Fields such as *parameters, returns,* and *side effects* seemed useful because they warned the programmer when the semantics of the routine were being changed. However, certain other fields, such as *history,* were generally not kept up to date. Since the usual cycle is edit, compile, test, it is unnatural for the programmer to go back and add a line in the history field, particularly if the change seems small. The final conclusion was that an out-of-date history is worse than none at all.

Fortunately, many fields, e.g., *globals, calls, called by,* and *history,* can be maintained automatically by language processors or source-code control programs. A sound rule is that any information that can be maintained automatically should be; manual maintenance is never as accurate and seldom as convenient. Fields such as *algorithm* are usually just a restatement of the code and should be eliminated in favor of comments interspersed in the code to explain what is happening. Such comments are easier to maintain and are more readily associated with the code they describe.

Tools. In order to maintain some internal documentation automatically, we have recently started using the Source Code Control System.[8] This package automatically keeps track of who makes changes and prompts for descriptive comments about each change. Furthermore, the code for both the old and new versions is available, so

backout is possible in case of disaster. The system has proved both effective and popular. It is far superior to comment blocks maintained by hand.

In general, we believe it is almost never a mistake to spend extra time investing in tools. We have made good use of the tools provided in the standard Unix environment, for example the parser generator YACC.[9] In addition, we spent considerable time importing tools such as the Vi text editor,[10] the "C-shell,"[11] and the Source Code Control System. We found these investments well worth the cost.

Support. There is a big difference between making Ingres work ourselves and enabling other people to make it work. The latter requires an enormous effort to eliminate bugs and provide user-level documentation, along with easy-to-follow installation procedures. Perhaps only a third of this total effort is required to get a large system to the stage where *we* can make it work.

Whether we like it or not, the Ingres project is in the support business. With over 125 installations, we get many phone calls that consume the time of key people. Originally, the calls gave valuable feedback about the system; today they tend to be less technical and more administrative. The fear of even more phone calls tended to inhibit changes to later versions of the code because changes inevitably introduce bugs or confuse users. Such a fear is counterproductive in our research environment.

With a system at this level of maturity, it appears necessary to engage a separate support organization if research and development are to continue. Realistically, support should be considered as the system is developed; reliability and maintainability are built in, not added on.

Hardware environment. Morale problems associated with unworkable hardware have been a serious project issue. They not only frustrate the programming team and slow progress, they also consume the time of key people who must cope with or remedy the situation. In retrospect, it is clear that if we had had twice our hardware budget at the right time, it would have been advantageous to buy all our hardware from one vendor. The Feldman report[12] may help in this regard.

Complexity. By setting high goals and embarking on distributed data base/operating system/network projects, we have created a software environment so complex that the project directors no longer have a good grasp of operational trade-offs. As a result, priorities are extremely difficult to set and often appear inconsistent from week to week. Moreover, the chief programmer and project directors spend a lot of time battling brush fires. This usually means that rational long-range planning is neglected. Consequently, maintenance and conversion efforts have been poorly planned and seem to go on forever. This creates a morale problem for the implementation team. Lastly, the presence of multiple networks and home-brew network hardware has created an unstable machine/operating system environment that amplifies any morale problems. The structure seems in danger of collapse at all levels.

The project directors and chief programmer are overloaded with work and beset with nontechnical details that interfere with useful research. The difficulties sometimes seem insurmountable, and the cost of making progress has become enormous. Other personnel are so bogged down with maintenance/conversion efforts (a new 32-bit machine, three new versions of Unix, and a new version of Ingres) that they see no progress at all.

We find the reward structure and support organization of a software house impossible to build within a university.

Earlier we used a throw-away-and-rewrite mechanism to deal with complexity. Recently, we have begun to act more like a software house, although we find the reward structure and support organization impossible to build within a university. We may well have reached a complexity barrier that we will not be able to penetrate with the limitations of the current environment. Certainly, the project appears technically out of control. Even more distressing is the question ''Where will the next generation of implementors come from?'' The complexity of our environment is such that it taxes undergraduates to the limit. Only juniors and seniors appear to have the background to successfully cope; hence, our previous strategy (hiring freshmen) appears unworkable. On the other hand, masters-level students are available for only one year, and it is widely recognized that implementations are not in the best interests of PhD students.

We are constrained by the limitations of our environment. Since the university supports neither a two-year master of software engineering program nor a significant implementation for a PhD dissertation, we cannot attract the necessary people. Also, without hiring professional managers, we are restricted to a one-level organizational hierarchy, sharply limiting the total size of the implementation.

Perhaps there is a meta-theorem here: ''Within our environment, one 75,000-line program can be written, but expanding it to a more complex 150,000-line program is impossible.'' No doubt all organizations have some fundamental limit; ours may simply be lower than others. To contradict the meta-theorem we would have to find a new way to deal with the complexity.

Conclusions

The Ingres system has gone through several stages of development. The initial stage produced poorly designed code, and little thought was given to maintenance or code sharing. This allowed individuals coding in their own process to exercise creativity to the utmost with a minimum of conflict. Later, to support users and make the system reliable, we were forced to write cleaner code. Recently, we have done less to support users, but the complexity of the system demands that we continue to write clean code.

Our largest mistake was probably in failing to clearly pinpoint the change from prototype to production system. At this point several procedural changes should have been implemented immediately; instead, they were slow to appear and frequently incomplete. We feel that system implementors should clearly identify this point in their development cycle.

In a research environment, any development effort involves problems whose solution is unknown. Under these circumstances, standard software development approaches, e.g. strict top-down design, do not always work, and rewriting code becomes a powerful development tactic. It is a serious mistake to believe that a piece of code is sacred because of the time taken to write it.

Throughout the development of Ingres, we made considerable use of the tools available in Unix. The cost and a few weeks spent setting up and learning to use a major tool are well worthwhile. It is nearly always a mistake to do a task by hand that can probably be performed better by a tool. ∎

References

1. M. Stonebraker et al., ''The Design and Implementation of INGRES,'' *Trans. Database Systems,* Vol. 2, No. 3, Sept. 1976.

2. M. Stonebraker, ''Retrospection on a Data Base System,'' *Trans. Database Systems,* Vol. 5, No. 3, Sept. 1980.

3. D. Ritchie and K. Thompson, ''The UNIX Time-Sharing System,'' *Comm. ACM,* July 1974.

4. L. Rowe and K. Birman, ''A Local Network Based on the UNIX Operating System,'' (submitted for publication), Sept. 1980.

5. M. Stonebraker, ''MUFFIN: A Distributed Data Base Machine,'' *Proc. 1st Int'l Conf. Distributed Computing,* Huntsville, Ala., Oct. 1979.

6. L. Rowe and K. Schoens, ''Data Abstraction, Views, and Updates in RIGEL,'' *Proc. 1979 ACM-SIGMOD Conf. Management of Data,* Boston, Mass., May 1979.

7. M. Astrahan et al., ''System R: A Relational Approach to Database Management,'' *TODS,* Vol. 1, No. 2, pp. 97-137.

8. L. E. Bonanni and A. L. Glasser, ''SCCS/PWB User's Manual,'' Bell Laboratories, Nov. 1977.

9. S. Johnson, ''YACC—Yet Another Compiler-Compiler,'' Computer Science Tech. Report No. 32, Bell Laboratories, Murray Hill, N.J., July 1975.

10. William Joy, ''An Introduction to Display Editing with Vi,'' University of California, Berkeley, Dec. 1979.

11. William Joy, ''An Introduction to the C-shell,'' University of California, Berkeley, Dec. 1979.

12. Jerome A. Feldman and William R. Sutherland, ''Rejuvenating Experimental Computer Science—A Report to the National Science Foundation and Others,'' *Comm. ACM,* Vol. 22, No. 9, Sept. 1979, pp. 497-502.

Eric P. Allman is currently employed by Britton-Lee, Inc., and works in the field of data base interfaces. He was a member of the implementation team for the Ingres data base system from 1975 through 1981, serving as chief programmer from 1977 to 1981. He received an MS in computer science in 1980 from the University of California at Berkeley.

Michael Stonebraker is a professor in the Department of Electrical Engineering and Computer Sciences, University of California at Berkeley. He is the author of many papers in the area of data base management and the principal architect of the Ingres relational data base system. Stonebraker received his PhD from the University of Michigan in 1971.

SOFTWARE—PRACTICE AND EXPERIENCE, VOL. 6, 293-299 (1976)

Software Malpractice—
A Distasteful Experience†

Software Malpractice—
A Distasteful Experience†

MICHAEL J. SPIER

Manager, Manufacturing Applications Systems Engineering, Digital Equipment Corporation
146 Main Street, Maynard, Massachusetts 01754, U.S.A.

SUMMARY

A sequence of events is described, leading to the severe deterioration of an initially well conceived and cleanly implemented compiler. It is shown how an initial "optimization" implanted a latent bug in the compiler, how the bug was subsequently activated through innocent compiler modification, and how the compiler then deteriorated because of the incompetent correction of the bug manifestation. This exceedingly negative case history is presented in the hope of conveying to the reader a better feeling for the complex problems inherent to industrial software production and maintenance. The difficulty in proposing any constructive (and complete!) software engineering methodology is known and acknowledged; the study of an episode such as described in this paper might help put the difficulties, with which we are confronted, into better perspective.

KEY WORDS: GOTO-less Programming, Program Correctness, Software Engineering Methodology, Software Production and Maintenance, Structured Programming.

PRE SCRIPTUM

We recognize nowadays that the more programs we write for applications of increasing complexity and sophistication, the more uncertain we become of our ability to write these programs such that they be as "good" as possible. It has become fashionable for our colleagues to propose various remedies—often dogmatic in nature—which are supposed to enhance the "goodness" of our programs. Thus, for example, we are encouraged to adopt "structured programming." Nobody *definitely* knows what it is—although popular myth has it that a total ban on GOTO statements will automatically impart beneficial "structure" to our code.

"Goodness", of course, is in the eyes of the beholder. I must confess to a nagging suspicion that some of the proposed remedies come from sources more concerned with classroom toy programs than with the realities of everyday software production. The suggested remedies are typically exemplified by means of some neat little exercise (*e.g.* enumeration of prime numbers, bubble sort, matrix inversion, eight queens problem),

---

† This paper describes a certain compound software bug which was encountered by the author at a certain point in his career. It must be emphasized that this case history relates neither to the author's present employment with Digital Equipment Corporation, nor to any DEC software product.

perhaps very suitable as a classroom illustration but a far cry from the real world programs where we hurt. It is nigh impossible to relate the sample program to the real one (*e.g.,* operating system monitor, airline reservation system, inventory control system, payroll program) such that the remedy might be evaluated in respect of its actual context of application.

What most proposed remedies have in common is their insistence on *how to write* the program. Little or no attention is paid to the remaining issues inherent to everyday software production. In reality, a program has to be designed, coded, debugged, verified for an acceptable level of reliability (I hesitate to use the word "correctness"), modified, improved both in the sense of functionality and in the sense of performance optimization, and all the while be kept at a stable level of lucidity in order to allow for its continued evolution.

The totality of issues which have to be taken into consideration is staggering. The development of a comprehensive software engineering methodology is a challenge whose immensity defies our bravest attempts. I suspect that too few of our academicians really grasp the larger implications of the problem, tending to polarize their attention on what in reality are insignificant issues (*e.g.,* the great GOTO controversy), while failing to see areas of difficulty which literally beg for attention (*e.g.,* how many of our experts in programming linguistics have ever designed a non-interpretive language where the symbolic debugging facility is an integral part of the language specification?)†

Old Chinese proverb say *"one picture worth thousand words."* It occurred to me that by describing an exceedingly negative—though, unfortunately typical—case study of how foolishness, compounded by ignorance and topped by incompetence resulted in a most incredible compound software bug, I might succeed in conveying a feeling for the problems that afflict the software industry.

I came across this bug a good many years ago. I doubt that the affected program, indeed the computer itself, are still in use. It happened well before I entered DEC's employment and is unrelated to DEC and its products. Still, he who sits in a glass house is wise not to cast stones. Thus the following has been fictionalized sufficiently to convey the essence of the story without pointing an accusing finger at any identifiable culprit.

THE STORY

Back in those days when core memory was scarce, random access disk storage was unknown and card readers and tape drives proliferated, there was a compiler. It consisted of 23 tape-to-tape subcompilation passes. The compiler was initially well designed and coded in as modular a fashion as could be expected under the circumstances.

Each pass was a distinct program, loaded from a library tape to overlay its predecessor in memory. A certain subset of memory was reserved as a common communications area between passes, containing both data and code. A software (*i.e.,* macro-) implemented CALL/RETURN mechanism existed. The CALL instruction would push the proper return address onto a software managed stack and transfer control to the designated subroutine. The RETURN instruction would transfer control to the locality indicated by top-of-stack, after having popped that datum from the stack to reveal the underlying return address. The stack resided in the common communications area; its size was barely sufficient to accommodate the collection of return addresses corresponding to the longest observed sequence of calls. There existed neither stack overflow nor stack underflow condition detection provisions.

---

† From a purely pragmatic point of view, I find little appeal in a miraculous new language, if the corresponding debugging tool talks back to me in octal or hexadecimal. If that is the only debugging tool available, then by sheer instinct of survival I would opt for machine language code, for else I would be penalized by having to learn the compiler's code generation idiosyncrasies.

Initial Coding

The compiler was modularly structured, having an iterative main program residing permanently in the common area:

```
main:   subroutine;
        prologue;
        while   (compilation is to proceed)
        begin
                load    (next program overlay);
                call    [current pass];
        end;
        epilogue;
end     main;
```

where a pass was of the general form

```
pass:   subroutine;
        perform necessary computation;
        return;
end     pass;
```

As can be seen, the above is the rudimentary representation of a well conceived program which, upon return from the current pass, would test certain common variables to determine whether or not the compilation should proceed. In the affirmative case it would bring in the next program overlay and call it.

Each logical database (*e.g.,* the symbol table) typically required two tape drives; an input tape containing the current version and an output tape onto which the updated version was copied. Two subroutines residing permanently in the common area were FLUSH and SWITCH, each parametrized for any given database. FLUSH guaranteed that the entire updated version of the relevant database was completely recorded on the corresponding output tape. SWITCH rewound the relevant tapes and made the necessary common variable updates to effect the functional permutation of the pair of tapes.

Initial Foolishness

Then, a bright programmer made a stupendous intellectual discovery whereby he could instill additional (subjective) "goodness" into the compiler. He observed that FLUSH and SWITCH were of the form

```
flush:   subroutine;
         perform flushing;
         call       switch;
         return;
end      flush;
switch:  subroutine;
         perform switching;
         return;
end      switch;
```

and decided to optimize the compiler by removing all space- and microsecond- "wasteful" calls, which in his judgement were functionally superfluous. In a recent article, Knuth[1] encouragingly recommends this foolishness, and even provides the recipe for its realization, to quote [*ibid.* pp. 280–282]: *"If the last action of a procedure p before it returns is to call procedure q, simply GOTO the beginning of procedure q instead."* And indeed, that is exactly what our wise guy did

```
flush:   subroutine;
         perform flushing
         goto switch;
end      flush;
switch:  perform switching;
         return
```

not merely with respect to these exemplified subroutines, but systematically throughout the entire compiler. With admirable perseverance, that anonymous optimizer invested a tremendous amount of work (to him, perhaps, a labor of love)† in order to save a few words of memory and an unmeasurable amount of CPU time. The unmeasurably "optimized" compiler continued to perform its function as reliably as ever.

Further Foolishness

Another "improvement" took place. Passes were no longer CALL-ed. Given that the end-of-pass locality was known, and that a pass always RETURN-ed to a fixed location in the main program, that program underwent transformation:

```
main:   subroutine;
        prologue;
        while   (compilation is to proceed)
        begin
                load   (next program overlay);
                goto   [current pass];
loop:   end;
        epilogue;
end     main;
```

where a pass was now of the general form
```
passi:   perform necessary computation;
         goto      loop;
```

Following this "improvement," the compiler continued to perform reliably. In view of the fact that this new modification is fraught with subtle traps (as will be demonstrated in the following), yet did not affect the compiler's reliability in any discernibly adverse manner, I suspect that this too was the handiwork of our original optimizer, whose professional competence (as distinct from his level of wisdom) must be acknowledged with the greatest respect.

Ignorance

Time passed. Our genial optimizer went on to accomplish bigger and better things in life. The compiler was now being maintained by programmers who were well below the optimizing wizard's level of technical competence. The programming language evolved—as programming languarges invariably do—and new linguistic features had to be incorporated into the compiler. Additionally, the compiler was gradually being improved, for both object code optimization and enhanced error detection facilities.

A continuous compiler recoding effort was underway. Certain passes were modified. Other passes were split in two and recoded from scratch. The programmers performing this work had no clear understanding of the compiler's underlying coding conventions, especially in respect of the magnificent "optimization" job which was done earlier. They did, however, assume that any systematically replicated pattern of code presented a safe way in which to program by mimicry. This is a most reasonable assumption which any seasoned programmer makes intuitively and typically follows through with success. In this case, our brave programmers innocently added the straw that broke the camel's back.

The recoding and/or modification effort inevitably required the services of "optimized" subroutine pairs such as FLUSH and SWITCH. For example, the modified compiler now evolved to the point where under certain circumstances SWITCH was to be invoked independently of FLUSH. If certain errors had been detected, a state variable was set to indicate that actual code generation was to cease, while further syntactic and semantic analysis should proceed for diagnostic purposes. The time consuming FLUSH-ing was then deemed unnecessary, however, a *pro forma* SWITCH-ing still had to be done to satisfy file system requirements. In fact, the analogous skipping of predecessor subroutines happened with respect to various other

---

such subroutine pairs. The technical problem confronting a program modifier was: "How is a label—such as SWITCH—attained?" The solution to the technical problem was obvious. Namely to look up existing code, and upon detection of a universal pattern of label reference to faithfully mimic that pattern. SWITCH and various other subroutines were all very clearly and systematically attained by a GOTO statement. Thus everybody invoked those subroutines *via* GOTO.

Unfortunately, the necessary underlying condition for the successful usage of the "optimization" technique described earlier is *that there exist at least one valid return address on the stack!*† The once reliable compiler started crashing when a sequence of GOTOs led to a single unmatched RETURN statement (*e.g.*, in SWITCH), provoking a stack underflow condition and sending control to the locality indicated by the value of the word which happened to immediately precede the base-of-stack locality.

Incompetence

This bug manifestation was extremely difficult to analyze. Not all CALLs were removed from the compiler. The optimizing wizard knew his business (proof: following his contribution, the compiler's reliability remained unaffected), and saw to it that each logical path contained a matching number of CALLs and RETURNs. Being unaware of this critical convention, the modifying programmers violated it by omission.

The stack was common to all passes. The actual violation of the implicit convention need not necessarily have happened when the stack was empty! Given that by virtue of the *Further Foolishness* LOOP was now attained *via* a GOTO statement, the possibility existed for a stack underflow in pass i to cause successor pass j > i to crash. The effect of the crash was clearly discernible; the cause of the crash may well have been located in an overlaid segment of code. These bug manifestations were highly capricious, depending upon the flow of control as dictated by specific input sequences.

Management became alarmed. Everybody went into frantic "debug mode," busily poring over memory dump listings. Eventually it was discovered that the crashes must be due to a stack underflow condition. Rather than analyze the problem to determine its cause, a quick and dirty solution was implemented to negate the problem's effect. The main program was modified in the following grotesque manner:

```
main:   subroutine;
        prologue
        goto  loop;
        while (compilation is to proceed)
        begin
                load  (next program overlay);
                goto  [current pass];
loop:   call  cont;
cont:   end;
        epilogue;
end     main;
```

where every passage through MAIN would push onto the stack a dummy return address pointing to CONT (which is functionally equivalent to LOOP) such that any extraneous RETURN would effect a transfer of control to CONT rather than cause a stack underflow.

---

† Another necessary condition is that the subroutine "invoked" with a GOTO statement not have any formal stack frame allocation, if such allocation is performed by the CALL instruction.

The bug manifestations known to be caused by the stack underflow condition were definitely "fixed." A new bug manifestation came into being when an *insufficient number* of the erroneous control paths was exercised. Specifically, the erroneous control paths produced a *deficiency* of return addresses on the stack. The new version of MAIN produced a *surplus* of return addresses on the stack, exactly equalling the number of times that control passed through LOOP. The stack was barely sufficient to accommodate the collection of return addresses corresponding to the longest observed sequence of CALLs. When an insufficient number of erroneous control paths was exercised, the stack would now *overflow*. The new symptom was recognized, and "fixed" by increasing the size of the stack by a number of words equalling the number of compiler passes! These extremely distateful modifications were made by someone who must have been a most incompetent programmer. Understanding neither the error's cause, nor the sheer asininity of his solution, he went ahead and "fixed the bug" to the general satisfaction of his superiors.

The Sorry Ending

The bug manifestations related to stack mismanagement were definitely "fixed" to preclude compiler crashes. Compilation would always terminate. The compiler's output ceased to be correct always, given that control would sometimes undertake certain quantum jumps in logic. The compiler produced esoteric code, and programmers were busy repairing the compiler at syntax analyzer, expression evaluator and code generator levels.

At this point I was called in to lend a helping hand. It took me a significant amount of detective work to reconstruct the sequence of events described above. I recommended that the compiler be written off as a loss, and that an effort be launched to remake the compiler, possibly using a very early version of it as a starting base. The recommendation was rejected. Firstly, the compiler was too widely used to be scrapped. Secondly, the management felt that if this compiler is impossible to maintain then any other compiler would be just as messy. Hence, they reasoned, there was no point in committing themselves to an unknown evil when they had finally resigned themselves to living with the current one.

POST SCRIPTUM

A software product has a lifespan during which it must undergo constant change. The "goodness" of the product must be maintained throughout that entire period of existence, of which the initial implementation is but a part (and a minor one, at that). The desired qualitative excellence is unfortunately subject to continuous modification; more regrettably, it is subject to practically unavoidable quantitative restrictions.

Concerning these quantitative restrictions; *volume of code* plays an exceedingly important role when it comes to large-scale software projects. The language chosen must allow for the independent compilation of program modules of manageable size. Consequently, global code quality can no longer be controlled by the language processor alone. Hence, no single "super compiler" would provide remedy. A possible solution would be to have a multi-level language where the linking of precompiled bodies of code would be treated as a semantically meaningful *post compilation* phase.

Similarly, *runtime efficiency* is as important a factor, as is—alas—the insistence on *memory usage minimization*, especially with regard to the ever more sophisticated expectations of small-scale minicomputer users. It is the quantitative aspect of the desire for the fastest possible execution within the smallest possible memory partition, which significantly contributes to the qualitative deficiencies of our software. The problem exists, and no amount of indifference to it will make it go away.

We have seen how a misdirected effort to "optimize" the compiler snowballed into catastrophe. Lest the proponents of GOTO-less programming gloat and proclaim: "See, I told you! You replaced some CALLs by GOTOs and God has inflicted just punishment upon you," let us reflect on the true meaning of this episode. GOTOs are but a tool, to be wielded incompetently or in a proficient, workmanlike manner. The act of replacing CALLs with GOTOs had—in itself—not the slightest deleterious effect upon the compiler, because the perpetrator knew his business and performed with commendable expertise. His successors did what they did and caused a *potential* bug to be activated. Yet potential bugs of similar severity lurk in practically all advocated programming languages. Consider FORTRAN, where the sequence of calls $X - Y - Z - X$ triggers a well known linguistic deficiency. And just in case some ALGOL *aficionado* grins and says: "Aha! Why don't you use an intelligently designed language which supports reentrant procedures," I would suggest that ALGOL and its derivatives have their own potential traps, the most blatant of which is the allowing of default references from a nested block to some outerblock variable, a notorious source of bugs of omission which are typically caused by innocent typos.

Give a bare machine to a programming wizard, and he will be up and running within a few weeks. Cast "pearls"† to swine, and you are no closer to that undefined Utopian "structured programming." I believe that the problem transcends the purely technical domain, and that its solution must encompass the managerial domain as well.[3] Such solution must comprise the methodologies, rules and conventions which have to be respected in order to impart certain engineering standards upon the programming profession (remember, the only *real* cause for the fiasco described earlier was the violation of a single unstated rule!). We may have paid too much attention to the way in which we express our algorithm; perhaps it is time to focus more attention on the technical and human engineering contexts within which the algorithm has to exist.

REFERENCES

1. D.E. Knuth, 'Structured Programming with GOTO Statements', *ACM Computing Surveys*, 6, No. 4, 261-301 (1974).
2. E.W. Dijkstra, 'Structured Programming', in 'Software Engineering Techniques,' *1969 NATO Conference Report*, J.N. Buxton and B. Randell (Ed.), NATO Scientific Affairs Division, Brussels 39, Belgium, April 1970.
3. M.J. Spier, 'A Pragmatic Proposal for the Impovement of Program Modularity and Reliability', *Int. J. Comput. Information Sci.*, 4, No. 2, 133-149 (1975).

---

† I hope that Dijkstra[2] will excuse the pun.

'KILL THAT CODE!'

A casual attitude toward program maintenance can have some deadly results for the organization.

By
Gerald M. Weinberg
founder
Weinberg & Weinberg
Lincoln, NE

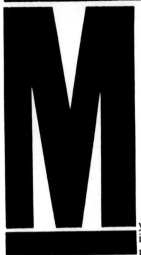

My wife, Dani, is an anthropologist by profession, but one of her hobbies is training dogs. The combination of the two produces some interesting ideas. The other day she described how to train attack dogs to keep them from being dangerous. As usual, the big problem with attack dogs is not the dogs, but the people.

When someone hears that a dog is attack trained, chances are about one in three that they'll turn to the dog and as a joke or just to see what the dog will do command: "Kill." To protect against this idiotic human behavior, trainers never use words like "kill" as the attack command. Instead, they use innocent words like "breathe" that would never be given in jest in a command voice.

This protection is needed because a trained dog is an information processing machine in some ways much like a computer. A single arbitrary command could mean anything to a dog, depending on how it was trained—or programmed. This arbitrariness doesn't matter much if it's not an attack dog. The owner may be embarrassed when Rover heels on the command to stay, but nothing much is lost. If the dog is trained to go for the throat, it's an entirely different matter.

It's the same with computers. Because they are programmed and many words in programs have arbitrary meanings, a single mistake can turn a helpful computer into one that can attack and kill an entire enterprise.

That's why I've never understood why management takes such a casual attitude toward program maintenance. Time and again, I hear managers explain that maintenance can be done by less intelligent people operating without all the formal controls of development because it's not very critical. And no amount of argument seems able to convince them differently. Until they have a costly maintenance blunder.

Most expensive errors

Fortunately, costly maintenance blunders are rather common. Managers are learning fast even though the tuition is high. I keep a confidential list of the world's most expensive programming errors. All of the top ten on the current list are maintenance errors. The top three cost their organizations $1,600,000,000, $900,000,000, and $245,000,000—and each one involved the change of a *single digit* in a previously correct program.

In all three cases, the change was "so trivial" it was instituted casually. A supervisor told a low-level maintenance programmer to change that digit without any written instructions, no test plan or nobody to read over the change. Indeed, no controls whatsoever existed between that one programmer and the day-to-day operations of the organization. It was exactly like having an attack dog trained to respond to "Kill," or perhaps to "Hello."

I've done some studies, confirmed by others, about the chances of a maintenance change being done incorrectly depending on the size of the change. Here's the first part of the table:

Lines changed	Chance of error
1	50%
2	60%
3	65%
4	70%
5	75%

Development programmers are often shocked for two reasons to see this high rate. In the first place, development changes are simpler. They involve cleaner, smaller, better structured code that has not been changed many times before. It does not have unexpected linkages. Such linkages were involved in each of my top three disasters.

Secondly, the consequences of an erroneous change during development are smaller. The error can be corrected without affecting real operations. Thus, development programmers don't take that much notice of their errors. They tend to underestimate their frequency.

In development, you simply fix errors and go on your merry way. Not so in maintenance where you must mop up the damage the error causes and spend countless hours in meetings explaining why it will never happen again—until the next time.

SOFTWARE/expo

Jerry Weinberg will deliver the keynote address at the Software/expo National conference in Chicago next month. He has over 25 years of experience as a consultant and researcher and is recognized as an accomplished teacher, lecturer and author. Among his several books are The Psychology of Computer Programming *and* An Introduction to General Systems Thinking.

Ignorant programmers

For these two reasons, development programmers interpret these frequent errors as indicative of the ignorance or inexperience of maintenance programmers. But if we continue the table down a few lines, it shows the cause cannot be either ignorance or inexperience.

Lines changed	Chance of error
10	50%
20	35%

The decrease in error rate as the size of change increases shows maintenance programmers perfectly capable of better work than their record with small changes indicates. My explanation of the higher rates for small changes is that they are not taken seriously. They are done carelessly and without controls. How many times have you heard a programmer say: "No problem! All I have to do is change one line!"?

And how many times have you heard their managers agree with them? Or even encourage them to work "quick and dirty" when it's only a small change?

That attitude would be sensible if "small" changes were truly small; if "maintenance" of a program were actually like maintenance of an apartment building. The janitor can change one washer in the kitchen sink without great risk of causing the building to collapse and bury all of its occupants. It's not safe to make the same assumption for a production program. But because we are so free and arbitrary with words, the word "maintenance" has been misappropriated from the one circumstance to the other.

Careless and unthinking

Whoever coined the term "maintenance" for computer programs was as careless and unthinking as the person who trains a dog to attack on the command "Kill."

With the wisdom of hindsight, I suggest that the "maintenance" programmer is more like a brain surgeon than a janitor. Opening up a working system is more like opening up a human brain and replacing a nerve than opening up a sink and replacing a washer. Would maintenance be easier to manage if it was called "Software Brain Surgery?"

Think about it this way. Suppose you had a bad habit like saying "Kill" to attack dogs. Would you go to a brain surgeon and say, "Just open up my skull, Doc, and remove that one little habit. And please do a quick and dirty job—it's only a small change. Just a little maintenance job." Ⓝ

IV. Strategies/Tools for Recognizing Structure

When software restructuring involves programmer actions, a question of what software structure is already present nearly always arises. Programmers look for structural guideposts to help them solve problems. The papers of part IV all concern how various aspects of software structure may be discovered.

In the first paper, "Assessing Software Maintainability," G.M. Berns gives a software metric for assessing how difficult a program is to understand. The approach is based on assigning weights to a program's statements, then summing the weights. The metric is a good example of a software metric whose basic computational framework should be tuned, before being used, to reflect the local views of software maintainability.

The next paper, "A Software Maintainability Evaluation Methodology" by D.A. Peercy, takes a much broader look at maintainability. Here, maintainability is not driven directly by source code statements (as in Berns' metric). Instead, modules are reviewed, using questionnaires, for the following six maintainability attributes: modularity, descriptiveness, consistency, simplicity, expandability, and instrumentation. Software maintainability is assessed by using the scores achieved for these attributes.

Some forms of software structure are easier to appreciate by simply extracting and displaying those program parts most relevant to the structure. In "MAP: A Tool for Understanding Software" by S. Warren, program structure is determined by using tools reflecting different views of the program. Sample views are display of procedures (in a system structure chart) which contain selected program statements; trace of the execution of selected statements; display of possible references or modifications to selected variables; and display of the differences between two versions of a source program. Tools like those available in MAP* are becoming increasingly common.

---

*Since publication of Warren's paper, MAP has been renamed and enhanced. It is available under the name VIA/INSIGHT, from VIASOFT, Phoenix, Arizona.

ASSESSING SOFTWARE MAINTAINABILITY

How easy is it to maintain a program? To a large extent, that depends on how difficult the program is to understand. A technique to measure program difficulty yields encouraging results.

"Assessing Software Maintainability" by G.M. Berns from *Communications of the ACM*, Volume 27, Number 1, January 1984, pages 14-23. Copyright 1984, Association for Computing Machinery, Inc., reprinted by permission.

GERALD M. BERNS

The job of software maintenance—correcting errors and changing program operation as requirements change—generally devolves upon personnel not involved in the original software development cycle who must learn how a program works before they can competently change it. Among the variables involved in this learning process are the accuracy, currency, and completeness of program documentation; programmer skill and experience; environmental factors such as urgency, the programming language, and especially, the attributes of the program itself.

Program maintainability and program understandability are parallel concepts: the more difficult a program is to understand, the more difficult it is to maintain. And the more difficult it is to maintain, the higher its maintainability risk. Since it is to the source program that maintenance staff must ultimately come, it would be useful to be able to quantify the relative magnitude of the task through an analysis solely of the attributes of the program.

Attempts have been made to quantify program difficulty by manipulating simple counts of *selected* program attributes, *e.g.,* lines of code, bifurcation points (cyclomatic number), and operations and operands (Halstead length). Although these manipulations may be informative, none has been persuasively shown to be a reliable measure of program difficulty [5].

This work was supported in part by the Department of the Navy. Opinions are those of the author and not necessarily those of the Department of the Navy.

This paper presents an approach based on the tenet that program difficulty represents the sum of the difficulties of its constituent elements, and that these elements can be quantified by the use of carefully selected weights and factors.

UNDERLYING CONCEPTS

A program can be thought of as a set of static definitional statements and a set of executable statements. The definitions establish the attributes and interrelationships of certain program elements, such as symbolic names. We are interested here in the difficulties of understanding how the dynamic portion of the program manipulates and controls the static elements.

Consider in exclusion the simple Assignment statement:

$$A = B + C$$

This statement is easy to understand because all of its symbolic name elements are implicitly defined to be local and unrelated. Now consider the following (using the Fortran language):

$$\text{COMMON } A$$
$$A = B + C$$

Without altering the executable statement, its difficulty has increased because changing A, now defined to be global rather than local, should affect other modules that share the blank common block. This definition of

A is more difficult than the definition of *A* in the preceding example. Now consider:

COMMON *A*
EQUIVALENCE (*B, D*)
A = *B* + *C*

Again the difficulty of the executable statement has increased without altering it, because now the definitions establish that *B* is an alias of *D*, and understanding the current value of *B* is not as straightforward as before. That is, because of this definition, *B* will be inherently more difficult to understand than it was before in *all* the executable statements in which it appears. In the following,

COMMON *A*
EQUIVALENCE (*B, D*), (*A, C*)
A = *B* + *C*

the executable statement still has not changed, but the definitions have altered the difficulty of its constituent symbolic name elements. Now *C* is not only Equivalenced into common, but it is also an alias of the variable that is being changed. Here again the static definitions of the elements affect the difficulty of understanding the executable statements that manipulate the elements.

In each example, the difficulty of understanding the executable part of the program—the "simple" Assignment statement—has increased in parallel with the difficulty of understanding the definitions of the elements in it. Thus, program difficulty is more than just a function of logical "complexity" since this is held constant in the unchanging Assignment statement. Furthermore, properly assessing program difficulty would seem to require more than simply counting and manipulating program attributes of one sort or another because functions of attribute counts do not capture the all-important definitional interrelationships.

The second part of our tenet is that the difficulty of understanding each element in a program can be represented by assigning each element a weight. Each syntactic *element*:

> parameter
> variable
> array
> function
> statement function
> subroutine
> common
> label
> constant
> operator

can be assigned a representative weight, and factors can be assessed for syntactic *attributes* such as:

> implicit definition
> name in common
> number of aliases
> value changed
> data type
> dummy argument

The various executable *statement types* in a language also have a hierarchy of difficulty of understanding. As a type, for example, Go To statements introduce more difficulty than do Assignment statements. Also, Go To statements that branch backward into a program (causing a loop) are more difficult than those that branch forward. Each statement element can be assigned a weight that is representative of its difficulty. Although specification statements establish some syntactic elements as well as their attributes and interrelationships, these statements are not themselves weighted. Only the *use* of these elements in executable statements contributes to the Index of Difficulty of the program.

Poor use of the programming language can add significantly to program difficulty. In the following Fortran statements:

PARAMETER (*I* = 10, *J* = 3*I)
INTEGER*2 *A*(100), *B*(200)
EQUIVALENCE (*A*((*I* + *J*)/2), *B*(3*J − *I*/2)), ···

parameter expressions establish the Equivalence relationship, making it very difficult to understand. Furthermore, other Equivalence relationships that involve *A* or *B* may also be affected by this relationship. Each poor usage of the language is therefore assigned a representative weight.

Program content itself is not the sole determining factor when the program is part of a set of intercommunicating modules. Deviations from an established interface can also make a program more difficult to understand and maintain than it need be, *e.g.*, by calling a subroutine with fewer arguments than the interface specifies, or including only part of a common block. Each interface exception can be assigned a weight to represent its relative contribution to total program difficulty.

By assigning weights of relative difficulty to each of the constituent elements, the concept is that the summation of these weights—the Index of Difficulty—will represent fairly the difficulty of understanding the program as a whole.

WEIGHTS AND FACTORS

To implement these ideas, weights and factors assigned to the program elements must be quantified. As with all weights, the values are tuned so that the results correlate with reality or a standard that represents reality. The problem in this case is that people do not agree on the relative difficulties of understanding programs, *i.e.*, there is no standard. In the absence of a standard, we traditionally rely pragmatically on what we and our co-workers believe to be correct based upon our knowledge, experience, and intuition.

Values for the weights and factors discussed in the preceding section were assigned by this method to elements of the Fortran language. Element weights are in the range 0–30. The values for the weights and factors currently in use are given in Tables I–VIII.

Table I shows the weights that are assigned to the various kinds of symbolic names in a Fortran program.

TABLE I.   Weights Assigned to Symbolic Name Elements

Symbolic Name Element	Weight
Parameter	1.00
Variable	0.85
Array	1.50
Function	2.00
Statement function	1.80
Subroutine	2.00
Common	0
Label	1.00

TABLE II.   Weights Assigned to Constant Elements

Constant Element	Weight
Logical	0
Integer	0
Real (all widths)	0.05
Hexadecimal	0.10
Octal	0.10
Character	0.10
Hollerith	0.10
Radix–50	0.10

TABLE III.   Weights Assigned to Operator Elements

Operator Element	Weight
EQV, NEQV, XOR	0.50
OR, AND	0.25
NOT	1.00
Relational	0.20
+ − //	0.20
/	0.30
*	0.25
**	0.50

The label "name" applies only to numeric labels, since Fortran does not support a label data type. That is, in the statement:

ASSIGN 100 TO *JACKB*

100 is a label and *JACKB* is a variable of the integer data type, not the label data type. Variables, arrays, and statement functions are assigned the basic weights of Table I in every non-specification statement in which they appear. The same is true of every reference to functions and subroutines. Functions that appear in parametric expressions are also weighted. Parameters receive weight in every statement in which they are used. Labels receive their weight when they are referenced, not when they are defined. Common block names are given a weight of zero because they only appear in specification statements.

The weights currently assigned to constant elements are given in Table II. Complex constants consist of two other constants which are weighted separately. Constants receive their specified weights in every executable statement in which they appear except the Stop and Pause statements. They also receive their weights in specification statements when they represent values that initialize symbolic names (*e.g.*, the Data statement).

TABLE IV.   Weights Assigned to Statement-Type Elements

Statement Type	Weight
ASSIGNMENT	0
ACCEPT	3.00
ASSIGN	2.00
BACKSPACE	4.00
BLOCK DATA	1.00
BYTE	0
CALL	1.00
CHARACTER	0
CLOSE	0.10
COMMON	0
COMPLEX	0
CONTINUE	0
DATA	0
DECODE	3.00
DEFINE FILE	0.10
DELETE	4.00
DIMENSION	0
DO	7.00
DOUBLE COMPLEX	0
DOUBLE PRECISION	0
DO WHILE	7.00
ELSE	0
ELSE IF	4.00
ENCODE	3.00
END	0.10
END DO	0
ENDFILE	1.00
END IF	0
ENTRY	10.00
EQUIVALENCE	0
EXTERNAL	0
FIND	1.00
FORMAT	0.10
FUNCTION	4.00
GO TO	10.00
IF	5.00
IMPLICIT	0
INCLUDE	0
INQUIRE	2.00
INTEGER	0
INTRINSIC	3.00
LOGICAL	0
OPEN	2.00
PARAMETER	0
PAUSE	0.10
PRINT	3.00
PROGRAM	0
READ	3.00
REAL	0
RETURN	
0.10 for first RETURN statement	
12.10 for other RETURN statements	
REWRITE	3.00
REWIND	1.00
SAVE	10.00
Statement Function Definition	0
STOP	0.10
SUBROUTINE	4.00
TYPE	3.00
UNLOCK	4.00
VIRTUAL	3.00
WRITE	3.00

TABLE V. Statement Types by Assigned Weights

Weight	Statement Types
12.10	RETURN (except the first Return statement)
10.00	ENTRY, GO TO, SAVE
7.00	DO, DO WHILE
5.00	IF
4.00	BACKSPACE, DELETE, ELSE IF, FUNCTION, SUBROUTINE, UNLOCK
3.00	ACCEPT, DECODE, ENCODE, INTRINSIC, PRINT, READ, REWRITE, TYPE, VIRTUAL, WRITE
2.00	ASSIGN, INQUIRE, OPEN
1.00	BLOCK DATA, CALL, ENDFILE, FIND, REWIND
0.10	CLOSE, DEFINE FILE, END, FORMAT, PAUSE, RETURN (first Return statement only), STOP
0	Assignment, BYTE, CHARACTER, COMMON, COMPLEX, CONTINUE, DATA, DIMENSION, DOUBLE COMPLEX, DOUBLE PRECISION, ELSE, END DO, END IF, EQUIVALENCE, EXTERNAL, IMPLICIT, INCLUDE, INTEGER, LOGICAL, PARAMETER, PROGRAM, REAL, Statement Function Definition

Operator elements are assigned the weights specified in Table III in every statement in which they appear. Some symbols can denote other elements besides operators (*e.g.*, the asterisk in INTEGER*2); weights are assigned only when the symbols are used as operators.

The weights assigned to statement types are given in Tables IV and V. (The statement types are those of VAX-11 Fortran [6].) Of the 23 statement types currently assigned the weight of zero, 16 are specification statements and six are considered non-executable. Only the Assignment statement in this group is executable, and it is given a weight of zero as a base point. All other statements are given progressively higher weights, culminating in a weight of 12.10 assigned to each Return statement after the first in a program. The relatively heavy weights assigned to Entry statements and multiple Return statements reflect the impact their use has on the idea of single-entry, single-exit, structured programming.

Table VI summarizes the weights assigned to other

TABLE VI. Weights Assigned to Other Program Elements

Element	Weight
Use of a dummy argument as the name of a function, subroutine, or entry point is assessed an additional weight	4.00
Reference to a "built-in" function (*e.g.*, %LOC)	15.00
Poor usage	30.00
Label definition that is not higher in value than the previous label defined	0.50 (up to a maximum of 75.00)
Interface exception	30.00

TABLE VII. Factors for Data Type of Symbolic Name Element

Data Type of Symbolic Name Element	Factor
LOGICAL*1	0.10
LOGICAL*2	0.05
LOGICAL*4	0
INTEGER*2	0.05
INTEGER*4	0
REAL*4	0.05
REAL*8	0
REAL*16	0.05
COMPLEX*8	0.20
COMPLEX*16	0.25

program elements such as dummy arguments and "built-in" functions.

Factors are used to increase the weight assigned to symbolic name elements (Table I) according to the attributes and interrelationships of the symbolic name. The weight assigned to a symbolic name element is multiplied by (1 + factor) for each of its attributes. Table VII gives the factors for data type, and Table VIII gives the factors for other attributes.

TABLE VIII. Factors for Other Attributes

Attribute	Factor
Changing a Value Applied whenever a statement causes the value associated with a symbolic name to change (*e.g.*, Assignment, Read, Data statements)	0.15
Dummy Argument The symbolic name is a dummy argument if it appears in a Subroutine, Function, or Entry statement	0.30
Call Argument Applied to a symbolic name if it is used as an argument in a Call statement	0.30
Implicit Applied to a symbolic name if it is implicitly defined	0.50
Common Applied to a symbolic name if it is defined or Equivalenced into a common block	1.00
Equivalence Applied to a symbolic name once for every explicit and implicit alias	0.50

EXAMPLE: EQUIVALENCE (A, B) gives A and B one alias each. In

      REAL*4 A, B, C, D(2)
      COMMON A, B, C
      EQUIVALENCE (B, D(1))

A has no alias, B and C have one alias, and D has two aliases, one explicit (B) and one implicit (C).

Attribute	Factor
Backward Reference Applied to a reference to a label that is defined earlier in the program (unless the label identifies a Format statement)	3.00

EXAMPLE

To demonstrate how these concepts are applied to a
Fortran program to assess its relative difficulty, the program given in Figure 1 is analyzed below on a line-by-line and element-by-element basis using the weights
and factors listed in Tables I through VIII.

line 1: Program statement has a weight of zero
Statement difficulty = 0.00

line 2: Integer statement has a weight of zero
Definitions have a weight of zero
Statement difficulty = 0.00

line 3: Common statement has a weight of zero
Definitions have a weight of zero
Statement difficulty = 0.00

line 4: Equivalence statement has a weight of zero
Equivalence relationships have a weight of zero
Statement difficulty = 0.00

line 5: Format statement has a weight of 0.10
Variable *A* has weight of
   0.85   for a variable
 ×1.05   for data type INTEGER*2
 ×2.00   for being in common
  = 1.79
Operator + has a weight of 0.20
Integer constant (2) has a weight of 0.05
Statement difficulty = 0.10 + 1.79 + 0.20 + 0.05 = 2.14

line 6: Read statement has a weight of 3.00
Integer constant (5) has a weight of 0.05
Label 100 has a weight of 1.00
Variable *A* has a weight of 1.79 (from line 5)
 ×1.15   for changing its value
  = 2.05
Variable *C* has a weight of
   0.85   for a variable
 ×1.15   for changing its value
 ×1.05   for data type INTEGER*2
 ×2.00   for being in common
 ×1.50   for having one alias
  = 3.08
Statement difficulty = 3.00 + 0.05 + 1.00 + 2.05 + 3.08 = 9.18

line 7: Do statement has a weight of 7.00
Label 200 has a weight of 1.00

Variable *I* has a weight of
   0.85   for a variable
 ×1.15   for changing its value
 ×1.00   for data type INTEGER*4
 ×1.50   for being implicitly defined and data typed
  = 1.47
Variable *A* has a weight of 1.79 (from line 5)
Variable *C* has a weight of 2.68
(3.08 from line 6 divided by 1.15 since its value is not changed)
Statement difficulty = 7.00 + 1.00 + 1.47 + 1.79 + 2.68 = 13.94

line 8a: If statement has a weight of 5.00
Function *IAND* has a weight of
   2.00   for a function
 ×1.00   for data type INTEGER*4
  = 2.00
Variable *I* has a weight of 1.47/1.15 = 1.28 (line 7)
Integer constant (1) has a weight of 0.05
Operator .EQ. has a weight of 0.20
Integer constant (0) has a weight of 0.05
Statement difficulty = 5.00 + 2.00 + 1.28 + 0.05 + 0.20 + 0.05 = 8.58

line 8b: Assignment statement has a weight of zero
Array *B* has a weight of
   1.50   for an array
 ×1.15   for changing its value
 ×1.05   for data type INTEGER*2
 ×2.00   for being Equivalenced into common
 ×1.50   for having one alias
  = 5.43
Variable *I* has a weight of 1.28 (line 8a)
Variable *I* has a weight of 1.28
Operator + has a weight of 0.20
Integer constant (2) has a weight of 0.05
Statement difficulty = 0.00 + 5.43 + 1.28 + 1.28 + 0.20 + 0.05 = 8.24

line 9: Assignment statement has a weight of zero
Variable *J* has a weight of
   0.85   for a variable
 ×1.15   for changing its value
 ×1.05   for data type INTEGER*2
  = 1.03
Variable *C* has a weight of 2.68 (line 7)
Operator + has a weight of 0.20

```
(1)          PROGRAM EXAMPLE
(2)          INTEGER*2 A, B(10), C, J
(3)          COMMON /DC/ A, C
(4)          EQUIVALENCE (C, B(1))
(5)  100     FORMAT (I5, I<A + 2>)
(6)          READ (5, 100) A, C
(7)          DO 200 I = A, C
(8)      .   IF (IAND(I, 1) .EQ. 0) B(I) = I + 2
(9)  200     ...J = C + I
(10)         CALL SUBR
(11)         STOP
(12)         END
```

FIGURE 1. Sample Fortran Program.

Variable *I* has a weight of 1.28 (line 8a)
Statement difficulty = 0.00 + 1.03 + 2.68 + 0.20 + 1.28
  = 5.19
line 10: Call statement has weight of 1.00
Subroutine name *SUBR* has a weight of 2.00
Statement difficulty = 1.00 + 2.00 = 3.00
line 11: Stop statement has a weight of 0.10
Statement difficulty = 0.10
line 12: End statement has a weight of 0.10
Statement difficulty = 0.10

The sum of the statement difficulties is 50. This is the Index of Difficulty of the sample program, not counting any weight for poor usage and interface checks. Later when MAT analyzes this program (Figure 2), it finds one poor usage (the reader is encouraged to find it if he or she can). Thus, the Index of Difficulty of this program is raised to 80.

THE IMPLEMENTATION

The Maintainability Analysis Tool [2] analyzes programs written in VAX-11 Fortran, a superset of Fortran 77. MAT consists of seven modules written in Flecs [4] and transformed via the Vflecs compiler [3] into VAX-11 Fortran [6].

To break a Fortran program into its constituent elements so that each can be weighted according to its difficulty, MAT has many of the characteristics of a Fortran compiler. This includes being able to parse full Fortran, to build a comprehensive identifier table, to provide full Equivalence and common block processing, and to interpret parametric expressions so that their current values are always known. Performing interface checking on the usage of common blocks, subroutines, and functions means that MAT also has many of the characteristics of a relocatable loader.

A ground rule of MAT is that sets of programs submitted to it for analysis should be source-error-free or "clean-compiling." Since a second ground rule is that users will inevitably forget or ignore the first rule, MAT is equipped with a defensive set of Fortran error diagnostics that it issues when appropriate. Generally, the Fortran errors detected and diagnosed are those that would cause MAT to cease operating correctly if they were not intercepted. Although fairly extensive, the Fortran diagnostic capability of MAT is less than that of a Fortran compiler.

MAT also produces extensive diagnostics for poor usage, interface checks, interface summaries, and cer-

tain other conditions, all of which are discussed in the following section.

Poor Usage Of Fortran
A poor use of Fortran is one that contributes unnecessarily to increased difficulty of understanding and maintenance. Here are Fortran constructions that MAT currently identifies as poor usage:

- A parameter expression is used in an Equivalence relationship.
- A parameter value is used that is difficult to understand, *e.g.*,

    PARAMETER (*A* = 3H123)
    INTEGER *X*(*A*)

- A subroutine (or subroutine entry point) is called with a different number of arguments than was used earlier in the module.
- An obsolete Fortran statement (*e.g.*, Find statement) or syntax is used.
- An Assignment statement is used that looks like another statement. For example:

    BACKSPACE(5) = *ABC*
    CLOSE(*K*) = 5

- Several Common statements are used to define the same common block. For example:

    COMMON /SET/ *A, B, C*
    .
    .
    COMMON /SET/ *D*
    .
    .
    COMMON /SET/ *E, F*

instead of:

    COMMON /SET/ *A, B, C,*
    − *D, E, F* (where − denotes continuation)

- A local variable or array is defined but not used.
- A local variable or array is set (given a value) but not otherwise referenced.
- A local variable or array is referenced but possibly not set. MAT assumes that arguments of a function call are not set by the function and that arguments of a subroutine call are set by the subroutine. This choice is somewhat arbitrary; hence the "possibly"

```
DIRECTORY FILE: NONE       MAINTENANCE ANALYSIS TOOL (MAT) V4.1      21-JUN-83   16:03:09       PAGE  1

SEQ                              -----RELATIVE-----  DIFFICULTY  EXEC  --COMMENT-- DEBUG  LABELS NOT  POOR
NUM  FILE NAME   MODULE NAME    RISK   SKILL   TIME  INDEX RATIO STMTS LINES STMTS STMTS  IN ORDER    USES

  1 EXAMPLE.FOR· PROG EXAMPLE   8( 5) 10( 6)  0( 0)   80   100    3     0     0     0        0          1
    ***POOR USAGE: LOCAL VARIABLES SET BUT NOT REFERENCED:  J
JOB COMPLETE
```

FIGURE 2   MAT Report for the Sample Fortran Program of Figure 1.

Reports and Articles

above. This diagnostic is labelled a "notice" and is not included in the count of poor usages.
- A parameter is not referenced.
- A statement function is not referenced.
- A label is not referenced.
- A common block is included in a program but not referenced by it.

For each of these Fortran constructions that have been identified as poor usage, MAT outputs a comprehensive diagnostic together with the Fortran line numbers and/or names of the elements, as appropriate.

Interface Checking
If the interface checking option is chosen, MAT examines how each module adheres to the interface so far established by the set of modules that is being analyzed. Among the interface violations that are detected are:

- A subroutine (or subroutine entry point) is called with a different number of arguments than was used by the module that first called it.
- The size of a common block differs from the way it appeared in the first module. For a named common block, this imperfection is an error according to the Fortran 77 specification [1].
- The kind of symbolic name (variable, array) in a given position in a common block differs from earlier usage.
- The data type of a symbolic name in a given position in a common block differs from earlier usage.
- The symbolic name in a given position in a common block differs from the symbolic name used in that position earlier.
- The number of dimensions of an array in a given position in a common block differs from earlier usage.
- The value of a dimension of an array in a given position in a common block differs from earlier usage.
- The lower dimensional bound of an array in a given position in a common block differs from earlier usage.
- A common block contains a different number of symbolic names than it did in an earlier usage.

Each interface violation is given a diagnostic by MAT, and each diagnostic contains the pertinent symbolic names.

Interface Summary
At the conclusion of each job for which the user has specified the interface checking option, MAT examines the interface established by the modules analyzed, searching for the following imperfections:

- A symbolic name in a common block is never set or referenced.
- A symbolic name in a common block is referenced (but not set) by just one module.
- A symbolic name in a common block is referenced but not set.

- A symbolic name in a common block is set (but not referenced) by just one module.
- A symbolic name in a common block is set but not referenced.
- A symbolic name in a common block is used by just one module.

All Equivalencing is taken into account in making these determinations. Each diagnostic is accompanied by the symbolic names, along with the suggestion that the names be removed from common.

MAT also reports on the subroutines, subroutine entry points, functions, and function entry points that are referenced by, but not included in, the module set. In so doing, MAT suppresses the names of the common system subroutines, the Generic functions, and the Fortran 77 Intrinsic functions that are referenced. MAT also reports the names of subroutines, subroutine entry points, functions, and function entry points that are included in the module set but not referenced.

Other MAT Diagnostics
Certain other conditions that interfere with program understandability are also detected and diagnosed by MAT—Include files that cannot be opened by the file name explicitly specified in the Include statement, and source files that cannot be opened or that exist but are empty (*e.g.*, contain only comments).

Another class of MAT diagnostic is the style error, which is considered to be a gross misuse of the Fortran language from the maintainability standpoint. Each of the following style errors generates a diagnostic that includes the Fortran listing line number:

- An Assignment statement looks so much like another statement that its presence causes confusion. Some examples:

      GO TO (100, 200, 300) = 10
      INTEGER A(10) = 5
      READ (5, 100) = ABC

- A symbolic name identifies more than one element in a module. Although the Fortran 77 standard [1] allows this usage in some cases, the use of the same name to mean two different things is considered bad practice. The diagnostic includes the symbolic name in question.
- The number of nested Include files exceeds three. This is not a limitation on the number of Include files in a module.
- A parameter expression contains a parenthetical nesting that is too deep. To determine the current value of each parameter and parameter expression, MAT compiles parameter expressions, generating value and operator stacks, and then executes the expression by interpreting the stacks. MAT's stacks are large enough that, if this diagnostic is displayed, the offending statement must be quite excessive in its parenthetical nesting.
- A Define File statement is used. This statement is wholly replaced by the Open statement.

First report excerpt

SEQ NUM	FILE NAME	MODULE NAME	RISK	SKILL	TIME	DIFFICULTY INDEX	RATIO	EXEC STMTS	COMMENT LINES	COMMENT STMTS	DEBUG STMTS	LABELS NOT IN ORDER	POOR USES
1	[IMSL83]DFMIN.FOR	SUBR ABNRMD	4	5	0	60	50	12	85	0	0	0	0
2	[IMSL83]DFMIN.FOR	SUBR ABNRMS	4	5	0	62	52	12	41	0	0	0	0
3	[IMSL83]DFMIN.FOR	SUBR CBNRMD	4	5	0	58	48	12	40	0	0	0	0
4	[IMSL83]DFMIN.FOR	SUBR CBNRMS	4	5	0	58	48	12	37	0	0	0	0
5	[IMSL83]DFMIN.FOR	SUBR CSORTD	6	8	1	381	85	45	36	0	0	0	0
6	[IMSL83]DFMIN.FOR	SUBR CSORTS	6	8	0	379	84	45	38	0	0	0	0
7	[IMSL83]DFMIN.FOR	SUBR DIFFD	8	10	0	30	100	3	38	0	0	0	0
8	[IMSL83]DFMIN.FOR	SUBR DIFFS	8	10	0	30	100	3	38	0	0	0	0
9	[IMSL83]DFMIN.FOR	SUBR IBNRMD	4	5	0	50	45	11	38	0	0	0	0
10	[IMSL83]DFMIN.FOR	SUBR IBNRMS	4	5	0	51	46	11	30	0	0	0	0

Second report excerpt

SEQ NUM	FILE NAME	MODULE NAME	RISK	SKILL	TIME	DIFFICULTY INDEX	RATIO	EXEC STMTS	COMMENT LINES	COMMENT STMTS	DEBUG STMTS	LABELS NOT IN ORDER	POOR USES
1	PLOTS.FOR	SUBR PLOT	7(6)	8(7)	4(3)	1065	78	137	15	4	0	0	2

***POOR USAGE: LOCAL VARIABLES SET BUT NOT REFERENCED: YPDEF XPDEF

| 2 | PLOTS.FOR | SUBR SYMBOL | 7(6) | 8(7) | 2(2) | 658 | 81 | 81 | 8 | 11 | 0 | 0 | 2 |

***INTERFACE CHECK: SIZE OF COMMON DIFFERS FROM EARLIER USAGE: KPLTS
***INTERFACE CHECK: COMMON HAS MORE ELEMENTS THAN IT HAD IN ITS EARLIER USAGE: KPLTS

| 3 | PLOTS.FOR | SUBR NUMBER | 7(6) | 8(7) | 2(1) | 459 | 82 | 56 | 4 | 7 | 0 | 0 | 2 |

***INTERFACE CHECK: SIZE OF COMMON DIFFERS FROM EARLIER USAGE: KPLTS
***INTERFACE CHECK: COMMON HAS MORE ELEMENTS THAN IT HAD IN ITS EARLIER USAGE: KPLTS

| 4 | PLOTS.FOR | SUBR SCALE | 7(6) | 8(7) | 3(2) | 793 | 77 | 103 | 14 | 19 | 1 | 0 | 2 |

***INTERFACE CHECK: SIZE OF COMMON DIFFERS FROM EARLIER USAGE: KPLTS
***INTERFACE CHECK: COMMON HAS MORE ELEMENTS THAN IT HAD IN ITS EARLIER USAGE: KPLTS

| 5 | PLOTS.FOR | SUBR AXIS | 7(6) | 8(7) | 4(4) | 1216 | 77 | 158 | 22 | 16 | 10 | 0 | 2 |

***INTERFACE CHECK: SIZE OF COMMON DIFFERS FROM EARLIER USAGE: KPLTS
***INTERFACE CHECK: COMMON HAS MORE ELEMENTS THAN IT HAD IN ITS EARLIER USAGE: KPLTS

| 6 | PLOTS.FOR | SUBR LINE | 6(6) | 7(7) | 3(3) | 1037 | 72 | 145 | 30 | 26 | 1 | 0 | 3 |

***INTERFACE CHECK: SIZE OF COMMON DIFFERS FROM EARLIER USAGE: KPLTS
***INTERFACE CHECK: DATA TYPE OF NAME IN COMMON DIFFERS FROM EARLIER USAGE: NEWGRF
***INTERFACE CHECK: COMMON HAS MORE ELEMENTS THAN IT HAD IN ITS EARLIER USAGE: KPLTS

Third report excerpt

DIRECTORY FILE: ERLS.MAT   MAINTENANCE ANALYSIS TOOL (MAT) V4.0   1-JUN-83 14:54:00   PAGE 1

SEQ NUM	FILE NAME	MODULE NAME	RISK	SKILL	TIME	DIFFICULTY INDEX	RATIO	EXEC STMTS	COMMENT LINES	COMMENT STMTS	DEBUG STMTS	LABELS NOT IN ORDER	POOR USES
1	DREH.FOR	SUBR ERROR_HANDLER	10(7)	10(9)	3(0)	775	861	9	58	0	0	1	23

***POOR USAGE: OLD LANGUAGE ELEMENT OR SYNTAX (TO BE AVOIDED IN NEW PROGRAMS) AT LINE 59
***POOR USAGE: PARAMETERS DEFINED BUT NOT USED: SQ_WAYPOINT_UNIT SQ_WARNING SQ_TRAJECTORY_UNIT SQ_TRACE_CAPTURE_UNIT SQ_TC_MAP_UNIT
  SQ_STOP_SAVE_RESTART_UNIT SQ_STATUS SQ_PLATFORM_CAL_CONST_UNIT SQ_OFS_CAL_CONSTANTS_UNIT
  SQ_OFS_LOAD_UNIT SQ_MDF_UNIT SQ_ISP_SCRIPT_MESSAGE_UNIT SQ_ISP_COMMAND_UNIT SQ_BULK_LOAD_UNIT SQ_FATAL
  SQ_ERROR_LOG_UNIT SQ_ERLS_CAPTURE_UNIT SQ_DISCRETES_CAPTURE_UNIT SQ_CAPTURE_PRINT_UNIT SQ_AVES_CAPTURE_UNIT
  SQ_NUCLEAR_EVENT_FLAG SQ_MKB2_INTERRUPT_FLAG QC_FP_INFINITY QC_FP_ZERO EQ_MEMORY_TOP
  EQ_OUTPUT_MODE EQ_NO_IO_MODE EQ_INPUT_MODE EQ_PC EQ_CARRY_FLAG EQ_PC_TRAPS_MASK EQ_WRITE_RANGE_TRAP_FLAG
  EQ_READ_RANGE_TRAP_FLAG EQ_WRITE_TRAP_FLAG EQ_READ_TRAP_FLAG EQ_PC_RANGE_TRAP_FLAG EQ_TRAP_PTR_FIELD
  EQ_INTERRUPT_TRAP_FLAG EQ_OPCODE_TRAP_FLAG EQ_PC_TRAP_EXIT_FLAG EQ_INTERRUPT_VECTOR_MASK EQ_EXTERNAL_IO_MASK
  EQ_TRACE_MODE_FLAG EQ_ADDRESS_TRAP_EXIT_FLAG EQ_OPCODE_TRAP_EXIT_FLAG EQ_INTERRUPT_TRAP_EXIT_FLAG
  ERATFG EMCMFG ERTCFG EQ_IO_EXIT_FLAG EQ_ERROR_EXIT_FLAG EQ_DMA_ENABLE
***POOR USAGE: LOCAL VARIABLES SET BUT NOT REFERENCED: M

| 2 | EREE.FOR | SUBR ERLS_EXECUTE | 10(9) | 10(9) | 10(10) | 5323 | 162 | 329 | 199 | 0 | 0 | 1 | 74 |

***POOR USAGE: OLD LANGUAGE ELEMENT OR SYNTAX (TO BE AVOIDED IN NEW PROGRAMS) AT LINES 40 164 213 214 215 216 217 218 219 220
  221 222 223 224
***POOR USAGE: LOCAL VARIABLES DEFINED BUT NOT USED: TEMP_R1 TEMP_R SIGN
***POOR USAGE: LABELS DEFINED BUT NOT REFERENCED: 900

FIGURE 3 Excerpts from Different MAT Reports.

- The number of different character lengths for variables, arrays, and functions exceeds 20. (This is not a limitation on the number of variables, arrays, and functions of the character data type in a module.)

MAT is heavily self-checked with both a set of more than 30 diagnostics that are displayed when MAT finds an error in itself, and a smaller set of "resource exhausted" diagnostics. Altogether MAT contains 116 diagnostic messages.

MAT Report

The MAT report displays the results for each module analyzed in occurrence order, followed by the interface summary. The report segment devoted to each particular module displays the file name, module name, Index of Difficulty, and other data in columnar format, followed by the diagnostics (Figure 3).

The data displayed include the number of executable statements. For executable modules (*i.e.,* not Block Data modules), this number excludes all specification statements and statements such as Continue, Else, and End If. Logical IF statements are counted as two statements. The "Difficulty Ratio" is computed as ten times the Index of Difficulty divided by the number of executable statements; it is considered a measure of the skill required to understand and maintain the module.

Dimensionless numbers in the range 0–10 are displayed as rough indices to three important maintainability properties of the module. The relative time to make a unit change or correction to the module is arbitrarily defined as the Index of Difficulty divided by 300. The relative skill required of the personnel who maintain the module is scaled from the Difficulty Ratio. The relative maintainability risk of the module is arbitrarily represented by a simple function of the previous two measures: three times the relative skill index plus the relative time index all divided by four. None of the indices is allowed to exceed ten. If MAT detects problems in the module, it displays two sets of these numbers: the unparenthesized set represents the module as it stands; the parenthesized set represents the module as if it were modified so as to correct the problems diagnosed by MAT. These rough guides have been tuned to approximate human perceptions.

For each module MAT also lists the number of comment lines, statements annotated by comments, debug statements, and label definitions that are not greater than the previous label defined.

Figure 2 presents the MAT report for the Fortran program illustrated in Figure 1. MAT finds that the local variable *J* was set but not referenced in this program. This instance of poor usage raises the Index of Difficulty to 80.

RESULTS

Although a relatively new program, MAT has already processed thousands of Fortran programs written by many people in many organizations. So far, no scientific study has been made comparing the results of MAT

maintainability analyses with human maintainability assessments for the same modules. What can be said is that the MAT maintainability results appear to correlate very well with human perceptions, after considerable tuning of the weights and factors used. No objections to MAT rankings and assessments have been received.

There have been several unexpected outcomes from MAT's use, among them the realization that many if not most Fortran programs, especially those including production programs, are cluttered with all kinds of unnecessary elements. These include defined but unreferenced variables, arrays, and labels; and variables and arrays that are set but never referenced. Many programs contain whole common blocks that are not used; one program was found that contained nine common blocks that were totally unused. Many common blocks contain symbolic names that are not used by at least two modules. In many cases, the names are probably in common because the functions of the program changed during its development, but the definition of the common blocks did not. It has been found that when a common block contains symbolic names that are not used in ways appropriate to their being in common, vestigial code manipulating these names exists as well and can also be eliminated.

Another revelation is the marked differences in programming style and proficiency that can be seen, for example, in the MAT reports shown in Figure 3. The largest total Index of Difficulty found so far by MAT is 13,812. This value was registered by a very long and involved module converted to Fortran by a pre-processor that generates inefficient code rich in Go To statements. The largest Index of Difficulty found to date for a handwritten Fortran program is 9,791. Good scores are now considered to be less than about 1,200.

The major surprise has been the number of errors MAT has discovered, even in production programs. For example, there is apparent confusion about the Fortran If-Then-Else structure. MAT has found several variations on the following theme:

```
    IF (e)
   −THENA = 0          (− denotes continuation)
    ELSEA = 10
```

This is equivalent to:

```
        IF (e) THENA = 0
        ELSEA = 10
```

which is not a structure at all but a Logical If statement followed by an Assignment statement. In this case, MAT reports that both *THENA* and *ELSEA* are set but not referenced. In one module examined, this construction occurred six times. Although legal, this usage produces a very different result than intended by the programmer. In none of the programs involved had testing been adequate to discover these errors.

Another class of errors found by MAT are typographical. One programmer reported that he needed to change the statement $PTR = 0$ to IF (ERR .EQ. 0) PTR = 0. Upon making the change he ran the program through MAT. To his surprise, MAT reported that the variable 0 "oh" was referenced but not set. Upon examination, he discovered that in making the modification he had typed an "oh" rather than a zero. MAT has reported similar findings in several modules, as well as many instances of the possible misuse of the variable I (possibly typed instead of 1, or vice versa).

MAT has also uncovered syntax errors not diagnosed by the VAX-11 Fortran compiler. For example, in the statement:

$$\text{IMPLICIT INTEGER*2 } I, J, K, L, M, N$$

the name list $I - N$ should be parenthesized.

Nearly every poor usage and interface violation that MAT can detect has been found in production programs. MAT's ability to examine Fortran source code for usage and to examine the interface between communicating sets of Fortran programs and diagnose exceptions to it may be unique. Because of its extensive diagnostic capabilities, MAT can be a potent debugging tool for use during program and system development.

REFERENCES

1. American National Standard Programming Language Fortran, X3, 9–1978. American National Standards Institute, New York, 1978.
2. Berns, G. M. Reference Guide to MAT, Maintenance Analysis Tool, Science Applications, Inc., Crystal City, Virginia, 1983.
3. Berns, G. M. Vflecs, a Fortran pre-processor that produces structured VAX-11 Fortran from Flecs and Fortran programs, Science Applications, Inc., Crystal City, Virginia, 1983.
4. Flecs: User's Manual, Department of Computer Science, University of Oregon, 1975.
5. Shen, V. Y., Conte S. D. and Dunsmore, H. E. Software Science Revisited: A Critical Analysis of the Theory and its Empirical Support, IEEE Trans. Software Engineer. 9, 2 (March, 1983), 155–164.
6. VAX-11 Fortran Language Reference Manual, Digital Equipment Corp. (Order No. AA-DO34B-TE), Maynard, Massachusetts, 1980.

CR Categories and Subject Descriptors: D.2.7 [**Software Engineering**]: Distribution and Maintenance; D.2.8 [**Software Engineering**]: Metrics—*software science*; D.2.5 [**Software Engineering**]: Testing and Debugging—*debugging aids*
General Terms: Measurement, Verification.
Additional Key Words and Phrases: program maintainability, maintainability measures, debugging aids, Fortran programs

Received 7/83; accepted 8/83

Author's Present Address: Gerald M. Berns, Science Applications, Inc., 2361 Jefferson Davis Highway, Suite 320, Arlington, VA 22202.

A Software Maintainability Evaluation Methodology

Abstract—This paper describes a conceptual framework of software maintainability and an implemented procedure for evaluating a program's documentation and source code for maintainability characteristics. The evaluation procedure includes use of closed-form questionnaires completed by a group of evaluators. Statistical analysis techniques for validating the evaluation procedure are described. Some preliminary results from the use of this methodology by the Air Force Test and Evaluation Center are presented. Areas of future research are discussed.

Index Terms—Evaluation by questionnaire, evaluation reliability, quality metrics, software engineering, software maintainability evaluation, software quality assurance.

I. INTRODUCTION

THE Air Force Test and Evaluation Center (AFTEC) has been developing a methodology for evaluating the quality of delivered software systems as part of its directed activity of operational test and evaluation (OT&E). Thayer [3] has reported the initial approach for a software maintainability evaluation methodology. The BDM Corporation has completed a technical directive for AFTEC to review this methodology, analyze the results of 18 different program evaluations which used the methodology, and recommend appropriate changes to the methodology. This paper summarizes the revised methodology from this effort.

Because of the number of software systems to be evaluated, the variability (language, computer, functions) of the software to be evaluated, and the limited state of the art in practical automated evaluation tools, AFTEC's software evaluation procedure has been based on the completion of closed-form questionnaires. The methodology defines a conceptual framework for the software characteristics from the user-oriented level to the software product level and an evaluation procedure whereby the identified product characteristics can be measured. The measures, or software metrics, are then normalized through evaluation-specific weights to provide the necessary evaluation maintainability measures.

The primary objective of the software maintainability evaluation is to collect enough specific information to identify for which parts of the software and for what reasons maintainability may be a problem. A secondary objective is to assess the effectiveness of the evaluation process itself. A future goal is to validate maintainability scores against an actual field maintenance level of effort.

Manuscript received February 4, 1980; revised January 21, 1981. This work was supported by AFTEC Technical Directive 120 of Contract F29601-77-C-0082.

The author is with the BDM Corporation, Albuquerque, NM 87106.

The major evaluation assumptions are as follows:
- maintainability considerations remain essentially the same from program to program,
- evaluators must be knowledgeable in software procedures, techniques, and maintenance, but need not have a detailed knowledge of the functional area of the program,
- a minimum of five independent evaluators will be used to provide acceptable confidence that the metrics (evaluator average scores) are a sound measuring tool,
- the random sampling of the program modules for evaluation provides conclusions which hold for the general population of all program modules.

The main features of the software maintainability evaluation are the following.
- The maintainability model is primarily based on the models in Thayer [3], Boehm [1], and Walters [4]. The evaluation process consists of a set of evaluators completing closed-form questionnaires on maintainability characteristics of program documentation and program source listings followed by automated processing of the evaluator responses and a careful manual analysis of all detected program and evaluation anomalies.
- The evaluation can be used at appropriate phases in the software development life cycle in addition to the operational maintenance phase.
- The evaluation is independent of any particular source language.
- The maintainability characteristics can be used as a quality assurance checklist.

The major results of this research effort have been to:
- provide a definitive evaluation methodology which is practical and immediately useful to AFTEC,
- reduce subjectivity and increase reliability of the evaluation,
- provide a conceptual framework which can be expanded both within maintainability and to other quality factors,
- provide a computer program for the automated processing and analysis of the evaluation data.

II. CONCEPTUAL FRAMEWORK

The software maintainability evaluation methodology has the conceptual framework shown in Fig. 1. The associated definitions are in Table I.

A. Quality Factors

The work of Boehm [1] and Walters [4] among others has established a set of user-oriented terms representing desired qualities of software. These terms, or quality factors, include maintainability, usability, correctness, human engineering,

Reprinted from *IEEE Transactions on Software Engineering*, Volume SE-7, Number 4, July 1981, pages 343-351. Copyright © 1981 by The Institute of Electrical and Electronics Engineers, Inc.

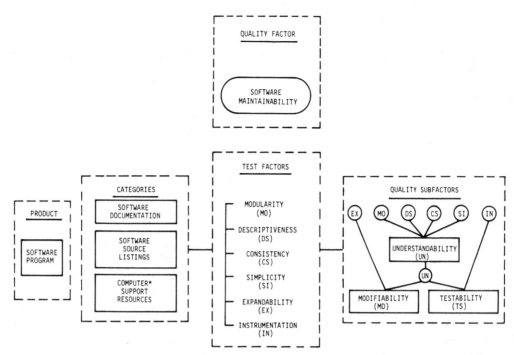

Fig. 1. Elements of software maintainability.

TABLE I
DEFINITIONS

SOFTWARE: _Software_ consists of the programs and documentation which result from a software development process.	objectives, assumptions, inputs, processing, outputs, components, revision status, etc.
SOFTWARE MAINTAINABILITY: _Software maintainability_ is a quality of software which reflects the effort required to perform the following actions: (1) Removal/correction of latent errors (2) Addition of new features/capabilities (3) Deletion of unused/undesirable features (4) Modification of software to be compatible with hardware changes Implicit in the above definition are the concepts that the software should be understandable, modifiable and testable in order to have effective maintainability.	CONSISTENCY: Software possesses the characteristics of _consistency_ to the extent the software products correlate and contain uniform notation, terminology and symbology. SIMPLICITY: Software possesses the characteristics of _simplicity_ to the extent that it lacks complexity in organization, language, and implementation techniques and reflects the use of singularity concepts and fundamental structures. EXPANDABILITY: Software possess the characteristics of _expandability_ to the extent that a physical change to information, computational functions, data storage or execution time can be easily accomplished.
UNDERSTANDABILITY: Software processes the characteristics of _understandability_ to the extent its purpose and organization are clear to the inspector.	INSTRUMENTATION: Software possesses the characteristics of _instrumentation_ to the extent it contains aids which enhance testing.
MODIFIABILITY: Software possesses the characteristics of _modifiability_ to the extent that it facilitates the incorporation of changes once the nature of the desired change has been identified.	SOFTWARE DOCUMENTATION: _Software documentation_ is the set of requirements, design specifications, guidelines, operational procedures, test information, problem reports, etc. which in total form the written description of the program(s) output from a software development process.
TESTABILITY: Software possesses the characteristics of _testability_ to the extent that it facilitates the establishment of verification criteria and supports evaluation of its performance.	SOFTWARE SOURCE LISTINGS: _Software source listings_ are the implemented representation (listing) described through a source computer language of the program(s) output from a software development process.
TEST FACTORS: _Software maintainability test factors_ are user-oriented general attributes of software which affect maintainability. The set of test factors includes: modularity, descriptiveness, consistency, simplicity, expandability, and instrumentation.	COMPUTER SUPPORT RESOURCES: _Computer support resources_ include all the resources (software, computer equipment, facilities, etc.) which support the software being evaluated.
MODULARITY: Software possesses the characteristics of _modularity_ to the extent that a logical partitioning of software into parts, components, and modules has occurred.	PROGRAM: A _program_ is a set of hierarchically related modules which can be separately compiled, linked, loaded and executed.
DESCRIPTIVENESS: Software possesses the characteristics of _descriptiveness_ to the extent that it contains information regarding its	MODULE: A _module_ is a set of "contiguous" computer language statements which has a name by which it can be separately invoked.

portability, reliability, and others. Although the quality factors may be the same syntactically among researchers, semantically they tend to have different interpretations. The definition in Table I of software maintainability reflects AFTEC's concern for acquiring software which is understandable (required locations for modifications can be easily established), modifiable (enhancements or corrections can be made), and testable (the software is properly instrumented for testing once modifications have been made).

B. Software Product/Categories

Each software program (product) is separately evaluated and consists of a set of components called modules. A module may, in general, be at any conceptual level of the program.

For each program there are three categories which are evaluated for characteristics which affect maintainability: software documentation, software source listings, and the computer support resources. Only program deliverables are considered in an evaluation.

1) Software Documentation: The primary documentation used in this evaluation consists of the documents containing program design specifications, program test plan information and procedures, and program maintenance information. These documents may have a variety of physical organizations depending upon the particular application, although software standards attempt to reduce the variability [22]-[28]. The documents are evaluated both for content and for general physical structure (format).

2) Software Source Listings: The source listings represent the program as implemented, in contrast to the documentation which represents the program design or implementation plan. Source listings are also a form of program documentation, but for this maintainability evaluation a distinction is made.

The source listing evaluation consists of a separate evaluation of each specified module's source listing and the consistency between the module's source listing and the related written module documentation. The separate module evaluations are accumulated into an overall evaluation of the software source listings.

3) Computer Support Resources: Attributes and procedures for the evaluation of computer support resources are being developed and will be detailed in a separate report.

C. Software Maintainability Test Factors

The maintainability of software documentation and source listings is a function of six attributes or test factors: modularity, descriptiveness, consistency, simplicity, expandability, and instrumentation. These test factors are defined in Table I. Discussions of their application in the evaluation of the documentation and source listings are given in the following paragraphs.

1) Modularity: It has been observed that software has been easiest to understand and change when composed of "independent" parts (sections, modules). Documentation and source listings are evaluated in relation to the extent their logical parts show only a few, simple links to other parts (low *coupling* [9]) and contain only a few easily recognizable subparts which are closely related (high *strength* [9]). Parnas [10], [11] has described these concepts in different, but relatively equivalent terms.

2) Descriptiveness: It is important that the documentation contain useful explanations of the software program design. The objectives, assumptions, inputs, and outputs are desirable in varying degrees of detail in both documentation and source listings. The intrinsic descriptiveness of the source language syntax and the judicious use of source commentary greatly aids efforts to understand the program operation.

3) Consistency: The use of some standards and conventions in documentation, flowchart construction, I/O processing, error processing, module interfacing, and naming of modules/variables are typical reflections of consistency. Consistency allows one to easily generalize understanding. For example, programs using consistent conventions might require that the format of modules be similar. Thus, by learning the format of one module (preface block, declaration format, error checks, etc.) the format of all modules is learned.

4) Simplicity: The aspects of software complexity (or lack of simplicity) that are emphasized in the evaluation relate primarily to the concepts of size and primitives. The use of high order language as opposed to assembly language tends to make a program simpler to understand because there are fewer discriminations which have to be made. There are certain programming considerations such as dynamic allocation of resources, recursive/reentrant coding which can greatly complicate the data and control flow. Real-time programs, because of the requirement for timing constraints and efficiency, tend to have more control complexity. The sheer bulk

of counts (number of operators, operands, nested control structures, executable statements, statement labels, decision parameters) will determine to a great extent how simple or complex the source code is [15]-[18].

5) Expandability: Software may be reasonably understandable but not easily expandable. If the design of the program has not allowed for a flexible timing scheme or a reasonable storage margin, then even minor changes may be extremely difficult to implement. Parameterization of constants and basic data structure sizes usually improves expandability. It is also very important that the documentation include explanations of how to make increases/decreases in data structure sizes or changes to the timing scheme. The limitations of such program expandability should be clear. The numbering schemes for documentation narrative and graphic materials must be carefully considered so that physical modifications to the documentation can be easily accomplished when necessary.

6) Instrumentation: For the most part, the documentation is evaluated by how well the program has been designed to include test aids (instruments), while the source listings are evaluated by how well the code seems to be implemented to allow for testing through the use of such test aids. The software should be designed and implemented so that instrumentation is imbedded within the program, can be easily inserted into the program, is available through a support software system, or is available through a combination of these capabilities.

D. Software Characteristics

Each test factor has a set of software-level characteristics which serve to define the test factor within the context of the software product category being evaluated. Characteristics were identified and grouped so as to minimize the overlap among the test factors and balance the number of characteristics across the test factors. Characteristics for the documentation and source listings were identified primarily from Thayer [3], Boehm [1], Walters [4], Kernighan and Plauger [7], Myers [9], Parnas [10], [11], Miller [19], Halstead [15], [16], McCabe [18], Yeh [12], and various documentation standards [22]-[28].

A fixed scale for all evaluation responses was chosen and closed-form questionnaires for documentation and source listings were designed based on the identified characteristics. In order to minimize subjectivity, increase the evaluation reliability, and provide for a more efficient evaluation process, a detailed evaluation guidelines handbook [33] was developed. The handbook contains background methodology, the evaluation questionnaires, and a set of guidelines for interpreting the terminology and potential responses for each question. A computer program was developed to aid the analysis of the evaluator responses.

III. Evaluation Procedure

The software evaluation procedure involves four distinct phases as shown in Fig. 2: planning, calibration, assessment, and analysis.

During the planning phase, the AFTEC Software Test Manager (STM) and the selected Software Assessment Team (SAT) Chairman establish evaluator teams, each consisting of

Test Planning

Software Test Manager (STM)/Software Assessment
Team (SAT) Chairman:

- Establishes Evaluation Structure
- Selects Modules for Evaluation
- Determines Test Factor Weights
- Establishes Time Frame for Evaluation

STM:

- Assigns Identification Information
- Completes Evaluator Briefing

Calibration Test

Each Evaluator:
- Completes One Documentation Questionnaire
- Completes Specified Module Questionnaire

STM:
- Reviews Completed Questionnaires
- Resolves Misunderstandings
- Debriefs Evaluators

Assessment

Each Evaluator:
- Updates Calibration Questionnaires
- Completes Remaining Questionnaires

Analysis and Reporting

STM:
- Accomplishes Automated Questionnaire Data Entry
- Produces Automated Preliminary Analysis
- Reviews Automated Analysis Results

SAT:
- Reviews Preliminary Analysis
- Performs Detailed Evaluation
- Prepares Evaluation Report

Fig. 2. Maintainability evaluation procedure.

TABLE II
TEST FACTOR QUESTION DISTRIBUTION

	MO	DS	CS	SI	EX	IN	GENERAL	TOTAL
Documentation	12	24	9	12	9	10	7	83
Source Listings	14	21	14	16	9	8	7	89

TABLE III
EXAMPLE QUESTIONS

(Documentation)

Format Modularity

Note: The following questions relate to how the documentation has been physically formatted into functional parts.

1. Program documentation includes a separate part for the description of program external interfaces.

2. Program documentation includes a separate part for the description of each major program function.

3. Program documentation includes a separate part for the description of the program global data base.

Processing Modularity

Note: The following questions relate to how the program control and data flow has been designed for functional use.

8. The program control flow is organized in a top down hierarchical tree pattern.

9. Program initialization processing is done by one (set of) modules(s) designed exclusively for that purpose.

(Source Listings)

Size Simplicity

Note: The following questions relate to various "counts" which reflect the amount of information which must be assimilated to understand a module.

62. The number of expressions used to control branching in this module is manageable.

63. The number of unique operators in this module is manageable.

64. The number of unique operands in this module is manageable.

65. The number of executable statements in this module is manageable.

General Questions

83. Modularity as reflected in this module's source listing contributes to the maintainability of this module.

at least five evaluators knowledgeable in software maintenance. The SAT chairman may or may not be one of the evaluators. The evaluators are preferably persons who will be responsible for maintaining some part of the software being evaluated. The program/module hierarchy is established and a set of representative modules is selected for each program to be evaluated. At least 10 percent of the modules in a program are randomly selected for evaluation. Specific test factor (attribute) weights are also determined at this time and the schedule for the evaluation is established. The software test manager briefs the evaluator teams on the procedures and assigns the necessary identification information for this specific evaluation.

The function of the calibration test is to ensure a reliable evaluation through a clear understanding of the questions and their specific response guidelines on each questionnaire. Each evaluator completes a documentation and module source listing questionnaire. The completed questionnaires are reviewed to detect areas of misunderstanding and the evaluation teams are debriefed on the problem areas.

In the assessment phase, the evaluation teams update their calibration test questionnaires based on the results of the calibration debriefing. The teams then complete the remainder of their assigned documentation and module source questionnaires. It is estimated that each evaluator will take 4–6 hours to complete the documentation questionnaire and 1–3 hours to complete each module questionnaire.

In the analysis phase, the software test manager accomplishes the conversion and initial data processing of the questionnaire data. This preliminary analysis is then reviewed and corrected, if necessary. The statistical summaries are then returned to the SAT for detailed evaluation and preparation of the final report.

A. Example Questions

Each evaluator is supplied with a documentation questionnaire, source listing questionnaire, evaluation response forms, and an evaluator guidelines handbook. The number of questions for each of the questionnaires and each of the test factors is summarized in Table II. Some of the questions are illustrated in Table III. Note the "general" question 83. Each test factor has such an associated general question. In future analysis of the methodology, test factor characteristics (scores) will be regressed against the general question (score) across all program modules and all programs. The guidelines for one of the sample questions are illustrated in Table IV.

B. Response Form

The form on which an evaluator records responses to questions is processed through an optical scanner. There are three "blocks" on this form: descriptive identification block, numerical identification block, and evaluator response

TABLE IV
EXAMPLE OF QUESTION GUIDELINES

```
                              Question Number S-62

QUESTION:      The number of expressions used to control branch-
ing in this module is manageable.

CHARACTERISTIC:  Simplicity (size simplicity).

Explanations:  The count of control expressions is closely related
to the number of independent cycles in a module.  The more control
expressions there are, the more complex the control logic tends to
be.

EXAMPLES:  The following examples indicate how to count the control
expressions:

CONTROL STRUCTURE     STATEMENT      CONTROL EXPRESSION     COUNT

Decision  IF (A.OR.B) GO TO 10           A;B                 2
          IF (A.AND.B) GO TO 10          A;B                 2
          IF (C.GT.D) GO TO 10           C.GT.D              1
          IF (A.AND.B).OR.(C.GT.D))
              GO TO 10                   A;B;C.GT.D          3
          CASE (I) OF                    I=1;I=2;I=3         2
            1: A                         (Alternatives)   (number of
            2: B                                          alternatives
            3: C                                          less one)
          END CASE

Iteration DO 10 I=1, 10                  I.LT.1
            A                            I.GT.10             2
         10 CONTINUE

GLOSSARY:  Control expression:  IF, CASE, or other decision control
expression.  DO, DO-WHILE, or other iterative control expression.

SPECIAL RESPONSE INSTRUCTIONS:  The following guidelines will anchor
A and F responses, but are fairly subjective (especially the F anchor).
The guidelines for the A response is suggested from other indepen-
dent research.  Remember to count all repetitions of the same control
expression also.

          Answer A if count < 10.
          Answer F if count ≥ 50.
```

block. The descriptive identification block contains information which identifies the particular questionnaire type, system, subsystem, program, module, evaluator, date, and time to complete. This block is only used for a visual identification check and is not processed by the optical scanner. The numerical identification block contains numeric codes for the same information contained in the descriptive identification block. The evaluator response block contains a set of 10 responses (A–J) for each question up to 90 questions.

C. Response Scale

The following response scale is used to answer each question:

a) completely agree,
b) strongly agree,
c) generally agree,
d) generally disagree,
e) strongly disagree,
f) completely disagree.

One of these responses *must* be given for each question. In addition, one or more of the following standardized comment responses can be selected:

i) I had difficulty answering this question,
j) a written comment has been submitted.

The responses g and h are not used. The responses a–f (equivalent numeric metric is 6 to 1) indicate the extent to which the evaluator agrees/disagrees with the question statement.

D. Analysis Techniques

The maintainability metrics are the average scores across evaluators, test factors, product categories, and programs. Test factors, product categories, and programs can be given

weights at the discretion of the AFTEC Test Manager and SAT Chairman, but raw scores will also be retained.

Assessment of the evaluation process itself is partially based on six measures: agreement, outliers, response distribution, standard deviation, regression, and question reliability.

Agreement on a question is calculated using the following formula:

$$AG = \frac{1}{NE} \sum_{i=0}^{NS} NR_i/2^i$$

where AG is the agreement factor, NS is the number of unit steps in the scoring scale, NR_i is the number of responses that are i steps from the mode, and NE is the number of evaluators (responses).

If there is no mode, then the scale value closest to the mean and with at least as many responses as any other scale value is used as the "mode." As an example, with five responses of B, C, C, C, E, the mode is C and $AG = \frac{1}{5}(3/2^0 + 1/2^1 + 1/2^2) = 0.75$.

Outliers are determined in a somewhat subjective (but logical) manner since neither the agreement factor nor standard deviation provide acceptably consistent measures. An outlier is any extreme response with a distance (DE) from the next closest response such that $DE/DT > 0.5$, where $DT = $ maximum distance between any two responses.

Response distribution is studied across all evaluations on a question-by-question basis to determine the validity of the general assumption of a normal response distribution. Such analysis can also be used to determine an experimental question weight. On an individual evaluation basis, the combination of agreement, outlier, and standard deviation analysis is used to pinpoint particular questions which have an unacceptable response distribution.

Regression analysis is used across all evaluations to study the validity of the test factor question groupings and to study the regression of test factor characteristic responses against the associated general test factor question response. Itzfeldt [2] presented some interesting related results using regression and factor analysis.

Reliability is a measure of consistency from one set of measurements to another. Reliability can be defined through error: the more (less) error, the lower (higher) the reliability. Since we can measure total variance, if we can estimate the error variance of a measure, we can also estimate reliability.

The statistical method for identifying error variance is Analysis of Variance (ANOVA). ANOVA allows the analyst to isolate the sources of variance within total variance. In the evaluation of module questionnaires, for example, the sources of variance are differences between the evaluators due to their differing backgrounds and expectations, differences in the characteristics of the modules, and unattributable differences due to error. Two-way analysis of variance allows a determination of all three variance sources. Mean-squares for raters, modules, and error are determined as measures of variance. Reliability is then calculated as 1.00 minus the proportion of mean-square error to mean-square modules.

If the reliability coefficient R is squared (R^2), it becomes a

TABLE V
EXAMPLE RELIABILITY COMPUTATIONS

EVALUATOR / MODULE	1	2	3	Σ	Σ²
1	C	C	C	12	48
2	C	A	C	14	68
3	D	A	C	13	61
4	C	A	B	15	77
Σ	15	22	17	54	
Σ²	57	124	73		254

NOTE: A = 6, B = 5, C = 4, D = 3, E = 2, F = 1

$V1 = (54)^2/(4)(3) = 243$

$V2 = 254$

$V3 = (15^2 + 22^2 + 17^2)/4 = 249.5$

$V4 = (12^2 + 14^2 + 13^2 + 15^2)/3 = 244.67$

$SSE = (V2-V4) + (V1-V3) = 2.83$

$SSR = V3-V1 = 6.5$

$MSE = SSE/(4-1)(3-1) = .47$

$MSR = SSR/(3-1) = 3.25$

$R = 1 - MSE/MSR = .86$

TABLE VI
SOFTWARE MAINTAINABILITY EVALUATION WEIGHTS

	OPERATIONAL SOFTWARE				SUPPORT SOFTWARE			
	P1	P2	P6	P7	P3	P4	P5	NON-CPCI
DOCUMENTATION CATEGORY	.40	.55	.40	.40	.50	.60	.60	.60
MODULARITY	.10	.15	.15	.14	.15	.15	.15	.14
DESCRIPTIVENESS	.35	.35	.25	.26	.25	.30	.30	.26
CONSISTENCY	.15	.11	.15	.15	.15	.15	.12	.18
SIMPLICITY	.20	.10	.18	.18	.18	.20	.20	.20
EXPANDABILITY	.10	.09	.12	.12	.14	.12	.15	.12
INSTRUMENTATION	.10	.20	.15	.15	.13	.08	.08	.10
SOURCE LISTING CATEGORY	.60	.45	.60	.60	.50	.40	.40	.40
MODULARITY	.20	.10	.12	.12	.15	.20	.20	.15
DESCRIPTIVENESS	.15	.30	.20	.39	.22	.18	.18	.25
CONSISTENCY	.15	.09	.18	.14	.13	.25	.25	.15
SIMPLICITY	.20	.11	.12	.12	.12	.17	.17	.15
EXPANDABILITY	.20	.21	.18	.23	.20	.12	.12	.20
INSTRUMENTATION	.10	.19	.20	0	.18	.08	.06	.10
CPCI WEIGHT	.15	.38	.37	.10	.35	.20	.35	.10
	OPERATIONAL .60				SUPPORT .40			

coefficient of determination. It gives us the proportion of the variance shared by the "true" score and the observed score. R^2 is interpreted as the proportion of observed variance which can be attributed to a true measurement. The expression $1 - R^2$ provides the proportion of total variance which can be attributed to error. If evaluators are focusing on different aspects of a question, then the resulting evaluator responses will have an associated error variance which is not explainable. Since the reliability squared indicates how much variance is explainable, the higher this value, the lower the possible unexplained error variance and hence, the less possibility the evaluators were misinterpreting the question. So, the higher the reliability, the more probable the question is a "good" question, at least from the viewpoint of not misinterpreting the question statement.

Table V illustrates the calculation of the reliability for a sample source listing question with 3 evaluators and 4 modules. Reliability is not calculated for the documentation questions since only one questionnaire is completed. If the same evaluators were to evaluate several programs, then by replacing "module" by "program" the reliability of each documentation question could be similarly computed. It is unlikely that the precise same set of evaluators will be used to evaluate very many programs. Box [26] and Kerlinger [27] have more detailed discussions of the ANOVA and reliability statistics involved in this type or analysis. The BMDP-77 [25] computer statistical package is a practical source for automated analysis.

IV. PRELIMINARY RESULTS

AFTEC has conducted several software evaluations using the methodology and procedures outlined in this paper. Results for one evaluation involving eight separate programs are summarized in Tables VI, VII, and VIII. A report, Program

Maintainability Scores, produced by the SMAP [34] computer program is illustrated in Fig. 3.

The average reliability from Table VIII is below the desired level of 0.9 in several of the evaluations. A reliability of 0.95 or greater is usually required by national testing services. The significance of the reliability (R) is in determining how well evaluators understood the questions (one source of error). Recall that $1 - R^2$ gives the unknown variance (error). Hence, if $R = 1$, there would be no error and the question would have been completely understood by the evaluators. From Table VIII with $R = 0.92$, slightly more than 15 percent of variance is due to error. When $R = 0.79$, then nearly 40 percent of the variance is due to error. After a significant number of evaluations those questions (26 from Table VIII) with reliability less than 0.80 will be carefully analyzed for better wording or perhaps elimination. As a comparison of reliability improvement over three stages of the methodology evolution, see Fig. 4. For example, the percentage of questions with reliability less than 0.75 has gone from 73 percent to 65 percent to 27 percent.

The evaluator agreement goal is 0.8 (e.g., five responses of B, C, C, C, D). The average agreement from Table VIII is somewhat under the goal, but there were only three evaluators available for most programs and there were some outlier problems as evidenced by the rather large standard deviation summarized in Table VIII. The desirable standard deviation of 0.5 may be difficult to reach, which simply means more careful analysis of the outliers and agreement is required to reach conclusions as to the validity of the evaluation scores.

One area of concern for AFTEC has been providing enough evaluators so that a larger number of evaluators would not significantly alter the evaluation results. That is, scores would remain within 0.5 units. The standard deviation helps to determine this "sample size" (of evaluators) for a given "confidence" level in the evaluation results. Briefly, a sample

TABLE VII
SOFTWARE MAINTAINABILITY SCORES

	OPERATIONAL								SUPPORT							
	OPERATING SYSTEM		TACTICAL APPLICATIONS		RADAR CONTROL		SIGNAL PROCESSING		SIMULATION		SOFTWARE SUPPORT TOOLS		DATA REDUCTION		NON-CPCI SOFTWARE	
	P1		P2		P7		P6		P3		P4		P5		P8	
	DOC	SRC	DOC	SRC	DOC	SRC	DOC	SRC	DOC	SRC	DOC	SRC	DOC	SRC	DOC	SRC
MODULARITY	4.33	5.15	4.00	4.54	3.78	4.57	4.69	5.77	3.36	4.51	3.97	4.84	3.92	5.21	5.28	4.86
DESCRIPTIVENESS	3.24	3.85	2.52*	2.59*	2.54*	2.86*	3.39	4.64	2.38*	2.16*	3.90	2.92*	3.81	3.73	4.14	3.43
CONSISTENCY	4.07	3.93	3.75	3.36	4.15	3.64	5.11	5.24	3.33	3.35	4.52	4.28	4.78	4.68	5.04	4.48
SIMPLICITY	3.58	4.68	3.35	4.07	3.53	4.35	3.89	4.50	3.14	3.91	4.53	4.77	4.33	4.84	4.53	4.38
EXPANDABILITY	3.93	4.33	2.78*	3.58	3.15	3.86	4.00	4.55	2.67*	3.47	4.52	4.81	4.37	4.83	4.59	4.33
INSTRUMENTATION	1.57*	2.79*	2.65*	2.71*	2.17*	2.61*	4.20	N/A	2.40*	2.58*	2.30*	3.54	2.67*	3.66	4.77	3.71
TEST FACTOR COMPOSITES	3.44	4.28	3.01	3.25	3.16	3.51	4.12	4.82	2.85*	3.22	4.08	4.24	4.04	4.58	4.66	4.08
CPCI COMPOSITES	3.94		3.12		3.37		4.54		3.03		4.14		4.25		4.23	
OPS/SUPPORT COMPOSITES	3.48								3.82							
SYSTEM COMPOSITE	3.62															

* Below Threshold

```
LEGEND:
   Goal       5.00          P1 - 3 Ev, 22 Mod     P5 - 3 Ev, 4 Mod
   Standard   4.15          P2 - 4 Ev, 15 Mod     P6 - 3 Ev, 19 Mod
   Threshold  3.00          P3 - 3 Ev, 4 Mod      P7 - 3 Ev, 4 Mod
                            P4 - 3 Ev, 10 Mod     P8 - 3 Ev, 1 Mod
```

TABLE VIII
SOFTWARE MAINTAINABILITY EVALUATION ASSESSMENT MEASURES

PROGRAM		AVE AGREEMENT	AVE STANDARD DEV	AVE RELIABILITY	1 GENERAL SCORES	2 TEST FACTOR COMPOSITE SCORE	3 TEST FACTOR RAW SCORES
D O C U M E N T A T I O N	P1	.76	.92	NA	3.43	3.44	3.42
	P2	.64	1.45	NA	2.93	3.01	3.08
	P3	.68	1.28	NA	2.95	2.85	2.80
	P4	.79	.82	NA	3.76	4.08	3.95
	P5	.79	.88	NA	3.62	4.04	3.94
	P6	.71	1.38	NA	3.14	3.16	3.11
	P7	.75	1.05	NA	3.95	4.12	4.06
S O U R C E L I S T I N G S	P1	.77	.90	.79	4.06	4.28	4.20
	P2	.70	1.11	.85	3.09	3.25	3.46
	P3	.76	.92	.80	3.07	3.22	3.29
	P4	.81	.71	.85	3.57	4.24	4.11
	P5	.77	.77	.79	3.92	4.58	4.48
	P6	.70	1.20	.90	3.21	3.51	3.66
	P7	.77	1.06	.92	4.50	4.82	4.64

```
# SOURCE LISTING QUESTIONS WITH RELIABILITY        NOTE:  NO DATA AVAILABLE FOR PROGRAM P8

            AVE RELIABILITY
        0          0-.49
        1          .50-.59
        5          .60-.69
       20          .70-.79
       32          .80-.89
       31          .90-1.0

CORRELATION (1,2) = .95
CORRELATION (1,3) = .93
```

size is desired which ensures that the imaginary population of all possible software raters is accurately represented by a randomly selected sample. There are two possible errors to guard against. The software is evaluated to be below (above) a criteria when a much larger sample would find that the software was above (below) a criteria. These are called Type I and Type II errors, respectively. Consequently, it is necessary to establish probabilities which are acceptable for each of the two possible error types. The probability of a Type I (Type II) error is termed alpha (beta). With alpha and beta defined, sample size n is given by

$$n = \left(\frac{Z_\alpha \sigma + Z_\beta \sigma}{\phi} \right)$$

where

	#Q	RS	WT	WS		#Q	RS	WT	WS
DOCUMENTATION	83.	3.01	.55	1.55	SOURCE LISTINGS	89.	3.25	.45	1.46
/-MODULARITY	12.	4.00	.15	.60	/-MODULARITY	14.	4.54	.10	.45
/ FORMAT	(5.	4.30	.42	1.79)	/ DATA/CONTROL	(4.	4.02	.29	1.15)
/ DATA	(2.	2.88	.17	.49)	/ PROCESSING	(10.	4.76	.71	3.40)
/ PROCESSING	(5.	4.15	.42	1.73)					
/-DESCRIPTIVENESS	24.	2.52	.35	.99	/-DESCRIPTIVENESS	21.	2.59	.30	.78
/ FORMAT	(6.	2.25	.25	.55)	/ PREFACE BLOCK	(9.	1.55	.38	.59)
/ CONSTRAINTS	(3.	2.33	.13	.29)	/ IMBEDDED COMMENTS	(7.	2.56	.33	.85)
/ MODULE	(5.	3.10	.21	.65)	/ IMPLEMENTATION	(6.	4.01	.29	1.15)
/ EXTERNAL INTERFACES	(5.	2.90	.21	.60)					
/ INTERNAL INTERFACES	(3.	1.75	.13	.22)					
/ MATH MODEL	(2.	2.38	.08	.20)					
/-CONSISTENCY	9.	3.75	.11	.41	/-CONSISTENCY	14.	3.36	.09	.30
/ FORMAT	(4.	3.81	.44	1.69)	/ EXTERNAL	(8.	3.03	.57	1.73)
/ DESIGN	(5.	3.70	.56	2.06)	/ INTERNAL	(6.	3.91	.43	1.63)
/-SIMPLICITY	12.	3.35	.10	.34	/-SIMPLICITY	16.	4.07	.11	.45
/ FORMAT	(4.	3.81	.33	1.27)	/ GENERAL CODING	(8.	4.29	.50	2.14)
/ DESIGN	(8.	3.13	.67	2.09)	/ SINGULAR CODING	(4.	4.31	.25	1.08)
					/ SIZE	(4.	3.40	.25	.85)
/-EXPANDABILITY	9.	2.79	.09	.25	/-EXPANDABILITY	9.	3.58	.21	.75
/ FORMAT	(3.	3.17	.33	1.05)	/ GENERAL	(4.	3.96	.44	1.76)
/ DESIGN	(6.	2.58	.67	1.72)	/ PROCESSING	(5.	3.27	.56	1.82)
/-INSTRUMENTATION	10.	2.65	.20	.53	/-INSTRUMENTATION	8.	2.71	.19	.51
/ FORMAT	(3.	3.08	.30	.93)	/ PROCESSING	(3.	2.95	.38	1.11)
/ DESIGN	(7.	2.46	.70	1.73)	/ CONTROL OF	(5.	2.56	.63	1.60)
/-GENERAL	7.	2.93	0.00	0.00	/-GENERAL	7.	3.09	0.00	0.00

Fig. 3. SMAP report: Program maintainability scores.

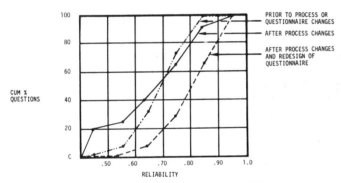

Fig. 4. Comparative questionnaire reliabilities.

Z_α = normal deviate at α,
Z_β = normal deviate at β,
  σ = standard deviation of the population scores,
  ϕ = not-to-exceed distance of the rater sample results from the hypothetical rater population results.

Values of Z_α and Z_β are found in Box [26] and Kerlinger [27], as well as most standard statistical tests. Using an alpha of 0.1 ($Z_\alpha = 1.28$), beta of 0.1 ($Z_\beta = 1.28$), ϕ of 0.5, and the goal standard deviation of 0.5, we get $n = 6.55$ or approximately seven evaluators are required. Since AFTEC has a general maximum of five evaluators available, the confidence level would have to be lowered from the above in order to use the goal standard deviation of 0.5.

The correlation between the test factor scores and the general question scores is significant. It indicates that the evaluators did seem to agree that the respective test factors as defined were represented by the test factor characteristics (the questions).

V. CONCLUSIONS AND FUTURE RESEARCH

The main conclusions of the research summarized in this paper are as follows.

• AFTEC has a viable software maintainability evaluation methodology which is cost-effective and reasonably implementable.

• The revisions to AFTEC's initial methodology should provide a substantial increase in the confidence of future evaluation results.

• The software maintainability questionnaires should be valuable as software quality assurance checklists for software contractors during initial development phases.

• Due to the nature of software state-of-the-art, the AFTEC methodology should be carefully and continually reassessed.

• The results of any metric measurement of software characteristics should be used as a *guide* to possible anomalies and not as absolute dictums.

Future research includes the need to

• correlate maintainability raw scores to actual maintenance level of effort,

• investigate even better response scales such as the Likert graphic response scale,

• correlate database of evaluator background data to evaluator response data,

• study cumulative database of responses to determine true distributions and the meaning of performance measures such as AFTEC's threshold, standard, goal.

ACKNOWLEDGMENT

Several AFTEC personnel were very supportive of this methodology research and have allowed the inclusion in this paper of some updated descriptions of the methodology and its use since completion of Technical Directive 120 in December 1978. In particular, Lt. Col. H. Arner, Capt. T. Brock, and P. Thayer have been very helpful. Within BDM, F. Ragland has contributed considerable research into the statistical foundation of this work. The referees also contributed several helpful suggestions which improved the original paper.

REFERENCES

[1] B. Boehm *et al.*, *Characteristics of Software Quality*. New York: North-Holland, 1977.

[2] W. Itzfeldt *et al.*, "User-perceived quality of interactive systems," in *Proc. 3rd Int. Conf. on Software Eng.*, May 1978, pp. 188–195.

[3] P. Thayer, "Software maintainability evaluation methodology," Air Force Test and Evaluation Cen. Rep., June 1978.

[4] G. Walters *et al.*, "Factors in software quality," RADC-TR-77-369, vol. I, II, III, Nov. 1977.

[5] *ACM Comput. Surveys*, "Special issue: Programming," vol. 6, Dec. 1974.

[6] E. Dijkstra, "Notes on structured programming," in *Structured Programming*, Dahl, Dijkstra, and Hoare, Eds. New York: Academic, 1972.

[7] B. Kernighan and P. Plauger, *The Elements of Programming Style*. New York: McGraw-Hill, 1974.

[8] H. D. Mills, "Mathematical foundations for structured programming," IBM Rep. FSC72-6012, Feb. 1972.

[9] G. Myers, *Reliable Software Through Composite Design*, 1st ed. New York: Petrocelli, 1975.

[10] D. Parnas, "Designing software for ease of extension and contraction," in *COMPSAC 1978 Tutorial, Software Methodology*, Nov. 1978, pp. 184–196.

[11] ——, "On the criteria to be used in decomposing systems into modules," *Commun. Ass. Comput. Mach.*, pp. 1053–1058, Dec. 1972.

[12] R. Yeh, Ed., *Current Trends in Programming Methodology: Vol. 1. Software Specification and Design*. Englewood Cliffs, NJ: Prentice-Hall, 1977.

[13] E. Yourdon, "Modular programming," in *Techniques of Program Structure and Design*. Englewood Cliffs, NJ: Prentice-Hall, 1975, pp. 93–136.

[14] T. Gilb, *Software Metrics*. Cambridge, MA: Winthrop, 1976.

[15] M. Halstead, *Elements of Software Science*. New York: Elsevier, 1977.

[16] ——, "Using the methodology of natural science to understand software," Purdue Univ., CDRTR 190, May 1976.

[17] T. Love *et al.*, "Measuring the psychological complexity of software maintenance tasks with the Halstead and McCabe metrics," *IEEE Trans. Software Eng.*, vol. SE-5, Mar. 1979.

[18] T. McCabe, "A complexity measure," *IEEE Trans. Software Eng.*, vol. SE-2, pp. 308–320, Dec. 1976.

[19] E. Miller, "Program testing techniques," presented at COMPSAC 1977 Tutorial, Nov. 1977.

[20] J. Bowen, "A survey of standards and proposed metrics for software quality testing," *Computer*, vol. 12, pp. 37–42, Aug. 1979.

[21] F. Buckley, "A standard for software quality assurance plans," *Computer*, vol. 12, pp. 43–50, Aug. 1978.

[22] Documentation Standards, "Structured programming series vol. VII and addendum," RADC-TR-300, Sept. 1974 and Apr. 1975.

[23] *DOD Manual for DOD Automated Data Systems Documentation Standards*, DOD Manual 7935.1S, September 1977.

[24] MIL-STD-483 (USAF), "Configuration management practices for systems, equipments, munitions, and computer programs, Dec. 1970.

[25] MIL-STD-490, "Specification practices," Oct. 1968.

[26] MIL-STD-1521A (USAF), "Technical reviews and audits for systems, equipments, and computer programs," June 1976.

[27] MIL-STD-1679 (Navy), "Weapon system software development," Dec. 1978.

[28] MIL-S-52779 (Army), "Software quality assurance program requirements," Apr. 1974.

[29] *BMDP-77*. Berkeley, CA: UCLA Press, 1977.

[30] G. Box, W. Hunter, and J. Hunter, *Statistics for Experimenters*. New York: Wiley, 1978.

[31] F. Kerlinger, *Foundations of Behavioral Research*, 2nd ed. New York: Holt, Rinehart and Winston, 1973.

[32] F. Ragland and D. Peercy, "Analysis of software maintainability evaluation process," BDM/TAC-78-698-TR, Dec. 1978.

[33] D. Peercy, "Software maintainability evaluation guidelines handbook," BDM/TAC-78-687-TR, Dec. 1978.

[34] D. Peercy and T. Paschich, "Software maintainability analysis program user's manual," BDM/TAC-78-697-TR, Dec. 1978.

David E. Peercy received the B.S. degree in applied mathematics from the University of Colorado, Boulder, in 1966, and the M.S. and Ph.D. degrees in a mathematics from New Mexico State University, Las Cruces, in 1967 and 1971, respectively.

From 1970 to 1972 he was a Post-Doctoral Fellow in the Department of Mathematics at West Virginia University, Morgantown, and from 1973 to 1977 he was a member of the Technical Staff of Texas Instruments performing research in software engineering methodology and development of real-time systems. In 1977 he joined the BDM Corporation, where he is currently a Senior Computer Scientist, serving as a Technical Consultant for the Computer Science Department. His research interests include software development methodology and software quality assessment.

Dr. Peercy is a member of the ANSI X3J9 Committee considering the standardization of the Pascal programming language.

MAP : a Tool for Understanding Software

Sally Warren

Amdahl Corporation
1250 East Arques Avenue
Sunnyvale, California 94086

Abstract

Maintenance of software is a major problem that the data processing industry faces today. This paper describes MAP, a tool, that addresses the problems of software maintenance by helping programmers to understand their programs.

Keywords and phrases: Maintenance, static analysis, understanding of programs, COBOL, control flow, data flow

1. INTRODUCTION

The Software Tools Development Department at Amdahl Corporation has constructed an automated tool, MAP, to assist people in the understanding of programs. The group's primary objective was to develop an automated tool that would improve programmer productivity.

In reviewing the tools and techniques used in maintenance programming we were impressed by the lack of attention given to the maintenance phase of programming relative to design and new program implementation. We decided to look for key problems that are associated with maintenance and focus our work there.

This paper describes how maintenance programmers understand their programs and how MAP supports their understanding, and includes some examples of how to use MAP.

1.1 DEFINING MAINTENANCE

Recent survey data, collected and reported by Lientz and Swanson [1], reinforced our own observation of many large data processing installations:

* Half or more of the application programmers at large DP installations work with production code--correcting, enhancing, and tailoring it.

* Approximately half of the production applications being maintained are written in COBOL.

This paper uses the term **maintenance**, in the same broad sense that Lientz and Swanson used in their book: maintenance is the activity of correcting, extending, and enhancing programs. This definition includes the increasingly important work of customizing or tailoring software application packages.

1.2 DEFINING UNDERSTANDING

The dictionary [2] definition of **understand** is "Grasp mentally, perceive the significance or explanation or cause or nature of, know how to deal with". We use the term "understanding of a program" in this sense, as applied to both the program's internal and external workings.

2. PROBLEMS WITH PROGRAM MAINTENANCE

The single most important problem associated with program maintenance is that before correcting or modifying a program the programmer must first understand it. Then, the programmer must understand the impact of the intended change. Although other documentation of varying utility and currency abounds, this learning process is usually tied to the program listing.

There are a number of complications to this problem:

* Often the program was written by another person or groups of people working over the years in isolation from each other.

* Often the program was changed by people who clearly did not understand it, resulting in a deterioration or smearing effect of the program's original organization.

* Program listings, even those that are well organized, are not structured to support reading for comprehension. We normally read an article or book straight through, but with listings the programmer rummages back and forth.

Understanding a program is a demanding mental

Reprinted from *Proceedings of the Sixth International Conference on Software Engineering*, 1982, pages 28-37. Copyright © 1982 by The Institute of Electrical and Electronics Engineers, Inc.

_ocess, which is presently supported by few effective aids. Holding the program listing, the programmer rummages through it, writes notes, highlights lines with markers, draws charts of data and logic flow. In effect he performs a mental simulation of the program's execution. As he is able to hold more detail of that simulation in his mind, he reaches a stage where his grasp of the program seems sufficient and assumes that he understands the program. Unfortunately, but frequently, his assumption is changed by the results of the next execution of the program.

This mental simulation that takes place while "reading" the listing constructs an understanding of the program that is based on a rearrangement of the program details. The programmer reaches a point where the arrangement of program statements or data flow can be visualized in possible execution sequences (as opposed to the linear textual layout of the source code).

Individual paths through the program are determined step by step as the programmer decides the outcome of conditional tests in control statements along the way. As his "reading" continues the burden of remembering these tests and their outcomes grows. By marking the listing or drawing charts of logic or data flow off to the side, the programmer modifies the information in the listing, changing it into forms more helpful to the job of simulating program execution.

3.   SIX TASKS TO UNDERSTAND A PROGRAM

In the understanding process described above the programmer performs specific tasks. We have identified six tasks that programmers do in order to understand a program. These tasks are briefly described in the following paragraphs. The seventh item in this section relates to the synthesis of the data from the other six items.

3.1   LOOK FOR STRUCTURE

Structuring a program is divide and conquer: If a program is broken into its component parts, then each part is smaller and therefore is easier to understand. It is on this premise that the "structured" design and programming methods are based. We have identified three aspects of the structure of a program:

a. Procedural Structure
    In the procedural languages of today, procedural structure is important. In COBOL the PERFORM and CALL statements give a program its procedural structure.

b. Data Interfaces
    Having split a program up into procedural sections, the programmer must then understand the data interfaces between the procedures.

c. Non-procedural structure
    There are other sorts of structure in a program. For instance, the I/O in a program forms structure. Some programs are well-structured with respect to I/O. For example, the writing to a particular file may be confined to just one procedure. On the other hand, a program that was badly structured with respect to I/O, would have its read or write statements littered all over the program.

3.2   FOLLOW CONTROL FLOW

Programmers follow the control flow of a program by reading through the listing or by browsing interactively. They ask themselves questions like "Can I get from this point to that point?" or "How do I take the abnormal exits from this subprogram?"

3.3   UNDERSTAND DATA ALIASING

Within one program many names can be given to one data cell. The programmer must know these aliases.

3.4   FOLLOW DATA FLOW

Once the programmer has understood control flow and data aliasing, he can start to follow data flow. When following data flow the programmer is looking at a particular line of source code and asking "Where did this value come from?" or "Where does this value go to?". In order to answer these questions, the programmer must follow the control paths, knowing all possible aliases for the data name, and trace the paths until all the answers have been found.

To answer the question "Where did this value come from?" the programmer must search backwards, counter to the flow of control of the program. Going backwards is often the important direction when hunting for a bug.

3.5   LOOK FOR TEXTUAL PATTERNS

A programmer may search the source code for textual patterns. Editors and browsers are commonly used for this.

3.6   LOOK FOR DIFFERENCES.

There are often two versions of a program, one version works in a specific instance and the other version does not. For example, two months ago the installation put up a new version of the report generating program, and it has produced the correct weekly report ever since; but now, in trying to produce the quarterly report, the program has failed.

The programmer needs to know the difference between the two versions of the same program. With this knowledge the process of understanding the change's impact can begin (and the first five items re-enter the picture).

3.7 SYNTHESIS OF INFORMATION

A programmer may combine the results of the previous six tasks as a fast way of locating specific entities. This may be considered looking for as a complex pattern within the program. In looking for these complex patterns, a programmer may want to apply:

1. Different searches to the same program.
   In this case the programmer wants to ask a complex question such as "I want an instance where this thing happens at the same time as this thing".

2. Similar searches to different programs
   Here the programmer must put the two programs side by side and apply the same search to each program.

4. DESCRIPTION OF MAP

MAP has features that assist in each of the six tasks described in section 3. An example of MAP use is given in the next section.

To help explain the operation of MAP, a high level data flow diagram of MAP is shown in Figure 1.

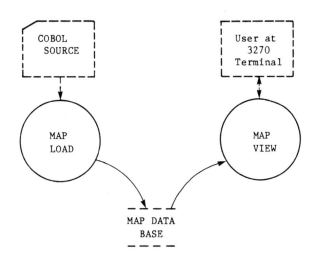

Figure 1. Data Flow of MAP Operation

The programmer gives MAP the COBOL source code-- exactly what is given to the COBOL compiler. The source code is analyzed by the MAP load process and the information about the program is stored in the MAP data base. MAP's analysis is like a compile except that MAP produces a data base rather than an object module.

Once there is a MAP data base for the program, the programmer may start viewing the program at a 3270 terminal. MAP has three formats for viewing programs: 1) the source code itself, 2) the structure charts and 3) the merged source of two versions of the same program. All of MAP's user documentation and tutorial information is on-line.

4.1 USABILITY ISSUES

4.1.1 INTERACTIVE

Having determined the programmer's tasks which need support, an automated tool for aiding a programmer's understanding of a program must also lighten the burden of storing and organizing detailed information. Producing a second "helpful" listing as large or larger than the program source would hardly promote this goal.

In many of the tasks listed above, the programmer is asking a question and must derive the answer for himself.

For these reasons, the analysis characteristics of MAP are combined with an interactive dialog. After analyzing the target program, MAP presents information about the program in response to commands expressed in its own query language.

4.1.2 SPECIAL PURPOSE COMMAND SEQUENCES

Having built a complex series of commands, the experienced programmer can save them in command files called **script** files. The commands in a script file may be executed as a single MAP command.

4.1.3 MULTIPLE VIEWS

MAP provides multiple sessions from one terminal so that a user can view more than one program at once or may view different aspects of the same program at once.

4.2 STRUCTURE

The items below correspond to the three aspects of the structure of a program mentioned in Section 3.1.

a. Procedural Structure
   To show procedural structure MAP draws structure charts [3]. Each box on the structure chart represents a unit of executable code which was PERFORMed or CALLed. The hierarchy of the boxes represents the calling structure.

   To see structure while looking at the source code, a feature called ZOOM allows the users to look at the source code being performed. ZOOM simulates the effect of a procedure call (the PERFORM statement in COBOL).

b. Data Interfaces
    MAP produces data interface charts to show the data flows between the procedures of the program.

c. Non-procedural Structure
    The other structures in a program are supported by the recognition of types of COBOL statements. Each COBOL statement is of one or more of the following types: I/O, assignment, control, comment, call, definition or label. For instance, a READ statement with an "AT END" clause is both an I/O AND a control statement. We call these types the COBOL Subsets.

The FINDSUB feature of MAP searches through the source code for a subset and highlights those boxes in the structure chart that contain statements of subset type, or if viewing the source code, the statements themselves are highlighted.

4.3   CONTROL TRACE

MAP's control trace commands are the PICK commands to support forward tracing, and the COMEFROM command to support backward tracing. Using the PICK statement the programmer builds a control path through the program. MAP also remembers the path which has been taken and gives advice on which branch is likely to be of most use.

4.4   DATA ALIASING AND DATA TRACING

The data trace commands answer the data flow questions of "Where does this value come from/go to?" There are six MAP commands: forward and backward searches on uses, modifications and references to variables. These searches consider all the paths to/from the start point and any data aliasing.

Data aliasing in COBOL can get complicated. In COBOL, group names may have subgroups within them and ultimately have elementary items within them. The REDEFINES statement makes the situation much more complex by allowing data names to refer to the same fields outside of the group structure.

MAP's data trace commands automatically take all data aliases into account.

4.5   TEXTUAL PATTERNS

The MAP command to perform a textual pattern search is FIND. FIND is similar to the FIND facility of an editor or browser, its pattern is similar to a regular expression [4]. MAP has these capabilities in it for ease of use--it would be very frustrating to have to exit MAP to do a simple textual search.

4.6   DIFFERENCES

MAP allows the user to view the differences between two versions of the same program in its source difference view. In this view two versions of source code are shown, merged together on the same screen. The user can manipulate the format of the screen to make the differences more apparent. To detect differences in source code, MAP uses the method of longest common subsequence which has received some attention in the literature [5, 6].

4.7   SYNTHESIS OF INFORMATION

MAP helps the programmer synthesize the results of the MAP commands.

1. Combining different searches on the same program
    To answer complex question such as: "I want an instance where this thing happens at the same time as this thing", MAP allows two commands to be hooked together in a filter. For instance "Show me the I/O statements" and then "show me only those that refer to 'OUTPUT-BUFFER'" may be posed as one MAP command.

2. Similar searches on different programs
    The programmer uses multiple sessions from one terminal to view more than one program at once and may apply the same set of commands, perhaps using a script file.

5.   AN EXAMPLE OF A USE OF MAP

All of the sample screens shown here were produced by MAP. They have been reduced in size to meet publication standards.

When the programmer first enters MAP, he sees the Primary Option Menu (see Figure 2). From this menu, the programmer selects a load, a view or the tutorial.

```
AMDAHL MAP R1.0
==>

              M    A    P

      P R I M A R Y   O P T I O N   M E N U


   LOAD SOURCE CODE
       1.1   Load for Examination      (load)
       1.2   Load for Comparison       (comp)

   THE VIEWS OF A PROGRAM
       2.1   Source Code               (source)
       2.2   Structure Chart           (schart)
       2.3   Source Code Difference    (diff)

   3    TUTORIAL                       (tutor)

   9    END (Current frame)            (end)
```

Figure 2.   Primary Option Menu

5.1 STRUCTURE CHART VIEW

If the programmer has not seen this program before, most likely he wants to see a picture of the program structure; so first he looks at a structure chart. This chart is automatically generated from analysis of the source code and is drawn on the full screen (see Figure 3). Each box on the structure chart represents a unit of executable code that was PERFORMed or CALLed. The hierarchy of the boxes represents the calling structure. The chart of a large program may be split into separate pages, and there are commands to move around the pages and the screens. See Figure 4 for an explanation of a structure chart box.

CG1030   Page 1 of 4
===>

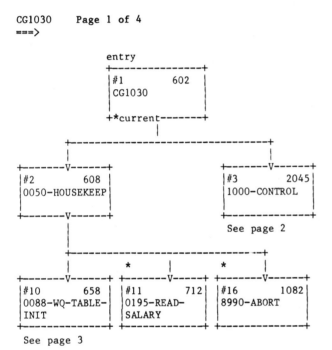

Figure 3. First Page of a Structure Chart

Words above the box:
  '*'--multiple superordinates.
  'entry'--ENTRY point.
  'declaratives'--a DECLARATIVES
      section that is never PERFORMed.

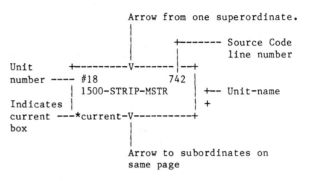

Words below the box:
  'see page nnn'--subordinates on another page.
  'external'--a CALLed unit.
  'recursive'--a recursively PERFORMed unit.

Figure 4. Explanation of Structure Chart Box

If the programmer is interested in how the data moves into and out of the program he looks at the interface chart at the program level. If he is interested in how the data flows between the different boxes (Paragraphs or Sections in COBOL), he looks at the interface chart at the interprogram level (see Figure 5). The interface chart shows which data is used or modified by the specified unit (program or interprogram). The data is classified as internal or external to the program.

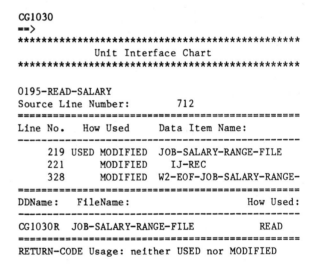

Figure 5.   An Interface Chart

The programmer uses the FIND and FINDSUB commands to search the source code and highlight the boxes whose source code contains a result of the search. For example, "FINDSUB IO" issued on a structure chart, highlights all the boxes whose source contains input or output statements. Similarly, "FIND TEXT" issued on a structure chart, highlights all the boxes whose source contains the text string TEXT. In this way the programmer begins to understand how the program holds together at the procedure level.

5.2   SOURCE CODE VIEW

When the programmer has pinpointed an area of concern from the structure chart, he might want to look at the source code itself. The example given here is from another COBOL program.

MAP shows the procedural structure of the program at the source code level too. When a trace command searches through a PERFORM statement and there is a result in the code being PERFORMed, MAP highlights the PERFORM statement rather than the actual statement within the procedure. The user must "ZOOMIN" on the PERFORM statement and reissue the trace command to see the actual statement itself. ZOOMIN is a control trace command (see below) and simulates the effect of the PERFORM. ZOOMIN may be retraced with a "ZOOMOUT" command.

The FIND and FINDSUB commands also work while viewing the source code; they highlight the actual source rather than the whole procedure which contains the statement as in structure chart. MAP has scrolling and highlight searching commands and allows exclusion of any lines or sets of lines from the screen. In this way, the user may align the screen to show those parts of the program which are of interest. See Figure 6 for an example.

Control Tracing

Before studying the control flow, the programmer might like to reformat the screen to exclude all lines but those which effect control flow. This can be achieved by the sequence of MAP commands:

```
FINDSUB CONTROL ALL
!NH | EXCLUDE
FINDSUB LABELS ALL
FINDSUB CALLS ALL
```

These commands mean:
* find all the control statements and highlight them,
* exclude from the screen those that are not highlighted (i.e. are not control statements),
* bring back into view the labels, and
* bring back into view the call statements (call subset includes PERFORMs and CALLs).

After these commands the MAP screen looks like:

```
CG920030
==>

000001   IDENTIFICATION DIVISION.
000002
000003   PROGRAM-ID.
000004      CG920030.
            ...               9  lines excluded
000014   ENVIRONMENT DIVISION.
            ...              11  lines excluded
000026   DATA DIVISION.
            ...            2510  lines excluded
002537   PROCEDURE DIVISION.
            ...              12  lines excluded
002550      IF VSAM-FILE-STAT NOT = NORMAL-RETURN
            ...               2  lines excluded
002553         GO TO CLOSE-FILES.
            ...               2  lines excluded
002556      CALL 'CG920WRT' USING COMMUNICATIONS-A
            ...              15  lines excluded
```

Figure 6.   Screen for Control Tracing

Working either with the abbreviated screen or with all the source showing, the programmer uses the forward control trace commands to pick his way through a program. MAP remembers the path and gives advice on which directions may be of most interest. For example, he has set a label ERROR-EXIT as a destination (using the DEST command) and is picking (using the PICK command) his way through some code which is suspected of transferring unexpectedly to that label. With a destination set, PICK ? indicates which paths lead towards the destination. For example, having reached line 4476 in Figure 7, he issues the command PICK ? to show the options on this altered GOTO. PICK ? responds with the screen in Figure 8.

```
CG920030
==>

004472   CALL-PCM00200.
004473      CALL 'PCM00200' USING HEX-DATE SW-DAT
            ...               1 line excluded
004475   SIGNPOST.
004476      GO TO.
004477   POL-ERR-RTN.
            ...               1 line excluded
004479      IF W-ERROR = 4 OR -1
004480         NEXT SENTENCE
004481         ELSE MOVE 1 TO ERROR-INDICATOR.
```

Figure 7.   Screen before PICK ?

```
PICK     MENU
==>

STORE-C        (MAY EVENTUALLY REACH DEST)
STORE-E        (MAY EVENTUALLY REACH DEST)
STORE-R1       (CANT REACH DEST-TRY PERFORMS)
CHECK-EFF      (CANT REACH DEST-TRY PERFORMS)
STORE-DUE      (CANT REACH DEST-TRY PERFORMS)
STORE-T        (CANT REACH DEST-TRY PERFORMS)
STORE-BTD      (MAY EVENTUALLY REACH DEST)
FALLTHROUGH    (CANT REACH DEST-TRY PERFORMS)
```

Figure 8.   Result of PICK ?

From the PICK ? menu, he selects a path and continues to the next branch in the path.

If the programmer wants to retrace his path, and start looking at other paths, MAP unwinds the path with a BACKUP command and shows the branch which was taken last time through this point.

MAP has a backward control trace command, COMEFROM which tells all the places which transfer control to that point in the code. Using Figure 7 as a starting point, and issuing the COMEFROM command on line 4472, and excluding all non-highlighted lines, MAP shows Figure 9.

```
CG920030
==>

002598       PERFORM CALL-PCM00200.
             ...           11  lines excluded
002610       GO TO CALL-PCM00200.
             ...            6  lines excluded
002617       GO TO CALL-PCM00200.
             ...            7  lines excluded
002632       GO TO CALL-PCM00200.
             ...           18  lines excluded
002651       PERFORM CALL-PCM00200.
             ...           92  lines excluded
002744       PERFORM CALL-PCM00200
```

Figure 9. Result of COMEFROM; !NH | EXCLUDE

Data Tracing

The programmer may be interested in following data flow, in particular he might want to ask the question "Where did this value come from?". He uses the command "PREVMOD <variable name>". Note that this command follows control paths through the program and takes data aliasing into account. There could possibly be more than one answer to this question; each answer is highlighted and highlight scrolling commands are used to examine each one.

Figure 10 is the result of the command "PREVMOD HLD-E", starting the search at line 2622. MAP tells that, despite the complex control flow at this point, variable HLD-E may have been set at line 2585. This is shown by highlighting "HLD-E" on line 2585. The message also indicates that there is a path from the beginning of the unit (procedure) to line 2622 which does not set HLD-E (bypassing line 2585), and that there may be a previous modification prior to PERFORMing this unit.

```
CG920030       1 Prev Mod(s).  Unit boundary reached.
==>

002584       MOVE DATE-CUTOFF TO HLD-C, HEAD-C-DATE.
002585       MOVE DATE-EARNED TO HLD-E, HEAD-E-DATE.
002586   PRINT-NEW-PAGE-2.
             ...          28  lines excluded
002615       MOVE HLD-C TO GREG-DATE.
002616       ALTER SIGNPOST TO PROCEED TO STORE-C.
002617       GO TO CALL-PCM00200.
002618
002619   STORE-C.
002620       MOVE DEC-DATE TO S-DEC-C.
002621       MOVE HEX-DATE TO S-C.
002622       MOVE HLD-E TO GREG-DATE.
002623       ALTER SIGNPOST TO PROCEED TO STORE-E.
002624       GO TO CALL-PCM00200.
```

Figure 10. Result of PREVMOD HLD-E

The other data trace commands work in a similar way. MAP has six data trace commands which work forwards and backwards and on uses, modifications and references.

The programmer uses control trace, data trace, FIND and FINDSUB commands on the source code to help build his understanding of how the program works.

5.3   SOURCE DIFFERENCE VIEW

If the programmer wants to view the differences between two versions (OLD and NEW) of a program, he uses source difference view. First MAP must analyze both versions of the program, then the merged source code may be viewed. The programmer may alter the screen to remove lines of lesser interest and so make the differences more apparent. FIND and FINDSUB commands are also available.

Figures 11 and 12, show the same two versions of a program but with different screen formats. In Figure 11, the screen shows the new version of the source code with indication where the old version differed from it. The lines that are unique to the old version are excluded from view. In Figure 12, the screen shows all of the differences between the old and new versions, but the lines which are common are excluded. A single command changed the format.

```
CS2030
==>
OLD      NEW
000110  000109   OPEN INPUT AMD580-NULLS-FILE.
        DELETE       ...            1 line excluded
000112  000110   IF W2-EOF-AMD580-NULLS-FILE ='1'
000113  000111       MOVE 'DD CS2032C, FILE EMPTY'
        FROM         ...            2 lines excluded
TO      000112   PERFORM 0195-READ-AMD580.
TO      000113   PERFORM 0196-COMPUTE-AMD580.
TO      000114   PERFORM 0197-CHECK-AMD580.
000116  000115   EXHIBIT IJ-NUM 'NOT NUMERIC'
        DELETE       ...            9 lines excluded
000126  000116   PERFORM 0195-READ-AMD580 UNTIL
```

Figure 11. Differences in Terms of New Version

```
CS2030
==>
OLD      NEW
000109 DELETE    SET WQ-NDX1 WQ-NDX2      TO +1.
...... ......              ...      1 line excluded
000111 DELETE    PERFORM 0195-READ-AMD580.
...... ......              ...     2 lines excluded
000114  FROM     PERFORM 0195-PROCESS-AMD580.
000115  FROM     IF IJ-NUMBERS IS ALPHANUMERIC
   TO  000112    PERFORM 0195-READ-AMD580.
   TO  000113    PERFORM 0196-COMPUTE-AMD580.
   TO  000114    PERFORM 0197-CHECK-AMD580.
...... ......              ...      1 line excluded
000117 DELETE    DISPLAY 'THIS IS FOR DEBUGING'
000118 DELETE    DISPLAY 'IJ-NUMBERS BEING'
```

Figure 12.   The Differences Themselves

6.   MAP IMPLEMENTATION

MAP runs as an application program under MVS/TSO or
UTS on an Amdahl 470 or other IBM compatible
hardware. UTS is the Amdahl version of UNIX* which
runs on 470 compatible hardware. UTS is the host
system for the development of MAP; MVS/TSO is the
first target system. MAP analyses COBOL programs
conforming to ANSI 74 and ANSI 68 standards and to
the extensions defined by IBM's VS COBOL compiler.
MAP supports IBM 3270 type terminals.

MAP has been running in a real programming environment since October 1981. The largest COBOL single
program processed is 27,000 lines. We have not
tried larger programs.

Since we thought that the maintenance problem was
most severe in COBOL, we chose COBOL as the
language for MAP to analyse. The concepts of MAP
are applicable to most programming languages, but
the concepts must be implemented correctly for each
language. For example, the concept of a MAP unit
as a callable block of code exists in many
languages Specific examples include SUBROUTINEs and
FUNCTIONs in FORTRAN; PROCEDUREs and FUNCTIONs in
PASCAL. In COBOL, MAP units are PERFORMed and
CALLed blocks of code. However, MAP required
correct implementation of the action of a specific
COBOL compiler. This last requirement is quite
complex. Looking forward to the day when MAP will
support other languages, we have tried to retain as
much language independence as feasible.

MAP assists people to understand programs in a way
somewhat analogous to Computer Aided Instruction.
The target program corresponds to the course topic;
MAP's static analysis corresponds to the preparation of a lesson plan and programmed instruction
material; and the programmer's MAP sessions
correspond to a student's progress through the
course.

---

*UNIX is a trademark of Bell Laboratories.

In the design of the first version of MAP we
avoided transformations of the source code in the
way MAP presents the program to the user (other
than the structure chart). Shneiderman [7]
discusses cognitive processes in the "comprehension" of programs. Since the programmer must ultimately modify the source code of a program, we
considered it better if his understanding was in
terms of the source code rather than, say, a
flowchart. An overview of the program obtained
from the structure chart, is important enough to be
worth having two visual forms (the structure chart
and source code). The additional information
gained by a new visual form must be valuable enough
to require the programmer to re-recognise his program.

The MAP development programmers made use of many
tools. One important tool is AMP which is
described in Warren, Martin and Hoch [8].

7.   MAP COMPARED TO OTHER TOOLS

Some maintenance programmers make use of on-line
text editors to browse their source listings and to
locate information as they build their understanding of programs. Tools that don't involve the execution of target programs are static. Included in
this category are tools that construct useful views
of the program, such as cross references and structure charts.

Instruction tracers and symbolic debugging tools
provide information collected from the execution of
the target program; they are dynamic tools.
Because reading a listing involves the mental gym-
nastics of translating textual arrangement of
information into a variety of execution arrangements, dynamic tools have been in a position to
offer direct assistance. But this source of assistance has been plagued by a keen difficulty. In
order to learn about a key path through the program, the user must establish the boundary conditions (i.e. data values in sometimes highly complicated interrelationships) that drive execution down
that path. In many cases, it is the boundary condition that is the unknown!

8.   CONCLUSION

MAP manages the details that a maintenance programmer must aquire in order to understand a program.
MAP is interactive to support the learning process
and is flexible to allow the experienced programmer
to be effective. By relieving the maintenance programmer of much of his clerical burden, we hope
that maintenance programming will become a fun job
which programmers will want to do.

MAP makes use of static analysis of programs to assist programmer understanding. MAP opens new possibilities for improving the human understanding of software.

9. ACKNOWLEDGEMENTS

The development of MAP has been a team effort. The author acknowledges the contribution of each team member, namely: John Hiles, Ron Tischler, Sushma Bhatia, Robin Schaufler, Marty Honda, Charles Hoch, Charlotte Payne, Y.C. Wang, John Spiller, Bruce Martin, Mikel Lechner, Nanda Nandkishore and Jim Voll.

References

[1] Leitntz, B. and Swanson, E. B., Software Maintenance Management. (Addison Wesley, 1980)

[2] Concise Oxford English Dictionary

[3] Yourdon, E. and Constantine, L., Structured Design, (Yourdon Inc, 1975).

[4] Kernighan, B., and Plauger, P., Software Tools (Addison Wesley, 1976), p 138.

[5] Aho, A., Hirschberg, D., and Ullman, J., Bounds on the complexity of the longest common subsequence problem. J. ACM 23, 1(Jan 1976), 1-12.

[6] Hirschberg, D., A linear space algorithm for computing maximal common subsequences. Comm ACM 18, 6(June 1975), 342-343.

[7] Shneiderman, B., Software Psychology (Winthrop Publishers,1980).

[8] Warren, S., Martin, B., Hoch, C., Experience. with a Module Package in Developing Production Quality PASCAL Programs. Sixth International Conference on Software Engineering, Sept 1982.

APPENDIX A.   SUMMARY OF MAP COMMANDS

MAP commands may be either primary commands or line commands. Line commands are entered over the line number field of the screen and duplicate the function of certain primary commands. For brevity only primary commands are described here.

Not all commands are available in all views, for instance the difference handling commands work in difference view only and the logical trace commands work only in source code view.

MAP **searching** commands produce a set of lines which is the result of the search. This set of lines is either passed on to the next command in the filter or if there is no further command in the filter, the tokens which were found by the search are displayed as highlights.

While viewing a structure chart, the results are shown by highlighting the boxes whose source code was found by the search. This leads to some subtle differences in options and actions which are not discussed in this summary.

Typically the information MAP provides will not fit on the standard screen (24 lines or longer). A MAP **virtual screen** may be much longer and wider than window viewable by the physical screen. The scrolling commands move the window about the virtual screen.

A.1   Commands that produce a set of lines

These commands are useful to get a MAP search started. MAP has mnemonics to identify sets of lines with particular characteristics; for example those with highlights on them, those which are common to both old and new versions of the program, those which are within the current PERFORMed section. Sets of lines may be remembered in a marker.

A.2   Searching the source sequentially

Command	Meaning
Find <pattern>	Find the lines which contain the regular expression
FindSub <type spec>	Find the lines which contain statements of type equal to type spec.

A.3   Searching the source along logical paths

A.3.1   Control Trace Commands

Command	Meaning
Comefrom	Find those lines which transfer control to this line.
Prevdec	Find the previous decision points (e.g. IF, GOTO, PERFORM) which effected transfer of control to this point.
Pick ?	1. Find to which lines control can transfer next, 2. If destination(s) are set, show which paths lead to the destination,

3. Remember which path is taken.

Pick \<path\> Short form of Pick ? when path is
already known, path is: a lable name,
THEN, ELSE, ZOOMIN, ZOOMOUT etc.

Dest   Set a destination for use with Pick.

Nodest   Remove any destinations.

Dest ?   Show which places are destinations.

Backup   Go back along the path just traversed
using Pick.

Repeated Backups unravel a path.

A.3.2   Data Trace Commands

Command	Meaning
Nextmod \<var\>	Search along the logical paths of the program for the next place where where variable \<var\> is overwritten regardless of the name used in the modification. This command can give zero, one or multiple results.
Nextref \<var\>	Like nextmod but look for references
Nextuse \<var\>	" " " " " uses
Prevmod \<var\>	" " " " backwards
Prevref \<var\>	" prevmod " " for references
Prevuse \<var\>	" " " " " uses

A.4   Showing data interfaces

Command	Meaning
Showintf program	Display the data interfaces for this program
Showintf unit	Display the data interfaces for the current unit and its caller

A.5   Reformatting the Screen

Source code screens may be reformatted to exclude
or reshow any lines. Structure chart screens may
be reformatted to different page and box size with
some control over the layout.

A.6   Scrolling

Map provides standard scrolling commands: Up, Down,
Left and Right and locating of markers. In addition, MAP provides scrolling to the first, last,
next or previous highlight and to the first, last,
next or previous difference between the old and new
version of the source code.

A.7   Hardcopy output

The user may get a hardcopy of any screen using the
Printwindow or Printscreen commands. The
Printchart command produces the complete structure
chart on hardcopy. The user obtains a hardcopy of
the users guide by the Printtutorial.

V. Infusing Software with Structure: Code Level Approaches

When software has little recognizable structure, restructuring approaches may be used to uncover structure in the software. The papers of part V concern restructuring at the code level. The approaches are driven by a view of structure at the programming language statement level and not by a view largely dependent on the software's specification. In Part VI we will see restructuring approaches in which software specifications play a larger role in determining how the software is structured.

In the first paper, "Help! I Have to Update an Undocumented Program" by S.D. Fay and D.G. Holmes, a practical approach to understanding someone else's code is given. Wherever possible, code should be understood before it is changed. With down-to-earth advice, the authors describe how up-to-date documentation for old code may be created.

In the next paper, "Improving Computer Program Readability to Aid Modification" by J.L. Elshoff and M. Marcotty, programs are made readable by manually applying transformations to improve coding style. A useful and instructive battery of code-improving transformations is presented.

In the paper, "Using Automated Techniques to Improve the Maintainability of Existing Software," K. Burns gives a useful approach to systematically restructuring one's code. The approach involves assessing alternatives to restructuring, establishing a maintainability measure to determine hard-to-maintain code and to track restructuring progress, tempering the use of metrics with concern for the payoffs of restructuring certain code portions, automating the restructuring process, accounting for actual costs of restructuring, and estimating restructuring effectiveness.

The last two papers concern commercially available restructuring tools. Since the tools described are commercially available and subject to change, the interested reader should contact the vendors concerning the latest capabilities of the tools. The reader should also consult tools directories for restructuring tools which have appeared from other vendors. Some of these tools are mentioned in this Tutorial's annotated bibliography: RECODER (from Language Technology) and COBOL Structuring Facility (from IBM).

In "Salvaging Your Software Asset (Tools Based Maintenance)," M.J. Lyons discusses the use of a COBOL restructuring tool as a way to circumvent totally rewriting poorly structured programs. The tool, Structured Retrofit, is available from Peat, Marwick, Mitchell & Co., The Catalyst Group, Chicago, Illinois.

In "Evolution of a Software Maintenance Tool," H.W. Morgan describes experiences that led to the current versions of a structure recognition aid (SCAN/370) and another COBOL restructuring tool (SUPERSTRUCTURE). SCAN/370* and SUPERSTRUCTURE are available from Group Operations, Washington, D.C.

---

*SCAN/370 has been renamed SCAN/COBOL.

HELP! I HAVE TO UPDATE AN UNDOCUMENTED PROGRAM

SANDRA D. FAY   DENISE G. HOLMES

LOCKHEED AIRCRAFT SERVICE COMPANY
SOFTWARE ENGINEERING DEPARTMENT (1-334)
ONTARIO, CALIFORNIA 91761

This paper discusses a method for documenting and maintaining an undocumented program. The paper provides guidance to junior personnel and management of areas that can alleviate the situation.

The paper specifically addresses:

> First Impressions
> Resources, Who and What
> Approaches
> Schedule Assessment

This paper is directed to those people in industry who are faced with documenting an undocumented program. However, it is also written with the hope that this will give the person supervising the maintainer a clearer view of the help which can be given by providing the resources and time necessary to maintain a program in the proper manner.

Introduction

It's your third week on the job and the boss decides you're the perfect candidate to update "The ABC System". First you don't know what the ABC System is, and worse, when you mention the name to anyone else, they give you a pitying look and say, "Oh, you're going to work on the ABC System." And, as you walk away, you hear snickering in the background.

Many of us in industry have been faced with this situation. There are numerous undocumented programs. Maintaining a program that is undocumented (or poorly documented) is a costly task. The authors' experience indicates that this is a young programmer's dilemma and one that can be improved. Assigning junior personnel to update undocumented programs only increases the cost of the task. In preparing this paper, we have drawn on the experience of senior as well as junior personnel. The consolidated opinions are that the programmers can help themselves: by their attitudes, their techniques, documenting as they go, and by giving visibility to management.

First Impressions--Use them to your Advantage

You've been barraged with all the facts: the original programmers are gone; everyone that is around and knows something about the program doesn't want anything to do with it; the few comments that are in the code aren't necessarily correct (although they might be); and the small amount of documentation that exists (if any) is not necessarily correct or complete--it hasn't been updated for the last who-knows-how-many code updates.

There you have it, everything appears to be against you. But, that's your first advantage. If everyone thinks it's a terrible program and you make something good out of it, you're going to look good. Also, if it's really that notorious, you'll get lots of visibility while doing it.

Most poorly written programs that will need to be updated probably have an infamous reputation which follows them. So your job is to let that reputation live on of its own accord. Don't encourage it because then you'll have a hard time working on the program yourself. But don't discourage it too much either because then you're hurting your chances of looking as good as possible. Be positive! You can improve the situation and also use this opportunity to increase your reputation.

Now what can be done to actually perform the update and, at the same time, improve the existing software documentation all within the schedule. Your next step is to gather the resources that you need to do your tasks.

Resources Available

The first step is to find out who your "friends" are. Who has worked on the program before? Who knows anything about it? There's usually at least one person in the company who has worked on the project before. That person may be hard to find but there's always someone who knows what's been happening in every department

Reprinted from *The Proceedings of the Conference on Software Maintenance —1985*, 1985, pages 194-202. Copyright © 1985 by The Institute of Electrical and Electronics Engineers, Inc.

(or at least in yours) for the past five years. Find that person and get all the background information you can. Try to get on their good side so that you can call whenever you need help. You can do this by making sure you don't call too often and when you do, being sure to give profuse thanks for the time taken to share experience and knowledge.

The next person to find is the one who can help you locate the other resources you need. This person is someone who is experienced in writing documents, experienced in working with people, and realizes how desperately documentation needs to be done. This person is a real "must" to your success. If you're lucky, the software department will have already hired someone like this. Ask around until this great resource is found. If you've looked everywhere and have come to the conclusion that one does not exist, let your manager and/or the manager of the software engineering department know how valuable a person with this knowledge can be.

Next, using the above-mentioned people's help and the help of any other people who are willing, find examples of documents written on similar projects. Look for a Program Description Document, a User's Manual, a Version Description Document, and any other documents you can get your hands on. There may actually be some documentation on the program you're working on. If so, be sure to get a copy of that. Try to determine how much of it is still fact and how much has turned into fiction. One of the best things you can find is a "data dictionary"[1]. This gives a brief description of all the variables, either in one module or in the whole program. When trying to understand a program, it is amazingly helpful to be able to understand the program's variable names.

But where do you find these documents? Most companies have libraries of past documentation. You'll probably need help from your "knowledgeable friend" to get the material you need. Sometimes people keep their own files of all the old projects they have worked on. Try to get at least one of these. One thing that is almost always done is testing. You should be able to find some test documentation for your program which will give you insight into the aspects of the program deemed important enough to test.

You might check to see if any automated tools exist within your company--tools for configuration management, testing, building structure charts, requirements analysis, source translation, etc.

The last, and possibly most important resource you will need is the most current listing of your program. This seems like it would be a given, but not necessarily so. Do a spot check to make sure that the source code you have matches the current executing system. It would be most discouraging to spend time updating a system that doesn't even exist anymore.

The main key in finding all the right resources is to keep your eyes and ears open. Each person who has been in the department since the last time your program was updated can be a source of help. Anyone who has worked with configuration management can be of help. Anyone who has ever written a document knows something about ways to approach documentation.

Approaches

Now you're over your first impressions and you've gathered all the resources you can possibly think of gathering. Although, believe it or not, you may discover more as you go, you have to start somewhere, so this is it. You have the code in front of you, you need to fix the bug or add the new feature, and your manager wants to know when the job will be done. Where to begin? The following are the steps we suggest:

STEP I. Learn the Structure and Organization of the Program

A. Start on the structure charts by going through the code and noting each time a module is called. Make sure to keep these notes accurately as they will be of use again later in step III. Figure 1 shows an example of a simplified structure chart (2,3) in the event that you are not accustomed to preparing them. What matters at this point is your need to understand the structure of the system--which modules call other modules, how the module is called, where data is set, where data is used, etc.

B. You may prefer to use data flow diagrams (DFDs)[3]. Figure 2 gives a simplified example. Our experience is that DFDs are more useful at the design or requirements level of programming. Other people find them very useful in understanding an existing program's organization so use whatever technique is comfortable. Remember, part of your job is to improve the program's documentation so use techniques and tools that conform to your company's standards. However, do not let the techniques

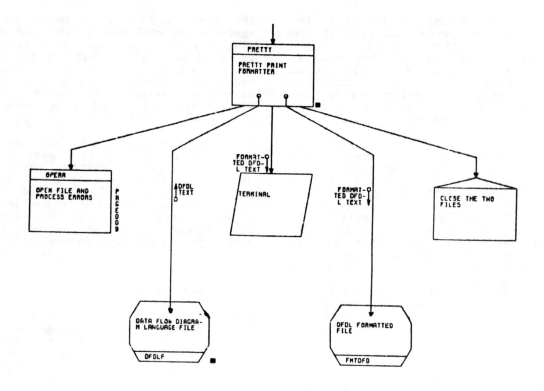

Figure 1.   Sample Structure Chart

get in your way of understanding the system.

C.   Skim through the source code once more. Make your structure charts (or data flow diagrams) as accurate as possible. Each time you go through the code, you should be writing down any questions that arise. Step II explains how your questions can be resolved.

STEP II.   Determine What the Program is Currently Doing

A.   Go through the code carefully (module by module) trying to grasp everything you can. Take diligent notes. You should be noting things such as: how is the module called/invoked; does the module have only one entry; does the module have only one exit; what are the data items the module operates on; what are the error conditions; what and why are other modules called. Write down every question you can think of. At this point, flowcharts may be of extreme help--especially if your code is written in assembly language. Make the boxes as big as you need them or as many as you need. Remember, the things you're doing now don't have to be beautiful. They are merely an aid to help increase your knowledge. If

you're not sure how to make flow-charts, go see your resource person. You may also consult reference 4 for details about flowcharts.

B.   Once you've gone entirely through the code, you should be able to answer many of your own questions. Answer what you can, then determine which of the remaining ones are the most important to understanding the overall flow of the program. Get the answers you need by using all of your resources.

C.   Now, go through the code again. Redo your flowcharts as you go. It could be that pseudo-code works better for you than flowcharts. Use the method that will help you the most in understanding the program. This time, comment as you go along. Remember how you felt on your first pass through the code and there were no comments. Try to make it so the next person who has to go through the code doesn't run into the same problems. Remove all old comments that no longer make sense. It is best to do this in pencil. Sometimes your next perusal of the code will require modification of something you have previously noted. Modify comments so they are current with your understanding, don't let them get out of date.

SYMBOLS   MEANINGS

            ⬭
         X.X.X   A process "bubble" represents the activity
        PROCESS   of transforming input data into output
                          data. PROCESS represents the name of the
                          process, and x.x.x represents the section
                          where it is defined.

         data name   A labeled arrow represents the flow of
         ⟶   data. The direction of the arrow
                          identifies the direction of flow.

        ═══════   Two horizontal bars with a name between
          STORE   them represents a "store". The store
        ═══════   identifies a mechanism for the storage of
                          data. It could be a file, dynamic storage
                          (e.g., buffers), or a database, for
                          example.

        ┌──────────┐   A box with a brief description inside
        │ SOURCE │   represents a "source" and/or "sink"
        │   │   (destination) of data.
        └──────────┘

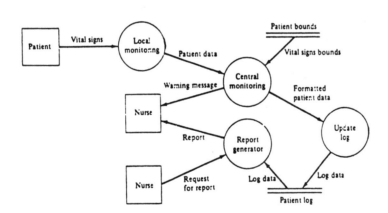

Figure 2.   Sample Data Flow Diagram

167

STEP III. Begin Documentation

A.   As you gain knowledge of the program's structure, begin developing module prologues[3]. Module prologues are an easy and helpful way to begin documenting. The prologue is a dedicated area that includes things such as the module name, description of module purpose, interface descriptions and version number of the module. Figure 3 gives an example of a module prologue. As you write your module prologues, you will discover more things about your program. Be sure to include as many of the module's variable definitions as possible. You can use your structure charts to help fill in the "How Called:" and "Subroutines and Functions Called:" areas. If the program already has prologues, be sure they are correct. Consult reference 3 for more details on module prologues.

NAME: TCOPY

VERSIONS:
    1.0   28 Jun 1984   Created as per CR 2234.

    1.1   7 Oct 1984   Created as per CR 2508.
             Modified the use of cartridge number (CRN) reference
             to handle all valid alphanumeric inputs for CRN.

DESCRIPTION:
    Copies a file off of an airplane transcribed tape into a
    disc file.

FILE DESCRIPTION:
    TCOPY creates a file with the following format:
        Record 1:
            Words 1-3 = the file name from the tape; if the
                        file name starts with anything except
                        "TR" then word 4 also applies
            Word   4 = number of words per subframe
        Records 2-N:
            the ID array of 1024 words off of the transcription
            tape

HOW CALLED:
    IF (IPROC.EQ.1) CALL TCOPY   [from TPDSC]

REMARKS:
    The module has been modified per customer request to allow
    a larger selection of operations.

SUBROUTINES AND FUNCTIONS CALLED:
    QIOMT,GTNAM,GTDNM

COMMON VARIABLES USED:
    ICRT - Terminal logical unit number
    ID(1024) - a record of data read from a tape or disc file
    LP - Line printer logical unit number
    MTLUN - Magtape drive logical unit number

LOCAL VARIABLE DEFINITIONS:
    ACSIZE - The actual size of the created file
    DFILE(3) - The user entered name of the disc file
    FLAG - Variable used in call to GTDNM; sent as 0 means
           need to create file; sent as 1 means need to open.
           Returned as 1 means an error occurred; returned as
           2 means file was opened; returned as 3 means file
           was created.
    LFILE(3) - The user entered name of the tape file
    NREC - The current record number

Figure 3.   Sample Module Prologue

B. If there are many global variables, it would be wise to begin a data dictionary or update the existing one. Create your data dictionary on the computer using a separate file in the same account as your working copy of the source code. Type in all of the global variable names and the definitions you know. This allows you to make necessary changes easily. Make use of Set/Use and/or cross-reference listings if they are available.

C. Check with your manager to see if the modifications that you are making should be placed under configuration management. If so, find out what paperwork needs to be done and do it now. If not, you may want to create your own configuration management system so that you will be able to track what changes you are implementing and why. It is recommended that each modification be kept until the task is completed. Multiple versions may be kept on the computer. If an existing listing is being marked up, we suggest using different colors for each day and noting the date for each color. It is important to keep a history of changes and the reasons for making them so the same error will not be made twice. This history will also help in completing the module prologues in the future when filling in the version numbers. Lastly, keeping a record of your implemented changes will be of great use when creating the Version Description Document discussed in Step V. Figure 4 gives an example of the type of paperwork you might use to keep track of the changes you make to the code.

D. If you have not made a copy of your master (original) source code, do it now. You will need to reference the unmodified version without your changes. If you made only one copy of the source listing, make a second one and don't mark it up!

STEP IV. Make the Required Update(s)

A. Be sure you know what is needed. Was the bug correctly reported? Are you solving the real problem or a peripheral one? Do you understand the requirements? Do you know or have a guess what the change will do to the program? Discuss any questions with your manager. Let it be known what you have done, what you are doing, and your expected completion date.

B. It's time now to solve the problem at hand. You understand the code (at least to a degree), so this part should be easy. You may still need a little help from the people who have worked on the program before. If you do, don't hesitate to call them. If the software is in use, discuss the change and its impact with the current users. Discuss your proposed modification. Determine if it is what they want and/or need. This is requirements analysis, and it's as important in a maintenance activity as it is in a development activity. Conduct a mini design review prior to modifying the code.

C. Repeat previous test procedures to see if you obtain the same results as documented in the test reports. You need to know if the unmodified code executes correctly so you can determine the impact of your modifications.

D. Determine where the update(s) should be implemented within the code. Be sure to note in the module prologues what changes are being made and the date of change. This is where an automated configuration control tool (such as UNIX Source Configuration Control System, DEC Configuration Management System, SOFTOOL Change and Configuration Control Systems, etc.) is helpful. Consult reference 5 for more details.

E. Type in the update(s) and compile. If you're lucky, it will compile the first time. However, this is not the norm, as we all know. Keep working on this step until you produce code that will execute.

F. Test the update(s) in every manner possible. This is important because you won't look good if you turn in a completed program that doesn't work. Beware of systems that contain self-modifying code--what you see in the listing may not be what is executing. Beware of the impact of your change on the other modules in the system that use the module you are modifying. Be sure you test all module combinations.

STEP V. Finish the Documentation

A. The first step is to make sure the code itself is well documented. Are the module prologues complete? Is the code commented in all the necessary places? Are the comments that exist correct?

B. Now it's time to start pulling together all those notes you've been keeping. Your notes (minus the

SCR
SOFTWARE CHANGE REQUEST

ORIGINATOR	DATE	PROJECT		SCR NO.
	DOCUMENT ONLY	SYSTEM VERSION		REF CR NO.

SCR TITLE

DESCRIPTION

AFFECTED DOCUMENTS		AFFECTED TEST
1.	4.	
2.	5.	
3.	6.	

COORDINATOR	RESPONSIBLE PROGRAMMER

PERFORMANCE EFFECT			IMPACT EFFECT		
INTERNAL ☐	CLASS I ☐	CLASS II ☐	EMERGENCY ☐	URGENT ☐	ROUTINE ☐

SCRB ACTION	SCCB APPROVAL SIGNATURES
DATE APPROVED	
DATE REJECTED	

LAS 4419   M2569C

Figure 4. Sample Configuration Management Form

<u>VERSION DESCRIPTION DOCUMENT FORMAT</u>

1.0   <u>INTRODUCTION</u>

2.0   <u>INVENTORY</u>

2.1   <u>DOCUMENTATION</u>

A list of documentation affected by this software version. If change pages are available, the change pages should be an Appendix to the VDD.

2.2   <u>SOFTWARE MEDIA</u>

This section will be an itemization of the entire release. It should include all the pieces of the release, formats of the media, version numbers, description (pictorial) of tapes, disk, and floppies should be provided.

3.0   <u>INCORPORATED CHANGES</u>

This section may be a table which shows per CPCR/ECR those modules modified and their current version number. If not applicable state, "Not applicable, an initial customer baseline release".

4.0   <u>KNOWN ERRORS</u>

If applicable to the release, a description or list by CPCR/ECR number of known errors.

If not applicable state, "Not applicable, no known errors".

5.0   <u>SYSTEM GENERATION</u>

This section will describe how the release is created. It should include the operating system, language processors, command files, utilities and their version numbers used in the generation process. A load map can be included here if applicable.

6.0   <u>ASSUMPTIONS</u>

If applicable, those assumptions made in building or creating this release. Detailed design decisions are not appropriate.

7.0   <u>RESTRICTIONS/LIMITATIONS</u>

If applicable to the system, examples would be: required memory to build or execute the system, required hardware, required number or type of peripherals.

Figure 5. Sample Version Description Document Table of Contents

configuration management information) will constitute the majority of a Program Description Document (PDD). The purpose of this document is to give an overview of the major program functions. The structure charts, data flow diagrams and/or flowcharts should be included. Anything that will make the program more under-standable to the next programmer should be included here.

C.   The Version Description Document (VDD) should contain all the information pertaining to this version (update) of your program. Included within should be your company's required configuration management information. Use the dated change descriptions you added to the module prologues to help write the descriptions needed in this document. Figure 5 gives a sample table of contents for a VDD. Consult reference 6 for more details on the contents of a VDD.

D.   If a User's Manual currently exists, it probably needs to be updated. If one does not exist, then one should be written. This document describes, from a user's standpoint, how to operate the system. Consult reference 6 for more details on User's Manuals.

E. It's possible that a new test document will need to be written or an existing one modified. This is totally at the discretion of your supervisor. The format of this document depends on the format officially determined by your organization. The one key to remember is to make the document precise--be sure it includes tests of all the necessary functions and the expected results.

Schedule Assessment

How can you determine what you can reasonably expect from yourself in the amount of time given? Remember, part of updating the undocumented program is to document it. This requires more time than just changing source lines of code. If you are new, consult with senior personnel to determine if your schedule is reasonable. If you feel your schedule is unreasonable, notify your manager and give details of the tasks that need to be done. Documenting now will save the next person who has to update this program time and mental duress. Be sure your manager realizes that you have to go through this learning experience anyway so it should be made as productive as possible. The things you're writing down now should be stored in a permanent document.

If you can't get agreement to the whole list of documents mentioned heretofore, try to narrow it down to the most important. Importance, of course, is relative. In our estimation, the most important thing is to document the code because it will never be lost. Next would be the Program Description Document, User's Manual, Version Description Document, and any test documentation.

A good maintenance activity follows sound engineering discipline. This is where management plays a key role. Managers, help yourself by accepting only well-documented programs. Enforced company coding standards are essential to obtaining well-commented and organized programs. Conformance to a known standard allows other programmers to easily understand an existing program, therefore saving the company time and money in maintenance. Reward your good maintainers--they are hard to find. A poor job of maintenance costs you many times over. Don't skip documenting due to schedule crunches or lack of recognition of what the maintenance activity entails (requirements analysis, design, implementation, verification, and documentation).

Remember, the whole point of the matter is to make this program understandable enough so that the next person who comes along won't have the frustrating time that you've had. The task effort will be considerably less: less time, less effort, less money. If the boss can't be convinced to give time for _any_ documentation, then at least be sure that what has been done (notes, charts, etc.) is saved in a library in a format that is retrievable for the next programmer or manager.

Best of luck, and through it all, when you think you will never be able to understand the program, keep telling yourself that lots of other people have been in the same situation that you're in and have come out okay in the end. When using the right techniques, there's no reason why your story can't have a very successful ending.

REFERENCES

1. IEEE, Software Engineering Standards, The Institute of Electrical and Electronics Engineers, Wiley - Interscience.

2. E. Yourdon and L. L. Constantine, Structured Design, Fundamentals of a Discipline of Computer Program and System Design, Prentice-Hall.

3. M. Page-Jones, The Practical Guide to Structured Systems Design, Yourdon Press.

4. H. Katzan, Jr., Systems Design and Documentation, Van Nostrand Reinhold Company, Computer Science Series.

5. Softool Corporation, SOFTOOL, Change and Configuration Control (CCC), an Overview with Examples, Softool Corporation.

6. Department of Defense, DoD-STD-2167, Software Development Standard, Department of Defense.

7. General Software Engineering How to Literature:

   R. Glass and R. A. Noiseux, Software Maintenance Guidebook, Prentice-Hall.

   J. Martin and C. McClure, Software Maintenance; The Problem and Its Solutions, Prentice-Hall.

   J. Wolberg, Conversion of Computer Software, Prentice-Hall.

COMPUTING
PRACTICES

"Improving Computer Program Readability to Aid Modification" by J.L. Elshoff and M. Marcotty from *Communications of the ACM*, Volume 25, Number 8, August 1982, pages 512-521. Copyright 1982, Association for Computing Machinery, Inc., reprinted by permission.

Improving Computer Program Readability to Aid Modification

James L. Elshoff and Michael Marcotty
General Motors Research Laboratories

1. The Modification Cycle

The modification of computer programs is a costly and constant job. An informal survey conducted at General Motors and reported on by Elshoff [6] concluded that about 75 percent of all programmer/analysts' time in a commercial data processing installation is spent on program modification. This conclusion agrees with independent assessments made by Liu [16], Boehm [2], and Lientz and Swanson [15]. Moreover, the reasons for modifying programs will not disappear. As pointed out by Lehman [14], all programs are models of some part of the real world and, as the world changes, programs must be modified to keep pace with these changes or they become progressively less relevant, less useful, and less cost-effective. As new software is developed, the inventory of programs to be maintained grows, and thus this high level of modification work is not expected to decrease.

The modification cycle is composed of a sequence of steps such as:

(1) The user requests that a program be changed.
(2) The specifications for the change are written and the cost of the change estimated.
(3) It is decided that the changes are worth being made.
(4) The program is changed to meet the new specifications.

Unfortunately, the modification environment is not as simple as this list. The frequency of change, the extent

CR Categories and Subject Descriptors: D.2.2 [**Software Engineering**]: Tools and Techniques; D.2.7 [**Software Engineering**]: Distribution and Maintenance—*documentation, enhancement, and restructuring*.
General Terms: Documentation, Human Factors, Languages
Additional Key Words and Phrases: software modification cycle.
Authors' present address: J.L. Elshoff and M. Marcotty, Computer Science Department, General Motors Research Laboratories, Warren, MI 48090-9055.

SUMMARY: Frequently, when circumstances require that a computer program be modified, the program is found to be extremely difficult to read and understand. In this case a new step to make the program more readable should be added at the beginning of the software modification cycle. A small investment will make (1) the specifications for the modifications easier to write, (2) the estimate of the cost of the modifications more accurate, (3) the design for the modifications simpler, and (4) the implementation of the modifications less error-prone.

of a change, the acceptable cost for a change, and other change attributes vary with the individual program. The one common denominator of the modification process is that it starts with an existing program and its documentation. In most cases this means a listing of the program's source text. The readability of that source text can have a great impact on the decisions made during the modification cycle.

2. Unreadable Programs

In a study of commercial programming practices by Elshoff [6], it was found that most programs were poorly written. They were very large, extremely difficult to read, and more complex than necessary. Furthermore, the study determined that programming language usage was poor and inconsistent. The results of the survey by Lientz and Swanson [15] show that the quality of programming is a generally perceived problem.

During the last five years and continuing today, there has been a major effort in data processing installations to improve programming practices. Programmer training and installation procedures are being upgraded through the use of better practices as described by Kernighan and Plauger [13], and Elshoff [4, 5]. The improvements achieved with better practices have been shown by Elshoff [7] to be significant and are supported by the experimental evidence of Sheppard et al. [21].

Nevertheless, most data processing installations still have large inventories of programs that are nearly impossible to read. Programs from this inventory must regularly be modified or replaced. Before this can be done, it is first necessary to understand exactly what that program currently does. In fact, the very decision whether to modify or completely replace a program may hinge on how well the program is understood. The need for readability is apparent and imperative in a communication medium like the source text of a computer program. The life of the program depends on it.

The thesis of this paper is that modifying a program simply to improve its readability is generally a worthwhile endeavor. With proper timing, the improvements in readability can be achieved at little or no cost. Furthermore, once the program is readable, the advantages of improved readability will accrue with each subsequent modification. Here, we present a method for improving the readability of a program through a set of specific transformations that can be applied directly to the program text. The effects of applying the transformations to a sample program are shown and discussed.

3. Readability

The readability of a computer program depends on many factors. The reader's familiarity with the program, knowledge of the application area, and own programming style are important factors that are mostly independent of the program to be modified. In this paper, we concentrate on those attributes of the program's text that impact its readability. Thus, we will take the pragmatic, realistic point of view of a programmer who is knowledgeable in the application area but who is seeing a particular program for the first time.

A readable program always seems to exhibit a common set of properties, as listed, for example, by Kernighan and Plauger [13], Yourdon [24], and Myers [19]. The program is well commented. The logical structure of the program is constructed of single-entry single-exit flow of control units. Variable names are mnemonic and references to them localized. The program's physical layout makes the salient features of the algorithm that is implemented stand out. It is true that a program may have all these properties and still be unreadable; however, the readability of a program is certain to suffer when it lacks one or more of the properties.

4. Program Transformations

There are many known source program transformations described by Kernighan and Plauger [13], and Standish et al. [22]. Algorithms have even been developed to perform the complete restructuring of programs;

these are described by Mills [18] and Ashcroft and Manna [1], and have also been implemented in computer programs. However, as Dijkstra pointed out in 1968 [3],

> The exercise to translate an arbitrary flow diagram more or less mechanically to a jumpless one, however, is not to be recommended. Then the resulting flow diagram cannot be expected to be more transparent than the original one.

This has been borne out in actual examples—for instance, Elshoff and Marcotty [8].

Our own experience with the manual restructuring of PL/I programs indicates that the use of the set of transformations listed in the next section is a key to making programs more readable. We have found that the actual text manipulation gives the programmer an increased understanding of the program and insights for further modifications. The understanding developed by the programmer is generally well beyond the capability of artificial intelligence, and the undesirable side-effects often introduced by automatic restructuring techniques can be avoided.

All the transformations described in the next section aim to simplify the program by modifying the executable statements and rearranging the sequence in which they are executed. As a result of these changes, the program may need to be reformatted and additional comments added. These operations are really program transformations that enhance readability without altering the program's execution and are discussed in this section. Reformatting and commenting should be done for each pass over the source text. As understanding increases, the programmer will be able to add more meaningful comments.

4.1 Add Comments

Programmers consistently state that few programs have documentation outside of the source text. Moreover, when there is external documentation, it is most frequently no longer in step with the program text. Since the source text represents reality, the final authority on what is executed, it should be self-documenting, which means it must be readable.

Comments should be used to make the source text of a program understandable. Block comments should be placed at the beginning of a program to describe the program's purpose, external interface, and how it works. The program should be divided into major sections, paragraphs, separated by blank lines or page boundaries. Block comments should also be used to describe the functions performed by the paragraphs.

Comments can be the most important contribution that a programmer makes. The programmer modifying a program must be able to read and understand it even though it is difficult. This difficulty can be reduced for all future modifications by adding appropriate comments as discoveries about the program are made. Surprisingly, adding comments is often one of the last tasks that can be done; the programmer just cannot understand the program text well enough to add comments early on.

COMPUTING PRACTICES

4.2 Reformat

Maintaining a consistent format adds greatly to the readability of a program. Just as paragraphing and sectioning help written English, so can indentation, key word positioning, and logical grouping aid a programming langauge. Using an automatic formatter such as the one on the IBM PL/I Checkout Compiler [12] can standardize style for an installation. However, even when the reformatting must be done by hand, it should be done consistently. Consistency of style is more important than the details of the style itself. The few extra minutes the programmer spends keeping a program consistently formatted will pay dividends the next time the program is read.

5. Readability Transformations

In this section, we describe a set of simple changes that can be made to a program to improve its readability. A programmer using a good editor can quickly apply these transformations. Where sample program text is provided as an illustration, the PL/I programming language is used. However, most of the transformations described have direct analogies in other programming languages. Some of the programming examples are accompanied by simple flowgraphs with the convention that at branch points, the true branch is *always* to the left.

The transformations are presented in approximately the order they will be applied, although the specific ordering will vary from program to program. Moving labeled blocks and adding ELSE clauses are easy transformations to apply and should be done early on. Frequently, the application of one transformation will change the pattern of the program text so that additional transformations may be applied. The recommended approach is to read the source code, apply a set of straightforward and obvious transformations, add comments, and readjust the indentation.

Since the programmer may make a mistake while applying a transformation, a policy of checking the program after each pass is recommended. The first simple check is to compile the program. The compiler will check the syntactical correctness of the program and produce a symbol table that can be easily compared with the symbol table produced for the preceding pass. A second check is to execute the program against a set of test data. The idea behind this testing is not to check all possible paths but to simply check the repeatability of results. An execution test can prevent an error in an early pass from being compounded in succeeding passes.

The modified program should then be reread to find the next set of transformations to apply. The process is thus an iterative one with the program's readability and the programmer's understanding increasing simultaneously. Depending on the size of the program and its unreadability, the number of passes will vary, but sooner or later the mainline of the program will begin to become obvious and the program will be understood by the programmer.

5.1 Move Single Entry Labeled Blocks

A structure frequently found in an unreadable program is the single-entry labeled block, called code-block. This consists of a sequence of statements that may only be entered at the first statement and, when executed, will be executed to the last statement without any other possible exit.

A quick check of a program's symbol table can usually be used to find labels that are only referenced once. After the programmer verifies that the code-block cannot be reached by normal sequential execution, the code-block is moved to its proper location.

There are many minor variations of this change. Often, the code-block must be embedded in statement blocking symbols such as the DO-END statements in PL/I. Frequently, the code-block ends with a GO TO statement and the additional GO TO label-2 statement is unnecessary. In any case, this modification removes a label and relocates a code-block physically closer to the decisions governing its invocation.

5.2 Duplicate Labeled Blocks

This transformation is directly analogous to the previous one except that the label on the block, i.e., label-1, is referenced more than once. When this is the case and the code-block is small (say, less than 10 statements), the code-block is simply duplicated at each of the locations where a GO TO label-1 statement occurs. If the code-block is large or invoked many times, consideration might be given to making it into a procedure, as described in a succeeding section. However, at this stage in the transformation process, we are expanding text in order to gain understanding. The fact that a sequence of code is repeated several times does not necessarily mean that it would be wise to make it into a procedure; the function that it performs must instead be considered. This usually cannot be done until understanding is reached.

5.3 Add ELSE Clauses

The addition of an ELSE clause to every IF statement clarifies a program immensely. In the simplest case, the programmer walks through the program finding each IF statement that has no ELSE clause and adds one with a null statement. The null ELSE clause is a construct that many programmers view as a waste of time. It takes a second to write, has no effect on a program's compilation or execution, and can save a reader hours of effort by making a program more explicit and thus easier to read. The presence of the ELSE clause on all IF statements resolves any ambiguity that might be present in the reader's mind because of the optional nature of the ELSE clause. The structure

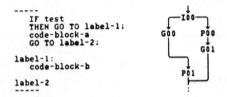

```
    -----
    IF test
    THEN GO TO label-1;
    code-block-a
    GO TO label-2;

label-1:
    code-block-b

label-2
    -----
```

is not uncommon. Its readability can be improved by making the relationship of the code-blocks to the IF test explicit in terms of THEN and ELSE clauses.

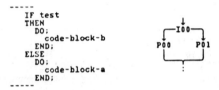

```
    -----
    IF test
    THEN
        DO;
            code-block-b
        END;
    ELSE
        DO;
            code-block-a
        END;
    -----
```

5.4 Renest IF Statements

After null ELSE clauses, as suggested in the previous section, have been inserted, it will become obvious in many instances that the ELSE clause is not really null. The pattern

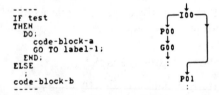

```
    -----
    IF test
    THEN
        DO;
            code-block-a
            GO TO label-1;
        END;
    ELSE
        ;
    code-block-b
    -----
```

is found in the program such that code-block-b is really the ELSE clause but is not packaged that way. Eliminating the null statement and putting code-block-b in a DO-END group make the program text more obvious. This change has the additional benefit of increasing the probability that the GO TO label-1 statement can be easily removed.

5.5 Make Loops Obvious

Using a GO TO statement to implement a loop greatly obscures a program. The program segment

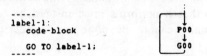

```
    -----
label-1:
    code-block

    GO TO label-1;
    -----
```

in which the code-block may be from one to several hundred statements long is not unusual. The problem is that the programmer reads the source text from top to bottom and does not realize the code-block is a loop body until the GO TO statement is read. Simply replacing the label and the GO TO with a DO WHILE as in

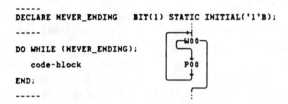

```
    -----
    DECLARE NEVER_ENDING   BIT(1) STATIC INITIAL('1'B);
    -----
    DO WHILE (NEVER_ENDING);
        code-block
    END;
    -----
```

establishes the fact that the program contains a loop structure at this point. This modification also alerts the reader to the existence of a loop whose termination condition is not yet understood, as will be described in the next section.

Experience has shown that making more than one of these modifications during a pass can sometimes result in intersecting loops. When this occurs, either the modification of one of the GO TO loops will have to be delayed until a subsequent pass or some sub-code-blocks will have to be interchanged.

5.6 Make Loop Termination Explicit

As discussed by Gries [10], one of the hardest programming constructs to understand is the loop. This difficulty is increased considerably when the conditions for terminating the loop are not explicit. This can arise when the loop itself is hidden, as discussed in the previous section. Another common fault is to use an iterative loop when it is not an intrinsic part of the process being performed. The third method is to use a LEAVE or GO TO statement to branch out of the loop, as will be discussed in the next section. The basic problem is that the reader cannot determine from the statement at the head of the loop the exact conditions that will cause termination of the loop and thus cannot determine the real reason for the loop.

Using an iterative loop when it does not apply, as in

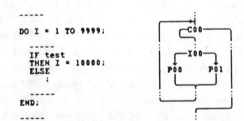

```
    -----
    DO I = 1 TO 9999;
    -----
    IF test
    THEN I = 10000;
    ELSE
        ;
    -----
    END;
    -----
```

is one example of a misleading loop termination. The programmer probably used the wrong form of the DO statement. If the index I is not used anywhere else in the body of the loop, a simple DO WHILE should have been used, as in the example

176

COMPUTING PRACTICES

```
-----
DECLARE CONTINUE_LOOP    BIT(1),
        YES              BIT(1) STATIC INITIAL('1'B),
        NO               BIT(1) STATIC INITIAL('0'B);
-----
CONTINUE_LOOP = YES;
DO WHILE (CONTINUE_LOOP);
   -----
   IF test
   THEN CONTINUE_LOOP = NO;
   ELSE
        ;
   -----
END;
-----
```

to clarify the loop termination condition. The selection of the name for the loop control variable, CONTINUE_LOOP above, can greatly improve the structure's readability. A name that makes the DO WHILE read in a straightforward manner, such as

```
DO WHILE (NOT_END_OF_FILE_A);
DO WHILE (OUTSIDE_ERROR_BOUNDS);
DO WHILE (MORE_CHARACTERS_IN_STRING);
```

should be used. When the programmer really understands the loop, the termination condition is obvious and the selection of a variable name follows naturally.

If the index I is referenced within the loop, the programmer can choose one of two ways to make the loop termination explicit. The variable I can be explicitly controlled by initializing it before entering the loop and incrementing it within the loop, or a more complicated form of the DO statement

```
DO I = 1 TO MAX WHILE (NOT_FOUND);
```

can be used. The latter approach should only be used when the loop may be terminated by either the indexing condition or the WHILE condition. This is a form of multiple loop termination that is examined more closely in the following section.

5.7 Remove Multiple Exits from Loops

It is not unusual to find a loop with more than one exit. In addition to the normal loop termination, the loop may be exited with a LEAVE statement, a GO TO statement, or an exception condition that is trapped by an ON unit. In order to change the multiple exit loop

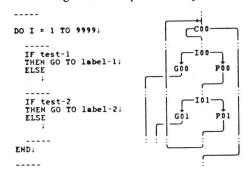

```
-----
DO I = 1 TO 9999;
   -----
   IF test-1
   THEN GO TO label-1;
   ELSE
        ;
   -----
   IF test-2
   THEN GO TO label-2;
   ELSE
        ;
   -----
END;
-----
```

to a single exit loop, the WHILE clause must usually be made into a compound conditional like

```
DO WHILE (NOT_END_OF_FILE_A & NO_ERROR_ENCOUNTERED);
```

using techniques like those discussed in the two previous sections. In some tougher cases, the introduction of a variable may be required. A SELECT statement or a nest of IF statements can then be used to maintain the proper logical flow. For example, the variable STATE could be used to modify the code above to

```
DECLARE STATE    CHARACTER(8);
-----
STATE = 'NORMAL';

DO WHILE (STATE = 'NORMAL');
   -----
   IF test-1
   THEN STATE = 'label-1';
   ELSE
      DO;
         -----
         IF test-2
         THEN STATE = 'label-2';
         ELSE
            DO;
               -----
            END;
      END;
END;

SELECT (STATE);
   WHEN ('label-1')
      GO TO label-1;

   WHEN ('label-2')
      GO TO label-2;

   -----
   OTHERWISE /* should not occur */
      SIGNAL ERROR;
END;
-----
```

A proper choice of names for the values assigned to STATE can further increase the readability of the program. Limited experience with this tougher case has shown that moving from loops with many exits to single-exit loops greatly clarifies the program text even though a multiple-exit SELECT structure is introduced. In fact, in all observed cases, the multiple-exit SELECT structure was quite easily transformed to a single-exit structure in subsequent passes over the program.

5.8 Remove Label Variables Used for Blocking

Label variables are used occasionally to simulate internal, nonparameterized procedures. For example, the code sequence

```
-----
   label-variable = label-1;
   GO TO label-2;
label-1:
-----
label-2:
   code-block
   GO TO label-variable;
-----
```

sends control to the code-block at label-2 and then returns control to the next sequential statement following label-1. Either the code-block should be made into a PROCEDURE that is called, or the code block should be distributed throughout the program. In either case, the labels, the GO TOs, and the label-variable with its multiway branch are removed and the program becomes more readable in a top-to-bottom fashion.

5.9 Remove Label Variables Used as Memory

Another common use for label variables is to remember a particular decision or path in a program by assigning a label to a label variable. In the code sequence

177

```
  -----
    label-variable = label-1;
  -----
    label-variable = label-2;
  -----
    label-variable = label-3;
  -----
    GO TO label-variable;
  -----
```

for example, the label-variable is used to remember which of three different paths was last executed in order to determine which path of the multiway branch is taken. The modification suggested in this case is the same as that recommended for the more difficult multiple-exit loops. Use a state variable as the memory device instead of a label variable. The resulting source text

```
  -----
  DECLARE STATE   CHARACTER(8) STATIC INITIAL('UNKNOWN');
  -----
    STATE = 'label-1';
  -----
    STATE = 'label-2';
  -----
    STATE = 'label-3';
  -----
  SELECT (STATE);
  WHEN ('label-1') GO TO label-1;
  WHEN ('label-2') GO TO label-2;
  WHEN ('label-3') GO TO label-3;
  OTHERWISE SIGNAL ERROR; /* should not occur */
  END;
  -----
```

may even appear slightly more complex initially. However, as with multiple-exit loops, experience has shown that removing label-variables is necessary to clarify the program text so that the multiple-exit SELECT structure can, in turn, be changed to a single-exit structure by applying other simple transformations within each WHEN clause. Although we appear to be swapping one kind of memory for another, this form makes the program easier to read and has the added advantage that its value can be printed for debugging purposes.

5.10 Use Status Variables to Track Execution

A frequently used programming form that contributes to unreadability is the use of long branches to a label that does standard error processing. Whether long branches are for error handling or other purposes, the introduction of a status variable is recommended to eliminate the branches and the resulting multiple-exit, multiple-entry code. As with the examples for multiple-exit loops and label variables, a character string variable is declared. Set the variable to 'NORMAL' and in the event an error is uncovered, set the variable to a value indicating the nature of the error. The variable can then be tested at the beginning of each major functional block within the program to determine whether that function should be performed or bypassed. The program text has a form like

```
  -----
  IF STATUS = 'NORMAL'
  THEN DO;
          major-function-1
        END;
  ELSE ;
  IF STATUS = 'NORMAL'
  THEN DO;
          major-function-2
        END;
  ELSE ;
  -----
```

and execution proceeds through the functions as long as everything is normal.

The judicious selection of the character string values assigned to a status variable can also make the program clearer by making it more self-documenting. A simple method is to maintain a block comment with the declaration for the status variable that indicates all of the values the status variable may have and what each value means.

5.11 Use Switches in ON-Units

The use of switches in ON-units can eliminate an excess of branching. In particular, switches should be used to control the program flow for conditions such as the end of file. A typical code sequence

```
  -----
  ON ENDFILE(file-a)                      O00-•••¬
      GO TO label-1;                             | G00
                                                 | ᶫ•••¬
  -----
  label-2:
                                              ┌──────┐
      READ FILE(file-a) ... ;                 │  P00 │
                                              │      │
      GO TO label-2;                          │  G01 │
                                              └──────┘
  label-1:
  -----
```

can be transformed to a sequence of single-entry, single-exit control structures like

```
  DECLARE MORE_RECORDS     BIT(1),
          YES              BIT(1) STATIC INITIAL('1'B),
          NO               BIT(1) STATIC INITIAL('0'B);
  -----
  ON ENDFILE(file-a)                      O00-•••¬
      MORE_RECORDS = NO;                         | P00
                                                 ᶫ•••¬
  MORE_RECORDS = YES;                     P00

  DO WHILE (MORE_RECORDS);              ┌──────W00
      READ FILE(file-a) ... ;          │
  ----                                 │     P01
                                       │
  END;                                 └──────┘
  ----
```

with the addition of a switch.

5.12 Localize References

The transformation implied here is to move statements around so that the references to a single variable or name are close together. The use of the file constant, FILE_A, in the source text

```
  -----
  ON ENDFILE(FILE_A)
      MORE_RECORDS = NO;
  -----
  many-statements
  -----
  OPEN FILE_A;
  -----
  many-statements
  -----
  MORE_RECORDS = YES;
  DO WHILE (MORE_RECORDS);
      READ FILE(FILE_A) ... ;
  END;
  -----
  many-statements
  -----
  CLOSE FILE_A;
  -----
```

is not uncommon. However, there is no rule that ON-units and OPEN statements must come first and CLOSE statements last in a program. Since the association between an input statement and its corresponding ON END-FILE statement is implicit, putting the two close together, as was done in the previous section, makes this association more obvious. Localizing the uses of the name FILE_A,

178

COMPUTING
PRACTICES

```
-----
OPEN FILE_A;
ON ENDFILE(FILE_A)
    MORE_RECORDS = NO;
MORE_RECORDS = YES;
DO WHILE (MORE_RECORDS);
    READ FILE(FILE_A) ... ;
END;
CLOSE FILE_A;
-----
```

means the reader does not have to keep details of that file in mind while reading other parts of the program. Moreover, if the reader is particularly interested in FILE_A, its uses are not spread all over the program. A pleasant side-effect of localizing references is that the execution efficiency of a program may be improved due to reduced paging.

5.13 Extract Common Code Sequences

The final area to be discussed is the extraction of common code sequences into procedures. Common code sequences may be labeled blocks that are either too large or too frequently referenced to be distributed throughout the program, as discussed earlier. They may be labeled blocks that are terminated by GO TO label variables, as discussed earlier. They may just be duplicate blocks of code that the reader discovers in the code. Finally, a common code sequence may simply be a single-entry, single-exit, functional block of code, in which case the extraction of the code block will make the main program easier to comprehend merely by making it smaller.

Just because a large block of code happens to appear many times is not sufficient grounds for making it into a procedure. In order to be of help in the readability and subsequent modifiability of the program, procedures should be constructed so that they each perform a specific logically self-contained task. The fact that an identical sequence of instructions happens to occur repeatedly does not mean that those instructions perform a cohesive task. Guidelines for recognizing and organizing code into functional procedures are described by Myers [19] and Stevens [23].

Once a sequence of instructions has been identified as suitable for transformation into a procedure, a simple method can be followed:

(1) Remove the common code sequence from the main program and wrap a set of PROCEDURE-END statements around it.

(2) Replace each reference to the common code sequence by a CALL statement in the main program.

(3) Recompile the main program and compile the common code sequence.

(4) Determine parameters by finding symbols common to both programs.

(5) Determine local variables for the common code sequence by finding symbols no longer referenced in the main program.

(6) Add a declaration for the new procedure in the main procedure. Update all CALL statements for the new procedure to use a proper argument list.

(7) Add a block comment to the new procedure describing its purpose and use.

(8) Move declarations for local variables into the new procedure.

6. Experience with the Transformations

Rather strange sections of source text may arise while transforming a program for readability. Some examples encountered in the past are (1) program text that cannot be reached via any execution path, (2) branches into the middle of loops, and even (3) an IF statement with identical code in its THEN and ELSE clauses. The wise programmer will go back and check the original program text when an odd section of code arises to make sure that a transformation has not been improperly applied, but the programmer will usually discover that the oddity really exists.

Often, the programmer will find other transformations to apply to make a program more concise and more readable. For example, statements common to both the THEN and ELSE clauses of an IF statement or common to all clauses of a SELECT statement can frequently be extracted to either immediately precede or follow the IF or SELECT statement. The programmer should make modifications whenever the readability of the program can be enhanced.

7. An Example Program

In this section the application of readability transformations to a production program is discussed. The particular program used here was selected because it was the smallest nontrivial program in a set of commercial data processing programs. The program turned out to be particularly unreadable. Multiple applications of every transformation mentioned above were used to make the program more readable. The program was modified in 13 separate passes. It began as a single PL/I procedure, P1, and finished as a program, P2, comprising six procedures, M1 through M6, with M1 identifying the residual mainline procedure. Table I shows some of the two program's basic statistical properties.

Although the lines of source text have increased by more than half, the program is actually smaller in many respects. Duplicate code in the form of header blocks of

Table I. Comparison of Basic Statistical Properties.

Property	P1	P2	M1	M2	M3	M4	M5	M6
Lines of source text	597	916	431	160	117	94	49	65
Identifiers	218	274	132	22	42	33	19	26
Non-DECLARE statements	270	336	176	83	29	23	8	17
CALL statements	3	48	25	12	5	2	1	3
Assignment statements	125	92	48	18	9	5	4	8
IF statements	24	39	21	11	3	3	0	0
DO statements	4	47	23	16	4	3	0	1
GO TO statements	80	0	0	0	0	0	0	0

179

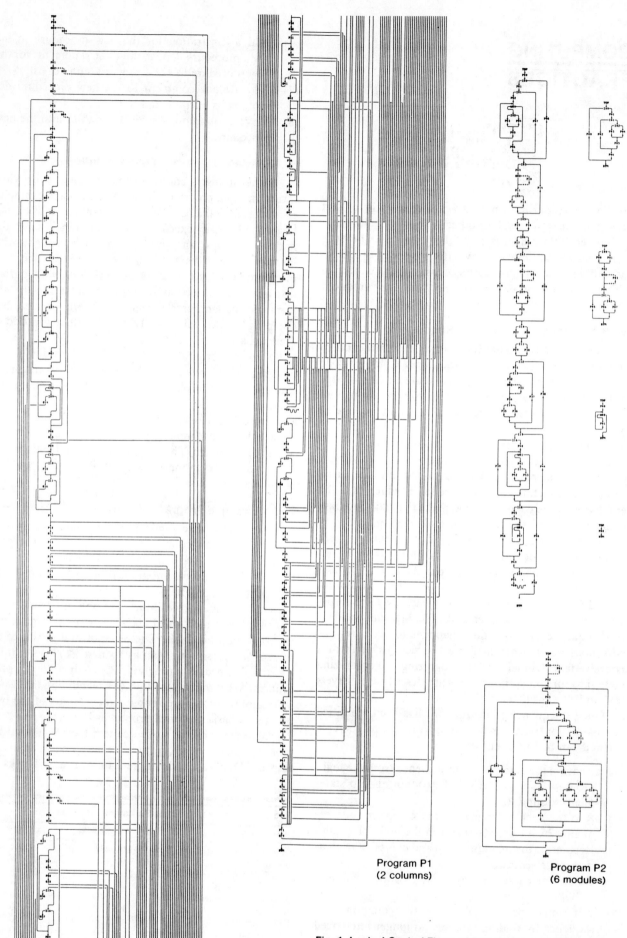

Program P1
(2 columns)

Program P2
(6 modules)

Fig. 1. Logical Control Flows of Two Versions of a Program.

comments and declarations accounts for most of the increase. Duplicate declarative information also accounts for the increase in identifiers. The extraction of subprocedures increases the number of CALL statements, while reducing the numbers of the type of statements extracted, such as assignment statements. All 80 GO TO statements were eliminated from the original program. The introduction of status variables and their testing account for the increase in IF statements. Introducing ELSE clauses and logically grouping blocks of code account for most of the increase in DO statements and a large increase in the total number of lines of text and total statements; 40 grouping DO-END blocks now exist in a program that started with none.

The load module increased in size from 8,800 bytes for P1 to 13,400 bytes for P2. This increase is due mostly to the additional prologue and epilogue code generated for the subprocedures. Execution measurements were not done for this program, but experience with other programs has shown that an improvement of 5 to 10 percent is not unusual.

The decrease in complexity of the logical flow was monitored as the program was modified. The cyclomatic complexity measure, introduced by McCabe [17] and discussed by Elshoff and Marcotty [8] and Myers [20], associated with the number of testable paths in the program was used. The results shown in Table II indicate that the complexity of the program was reduced by more than 40 with respect to its flow of control. The logical flow of the program was also mapped using the same conventions as were used in the flowgraphs illustrating the program samples earlier in this paper. Figure 1 is a photo-reduced picture of the logical flow of control for the program's two versions. The reader can readily observe the difference.

An experimental measure of program clarity described by Gordon [9] was also applied to the program after each pass. This clarity measure theoretically determines the effort required to understand the program.

With a factor of 43,200 (12 units/second, as suggested by Halstead [11]) used to convert the effort units to hours, the results are listed in Table III. Although this measurement indicated that the program grew slightly more complicated after a few initial passes, the end-result of applying the readability transformations represents a large reduction in the estimated effort required to understand the program.

Although the clarity measure has not been validated and must be treated as an average for any programmer, the relative difference seems to understate the case for the readable version of the program. In our opinion, the original program could not be fully understood in 24 hours. On the other hand, the program module M1, because of its use of status variables and the similarity of several sections of source text, should not require 8 hours to understand. The 13 passes to improve the program's readability required 16 hours to complete. A single pass took from 15 minutes to two hours. Thus, if we view the clarity measure as an absolute value, the total time to understand this program was increased by about four hours, a small amount of time that should easily be recouped when the program is modified. Real net benefits should then accrue on all subsequent modifications since the program will be more readable from the start.

8. Recommendation—A New Modification Cycle

A new step should be added to the modification cycle: modifying the program to make it readable. If the new program is judged to be already readable, this new step may be skipped. However, when the program is judged to be difficult to read, readability transformations should be applied to make it more readable.

The time to make a program readable is at the beginning of the modification cycle. The small investment will start paying dividend by making (1) the specifications for the modifications easier to write, (2) the estimate of the cost of the modifications more accurate, (3) the design for the modifications simpler, and (4) the implementation of the modifications less error-prone. Once the program is made readable, these benefits should apply to all future modifications as well. In fact, doing a better job on one modification cycle may eliminate the need for some future cycles.

Table II. Comparison of the Flow of Control.

Program	Cyclomatic complexity
P1 (before)	91
P2 (after)	52
M1	25
M2	16
M3	4
M4	4
M5	1
M6	2

Table III. Clarity—Time to Understand the Program.

Program	Time (hours)
P1 (before)	23.6
P2 (after)	11.4
M1	7.5
M2	2.8
M3	0.3
M4	0.4
M5	0.1
M6	0.3

The effective application of good programming practices to new program development and the application of readability transformations during the modification cycle should eventually result in an inventory of readable programs. However, until all the programs in an installation's inventory are readable, the modification cycle introduced in the first section of this report should be changed to the five-step cycle listed below, where step 2 has been inserted.

(1) The user requests that a program be changed.
(2) The source text of the program is made readable.
(3) The specifications for the change are written and the cost of the change estimated.
(4) It is decided that the changes are worth being made.
(5) The program is changed to meet the new specifications.

References

1. Ashcroft, E., and Manna, Z. The translation of 'GOTO' programs to 'WHILE' programs. Proc. 1971 IFIP Congress, Ljubljana, Yugoslavia, Aug. 1971, pp. 250–255. Demonstrates that every flowchart program can be written without GO TO statements by using WHILE statements.

2. Boehm, B. Software engineering. *IEEE Trans. Comptrs. C-25*, 12 (Dec. 1976), 1226–1241. Provides a definition of the term "software engineering" and a survey of the state of the art of software production in 1976. Contains an extensive set of references.

3. Dijkstra, E.W. GO TO statement considered harmful. *Comm. ACM 11*, 3 (March), 147–148. This famous letter contends that the quality of programmers is a decreasing function of the density of GO TOs in the programs they produce, and advocates the abolition of the GO TO from high-level languages because it is too primitive a construct.

4. Elshoff, J.L. A case study of experiences with top down design and structured programming. GMR-1742, Comptr. Sci. Dept., General Motors Res. Labs., Warren, Mich., Oct. 1974. Describes the author's personal experiences in consciously using top down development techniques and structured programming techniques.

5. Elshoff, J.L. Defensive programming. GMR-1799, Comptr. Sci. Dept., General Motors Res. Labs., Warren, Mich., Feb. 1975. Presents a description of the techniques of defensive programming and some of the trade-offs that should be considered by programmers using them.

6. Elshoff, J.L. An analysis of some commerical PL/I programs. *IEEE Trans. Software Eng. SE-2*, 2 (June 1976), 113–120. Presents the results of studying 120 commercial PL/I programs with respect to their size, readability, complexity, programming discipline, and use of programming language.

7. Elshoff, J.L. The influence of structured programming on PL/I program profiles. *IEEE Trans. Software Eng. SE-3*, 5 (Sept. 1977), 364–368. Studies two sets of commercial PL/I programs representing programming practice before and after the introduction of structured programming techniques.

8. Elshoff, J.L., and Marcotty, M. On the use of the cyclomatic number to measure program complexity. *SIGPLAN Notices 13*, 12 (Dec. 1978), 29–40. Further discussion of the cyclomatic complexity measure of McCabe [17] and its extension by Myers [20].

9. Gordon, R.D. Measuring improvements in program clarity. *IEEE Trans. Software Eng. SE-5*, 2 (March 1979), 79–90. A functional relation between the clarity of a program and the number and frequency of operators and operands in the program is presented. This measure of program clarity gives an estimate of the amount of mental effort required to understand the program.

10. Gries, D. *The Science of Programming*. Springer-Verlag, New York, 1981. Describes with many examples and exercises the basic principles behind the construction of programs that can be demonstrated to be correct through reasoning.

11. Halstead, M.H. *Elements of Software Science*. Elsevier North-Holland, New York, 1977. Halstead investigates the natural laws that govern the construction of programs and presents some measures of the effort required to write and understand programs.

12. IBM. *OS PL/I Checkout Compiler: Programmer's Guide*. Pub. SC33-0007, IBM Corp., White Plains, New York, Oct. 1976, 4th edition.

13. Kernighan, B.W., and Plauger, P.J. *The Elements of Programming Style*. McGraw-Hill, New York, 1974. A study of programming style that discusses the shortcomings of examples drawn from programming textbooks. General rules of style are then used to rewrite the examples for readability.

14. Lehman, M.M. Laws and conservation in large-program evolution. Proc. 2nd Software Life Cycle Management Workshop, Atlanta, Georgia, 1978 (IEEE Pub 78CH1390-4C, pp. 140–145). Lehman describes natural phenomena observed about the way in which the maintenance and evolution of large programs are planned, managed, and implemented.

15. Lientz, B.P., and Swanson, E. B. *Software Maintenance Management*. Addison-Wesley, Reading, Mass., 1980. The results of the authors' survey of almost 500 companies to compare software maintenance and costs.

16. Liu, C.C. A look at software maintenance. *Datamation 22*, 11 (Nov. 1976), 51–55. Investigates the problems of software maintenance and describes some improvements, in particular, in the areas of documentation and testing.

17. McCabe, T.J. A complexity measure. *IEEE Trans. Software Eng. SE-2*, 4 (Dec. 1976), 308–320. McCabe describes a graph-theoretic program complexity measure that depends only on the decision structure of the program. The use of this measure to manage and control program complexity is described.

18. Mills, H.D. Mathematical foundations for structured programming. Doc. FSC72-6012, IBM Federal Syst. Div., Gaithersburg, Md., Feb. 1972. The programming process is formulated as a step-by-step expansion of mathematical functions. A structure theorem guaranteeing that any program that can be represented as a flowgraph can be transformed into one containing only three types of structures—sequence, conditional, and iterative—is proved.

19. Myers, G.J. *Software Reliability*. John Wiley, New York, 1976. Defines software reliability, analyzes the major causes of unreliability, discusses the design and testing of reliable software, and touches on other factors in the production of reliable software such as project organization.

20. Myers, G.J. An extension to the cyclomatic measure of program complexity. *SIGPLAN Notices 12*, 10 (Oct. 1977), 61–64. Discusses anomalies found when calculating the complexity of a program under the assumption that it depends only on the program's decision structure and describes a simple extension to McCabe's complexity measure [17] to eliminate the anomalies.

21. Sheppard, S.B., et al. Modern coding practices and programmer performance. *IEEE Computer 12*, (Dec. 1979), 41–49. Describes the results of a series of experiments on the effects of modern coding practices on programming comprehension, program modification, and debugging performance.

22. Standish, T.A., et al. *The Irvine Program Transformation Catalogue*. Dept. Inform. and Comptr. Sci., Univ. of Calif. at Irvine, Irvine, Calif., 1976. A source book of ideas for improving programs through source-to-source transformations.

23. Stevens, W.P. *Using Structured Design*. Wiley-Interscience, New York, 1981. Illustrates the techniques of structured design with numerous examples that demonstrate guidelines for splitting a program into separate modules.

24. Yourdon, E. *Techniques of Program Structure and Design*. Prentice-Hall, Englewood-Cliffs, N.J., 1975. Discusses program design philosophies and methods; presents practical strategies for developing modular programs that are clear and readable.

USING AUTOMATED TECHNIQUES TO IMPROVE
THE MAINTAINABILITY OF EXISTING SOFTWARE

By KEVIN BURNS
Executive Vice President
Sage Software Products, Inc.

Reprinted with permission from *ISSD User's Conference/6—Maintenance*, 1981, pages 33-39. Copyright © 1981 by Ken Orr & Associates.

Since my presentation deals with automated techniques to improve the maintainability of existing software, I've selected a project recently completed by Sage as a case example. I think you will find it both interesting and informative. I selected this project because it shows a variety of alternative techniques applied on an integrated basis within a single project.

The Case Problem

A manufacturing oriented Fortune 500 company had contracted with an outside firm to build a state-of-the art material requirements planning system. The system was completed on-time and from the users' point of view was a booming success. In fact, the corporate vice president of manufacturing wanted to install the system at all computerized manufacturing facilities worldwide. That was the good news. The bad news was that from a data processing point of view, the source code was difficult to understand and almost impossible to maintain. The system consisted of 225,000 lines of unstructured, undocumented COBOL code. There were 85 separate modules and it was obvious that at least 15 different programmers had worked on the project; each with a slightly different flavor of programming style and naming conventions. To add insult to injury, the contract used a popular DBMS but did not use the companion Data Dictionary facility and each programmer used different internal data names for the same data element.

As you can imagine, DP management was extremely concerned about the cost of enhancing and maintaining the system given the current condition of the code, and the wide use planned. Nevertheless, the system had one redeeming quality; it worked and the users liked it.

While this is perhaps an acute case, I don't think it is completely atypical of the situation facing many DP organizations today. Most organizations have operational systems that meet the corporation's requirements, but are excessively expensive to maintain. The dilemma is what to do with these types of systems. Traditionally, the alternatives have not been very appealing. On one hand, solutions that superficially address the symptoms rarely produce any significant reduction in maintenance costs. Experience has shown the only way to significantly improve maintainability is to upgrade the quality of the source code and its associated documentation. On the other hand, rewriting existing systems is usually unpopular, risky, and expensive.

Assessment of Alternatives

In this particular case the company considered the following alternatives:

1. Sue the contractor.
2. Rewrite the system in house from the functional specs.
3. Live with the situation and perform maintenance by "brute force".
4. Inform users that no changes would be allowed.

Rewriting the system was conceptually the most appealing alternative, but was rejected for cost, lack of programmers to put on the project, and political reasons. After much analysis, the decision was made to retrofit structured code, documentation and the Dictionary from the inherited code. All factors considered, this was the only practical and feasible approach.

Measuring Maintainability

Many organizations can not even begin to improve maintainability, simply because they do not have both a clear definition of maintainability and a vehicle for measuring progress.

At Sage we use two concepts that may be helpful. Let's cover them so we can use them in discussing the case. The first is "Programmer Span of Control". Studies have shown that given the quality of a system, there is a finite number of lines of code a single programmer can effectively maintain. You may be shocked to hear that for unstructured code in a typical commercial system written in COBOL, average Span of Control is between 15-20,000 lines. When programmers are assigned work loads over the span of control threshold, maintainability deteriorates, getting worse over time. This phenomenon is called entrophy or introducing "noise".

The second key concept is the "Maintainability Index". Since Span of Control is a function of the quality of the code, it is essential to have a way to measure the quality. Our concept is to express the index on a relative scale of zero (impossible to maintain) to 10 (relatively easy to maintain). Actual scores are assigned to programs by applying a rating scheme which takes the following criteria into consideration:

*Degree to which the program meets a consistent style standard
*Correlation between program level documentation and the source code
*Average length of data names and labels
*Number of crossing GO TOs per program
*Number of overlapping PERFORMs per program
*Number of GO TOs that transfer out of the range of a PERFORM
*Consistency of data naming conventions across program boundaries
*Incidence of "dead code"
*Correlation of the paragraph ordering scheme against a **top-down** model

For the purpose of our discussion, the concept of the Maintainability Index is more important than the details. So I won't clutter things up by going over the actual algorithms that map these criteria to an actual score. The important message here is that you must have a way to measure maintainability. Your maintainability index must measure how easily a nonauthor could understand the program logic, identify where to make a change, and make the change without breaking another part of the program or system. The Maintainability Index combined with a reading on current and anticipated demand for changes will help you identify high payback candidates for retrofitting.

Project Goals

At the beginning of the project, the code had a Maintainability Index of 1.5. Based on this score the Span of Control can be projected to be approximately 15,000 lines of code per programmer. It is easy to see that to be effective, the company would require a maintenance staff of 15 people (225,000 lines/15,000), to handle the anticipated high demand for changes typical of a new system. This particular company has a standard cost for programmers of $40,000 including overhead. Personnel costs for system maintenance prior to upgrading were estimated at $600,000 for the first year. The overall goal of the upgrade project was to increase the Index to at least 7.0 and thereby reduce the maintenance staff to 4 people and decrease the cost to $160,000.

Automated Software Tools Assembled for the Retrofit

1. Analysis module to document and monitor the Maintainability Index.

2. Program Reformat Utility to invoke a consistent style (e.g., one verb per line, indentation conventions, etc.).

3. Automatic Dictionary Development facility to automate source code analysis and create an input stream for the Dictionary loader.

4. Structured Upgrade Facility which reads arbitrary COBOL source code and outputs structured block diagram pseudo code.

5. Structured Preprocessor Facility that will read the pseudo code and generate structured COBOL as output.

6. Intelligent Compare facility to ensure that retrofitted programs are, in fact, functionally equivalent to their predecessor.

Without these types of tools, the only way to accomplish the project goals would have been a manual rewrite.

Application of the Tools in the Retrofit Process

1. **Baseline statistics and analysis** All code was processed through the Analysis Module in order to document the Maintainability Index and chart an appropriate upgrade plan. At this stage, we determined that three steps would have to be accomplished. These were: A) resolve data name inconsistencies and populated the Dictionary, B) reformat the code to a consistent style standard and, C) regenerate the code in **top–down - structured programming** format.

2. **Dictionary Analysis** The analysis module from No. 1 above saved program level cross-reference information in an output file. By inputting the common data structures at the "01" level, the Automatic Dictionary Development facility produced an alphabetical report of data names, aliases and their usage on a system-wide basis. Through a series of intermediate review and edit steps, an accurate picture of data

names, aliases and the defacto data model was created and stored on disk.

3. **Dictionary Population** The output from the Automatic Dictionary Development step was then converted to the required format of the Dictionary loader utility. Once this information was populated in the Dictionary, the DBA nominated standard data names for internal program references.

4. **Standardization of Datanames** New Data Divisions of the 10 programs were generated with the standard data names using the DD/DB preprocessor. The programs were then run through the Structured Upgrade Facility. During this process, the parser identified the usage of the old data names in the Procedure Division and replaced them with the new standard names.

5. **Style Reformat** The test programs were then reformatted. The style standard was one verb per line and indentation to show the hierarchy of data names and conditional logic. At this stage the programs had consistent, meaningful data names and were significantly easier to read. The Maintainabiltiy Index was checked and found to be 3.25. While substantially improved, the programs were still lacking because of their internal structural complexity. Reformatting prior to structured upgrade also improves the quality of the upgrade output.

6. **Structured Upgrade** The Structural Upgrade Facility was used to unwind the logic of the code and generate a functionally equivalent program written in **top-down** structured pseudo. The pseudo code has the following characteristics:

    *   The pseudo code is a block diagram outline of the program logic expressed in a COBOL-like syntax

    *   Paragraphs have a single entry and exit point

    *   Paragraphs are ordered in **top-down** sequence. Paragraphs which are the target of a PERFORM fall below the **performing** paragraph

    *   Indentation actually controls the conditional logic of the program

    *   The COBOL loop mechanism GO TO and PERFORM. . . VARYING) is expressed with a new verb combination i.e., REPEAT. . . UNTIL

* ELSE-IF is used to express the COBOL **case** statement

* Any construction can be indented under any conditional expression thus eliminating the need for GO TOs to do complex logic

* PERFORM THRU is not necessary since paragraph names are only used as names of paragraphs and not as destination of GO TOs

7. **Map to Native COBOL** Final test code was generated from the pseudo code using the Structured Preprocessor. If the Structured Upgrade Facility generated the native COBOL code directly, then there would be no way to ensure that upgraded code stays in the structured format as future maintenance occurs. This particular client made the decision to perform all future maintenance at the pseudo code level.

8. **Testing** The sample COBOL job stream was compiled and executed against baseline test data-output results were compared against a "before" run using the Intelligent Compare facility. Three iterations of steps four thru seven were required before satisfactory results were achieved.

9. **Check on Maintainability Index** The Maintainability Index was checked and found to be 6.75 as an average. Although the Index was slightly under the project goal of 7.0 the decision was made to accept this level of maintainability. Further improvement would have required a redesign of some of the larger modules.

10. **Production Run of the Entire Process** The remaining 75 programs were run through steps one thru nine. Prior to upgrading, the best program had an Index of 4.25 the worst one scored .5. Six programs required manual editing in order to fit into the production process.

Summary and Conclusions

The entire project took 90 calendar days. The overall cost to the client was $167,000 including software license fees, and technical support. The firm had three estimates of the cost of rewriting the system. The lowest was $1.85 million.

Today this organization is effectively making major enhancements to the MRP system with a staff of three maintenance programmers. An interesting side benefit was that performance measured in terms of wall clock execution time was improved by 15 percent.

Thank you for your attention. I hope in reviewing the case, I have spared some ideas on how automated techniques might assist you in coping with your own in-house maintenance requirements.

Salvaging your software asset (tools based maintenance)

by MICHAEL J. LYONS

The Catalyst Corporation
LaGrange, Illinois

"Salvaging Your Software Asset (Tools Based Maintenance)" by M.J. Lyons. This material appears in *AFIPS Conference Proceedings Volume 50, 1981 National Computer Conference*, pages 337-341.

ABSTRACT

Software is a valuable asset embodying decision processes of an organization and contributing directly to the means of production. Maintenance is the mechanism for combating deterioration of that software asset, which over time tends to become arthritic and inflexible to change. Maintenance, though extremely costly, is essential to insuring the viability of the organization. Both rewrites and purchased software, with ensuing conversions, are usually not a cost-effective solution to software decay. Structured retrofit is an effective alternative, using a software tools-based methodology for combating decay and the high costs of maintenance. The critical tool is the COBOL structured programming engine. With it, spaghetti code software is mechanically transformed to well-structured programs, whose ongoing maintenance reaps the benefits of the structured programming methodologies.

INTRODUCTION

Software is an asset. It is an owned resource that contributes to the means of production. It is costly to acquire and even more costly to replace. To insure maximum return on one's software investment requires prolonging software's usable life and making best use of that life. It is essential to mine that software asset in order to maximize its role as a major contributor to the means of production and overall organizational productivity.

The function of software is to embody a subset of the enterprises's decision processes and to enable them to be carried out by computer machinery. It is the decision processes of the enterprise that are at issue. They are unique to the organization and vital to its prosperity. It is software's embodiment of the organization's decision processes that makes it a direct contributor to the means of production. Indeed, one might say that the survival of the organization depends on insuring the vitality of software.

Software is not a physical machine, and it therefore does not wear out. By the same token, it is not like a small child, which can improve its capabilities or change its attitudes over time. Therein lies the cause of software deterioration: its inability to change itself to match the changing decision processes of the enterprise. Software progressively loses its pro-

ductive capacity unless it is continually infused with the ongoing changes in the enterprise's decision system. This process of adaptation and enhancement is called software maintenance. Whether it corrects bugs, changes the specifications, or improves efficiency, *maintenance* for the purposes of this paper is any change to any system for any reason. The process of maintaining software is unexpectedly difficult and expensive. The typical Fortune 500 company today spends 70% of its (non-operations) data processing budget on maintenance.[1] I have already said that software, unlike a child, does not grow smarter and more capable; unfortunately, it does seem to grow old and cranky. The very act of changing it tends to destroy or obscure its structure[2,3] (spaghetti code and untrustworthy documentation) and make it progressively more resistant to change. I sometimes call this condition *software arthritis*—the buildup of deposits in the joints of the organism that make it less and less flexible. Remember that flexibility is the characteristic required to preserve the productivity of the asset. Therefore, preserving flexibility—combating software arthritis—is the key element in protecting the asset; and it is the subject of this paper.

Before a discussion on combating software arthritis, let me first point out why the maintenance function will not go away, and, furthermore, why its costs and complexity are on the increase.

IS REWRITE A SOLUTION?

If software deteriorates over time, why don't we rewrite it? Software rewrite is economically unacceptable. An inventory of one Fortune 500 company's software library, shown in Table I, points out why. These statistics were taken from a Chicago-based diversified manufacturing firm.[18] They point out some interesting facts. First, in this case, software represents a very substantial one-third-billion-dollar asset, assuming a cost of $10/line to rewrite. Note that this figure is the most conservative one we could find. A more commonly quoted figure is $25/line.[4,5]

Second, since all programs are not equal, let us assume a strategic approach to a rewrite. The 80/20 rule states that "20% of the programs cause 80% of the problems and corresponding costs." Assuming the ability to weed the good from the bad, in this case we are left with 10,000 tin gods—my term

TABLE I—Appraisal of a software rewrite

Number of COBOL programs:	50,000
Average number of lines/program:	750
Total lines of COBOL code:	37,500,000
Replacement value of code:	$375 million

ASSUME 80/20 RULE:
50,000 × 80% programs = 40,000 programs
50,000 × 20% programs = 10,000 programs

COST TO REWRITE THE 20% HIGH-PAYOFF CANDIDATES
10,000 programs × 750 lines = 7,500,000 lines
7,500,000 lines × $10/line = $75 million

LABOR TIME FOR HIGH-PAYOFF REWRITE
7.5 million lines/(15 good lines/day × 240 productive days/year) = 2,015 RESOURCE YEARS

for any program most often described as "My god, don't touch that or it'll blow up." If we decided to rewrite the tin gods at an average rate of 15 good-debugged lines/day[6] it would cost $75 million. Even if funding were available, it would take over 2,000 resource-years to do the job. When 13% of the data processing jobs in America today are open and there is no one to fill them, when there is a current shortfall of 58,000 programmers,[1,7] who is going to do such a rewrite? In short, a rewrite is not a viable alternative! It might be worth noting that although the example used here represents a large company, the circumstances are linear. That is, if your particular company is small, then your library is smaller and your rewrite task is smaller, but so is your budget and staff.

THE MAINTENANCE DILEMMA

Notwithstanding the criticality of software to the organization, arthritic software is a special maintenance headache for management. Spaghetti code and untrustworthy documentation are not new; management has been facing them for years. Familiarity, however, is not control. The exponential growth in maintenance costs is directly attributable to our inability to control or improve on the quality and human maintainability of our systems. In 1960 the typical data processing organization spent 30% of its nonoperations budget on maintenance; in 1970 it spent 50%; today it spends 70%.[1] The primary reasons for high maintenance cost are

1. Maintenance is a people-intensive activity. While the cost of hardware plummets, the cost of people is rising. By 1985 the cost of hardware will be at 1/10 the 1979 rate, and people will be at twice the 1979 rate.[8]
2. The number of systems in our inventory has increased substantially, correspondingly increasing the maintenance load. Average systems life has increased from three years in 1960 to five in 1970 and eight today.[18]
3. Existing systems were designed to operate in a stand-alone fashion, but today we have new requirements from

TABLE II—The structured programming methodologies

CHIEF PROGRAMMER TEAM
DEVELOPMENT SUPPORT LIBRARIES
TOP-DOWN DESIGN
STRUCTURED PROGRAMMING
STRUCTURED WALKTHROUGHS
STRUCTURED TESTING

middle and top management. We are trying to revise existing operational-level systems in order to support control and planning-level systems.[9,10]

This last point is the one that most influences maintenance costs for the 1980's.[9,10] The primary reason 7 out of 10 programmers are involved in maintenance today is that those lower-level operational systems were designed for hardware efficiency and not human maintainability. Costs of maintenance have become alarming because the lower-level systems can not easily support the higher-level systems demanded today.

Should we scrap existing code and start again? There is little argument that code in most operational level systems today is difficult to maintain, but that difficulty does not make the programs bad. Bad code is not the same as bad programs. It is critical to remember that all code, even spaghetti, meets operational-level user requirements but is now subject to sweeping changes mandated to support control and planning-level systems.[9] The basic logic is sound and proven; the code reflecting it is not. The question here is whether the structured programming methodologies can be employed to advantage in improving the code (see Table II).

These methodologies are being introduced into new systems every day and have had a substantial impact on subquent costs of maintenance. Normally, when the structured programming methodologies are used in development, subquent maintenance costs and effort are reduced by a 3:1 ratio.[11,12,20] However, it is usually uneconomic to rewrite or convert operational-level systems in order to facilitate development of new control- and planning-level systems.

Fortunately, there is an alternative that preserves the logal integrity of the operational-level systems and at the same time provides a well-structured basis for comprehensive maintenance and future systems growth. It involves introducing the structured programming methodologies and their benefits to existing systems reliably and promptly, *after the fact,* through the use of software tools. It is called *structured retrofit.* Structured retrofit is the application of today's structured proming methodologies to yesterday's systems in order to meet tomorrow's demand. Through this method the organization can combat software arthritis, continue to get payback from existing systems, and still meet demands to build on them, thereby salvaging its software asset.

The remainder of this paper presents a software-tools-based methodology for introducing structured programming into existing code. The structured-retrofit procedures, methodologies, and software tools have all come together for beta testing at FMC Corporation for the past year. FMC Corporation is a 3.5-billion-dollar-a-year diversified corporation. Its data processing facilities involve a worldwide network tied into large IBM mainframes, supporting a library of approximately 35,000 COBOL programs, from which we have drawn our testing sample population. The procedures for structured retrofit used during beta testing at FMC are described in the remainder of this paper.[18]

STRUCTURED RETROFIT

Structured retrofit, a concept and methodology pioneered by Jon Cris Miller,[13,14,15,16,17] involves the establishment of a task force made up along the lines of a chief programmer team. This team has responsibility for scoring the existing software library, isolating high-payoff candidates for retrofit, conducting the retrofit, and finally, validating its success. The task force has a basic arsenal, made up of the following software tools, assembled from various organizations around the United States: Code evaluators, formatter, structuring engine, optimizer, and file-to-file compare utility. (Other software tools are being considered for future use, including but not limited to automated documenters, job schedulers, and test vehicles.) Their use, described below, minimizes human clerical activity and maximizes mechanical processes.

Scoring

Scoring combines both objective evaluation of the software through the use of code evaluation tools and subjective input from managers and users. The objective evaluation determines the degree of structure in a program, the level of nesting, the degree of complexity, the breakout of verb utilization, and failure analysis; and it presents a concise trace of control logic. With it, we have a clear appraisal of the quality of the code.[14,18] However, no matter how low a piece of code rates during the objective evaluation, if that code runs week after week without problems and never requires enhancement, then obviously it is a low-priority candidate for retrofit. In short, scoring must involve more than just an appraisal of code. It must also be a predictor of upcoming maintenance, enhancements, and planned replacement. There is no substitute for subjective input from management and users.

Compilation

Once the high-payoff candidates have been strategically isolated, they are compiled. One of the fundamental assumptions behind a retrofit is that programs must compile cleanly and be currently operational. Those that do not compile cleanly are referred to the appropriate department for cortion. The retrofit procedures are not a mechanism for making nonoperational systems operational.

Restructuring

The source code is then put through a structured proming engine. For purposes of this presentation, a structuring engine is a software tool with two properties:

- It transforms an executable program written in a given language, but of undetermined structure, into another program written in the same language with a well-defined structure.
- The resulting program produces the same transformation on any set of input data as does the original program.

Further discussion of structured programming and of a structured programming engine will follow shortly.

Formatting

Once restructured, the source code is then put through a formatting package in order to enhance the visuals and readability. Following formatting, the newly transformed code is then recompiled to insure that there are no syntactic errors. A formatting package can be expected to substantially enhance the visuals. Standard features of a good formatting package can be seen in Table III. I am also aware of development on a formatting package that will eliminate qualification of data names. For move corresponding, it currently requires that the user manually expand each qualified move before eliminating qualification mechanically.

Validation

Once recompiled, the validation mechanism begins. A set of input data is processed through the old program, then through the new program. The resulting outputs are then compared by a file-to-file compare utility. One certainly does not want to employ a visual scan of output reports to insure that they are identical. A mechanical bit-for-bit comparison is far more accurate, simple, and fast. Ideally, one uses copies of live files for a comprehensive validation.

Optimization

In conjunction with compilation, the program passes through an object code optimizer. Whether restructuring is done manually or through automated mechanisms, one expects to introduce some overhead as a consequence of restructuring. However, experience to date indicates that little net overhead remains if an optimizer is used. Initial experimentation resulted in a 20% increase in core requirements from optimized original code compared to optimized restructured code. However, recent improvements in the structuring engine algorithms indicate only an average of 8% overhead and suggest the possibility of absolute improvements.

Retrofit Results

Retrofit goes beyond description and prescription to produce a completed product: well-structured source code logically equivalent to the original. It cannot, however, eliminate logic errors; determine intent; or react to user requirements, demands, and complaints. It does not solve the maintenance problem, but it does simplify the solution. It provides a base-

TABLE III—Features of a formatter

- Indents and formats code
- Standardizes paragraph prefixes
- Relevels data division
- Standardizes field alignment
- Standardizes reserved words
- Restricts verbs to one per line
- Provides global name substitution

line for cost-effective maintenance by making existing systems understandable.

WHAT IS STRUCTURED PROGRAMMING?

If I were to ask 10 different people for a definition of structured programming, I would probably get 10 different answers. But, suffice it to say for our purposes, structured programming is a method of programming according to a set of rules that enhance a program's readability and maintainability. Structured programming centers around the concept of a module having a single entry point and a single exit point. Structured programming involves the separating of control from action so that the logic flow becomes clearer to human beings, even though a computer obviously doesn't care.

STRUCTURED PROGRAMMING ENGINES

Structured programming engines could theoretically be developed for any programming language. However, to my knowledge, the only two languages for which they currently exist are FORTRAN and COBOL. The FORTRAN engine, developed by Caine, Farber & Gordon, Inc., has been in existence since 1975 and is used in conjunction with a superset of FORTRAN.[19] The only commercially available COBOL structured programming engine, to my knowledge, is the one developed at the Catalyst Corporation by Jon Cris Miller.[18] A structured programming engine accomplishes two things. First, it cleans up existing language and verb usage; second, it introduces consistent structure to the code. Table IV shows what you can expect from a COBOL structured programming engine. A structured programming engine and a good formatting package cover and correct a multitude of sins. The most important result is an isolated control hierarchy. Isolating control provides clear visibility of the algorithms used in that program. In COBOL, the primary control structures used are loops and decision trees.

Unfortunately, most programs employ them on a global rather than a local basis, to construct algorithms. Being able to see control in tight, small modules allows clear visibility and understanding of the program and its component algorithms. If one ever really expects to introduce the concept of reusability of code, there is no better asset to mine than an operational software library. Structured retrofit potentially leads to an inventory of existing algorithms and a practical mechanism for the reusability of code.

TRANSFORMATION RATE

Can a structuring engine handle any program? Judging from personal experience and the results obtained from the beta testing, our engine can process 60% of programs offered immediately and an additional 20% with some manual intervention. The other 20% we cannot handle cost-effectively now. These percentages seem to be consistent with those of Caine, Farber & Gordon.[19] One example of code that requires manual manipulation in order to restructure it is structurally recursive code. Technically, COBOL does not support recursive code. However, some programmers have discovered that by using switches they can terminate a seemingly endless chain of PERFORM flip-flops. It is sometimes difficult to determine compiler tolerances to syntax violations, as in the case of delimiters, reserved words, and margin alignment. When in doubt, we have always elected to follow the ANS COBOL standards.

NON-TASK-FORCE RESPONSIBILITIES

In addition to tasks performed by the retrofit task force, there are tasks to be done by other members of the participating organization:

1. Provide source code for retrofit.
2. Provide copies of live test data for validation of the retrofit. If already available, comprehensive artificial test data may be employed.
3. Review the dead code list to verify that code is not required.
4. Provide on-site computer time.

While the process is primarily mechanical, there is still a substantial amount of work for the retrofit task force and selected members of the host organization. However, the process offers *no* disruption to the user community.

TABLE IV—Features of a COBOL structuring engine

Cleans up language	Removes alters
	Eliminates perform through overlap
	Reduces go tos
	Increases performs
	Converts notes to comments
	Eliminates drop through confusion
	Removes dead code
Structures	Isolates control hierarchy
	Highlights looping conditions
	Bounds action modules
	Physically groups and standardizes all I/O
	Consolidates all program termination to a single goback
	Does not remove logic errors

TABLE V—Reasons to retrofit

- Cut maintenance costs substantially.
- Divert maintenance resources to new development.
- Meet user requirements on a timely basis.
- Decrease programmer turnover.
- Decrease the number of systems designated incapable of cost-effective maintenance.
- Increase the number of systems capable of sustaining major enhancements without a rewrite or extensive testing.
- Limit the need for a specialized person to maintain each system.
- Simplify tuning, reconfiguring, and rewrites to take advantage of cost and technological opportunities.
- Standardize the multiple programming styles found in a program written or maintained by more than one programmer.
- Cut research costs when the user says, "I suspect something is wrong."
- Insure consistency with mechanically verifiable standards

SUMMARY

In this paper I have introduced structured retrofit, a complex process. It is not a new process in other production areas of the business world, but it is new to data processing. Table V reviews the primary benefits of retrofit.

In closing, let me emphasize two very important points:
- Software, of all ages, shapes and sizes, is a valuable asset to a corporation.
- The corporation can reap the benefits of the structured programming methodologies from currently unstructured systems, thereby salvaging its software asset.

Structured retrofit of application systems decreases costs, increases productivity, and improves morale. As compared to a manual rewrite, it is virtually 100% mechanical, requires little elapsed time, makes minimal demands on managerial and technical staffs, and is completely transparent to the user. Structured retrofit fights software decay.

ACKNOWLEDGMENTS

Putting pen to paper is a difficult chore for me. I owe thanks to many for contributing to this paper: To Jon Cris Miller, who not only acted as editor, but, more important, introduced me to retrofit concepts. To FMC Corporation, our retrofit beta test site, which has endured our failures and enjoyed our success. To Nicholas Zvegintzov, for his insights on software as an asset. Last, to my wife, without whose support there would be nothing. The errors and omissions remain my own.

REFERENCES

1. Cooper, J.J. "Software Factory." *Raytheon Data Services.* Burlington, Massachusetts, 1980 p. 13.
2. Brooks, F.P., Jr. *The Mythical Man-Month* (3rd ed.) Reading, Massachusetts: Addison-Wesley, 1975.
3. Belady, L.A., and Lehman, M.M. "A Model of Large Program Development". *IBM Systems Journal,* (Vol. 15, No. 3), 1976, pp. 225-252.
4. Lehman, J.H., "How Software Projects Are Really Managed." *Datamation,* 25 (1979), pp. 118-129.
5. Jones, C. "Optimizing Program Quality and Programmer Productivity." *Proceedings of GUIDE 45,* 2 (1977), pp. 689-705.
6. Yourdon, E.N. *Techniques of Program Structure and Design.* Englewood Cliffs, New Jersey: Prentice-Hall, 1975.
7. Editors of Business Week. "Missing Computer Software." *Business Week,* No. 2652 (Sept. 1, 1980), pp. 46-56.
8. Diebold, J. "The Annual Diebold Technology Scan 1979." *The Diebold Computer Planning and Management Service,* 1979, 89pp.
9. Nolan, R.L. "Managing the Crisis in Data Processing." *Harvard Business Review,* 57 (1979), pp. 115-126.
10. Danziger, J., Kraemer, K., and King, J. "An Assessment of Computer Technology in U.S. Local Government." *Urban Systems 3,* 1978, pp. 21-37.
11. Diebold, J. "Improving the Utilization of Personnel Resources." *The Diebold Computer Planning and Management Service,* August, 1979, pp. 44-46.
12. Ryan, H.W. "Structured Methods." *Computerworld* 13 (1979), pp. INDEPTH/1-24.
13. Miller, J.C. "Some thoughts on Structured and Traditional Programming." Unpublished paper, Montgomery Wards Corporate Systems Division, 1975, 4pp.
14. Miller, J.C. "Improved Programming Technologies Retrofit (A Study of the Application of Improved Programming Technologies to Systems Developed without Improved Programming Technologies." Unpublished report, Montgomery Wards Corporate Systems Division, 1976, 46pp.
15. Miller, J.C. "Sow's Ear: The Structuring Engine (COBOL)." *Yink, The Weekly Memo to Yourdon Instructors,* Nov. 18, 1977. pp. 1-3.
16. Miller, J.C. "S.E.—The Structuring Engine." Unpublished paper, 1979, 14 pp.
17. Miller, J.C. "Structured Retrofit." *Techniques of Program and System Maintenance.* Lincoln, Nebraska: Ethnotech, 1980, pp. 85-86.
18. Lyons, M.J. "Structured Retrofit—1980." *Proceedings of SHARE 55,* (1980), pp. 263-265.
19. de Balbine, G. "Better Manpower Utilization Using Automatic Restructuring." Caine, Farber and Gordon, Inc., *AFIPS Proceedings of the National Computer Conference,* 1975, pp. 319-327.
20. Daly, E.B. "Organizing for Successful Software Development." *Datamation,* 25 (1979), pp. 106-120.

EVOLUTION OF A SOFTWARE MAINTENANCE TOOL

Henry W. Morgan

It has been said that the best products of man's creativity are those born of necessity. The emergence of two related software maintenance tools, exemplify this observation.

We are going to discuss the succession of events, including successes and failures, which led to the evolution of these tools.

Recognizing the need

Since 1969, Group Operations, Incorporated has been in the business of developing and maintaining EDP systems for its clients. In many instances these efforts involved taking over an existing system that our programmers and analysts had never seen before.

The first thing we would always ask for was the program documentation. As you would probably guess, this request was almost always met with a blank stare. In a few instances where documentation was available it was invariably out of date. If there is one thing that is worse than no documentation it is documentation that is wrong. And there are good reasons for this situation. In the course of bouncing from one crisis to another there really isn't time to document. Plus the fact that it is no fun. When was the last time you heard a programmer say "Boy, I can't wait to finish this program so I can start on the documentation!". So the problem with documentation is that nobody has time to do it, nobody wants to do it, and so it doesn't get done. And if it ever did exist when the program was first developed the code has probably been modified so many times that the original documentation is wrong anyway.

So where does all this leave the poor soul who suddenly finds himself having to work on an bunch of programs he has never seen before. Obviously there has to be a feeling of helplessness and frustration.

The time required to learn what our client's programs do and how they work represented a sizeable cost to Group Operations, Incorporated. How do you cut these costs and help our people do a better job? That was the challenge.

The anwser? Develop a static analyzer.

The Solution - SCAN/370

The first step was to develop a simulator that simulates the execution of a COBOL program in such a way as to exercise every possible data condition which could ever occur at run time - without actually executing the program itself. This approach assures that every possible logic path is included in the analysis - a capability which a run time analyzer cannot provide.

Conciseness

Once the simulator was completed the next questions was "What do we do with the plethora of information which was collected during the simulation process?"

Reprinted with permission from *The Proceedings of the Second National Conference on EDP Software Maintenance*, 1984, pages 268-278. Copyright © 1984 by H.W. Morgan.

The first decision was that the information generated by SCAN/370 had to be concise. Past experience with reams of output generated by automatic flowcharters led us to the following conclusion:

"The usefulness of any analysis tool is inversely proportional to the volume of its output."

To meet this requirement a hierchical charting technique was developed which graphically describes every possible processing path which can ever occur at run time - and yet require 80% less output than the listing of the program itself.

S C A N / 3 7 0				**HIERARCHICAL PROCESSING CHART**	**THRU LEVEL 99**	**PROGRAM-ID - USER**												
LINE NBR	BRANCH AT	TO	BRANCH TYPE	**T O P D O W N L E V E L S T R U C T U R**														
				1	2	3	4	5	6	7	8	9	10	11	12	13	14	
1	00145	00145	ENTRY	PROCEDURE/DIVISION.														
2	00148	00165	PERFORM	<-->PAR-IN.														
3	00154	00167	PERFORM	<-->LOCATR.														
4	00168	00174	PERFORM	<-->LOAD-LOC-TABLE.														
5	00176	00176	FALL THRU	NXT-LOC.														
6	00177	00165	PERFORM	<-->PAR-IN**2.														
7	00179	00190	CDTL GO TO	?-->LOAD-LOC-EXIT.														
8	00184	00176	CDTL GO TO	?-->NXT-LOC--->5.														
9	00188	00159	PERFORM	<-->WRITE-RPT.														
10	00189	00156	GO TO	CLOSE-FILES.*RANGE														
11	00158	00158	STOP	STOP.														
12	00169	00169	CALL	'TBLSORT'.														
13	00173	00197	PERFORM	<-->LOC-RPT.														
14	00198	00203	PERFORM	<-->BLD-PG-HDG.														
15	00209	00159	PERFORM	<-->WRITE-RPT**9.														
16	00211	00159	PERFORM	<-->WRITE-RPT**9.														
17	00199	00214	PERFORM	<-->BLD-PAGE.														
18	00216	00219	PERFORM	<-->FIND-COL-B.														
19	00223	00223	FALL THRU	FIND-NXT.														
20	00226	00240	CDTL GO TO	?-->FOUND-COL-B.														
21	00235	00240	CDTL GO TO	?-->FOUND-COL-B**20														
22	00239	00223	GO TO	FIND-NXT--->19.														
23	00218	00245	PERFORM	<-->BLD-LINES.														
24	00247	00253	PERFORM	<-->LOAD-A.														
25	00258	00258	FALL THRU	NXT-X.														
26	00264	00268	CDTL GO TO	?-->LOAD-A-EXIT.														
27	00266	00268	CDTL GO TO	?-->LOAD-A-EXIT**26.														
28	00267	00258	GO TO	NXT-X--->25.														
29	00250	00289	PERFORM	<-->LOC-DTL-OUT.														
30	00296	00159	PERFORM	<-->WRITE-RPT**9.														
31	00252	00245	CDTL GO TO	?-->BLD-LINES--->23.														
32	00200	00297	PERFORM	<-->BLD-PAGE-CLOSE.														
33	00299	00159	PERFORM	<-->WRITE-RPT**9.														
34	00302	00302	FALL THRU	BLD-PAGE-END.														
35	00303	00176	PERFORM	<-->NXT-LOC.														
36	00177	00165	PERFORM	<-->PAR-IN**2.														
37	00179	00190	CDTL GO TO	?-->LOAD-LOC-EXIT.														
38	00184	00176	CDTL GO TO	?-->NXT-LOC--->35.														
39	00188	00159	PERFORM	<-->WRITE-RPT**9.														
40	00189	00156	GO TO	CLOSE-FILES.*RANGE														
41	00158	00158	STOP	STOP.														
42	00305	00197	CDTL GO TO	?-->LOC-RPT--->13.*RANGE														
43	00307	00310	CDTL GO TO	?-->TERM-RT.														
44	00312	00176	CDTL PERFORM	?<-->NXT-LOC**35.														
45	00313	00313	CDTL STOP	?-->STOP.														
46	*****	*****	***********	*RUNAWAY PATH TERMINATED.														
47	00308	00308	FALL THRU	BLD-PAGE-SWITCH.														
48	00308	00302	ALTER GO TO	?-->BLD-PAGE-END--->34.														
49	00309	00297	GO TO	BLD-PAGE-CLOSE--->32.														
50	00202	00197	CDTL GO TO	?-->LOC-RPT--->13.														
51	00156	00156	FALL THRU	CLOSE-FILES.														
52	00158	00158	STOP	STOP.														

0   1   2   3   4   5   6   7   8   9   10   11   12   13   14   15

Convenience

While the SCAN/370 Hierarchical Processing Charts proved to be very useful to our programmers in comprehending the logical flow of the program, one major criticism surfaced again and again. When a programmer was immersed in the source listing of the program it was inconvenient to have to flip to a separate document to determine the logical relationships of a given paragraph to other paragraphs within the program. This problem was analyzed and it was determined that the best solution was to put the pertinent information from the charts right at the programmer's fingertips as in-line narrative comments within the source listing.

```
00176    SCAN****-------------------------------------------------------------*
00176    SCAN***| 1. FALL THRU FROM 00174 LOAD-LOC-TABLE.                      |
00176    SCAN***| 2. PERFORMED THRU LOAD-LOC-EXIT BY 00302 BLD-PAGE-END,       |
00176    SCAN***|    00310 TERM-RT.                                            |
00176    SCAN***| 3. BEGINS PROCESSING LOOP RETURNING FROM 00176 NXT-LOC.      |
00176    SCAN****-------------------------------------------------------------*
00176    044700 NXT-LOC.
00177    044800     PERFORM PAR-IN
00178    044900     IF EOF-SW = 1
00179    045000         GO TO LOAD-LOC-EXIT.
00180    045100     MOVE PAR TO LOC-SEQ (L)
00181    045200     MOVE ST  TO LOC-REF (L)
00182    045300     SET L UP BY 1
00183    045400     IF L NOT > L-LIM
00184    SCAN***                      FOLLOWING CREATES PROCESSING LOOP ***********
00184    045500         GO TO NXT-LOC.
00185    045600     MOVE 'LOCATOR TABLE EXCEEDED. LOCATOR REPORT BYPASSED.'
00186    045700     TO RPT-BDY
00187    045750     MOVE +12 TO RETURN-CODE
00188    045800     PERFORM WRITE-RPT
00189    SCAN***                      FOLLOWING EXCEEDS PERFORM RANGE ***********
00189    045900     GO TO CLOSE-FILES.
00190    SCAN****-------------------------------------------------------------*
00190    SCAN***| 1. ALTERNATIVE PATH FROM 00176 NXT-LOC.                      |
00190    SCAN****-------------------------------------------------------------*
00190    046000 LOAD-LOC-EXIT.
00191    046100     IF L NOT = 1
00192    046200         SET L DOWN BY 1.
00193    046300     SET L-LIM TO L.
00194    046350     MOVE L-LIM TO SORT-ENTRIES
00195    046400     SET L, L-A, L-B TO 1
00196    046500     MOVE ZERO TO LST-LOC-A, LST-LOC-B.
0019?    SCAN****-------------------------------------------------------------*
00197    SCAN***| 1. PERFORMED BY 00167 LOCATR.                                |
00197    SCAN***| 2. BEGINS PROCESSING LOOP RETURNING FROM 00197 LOC-RPT,      |
00197    SCAN***|    00302 BLD-PAGE-END.                                       |
00197    SCAN****-------------------------------------------------------------*
00197    046600 LOC-RPT SECTION.
00198    046700     PERFORM BLD-PG-HDG
00199    046800     PERFORM BLD-PAGE
00200    046900     PERFORM BLD-PAGE-CLOSE
00201    047000     IF END-B = '0'
00202    SCAN***                      FOLLOWING CREATES PROCESSING LOOP ***********
00202    047100         GO TO LOC-RPT.
00203    SCAN****-------------------------------------------------------------*
00203    SCAN***| 1. PERFORMED BY 00197 LOC-RPT.                               |
00203    SCAN****-------------------------------------------------------------*
00203    047200 BLD-PG-HDG SECTION.
00204    047300     MOVE HDG-AA TO RPT-BDY
00205    047400     WRITE PRT-REC AFTER PG-TOP
00206    047500     ADD 1 TO PG-CT
00207    047600     MOVE PG-CT TO LOC-PG-NBR
00208    048100     MOVE HDG-DD TO RPT-BDY
00209    048200     PERFORM WRITE-RPT
00210    048300     MOVE HDG-EE TO RPT-BDY
00211    048400     PERFORM WRITE-RPT
00212    048500     SET L-A TO L-B
00213    048600     MOVE 0 TO LN-CT.
```

Exception Reporting

In using the graphic charts and narratives comments, our programmers were able, in many instances, to spot potential problems areas in programs before they showed up in testing or production. The only problem was that a thorough review of the SCAN/370 outputs might be required to avoid missing anything and if the program was large this could be time consuming.

The solution - create a series of exception reports which the programmer could review quickly and easily to detect these danger spots.

If you're maintaining an unfamiliar program, the report will show you any dead procedures so you won't have to spend time trying to figure out how they're executed. And after you've made the changes it will let you certify that no other procedures have been inadvertently crippled in the process.

If you're developing a program, you can quickly detect those logic errors which cause any procedure to become inoperative - and take corrective action before testing.

```
SCAN/370 EXCEPTION ANALYZER REPORTS*********************************PROGRAM USERDEMO


************************ UNENTERED PROCEDURE ANALYZER ************************
SEQ    PROCEDURE NAME
---    --------------

00270  LOAD-B
00277  NXT-Y
00287  LOAD-B-EXIT
```

The Runaway Path Analyzer allows you to 1) verify that none exist or 2) refer to the line number(s) in the graphic chart where the situation(s) were encountered and flagged. The graphic chart will then show you the entire path which led to each runaway situation, including all decision points and branches which created the path.

```
************************** RUNAWAY PATH ANALYZER ****************************
CHART LINE NUMBER
-----------------

00046
```

Any GOTO which branches outside the range of an active PERFORM is flagged and described.

In certain situations, such as branching to an end-of-job routine, exceeding a PERFORM range is perfectly harmless. When the range is exceeded inadvertently, however, the result can be disastrous - falling through to global routines creating wild, uncontrolled paths.

This report will allow you to determine that 1) no PERFORM range exceptions exist, 2) those which do exist are intentional with no possible adverse effect or 3) dangerous logic is present.

```
*********************** PERFORM RANGE EXCEPTION ANALYZER ***********************

BRANCH FROM                              TO
-----------                              --

00189 NXT-LOC .......................... 00156 CLOSE-FILES
00305 BLD-PAGE-END ..................... 00197 LOC-RPT
```

An errant fall through can be one of the most serious and elusive bugs in a COBOL program. Serious - because it often results in wild, uncontrolled logic paths. Elusive - because the point of failure is usually far downstream from the bug which caused it.

This report documents every fall thru situation so that you can quickly spot any which are errant.

```
*************************** FALL THRU ANALYZER ***************************

FALL THRU TO                             FROM
------------                             ----

00156 CLOSE-FILES ..................... 00145 PROCEDURE/DIVISION
00176 NXT-LOC ......................... 00174 LOAD-LOC-TABLE
00223 FIND-NXT ........................ 00219 FIND-COL-B
00258 NXT-X ........................... 00253 LOAD-A
00302 BLD-PAGE-END .................... 00297 BLD-PAGE-CLOSE
00308 BLD-PAGE-SWITCH ................. 00302 BLD-PAGE-END
```

All logic loops are documented showing the procedure where each loop begins and the procedure(s) from which the loop(s) return.

Erroneous loops and/or missing loops can be spotted and corrected before they are encountered during execution.

```
***************************** LOGIC LOOP ANALYZER *****************************

LOOP BEGINS AT                              RETURNS FROM
--------------                              ------------

00176 NXT-LOC ......................... 00176 NXT-LOC
00197 LOC-RPT ......................... 00197 LOC-RPT
                                            00302 BLD-PAGE-END
00223 FIND-NXT ........................ 00223 FIND-NXT
00245 BLD-LINES ....................... 00245 BLD-LINES
00258 NXT-X ........................... 00258 NXT-X
00297 BLD-PAGE-CLOSE .................. 00308 BLD-PAGE-SWITCH
00302 BLD-PAGE-END .................... 00308 BLD-PAGE-SWITCH
```

While the use of the COBOL ALTER statement is discouraged or even forbidden in most shops, this insidious feature sometimes crops up in older programs undergoing maintenance. If you are faced with having to maintain an older program, this report will 1) certify that no ALTER's exist and relieve you of any concern in that regard or 2) point out every alternative path resulting from ALTER statements.

```
****************************** ALTER ANALYZER ******************************

PROCEDURE ALTERED                           TO PROCEED TO
-----------------                           -------------

00308 BLD-PAGE-SWITCH ................. 00302 BLD-PAGE-END
```

Availability

While the effort required to invoke SCAN/370 to statically analyze a
program was very simple, another problem surfaced. The time required to
put in a job and get the results back was sometimes inconvenient and
often the work that had to be done just could not wait.

So the challenge was to come up with a way to eliminate that extra
step so that the SCAN/370 outputs were automatically available to
the programmer without the inconvenience and time delay of going through
an extra step.

The answer - provide the option of invoking SCAN/370 automatically
with each clean compile and include the SCAN/370 outputs as a part of
the compiler outputs. The narrative comments become an integral part of
the compile listing and the charts and exception reports tag along with
other compiler output options such as the CLIST, PMAP, XREF, etc.

Using this technique the SCAN/370 outputs are always available and
as current as the last clean compile.

Taking SCAN/370 to the marketplace

While SCAN/370 was developed to assist our own programmers and
analysts in the performance of their jobs, the results ended up in the
hands of our clients in the form of deliverables. The typical reaction
from our cients was "This stuff is great - but now how do we keep it up
to date?" Being nice guys we decided we would allow our clients to
license the product for use at their own site.

Thus was born the commercial exploitation of SCAN/370 as a
proprietary software product.

The spaghetti code legacy

Over the last eight to ten years, structured programming has brought
to the EDP industry a methodology which, according to industry studies,
reduce the cost of program maintenance by a factor of 3 to 1. Most
companies have taken advantage of this methodology in recent years and
structured program development has resulted in substantial benefits in
program maintainability.

But what about those old spaghetti code programs that have been
around for ten or fifteen years and have gone through a multitude of
revisions?

SCAN/370 provided a partial solution by simplifying the analysis of
these programs. But we kept getting hit with the same plea "SCAN/370
may help but it is only relieving the symptom. What we need is
something that will cure the illness!".

SUPERSTRUCTURE - a cure for the illness

How do you take a spaghetti code program and, completely automatically, transform it into a structured program that is functionally 100% indentical?

The biggest problem in achieving 100% identical functionality is being able to precisely identify every possible logical path combination in the spaghetti code version. Enter the simulator from SCAN/370. Not only does the SCAN/370 simulator figure out every logical path combination, but it has gone through years of use involving many thousands of programs and, hence, extensive refinement and elimination of program bugs.

The SCAN/370 simulator was used as the nucleus of SUPERSTRUCTURE giving us a running start with well tested code.

The development of SUPERSTRUCTURE then boiled down to creating a restructuring algorithm using as input the intelligence gathered by the simulator.

The Structuring Criteria

In developing the structuring algorithms it was necessary to establish a structuring criteria. Since there are numerous variations of criteria in structured programming, we had to use our own judgement in coming up with a criteria that would offend as few people as possible.

- o All of the PROCEDURE DIVISION code is comprised of independent modules.
- o Each module has a single entry point and single exit point.
- o Modules are invoked only by PERFORM statements linked hierarhically to the main-line routine.
- o All interparagraph GOTOs are eliminated. The only GOTOs allowed are those which loop back to the paragraph in which they reside or to the paragraph exit.
- o Fall-throughs between modules are eliminated.
- o Dead code is identified and converted to comments.
- o PERFORM range violations are eliminated.
- o ALTER statements and altered GOTOs are removed.

Functionality

Our greatest concern in creating SUPERSTRUCTURE was the degree of success we would achieve in creating programs which were 100% functionally equivalent. When you are selling a package, rather than a service, this aspect is critical. Since the client does not have detail knowledge of the structuring algorithms used by the product, manual intervention to achieve functionality is simply not feasible.

Fortunately, functionality did not turn out to be a problem. What did turn out to be a problem, however, was something we had never anticipated.

Cosmetics

In the process of building a new program SUPERSTRUCTURE follows a given formatting convention to assure such things as one statement per line and proper indentation for IF and ELSE.

In situations where the spaghetti code was poorly formatted the user gladly accepted the formatting conventions of SUPERSTRUCTURE. However, if the user had spent a lot of time and effort to apply a specific formatting technique to achieve his own desired cosmetic appearance for the spaghetti code version, any deviation in the formatting conventions used by SUPERSTRUCTURE was often met with a degree of resentment which was hard for us to believe.

After being bloodied by this on numerous occasions we finally decided to add an option to allow the user to retain the formatting of the orignal spaghetti code in the new program created by SUPERSTRUCTURE. This decision overcame the largest obstacle we have encountered with SUPERSTRUCTURE.

SUPERSTRUCTURE scorecard

In addition to the restructured version of the original spaghetti code program, SUPERSTRUCTURE also generates a scorecard comparing the structure characteristics of the original program with those of the restructured program.

SUPERSTRUCTURE SCORECARD		
STRUCTURE PROFILE	ORIGINAL	RESTRUCTURED
GOTO BRANCHES (INTER-PARAGRAPH)	708	0
GOTO ... DEPENDING BRANCHES	5	0
ALTER STATEMENTS	9	0
ALTERED GOTO BRANCHES	3	0
FALL-THROUGHS	237	0
DEAD CODE (LINES)	90	0
PERFORMED PROCEDURES	54	421

Conclusion

SCAN/370 and SUPERSTRUCTURE now represent the backbone of the Proprietary Software Division of Group Operations, Incorporated.

HENRY W. MORGAN - BIOGRAPHICAL SUMMARY

Mr. Morgan is currently Vice President of Group Operations, Incorporated, a Washington, D.C. based company involved in data processing consulting and the development and sale of proprietary software products.

Mr. Morgan is the author of three proprietary software products marketed by Group Operations, Incorporated:

1. SCAN/370

    A static analyzer for COBOL programs

2. EDITOR II

    A COBOL program generator

3. SUPERSTRUCTURE

    A system that turns COBOL spaghetti code into structured code - automatically.

Prior to joining Group Operations, Incorporated, Mr. Morgan was Vice President of PSI-TRAN Corporation where he authored the DCD II proprietary software product - a system that documents COBOL programs automatically.

Mr. Morgan spent thirteen years in marketing for the IBM Corporation before joining PSI-TRAN Corporation.

Prior to joining IBM Corporation, Mr. Morgan graduated from the University of Maryland with a bachelor of science degree in Mechanical Engineering.

VI. Infusing Software with Structure: System Level Approaches

System level restructuring approaches may be distinguished from code level restructuring approaches in that software specifications, or recovering software specifications, are more prominent in guiding the restructuring. Since software specifications are usually kept informally, system level restructuring requires more manual effort. Few automatic restructuring tools are available.

The first two papers concern redocumenting systems that have become difficult to understand. In the first paper, "Software Renewal: A Case Study" by H.M. Sneed, a 24,000 line PL/1 subsystem is redocumented using automated tools. The tools were critical to the project's success, but the work remained labor intensive. Because of the great effort needed to respecify, redocument, and retest the subsystem, the paper gives a stark example of the relatively great effort needed to recreate up-to-date documentation.

This theme is echoed in the second paper. In "Creating a Baseline for an Undocumented System—or What Do You Do with Someone Else's Code?" J.C. Philips gives a horror story of how a 20,000 line FORTRAN system was arduously analyzed and redocumented. The paper illustrates that if documentation is allowed to become totally out-of-date, recovering a new documentation baseline can be expensive.

The next paper, "Upgrading Aging Software Systems Using Modern Software Engineering Practices: IBM-FSD's Conversion of FAA's National Airspace System (NAS) En Route Stage A Software from 9020's to S/370 Processors" by B. Britcher and J. Craig, gives a practical application of software restructuring based on mathematical formalisms. The paper describes how 100,000 lines of twenty-year-old software was restructured using the ideas of a state machine and a function, both standardized internally within IBM Federal Systems Division.

The next paper, "Software Improvement Program (SIP): A Treatment for Software Senility" by C. Houtz, outlines an ambitious plan for not only improving software at the system and code levels, but also for improving the practices that may have led to poor structure. The paper defines a SIP as a plan to "preserve the value of past software investments as much as possible, and provides an incremental and evolutionary approach to modernizing the existing software to maximize its value, quality, effectiveness, and efficiency." An essential support for the SIP is a local definition of a software engineering technology (SET), a collection of procedures, guidelines, and tools governing the production of software.

The next paper, "Designing Software for Ease of Extension and Contraction" by D.L. Parnas, gives principles for partitioning a system into modules to increase its maintainability. The principles apply equally to repartitioning an existing system. The benefit gained with repartitioning is increased flexibility, which can ease enhancements, reduce errors, and reduce the need for restructuring later on. The paper discusses the issues of (1) identifying functionally independent and complete subsets of requirements, (2) hiding changeable aspects of a design within a module and making module interfaces insensitive to these changes, (3) viewing software as a virtual machine that supplies building block operations for constructing a system, and (4) making precise the virtual machine approach to partitioning by examining the "uses" relation among modules in the system.

When code is salvaged from one system for use in others, the code must be restructured to supply the operations most likely needed in other systems. Similarly, existing code that is to receive a reusable code module must be changed to accommodate the module. Restructuring code for reusability may not cause actual restructuring of the system from which the code came, but it is a restructuring approach nonetheless. In "Software Engineering with Reusable Designs and Code" by R.G. Lanergan and C.A. Grasso, a strategy for the recognition, definition, and reuse of functional modules is presented. The paper illustrates the potential economic benefits of restructuring followed by reuse of commonly used software functions.

Software Renewal: A Case Study

Harry M. Sneed, Software Engineering Service

Reprinted from *IEEE Software*, Volume 1, Number 3, July 1984, pages 56-63. Copyright © 1984 by The Institute of Electrical and Electronics Engineers, Inc.

> **Error-free software in large applications may be possible only by respecifying the original design—and may be affordable only when automatic tools become available.**

The data processing community needs to apply software engineering techniques and tools to real projects to determine their practical usefulness. Such an opportunity was provided by the Bertelsmann Publishing Corporation of Gütersloh, West Germany, during a two year period from 1981 to 1983. This article reports the results of that project and the experience gained from it.

The application

In 1981 Bertelsmann, the world's second largest publishing company, completed a commercial application system for distributing books and other publications throughout the world. The system, which includes ordering, billing, packing, and distributing, runs on line during the day and in batch mode during the night. It is made up of eight subsystems, with more than 1000 modules and 300,000 PL/I source statements. The system was developed with the help of IBM analysts using the HIPO method for design[1] and a decision table generator, Dectab, for coding.[2] The database, which contains some 5000 data items, was constructed using the Adabas database system.[3]

Testing and documenting such a large system proved to be a problem. Due to application size and complexity, the modules needed to be tested individually, but at the time of development no adequate test tools were available. The original documentation, in the form of HIPO charts, was soon outdated as the programs were altered during testing. So great was the difference between the original design documentation, which was never fully completed, and the final programs that the design had to be discarded.

This left the system without a baseline documentation. The only true description of the application was the programs themselves, but these were in a constant state of fluctuation as there were numerous error reports, at the rate of one error per 175 source lines, and user change requests, at the rate of one change per two and a half modules, during the installation phase.

At this critical point, after one year of operation, Bertelsmann decided to try and reconstruct a requirements specification from the programs themselves, and to systematically test the modules with the aid of automated tools. One subsystem of the total system was chosen: the mailing system with 232 modules and some 24,000 lines of PL/I source code. By respecifying, redocumenting and reverifying this one subsystem we hoped to determine whether or not the entire system could be reconstructed in accordance with the principles of software engineering. Like urban renewal, we wanted to find out whether software systems could be economically renovated.

Project strategy

The strategy of the project was to proceed in four stages. In the first stage, the modules were to be statically analyzed and redocumented with the aid of an automated static analyzer. In the second stage, the programs and data structures were to be formally specified using an automated specification tool based on the structured analysis method[4] and the documents produced by the static analyzer. In the third stage, the module test cases were to be written in a test specification language based on the assertion method[5] and executed by a module test system

EH0244-4/86/0000/0206$01.00 © 1984 IEEE

with the objective of achieving 90-percent branch coverage.[6] In the fourth and final stage, the test specification, in the form of assertion procedures, was to be merged with the functional specification of the programs and their data structures to create a production environment for maintenance and further development[7] (Figure 1).

The final result was to be a formal specification of the processes, data objects, and their relationships, as well as a set of test procedures for testing new module versions against the evolving specification.

The process specification was to consist of

- a process description,
- a function tree,
- an input/output diagram for each function,
- a decision table for each group of conditional functions,
- a function tree for each process,
- a description for each function, and
- the assertions on the pre- and postconditions of each elementary function.

The object specification was to consist of

- an object description,
- a data tree,
- a data usage diagram for each data item,
- a description of each data item, and
- the assertions on the input/output domains of each elementary data item.

In addition, the relationships between the processes, between the objects, and between the objects and processes were to be specified in accordance with the entity/relationship model.[8] Finally, there was to be a data test procedure for each of the 78 data interfaces, that is, data capsules, and a module test procedure for each of the 232 PL/I procedures, that is, modules.

The project was planned to last a year and to involve two testers and two specifiers besides the personnel developing the automated tools. As it turned out, this proved to be a gross underestimation, mainly because of the effort required to refine the tools. However, without tools the task of renovation was deemed impossible.

The rationale for employing automated tools was one of sheer economic necessity. A human being can only understand and document a few hundred lines of code per week. With the aid of a tool, this can be increased to several thousand. The ratio is at least one to ten. The same applies to testing. Without the help of a tool, it is not possible to trace the test paths and to document the test coverage. Besides, the tool is what generates the test data and verifies the test results. So it was clear from the beginning that the

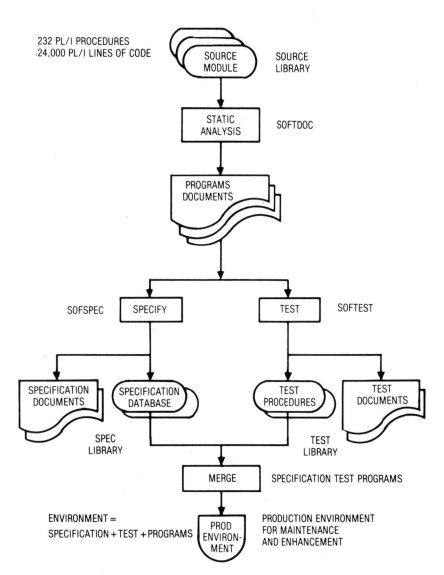

Figure 1. Renovation project strategy.

207

postdocumentation and the testing of the programs had to be done automatically.

The least help from tools was expected in respecifying what the programs should be doing. But even here a tool was found to be indispensable. The business analysts, who generally are not trained to make precise specifications, were encouraged by the specification tool to be precise and formal. If for no other reason, a specification tool can be justified on this basis. The resulting specification would have been valueless if the discipline enforced by the tool had been missing. In fact, an argument might be made that the lack of discipline on the part of the original developers was a major reason for having to renovate the Bertelsmann system.

Static analysis

The first stage of the project involved the static analysis of the selected programs. This stage proceeded bottom up in three steps: (1) module analysis, (2) program analysis, and (3) system analysis.

The tool for this purpose was Softdoc, a static analyzer for Cobol, PL/I, and assembler programs.[9] Softdoc processed the source code in order to produce four tables for each module: a data description table, a data flow table, a control flow table, and an interface table.

The data description table described the attributes and usage of each data item referenced by the module in question. The data flow table depicted in which statements each data item was used and how it was used, either as a predicate in a condition, an argument, or a result. The control flow table encompassed each PL/I control command, such as PROC, DO-WHILE, SELECT, and IF, including their conditions, as well as all comments contained in the procedure. The interface table consisted of all entries, calls and I/O operations, with their respective parameters (Figure 2).

With the aid of these tables, it was possible to automatically generate a series of documents from the programs themselves, at three different levels of aggregation. At the module level, the following documents were generated:

- a tree of internal procedures and begin blocks,
- an input/output diagram for each internal procedure and begin block,
- a data description list,
- a pseudo code listing,
- a control graph,
- a path analysis report, and
- an intramodular data flow table.

At the program level, the modules of each of the eight programs were aggregated to produce:

- a module tree,
- a calling hierarchy list,
- an input/output diagram for each module,
- an interface description list, and
- an intermodular data flow table.

At the system level, the program tables were aggregated to produce a document of the interprogram relationships. In all, five documents were produced at this level:

Without a tool, it would have taken at least three man years to document the programs at the same level of detail.

- a table of module references,
- an input/output diagram for each program,
- a file reference table,
- an interprogram data flow table, and
- a system data dictionary.

The whole analysis took no more than one week to complete. Altogether some 1624 module documents, 40 program documents, and five system documents were produced, giving an approximately one to one and a half ratio of code to program documentation. Thus, it was possible to analyze 5000 lines of code per day. Without a tool, it would have taken at least three man-years to document the programs at the same level of detail. This showed that for the postdocu-

mentation of programs, automated tools are indispensable. There can be no adequate and reliable description of the programs without them. However, it should be noted that the documentation of the programs is no substitute for a requirements specification. This work remained to be done.

Requirement specification

Following the production of the program documentation, it was possible to commence with the respecification of the application. In contrast to the program analysis, the specification proceeded top down. In all, 10 steps were involved (Figure 3):

(1) describing the data objects,
(2) describing the processes,
(3) depicting the object/process relationships,
(4) depicting the user interfaces,
(5) depicting the data trees,
(6) depicting the function trees,
(7) depicting the decision logic,
(8) depicting the data flow,
(9) describing the functions, and
(10) describing the data.

The tool used was Sofspec, a system for the interactive submission of an application using 12 different CRT forms and their storage in a specification database based on the entity/relationship model.[10] Sofspec allows the user to submit the specification in interactive mode under the IBM TSO/SPF monitor in a tabular format. At any time during a terminal session it can be asked to produce a certain specification document, or it can be requested to verify a certain aspect of the specification.

The specification work began by examining the files, databases, and data communication interfaces documented by the static analysis. Data objects could be derived from the file reference table. Each object was defined in terms of its meaning, occurrence, periodicity, space requirements, and description. Processes could be taken from the interprogram data flow table. Each process was also defined in terms of is meaning, occurrence, periodicity, time requirements, and description.

Following the description of the objects and processes, the relationships were defined. The process/object relationships (input, output, I/O) could be taken from the input/output diagrams produced by the static analysis. The Adabas search keys for each access had, however, to be taken from the database design. The object/object relationships (1:1, 1:N, M:1, M:N) were obtained by inverting the process/object relationships. The process/process relationships (predecessor, successor, parallel task, invoker, invokee), that is, the process control flow, could be derived from the system data flow table.

Thus, it proved possible to recreate an abstract conceptual model of the system represented by objects, processes, and their relationships, but only partially from the information obtained from the existing programs. A great deal of information had to be collected from the original designers. This was due to the large semantic gap between the view of the system as a whole, in terms of objects and processes, and the view of the individual programs. The specification process proceeded top down. The fourth and fifth steps were to document the data structures. These were found to be of two types: user interfaces, that is, forms, and data sets. The user interfaces were described in terms of sample forms with references to the variables contained in them. The data sets were defined as data trees in accordance with the Jackson notation using sequence, selection, repetition, grouping, and search key identification.[11] Sofspec supported both notations. The information for the data structuring was taken from the actual listing and CRT panels, as well as from the data dictionary generated through the static analysis of the programs by Softdoc.

In the following two steps, the function structures and decision logic tables were specified from the module tree diagrams and the pseudo code generated by Softdoc. The function trees in Sofspec were also defined in terms of the Jackson methodology. For every repetitive and selective func-

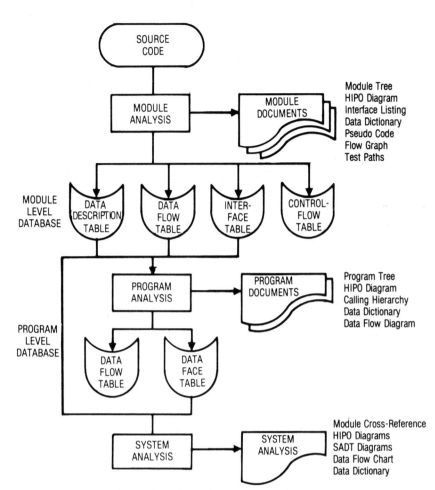

Figure 2. Static analysis with Softdoc.

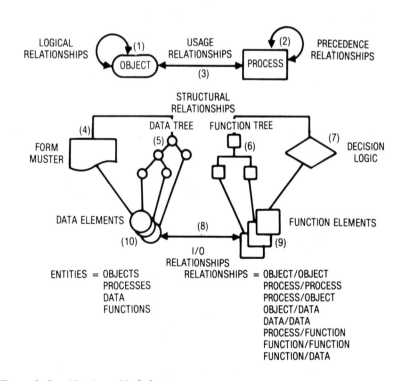

Figure 3. Specification with Sofspec.

tion it was necessary to define the condition. This was done using either a terminal-supported decision table or a decision tree. Later in the documentation the function trees and decision trees, that is, decisions tables, were merged to produce a single specification document, which also included the detailed data flow.

The detailed data flow description was the eighth step. Here the module input/output diagrams derived from the code were used to specify the inputs and outputs of each function. The new data flow diagrams, at the functional level, were then generated by the specification tool.

The ninth step was to describe each function based on the comment block contained in the code. Where the comment blocks were missing, it was necessary to examine the code itself in order to describe the algorithm in

---

There were several deviations between the assumption of the user and the actual construction of the programs.

---

natural language. A function was defined to correspond to a PL/I procedure. These procedures ranged from 50 to a maximum of 500 executable PL/I statements.

The tenth and final step in the respecification phase was actually the first step of the testing phase. Each data element in the system had to be defined in terms of is attributes. These were taken from the Softdoc data dictionary. In addition, the domain of each data item had to be defined. But since this was related to the program test it was postponed until after the test phase.

The task of respecifying the application programs took 17 man-months to complete. This amounted to one man-month of specification per 1400 lines of code. The ratio of program code to specification documentation was on the average of three to one; for example, for every three pages of code there was one page of specification documentation.

When the specification documentation was finished, it was possible to discuss it with the user, who up to this point was not sure what the system was doing. Insofar as the user became familiar with the formal specification techniques, this discussion proved very fruitful. As a result of the discussion, it became clear that there were several deviations between the assumptions of the user and the actual construction of the programs. Because of that it became necessary to revise the specification to accommodate the user's view. This took another four man-months.

Program testing

The final stage of the project turned out to be the most difficult and time-consuming. It entailed testing the programs against the newly constructed specification. Twenty-two man-months were required to specify all of the data, and another six man-months were necessary to conduct the tests themselves. Each module had to be tested independently until at least 90 percent of its branches were covered.

The basis of the test was the program documentation produced by the static analyzer. Among the documents produced were a diagram of the module inputs and outputs and a list of the paths through the module, together with the conditional operands, that is, predicates associated with each path. The person responsible for the test had to analyze each module to determine what inputs would lead to the execution of what paths through the module. They also had to predict which results would occur from each path. A test case table was used to record the inputs and outputs of each path as well as the branches traversed by that path (Figure 4).

Unfortunately, the modules had originally been generated by a decision table generator and then expanded by hand. Thus, they were very badly structured. GOTO instructions were the rule instead of the exception. This made it difficult to trace the paths and predict the results. A module of 300

statements took two man-days to analyze. A module of 600 statements took seven to eight days to analyze. The largest module with some 760 statements took 11 days to analyze. We began to see that the effort involved in defining a program-based test increased exponentially in relation to the number of instructions, the number of decision nodes, and the number of arguments, that is, inputs.

Linear code with sequences of IF and WHILE statements was easier to handle than highly nested code with conditions within conditions and loops within loops. As might be expected, the worst case was that of overlapping GOTOs. Modules with few arguments, especially those with few conditional arguments or predicates, were easier to test than those with many such arguments. All of this further demonstrated that there was a definite relationship between program and complexity—in terms of program length,[12] decision nodes,[13] and data usage[14]—and test effort.

Having designed a test case table for a module, the inputs and outputs were then transformed into an assertion procedure. The assertion language consisted of an IF statement along with four types of assertions: set assertions, range assertions, function assertions, and relational assertions.[15]

Alphanumeric and coded values were usually defined by means of a set assertion. Numeric values were defined as ranges. Address and length information was defined by function. Relationships between input and output values were defined by the relational assertion. The writing of assertions proved to be a simple and easily learned task. The problem was in knowing what assertions to write.

The assertion procedures written were of two types, driver procedures and stub procedures. Driver procedures initialized the preconditions of a module under test and initiated the test cases. After each test case they verified the postconditions of the module. Stub procedures simulated either submodules or files. They verified the outputs and generated inputs to the module under test wherever a call or

I/O operation was performed. In all, over 300 assertion procedures were written with total of some 7000 assertions (Figure 5).

The actual execution of the test lasted less that three months. With two testers working in parallel it was possible to test 20 modules per week, that is, each tester tested approximately two modules a day. This was due to the use of the tool Softest, which compiled the test procedures into test tables, which were then interpreted to test the modules.[16] The testbed was automatically generated. In the testbed all procedure calls and I/O operations were simulated. For coupling the module under test with the test procedures, the module symbol table was used. In this way, the input variables were assigned, and the output variables verified. Concurrently, the paths traversed were traced, the branch coverage registered, and the data flows followed.

After each test a postprocessor produced a series of reports: a test path report, a data usage report, and a branch coverage report. The branch coverage report indicated the coverage ratio and the test branches not tested. Each test was continued until at least 90-percent branch coverage was attained, as prescribed in the contract (Table 1).

In most cases where 90-percent coverage was not reached, it was due to erroneous or incomplete assertion procedures. Modules with more than 500 statements and a highly nested logic proved to be the most difficult to cover. The test had to be repeated as many as 10 times before the adequate coverage was reached. Following each test the assertions had to be adjusted or enhanced to invoke different paths. An average of five to eight test cases were needed to test the smaller modules but as many as 26 test cases were necessary to test larger modules.

Minor errors were discovered in 55 of the 232 modules. These had to be corrected by the responsible programmers before the test could continue. Most of these errors were related and were the result of design decisions. The low level of errors found was due to the fact that the programs had already been in operation for a year before they were submitted to this test. So most of the critical errors had already been removed. In addition, since the modules had, to a great extent, been generated from decision tables, all the errors were of a common nature and the patterns could be easily recognized. Over 75 percent of the errors were discovered while analyzing the code. The test only documented their existence. The other 25 percent were exposed at execution time by either not being able to reach

	DATA	1	2	3
	FIELD1	'XXX'	'YYY'	'ZZZ'
	FIELD2	100	200	300
	FIELD3	−5	0	5
INPUTS	FIELD4	X'FF'	X'F1'	X'FO'
	FIELD5	11	10	9
	FIELD6	B'0'	B'0'	B'1'

	DATA	1	2	3
	FIELD11	'XXX'	'YYY'	'ZZZ'
	FIELD12	95	200	305
OUTPUTS	FIELD13	26	10	4
	FIELD14	X'FF'	X'F1'	X'FO'
	FIELD15	B"1'	B'1'	B'0'

	MODULE	1	2	3
	Y6651	1	1	1
		3	2	5
		7	4	8
		9	6	9
PATHS		12	10	11
		15	14	13
		16	17	17
		17		

Figure 4. Test case tables.

```
MODULE: V665A, STAT
    ASSERT PRE FIELD1      SET ('XXX − , 'YYY', 'ZZZ');
    ASSERT PRE FIELD2      RANGE (100 + 100);
    ASSERT PRE FIELD3      RANGE ( − 5:5);
    ASSERT PRE FIELD4      SET (X'FF', 'F1', 'FO');
    ASSERT PRE FIELD5      RANGE (11 − 1);
    ASSERT PRE FIELD6      SET (B'0'(2), '1 − );

    ASSERT POST FIELD11    = FIELD1;
    ASSERT POST FIELD12    = FIELD2 + FIELD3;
    ASSERT POST FIELD13    = FIELD5 − FIELD3;
    ASSERT POST FIELD14    = FIELD4;
    ASSERT POST FIELD15    = NOT (FIELD6);

END V665A;
```

Figure 5. Assertion procedure.

> **Those errors found were almost all on exceptional functions which had not been used in production.**

certain branches or by the control flow following paths other than those predicted. Only three errors were found by violating output assertions. This was probably because the programs had already been exposed to extensive system testing. Those errors found were almost all on exceptional functions that had not yet been used in production. This only underlines the fact that programs do not have to be error free to be useful. It all depends on how they are used.

The total effort of 22 months to test 24,000 lines of PL/I code to find 55 minor errors and three major ones could certainly not be economically justified. The main value of the testing project was in establishing a testbed for future testing. It did, however, demonstrate that systematic module testing on a large scale was feasible, and that with new untested modules it could even be economical, but only if adequate tools are available. The test effort amounted to an average of one man-day per 54 instructions. Considering the fact that this was the first experience with a new test specification language, it should be possible in the future to increase this productivity.

Although we were successful, the move from conventional development and maintenance practices to systematic software engineering was expensive. The effort cost two thirds of the original cost, and, without the support of highly sophisticated tools, was not economically justified.

In the long run, to reduce costs and make systematic maintenance more attractive, companies will have to invest in developing adequate tools and ways to automatically bridge the gap between programs and their specification. Our work at Bertelsmann convinced us that automation is the only true solution to the maintenance problem. ∎

References

1. "HIPO—A Design Aid and Documentation Technique," IBM Corp., Manual No. GC-20-1851, White Plains, N.Y., 1974.

2. "IBM Decision Table Translator, User-Guide," IBM Form No. 79974, Stuttgart, Germany, 1973.

3. "ADABAS Introduction," *Software AG of North America,* Reston, VA., 1976.

4. T. DeMarco, *Structured Analysis and System Specification,* Yourdon Press, New York, 1978.

5. C. V. Ramamoorthy, S. F. Ho, and W. T. Chen, "On the Automated Generation of Program Test Data," *IEEE Trans. Software Eng.,* Vol. SE-2, No. 4, 1976, pp. 293-300.

6. J. C. Huan, "An Approach to Program Testing," *ACM Computing Surveys,* Sept., 1975.

7. H. M. Sneed and A. Merey, "Automated Software Quality Assurance," *Proc. Compsac 82,* Computer Society Press, Los Alamitos, Calif., 1982, pp. 239-247.

8. P. Chen, "The Entity-Relationship Model: A Basis for the Enterprise View of Data," *AFIPS Conf. Proc.,* Vol. 46, 1977 NCC, Dallas, Tex., 1977, pp. 77-84.

9. G. Jandrasics, "SOFTDOC—A System for Automated Software Analysis

Table 1.
Test coverage measurement.
(Total branches, 17; executed branches, 16; coverage ratio, 94 percent)

MODULE	BRANCH	STATEMENT	LAST TEST	TOTAL TEST
V665A	1	1	3	3
	2	50	1	1
	3	54	1	1
	4	58	1	1
	5	62	1	1
	6	64	1	1
	7	68	1	1
	8	72	1	1
	9	76	2	2
	10	80	1	1
	11	84	1	1
	12	88	1	1
	13	92	1	1
	14	96	1	1
	15	100	1	1
	16	104	(Not executed.)	
	17	108	3	3

and Documentation," *Proc. ACM Workshop Software Quality Assurance,* Gaithersburg, Md., Apr., 1981.

10. Nyary and H. M. Sneed, "SOFSPEC—A Pragmatic Approach to Automated Specification Verification," *Proc. Entity/Relationship Conf.,* Anaheim, Calif., Oct., 1983.

11. M. Jackson, *Principles of Program Design,* Academic Press, London, 1975.

12. M. Halstead, *Elements of Software Science*, Elsevier Computer Science Library, New York, 1977.

13. T. McCabe, "A Complexity Measure," *IEEE Trans. Software Eng.,* Vol. SE-2, No. 4, Dec. 1976, pp. 308-320.

14. S. Henry and O. Kafura, "Software Structure Metrics Based on Information Flow," *IEEE Trans. Software Eng.,* Vol. SE-7, No. 5, Sept. 1981, pp. 510-518.

15. M. Majoros and H. M. Sneed, "Testing Programs Against a Formal Specification," *Proc. Compsac 83,* Computer Society Press, Los Alamitos, Calif.,.1983, pp. 512-520.

16. M. Majoros, "SOFTEST—A System for the Automated Verification of PL/I and Cobol Programs," *J. Systems & Software,* New York, Dec. 1982.

Harry M. Sneed is the technical manager at Software Engineering Service, a Munich, West Germany, software house. Before joining SES in 1978, he was a systems programmer for Siemens, and before that he was with the Volkswagen Foundation. From 1967 to 1970 he worked as a programmer/analyst for the US Navy Department.

Sneed received his BA and MS degrees from the University of Maryland in 1967 and 1969. He is a member of the ACM and IEEE.

His address is Software Engineering Service GmbH, Pappelstrasse 6, 8014 Neubiberg, West Germany.

CREATING A BASELINE FOR AN UNDOCUMENTED SYSTEM

- OR WHAT DO YOU DO WITH SOMEONE ELSES CODE?

Jane C. Philips

The BDM Corporation
Columbia, Maryland

ABSTRACT

This article describes an Independent Software Review of a complex computer simulation. A computer simulation must have the confidence of the users; however, this system did not. This particular model was delivered to the Government under contract. During the course of the contract no independent validation and verification agent reviewed the software development activities to provide quality assurance and to establish that design requirements were met. The purpose of this work was to review critically the delivered software source code and documentation. Additionally, the evaluators were to determine the current state of development and to identify potential problem areas that may adversely affect the operation or validity of the model. The result of this Independent Software Review is a baseline for further system enhancements and configuration management.

A team of computer scientists, operations researchers, and mathematicians were given the opportunity to complete an Independent Software Review of a large computer simulation. This multidisciplinary team had to create the goals and methodology for the analysis of this model. The team was unfamiliar with the model and its limitations and capabilities. The question that these team members had to answer were: What do you do with code that is not even compilable, has few correct comments, and has only a sprinkling of backup documentation?

The goal of this Independent Software Review was to decipher the software, determine the model's capabilities, and to develop a set of possible specific requirements for the system. This goal was set to provide the knowledge required to use the model effectively and efficiently. The means to achieve these goals were yet to be determined. The Team realized that many different approaches could be used to analyze this model. This task was a challenge because the tools for documenting a software system are designed for development use, during the design of the system. The problem was also complicated because there was no access to the computer system to run the simulation. The

developers of this model were no longer available for consultation. To attempt to document a completed system, without the aid of the developers or a computer system, seemed an awesome task.

The available documentation and source code for the model were very unstructured. The first task was to take an inventory of the available reference materials. After the initial inventory, the material had to be evaluated. Determining the most current source code and documentation for each module was a sizable task since many versions existed.

An analysis of the existing requirements was needed to determine what capabilities were expected of the model. This requirements analysis set up the framework for tracing the existing requirements through source code, acceptance criteria, and testing. A few problems that surfaced during this step:

(1) Requirements at different levels,
(2) Contradictory requirements, and
(3) Incomplete requirements.

After the requirements were analyzed, the software could then be analyzed. The software analysis was the real challenge. Since multiple versions of the software existed, the first step was to establish a set of code as the baseline from which to work. Each subroutine had to be evaluated and agreed upon with the customer.

The model code was not available on a computer; as a result, only the reduced listings of the code could be analyzed. The methodology to do this analysis consisted of the following tools:

(1) System Flow Chart,
(2) Hierarchy Chart,
(3) Data Flow Diagrams,
(4) Program Structure Charts,
(5) Subroutine Interaction Tables,
(6) Data Definition Tables,
(7) Updated Detailed Design,
(8) Program Design Language (PDL), and
(9) Data Dictionary.

In order to use some of these tools, i.e., Data Flow Diagrams, the testers had to think

Reprinted from *The Record of the 1983 Software Maintenance Workshop*, 1983, pages 63-64. Copyright © 1983 by The Institute of Electrical and Electronics Engineers, Inc.

both as reviewers and as developers. On one hand, they wanted to document the system as it currently existed while pretending to use the tool as a developer of a new system. This split personality was required to accurately document without letting the end result of the system cloud their thinking.

Each tool had a purpose that ranged from becoming familiar with the system to finding software inconsistencies and errors. The results became a building block process: laying the foundation and building a system baseline.

A tremendous amount of documentation was created from the source code analysis. This documentation included:

(1) Eleven Unit Development Folders,
(2) Revised Requirements,
(3) Capabilities Report,
(4) Problem Report,
(5) Test Plan Analysis,
(6) Users Guide,
(7) Program Maintenance Manual, and
(8) Data Dictionary.

This documentation provides knowledge of the model from a high level, Data Flows, to a low level, Program Design Language. The module information was separated by modules into Unit Development Folders. This provided all the information about a module in one location. Reports were also written to detail the model capabilities and limitations. A problem report was written detailing the known problems of the model found in the analysis. The existing test plan was studied to reveal the deficiencies of the test plan.

The original requirements of the model continued to be a problem throughout the project. It was determined that a new set of requirements would be written based on the model's current or intended capabilities. Clear traceability from the original requirements to the new requirements was maintained. This provided the customer with the means to determine what the final requirements should be.

At the completion of the analysis a Users Guide and Program Maintenance Manual were created. These documents will not be totally completed until the code is compiled and executed. The existing documents contain adeqaute instructions for using the model.

The Independent Software Review also resulted in an evaluation of the software analysis tools and their functions. This methodology proved to be successful with few exceptions.

This project required a team of six people for one year to do this Independent Software Review. The computer simulation consisted only of 20,000 lines of executable FORTRAN code. This is an extreme case for the statement: "An ounce of development documentation is worth a pound of cure".

UPGRADING AGING SOFTWARE SYSTEMS USING
MODERN SOFTWARE ENGINEERING PRACTICES:
IBM-FSD's Conversion Of FAA's National Airspace System (NAS)
En Route Stage A Software From 9020s To S/370 Processors

Bob Britcher
Jim Craig

IBM Corporation
Federal Systems Division
Gaithersburg, Maryland

ABSTRACT

In July 1965, IBM's Federal Systems Division (FSD) was awarded a contract by the Federal Aviation Administration (FAA) to develop the software for its National Airspace System (NAS) en route system, an effort that ran to over two million lines of source code.

Twelve years later, in October 1977, John Jackson, president of IBM-FSD, committed the division to a software engineering program, the cornerstone of which is a design approach that models computer programs as mathematical objects, functions and state machines, so that they can be developed correctly through stepwise decomposition and verification.

In October 1983 IBM-FSD was awarded a contract to upgrade the NAS en route system from vintage S/360 computers (9020s) to S/370 computers. This paper describes how IBM-FSD successfully used today's software engineering principles to redesign portions of that software system, written almost 20 years ago.

INTRODUCTION

One of the major challenges facing software system managers in the 1980s is how to upgrade large, complex embedded systems, written a decade (or more) ago using unstructured languages and designed in a way that makes modification difficult. This paper draws on the authors' experience with one of those systems -- the FAA's National Airspace System (NAS) en route air traffic control system.

In 1981 the FAA announced its plan to modernize its entire air traffic system, including its tower, approach control, and en route centers. The plan would upgrade air traffic controller suites (work stations), the computers and their software, and the support system that maintains them.

The first step of the plan calls for the upgrading of the NAS en route system computers, from S/360 9020s[1] to S/370 processors. The 9020s are now more than 20 years old; their processing capacity is limited (by today's standards) and the reservoir of spare parts is diminishing. Replacing the 9020 host computer and its peripherals (tapes, disks, printers, etc.), without changing its interfaces to the radar acquisition system, the air traffic controller display and data entry sys-

tem, and, of critical importance, without changing the controller's interface, requires careful modification of portions of the host's software.

In October 1983 FAA awarded to IBM-FSD one of two contracts to participate in the Design Competition Phase (DCP) of the host replacement, referred to as the Host Computer System (HCS). IBM-FSD successfully completed the DCP in June 1985, developing 52,000 lines of new software (to build FAA an automated software development lab), and modifying 100,000 lines of the 1.5 million lines of existing FAA software.

Our paper asserts that the modern software engineering practices, specifically software design practices, developed in the late 1970s by IBM-FSD [2,3], and used by IBM-FSD and its subcontractors on the HCS, are central to that program's success. Although the practices are aimed at writing new software, the HCS software designers successfully applied them to modifying software; software that supports a system that has reliably controlled air traffic for more than a dozen years.

Following a summary of the FAA's NAS software and IBM-FSD's software engineering practices, the paper describes how those practices were applied to the FAA software. An example from the FAA's support software, OBJEDT, provides the details of our approach.

FAA's NAS SOFTWARE

The FAA's NAS en route software was developed and acquired (although there was very little off-the-shelf software) in the late 1960s and early 1970s by IBM-FSD and FAA. The entire software library, including operational, support, and hardware diagnostic software, runs to over 1.5 million source lines. In its fifteen- to twenty- year lifetime, virtually every program has been modified; even once-commercial software has been changed by FAA and its subcontractors, including IBM's operating system, MVT, and the original languages, JOVIAL and Basic Assembly Language (BAL).

The NAS software runs on the 9020 computer and its peripherals[1]. The 9020 -- there are two models, the 9020A and the more powerful 9020D -- was developed by IBM in the early 1960s. It is a S/360 multiprocessor comprising two or three computing elements (modified S/360 Model 50s for the 9020A, and Model 65s for the 9020D), two computing elements dedicated to I/O, and a set of storage ele-

Reprinted from *The Proceedings of the Conference on Software Maintenance —1985*, 1985, pages 162-170. Copyright © 1985 by The Institute of Electrical and Electronics Engineers, Inc.

ments, each containing a quarter or a half megabyte of storage, depending on the 9020 model. The 9020 peripherals are second-generation disks, tapes, printers and teletypewriters. The FAA relies heavily on punch cards, both in the operational system and the support system.

The 9020 interfaces with the air traffic controller displays through either a Raytheon CDC 730, from the 9020A, or a 9020E (another version of the 9020 containing a modified NAS Monitor and display applications), from the 9020D. A modified IBM 2703 communications controller, called a Peripheral Adaptor Module (PAM), allows the 9020 to communicate with the array of air traffic devices.

The 9020s are installed at each of this country's 20 en route air traffic control centers (the centers burdened with heavy traffic have the 9020Ds), at the FAA Training Academy in Oklahoma City, and at the FAA Technical Center (FAATC) in Pomona, New Jersey.

The operational software has three parts: the NAS Monitor, consisting of about 240,000 lines of source; the applications, about 280,000 lines; and a COMPOOL containing 15,000 data definitions.

The primary functions of the NAS applications are to process flight plans and digital radar returns, including weather, and to output to the controllers' displays: symbol data, such as map projections, and icons that identify an aircraft's position in the projected airspace; and alphanumeric data that identify an aircraft's transponder code, its ground speed, altitude and status (in handoff, or holding, for example), etc.

In addition to the operating system, language processors and utilites, the support software contains programs that build, test, and reduce the data generated by the operational software. The hardware diagnostic software includes an FAA-written operating system and hundreds of applications to test the 9020 and peripherals and the air traffic equipment and their interfaces.

The HCS Design Competition Phase called for IBM-FSD to demonstrate at the FAA Technical Center the replacement of the 9020s and peripherals with fourth-generation equipment, without changing the air traffic control interface.

In IBM-FSD's proposed configuration the operational software (the NAS Monitor and NAS applications) runs in a single S/370 3083, referred to as the primary processor. A standby 3083 hosts VM and several guest virtual machines, including

- interactive users developing or modifying software and running tests

- MVS (replacing the FAA-modified MVT) running the FAA's support applications

- the FAA's equipment diagnostic operating system and its applications

- IBM's commercial equipment diagnostics operating system and its applications

- test versions of the operational software

- the NAS Monitor in standby mode, communicating through a shared disk with the NAS Monitor in the primary processor, ready to take over if the primary fails.

IBM-FSD modified about 63,000 lines of the NAS operational software (60,000 lines in the NAS Monitor) and about 37,000 lines of support and diagnostics software. IBM-FSD wrote 52,000 lines of new software to provide FAA a modern software development lab, including automated systems for design tracking, change proposals, trouble reporting and software accounting. This paper is primarily concerned with the modification of the 100,000 lines of twenty-year-old FAA software.

The FAA provided IBM-FSD with the software source code and documentation, including functional specifications, design data, and operations and training manuals.

The NAS Monitor is written in BAL without psuedocode. The NAS applications are written in JOVIAL. Neither language is standard. Some of the support programs are written in FORTRAN and in Assembler F. The completeness, depth, and accuracy of the software documentation, including design specifications and code commentary, varies considerably. Although the low-level software design, depicted in flow charts, proved unreliable, the well-maintained COMPOOL table specifications were quite helpful. Ultimately, the job of re-engineering the FAA software started with the source code.

The greatest obstacle to successfully modifying the operational software is its structure. The NAS Monitor and the applications are tightly coupled through the COMPOOL, and the entire software system is built as a single executable entity; a change to one table can affect hundreds of programs. Programmers enhancing or repairing NAS software must read and understand source code covering a much wider domain than that subtended by the lines of code they are changing.

FSD's SOFTWARE ENGINEERING PRACTICES

In 1978 IBM-FSD began a software engineering program to transfer software development technology from its outcroppings in academia to full industrial use. The program has three aspects

a. After considerable research and analysis of its own projects and business objectives, IBM-FSD published its unified approach to software development as a set of software standards and practices.

b. To formally train all IBM-FSD software engineers and managers in the use of the standards, IBM-FSD established a software engineering education program[8].

c. To measure each IBM-FSD project's adherence to the standards, the division chartered a division-level software technology steering group.

The program reached its stride in the early 1980s: more than 3,000 IBM-FSD engineers and managers had attended the software engineering workshops, a core curriculum taught by certified instructors; the training program was exported to the corporation at large (centered at IBM's Software Engineering Institute); the software standards and practices were approved and in use on every IBM-FSD software program; and software engineering had become an integral part of strategic operations at both the division and corporate levels.

The rationale for the program is to improve the management of complex software systems by strengthening intellectual control of software development. The cornerstone of the program is the designing of defect-free software. Although the IBM-FSD software standards[3] cover every aspect of software development, from requirements analysis and cost management to integration and testing, the bulk of the standards, and the bulk of the entire program, is devoted to software design.

Structured programming, that is, using a fixed-basis set of control structures (for example, sequence: f1, f2; conditional: IF p THEN f; and iteration: WHILE p DO f) to develop programming logic, began to enjoy comfortable and widespread practice in the early and mid-1970s. From a procedural, or coding, point of view, "GOTO-less programming" encourages thinking-through algorithms and simplifies their expression as computer programs. But control structures alone do not reduce the complexity of large programming problems; some means are needed to ensure that problems and our solutions to them, our designs, do not overreach our ability to verify their correctness. The means are abstractions.

In the late 1970s, Dr. Harlan Mills and his staff developed an approach to designing software that builds correctness into programs by modeling them as mathematical abstractions -- either as a Cartesian function (function abstraction) or as a state machine[5] (data abstraction) -- and defining formal verification rules to prove their correctness. See Figure 1.

A function abstraction (f) is purely transformational: a given value from the input (i) domain always yields the same value in the output (o) range on every execution of the function rule (algorithm); it can be expressed as a set of ordered pairs: $f=(i,o)$.

A data abstraction (d) retains data between executions: its input (I) domain is a set of ordered pairs $(i,s(i))$, where $s(i)$ is the state of its retained data before execution; and its output (O) range is a set of ordered pairs $(o,s(o))$, where $s(o)$ is the state of its retained data after execution. Thus $d=(I,O)$.

In both function and data abstractions, the software designer models an algorithm by describing its intended behavior. The intended behavior is a formal specification from which further refinement of the algorithm is derived. For example, the intended function, TYPE x,y,z=INTEGER and z:=MAX(x,y), specifies "assign to the variable z the larger of x or y." Stated as a function rule, MAX=((x,y),z). The programmer may not need to describe this algorithm in more detail; providing a mapping of the input to the output may be enough to gain intellectual control.

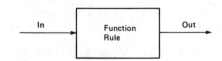

The Cartesian Function

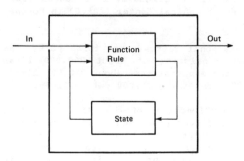

The State Machine

Figure 1. Function and State Machine Models

As each successive level of refinement is developed, the functional equivalence of the more concrete representation and its specification must be verified. In the example, z:=max(x,y), one refinement might be

```
IF              (p)
  x>y
THEN
  z:=x          (g)
ELSE
  z:=y          (h)
FI
```

To verify the correctness of this conditional assignment statement with respect to the intended function, the designer would partition the input domain, i=(x,y), into the TRUE part and the FALSE part, and evaluate, for all values of x and y, the correctness of (g) if (p) is true, and the correctness of (h) if (p) is not true. (Detailing the verification rules for sequences and loops, and for data abstractions, is beyond the scope of our paper. However, Shankar's paper, "A Functional Approach to Module Verification," provides an excellent tutorial on the verification of data abstractions.)

The example above builds a program from a function abstraction. A data abstraction behaves like a state machine, but, as described above, it can be defined as a set of ordered pairs, like the function. A data abstraction consists of a class of data objects, and a set of operations performed on them; it can be viewed by its user as an abstract data type. Developing the design of a data abstraction is similar to developing the design of a function abstraction. The designer specifies an intended state machine by specifying the data objects (state data) as abstract types, such as sets, lists and sequences, and the operations as intended functions, i.e., function rules (see the example above), and then refines the design in terms of more concrete types and rules, verifying, at each step, that the composite behavior of the successor design satisfies the original intended state machine specification.

To record in a formal notation the designs of its programs, IBM-FSD developed a design language called Process Design Language (PDL). The syntax supports data typing, abstract types (such as sequences), control structures, and the function and data abstraction models. Figure 3 describes the PDL template used on the FAA Host Computer System.

IBM-FSD's approach to software design has been used successfully on a number of large, complex projects, including the Global Positioning System (GPS), Data System Modernization (DSM) and SACDIN[7], all for the U.S. Air Force. The software written for these projects was developed from scratch. The FAA HCS is the first full-scale application of IBM-FSD's design standards to an **existing** software system.

APPLYING THE PRACTICES TO FAA's SOFTWARE

In redesigning parts of existing FAA programs, written in languages that do not support structured programming, and whose topology makes dissecting them very tedious (programs are tightly coupled in terms of both data and control), the use of function and data abstractions proved vital.

Working from source code, the HCS software designers applied stepwise abstraction, using what Mills calls the Axiom of Replacement[4]. Complicated programs, or segments of programs, were reduced to simple programs using PDL. For example, a paragraph of code to fill an array, written in 20 or 30 lines of BAL, and using indexing and register manipulation, was replaced by

```
TYPE table_in,table_out=SEQ_OF_INTEGER
RESET table_in,table_out
WHILE
   table_out¬=EMPTY
DO
   NEXT(table_out):=NEXT(table_in)
OD
```

Abstracted programs (now in PDL) were redesigned, coded, and spliced into the NAS software.

New programs and existing programs requiring major changes were designed as data abstractions. However, modeling existing programs as state machines demanded that assumptions be made about data ownership, since, in the current NAS software, programs and tables are tightly coupled: no one program owns any one table. For example, program RIN, the radar front-end processor, uses table RH.

RH is used by other programs. In modeling RIN as a state machine, the designer declared table RH as owned, exclusively, by RIN; for design purposes only, RH resides in RIN's data space. Stepwise abstraction mines the essential properties of a program and allows designers to defer grappling with the particulars of its implementation.

THE PROCESS

The HCS software designer relied on the source code to learn the software. FAA-furnished design specifications describe the processing of each module (we use the term module to describe a compilable program; a NAS module is defined according to no specific design schema or model) and its place in the subsystem; but the specifications are not detailed. The designer used the subsystem and module design documents primarily to assess the scope of a change and the impact it might have. Typically, one designer was responsible for one subsystem; as the designer gained experience with a subsystem, the design documents became less important to him.

Figure 2 illustrates the module redesign process. The figure shows the work products created, and describes the steps that transform each work product into the next, beginning with the original source (upper left) and concluding with the updated source (lower left).

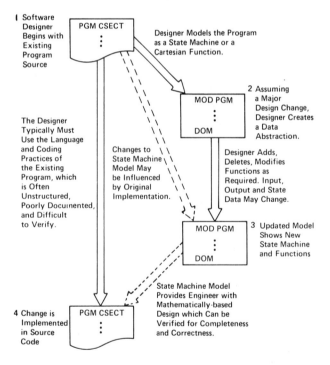

Figure 2. Process Used to Redesign a Module

From the source code, the designer abstracted the module design and recorded it using PDL. He chose the level of abstraction based on the module, the change required, and personal preference. Sometimes this was an iterative process; the designer abstracted a detailed design from the code, then generated another less detailed (yet still precise) abstraction from that design. The iteration continued until the designer was comfortable with the level of abstraction. If only a portion of the module needed redesign, and it could be isolated from the rest of the code, only that piece was recorded (a typical NAS Monitor module comprises between 1,000 and 2,000 lines of source code, including instructions, data, and comments; some modules are smaller, some much larger).

The module was modeled as a state machine (a data abstraction) if it retained data (usually COMPOOL data) across invocations, or a Cartesian function (a function abstraction) if it did not retain data. When only a portion of a module was abstracted, the designer usually modeled it as a function, because state data cannot easily be isolated for a disjointed program segment. (Figure 2 assumes a design modeled as a state machine.)

The abstracted design recorded in PDL served two purposes: it provided a uniform means for understanding and communicating about the original design of a module; and it expressed the design as a mathematical object, with its attendant attributes of formality and verifiability. Abstracting the design from the code was often the most difficult task in redesigning a module, and the most important. No formal procedures or techniques were employed to derive the design from the code; the designer relied on intuition and experience.

Using the design model, the software designer added, deleted, and updated functions as needed, recording all function rules, inputs, outputs, and state data. The designer used IBM-FSD's software engineering practices and techniques to develop and record new design, but since changes had to be integrated into existing code, the original implementation often influenced the design. For example, the NAS Monitor module MML branches to a subroutine, based on a return code; the designer created a CASE statement to model a branch table. (We extracted the PDL below from the MML design.)

```
"process Monitor output block (OMIB)"
"based on return code"
CASE
   retcode =
PART (01)
   RUN cod01 (IN omib OUT ereprec1)
PART (02)
   RUN cod02 (IN omib OUT ereprec1, ereprec2)
   .
   .
ESAC
```

The designer may not have chosen this design in creating a new module, but it was well suited to the existing implementation.

All HCS design was inspected. Representatives from the quality assurance and the software test organizations attended the inspections. Because modules were abstracted and recorded in a standard design language, all inspection attendees could comprehend the design without having to decipher the original code.

The function and state machine models provided the designer a specification from which to make the changes to the source code. In the final transformation, the designer had to consider the mapping to the target language and the contours and coding conventions of the original module. Updating the source required great care -- many pitfalls were encountered -- as might be expected in twenty-year-old software; but using stepwise abstraction and recording the design in PDL reduced the risk of a faulty implementation significantly.

RECORDING THE PROCESS

IBM delivered two documents to the FAA for each module with a design impact: a HCS Design Document (HDD), a textual description of the module's design; and the PDL for the changed parts of a module or a new module. PDL written and used only for analysis was not delivered.

Both the HDD and PDL were stored in an online library, available to all HCS project personnel. The software designer responsible for a module maintained a member in the HDD and PDL library for each module that changed. An outline organized the members into a single document.

In addition to verifying the new design, inspecting the HDD and PDL forced the designer to keep the design documents up-to-date. At code inspections, the software designers verified that the updated source code matched the HDD and PDL to ensure that implementation matched design. After verification the HDD and PDL were promoted to write-protected libraries to preserve their integrity.

All HDDs are written in the same format. An overall module description provides a functional view of the module. The high level design section describes the inputs, processing, outputs, and state data at a level of abstraction that allows a reader to gain intellectual control over the design without absorbing too much detail. For instance, if the designer knew the exact format of an input, he described it in the HDD; otherwise the precise specification was deferred to the PDL. Any procedural changes resulting from the new design were also documented in the high level design section. The final sections of the HDD describe the module's relationship to the subsystem (which programs call it, which programs it calls, how it is invoked) and any external interfaces.

All HCS PDL was developed using the same template (the state machine), whether a module behaved as a state machine or a function; if a module was modeled as a Cartesian function it was recorded as a state machine with no state data. The HCS project procedures specified a standard format to make reading the design documents easier and to aid the verification process for programmers and for the customer.

Figure 3 illustrates the HCS module design template. The PDL consists of three parts: definitions (the DEF section on the template); the intended state machine (the ISM section); and the

```
MOD module_name
DEF                             "Define data types and abstract operations"
ISM                             "THE SPECIFICATION PART (Intended State  "
                                "                             Machine)    "

   INPUT                        "Define machine's inputs                  "
   OUTPUT                       "Define machine's outputs                 "
   STATE                        "Define machine's state (retained) data   "
   INIT                         "Define machine's initial state           "
   TRANS                        "Define machine's state transitions       "
     ENTRY mmmm (IN x OUT y)    "Define domain range and function rule    "
            x>=0 --> y:=0       "x greater than 0 implies return a 0 in y "
            x<0  --> y:=x       "x less than 0 implies return x in y      "

     ENTRY nnnn (IN x OUT y)    "A second function                        "
       .
       .
       .

DES                             "THE DESIGN PART                          "
   PGMS                         "Refine functions as procedures           "
     PROC mmmm (IN x OUT y)     "Define variables and control logic       "
        VAR x : INTEGER
        VAR y : INTEGER
        y:=0                    "Initialize y to zero.                    "
        IF x<0 THEN y:=x FI     "Store x in y if x is negative.           "
     CORP

     PROC nnnn (IN x OUT y)
       .
       .
       .
     CORP
DOM
```

Figure 3. HCS Module Design Template

design part (the DES section). The definition
section allows the user to type data, and to define abstract operations, such as FIND and STOW
(see the PDL for OBJEDT below). On the HCS
project, most design changes required new or
changed data types, the result of new I/O devices
and greatly expanded storage capacity. The intended state machine part describes the specification: the input, output, state data and the operations performed on the data; the state
transitions. Each state transition is defined as
a function rule. The final part, the design part,
refines the intended state machine, developing
procedures which describe the function variables
and control logic. See Figure 5 as an example.

OBJECT EDIT (OBJEDT): AN EXAMPLE

OBJEDT is one of the FAA support programs that
build the NAS operational software. It allows
programmers and testers at the air traffic control
centers to update the software without changing
the source code.

New versions of NAS software are created at the
FAA Technical Center (FAATC) in Pomona, New
Jersey. The FAATC support staff distributes the
system to each of the air traffic control centers
on tape, in object form. To maintain system integrity at each of the centers, no source code is
delivered with the system. The air traffic control centers customize the standard NAS system
with adaptation data, a set of parameters that describes the center's processing environment, air

space, air traffic requirements, radar facilities,
etc. When a system is built, the adaptation data
initialize the COMPOOL, the COMPOOL is integrated
with the object modules, and an IPL system (essentially a large load module) is created on disk.

When a center must change NAS because of errors,
or unusual operational requirements, the change is
made using a patch (since the source code is not
available). A patch overlays an area of storage
(either instruction or data), and is applied while
the system is in startup mode. When a center
patches the system, it reports the change and reason for it to the FAATC staff, who incorporate it
into a future release. Because of the length of
time between releases, each center typically has
many patches that must be applied every time the
system is IPL'd.

The FAA wrote OBJEDT to reduce startup time by applying the patches to the object modules at system
build time, eliminating the need to apply them every time the system is IPL'd. OBJEDT reads a set
of patch records, locates the object modules to be
patched, applies the patches to each, and replaces
the updated object modules. The system build procedures use the updated object modules; additional
patches can still be applied at startup in the
conventional manner.

In the original implementation, OBJEDT processes
the modules entirely from tape. The object modules are distributed on tape, and the tape is input to the system build programs. The patch records are on punch cards. OBJEDT reads the cards

and creates a patch table in main storage. It then reads each object module sequentially from the tape, searches the patch table for any patches for that module, applies them, and writes the module to an output tape. On the 9020, an average OBJEDT run takes 20-30 minutes.

In the HCS implementation, the system build software processes the object modules from partitioned data sets on disk. OBJEDT reads the patch records and creates a patch table in main storage (as before, except that the patch records are a virtual card deck in a disk file). It locates (on disk) each object module to be patched, reads it, applies the patches for the module, and writes the module back to disk. In the new implementation, an average OBJEDT run takes 5-10 minutes.

The software designer began the OBJEDT conversion by recording the original version in PDL. Only that part of the code that reads and stores object modules was abstracted (although the designer had to understand the function of the entire program).

The designer modeled the tape input and output as a _sequence_ of object modules, and modeled an object module as a _sequence_ of records. The algorithm requires a WHILE-DO control structure to process the object modules one at a time. The parts of the code within the WHILE-DO structure that did not change (for instance applying the patches) in the new implementation were abstracted at a very high level. See Figure 4 and Figure 5.

In redesigning OBJEDT for the HCS, the designer changed the data specifications to reflect NAS object modules residing on disk as partitioned data sets, rather than on tape, modeling the partitioned data sets as _sets_ in the new design. Two operators were defined for the new data type: FIND, which located object modules in the set and retrieved them; and STOW, which replaced object modules back into the set. Using the new data type, the designer wrote an algorithm to determine which programs to patch, FIND the object module, apply all the patches for that module, and STOW the module.

```
        MOD OBJEDT

        DEF
          TYPE pgms = SEQ OF pgm_name        "Table of programs to edit      "
          TYPE pgm_name = SEQ OF CHAR        "8-byte program name            "
          TYPE pds = SET OF members          "partitioned data set           "
          TYPE members = SEQ OF block        "an object module               "
          TYPE block = SEQ OF card           "a partition of a member        "
          TYPE card = SEQ OF CHAR            "80-byte card image             "

          FIND(x,y) = get the member identified by x from set y
          STOW(x,y) = replace the member identified by x in set y

        ISM
          INPUT
            VAR names : SEQ OF pgm_name        "entries in name table        "
            VAR mods : SEQ OF patch            "entries in patch table       "

          OUTPUT
            VAR names : SEQ OF pgm_name        "updated name table entries "

          STATE
            VAR data_set : pds                 "data set containing programs"
            VAR blocksize : INTEGER            "size of members partition  "
            VAR in_buf : block                 "input buffer               "
            VAR out_buf : block                "output buffer              "

          INIT
            data_set := "This set is created by other modules         "
            blocksize := "A characteristic of the physical storage device   "
            in_buf, out_buf := EMPTY

          TRANS
            ENTRY ESD01 (IN names, mods OUT names)
              "Get programs to be patched from name table and apply patches   "
        DES
          PGMS
            "The procs listed here are defined below"

            PROC ESD01 (IN names, rmods OUT names)
            PROC GET( IN in_buf OUT text_card, eof )
            PROC PUT( IN text_card, buf_size OUT out_buf, buf_size )

        DOM
```

Figure 4.   OBJEDT Overall State Machine Design

```
        PROC ESD01 (IN names,mods OUT names)

        "Get programs to be patched from name table and apply patches   "
        "from mods table                                                "

        VAR names : SEQ OF pgm_name        "entries in name table       "
        VAR mods : SEQ OF patch            "entries in patch table      "
        VAR pgm : pgm_name                 "program name                "
        VAR eof : BOOLEAN                  "End-of-file indicator        "
        VAR text_card : card               "one record of object member"
        VAR buf_size : INTEGER             "amount of out_buf used       "

          names := RESET
          WHILE
            names ¬= EMPTY
          DO
            buf_size := 0
            eof := FALSE
            pgm := NEXT( names )
            member := FIND( pgm, data_set )
            member := RESET
            RUN get( IN in_buf OUT text_card, eof )
            WHILE
              ¬eof
            DO
              "Apply patches from mods table to text_card        "
              "(existing code builds ESD, TXT, and RLD cards from "
              "the patches and inserts them in the object deck)   "

              RUN put( IN text_card, buf_size OUT out_buf, buf_size )
              RUN get( IN in_buf OUT text_card, eof )
            OD
            IF
              out_buf ¬= EMPTY
            THEN
              CURRENT( member ) := out_buf
              out_buf := RESET
            FI
            data_set := STOW( pgm, dataset )
          OD

        CORP


PROC GET( IN in_buf OUT text_card, eof )          PROC PUT( IN text_card, buf_size OUT out_buf, buf_size )

"Read object into input buffer from dataset"      "Put text_card into output dataset"

VAR in_buf : block                                VAR text_card : card
VAR text_card : card                              VAR out_buf : block
VAR eof : BOOLEAN                                 VAR buf_size : INTEGER
                                                  CONST rec_len = 80
  IF
    in_buf = EMPTY                                  NEXT( out_buf ) := text_card
  THEN                                              buf_size := buf_size + rec_len
    in_buf := NEXT( member )                        IF
    IF                                                buf_size = blocksize
      in_buf = EMPTY                                THEN
    THEN                                              CURRENT( member ) := out_buf
      eof := TRUE                                     buf_size := 0
    ELSE                                              out_buf := RESET
      text_card := NEXT( in_buf )                   FI
    FI
  ELSE                                            CORP
    text_card := NEXT( in_buf )
  FI

CORP
```

Figure 5. OBJEDT Procedures

The completed and inspected PDL served as the specification for revising the OBJEDT source code. To date, no errors have been found in the HCS OBJEDT.

OBJEDT is representative of many of the changes made to NAS; the change to the algorithm was driven by a change to the data. In OBJEDT, disk data sets replaced tape input and output. Once the designer created a data abstraction from the code, he changed the appropriate data specifications, and redesigned the program to use them. While many programs required more extensive and more difficult changes, the basic methods used to develop the new design were the same.

CONCLUSIONS

The process of modifying a large, complex software system is exacting. Software designers must read and understand parts of the software without understanding the whole, then modify the parts and insert them without degrading the system's performance. And the modifications, whether a result of a new capability or a changed hardware interface, frequently do not follow the contours of the original software structure.

Thinking about and recording programs in an abstract -- yet precise -- way is fundamental to IBM-FSD's software design methods. These methods were decisive in the successful re-engineering of the NAS en route software. The example program, OBJEDT, is one of over 60 redesigned for the Host Computer System. Its correct execution, and the correct execution of all the NAS en route software on S/370 processors has been demonstrated to the FAA. The entire HCS effort, hosting more than 1.5 million lines of code, while adding or modifying 152,000 lines, was completed on schedule (21 months) and under cost, with a staff of junior and intermediate (five to seven years experience) level programmers.

As a result of our experience on the FAA HCS project we feel that software design methods that treat programs as mathematical objects -- whose behaviors are predictable and verifiable -- may turn out to be more valuable in modifying existing software than in creating new software.

ACKNOWLEDGEMENTS

The authors gratefully acknowledge the work done by Sarah Peterson in developing the OBJEDT design and the efforts of Kevin Blanc in preparing this paper for publication.

REFERENCES

1. Keeley J. F., Blakeney G. R., Cudney L. F., Eickhorn C. R., Devereaux J. A., Lancto D. C., Rockefeller, R. L., Suda R. and Seward, F. K., "An Application-oriented Multiprocessing System," IBM Systems Journal, Volume 6, Number 2, 1967.

2. Mills, H. D. and O'Neill, D. and Linger, R. C. and Dyer, M. and Quinnan, R. E., "The Management Of Software Engineering," IBM Systems Journal, Volume 19, Number 4, 1980, pages 414-417.

3. Britcher, R. N., Moore, A. R. and Segal, M. A., "Technology Transfer: The Key To Software Engineering Standards," IEEE Computer Society Second Software Engineering Standards Application Workshop (SESAW), May 1983, pages 33-36.

4. Linger, R. C., Mills, H. D., and Witt, B. I. Structured Programming Theory and Practice, Addison-Wesley, 1979.

5. Ferrentino, A. B. and Mills, H. D., "State Machines And Their Semantics In Software Engineering," Proceedings, IEEE Computer Society First International Computer Software and Applications Conference (COMPSAC), 1977, pages 242-251.

6. Shankar, K. S., "A Functional Approach To Module Verification," IEEE Transactions On Software Engineering, Volume SE-8, March 1982, pages 147-160.

7. Britcher, R. N., and Moore, A. R. , "Increased Productivity Through the Use of Software Engineering In An Industrial Environment," Proceedings, IEEE Computer Society Fifth International Computer Software and Applications Conference (COMPSAC), November 1981, pages 199-205.

8. Moore, A. R. and Kopp, R. S., "Educational Experiences In Industrial Software Engineering," Proceedings of the ACM, 1980, pages 118-122.

SOFTWARE IMPROVEMENT PROGRAM (SIP): A TREATMENT FOR SOFTWARE SENILITY

Carol A. Houtz

PRC Government Information Systems
1500 Planning Research Drive
McLean, VA 22102

ADP organizations are plagued with high maintenance costs, long delays in responding to users' changing needs, and continued development and maintenance of antiquated, outmoded, and relatively obsolete software. This software can be thought of as being in an advanced state of software senility, a degenerative condition, which if not corrected, will eventually render the software totally useless. A reversal of this situation requires a Software Improvement Program (SIP), which is a treatment for the ills of software senility, and offers a cure for many of the software problems from which most ADP organizations are suffering. A SIP is an incremental and evolutionary approach to modernizing software to maximize its value, quality, efficiency, and effectiveness, while simultaneously preserving the value of past software investments and enabling the organization to capitolize on today's modern ADP technology, as well as future technological advances in the field. This paper describes the SIP philosophy and presents a strategy for implementing a dynamic, ongoing SIP coupled with a sound Software Engineering Technology (SET), to attack the causative factors of the ever-growing software crisis.

Key Words: Software Engineering Technology (SET); software improvement; Software Improvement Program (SIP); software obsolescense; stepwise refinement.

1. Need for Software Improvement

Over the past several decades there have been substantial changes in the automatic data processing (ADP) industry. There have been dramatic increases in hardware productivity, with a significant decrease in the footprint of the hardware configuration due to its reduced size, component modularity, and lowered air-conditioning and electrical consumption. Simultaneously, total ADP costs have continued to rise with the largest costs shifting from hardware to software. This shift in costs is primarily due to substantial automatic data processing equipment (ADPE) price reductions, coupled with increased personnel costs for software development and maintenance activities.

During this same period of high-powered, low-cost, rapidly-advancing ADPE, many ADP organizations are facing a software crisis. Software activities are still labor intensive, with little increases in productivity being realized in software production and maintenance. Resource utilization has shifted from software

development activities to maintenance, with over half of all software personnel involved in correcting software errors, modifying software to change its functions or extend its life, and simply keeping the software operational [1].

Most existing government software is well over a decade old, with some as much as twenty to twenty-five years old. Much of the software was originally written on second-generation hardware and operating systems, in machine-dependent and nonstandard languages, and have undergone several hardware, operating system, and language conversions. Most of this software was written with little or no utilization of software design, programming, or testing standards, guidelines, or procedures; required substantial operator intervention; utilized sequentially accessed card and tape input and output files; and had minimal, inadequate, or in some cases, a total lack of documentation.

---

[1]Figures in brackets indicate the literature references at the end of this paper.

Reprinted from *The Proceedings of the 19th Computer Performance Evaluation Users Group*, National Bureau of Standards Special Publication 500-104, October 1983, pages 92-107. U.S. Government work. Not protected by U.S. copyright.

Embedded in this aging software were home-grown system utility and operating system features such as sorts, merges, record buffers, copies, and manual restarts. These features were included, of necessity, in the software because most of the features of modern software package utilities and operating systems, which we now take for granted, were not available as packages or in operating systems of that day. Many of these home-grown utilities and operating systems are no longer supported by the developing organization or the vendor, nor is there a readily available and adequate pool of programmers for maintenance of this software.

In the past, bigger or more powerful ADPE configurations, or emulation or simulation has been a quick fix for these software problems. But increasingly, the hardware fix for the software aches and pains has been found to be a fleeting panacea, or a temporary solution at best; and today's modern systems cannot, and do not, support emulation or simulation of the older programming features and practices.

Coupled with these problems of aging software, ADP organizations are plagued with high maintenance costs, long delays in responding to users' changing needs, and continued development and operation of antiquated and underpowered computer software. Productivity increases for ADP organizations with these problems are severely limited, if not impossible to attain, due to the proliferation of archaic software analysis, design, coding, and testing features and techniques; low-level and nonstandard languages; machine or environment dependencies; and custom-written utilities.

This antiquated, aging, outmoded, and relatively obsolete software is in need of modernization. While this software cannot be termed totally obsolete, because it is still operational, it can be thought of as being in an advanced state of software senility. Software senility is a degenerative condition, which if not corrected, will eventually render the software totally useless.

In view of the many and complex, aforementioned software problems, and the emerging trend that the software crisis will continue to grow and worsen, a quick fix or single solution to the problems is not feasible, and a direct conversion from the problem environment to a modern ADPE system and environment is virtually impossible. To solve these problems and combat the software crisis, a program must be instituted to preserve the value of past software investments as much as possible, and provide an incremental and evolutionary approach to modernizing the existing software to maximize its value, quality, effectiveness, and efficiency.

Such a software improvement program (SIP) is described herein as a treatment for the ills of software senility, and offers a cure for many of the software problems from which today's

government ADP organizations are suffering. Institutionalization of a sound software engineering technology (SET), coupled with a dynamic, ongoing SIP, can attack the causative factors of the software crisis; and provide the government with viable, modernized, effective, efficient, and high quality ADP systems, capable of capitolizing on today's modern ADP technology, as well as future technological advances in the field.

2. Goals of a SIP

There are many goals for a SIP to achieve. The most important of them being to-

. improve software maintenance and control;

. reduce delays in responding to users' needs;

. improve software quality;

. increase programmer productivity;

. decrease software maintenance costs;

. institutionalize processes;

. change software from a reactive to proactive state;

. extend the software's life; and

. put the organization in a position to take advantage of new and emerging technology.

However, the end goals of a SIP are not only to improve software maintenance and control, but also to achieve as much isolation of function and standardization of interfaces within the software systems as possible. The achievement of these goals is attained through-

. isolating system functions;

. allowing for interchangeability of system functions; and

. facilitating change of elements within function.

Isolating system functions through modularization is a natural step towards avoiding reliance upon one architecture or environment, and increases software maintainability and understandability. As functions are isolated, more design alternatives present themselves and further possibilities of segmentation emerge. Thus, isolation of function holds the key to selecting cost-effective and efficient system alternatives in the future.

Functions should also be interchangeable with alternative design realizations to facilitate functional interfaces. This interchangeability of function, usually achieved through the use of reuseable and standardized modules of code, ensures an easier change in the means of performing a function. For example, exchanging a called module that accesses a tape file for a called module that accesses a disk data set.

Facilitating the change of elements within functions refers to the software's portability and maintainability. Better portability and easier maintainability through the use of single-function, standardized, and reuseable modules of code is paramount to achieving the goals of a SIP. Easier changeability of the software and its functions, increases and ensures more efficient use of the key data processing resources, especially people and machines. Standardizing, modularizing, parameterizing, and documenting the software are several techniques that aid in facilitating the change of elements within functions.

Improving the software's quality (i.e., making the software better), is probably the best available means of achieving the SIP's goals. Software quality is a measure of its excellence, worth, or value against some ideal or standard. Although quality is an ill-defined term, there are many specific properties, or attributes, by which it can be defined or measured [2]. Figure 1 illustrates a proposed hierarchy of the major software quality attributes and their subordinate attributes. Although the subattributes are listed under only one major attribute, it must be stressed that several of them could conceivably be listed under more than one major attribute. For the sake of clarity and to minimize misunderstandings, each subattribute has been listed only once, under the major attribute with which it is most often associated.

It must be noted that it is rarely possible for all software quality attributes or subattributes to be implemented. It is first necessary to define the SIP's goals, and then the improvement objectives for each individual software application. Appropriate tradeoff decisions must then be made among the various quality attributes and subattributes, and the goals and objectives to be achieved. For example, some processing efficiency may have to be sacrificed to achieve more maintainability, and vice versa.

3. Description of a SIP

A SIP can be thought of as a preventive maintenance program for software. Like ADPE preventive maintenance, software must also be periodically and systematically cleaned-up, fine-tuned, optimized, and enhanced to keep it in working order and capable of fulfilling its current and future requirements.

The concept of software improvement is not new, rather it is an outgrowth of normal day-to-day software maintenance projects and an extension of conversion projects. Some types of software improvement, such as realigning code and implementing naming conventions, are presently performed concurrently with such everyday tasks as software modification or maintenance, or for conversion from one computer configuration to another. However, these improvements are traditionally performed on a random, piecemeal basis, without structure or overall software or organizational considerations.

Such improvement decisions are usually made by the individual programmer without the benefit of managerial input. This bottom-up, piecemeal approach to software improvement is unstructured, and usually results in an unsuccessful attempt to cohesively improve the current software and acquire and use modern tools and techniques.

In contrast to the traditional, single-purpose software improvement approach, the modern software improvement approach, as described hereinafter, actually serves multiple purposes. Under the modern software improvement approach, improvements are not performed to meet only a single need or objective, but rather to accomplish several objectives and reconcile multiple problem areas. Also, the decisions as to when software improvement is needed and what types of improvements are needed are not left to the individual programmer or analyst, and the improvements are not performed in a casual manner. Rather, these decisions and the improvement performance are institutionalized as a formal process to which all programmers and analysts must adhere.

While the software improvement concept may not be new, the software improvement approach to building or improving systems, is innovative and more sophisticated than the conventional and more simplistic software life-cycle approach. The software improvement approach to building and improving systems [1] is built on the key assumptions that—

. most major ADP organizations have a decade or more of investment in software;

. most Federal organizations are almost entirely dependent on their software to meet their mission;

. keeping software operational is difficult enough without deviating from that baseline of software to add enhancements or change functions through major redesign or new development, which is thought to be an uncertain and risky business; and

. there is a need to support new applications to keep ADP costs low and service levels high.

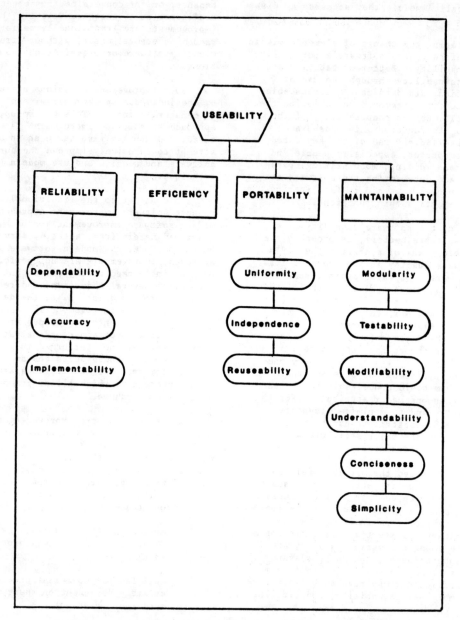

Figure 1. Hierarchy of Software Quality Attributes

The software improvement approach to improving existing systems, or building new systems from existing software, is different from the conventional system development approach in that it recognizes-

. the existence and characteristics of the current systems that support day-to-day operations;

. the existence of other operational systems that may be integrated to replace functions in an existing system;

. the inherent problems in engineering new code in any quantity;

. that existing systems are frequently the only specification of existing processes;

. the need to preserve the testing integrity of the current system while moving to a new or improved system;

. that many faults or deficiencies in an existing system can be accurately and cost-effectively corrected by improving it;

. the need for an orderly, incremental approach to the building or improving of a system that allows for adequate testing, manageable pieces, constant achievement and growth, and progress feedback;

. the need for a useable version of the new or improved system at each stage of development or improvement, allowing for rapid capitalization upon the new system and its components; and

. the virtual impossibility of completely re-engineering or redeveloping very large systems within a reasonable time frame [3].

The universe of software, from which a desired application can be built or improved on, can be conceived as a triangle, as illustrated in Figure 2.

At the apex of the triangle is all of the "software that currently exists" in production today. This software performs the functions that the organization needs to conduct its day-to-day business. Because this software is already working and tested, it has an intrinsic value to the organization and represents the vested interest an organization has in its own software applications. Existing software is usually salvaged, transferred, and incorporated into a new or improved system by purging any undesirable or unnecessary software, leaving some of the software as it is, and improving the remaining software through conversion, refine-

ment, and enhancement activities. While it is typically the easiest and most accurate to test and the least costly to produce, this software is often the most expensive code to maintain because it is usually undocumented and built in a "patchwork" fashion.

At the bottom left-hand corner of the triangle is "other operational software that exists" in other organizations. This external software represents the software packages available from industry or other ADP organizations. While this software may suffer from some deficiencies, it may be modified to fit the organization's needs. Also, many software packages are highly maintainable, well documented, and quite portable, and may not require extensive, if any, modification. External software is usually incorporated into a system by replacing existing code with an existing package. This software is typically somewhere between existing and new software in cost, accuracy, and maintainability, depending on the package's functions and its level of sophistication.

Finally, at the bottom right-hand corner is "new software," which does not yet exist and must therefore be engineered. While this code is typically the easiest to maintain because it is state-of-the-art and newly documented, in terms of accuracy it is normally the most difficult to engineer and the most risky to undertake because there is no existing baseline from which to test or measure. It is also the most costly to produce because it must be engineered from "scratch." This software should be incorporated into a system as a last resort, if transfer of the existing software or replacement with a package is not feasible. Nevertheless, any new software should be engineered using modern programming practices to ensure software that is well documented; fits the application better; is easy to support, read, understand, modify, and enhance; and is less expensive and time consuming to maintain.

The software improvement approach to improving an existing system or constructing a new one, thus is one of-

. determining on a case-by-case basis, the source (e.g., existing internal software, existing external software package, or new software) of the software or software subpiece;

. determining the actions required to modify and/or implement the software (e.g., purge the software from the system; salvage the current software by leaving it alone and moving it as it is; salvage the current software by improving it through conversion, refinement, and/or enhancement; replace the current software with an external software package; or redesign/newly develop the software);

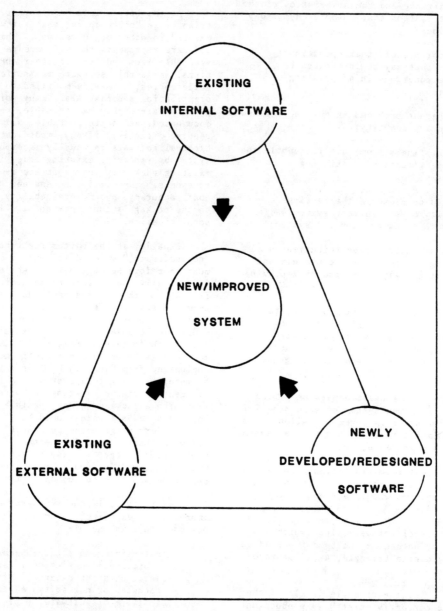

Figure 2. Software Improvement Approach

. assessing the software's source and actions required against the costs, benefits, and risks of each; and, then

. developing a strategy or plan for the software's purge, transfer, improvement, integration, and/or redesign/new development into the improved or newly constructed system.

In summary, four basic advantages of the software improvement approach to improving or building a system over the conventional system development approach are that it—

. minimizes uncertainty and risk by maximizing the utilization of testable components;

. preserves the value of past software investment as much as possible and avoids the dangers of failure inherent in the "tear-it-down-and-start-anew" approach;

. enables the project to be broken into small, manageable pieces with an operational system at each phase; and

. is iterative in nature, which allows for the tasks performed to be repeated in an orderly, incremental fashion with constant achievement, growth, and feedback, until the overall objectives of the project are met.

4. Stepwise Refinement

Because of the large amount of software that exists in most ADP organizations, most software can't be improved in one "lump sum." Thus, the software must be divided into smaller, more manageable increments, that progress through the software improvement process as a work unit. Increments can be based on system, subsystem, or project boundaries, or by functional areas (e.g., input, edit, file update, report generation, or error handling). The key is to subdivide the software minimizing the interfaces between the groups. The absense, or minimization, of increment interfaces makes the improvements for each increment more independent, and allows the concurrent improvement of several increments at a time.

Also, because of the vast differences that may exist between the current and desired software environments, most needed improvements can't be accomplished in one "quantum leap." Thus, the improvements for each increment are accomplished in multiple steps or releases [3] of logically related sets of improvement activities that are performed at one time. Improvements are normally subdivided by activity type into the three basic releases of conversion, refinement, and enhancement as depicted in Figure 3.

As illustrated in Figure 3, the software improvement activities under these three releases range from simple translation of code to complete re-engineering of existing systems. The software improvement activities flow from one release to the next; thus, there is no "clear cut" dividing line between each release, and some functional overlap is inevitable.

The decisions as to the number of releases necessary to improve each increment, and the improvement activities to be performed in each release, are dependent on the size of the increment, overall number and type of improvements required, and priority of the improvements. Improvement activities can be combined into one large release, or further subdivided into multiple mini-releases as illustrated in Figure 4. Figure 4 also illustrates the stepwise refinement approach to upgrading and modernizing the software, with continual advancement and the opportunity between each stp to reevaluate the SIP plans and results, and to introduce changes as necessary.

Software improvement conversion activities transform the software, without functional change, standardizing it and making it environment independent. Without standardization and independence, the next two releases, refinement and enhancement, would be extremely difficult, if not impossible, to accomplish. Standardized software, that is as independent as possible, lends itself to manipulation by automated means and proceduralized processes, and facilitates flexibility for future requirements (e.g., moving to a new environment).

Software improvement refinement activities modernize the software to a state-of-the-art status and improve software maintainability and programmer productivity. Refinement is a prerequisite for software enhancement to ensure enhancements are not being made to unmaintainable software with obsolete coding features (e.g., EXAMINE or ALTER statements in COBOL), or outdated or incorrect functional requirements.

Software improvement enhancement activities optimize the value, quality, efficiency, and effectiveness of the software enabling easier technical redesigns, easier addition of modern "technological" features and capabilities, and more efficient and effective use of resources. Without enhancement, the standardized and modernized software may still not function efficiently or effectively, or fulfill the user's desired requirements.

Improvement activities do not have to be subdivided into these three basic releases or follow the suggested release flow. They can be combined into one large release, or further subdivided into multiple mini-releases. The decisions as to the number of releases necessary to improve each increment, and the improvement activities to be performed in each release, are dependent on the size of the increment, overall

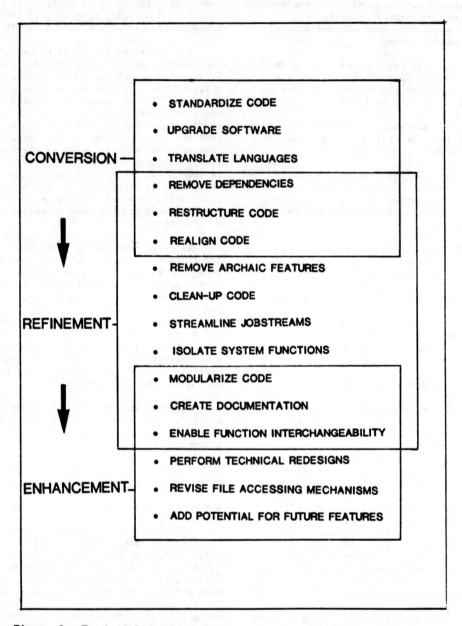

CONVERSION —
- STANDARDIZE CODE
- UPGRADE SOFTWARE
- TRANSLATE LANGUAGES
- REMOVE DEPENDENCIES
- RESTRUCTURE CODE
- REALIGN CODE

REFINEMENT -
- REMOVE ARCHAIC FEATURES
- CLEAN-UP CODE
- STREAMLINE JOBSTREAMS
- ISOLATE SYSTEM FUNCTIONS
- MODULARIZE CODE
- CREATE DOCUMENTATION
- ENABLE FUNCTION INTERCHANGEABILITY

ENHANCEMENT-
- PERFORM TECHNICAL REDESIGNS
- REVISE FILE ACCESSING MECHANISMS
- ADD POTENTIAL FOR FUTURE FEATURES

Figure 3. Typical Software Improvement Release Flow and Activities

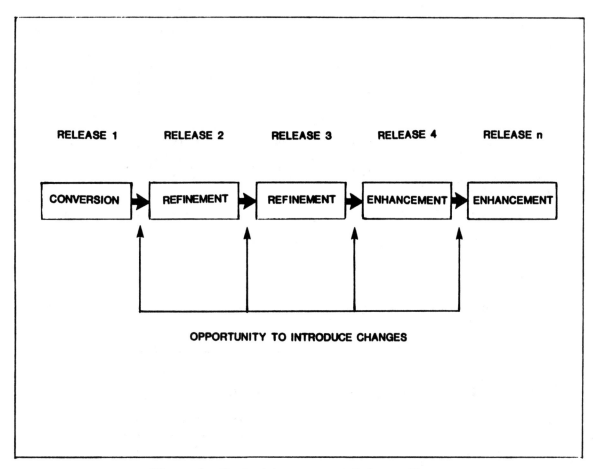

Figure 4. Typical Incremental Release Flow

number and type of improvements required, and priority of the improvements.

5. Major Benefits of a SIP

The tasks required during the software improvement process encompass a broad range of activities, and at a minimum include-

. performing a software inventory and analysis;

. developing SIP plan(s);

. establishing engineering elements;

. preparing work packages;

. preparing test data sets;

. developing software improvement release specifications;

. improving the software;

. unit and system testing the improved software;

. documenting the software;

. acceptance testing the improved software; and

. transitioning the improved software into production.

From this list of tasks, it is clear that a SIP is labor, management, machine-resource, and, possibly, deadline intensive. However, in spite of the problems that will inevitably arise, a SIP can be successfully engineered and prove highly beneficial to the organization.

The advantage of utilizing state-of-the-art technological advances, such as teleprocessing, data base management systems (DBMS), and mass storage, is one such benefit. Also, a SIP provides the capability to use this modern technology without being "locked in" to architectural or environmental dependencies.

Another benefit is the potential for more efficient and effective programmer productivity. Existing software, after improvement, can be maintained much more efficiently and the programmer's span of control should be greatly increased. That is, after software improvement, a programmer can maintain significantly more lines of code or system functions due to the increased maintainability and understandability of the improved software. The result is increased availability of an organization's most scarce resource -- skilled programmers. A SIP more efficiently uses key resources, both people and machines. More readily available junior personnel can be used for both new development and maintenance, with improved productivity, lower risk, and less training. The more senior

personnel can be used for more advanced tasks such as systems design or analysis, or tool evaluation and selection.

Additionally, the incorporation of a Software Engineering Technology (SET), consisting of a synchronized set of software standards and guidelines, procedures, tools, quality assurance, and training implemented through and coupled with a dynamic, ongoing SIP, simplifies the learning required of programmers and analysts. The simplified learning enables the institutionalization of a single training program for a common methodology and consolidated goals and objectives.

More efficient use of the ADPE is also possible because the state-of-the-art ADPE will not simply emulate obsolete or out-of-date functions. Rather, it will perform the technologically advanced activities for which it was designed.

Many additional benefits can be achieved with a thorough, comprehensive, and well-planned, -analyzed, and -managed SIP. Some of these include-

. improved user service levels;

. more flexibility for future requirements;

. the capability for automatic documentation and/or code generation;

. enhanced error recovery, system debugging, testing, data integrity, and security features;

. increased software quality (i.e., reliability, efficiency, portability, and/or maintainability);

. improved quality of software end-products (e.g., reports, statistics, and programs); and

. a synchronized, formalized, and tested SET for the SIP.

6. SIP and SET Interrelationship

As previously discussed, the SIP works closely, and in tandem with a SET. A SET, as depicted in Figure 5, consists of a synchronized group of five equally important software engineering elements:

. standards and guidelines;
. procedures;
. tools;
. quality assurance (QA); and
. training.

These five software engineering elements direct and control all software activities throughout the software's life cycle [4], and

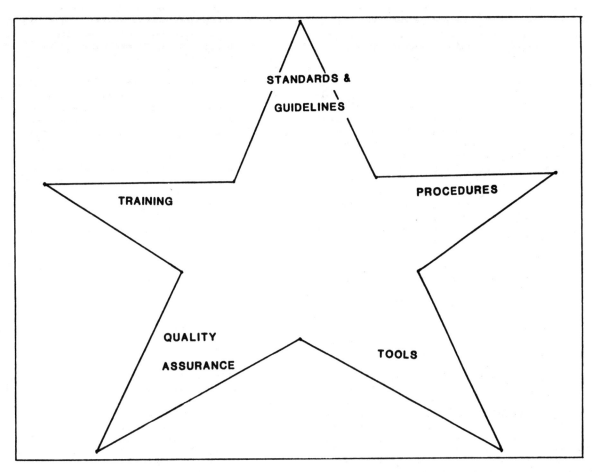

Figure 5. Software Engineering Technology Engineering Elements

for different software engineering or
re-engineering purposes (e.g., software development, maintenance, improvement, conversion, or
redesign). Thus, the SET addresses, on an
organization-wide basis, the software engineering methods, metrics, and latest controls
for managing an installation's software activities, while the SIP addresses the upgrading of
the existing software (i.e., programs, modules,
job streams, files, and documentation) with
regard to the SET baseline.

The same five engineering elements of a SET
are required, in a specialized sense, for a SIP.
The establishment of these five engineering
elements as a formalized SET is paramount to the
successful implementation of a SIP. Improvement
and installation standards, guidelines, and
procedures are required to standardize the
software activities and the software, so they
can be measured, controlled, and improved.
Specialized improvement tools are both necessary
and desirable to increase programmer productivity, enforce systemization, and improve
controls. QA is required to quantitatively prove
that the SIP is a viable and worthwhile effort,
ensure that the improvements made actually
resolve the problems, identify and measure the
resultant improvements and benefits, and control
and enforce the quality of the software and the
improvement performance. Finally, training and
retraining are also necessary, for without them
successful accomplishment of the SIP would be
next to impossible and the improved software and
methodologies would quickly degrade.

The establishment of a SIP and a SET are
separate, but interrelated and coordinated
processes. Each can be established independently of the other, but each has a controlling
or influencing effect on the other. That is,
the standards and guidelines, procedures, tools,
QA, and training established for the installation as a SET, define the framework for, and
provide a baseline from which, the SIP can
operate. In this sense, the SIP cannot, for
example, set standards that oppose those
instituted in the SET, or use tools that
conflict with the tool's technology chosen for
the organization and established in the SET.

Conversely, standards and guidelines,
procedures, tools, QA, and training, when established in a SIP; limit the choices of the SET.
For example, the SET cannot institute software
or installation standards different from those
just implemented by a SIP, or maintained and
enforced by the improvement tools. If either
the SIP or SET institute engineering elements
without considering the organizational impact,
or short- and long-term consequences, the
resulting software and engineering activities
will, at best, be chaotic and consist of a
"patchwork" of styles, structure, and standards.

A SIP and a SET should be established
together, one complementing the other. This
double-barreled approach to resolving software

problems can be thought of as a Software and
Technology Modernization Program (STMP). Figure
6 illustrates a typical interrelationship of the
SIP and SET as integral parts of a STMP.
Implementing a STMP thus becomes an effort to-

. identify needed program-unique or
  organization-wide engineering elements
  (i.e., standards and guidelines, procedures, tools, QA mechanisms, and
  training);

. consider long-term software activities
  and consequences (e.g., ADPE and
  software compatibility, the upward
  compatibility of software changes, and
  technological advancements), and analyze
  the full spectrum of impact (e.g.,
  across engineering activities, or
  between projects), before adopting any
  specific standards, procedures, etc.;

. isolate the program-unique engineering
  elements for the SIP from the
  organization-wide engineering elements
  for the SET;

. adopt and institute as part of the SIP,
  the program-unique engineering elements;
  and

. adopt and institute as part of the SET,
  the organization-wide engineering
  elements.

7. Synosis of a SIP

A synopsis of the six key principles of a
SIP are:

. Evolutionary Growth: That is, build on
  your past software investment as much as
  possible by purging some of the software, leaving some of it alone,
  replacing some software with packages,
  improving most of the software, and
  redesigning or newly developing only
  that which is absolutely necessary.

. Incremental Improvement: Minimize the
  risk of failure and make the SIP more
  manageable by grouping the software,
  through functional decomposition, into
  smaller, logical subpieces with minimal
  interfaces.

. Top-Down Planning with Bottom-Up Input:
  Plan in a hierarchical manner, from a
  general, overall SIP level, progressing
  to more specific, increment levels.
  Allow for continual feedback, analysis,
  and evaluation of improvement plans,
  results, and methodologies.

. SIP Pilot Project: Prototype the
  improvements, engineering elements, and
  methodologies on a small scale to
  empirically demonstrate the feasibility

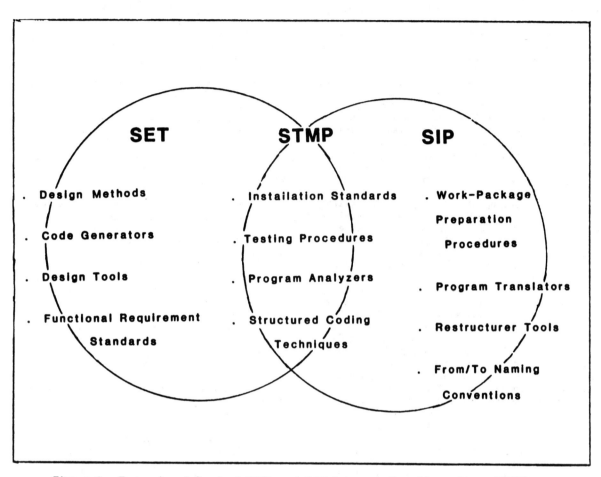

SET

. Design Methods

. Code Generators

. Design Tools

. Functional Requirement
  Standards

STMP

. Installation Standards

. Testing Procedures

. Program Analyzers

. Structured Coding
  Techniques

SIP

. Work-Package
  Preparation
  Procedures

. Program Translators

. Restructurer Tools

. From/To Naming
  Conventions

Figure 6. Example of Typical SET and SIP Interrelationship under a STMP

and success of the improvements, methodologies, and plans; and to help solve, early in the SIP life cycle, any technical problems that may occur.

. Release Specifications: Subdivide the improvements required for each increment into logically related sets of improvement activities that can be performed at one time (e.g., conversion, refinement, and enhancement). Develop release specifications which direct and control the improvements to be performed for each release of an increment. Be sure to include in the specifications the specific improvements required for each individual system, subsystem, program, module, job stream, and/or file in the increment, as well as the required deliverables, standards of performance, and acceptance criteria.

. Engineering Elements (SET): Establish within the SIP, or as a baseline SET, formalized engineering elements (i.e., standards and guidelines, procedures, tools, QA, and training) to be implemented, employed, and enforced by the SIP.

While the SIP guidelines presented here may not seem to be "earthshaking," they are a less risky, more formalized means of modernizing the organization's information processing, and have been found to be "tried-and-true." The use of these SIP guidelines is strongly encouraged, and in concert with a strong SET, will promote more uniform, thorough, cost-effective, and efficient software and software engineering activities.

8. SIP Case Studies

The most successful organizations have recognized that their software is a key asset, which must be developed, managed, controlled, and maintained with as much care and attention as their other important assets. That is why these organizations have invested, or are investing, significant resources into SIP's, using principles similar to those described here.

The experiences of these organizations should not be considered unique. The concept of a SIP is indeed a valid alternative to the two traditional choices of "don't-touch-it-or-it-will-fall-apart" and "tear-it-down-and-start-anew." Unless the functions are changing, substantial redesigns may not be necessary, and a SIP may solve immediate, as well as long-range ADP problems. It is an alternative with principles and procedures applicable to most government agencies, and must be given serious consideration.

Several organizations have successfully established and undertaken SIP's. Some examples of these organizations are the Office of

Personnel Management (OPM) in Washington, DC; Raytheon Service Company in Boston, MA; NCR Corporation in San Diego County, CA; and the San Diego County Department of Education in San Diego, CA.

Several years ago, OPM undertook a SIP with gratifying results. Many of its ADP systems were developed in Assembler language for an RCA Spectra 70/45, and when converted to COBOL, still reflected the second generation logic of the earlier Assembler code. OPM decided to adopt a controlled system improvement approach, migrating in steps from a second to third generation system. The decision was also made to convert the Assembler code to ANSI COBOL to simplify maintenance and enhance portability considerations [5].

Similarly, in the late seventies and early eighties, Raytheon undertook a SIP with the primary objective of developing, implementing, and perfecting a reuseable code methodology for accelerating applications development. By using reuseable code, 40 to 60 percent of the redundancy in their business applications development was eliminated, and maintenance was substantially improved [6].

In late 1976, the NCR Corporation undertook a large scale Quality Improvement Program (QIP) for a major set of systems software for over 103 separate products. This software set included operating systems, compilers, peripheral software, data utilities, and telecommunications handlers, and totaled over 1.3 million lines of source code. The QIP was initiated to provide improvements in the software base and to take advantage of recent advances in the state-of-the-art of software engineering. NCR found several major favorable effects resulting from the QIP, such as a substantial reduction in outstanding problems in the software base, a reduction in the average number of error reports per month, total elimination of problem backlogs, and a significant reduction in late responses to problem reports. All of these improvements are reflected in an improved perception of the quality of the software, and allowed NCR to make a very substantial redirection in funds from support of existing products to the development of new ones [2].

Finally, the San Diego County Department of Education's ADP data center cut its maintenance time by 70 percent as a result of a SIP. This startling reduction in the data center's program-maintenance load has resulted primarily from the decision to adopt and convert to structured design and programming techniques, with ongoing and formalized ADP training in these same areas. While the primary emphasis in this effort was on redesigning and replacing the existing systems, rather than salvaging the existing systems, the six key principles of a SIP were basically adhered to [7].

Besides the organizations that have established and undertaken successful SIP's, several Federal organizations are currently in the initial steps of establishing SIP's. Several of these organizations include the Social Security Administration (SSA) in Baltimore, MD; Veterans Administration's (VA) Data Processing Center (DPC) in Austin, TX; and Defense Mapping Agency (DMA) in Washington, DC.

The SIP being established by the SSA is a key example where the two traditional alternatives are infeasible. SSA is in the process of transitioning its more than 16,689 computer programs, containing over 11 million lines of code, from a "survival" mode to a state-of-the-art environment. To leave the systems alone will only result in further ADP system deterioration and seriously jeopardize the agency's ability to perform its basic mission. Conversely, to redesign all software would be extremely risky, require maximum reinvestment of resources, and require more time than SSA has to survive the current crisis. Thus, the key is an incremental, evolutionary improvement approach, aimed at a recovery of SSA's heavy investment in its software, and the ability to take advantage of new ADP technological advances [8].

The VA's Austin DPC is another example where top management has recognized that the efficiency and effectiveness of their mission is a function of their software. The Austin DPC has over three million lines of code of application software. Like software in most government agencies and industry, this software was not developed overnight; rather it has evolved over many years, with layer upon layer of modification making it even more complex, unmangeable, and unmaintainable. Together with a hardware-upgrade and SET initiative, the Austin DPC is initiating a SIP to cut escalating ADP costs, improve the quality of service to the veteran, and better support far-reaching management decisions [9].

The DMA is currently in the initial stages of a five-year program to upgrade its software and modernize it software production practices. The ultimate objectives of this SIP are to increase productivity, improve software quality, and standardize software development practices. DMA's SIP encompasses the three major areas of introducing of a modern programming environment, improving existing software, and upgrading development and management skills to support the new environment [10].

Several more organizations establishing SIP's are Tupperware in Orlando, FL; Ford Aerospace and Communications Corporation in Sunnyvale, CA; and New Jersey State Government.

From the preceeding discussion, it should be clear that organizations who can no longer afford outdated and inefficient information processing, want to combat the software crisis, want to stop "software "senility" in its tracks,

and, on the whole, need to modernize their software and software engineering technologies must establish a SIP. A commitment to undertake a SIP begins with top management, progresses through the ADP organization, and, ultimately, ends with the user. Top management commitment to the SIP is a major factor for its success, and manifests itself in three forms:

. First, top management must acknowledge that a software problem really exists, and resolve to correct it.

. Second, top management must be willing to "put their money where their mouth is." That is, they must not offer only "lip service," but be willing to devote the resources necessary to implement the SIP. Resources include people, dollars, time, ADPE, tools, and other miscellaneous supplies and materials.

. Third, top management must actively support the SIP and ADP organization by helping to advertise the SIP goals, objectives, benefits, and achievements, and by gaining user involvement and support.

There are three documents currently published on the subject of software improvement that may be of further interest to organizations contemplating a SIP. These documents are listed in the references [1, 11, 12] and contain more detailed information on the need for software improvement, planning and implementing a SIP, and the actual software improvement process.

References

[1] Office of Software Development, General Services Administration, Software Improvement - A Needed Process in the Federal Government, Report No. OSD-81-102, June 3, 1981.

[2] Woodmancy, Donald A., "A Software Quality Improvement Program," NCR Corporation, San Diego, CA, IEEE Catalog No. 79CH1479-5/C, 1979.

[3] Office of Software Development, General Services Administration, Long Range Plan, Report No. OSD-82-104, April 9, 1982.

[4] Federal Software Testing Center, General Services Administration, Establishing a Software Engineering Technology (SET), Report No. OSD/FSTC-83/014, June 1983.

[5] Cooper, Roger, "Upgrading Federal Computers Through Existing Systems," Government Executive, August 1979.

[6] Lanergan, Robert G. and Poynton, Brian A., "Reusable Code: The Application Development Technique of the Future," Raytheon Service Company.

[7]   Beeler, Jeffry, "Manager Cuts Maintenance
      Time by 70%," Computerworld, January 31,
      1983.

[8]   Social Security Administration, U.S.
      Departmetn of Health and Human Services,
      Systems Modernization Plan, February
      1982.

[9]   Austin, Texas Data Processing Center,
      Veterans Administration, Software Improve-
      ment Program (SIP) Macroplan, August 1983.

[10] Stroup, Opal R., DMA Software Improvement
      Program, Talking Paper for Federal DP Expo
      (Session E-2) "Dealing with Obsolescence:

      Conversion and Upgrading," DMA, U.S. Naval
      Observatory, Washington DC, April 12,
      1983.

[11] Federal Conversion Support Center, General
      Services Administration, Guidelines for
      Planning and Implementing a Software
      Improvement Program (SIP), Report No.
      OSD/FCSC-83/004, May 1983.

[12] Federal Conversion Support Center, General
      Services Administration, The Software
      Improvement (SI) Process --Its Phases and
      Tasks, Report No. OSD/FCSC-83/006, July
      1983.

Designing Software for Ease of Extension and Contraction

DAVID L. PARNAS

Abstract – Designing software to be extensible and easily contracted is discussed as a special case of design for change. A number of ways that extension and contraction problems manifest themselves in current software are explained. Four steps in the design of software that is more flexible are then discussed. The most critical step is the design of a software structure called the "uses" relation. Some criteria for design decisions are given and illustrated using a small example. It is shown that the identification of *minimal* subsets and *minimal* extensions can lead to software that can be tailored to the needs of a broad variety of users.

Index Terms – Contractibility, extensibility, modularity, software engineering, subsets, supersets.

Manuscript received June 7, 1978; revised October 26, 1978. The earliest work in this paper was supported by NV Phillips Computer Industrie, Apeldoorn, The Netherlands. This work was also supported by the National Science Foundation and the German Federal Ministry for Research and Technology (BMFT). This paper was presented at the Third International Conference on Software Engineering, Atlanta, GA, May 1978.

The author is with the Department of Computer Science, University of North Carolina, Chapel Hill, NC 27514. He is also with the Information Systems Staff, Communications Sciences Division, Naval Research Laboratory, Washington, DC.

I. INTRODUCTION

THIS paper is being written because the following complaints about software systems are so common.

1) "We were behind schedule and wanted to deliver an early release with only a <proper subset of intended capabilities>, but found that that subset would not work until everything worked."

2) "We wanted to add <simple capability>, but to do so would have meant rewriting all or most of the current code."

3) "We wanted to simplify and speed up the system by removing the <unneeded capability>, but to take advantage of this simplification we would have had to rewrite major sections of the code."

4) "Our SYSGEN was intended to allow us to tailor a system to our customers' needs but it was not flexible enough to suit us."

After studying a number of such systems, I have identified some simple concepts that can help programmers to design software so that subsets and extensions are more easily obtained. These concepts are simple if you think about software in the way suggested by this paper. Programmers do not commonly do so.

Reprinted from *IEEE Transactions on Software Engineering*, Volume SE-5, Number 2, March 1979, pages 128-138. Copyright © 1979 by The Institute of Electrical and Electronics Engineers, Inc.

II. Software As a Family of Programs

When we were first taught how to program, we were given a specific problem and told to write one program to do that job. Later we compared our program to others, considering such issues as space and time utilization, but still assuming that we were producing a single product. Even the most recent literature on programming methodology is written on that basis. Dijkstra's *A Discipline of Programming* [1] uses predicate transformers to specify *the* task to be performed by *the* program to be written. The use of the definite article implies that there is a unique problem to be solved and but one program to write.

Today, the software designer should be aware that he is not designing a single program but a family of programs. As discussed in an earlier paper [2], we consider a set of programs to be a program family if they have so much in common that it pays to study their common aspects before looking at the aspects that differentiate them. This rather pragmatic definition does not tell us what pays, but it does explain the motivation for designing program families. We want to exploit the commonalities, share code, and reduce maintenance costs.

Some of the ways that the members of a program family may differ are listed below.

1) They may run on different hardware configurations.

2) They may perform the same functions but differ in the format of the input and output data.

3) They may differ in certain data structures or algorithms because of differences in the available resources.

4) They may differ in some data structures or algorithms because of differences in the size of the input data sets or the relative frequency of certain events.

5) Some users may require only a subset of the services or features that other users need. These "less demanding" users may demand that they not be forced to pay for the resources consumed by the unneeded features.

Engineers are taught that they must try to anticipate the changes that may be made, and are shown how to achieve designs that can easily be altered when these anticipated changes occur. For example, an electrical engineer will be advised that the world has not standardized the 60-cycle 110-V current. Television designers are fully aware of the differing transmission conventions that exist in the world. It is standard practice to design products that are easily changed in those aspects. Unfortunately, there is no magic technique for handling unanticipated changes. The makers of conventional watches have no difficulty altering a watch that shows the day so that it displays "MER" instead of "WED," but I would except a long delay for redesign were the world to switch to a ten day week.

Software engineers have not been trained to design for change. The usual programming courses neither mention the need to anticipate changes nor do they offer techniques for designing programs in which changes are easy. Because programs are abstract mathematical objects, the software engineers' techniques for responding to anticipated changes are more subtle and more difficult to grasp than the techniques used by designers of physical objects. Further, we have been led astray by the other designers of abstract objects—mathematicians who state

and prove theorems. When a mathematician becomes aware of the need for a set of closely related theorems, he responds by proving a more general theorem. For mathematicians, a more general result is always superior to a more specialized product. The engineering analogy to the mathematician's approach would be to design television sets containing variable transformers and tuners that are capable of detecting several types of signals. Except for the U.S. armed forces stationed overseas, there is little market for such a product. Few of us consider relocations so likely that we are willing to pay to have the generality present in the product. My guess is that the market for calendar watches for a variable length week is even smaller than the market for the television sets just described.

In [2] I have treated the subject of the design of program families rather generally and in terms of text in a programming language. In this paper I focus on the fifth situation described above; families of programs in which some members are subsets of other family members or several family members share a common subset. I discuss an earlier stage of design, the stage when one identifies the major components of the system and defines relations between those components. We focus on this early stage because the problems described in the introduction result from failure to consider early design decisions carefully.

III. How Does the Lack of Subsets and Extensions Manifest Itself?

Although we often speak of programs that are "not subsetable" or "not extensible," we must recognize that phrase as inaccurate. It is always possible to remove code from a program and have a runable result. Any software system can be extended (TSO proves that). The problem is that the subsets and extensions are not the programs that we would have designed if we had set out to design just that product. Further, the amount of work needed to obtain the product seems all out of proportion to the nature of the change. The obstacles commonly encountered in trying to extend or shrink systems fall into four classes.

A. Excessive Information Distribution

A system may be hard to extend or contract if too many programs were written assuming that a given feature is present or not present. This was illustrated by an operating system in which an early design decision was that the system would support three conversational languages. There were many sections of the system where knowledge of this decision was used. For example, error message tables had room for exactly three entries. An extension to allow four languages would have required that a great deal of code be rewritten. More surprisingly, it would have been difficult to reduce the system to one that efficiently supported only two of the languages. One could remove the third language, but to regain the table space, one would have had to rewrite the same sections of code that would be rewritten to add a language.

B. A Chain of Data Transforming Components

Many programs are structured as a chain of components, each receiving data from the previous component, processing it (and changing the format), before sending the data to the next program in the chain. If one component in this chain is not needed, that code is often hard to remove because the output of its predecessor is not compatible with the input requirements of its successor. A program that does nothing but change the format must be substituted. One illustration would be a payroll program that assumed unsorted input. One of the components of the system accepts the unsorted input and produces output that is sorted by some key. If the firm adopts an office procedure that results in sorted input, this phase of the processing is unnecessary. To eliminate that program, one may have to add a program that transfers data from a file in the input format to a file in the format appropriate for the next phase. It may be almost as efficient to allow the original SORT component to sort the sorted input.

C. Components That Perform More Than One Function

Another common error is to combine two simple functions into one component because the functions seem too simple to separate. For example, one might be tempted to combine synchronization with message sending and acknowledgment in building an operating system. The two functions seem closely related; one might expect that for the sake of reliability one should insist on a "handshake" with each exchange of synchronization signals. If one later encounters an application in which synchronization is needed very frequently, one may find that there is no simple way to strip the message sending out of the synchronization routines. Another example is the inclusion of run-time type-checking in the basic subroutine call mechanism. In applications where compile-time checking or verification eliminates the need for the run-time type-check, another subroutine call mechanism will be needed. The irony of these situations is that the "more powerful" mechanism could have been built separately from, but *using*, simpler mechanisms. Separation would result in a system in which the simpler mechanism was available for use where it sufficed.

D. Loops in the "Uses" Relation

In many software design projects, the decisions about what other component programs to use are left to individual systems programmers. If a programmer knows of a program in another module, and feels that it would be useful in his program, he includes a call on that program in his text. Programmers are encouraged to use the work of other programmers as much as possible because, when each programmer writes his own routines to perform common functions, we end up with a system that is much larger than it need be.

Unfortunately, there are two sides to the question of program usage. Unless some restraint is exercised, one may end up with a system in which nothing works until everything works. For example, while it may seem wise to have an operating system scheduler use the file system to store its data (rather than use its own disk routines), the result will be that the file system must be present and working before any task scheduling is possible. There are users for whom an operating system subset without a file system would be useful. Even if

one has no such users, the subset would be useful during development and testing.

IV. Steps Towards a Better Structure

This section discusses four parts of a methodology that I believe will help the software engineer to build systems that do not evidence the problems discussed above.

A. Requirements Definition: Identifying the Subsets First

One of the clearest morals in the earlier discussion about "design for change" as it is taught in other areas of engineering is that one must anticipate changes before one begins the design. At a past conference [3] many of the papers exhorted the audience to spend more time identifying the actual requirements before starting on a design. I do not want to repeat such exhortations, but I do want to point out that the identification of the possible subsets is part of identifying the requirements. Treating the easy availability of certain subsets as an operational requirement is especially important to government officials who purchase software. Many officials despair of placing strict controls on the production methods used by their contractors because they are forbidden by law to tell the contractor how to perform his job. They may tell him what they require, but not how to build it. Fortunately, the availability of subsets may be construed as an operational property of the software.

On the other hand, the identification of the required subsets is not a simple matter of asking potential users what they could do without. First, users tend to overstate their requirements. Second, the answer will not characterize the set of subsets that might be wanted in the future. In my experience, identification of the potentially desirable subsets is a demanding intellectual exercise in which one first searches for the *minimal* subset that might conceivably perform a useful service and then searches for a set of *minimal* increments to the system. Each increment is small—sometimes so small that it seems trivial. The emphasis on minimality stems from our desire to avoid components that perform more than one function (as discussed in Section III-C). Identifying the minimal subset is difficult because the minimal system is not usually a program that anyone would ask for. If we are going to build the software family, the minimal subset is useful; it is not usually worth building by itself. Similarly, the maximum flexibility is obtained by looking for the smallest possible increments in capability: often these are smaller increments than a user would think of. Whether or not he would think of them before system development, he is likely to want that flexibility later.

The search for a minimal subset and minimal extensions can best be shown by an example. One example of a minimal subset is given in [4]. Another example will be given later in this paper.

B. Information Hiding: Interface and Module Definition

In an earlier section we touched upon the difference between the mathematician's concept of generality and an engineer's approach to design flexibility. Where the mathematician wants his product, a theorem or method of proof, to be as general as possible, i.e., applicable, without change, in as many situations as possible, an engineer often must tailor his product to the situation actually at hand. Lack of generality is necessary to make the program as efficient or inexpensive as possible. If he must develop a family of products, he tries to isolate the changeable parts in modules and to develop an interface between the module and the rest of the product that remains valid for all versions. The crucial steps are as follows.

1) Identification of the items that are likely to change. These items are termed "secrets."

2) Location of the specialized components in separate modules.

3) Designing intermodule interfaces that are insensitive to the anticipated changes. The changeable aspects or "secrets" of the modules are not revealed by the interface.

It is exactly this that the concept of information hiding [5], encapsulation, or abstraction [6] is intended to do for software. Because software is an abstract or mathematical product, the modules may not have any easily recognized physical identity. They are not necessarily separately compilable or coincident with memory overlay units. The interface must be general but the contents should not be. Specialization is necessary for economy and efficiency.

The concept of information hiding is very general and is applicable in many software change situations—not just the issue of subsets and extensions that we address in this paper. The ideas have also been extensively discussed in the literature [5]-[9]. The special implications for our problem are simply that, as far as possible, even the presence or absence of a component should be hidden from other components. If one program uses another directly, the presence of the second program cannot be fully hidden from its user. However, there is never any reason for a component to "know" how many other programs use it. All data structures that reveal the presence or number of certain components should be included in separate information hiding modules with abstract interfaces [10]. Space and other considerations make it impossible to discuss this concept further in this paper; it will be illustrated in the example. Readers for whom this concept is new are advised to read some of the articles mentioned above.

C. The Virtual Machine (VM) Concept

To avoid the problems that we have described as "a chain of data transforming components," it is necessary to stop thinking of systems in terms of components that correspond to steps in the processing. This way of thinking dies hard. It is almost certain that your first introduction to programming was in terms of a series of statements intended to be executed in the order that they were explained to you. We are goal oriented; we know what we start with and what we want to produce. It is natural to think in terms of steps progressing towards that goal. It is the fact that we are designing a family of systems that makes this "natural" approach the wrong one.

The viewpoint that seems most appropriate to designing soft-ware families is often termed the virtual machine approach. Rather than write programs that perform the transformation from input data to output data, we design software machine extensions that will be useful in writing many such programs. Where our hardware machine provides us with a set of instructions that operate on a small set of data types, the extended or virtual machine will have additional data types as well as "software instructions" that operate on those data types. These added features will be tailored to the class of programs that we are building. While the VM instructions are designed to be generally useful, they can be left out of a final product if the user's programs do not use them. The programmer writing programs for the virtual machine should not need to distinguish between instructions that are implemented in software and those that are hardware implemented. To achieve a true virtual machine, the hardware resources that are used in implementing the extended instruction set must be unavailable to the user of the virtual machine. The designer has traded these resources for the new data elements and instructions. Any attempt to use those resources again will invalidate the concept of virtual machine and lead to complications. Failure to provide for isolation of resources is one of the reasons for the failure of some attempts to use macros to provide a virtual machine. The macro user must be careful not to use the resources used in the code generated by the macros.

There is no reason to accomplish the transformation from the hardware machine to a virtual machine with all of the desired features in a single leap. Instead we will use the machine at hand to implement a few new instructions. At each step we take advantage of the newly introduced features. Such a step-by-step approach turns a large problem into a set of small ones and, as we will see later, eases the problem of finding the appropriate subsets. Each element in this series of virtual machines is a useful subset of the system.

D. Designing the "Uses" Structure

The concept of an abstract machine is an intuitive way of thinking about design. A precise description of the concept comes through a discussion of the relation "uses" [11], [12].

1) The relation "uses": We consider a system to be divided into a set of programs that can be invoked either by the normal flow of control mechanisms, by an interrupt, or by an exception handling mechanism. Each of these programs is assumed to have a specification that defines exactly the effect that an invocation of the program should have.

We say of two programs A and B that A *uses* B if correct execution of B may be necessary for A to complete the task described in its specification. That is, A *uses* B if there exist situations in which the correct functioning of A depends upon the availability of a correct implementation of B. Note that to decide whether A *uses* B or not, one must examine both the implementation *and* the specification of A.

The *"uses"* relation and "invokes" very often coincide, but *uses* differs from *invokes* in two ways:

a) Certain invocations may not be instances of *"uses."* If A's specification requires only that A *invoke* B when certain conditions occur, then A has fulfilled its specification when it has generated a correct call to B. A is correct even if B is incorrect or absent. A proof of correctness of A need only make assumptions about the way to invoke B.

b) A program A may use B even though it never invokes it. The best illustration of this is interrupt handling. Most programs in a computer system are only correct on the assumption that the interrupt handling routine will correctly handle the interrupts (leave the processor in an acceptable state). Such programs use the interrupt handling routines even though they never call them. "*Uses*" can also be formulated as "*requires the presence of a correct version of*."

Systems that have achieved a certain "elegance" (e.g., T.H.E. [5], Venus [6]) have done so by having parts of the system "*use*" other parts in such a way that the "user" programs were simplified. For example, the transput stream mechanism in T.H.E. *uses* the segmenting mechanism to great advantage. In contrast, many large and complex operating systems achieve their size and complexity by having "independent" parts. For example, there are many systems in which "spooling," virtual memory management, and the file system all perform their own backup store operations. Code to perform these functions is present in each of the components. Whenever such components must share a single device, complex interfaces exist.

The disadvantage of unrestrained "usage" of each others facilities is that the system parts become highly interdependent. Often there are no subsets of the system that can be used before the whole system is complete. In practice, some duplication of effort seems preferable to a system in which nothing runs unless everything runs.

2) The uses hierarchy: By restricting the relation "*uses*" so that its graph is loop free we can retain the primary advantages of having system parts "*use*" each other while eliminating the problems. In that case it is possible to assign the programs to the levels of a hierarchy by the following rules:

a) level 0 is the set of all programs that *use* no other program;

b) level i (i ≥ 1) is the set of all programs that *use* at least one program on level i - 1 and no program at a level higher than i - 1.

If such a hierarchical ordering exists, then each level offers a testable and usable subset of the system. In fact, one can get additional subsets by including only parts of a level. The easy availability of these subsets is very valuable for the construction of any software systems and is vital for developing a *broad* family of systems.

The design of the "uses" hierarchy should be one of the major milestones in a design effort. The division of the system into independently callable subprograms has to go on in parallel with the decisions about *uses*, because they influence each other.

3) The criteria to be used in allowing one program to use another: We propose to allow A "*uses*" B when all of the following conditions hold:

a) A is essentially simpler because it uses B;

b) B is not substantially more complex because it is not allowed to use A;

c) there is a useful subset containing B and not A;

d) there is no conceivably useful subset containing A but not B.

During the process of designing the "uses" relation, we often find ourselves in a situation where two programs could obviously benefit from using each other and the conditions above cannot be satisfied. In such situations, we resolve the apparent conflicts by a technique that we call "sandwiching." One of the programs is "sliced" into two parts in a way that allows the programs to "use" each other and still satisfy the above conditions. If we find ourselves in a position where A would benefit from using B, but B can also benefit from using A, we may split B into two programs: B1 and B2. We then allow A to use B2 and B1 to use A. The result would appear to be a sandwich with B as the bread and A as the filling. Often, we then go on to split A. We start with a few levels and end up with many.

An earlier report [11] introduced many of the ideas that are in this paper and illustrated them by proposing a "uses" relation for a family of operating systems. It contains several examples of situations where "sandwiching" led us from a "T.H.E.-like structure" [14] to a structure with more than twice as many levels. For example, the virtual memory mechanism was split into address translation and dynamic allocation of memory areas to segments.

The most frequent instances of splitting and sandwiching came because initially we were assuming that a "level" would be a "module" in the sense of Section IV-B. We will discuss this in the final part of this paper.

4) Use of the word "convenience": It will trouble some readers that it is usual to use the word "convenience" to describe a reason for introducing a certain facility at a given level of the hierarchy. A more substantial basis would seem more scientific.

As discussed in [11] and [13], we must assume that the hardware itself is capable of performing all necessary functions. As one goes higher in the levels, one can lose capabilities (as resources are consumed)—not gain them. On the other hand, at the higher levels the new functions can be implemented with simpler programs because of the additional programs that can be used. We speak of "convenience" to make it clear that one could implement any functions on a lower level, but the availability of the additional programs at the higher level is useful. For each function we give the lowest level at which the features that are useful for implementing that function (with the stated restrictions) are available. In each case, we see no functions available at the next higher level that would be useful for implementing the functions as described. If we implemented the program one level lower we would have to duplicate programs that become available at that level.

V. Example: An Address Processing Subsystem

As an example of designing for extensibility and subsets, we consider a set of programs to read in, store, and write out lists of addresses. This example has also been used, to illustrate a different point, in [10] and has been used in several classroom experiments to demonstrate module interchangeability. This

```
The following items of information will
be found in the addresses to be processed
and constitute the only items of relevance
to the application programs:

  •Last name
  •Given names (first name and possible
     middle names)
  •Organization (Command or Activity)
  •Internal identifier (Branch or Code)
  •Street address or P.O. box
  •City or mail unit identifier
  •State
  •Zip code
  •Title
  •Branch of service if military
  •GS grade if civil service

Each of the above will be strings of
characters in the standard ANSI alphabet,
and each of the above may be empty or blank.
```

Fig. 1.

example is intended as an integral part of this paper; several statements in the final summation are supported only in this section.

A. Our Basic Assumptions

1) The information items discussed in Fig. 1 will be the items to be processed by all application programs.

2) The input formats of the addresses are subject to change.

3) The output formats of the addresses are subject to change.

4) Some systems will use a single fixed format for input and output. Other systems will need the ability to choose from several input or output formats at run-time. Some systems will be required in which the user can specify the format using a format definition language.

5) The representation of addresses in main storage will vary from system to system.

6) In most systems, only a subset of the total set of addresses stored in the system need be in main storage at any one time. The number of addresses needed may vary from system to system, and in some systems the number of addresses to be kept in main memory may vary at run-time.

B. We Propose the Following Design Decisions

1) The input and output programs will be table driven: the table will specify the format to be used for input and output. The contents and organization of these format tables will be the "secrets" of the input and output modules.

2) The representation of addresses in core will be the "secret" of an address storage module (ASM). The implementation chosen for this module will be such that the operations of changing a portion of an address will be relatively inexpensive, compared to making the address table larger or smaller.

3) When the number of addresses to be stored exceeds the capacity of an ASM, programs will use an address file module (AFM). An AFM can be made upward compatible with an ASM; programs that were written to use ASM's could operate using an AFM in the same way. The AFM provides additional commands to allow more efficient usage by programs that do not assume the random access properties of an ASM. These programs are described below.

4) Our implementation of an AFM would use an ASM as a submodule as well as another submodule that we will call block file module (BFM). The BFM stores blocks of data that are sufficiently large to represent an address, but the BFM is not specialized to the handling of addresses. An ASM that is used within an AFM may be said to have two interfaces. In the "normal interface" that an ASM presents to an outside user, an address is a set of fields and the access functions hide or abstract from the representation. Fig. 2 is a list of the access programs that comprise this interface. In the second interface, the ASM deals with blocks of contiguous storage and abstract from the contents. There are commands for the ASM to input and output "addresses" but the operands are storage blocks whose interpretation as addresses is known only within the ASM. The AFM makes assumptions about the association between blocks and addresses but not about the way that an address's components are represented as blocks. The BFM is completely independent of the fact that the blocks contain address information. The BFM might, in fact, be a manufacturer supplied access method.

C. Component Programs

1) Module: Address Input

INAD: Reads in an address that is assumed to be in a format specified by a format table and calls ASM or AFM functions to store it.

INFSL: Selects a format from an existing set of format tables. The selected format is the one that will be used by INAD. There is always a format selected.

INFCR: Adds a new format to the tables used by INFSL. The format is specified in a "format language." Selection is *not* changed (i.e., INAD still uses the same format table).

INTABEXT: Adds a blank table to the set of input format tables.

INTABCHG: Rewrites a table in the input format tables using a description in a format language. Selection is not changed.

INFDEL: Deletes a table from the set of format tables. The selected format cannot be deleted.

INADSEL: Reads in an address using one of a set of formats. Choice is specified by an integer parameter.

INADFO: Reads in an address in a format specified as one of its parameters (a string in the format definition language). The format is selected and added to the tables and subsequent addresses could be read in using INAD.

2) Module: Address Output

OUTAD: Prints an address in a format specified by a format table. The information to be printed

MODULE: ASM

NAME OF ACCESS PROGRAM*	INPUT PARAMETERS						OUTPUT	
*ADDTIT:	asm	X	integer	X	string	→	asm	•
ADDGN:	asm	X	integer	X	string	→	asm	•
ADDLN:	asm	X	integer	X	string	→	asm	•
ADDSERV:	asm	X	integer	X	string	→	asm	•
ADDBORC:	asm	X	integer	X	string	→	asm	•
ADDCORA:	asm	X	integer	X	string	→	asm	•
ADDSORP:	asm	X	integer	X	string	→	asm	•
ADDCITY:	asm	X	integer	X	string	→	asm	•
ADDSTATE:	asm	X	integer	X	string	→	asm	•
ADDZIP:	asm	X	integer	X	string	→	asm	•
ADDGSL:	asm	X	integer	X	string	→	asm	•
SETNUM:	asm	X	integer	→	asm	•		
FETTIT:	asm	X	integer	→	string			
FETGN:	asm	X	integer	→	string			
FETGN:	asm	X	integer	→	string			
FETLN:	asm	X	integer	→	string			
FETSERV:	asm	X	integer	→	string			
FETBORC:	asm	X	integer	→	string			
FETCORA:	asm	X	integer	→	string			
FETSORP:	asm	X	integer	→	string			
FETCITY:	asm	X	integer	→	string			
FETSTATE:	asm	X	integer	→	string			
FETZIP:	asm	X	integer	→	string			
FETGSL:	asm	X	integer	→	string			
FETNUM:	asm	→	integer					

*These are abbreviations: ADDTIT = ADD TITLE; ADDGN = ADD GIVEN NAME, etc.

Fig. 2. Syntax of ASM functions.

is assumed to be in an ASM and identified by its position in an ASM.

OUTFSL: Selects a format table from an existing set of output format tables. The selected format is the one that will be used by OUTAD.

OUTTABEXT: Adds a "blank" table to the set of output format tables.

OUTTABCHG: Rewrites the contents of a format table using information in a format language.

OUTFCR: Adds a new format to the set of formats that can be selected by OUTFSL in a format description language.

OUTFDEL: Deletes a table from the set of format tables that can be selected by OUTFSL.

OUTADSEL: Prints out an address using one of a set of formats.

OUTADFO: Prints out an address in a format specified in a format definition language string, which is one of the actual parameters. The format is added to the tables and selected.

3) Module: Address Storage (ASM)

FET: (Component Name): This is a set of functions used to read information from an address store. Returns a string as a value. See Fig. 2.

ADD: (Component Name): This is a set of functions used to write information in an address store. Each takes a string and an integer as parameters. The integer specifies an address within the ASM. See Fig. 2.

0BLOCK: Takes an integer parameter, returns a storage block as a value.

1BLOCK: Accepts a storage block and integer as parameters. Its effect is to change the contents of an address store—which is reflected by a change in the values of the FET programs.

ASMEXT: Extends an address store by appending a new address with empty components at the end of the address store.

ASMSHR: "Shrinks" the address store.

ASMCR: Creates a new address store. The parameter specifies the number of components. All components are initially empty.

ASMDEL: Deletes an existing address store.

4) Module: Block File Module

BLFET: Accepts an integer as a parameter and returns a "block."

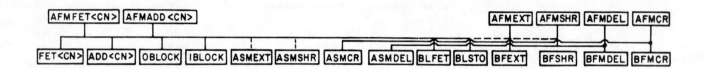

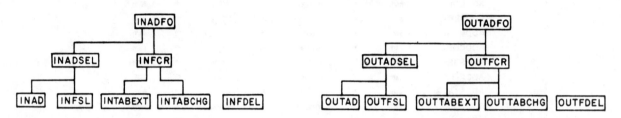

Fig. 3.

BLSTO: Accepts a block and an integer and stores the block.

BFEXT: Extends BFM by adding additional blocks to its capacity.

BFSHR: Reduces the size of the BFM by removing some blocks.

BFMCR: Creates a file of blocks.

BFMDEL: Deletes an existing file of blocks.

5) Module: Address File Module

This module includes implementations of all of the ASM functions except OBLOCK and IBLOCK. To avoid confusion in the diagram showing the uses hierarchy we have changed the names to:

AFMADD (Component Name) defined as in Fig. 2
AFMFET (Component Name) defined as in Fig. 1
AFMEXT defined as in BFM above
AMFSHR defined as in BFM above
AFMCR defined as in BFM above
AFMDEL defined as in BFM above.

D. Uses Relation

Fig. 3 shows the *uses* relation between the component programs. It is important to note that we are now discussing the implementation of those programs, not just their specifications. The *uses* relation is characterized by the fact that there are a large number of relatively simple, *single-purpose* programs on the lowest level. The upper level programs are implemented by means of these lower level programs so that they too are quite simple. This *uses* relation diagram characterizes the set of possible subsets.

E. Discussion

To pick a subset, one identifies the set of upper level programs that the user needs and includes only those programs that those programs use (directly or indirectly). For example, a user who uses addresses in a single format does not need the component programs that interpret format description lan-guages. Systems that work with a small set of addresses can be built without any BFM components. A program that works as a query system and never prints out a complete address would not need any Address Output components.

The system is also easily extended. For example, one could add a capability to read in addresses with self-defining files. If the first record on a file was a description of the format in something equivalent to the format description language, one could write a program that would be able to read in that record, use INTABCHG to build a new format table, and then read in the addresses. Programs that do things with addresses (such as print out "personalized" form letters) can also be added using these programs and selecting only those capabilities that they actually need.

One other observation that can be made is that the upper level programs can be used to "generate" lower level versions. For example, the format description languages can be used to generate the tables used for the fixed format versions. There is no need for a separate SYSGEN program.

We will elaborate on this observation in the conclusion.

VI. SOME REMARKS ON OPERATING SYSTEMS: WHY GENERALS ARE SUPERIOR TO COLONELS

An earlier report [11] discusses the design of a "uses" hierarchy for operating systems. Although there have been some refinements to the proposals of that report, its basic contents are consistent with the present proposals. This section compares the approach outlined in this paper and the "kernel" approach or "nucleus" approach to OS design [18]-[20]. It is tempting to say that the suggestions in this paper do not conflict with the "kernel" approach. These proposals can be viewed as a refinement of the nucleus approach. The first few levels of our system could be labeled "kernel," and one could conclude that we are just discussing a fine structure within the kernel.

To yield to that temptation would be to ignore an essential difference between the approaches suggested in this paper and the kernel approach. The system kernels known to me are such that some desirable subsets cannot be obtained without major surgery. It was assumed that the nucleus must be in every system family member. In the RC4000 system the inability to separate synchronization from message passing has led some users to bypass the kernel to perform teletype handling functions. In Hydra as originally proposed [19], "type checking" was so intrinsic to the call mechanism that it appeared impossible to disable it when it was not needed or affordable.[1]

Drawing a line between "kernel" and the rest of the system, and putting "essential" services of "critical programs" in the nucleus yields a system in which kernel features cannot be removed and certain extensions are impractical. Looking for a *minimal* subset and a set of *minimal* independent incremental function leads to a system in which one can trim away unneeded features. I know of no feature that is always needed. When we say that two functions are *almost* always used together, we should remember that "almost" is a euphemism for "not."

VII. SUMMATION

This paper describes an approach to software intended to result in systems that can be tailored to fit the needs of a broad variety of users. The points most worthy of emphasis are as follows.

1) The Requirements Include Subsets and Extensions: It is essential to recognize the identification of useable subsets as part of the preliminaries to software design. Flexibility cannot be an afterthought. Subsetability is needed, not just to meet a variety of customers' needs, but to provide a fail-safe way of handling schedule slippage.

2) Advantages of the Virtual Machine Approach: Designing software as a set of virtual machines has definite advantages over the conventional (flowchart) approach to system design. The virtual machine "instructions" provide facilities that are useful for purposes beyond those originally conceived. These instructions can easily be omitted from a system if they are not needed. Remove a major box from a flowchart and there is often a need to "fill the hole" with conversion programs.

3) On the Difference Between Software Generality and Software Flexibility: Software can be considered "general" if it can be used, *without change*, in a variety of situations. Software can be considered flexible, if it is *easily changed* to be used in a variety of situations. It appears unavoidable that there is a run-time cost to be paid for generality. Clever designers can achieve flexibility without significant run-time cost, but there is a design-time cost. One should incur the design-time cost only if one expects to recover it when changes are made.

Some organizations may choose to pay the run-time cost for generality. They build general software rather than flexible software because of the maintenance problems associated with maintaining several different versions. Factors influencing this decision include a) the availability of extra computer resources,

b) the facilities for program change and maintenance available at each installation, and c) the extent to which design techniques ease the task of applying the same change to many versions of a program.

No one can tell a designer how much flexibility and generality should be built into a product, but the decision should be a conscious one. Often, it just happens.

4) On the Distinction Between Modules, Subprograms, and Levels: Several systems and at least one dissertation [14]-[17] have, in my opinion, blurred the distinction between modules, subprograms, and levels. Conventional programming techniques consider a subroutine or other callable program to be a module. If one wants the modules to include all programs that must be designed together and changed together, then, as our example illustrates, one will usually include many small subprograms in a single module. If does not matter what word we use; the point is that the unit of change is not a single callable subprogram.

In several systems, modules and levels have coincided [14], [15]. This had led to the phrase "level of abstraction." Each of the modules in the example abstract from some detail that is assumed likely to change. In our approach there is no correspondence between modules and levels. Further, I have not found a relation, "more abstract than," that would allow me to define an abstraction hierarchy [12]. Although I am myself guilty of using it, in most cases the phrase "levels of abstraction" is an abuse of language.

Janson has suggested that a design such as this one (or the one discussed in [11]) contain "soft modules" that can represent a breach of security principles. Obviously an error in any program in one of our modules can violate the integrity of that module. All module programs that will be included in a given subset must be considered in proving the correctness of that module. However, I see no way that allowing the component programs to be on different levels of a "uses" hierarchy makes this process more difficult or makes the system less secure. The boundaries of our modules are quite firm and clearly identified.

The essential difference between this paper and other discussions of hierarchically structured designs is the emphasis on subsets and extensions. My search for a criterion to be used in designing the *uses* hierarchy has convinced me that if one does not care about the existence of subsets, it does not really matter what hierarchy one uses. Any design can be bent until it works. It is only in the ease of change that they differ.

5) On Avoiding Duplication: Some earlier work [21] has suggested that one needs to have duplicate or near duplicate modules in a hierarchically structured system. For example, they suggest that one needs one implementation of processes to give a fixed number of processes at a low level and another to provide for a varying number of processes at a user's level. Similar ideas have appeared elsewhere. Were such duplication to be necessary, it would be a sound argument against the use of "structured" approaches. One can avoid such duplication if one allows the programs that vary the size of a data structure to be on a higher level than the other programs that operate on that data structure. For example, in an operating system, the programs to create and delete processes need not be on the

[1] Accurate reports on the current status and performance of that system are not available to me.

same level as the more frequently used scheduling operations. In designing software, I regard the need to code similar functions in two separate programs as an indication of a fundamental error in my thinking.

6) Designing for Subsets and Extensions Can Reduce the Need for Support Software: We have already mentioned that this design approach can eliminate the need for separate SYSGEN programs. We can also eliminate the need for *special-*purpose compilers. The price of the convenience features offered by such languages is often a compiler and run-time package distinctly larger than the system being built. In our approach, each level provides a "language extention" available to the programmer of the next level. We never build a compiler; we just build our system, but we get convenience features anyway.

7) Extension at Run-Time Versus Extension During SYSGEN: At a later stage in the design we will have to choose data structures and take the difference between run-time extension and SYSGEN extension into consideration. Certain data structures are more easily accessed but harder to extend while the program is running; others are easily extended but at the expense of a higher access cost. These differences do not affect our early design decisions because they are hidden in modules.

8) On the Value of a Model: My work on this example and similar ones has gone much faster because I have learned to exploit a pattern that I first noticed in the design discussed in [11]. Low level operations assume the existence of a fixed data structure of some type. The operations on the next level allow the swapping of a data element with others from a fixed set of similar elements. The high level programs allow the creation and deletion of such data elements. This pattern appears several times in both designs. Although I have not designed your system for you, I believe that you can take advantage of a similar pattern. If so, this paper has served its purpose.

ACKNOWLEDGMENT

The ideas presented in this paper have been developed over a lengthy period and with the cooperation and help of many collaborators. I am grateful to numerous Philips employees for thought provoking comments and questions. Price's collaboration was invaluable at Carnegie-Mellon University. The help of W. Bartussek, G. Handzel, and H. Wuerges at the Technische Hochschule Darmstadt led to substantial improvements. Heninger, Weiss, and J. Shore at the Naval Research Laboratory helped me to understand the application of the concepts in areas other than operating systems. B. Trombka and J. Guttag both helped in the design of pilots of the address process system. Discussions with P. J. Courtois have helped me to better understand the relation between software structure and run-time characteristics of computer systems. Dr. E. Britton, H. Rettenmaier, L. Belady, Dr. D. Stanat, G. Fran, and Dr. W. Wright made many helpful suggestions about an earlier draft of this paper. If you find portions of this paper helpful, these people deserve your thanks.

REFERENCES

[1] E. W. Dijkstra, *A Discipline of Programming.* Englewood Cliffs, NJ: Prentice-Hall, 1976.

[2] D. L. Parnas, "On the design and development of program families," *IEEE Trans. Software Eng.*, vol. SE-2, pp. 1-9, Mar. 1976.

[3] 2nd Int. Conf. Software Engineering, Oct. 13-15, 1976; also, *IEEE Trans. Software Eng.*, (Special Issue), vol. SE-2, Dec. 1976.

[4] D. L. Parnas, G. Handzel, and H. Würges, "Design and specification of the minimal subset of an operating system family," presented at the 2nd Int. Conf. Software Engineering, Oct. 13-15, 1976; also, *IEEE Trans. Software Eng.*, (Special Issue), vol. SE-2, pp. 301-307, Dec. 1976.

[5] D. L. Parnas, "On the criteria to be used in decomposing systems into modules," *Commun. Ass. Comput. Mach.*, Dec. 1972.

[6] T. A. Linden, "The use of abstract data types to simplify program modifications," in *Proc. Conf. Data: Abstraction, Definition and Structure*, Mar. 22-24, 1976; also, *ACM SIGPLAN Notices* (Special Issue), vol. II, 1976.

[7] D. L. Parnas, "A technique for software module specification with examples," *Commun. Ass. Comput. Mach.*, May 1972.

[8] —, "Information distribution aspects of design methodology," in *1971 Proc. IFIP Congr.* Amsterdam, The Netherlands: North-Holland, 1971.

[9] —, "The use of precise specifications in the development of software," in *1977 Proc. IFIP Congr.* Amsterdam, The Netherlands: North-Holland, 1977.

[10] —, "Use of abstract interfaces in the development of software for embedded computer systems," Naval Res. Lab., Washington, DC, NRL Rep. 8047, June 1977.

[11] —, "Some hypotheses about the 'uses' hierarchy for operating systems," Technische Hochschule Darmstadt, Darmstadt, West Germany, Tech. Rep., Mar. 1976.

[12] —, "On a 'buzzword': Hierarchical structure," in *1974 Proc. IFIP Congr.* Amsterdam, The Netherlands: North-Holland, 1974.

[13] D. L. Parnas and D. L. Siewiorek, "Use of the concept of transparency in the design of hierarchically structured systems," *Commun. Ass. Comput. Mach.*, vol. 18, July 1975.

[14] E. W. Dijkstra, "The structure of the "THE"-multiprogramming system," *Commun. Ass. Comput. Mach.*, vol. 11, pp. 341-346, May 1968.

[15] B. Liskov, "The design of the Venus operating system," *Commun. Ass. Comput. Mach.*, vol. 15, pp. 144-149, Mar. 1972.

[16] P. A. Janson, "Using type extension to organize virtual memory mechanisms," Lab. for Comput. Sci., M.I.T., Cambridge, MA, MIT-LCS-TR167, Sept. 1976.

[17] —, "Using type-extension to organize virtual memory mechanisms," IBM Zurich Res. Lab., Switzerland, Res. Rep. RZ 858 (#28909), August 31, 1977.

[18] P. Brinch Hansen, "The nucleus of the multiprogramming system," *Commun. Ass. Comput. Mach.*, vol. 13, pp. 238-241, 250, Apr. 1970.

[19] W. Wulf, E. Cohen, A. Jones, R. Lewin, C. Pierson, and F. Pollack, "HYDRA: The kernel of a multiprocessor operating system," *Commun. Ass. Comput. Mach.*, vol. 17, pp. 337-345, June 1974.

[20] G. J. Popek and C. S. Kline, "The design of a verified protection system," in *Proc. Int. Workshop Prot. In Oper. Syst.*, IRIA, pp. 183-196.

[21] A. R. Saxena and T. H. Bredt, "A structured specification of a hierarchical operating system," in *Proc. 1975 Int. Conf. Reliable Software.*

David L. Parnas received the B.S., M.S., and Ph.D. degrees in electrical engineering—systems and communications sciences from the Carnegie Institute of Technology, Pittsburgh, PA.

He held the position of Assistant Professor of Computer Science at the University of Maryland and at Carnegie-Mellon University. During the period 1969-1970 he was employed by Philips-Electrologica, Apeldoorn, The Netherlands, and at the MBLE Research Laboratory, Brussels, Belgium. He then returned to Carnegie-Mellon

University where he held the rank of Associate Professor until 1973. In June of 1973 he was appointed Professor and Head of the Research Group on Operating Systems I at the Technical University of Darmstadt, Germany, where he remained through August 1976. He is presently Professor in the Department of Computer Science, University of North Carolina, Chapel Hill. He is also with the Information Systems Staff, Communications Sciences Division, at the Naval Research Laboratory, Washington, DC. He has published papers in the areas of computer design languages and simulation techniques. His current interests are in the field of software engineering methods, computer system design, abstract specification for programs, verification that a program meets its specifications, and cooperating sequential processes.

Software Engineering with Reusable Designs and Code

ROBERT G. LANERGAN AND CHARLES A. GRASSO

Abstract—For over six years Raytheon's Missile Systems Division, Information Processing Systems Organization has used a successful approach in developing and maintaining business software. The approach centers on the fact that 60 percent of all business application designs and code are redundant and can be standardized and reused. This approach has resulted in significant gains in productivity and reliability and improved end-user relations, while providing better utilization of data processing personnel, primarily in the maintenance phase of the software life cycle.

INTRODUCTION

IT is common practice when writing scientific programs to use prewritten subroutines or functions for common mathematical operations. Examples of these logarithmic or trigonometric subroutines. The computer manufacturer usually writes, supplies, and documents these subroutines as part of his software. For instance, they usually come with the Fortran compiler. The functions are universal. Square root is square root regardless of the computer, company, or application.

In business programming it is common belief that each system application is so unique that it must be designed and coded from the beginning. For instance, it has been the belief that the coding scheme that our company, even our plants, use for material classification code or make or buy code, or vendor code or direct labor code, and the algorithms used for processing these data elements are unique to the company or plant. Therefore, prewritten reusable modules cannot be designed, coded, and reused.

A close examination of this reasoning has led us to believe that there are two fallacies in it. The first is that, contrary to common belief, there are at least a few business functions that are sufficiently universal to be supplied by the manufacturer of a Cobol compiler. There are many others applicable to a company, plant, functional area, or application area that could be prewritten.

How many manufacturers supply a Gregorian date edit routine with their compilers?

How many manufacturers supply a Gregorian to Julian date conversion routine or vice-versa, with their compiler?

How many manufacturers supply a date aging routine for such applications as acounts receivable?

In every one of the above cases the application is probably written and rewritten in every business shop in North America.

Manuscript received August 1, 1983.

The authors are with the Missile Systems Division, Raytheon Company, Bedford, MA 01730.

In addition to universal routines, there are company-wide applications. Examples in our company include:

- part number validation routines,
- manufacturing day conversion routines,
- edits for data fields used throughout the company, such as employee number.

Within a functional area in any company, such as manufacturing or accounting, there are routines that can be prewritten, tested, documented, and then copied into a program.

Within a system such as payroll there are often routines that also can be prewritten, such as tax routines.

Yet we believe that the false notion of uniqueness still persists to such a degree that this approach is used at about one-tenth of its potential. We will discuss later the way we have used this concept to produce programs that have an average of 60 percent reusable code.

The second fallacy, in our opinion, involves the program as a whole. It is commonly believed that each business program (as well as each data field) is so unique that it must also be designed and developed from the start. In our opinion there are only six major functions you can perform in a business application program. You can sort data, edit or manipulate data, combine data, explode data, update data, or report on data. By identifying the common functions of these six types of programs, we have produced seven "logic structures." These logic structures give the programmer a head start and provide a uniform approach that is of value later in testing and maintenance.

REUSABLE MODULE DESIGN APPROACH

Our reusable module design approach strategy separates reusable modules into two distinct categories, functional modules and Cobol program logic structures.

Functional Modules

Functional modules are designed and coded fro a specific purpose. Then they are reviewed, tested, documented, and stored on a standard copy library. As mentioned earlier, some of the business routines have universal application, such as date aging; tax routines and others have more limited application to a company, plant, functional area, or system application.

Within our company we classify these functional modules in several Cobol language categories. These categories are:

- file descriptions, i.e., FD's
- record descriptions, i.e., 01 levels in an FD or in working storage

Reprinted from *IEEE Transactions on Software Engineering*, Volume SE-10, Number 5, September 1984, pages 498-501. Copyright © 1984 by The Institute of Electrical and Electronics Engineers, Inc.

- edit routines, i.e., the data area and procedure code to edit a specific data field
- functional routines, i.e., the data area and procedure code to perform some function, such as left justify and zero fill data elements
  - database I/O areas
  - database interface modules
  - database search arguments
  - database procedure division calls.

As can be seen from the above list, we have some modules that are solely data related, such as 01 level record descriptions. The majority of the modules involve both data areas and procedure code. For instance, a database call paragraph, designed to retrieve a specific series of segments, works in conjunction with a program control block module, a segment search argument module, and a database I/O module.

There are approximately 3200 modules in the above categories, supporting over 50 system applications at three plants. By using these functional modules and logic structures, we have been producing programs that average 60 percent reusable code. This produces more reliable programs, with less testing and coding. The maintainability and documentation associated with these applications has also improved substantially because the code is not physically contained in each program.

Cobol Program Logic Structures

A Cobol program logic structure has a prewritten identification division, environment division, data division, and procedure division. It is not a complete program because some paragraphs contain no code, and some record descriptions are also empty, consisting only of the 01 level. It does not however, contain many complete 01 levels and procedure paragraphs.

To illustrate the concept behind logic structures we will describe three types.

The *update* is designed for the classical, sequential update. There is a version with an embedded sort and a version without. The update is designed for situations where the transaction record contains a transaction type field (add, change, or delete). The update logic structures is also designed to accommodate multiple transactions per master record. Error messages to a transaction register are provided for standard errors such as an attempt to add an already existing record. Final totals are also provided, as well as sequence checking.

The *report* logic structure is also written in two versions, one with and one without a sort of the input records prior to report preparation. Major, intermediate, and minor levels of totals are provided for, but more may be added if needed. If multiple sequences of reports are desired, the record can be released to the sort with multiple control prefixes. Paragraphs are also provided for editing, reformatting and sequence checking.

The *edit* logic structure is also written in two versions, with or without a sort of the input records. This logic structure was designed for two purposes. One is the editing of input records. In effect the input records are examined based on some criteria and written to the selected (good records) or nonselected (error) files. Another use for this logic structure is the selection of records from a file, based on some criteria, for later use in a report.

CONSTRUCTION OF LOGIC STRUCTURES

For each type of logic structure there is a central supporting paragraph.

- For the update program it is the high-low-equal comparison.
- For the report program it is the paragraph that determines which level of control break to take.
- For the selection program it is the select/nonselect paragraph.

Let us consider the report program as an example.

Prior to the control beak paragraph we can identify support functions that must occur in order for the control break paragraph to function. Examples are: get-record, sequence-check-record, edit-record-prior-to-sort, and build-control-keys. These are supporting functions. Other functions such as major-break, intermediate-break, minor-break, roll-counters, build-detail-line, print-detail-line, page-headers, etc., are dependent on the control break or central paragraph.

Obviously many of these paragraphs (functions) can be either completely or partially prewritten.

Our report program logic structure procedure division contains 15 paragraphs in the version without a sort, and 20 paragraphs in the version with a sort.

To further clarify what we mean when we talk about logic structures, it might be helpful to specify some data and procedure division areas in a report logic structure, without an embedded sort.

```
Identification Division
Environment Division
Data Division
    File Section
    Working Storage Section
        01  AA1 – CARRIAGE-CONTROL-SPACING
        01  BB1 – CONSTANTS- AREA
        01  BB2 – TRANSACTIONS- STATUS
        01  BB4 – FILES-STATUS
        01  CC1 – COUNT-AREA
        01  DD1 – MESSAGE-AREA
        01  EE1 – TRANSACTION-READ-AREA
        01  FF1 – KEY-AREA
        01  GG1 – HEAD-LINE1
        01  GG2 – HEAD-LINE2
        01  GG3 – HEAD-LINE3
        01  HH1 – DETAIL -LINE
        01  LL1 – TOTALS-AREA
        01  SS1 – SUBSCRIPT-AREA
        01  TT1 – TOTAL-LINE-MINOR
        01  TT2 – TOTAL LINE-INTER
        01  TT3 – TOTAL-LINE-MAJOR
        01  TT4 – TOTAL-LINE-FINAL
    Procedure Division
        0010 – INITIALIZE
        0020 – MAIN-FLOW
        0030 – WRAP-IT-UP
        0040 – CHECK-CONTROLS
```

```
0050 – FINAL-BREAK
0060 – MAJOR-BREAK
0070 – INTER-BREAK
0080 – MINOR-BREAK
0090 – PRINT-TOTAL
0100 – ROLL-COUNTERS
0110 – FILL-DETAIL-LINE
0120 – WRITE-PRINT-LINE
0130 – NEW-PAGE-HEADING
0140 – GET-TRANSACTION-RECORD
0150 – TRANSACTION-FORMAT-OR-EDIT
0160 – SEQUENCE-CHECK
```

The above area, combined together as a program, provide the programmer with a modular functional structure on which to build a report program very easily.

For the update logic structure, the central paragraph is the hi-low-equal control paragraph. Prior to the central control paragraph there must be supporting functions such as get-transaction, sequence-ckeck-transaction, edit-transaction, sort-transaction, get-master, sequence-check-master, build-keys, etc. As a result of this central paragraph you will have functions such as add-a-record, delete-a-record, change-a-record, print-activity-register, print-page-heading, print-control-totals, etc.

Our update logic structure procedure division contains 22 paragraphs in the nonsort version and 26 paragraphs in the version with an embedded sort.

BENEFITS OF LOGIC STRUCTURES

We believe that logic structures have many benefits.
• They help clarify the programmer's thinking in terms of what he is trying to accomplish.
• They make design and program reviews easier.
• They help the analyst communicate with the programmer relative to the requirement of the system.
• They facilitate testing.
• They eliminate certain error-prone area such as end of file conditions since the logic is already built and tested.
• They reduce program preparation time, since parts of the design and coding are already done.

However, we believe that the biggest benefit comes after the program is written, when the user requests modifications or enhancements to the program. Once the learning curve is overcome, and the programmers are familiar with the logic structure, the effect is similar to having team programming with everyone on the same team. When a programmer works with a program created by someone else, he finds very little that appears strange. He does not have to become familiar with another person's style because it is essentially his style.

RESEARCH STRATEGY USED TO TEST THE CONCEPT OF REUSABILITY

In August 1976 a study was performed at Raytheon Missile Systems Division to prove that the concept of logic structures was a valid one. Over 5000 production Cobol source programs were examined and classified by type, using the following procedure.

Each supervisor was given a list of the programs that he was responsible for. This list included the name and a brief descrip- of the program along with the number of lines of code.

The supervisor then classified and tabulated each program using the following categories:

edit or validation programs
update programs
report programs

If a program did not fall into the above three categories, then the supervisor assigned his own category name.

The result of classification analysis by program type was as follows:

```
1089  edit programs
1099  update programs
2433  report programs
 247  extract programs
 245  bridge programs
 161  data fix programs
5274  total programs classified
```

It should be noted that the bridge programs were mostly select (edit and extract) types, and the data fix programs were all update programs. The adjusted counts were as follows as a result of this adjustment.

```
1581  edit programs
1260  update programs
2433  report programs
5274  adjusted total programs classified.
```

The average lines of code by program type for the 5274 programs classified were as follows:

```
626  lines of code per edit program
798  lines of code per update program
507  lines of code per report program
```

The supervisors then selected over 50 programs that they felt would be good candidates for study. Working with the supervisors, the study team found that approximately 40–60 percent of the code in the programs examined was redundant and could be standardized. As a result of these promising findings, three prototype logic structures were developed (select, update, and report) and released to the programming community for selective testing and feedback. During this time a range of 15–85 percent reusable code was attained. As a result of this success, it was decided by management to make logic structures a standard for all new program development in three data processing installations. To date over 5500 logic structures have been used for new program development, averaging 60 percent reusable code when combined with reusable functional modules. It is felt at this time that once a programmer uses each logic structure more than three times, that 60 percent reusable code can easily be attained for an average program. We believe this translates into a 50 percent increase in productivity in the development of new programs.

In addition, programmers modifying a logic structure written by someone else agree that, because of the consistent style, logic structure programs are easier to read and understand.

This is where the real benefit lies since most data processing installations are using 60–80 percent of their programming resource to support their maintenance requirements.

To summarize: the basic premise behind our reusability methodology is that a large percentage of program code for business data processing applications is redundant and can be replaced by standard program logic.

By supplying the programmer standard logic in the form of a logic structure we can eliminate 60 percent of the design, coding, testing, and documentation in most business programs. This allows the programmer to concentrate on the unique part of the program without having to code the same redundant logic time and time again.

The obvious benefit of this concept is that after a programmer uses a structure more than three times (learning curve time) a 50 percent increase in productivity occurs. The not so obvious benefit is that programmers recognize a consistent style when modifying a program that they themselves did not write. This eliminates 60–80 percent of the maintenance problem that is caused by each programmer using an individual style for redundant functions in business programs. This is one of the basic problems in maintenance programming today and is causing most programming shops to spend 60–80 percent of their time in the modification mode instead of addressing their new application development backlog.

CONCLUSION

After studying our business community for over six years, we have concluded that we do basically the same kind of programs year in and year out and that much of this work deals with redundant programming functions. By standardizing those functions in the form of reusable functional modules and logic structures, a 50 percent gain in productivity can be attained and programmers can concentrate on creative problems rather than on redundant ones. In addition to the one time development benefit, the data processing organizations can redeploy 60–80 percent of their resources to work on new systems development applications.

REFERENCES

[1] R. M. Armstrong, *Modular Programming in COBOL*. New York: Wiley, 1973.
[2] R. Canning, "The search for reliability," *EDP Analyzer*, vol. 12, May 1974.
[3] G. Kapur, "Toward software engineering," *Computerworld*, In-Depth Section, Nov. 1979.
[4] R. Lanergan and B. Poynton, "Reusable code—The application development technique of the future," in *Proc. IBM GUIDE/ SHARE Application Symp.*, Oct. 1979, pp. 127–136.
[5] D. Leavit, "Reusable code chops 60% off creation of business programs," *Computerworld*, pp. 1–4, Oct. 1979.
[6] D. Schechter, "The skeleton program approach to standard implementation," in *Computer Programming Management*. Pennsauken, NJ: Auerbach, 1983.

Robert G. Lanergan attended Northeastern University, Boston, MA, from 1964 to 1967.

He developed and implemented a highly successful software reusability methodology that resulted in a significant reduction in the time and effort required to develop and maintain business systems. At present he is Manager of Information Services with Raytheon Missile Systems Division, Bedford, MA. He presented papers and lectured on the subject of reusability to many national and international organizations (ACM, DPMA, NCC, ACPA, DOD, IBM Guide and Share). In 1980 he was selected as a key employee by Raytheon's Board of Directors for software productivity contributions. His research interests include software productivity, reliability and maintenance issues. He is in the process of authoring a book entitled *How to Alleviate The Software Maintenance Dilemma: Past–Present and Future*.

Charles A. Grasso received the B.A. degree in business from New Hampshire College, Manchester.

He is currently the Manager of the Missile System Division Systems and Programming Organization, Raytheon Company, Bedford, MA. He has been instrumental in the development of major computer applications employing a reusable code/program generator methodology created internally at Raytheon. He is affiliated with the University of Lowell, Lowell, MA, where he teaches advanced structured Cobol.

VII. Restructuring Criteria and Cost Models

Choosing when to restructure software and what the returns will be is just as important as choosing a restructuring approach itself. Ideally, before a restructuring approach is applied to software, one should know the underlying structural problem being resolved by the approach, how much the expected return will be (maintenance cost savings plus future software development cost savings), and when this return will become visible.

In "System Maintenance vs. System Redesign" by R.J. Martin and W.M. Osborne (*Federal Information Standards Publication 106: Guideline on Software Maintenance,* chapter 5), sample symptoms are given of software due for a restructuring audit. The paper suggests that symptoms such as frequent system failures, code over 7 years old, code written for previous generation hardware, very large modules, and so on, may imply the need for system redesign. The paper presents a useful checklist of redesign decision factors which the reader may augment for his or her environment.

The illuminating concept of software spoilage is presented in the next paper, "Seeking Remedies for Software Spoilage" by W. E. Perry. The paper suggests that modifying software also carries with it an engineering support cost. If this cost is not shouldered, the basis for maintaining software quality deteriorates in addition to deterioration of the software structure itself.

The cost of current maintenance vis-á-vis the cost of restructuring followed by maintenance are presented in the next paper, "Existing Computer Applications. Maintain or Redesign: How to Decide?" by Linda Brice Shafer. (The paper was published under the author's previous name, Linda Brice.) Using equations that quantify maintenance costs and restructuring costs, the paper illustrates how a breakeven point may be calculated. A breakeven point is that point in the future (if ever) when the costs of continued maintenance equal the costs of restructuring plus maintenance. One surprising result of the cost illustrations in this paper is the long calendar time needed to reach the breakeven point. The only example given where this is reached still took 13 months from the start of restructuring!

The reader has probably suspected that software restructuring and software conversion are related. They are. Software restructuring is a typical first step in preparing a system for conversion. In a sense, restructuring the software converts the software to run on a new virtual machine which makes the software's operations easier to understand and therefore easier to convert. Studying the economics of software conversion can be helpful in calculating software restructuring costs. Such economics are described in the final paper, "Conversion Economics" by J.R. Wolberg. The paper, among other valuable results, compares cost equations for software redesign, reprogramming, and conversion.

5. SYSTEM MAINTENANCE VS SYSTEM REDESIGN

Although maintenance is an ongoing process, there comes a time when serious consideration should be given to redesigning a software system. A major concern of managers and software engineers is how to determine whether a system is hopelessly flawed or whether it can be successfully maintained. The costs and benefits of the continued maintenance of software which has become error-prone, ineffective, and costly must be weighed against that of redesigning the system.

Reprinted from *Federal Information Processing Standards Publication 106: Guideline on Software Maintenance*, Section 5, National Bureau of Standards, June 15, 1984, pages 14-17. U.S. Government work. Not protected by U.S. copyright.

When a decision has been reached to redesign or to stop supporting a system, the decision can be implemented in a number of ways. Support can simply be removed and the system can die through neglect; the minimum support needed to keep it functioning may be provided while a new system is built; or the system may be rejuvenated section by section and given an extended life. How the redesign is affected depends on the individual circumstances of the system, its operating environment, and the needs of the organization it supports.

While there are no absolute rules on when to rebuild rather than maintain the existing system, some of the factors to consider in weighing a decision to redesign or maintain are listed in figure 4. These characteristics are meant to be general "rules of thumb" which can assist a manager in understanding the problems in maintaining an existing system and in deciding whether or not it has outlived its usefulness to the organization. The greater the number of characteristics present, the greater the potential for redesign.

```
 1.   Frequent system failures
 2.   Code over 7 years old
 3.   Overly complex program structure and logic flow
 4.   Code written for previous generation hardware
 5.   Running in emulation mode
 6.   Very large modules or unit subroutines
 7.   Excessive resource requirements
 8.   Hard-coded parameters which are subject to change
 9.   Difficulty in keeping maintainers
10.   Seriously deficient documentation
11.   Missing or incomplete design specifications
```

Figure 4. *Characteristics of systems which are candidates for redesign*

Frequent System Failures

A system which is in virtually constant need of corrective maintenance is a prime candidate for redesign. As systems age and additional maintenance is performed, many become increasingly fragile and susceptible to changes. The older the code, the more likely frequent modifications, new requirements, and enhancements will cause the system to break down.

An analysis of errors should be made to determine whether the entire system is responsible for the failures, or if a few modules or sections of code are at fault. If the latter is found to be the case, then redesigning those parts of the system may suffice.

Code Over 7 Years Old

The estimated lifecycle of a major application system is 7-to-10 years. Software tends to deteriorate with age as a result of numerous fixes and patches. If a system is more than 7 years old, there is a high probability that it is outdated and expensive to run. A great deal of the code in use today falls into this category. After 7-to-10 years of maintenance, many systems have evolved to where additional enhancements or fixes are very time-consuming to make. A substantial portion of this code is probably neither structured, nor well-written. While this code was adequate and correct for the original environment, changes in technology and applications may have rendered it inefficient, difficult to revise, and in some cases obsolete. On the other hand, if the system was designed and developed in a systematic, maintainable manner, and if software maintenance was carefully performed and documented using established standards and guidelines, it may be possible to run it efficiently and effectively for many more years.

Overly Complex Program Structure and Logic Flow

"Keep it simple" must be the "golden rule" of all programming standards and guidelines. Too often, programmers engage in efforts to write a section of code in the least number of statements or utilizing the smallest amount of memory possible. This approach to coding usually results in complex code which is virtually incomprehensible. Poor program structure contributes to complexity. If the system being maintained contains a great deal of this type of code and the documentation is also severely deficient, it is a candidate for redesign.

Complexity also refers to the level of decision making present in the code. The greater the number of decision paths, the more complex the software is likely to be. Additionally, the greater the number of linearly independent control paths in a program, the greater the program complexity. Programs characterized by some or all of the following attributes are usually very difficult to maintain and are candidates for redesign:

- excessive use of DO loops
- excessive use of IF statements
- unnecessary GOTO statements
- embedded constants and literals
- unnecessary use of global variables
- self-modifying code
- multiple entry or exit modules
- excessive interaction between modules
- modules which perform same or similar functions.

Code Written for Previous Generation Hardware

Few industries have experienced as rapid a growth as the computer industry, particularly in the area of hardware. Not only have there been significant technological advances, but, the cost of hardware has decreased dramatically during the last decade. This phenomenon has generated a variety of powerful hardware systems. Software written for earlier generations of hardware is often inefficient on newer systems. Attempts to superficially modify the code to take advantage of the newer hardware is generally ineffective, time-consuming and expensive.

Running in Emulation Mode

One of the techniques used to keep a system running on newer hardware is to emulate the original hardware and operating system. Emulation refers to the capability of one system to exhibit behavior characteristic of another machine. In effect, it makes the host machine imitate the emulated machine. Emulation is normally used when resources are not available to convert a system, or the cost of doing so would be prohibitive. It frequently prevents utilization of the total capabilities and full power of the newer system. Emulated systems run a very fine line between functional usefulness and total obsolescence.

Very Large Modules or Unit Subroutines

"Mega-systems" which were written as one or several very large programs or sub-programs (thousands or tens-of-thousands of lines of code per program) can be extremely difficult to maintain. If the large modules can be restructured and divided into smaller, functionally related sections, the maintainability of the system will be improved.

Excessive Resource Requirements

An application system which requires a great deal of CPU time, memory, storage, or other system resources can place a very serious burden on all ADP users. Issues which must be addressed include whether it is cheaper to add more computer power or to redesign and reimplement the system, and whether redesign will reduce the resource requirements.

Hard-Coded Parameters Which Are Subject To Change

Many older systems were designed with the values of parameters used in performing specific calculations "hard coded" into the source code rather than stored in a table or read in from a data file. When changes in these values are necessary, (withholding rates, for example) each program in the system must be examined, modified and recompiled as necessary. This is a time-consuming, error prone process which is costly both in terms of the resources necessary to make the changes and the delay in getting the changes installed.

Whenever possible, the programs should be modified to handle the input of parameters in a single module or to read the parameters from a central table of values.

Difficulty in Keeping Maintainers

Programs written in low level languages, particularly assembler, require an excessive amount of time and effort to maintain. Generally, such languages are not widely taught or known. Therefore, it will be increasingly difficult to find maintainers who already know the language.

Seriously Deficient Documentation

Too often, documentation ranges from nonexistent to out-of-date. Even if the documentation is good when delivered, it often steadily and rapidly deteriorates as the software is modified. In some cases, the documentation is up-to-date, but still not useful. This can result when the documentation is produced by someone who does not understand the software or what is needed.

The worst documentation is that which is well-structured and formatted but which is incorrect or outdated. If there is no documentation, the maintainer will be forced to analyze the code in order to try to understand the system. If the documentation is physically deteriorated, the maintainer will be skeptical of it and verify its accuracy. If it looks good on the surface, but is technically incorrect, the maintainer may mistakenly believe it to be correct and accept what it contains. This will result in serious problems over and above those which originally necessitated the initial maintenance.

Missing or Incomplete Design Specifications

Knowing "how and why" a system works is essential to good maintenance. If the requirements and design specifications are missing or incomplete, the task of the maintainer will be more difficult. It is very important for the maintainer to not only understand what a system is doing, but how it is implemented, and why it was designed.

Seeking Remedies for Software Spoilage

DP Issues

By William E. Perry

Major libraries throughout the world are realizing that many of their books are deteriorating. When the paper-making process moved from a rag-based paper to a pulp-based paper, a deterioration timeclock was set into motion. Thus, many of the books published within the last 100 years are literally crumbling when touched.

Many computer programs built 20 to 25 years ago are also crumbling. The term used for this deterioration in data processing is spoilage. Spoilage is a measure of the rate by which computer software is deteriorating.

Librarians are performing research in ways to preserve old books. One of the ways that has proved effective is to subject the books to a gas that neutralizes the acid in the paper. This process reduces deterioration, and it is believed it can increase the life of the book by a few hundred years.

Data processing professionals are looking for the "gas" that will preserve old code. Organizations such as the Social Security Administration are paying the high cost today of DP spoilage. Thus, data processing is learning the same lessons about software that librarians learned about books — if the product deteriorates too much it cannot be saved.

The Cause of Software Deterioration

The definition of "spoilage" is the cost required to maintain the operational currentness of software. The types of costs that are categorized as spoilage include:

■ Modifications required by new versions of operating systems.
■ Changes caused by upgrading of hardware.
■ Compliance with new data processing standards.
■ Maintaining currentness of documentation.
■ Completing documentation required by current design methodologies
■ Maintaining test plans and test conditions

The cost of spoilage can range from 10 to 50 percent of the development cost per year. Many organizations do not want to pay this cost. The alternative is to delay the absolutely unnecessary spoilage costs. For example, we can permit our testing criteria to deteriorate, documentation to deteriorate, and not require compliance with standards.

The damage caused by spoilage may be irreversible. For example, if the test plan and conditions are not maintained, the cost of reconstructing a test plan several years after the system has gone into operation may be cost-prohibitive.

One of the main causes of spoilage is the transfer of budgetary responsibility to users, without transferring the responsibility for technological currentness. Users have been allowed to make the choice on budgetary expenditures. What users have not been told is the potential cost of these budgetary decisions. In the case of the Social Security Administration the cost is a minimum of $500 million.

Spoilage Countermeasures

Organizations recognize the challenge of spoilage and attempt to address it. The two most common strategies for salvaging systems that are becoming technically obsolete are:

1. Rewrite. This is the approach taken by the Social Security Administration. Its Systems Modernization Plan is designed to rewrite the majority of the system to upgrade it technically. In the rewrite, it is expected to utilize current technology, such as data base.

2. Retrofitting. This approach attempts to upgrade the program code using a retrofitting methodology. Generally, this involves using software to help restructure software. The proponents of retrofitting claim to take "spaghetti code" and turn it into structured code. In available retrofitting systems, the language that can be upgraded is limited to COBOL.

Neither of these approaches addresses the real problem of spoilage. Spoilage is attributable to the lack of a defined software maintenance process. The real solution to spoilage is a management solution and not a technical solution.

Solving Software Spoilage

The solution to software spoilage is a three-part solution as follows:

1. Recognition of the problem. Spoilage has, is, and will continue to be a major threat to the longevity of software. Accounting systems recognize depreciation of assets, but many have not yet recognized that software wears out. Until management recognizes that it is a problem, it will not be addressed as a problem.

2. Assign spoilage accountability. The physical assets of an organization are under the direction of an asset management group. People do what that they are responsible for. Users believe they are responsible only for the functional characteristics of the software, and the data processing people believe they are only responsible for performing user requests. Someone must be accountable for the technological currentness of software.

3. Develop a software maintenance plan. The continued technological currentness of software will not happen until a plan is developed and put into place to make it happen. People will have to decide what needs to be done to maintain the technological currentness of software, determine how it can be performed, and then allocate the resources necessary to make it happen. Unfortunately, the plan will not occur until the problem is recognized, and people are assigned the responsibility for addressing the software spoilage facts of life.

Perry is director of the Quality Assurance Institute, Orlando, Fla.

EXISTING COMPUTER APPLICATIONS
MAINTAIN OR REDESIGN: HOW TO DECIDE?

Linda Brice
Los Alamos National Laboratory

ABSTRACT

Maintainence of large applications programs is an aspect of performance management that has been largely
ignored by those studies that attempt to bring structure to the software production environment.
Maintenance in this paper means: fixing "bugs", modifying current design features, adding enhancements,
and porting applications to other computer systems. It is often difficult to decide whether to maintain
or redesign. One reason for the difficulty is that good models and methods do not exist for
differentiating between those programs that should be maintained and those that should be redesigned.

This enigma is illustrated by the description of a large application case study. The application was
monitored for maintenance effort, thereby providing some insight into the redesign/maintain decision.
Those tools which currently exist for the collection and measurement of performance data are highlighted.
Suggestions are then made for yet other categories of data, difficult to collect and measure, yet
ultimately necessary for the establishment of accurate predictions about the value of maintaining versus
the value of redesigning.

Finally, it is concluded that this aspect of performance management deserves increased attention in order
to establish better guidelines with which to aid management in making the necessary but difficult
decision: maintain or redesign.

INTRODUCTION

There is no longer any doubt that some form(s) of
structured specification, design, and implementation
will be used to control major software projects of
the eighties and beyond. The value to be gained from
these approaches is well documented [1]. Unfortunately, many data processing departments will
derive little benefit from these advances for years
to come since most of the DP software budget is spent
maintaining code that was not designed with these
techniques.

How does management decide when to invest precious
resources in the redesign of an existing, working
application? Put another way, how do you quantify
change that may result from cleaner, better implementation? Quantifiable costs associated with an
application include: computer resources utilized by
the application, programmer staff time plus computer
resource costs expended to maintain the application,
and associated user time spent trying to learn and to
use the end product. Other costs which are harder to
quantify include: net effects of frustration among
users and maintainers of the existing application,
possible increases in user productivity, overall
improvements in operations resource consumption, and
those expenditures associated with redesign and
re-implementation.

Several semi-formal systems of rules have been
developed with the goal of avoiding poor designs and
implementations. Further, a type of folk wisdom has
evolved that allows applications to be classified as
generally good or bad, often based upon their
resource consumption and/or the quality of the user
interface. Tools exist [2, 3, 4, 5] for quantifying
expected improvements in resource consumption
resulting from specific design changes. While some
recent studies have shown the value of the concept of
software engineering, most design methods ignore
performance, thus devaluating these tools. Furthermore, the actual maintenance costs are often much
greater than the total computer costs associated with
use of an application.

Less attention has been focused on quantifying just
how costly an application is by utilizing as a base
the human time invested in maintainence, an activity
that consumes large fractions of a typical budget.

It is necessary but insufficient to know how many man
hours per month are invested in maintainence of an
application. It is also necessary, but insufficient
to understand why and how the maintainence was done.
Other metrics are needed if good models are to be
produced that allow a quantification of the benefits
that might accrue from a complete redesign of the
application.

In what follows, the performance metrics which were
developed for evaluating an applications maintenance
effort are described. The case study is a beginning
towards providing management with decision making
tools, but it is not totally adequate.

Presented here is the following:

● sample values of data collected for in-house
   maintenance effort,

● rewrite payoff estimates using only collected
   data,

● other, known approaches for collecting additional
   data which could improve predictions,

● suggestions for data which, given ideas for
   collection, would enhance the metrics necessary
   to parameterize models.

CASE STUDY

Maintenance work can be divided among three categories: fixing "bugs", adding minor enhancements or
altering features, and developing new features for an
existing system. The latter of these three categories may include, for example, a new output report
which must rely on existing subroutines and file
structures.

Described here in detail is the analysis of all
maintenance work done for a large application that
was ported (straight conversion) from a CDC 6600 to a
Hewlett Packard 3000 mini-computer. The data was
collected over a 13 month period. There are
approximately 120 programs and subroutines written
primarily in the Fortran language (with a few COBOL
codes), consisting of approximately 43,000 lines of
code. The application is used interactively by
80-100 users. Batch production cycle output is

Reprinted from *The Proceedings of the Computer Measurement Group*,
December 1981, pages 20-28.

distributed to about 2,000 users. Nearly 140mb of disk storage is consumed for program source, binaries and data files. The basic function of the application is to provide a subset of users with a method of interactively entering forecast data and iterating that data, and subsequently to provide all users with hard-copy reports depicting the current status of forecasts versus actual costs to date.

The maintenance programming effort is subdivided according to three main categories: pure corrective maintenance ("fixes" to performance or implementation failures), enhancements or optimization (changes in the processing environment), and development or extension (addition of new features for increased performance). Table 1 reflects the number of person hours of effort expended for each of these three categories. While "development" effort is the largest of the categories, it should be noted that 85% of the development was expended on only two requests: documentation of the system and a series of new output reports. The largest number of changes fell into the "enhancement" category, as illustrated in Figure 1. Service Request numbers, the documentation form used to log changes, are not chronological in this figure, but represent grouping of effort. For example, in the curve labeled "E" for enhancement, the x-axis point labeled "2" indicates that one enhancement request required 150 hours of effort. On the enhancement curve, the x-axis points labeled "6", "7", "8" and "9" indicate that each of four changes required 50 hours of effort. Similarly, on the "development" curve, it is shown that only one request (the one for new output) required 1,000 hours. Figure 1 shows that the number of development changes was five, the number of enhancement changes was 40, and the number of maintenance changes was 25, totaling 70 service requests. Figure 2 makes no distinction among development, enhancement or maintenance, but shows, as one curve, that the majority of changes were small in terms of effort hours. For example, 26 changes required 10 or fewer than 10 hours, 15 changes required 20 or fewer than 20 hours, etc. Compared to development, where one change took over 1,000 hours, maintenance and enhancement changes requiring less than 125 hours numbered 65. It can be inferred from this data that the "quick fix" or "patch" consumed over one-half of all effort expended during the time period. That is, enhancement and maintenance consumed 3,100 hours while development consumed 2,500 hours.

The two easily quantifiable costs associated with an application are computer resources for use and maintenance, and personnel resources for maintenance. Computer costs in this case study are fixed - approximately $5,900 per month for lease price plus approximately $1,100 per month for hardware maintenance, the total approximating $7,000 per month. The total number of person hours expended in maintaining the operation over the 13 month period is 5,639 - when overhead factors are added, the figure escalates to 7,933, or an effective average of 3.8 full time professional employees. Average cost per employee, including salary, overhead costs and fringe benefits exceeds $100,000 per year or $8,333 per month.

Total manpower cost is then calculated in Equation (1):

$$Tm = Ne * Na * A \qquad (1)$$
or
$$Tm = 3.8 * 13 * \$8,333$$
$$Tm = \$411,650$$
where Tm = total manpower cost
Ne = number of employees
Na = number of months elapsed
A = Average monthly cost per employee

Equation (2) gives total computer costs.

$$Tc = (Pl + Pm) * N \qquad (2)$$
or
$$Tc = (\$5,900 + \$1,100) * 13$$
$$Tc = \$91,000$$
where Tc = total computer cost
Pl = computer lease price
Pm = computer hardware maintenance price
N = number of months elapsed.

Comparison of computer costs of $91,000 to personnel costs of $411,650 points out that, in at least some applications, the ease of maintaining and using a system is more important than machine resource utilization.

Note that only programmer effort was included in these calculations. Management time, an even higher cost, was not considered, nor was production operations staff time. It is not known how many hours of effort were expended by users of the application, a metric which would be useful in the redesign decision. Based on informal observation, the user interface could be improved, but that kind of time-consuming survey has not yet been conducted in this case study.

Those who maintain the application would like to see it redesigned and rewritten to make the maintenance load easier. Yet the application is "working", thus creating the need to prove to management that a redesign using modern methods would result in a smaller maintenance effort and improved overall costs. Quantifying a "payoff" to be gained from a rewrite is the key. The following three figures are an attempt to use the collected data to indicate payoff possibilities.

In strictly monetary terms, the current and anticipated expenditures of maintenance, both staff and hardware, can be plotted as a function of time. In figures 3, 4, and 5:

$$Tl = t * (C + P) \qquad (3)$$
where Tl = total expenditures without rewrite
t = elapse time, in months
C = computer costs, defined as constant \$7,000/month
P = personnel costs
$= Ne * A$
$= 3.8 * \$8,333$
$\approx \$31,000$
where Ne = number of employees
A = average monthly cost per person

Figure 3 is a realistic estimate, assuming that the application can be rewritten by three people in a nine-month period. Figure 4 is an optimistic estimate, assuming that the applcation can be rewritten by two people in a six-month period. Figure 5 is pessimistic, assuming it would take four people one year to accomplish a rewrite. Figures 3, 4, and 5 use the line T2 to indicate redesign costs. In all figures the following assumptions are standard:

1) computer resource costs will remain constant,
2) following a rewrite, maintenance programmer costs will be significantly reduced (it will take only two people to support the maintenance effort, instead of the current 3.8),
3) the maintenance, enhancement and development load (number of service requests) will remain constant.

264

Costs, given a rewrite is calculated:

$$T2 = t * (C + P/p) + R \qquad (4)$$

where t = elapse time, in months
C = computer costs, defined as constant $7,000/month
P = personnel costs
= Ne * A
= 3.8 * $8,333
≃ $31,000

where Ne = number of employees
A = average monthly cost per person
p = reduction factor (assume 1.9)
R = rewrite costs
= Nr * A * t

where Nr = number of employees required for rewrite
A = average monthly cost per person
t = elapse time, in months, for rewrite.

In every case, costs are higher during the rewrite period when the project utilizes additional staff.

Also, in every case, costs recede following completion of the rewrite, and the payoff period begins some time after the rewrite. Figure 4 shows the savings effected - it can be seen that about $160,000 is the savings by the 24th month for the optimistic case. Payoff for the realistic and pessimistic cases will not begin until sometime after the 24th month following start of rewrite. The total savings is the difference of T1 - T2. In Figure 4 (optimistic) the payoff is shown to begin seven months after the rewrite.

These figures are a good indication of the positive effects of a rewrite, but they are incomplete without incorporating another needed metric - user interface. If user costs were added, T1 would shift upward, and T2 would shift upward, at least until the time of rewrite completion. If, however, there was some mechanism for predicting improved ease of use after rewrite (and therefore lower user costs), it could possibly be shown that T2 would dramatically shift downward after rewrite, creating greater overall savings.

Another metric needed to accurately forecast payoff possibilities is the cost of re-implementation. Guessing at the number of people and the time required for the project is not a good tool. The estimates used in this case study were deemed reasonable by all who were associated with the project, yet there is no guarantee that the application can be recreated and improved on a predetermined schedule.

OTHER APPROACHES

It has been said that "Maintenance-oriented design constraints are essential for continued reliability and correctness in a changing environment. The pressure for change results from the economic advantages of new hardware and the service advantages of new function. Since these advantages develop frequently, reflecting the rate of technological improvement and new applications, the pressure for change is persistent. Without the support of maintainability in such an environment, reliability and

correctness are fragile properties which can be quickly lost to either error or obsolescence. Therefore, in a changing environment, maintenance-oriented design constraints become as important as those of presently-required function." [6]

Some directly measurable maintainability factors have been defined as:

● problem recognition time,

● administrative delay time,

● maintenance tools collection time,

● problem analysis time,

● change specification time,

● active correction time,

● local functional correctness test time,

● global correctness test time,

● independent change - audit time,

● recovery time or correction implementation time [7].

In the case study, the above ten factors were measured as one, although each of the ten could have been measured independently. What was not measured, due in part to lack of tools, were the potentially highest cost savers: possible increase in user productivity and an accurate figure for decreased maintenance cost after rewrite. Decreased maintenance costs were merely guesses, while user interface was left constant due to absence of data. For example, if the programs were redesigned with better user features, the enhancement load (number of service requests) could be expected to drop sharply.

While maintenance for the application is expected to improve following a rewrite, publication of an accurate expectation requires both additional data and additional measurement tools for projections.

Additional data might include:

● distribution of user time spent exercising each interactive feature,

● distribution of user time spent exercising each batch report feature,

● prioritization of the usefulness of the features by the users of the application (frequency of use is often not indicative of importance - many reports produced only at month end carry heavy significance),

● prioritization of future enhancements desired by users.

UNOBTAINABLE (?) DATA

Projections which, made accurately, would aid in the maintain/redesign decision might include:

● cost to redesign and re-implement,

● resource consumption of the rewritten version of the application,

● improvements in interactive user productivity,

● improvements in batch report user productivity,

- improvements in operations staff application use,

- improvements in production control.

CONCLUSION

Applications which are difficult to maintain or use are often considered candidates for redesign, even though they exist in working status. Many DP shops are handicapped by too few available methods for deciding when an application should be left in maintenance mode with known, fixed costs, and when it should be rewritten. Some advantages of a rewrite are:

- improved user features,

- improved maintainability due to structured specification, design and implementation,

- improved user and maintenance costs.

Redesigns are expensive as most applications must continue to serve the user with a maintenance staff during the rewrite period. Management requires tools for estimating the cost of redesign and plotting it against the potential cost savings of a new version.

Maintenance effort and computer resource consumption are easily quantified and were done so in the case study. Other metrics such as frequency of the use of an application feature by users and user satisfaction survey could be used in the study, yet they still would not provide enough information for an intelligent decision. Performance management aspects which need to be addressed in order to aid in the maintain /redesign decision are:

- how to accurately estimate programmer time associated with redesign

- how to accurately predict resource consumption after rewrite if the end product remains the same, and if it does not,

- how to accurately estimate user productivity following rewrite,

- how to accurately estimate maintenance effort required for a new version.

Until each of these metrics are considered in the comparision of maintenance costs versus redesign costs, a proper decision cannot be clear.

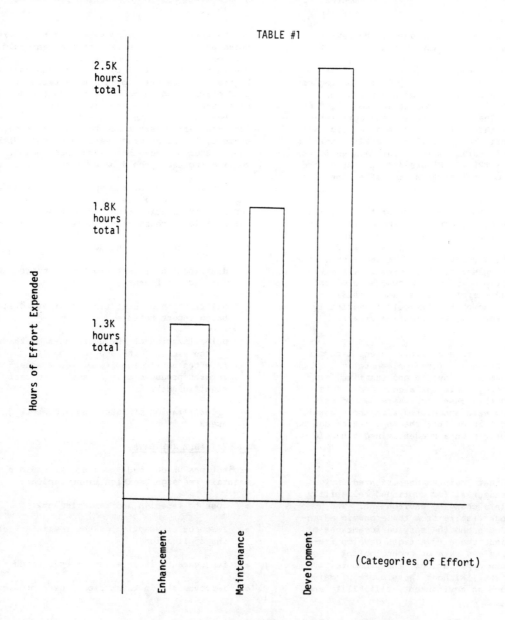

TABLE #1

266

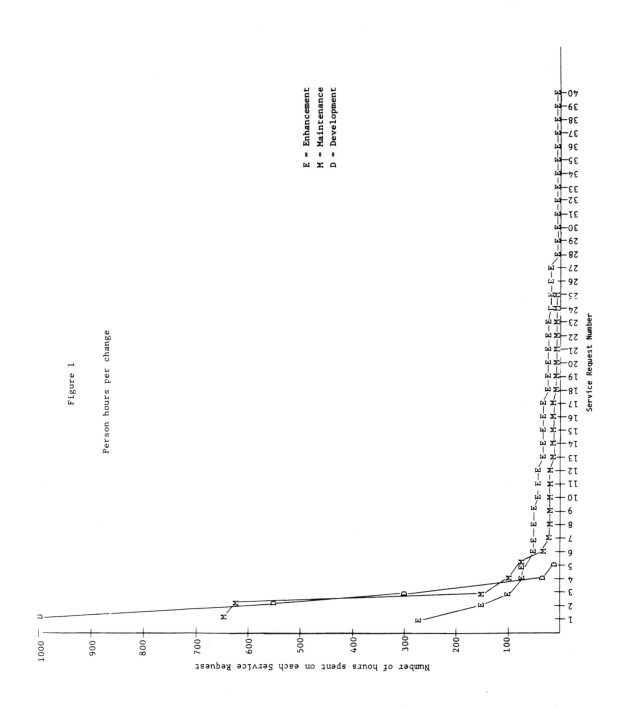

Figure 1

Person hours per change

E = Enhancement
M = Maintenance
D = Development

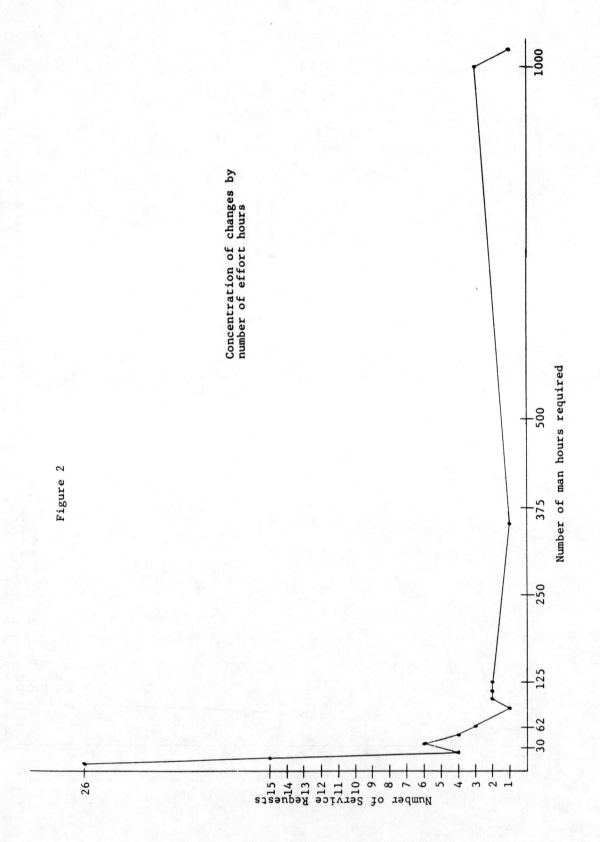

Figure 2

Concentration of changes by
number of effort hours

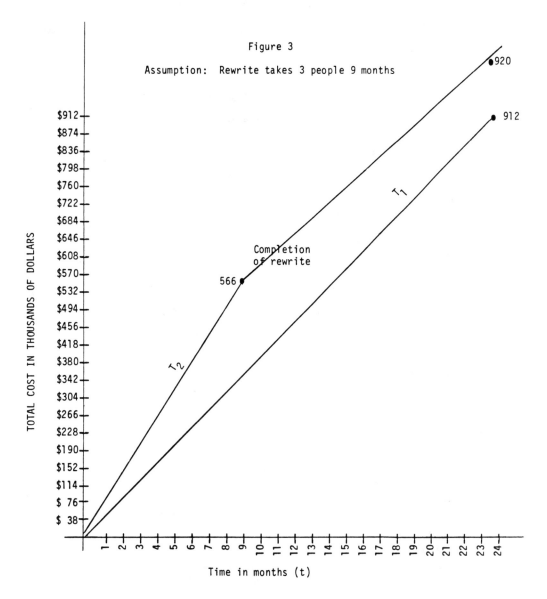

Figure 3

Assumption: Rewrite takes 3 people 9 months

T₁ = Current cost of maintenance

T₂ = Rewrite cost plus maintenance cost

269

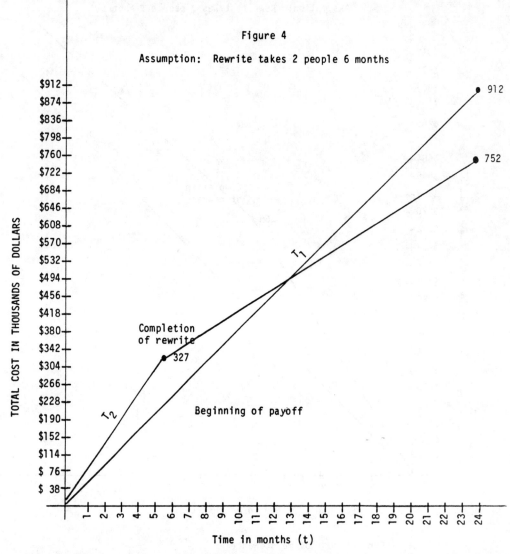

Figure 4

Assumption: Rewrite takes 2 people 6 months

T_1 = Current cost of maintenance

T_2 = Rewrite cost plus maintenance cost

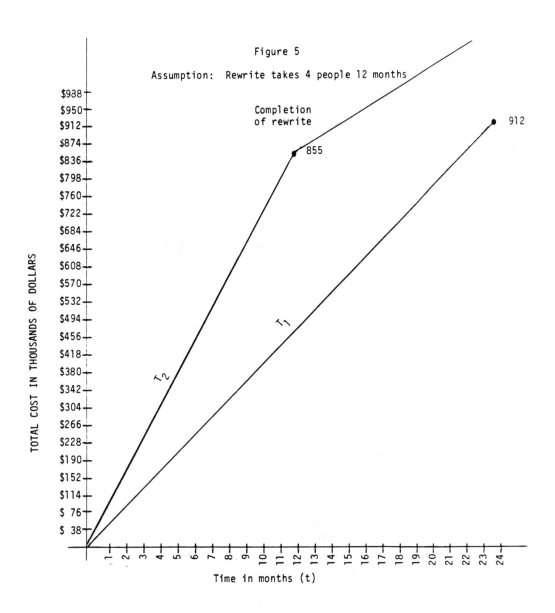

Figure 5

Assumption: Rewrite takes 4 people 12 months

Completion of rewrite

855

912

T_1

T_2

TOTAL COST IN THOUSANDS OF DOLLARS

$938
$950
$912
$874
$836
$798
$760
$722
$684
$646
$608
$570
$532
$494
$456
$418
$380
$342
$304
$266
$228
$190
$152
$114
$ 76
$ 38

Time in months (t)

T_1 = Current cost of maintenance

T_2 = Rewrite cost plus maintenance cost

1. Kleine, Karl, "Selected Annotated Bibliography on Software Engineering", ACM SIGSOFT, Software Engineering Notes Vol. 3, No. 1, January 1978.

2. C. U. Smith, J. C. Browne, "Aspects of Software Design Analysis: Concurrency and Blocking", Proc. Symposium on Computer Performance, Modeling, Measurement and Evaluation, Toronto, Ontario, Canada, May 1980.

3. C. U. Smith, J. C. Browne, "Performance Specifications and Analysis of Software Designs", Proc. Conference on Simulation, Measurement and Modeling of Computer Systems, Boulder, August 1979.

4. C. U. Smith, J. C. Browne, "Modeling Software Systems for Performance Predictions", Proc. Computer Measurement Group X, Dallas, December 1979.

5. T. J. Gilkey, F. R. White, and T. L. Booth, "Performance Analysis as a Software Design Tool", Proc. COMPSAC77, IEEE Computer Society, November 1977.

6. D. Gelperin, "Testing Maintainability,", ACM SIGSOFT, Software Engineering Notes, Vol. 4, No. 2, April 1979.

7. T. Gibb, "A Comment on 'The Definition of Maintainability'", ACM SIGSOFT, Software Engineering Notes, Vol. 4, No. 3, July 1979.

Conversion Economics

2.1 INTRODUCTION

The decision to convert is invariably an economic decision. A set of circumstances requires a change in the basic computing system. For some situations existing software will not be compatible with the new system. The three alternative lines of action are to convert the software, replace the software, or discard the software. A choice among these alternatives is usually made by considering the economic implications of the various lines of action.

To make intelligent decisions, one requires a methodology for estimating the costs, personnel requirements, and time required for the various alternatives. One method of estimation is to use correlations based on past experience. Estimation equations are discussed in Sections 2.2 to 2.4.

If a decision has been made to convert, for most conversions (except the most trivial), some attempt will be made to partially automate the process. Clearly, an investment is required in conversion aids and tools, so one is confronted with an optimization problem. By investing more in automation, one reduces the manual effort required in a conversion. But clearly, one reaches a point where the savings are no longer commensurate with the additional investment. This optimization problem is analyzed in Sections 2.5 and 2.6.

The number of paramount importance when attempting to estimate conversion costs is the cost per line. Clearly, if we had a value for the

Wolberg, *Conversion of Computer Software*, © 1983, pp. 35-59. Reprinted by permission of Prentice-Hall, Englewood Cliffs, New Jersey.

conversion cost per line of source code, a simple multiplication yields the total cost of the conversion. Some numbers are available and can be used to give rough estimates. An analysis of some available data is presented in Section 2.7.

2.2 CONVERSION ESTIMATION EQUATIONS

The first step in estimating the cost of a conversion project is to use the equation developed in Section 1.5 [i.e., Equation (1.3)]. This equation yields an estimate for E (person-months) as a function of L (thousands of lines of code). By using an average cost per hour or cost per month, the total cost of conversion can be computed. For example, RIS used a figure of $30 per hour to make cost estimations [1].

There is, of course, an additional cost for computer usage that must be included in any estimate of the total cost of a conversion project. However, this cost is dependent on the specific arrangements for computer usage for each project. For example, computer time might be supplied free of charge for the purposes of conversion by the vendor of the target machine. Alternatively, one might have to buy time at commercial rates. If an in-house computer is used, the usage charge can be set at any level decided upon by management. An extremely rough estimate for average computer usage for a conversion project is that computer usage cost is equal to personnel cost.

The cost per statement (exclusive of computer usage) is computed in Table 2.1 for the nine RIS conversion projects summarized in Table 1.8. The cost per statement values range from $0.53 to $9.59 (based on $30 per hour). Equation (1.3) yields a value of E for any value of L based on these nine projects. Examining Figure 1.1 we see that the nine data points are widely scattered about the least-squares line. The two most widely scattered points are at $L = 160$ and $L = 179$. These points are 57% below and 155% above the line, respectively. If we take these values as very rough upper and lower limits, the estimation that is obtained using Equation (1.3) is accurate to a factor of 2 to 3. If we arbitrarily choose a value of 2.5, we can assume the following limits:

$$\frac{E_c}{2.5} < E < 2.5 \times E_c \qquad (2.1)$$

where E is the expected value of effort (person-months) for a given conversion project of length L (thousands of lines) and E_c is the value of E computed using Equation (1.3) (i.e., $E = 7.14L^{0.47}$).

A more accurate method of estimation is to use a value obtained from a similar conversion but scaled using the 0.47 exponent:

$$E = E_i \left(\frac{L}{L_i}\right)^{0.47} \tag{2.2}$$

For example, assume that we wish to convert a 300,000-line system written in IBM 370 COBOL to Burroughs B6700 COBOL. An examination of Table 1.8 shows that the third entry in the table is for this particular type of conversion. The values of E_3 and L_3 are 35,532 and 500, respectively. Substituting these values into Equation (2.2), we calculate an expected value for E:

$$E = 35,532 \left(\frac{300}{500}\right)^{0.47} = 27,948 \text{ hours}$$

Based on a cost per hour rate of $30, the estimated cost per statement is

$$\text{cost per statement} = \$30 \times 27,948/300,000 = \$2.79$$

As expected, this cost per statement is greater than the cost for the 500,000-line conversion (as shown in Table 2.1).

TABLE 2.1   Cost per Statement for RIS Conversion Projects

Project	Number of Programs	Thousands of Statements	Person-Hours	Hours/Program	Statements/Hour	Cost/Statement[a]
1	1,673	2,000	35,146	21	57	$0.53
2	1,620	1,300	59,376	37	22	1.37
3	1,500	500	35,532	24	14	2.13
4	729	571	24,657	34	23	1.30
5	382	308	12,384	32	25	1.21
6	344	311	38,987	113	8	3.76
7	213	32	10,236	48	3	9.59
8	200	179	37,014	185	5	6.20
9	157	160	5,819	37	27	1.09

[a]Based on a rate of $30 per hour. Note that this cost does not include computer usage.

Instinctively, it is more accurate to use Equation (2.2) rather than (1.3); however, this can be done only if one can find relevant data. Even if the exact conversion of interest is not included in Table 1.8, we can sometimes use the existing data to advantage. For example, we see that the cost per statement is high for interlanguage conversions (note projects 6 and 7 in Table 2.1). Thus if the conversion is to be from one language to another (not merely from one version to another version of the same language), we might use Equation (2.2) and the data from project 6 or 7 or an average. Similarly, for projects with multiple source and target machines, the data from project 8 might be relevant.

An estimation equation for project duration was presented in Section 1.5 [i.e., Equation (1.4)]. An equation analogous to (2.2) can be used for scaling from existing data:

$$D = D_i \left(\frac{L}{L_i}\right)^{0.22} \qquad (2.3)$$

For example, for the case discussed above (i.e., a 300,000-line conversion from IBM 370 COBOL to Burroughs B6700 COBOL), the values of D_3 and L_3 are 12 months and 500,000 lines, respectively (see Table 1.8). Substituting these values into Equation (2.3), we calculate an expected value for D:

$$D = 12 \left(\frac{300}{500}\right)^{0.22} = 10.7 \text{ months}$$

The value of D computed using Equation (1.4) is

$$D = 4.1 \times 300^{0.22} = 14.0 \text{ months}$$

The value of 10.7 months is a more reasonable estimate for the project duration because it is based on data from a similar project. The value of 14 months is based on the overall correlation of all the RIS data.

2.3 REPROGRAMMING AND REDESIGN ESTIMATION EQUATIONS

The alternative to the conversion of software is the replacement of software. Two replacement options are *reprogramming* and *redesign*. Oliver makes the following distinction [2]:

1. *Reprogramming* may entail a system redesign (e.g., batch to on-line) but no significant functional redesign. The process is manual and not based on a line-by-line translation of the original system.
2. *Redesign* involves functional redesign and is therefore akin to new development.

Oliver considers both reprogramming and redesign to fall within the realm of conversion technology; however, I prefer to consider them as alternatives to conversion. They are both manual options and are governed by the rules of general software development. (In my terminology the conversion option implies that some degree of automation is possible because the new code will be based to a large extent on the original code.)

The distinction between reprogramming and redesign is not clear. At what point do the functional changes become "significant"? Clearly, reprogramming implies a smaller effort than redesign, however, it is difficult to place quantitative criteria on the degree of savings. For the purposes of the following analysis, the savings is arbitrarily assumed to be 50%. To develop equations similar to (1.3) and (1.4), the following assumptions are made:

1. *Redesign* of an existing system requires an effort comparable to the development of a new system of the same size.
2. *Reprogramming* of an existing system requires an effort equal to one-half the effort required for redesign.

Several correlations are available for new system development projects. Walston and Felix analyzed a data base of 60 completed software development projects with delivered source lines ranging from 4000 to 467,000 [3]. The programming effort ranged from 12 to 11,758 months. The overall correlation is

$$E = 5.2L^{0.91} \tag{2.4}$$

An assumption that redesign is equivalent to new system development thus leads us to the following relationship:

$$E_{rd} = 5.2L^{0.91} \tag{2.5}$$

where E_{rd} is the effort in person-months required to redesign a system of L thousands of lines.[1] Our assumption that reprogramming requires approximately one-half the effort of redesign yields the following relationship:

$$E_{rp} = 2.6L^{0.91} \tag{2.6}$$

where E_{rp} is the effort in person-months to reprogram a system of L thousands of lines.

Walston and Felix partitioned their data base into several classes of programs and noted that the exponent for L was in all cases nearly 1. Thus the development of new systems (and redesigning or reprogramming of old systems) is not appreciably helped by a scaling effect. Doubling the value of L will on average increase E by a factor of $2^{0.91} = 1.88$. This increase is significantly greater than the increase in E one would expect from a conversion project. [From Equation (1.3) we note an increase in E by a factor of $2^{0.47} = 1.39$ if L is doubled.]

Schneider analyzed data prepared by the Rome Air Development Center (RADC) consisting of 400 software projects [4]. He used a more sophisticated model which includes N (the number of programs)

---

[1] Boehm [9] suggests the correlation $E = 2.4L^{1.05}$.

as well as L. The suggested overall correlation for programs written in higher-level languages is

$$E = 28 \times N\left(\frac{L}{N}\right)^{1.83} \tag{2.7}$$

The ratio L/N is the average size of a program divided by 1000 and is relatively constant. Thus Schneider's results suggest that E is approximately proportional to N, which is approximately proportional to L. The close-to-linear relationship noted by Walston and Felix is thus verified by Schneider.

Using Equations (2.4) and (2.7), we can recalculate E for the nine points included in Table 2.1. The results are shown in Table 2.2. Analyzing the results leads one to the immediate conclusion that conversions are much cheaper than new system development. For the same values of L, Equation (2.4) yields values that range from 2.1 to 25.8 times the conversion project efforts. The ratio increases as L (the project size) increases. The results obtained using Equation (2.7) and the same values of L and N yield values that range from 7.4 to 320 times the conversion project efforts.

It is interesting to compare the results from Equations (2.4) and (2.7), as shown in Table 2.2. The results from (2.7) are consistently higher (from a factor of 3.6 to a factor of 12.3 higher). The large differences are at first glance suprising because both correlations are for new system development. The most probable explanation is the difference in complexity among the two data bases. Although Schneider does not describe the nature of the systems included in the RADC

TABLE 2.2 Comparison of Conversion Effort and New System Development Effort

Project	L	N	Conversion		New Development	
			Actual[a]	Eq. (1.3)	Eq. (2.4)	Eq. (2.7)
1	2,000	1,673	203	254	5,247	64,945
2	1,300	1,620	343	208	3,546	30,323
3	500	1,500	205	132	1,486	9,222
4	571	729	142	141	1,677	14,571
5	308	382	71.5	105	956	7,947
6	311	344	225	106	965	8,381
7	32	213	59.1	36.4	122	436
8	179	200	215	81.8	584	4,805
9	160	157	33.6	77.6	527	4,512

[a]Computed from person-hours in Table 2.1 divided by 173.2 hours per month.

study, one can assume that many of the systems were highly sophisticated (and indeed, the results indicate a very high level of effort per line of code). One might expect that the RADC study includes a large number of real-time applications fine tuned for performance for a given hardware configuration and operating system. Such systems are rarely converted. If the system for some reason must be moved to a new environment, it would most probably be redesigned. Thus for purposes of comparison with conversion effort, the Walston and Felix correlation [i.e., Equation (2.4)] is probably more relevant than Equation (2.7).

2.4 COMPARING CONVERSION, REDESIGN, AND REPROGRAMMING

The results from Sections 1.5, 2.2, and 2.3 can be used to develop equations for computing the relative efforts required to redesign, reprogram, or convert a given system [5]. The relevant equations are summarized in Table 2.3. The equations are shown graphically in Figure 2.1.

TABLE 2.3   Correlations for Redesign, Reprogramming, and Conversion

	Equation Number	Equation
Redesign	(2.5)	$E_{rd} = 5.2L^{0.91}$
Reprogramming	(2.6)	$E_{rp} = 2.6L^{0.91}$
Conversion	(1.3)	$E_c = 7.14L^{0.47}$

From the graph we see that if it is decided to convert a system rather than redesign or reprogram the system, there should be a significant savings in effort for systems of several tens of thousands of lines of code. The proportional savings increases as L increases.

It should be understood that for smaller systems conversion might also be the cheapest option; however, the analysis was based on the RIS data (see Table 1.8) and the smallest system in the data base was 32,000 lines. Thus the RIS data are not applicable for making conclusions regarding smaller conversions. The author is familiar with conversion projects for systems with fewer than 10,000 lines which were completed in a matter of days. The speed of the projects can be explained by the availability of automatic converters, which accomplished over 90% of all necessary changes automatically. For smaller conversions for which automatic converters are unavailable, it is not obvious which option is the cheapest and fastest.

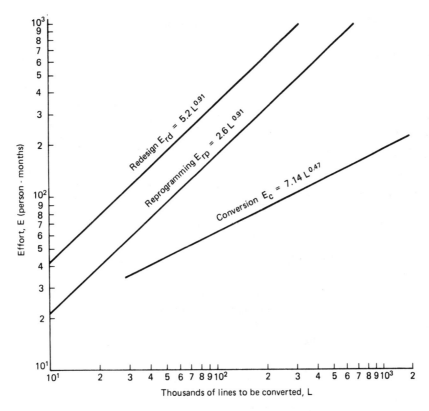

Figure 2.1   Redesign, reprogramming, and conversion efforts.

Ratios for redesign and reprogramming compared to conversion efforts can be obtained by dividing Equations (2.5) and (2.6) by (1.3):

$$\frac{E_{rd}}{E_c} = 0.728L^{0.44} \tag{2.8}$$

$$\frac{E_{rp}}{E_c} = 0.364L^{0.44} \tag{2.9}$$

(Note that we have assumed that $E_{rp}/E_{rd} = 0.5$.) Similar equations can be developed for project duration. Walston and Felix include a correlation for a project duration D (person-months) as a function of L (thousands of lines) for new system development:

$$D = 4.1L^{0.36} \tag{2.10}$$

If we assume that the duration for redesign is the same as new system development, and (very arbitrarily) assume that duration for reprogram-

[1] Boehm [9] suggests a similar equation: $D = 3.48L^{0.40}$.

ming is 80% of the new system development, we obtain the following two equations:

$$D_{rd} = 4.1L^{0.36} \qquad (2.11)$$

and

$$D_{rp} = 3.3L^{0.36} \qquad (2.12)$$

Using Equation (1.4) for project duration of conversion projects, we obtain the following ratios:

$$\frac{D_{rd}}{D_c} = 1.0L^{0.14} \qquad (2.13)$$

$$\frac{D_{rp}}{D_c} = 0.8L^{0.14} \qquad (2.14)$$

In Table 2.4 four projects of varying L are compared. We note that estimated effort for redesign increases from 3.25 to 15.2 times the effort for conversion as the project size increases from 30,000 to 1,000,000 lines. The estimated project duration will also increase, but we note that the increase is much less than the increase in effort.

TABLE 2.4   Comparing Projects of Various Sizes by Effort and Duration for Redesign, Reprogramming, and Conversion[a]

L	Effort Ratio		Duration Ratio	
	E_{rd}/E_c	E_{rp}/E_c	D_{rd}/D_c	D_{rp}/D_c
30	3.25	1.63	1.61	1.29
100	5.52	2.76	1.91	1.15
300	8.95	4.48	2.22	1.78
1000	15.2	7.61	2.63	2.10

[a]The subscript rd refers to redesign, rp to reprogramming, and c to conversion.

2.5 OPTIMIZING A CONVERSION PROJECT

The term *optimization* has different meanings in different situations. However, regardless of how we define optimization, the fundamental concept is that some objective must be minimized or maximized. When applied to the conversion problem, the usual objective is to minimize cost. We can reduce the manual effort associated with a conversion by investing in conversion tools and aids; however, we reach a point where the additional cost cannot be justified on the basis of the potential saving. The following analysis yields insight into the trade-off between the automatic and manual portions of the conversion.

A conversion project can be subdivided into five phases. Although the percentage of cost spent for each phase varies from conversion to conversion, the values shown in Table 2.5 are representative. Brandon suggests a slightly different set of values [6] (i.e., 15% for language translation, 25% for data preparation, 50% for testing, and 10% for installation); however, the differences are not important. What is important to note is that more than 50% of the cost of a conversion project is associated with conversion and testing of the source code. All the costs in Table 2.5 can be included in one of three categories [7]:

1. *Automatic cost, C_a.* This category includes the cost for purchasing and/or developing conversion software (i.e., converters and/or conversion aids) and the cost associated with running the conversion software. A fraction of the phase 3 (i.e., conversion) cost can be attributed to C_a.

2. *Manual cost C_m.* This category includes the remainder of the phase 3 (i.e., conversion) cost and the phase 4 (i.e., testing) cost. This work requires programmer intervention and interpretation; however, some of the tasks can be simplified using additional conversion software (e.g., file comparison software).

3. *Fixed cost C_f.* This category includes those cost items that do not vary regardless of the level of automation used in the conversion phase. The costs for phases 1, 2, and 5 (i.e., planning, data preparation, and implementation) are included in C_f. Conversion software can be used to simplify various tasks included in C_f (e.g., management planning tools, data preparation tools, etc.); however, the cost C_f is independent of C_a.

TABLE 2.5   Representative Cost Percentages for the Various Phases in a Conversion Project

Phase	Description	Cost Percentage
1	Planning	5
2	Data preparation	10
3	Conversion	25
4	Testing	45
5	Implementation	15
		100

The total cost of the project C_t is the sum of the three costs described above:

$$C_t = C_a + C_m + C_f \qquad (2.15)$$

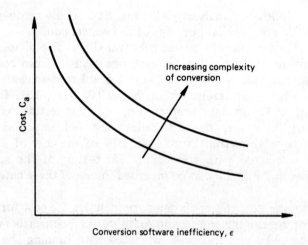

Figure 2.2   Automatic cost of conversion C_a as a function of the conversion software inefficiency ϵ.

Let us define a parameter ϵ as the *inefficiency* of the conversion software. (The parameter ϵ might, for example, be the fraction of lines of code that must be manually altered after the code has been processed by the conversion software.) A value of $\epsilon = 0$ means that the software performs perfectly (i.e., the resulting software is completely error-free if the source code is also error-free). For some conversions it is possible to develop perfect conversion software, but in general, the cost C_a becomes very large as ϵ approaches zero. We can see this phenomenon qualitatively in Figure 2.2.

The manual cost of conversion C_m is also a function of ϵ; however, it increases as ϵ increases (see Figure 2.3). Even if ϵ is zero, some cost

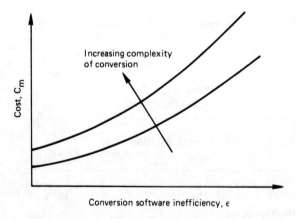

Figure 2.3   Manual cost of conversion C_m as a function of the conversion software inefficiency ϵ.

must be allocated to testing (if only to prove that the automatic conversion procedures have been executed properly). As ϵ increases, we can expect a greater number of problems to be associated with the code generated in the automatic phase. The greater the number of problems (i.e., bugs) included in the converted code, the greater the cost C_m.

For a given conversion we can plot the three cost components and the total cost C_t as functions of ϵ and we see in Figure 2.4 that an optimum value of ϵ (i.e., ϵ_{opt}) is obtained. The implication of Figure 2.4 is clear: There is an optimum level of automation associated with a given conversion project. Investing in conversion software reduces C_t until ϵ_{opt} has been achieved. Beyond this point additional investment results in an increase in C_t.

We can carry our analysis one step further by considering the influence of the size of the conversion (i.e., L thousands of lines) on the various cost components. Clearly, all components (including C_f) increase as functions of L; however, only C_a and C_m are affected by ϵ. The cost components are shown in Figure 2.5 for two values of ϵ (where ϵ_1 is greater than ϵ_2). The important point to note in Figure 2.5 is that C_m increases more rapidly than C_a as L increases. The explanation for this phenomenon is simple: The initial investment in conversion software is independent of the size of the conversion, whereas the manual effort is size dependent. The implication of Figure 2.5 is subtle: the optimum value of ϵ_{opt} decreases as L increases (see Figure 2.6). Re-

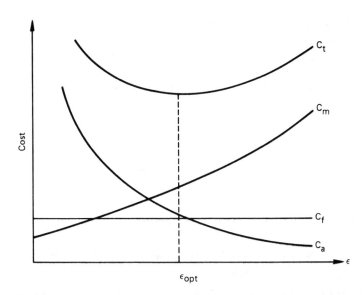

Figure 2.4   Cost components and total cost C_t as functions of the conversion software inefficiency ϵ.

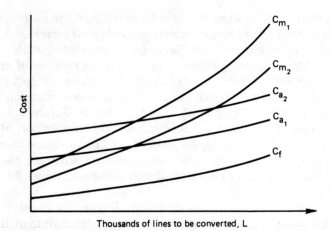

Figure 2.5 Cost components as functions of L (thousands of lines) for two levels of conversion software (ϵ_1 and ϵ_2). ϵ_1 is greater than ϵ_2, which means that level 2 uses better conversion software.

stating this conclusion in practical terms: As the size of the conversion increases, it is worthwhile to increase the investment in conversion software.

The conclusions from Figure 2.2 through 2.6 can be summarized as follows:

1. Conversion software of varying quality can be obtained or developed for a given conversion. A measure of the quality is ϵ, the *conversion software inefficiency*. Perfect software has a value of ϵ equal to zero.

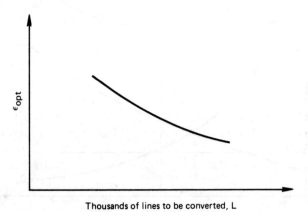

Figure 2.6 Influence of the size of the conversion on the optimum value of converter inefficiency ϵ. (Decreasing ϵ_{opt} is obtained by increasing the investment in conversion software.)

2. For a given conversion there is an optimum value of ϵ. If ϵ is less than the optimum, the investment in conversion software is excessive. If ϵ is greater than the optimum, the investment in conversion software is inadequate and money is being wasted in the manual effort associated with conversion and testing.

3. As the size of the conversion increases, the optimum value of ϵ decreases. Thus it becomes increasingly worthwhile to develop or obtain high-performance conversion software.

2.6 A MATHEMATICAL MODEL FOR CONVERSION OPTIMIZATION

The analysis presented in Section 2.5 regarding optimization of a conversion project is entirely qualitative. The primary conclusion of the analysis is that there is an optimum level of automation associated with any conversion project. It is cost-effective to invest in conversion software up to a point, but beyond this point, the additional cost is greater than the saving associated with the improved software.

When we attempt to quantify the analysis we are faced with some basic problems:

1. How do we actually measure the converter inefficiency ϵ?
2. How do we obtain the functional dependence of C_a and C_m on ϵ? (See Figures 2.2 and 2.3.)
3. How do we obtain the functional dependence of C_a, C_m, and C_f on L? (See Figure 2.5.)

If we assume that ϵ is the fraction of lines of code that remain to be manually altered upon completion of processing by the conversion software, how do we relate the various costs to ϵ? Clearly, ϵ must be an average value, and will vary considerably from program to program. To complicate matters further, for two programs of the same size and the same number of lines that remain to be altered manually, the cost associated with completing the conversion is not necessarily the same. These problems are typical of the problems associated with mathematical modeling. Our procedure will be to assume an idealized model which we know is not entirely accurate. We will then use the model in an attempt to gain some insight into the optimization problem. Clearly, interpretation of the results should be tempered by our awareness of the assumptions made in developing the model.[1]

[1] For those readers who have a basic abhorrence of mathematics, the remainder of this section can be skipped without any loss of continuity.

Let us assume the following model for C_a:

$$C_a = C_{a_1} + C_{a_2} N + C_{a_3} L \qquad (2.16)$$

where C_{a_1} is the cost for developing or obtaining the conversion software, C_{a_2} is the initial cost for running the software per program, and C_{a_3} is the incremental running cost per thousand lines of code. The parameter N is the number of programs and L is the total number of lines (in thousands of lines). Equation (2.16) is based on the assumption that the cost of running conversion software varies approximately linearly with the number of lines of code. This linear relationship has been observed for a variety of converters [8]. The cost coefficients C_{a_2} and C_{a_3} are based primarily on three factors:

1. The complexity of the conversion.
2. The quality of the conversion software (e.g., the parameter ϵ is a measure of quality).
3. The computer costs for the machine on which the software is to be used.

If one is purchasing a conversion service based on existing conversion software, the cost coefficients should be relatively easy to obtain. However, if one is undertaking the development of the necessary software, it is difficult to estimate these cost coefficients. For lack of a better approach, for such cases one can base cost estimates on results for comparable conversion software.

Let us assume the following models for C_{a_1}, C_{a_2} and C_{a_3}:

$$C_{a_i} = \frac{K_{a_i}}{\epsilon^{\alpha_i}} \qquad (2.17)$$

where the K_{a_i}'s and the α_i's are constants. To simplify the analysis, let us assume that α_1, α_2, and α_3 are all equal to the same value α:

$$C_{a_i} = \frac{K_{a_i}}{\epsilon^{\alpha}} \qquad (2.18)$$

It is reasonable to use a value of α greater than zero, which therefore causes C_a to approach infinity as ϵ approaches zero (see Figure 2.2).

Let us assume the following model for C_m:

$$C_m = C_{m_1} N + C_{m_2} L + C_{m_3} \epsilon^{\beta} L^{\gamma} N^{\delta} \qquad (2.19)$$

where C_{m_1} is the initial cost per program for running the testing phase, C_{m_2} is the incremental cost per thousand lines for running the testing phase (for the case where there are no errors in the code generated by the conversion software), and C_{m_3} is the coefficient for the final term, which is a measure of the cost associated with errors generated by the conversion software. The parameters β, γ, and δ are all positive coefficients. If $\epsilon = 0$, there are no errors and the last term goes to zero.

Let us assume the following model for C_f:

$$C_f = C_{f_1} N^\eta L^\nu \tag{2.20}$$

where C_{f_1} is a constant and η and ν are positive constant coefficients. This model implies that C_f will be different for two conversions of the same L but different values of N. This implication is certainly reasonable.

We can derive an equation for C_t (the total cost) as a function of ϵ, L, and N by substituting (2.16), (2.18), (2.19), and (2.20) into (2.15):

$$C_t = \epsilon^{-\alpha}(K_{a_1} + NK_{a_2} + LK_{a_3}) + NC_{m_1} + LC_{m_2} + C_{m_3}\epsilon^\beta L^\gamma N^\delta + C_{f_1}N^\eta L^\nu \tag{2.21}$$

To find the value of ϵ_{opt}, we must set the derivative $\partial C_t / \partial \epsilon$ to zero and solve for ϵ:

$$\frac{\partial C_t}{\partial \epsilon} = -\alpha\epsilon^{-\alpha-1}(K_{a_1} + NK_{a_2} + LK_{a_3}) + \beta\epsilon^{\beta-1}C_{m_3}L^\gamma N^\delta = 0 \tag{2.22}$$

$$K_{a_1} + NK_{a_2} + LK_{a_3} = \frac{\beta}{\alpha}\epsilon^{\alpha+\beta}C_{m_3}L^\gamma N^\delta \tag{2.23}$$

$$\epsilon_{\text{opt}} = \left(\frac{K_{a_1} + NK_{a_2} + LK_{a_3}}{\frac{\beta}{\alpha}C_{m_3}L^\gamma N^\delta}\right)^{1/(\alpha+\beta)} \tag{2.24}$$

To simplify the analysis, let us assume that all the coefficients (i.e., α, β, γ and δ) are equal to 1. Equation (2.24) reduces to the following:

$$\epsilon_{\text{opt}} = \sqrt{\frac{K_{a_1} + NK_{a_2} + LK_{a_3}}{C_{m_3}LN}} \tag{2.25}$$

Let us assume that L/N is approximately constant (i.e., all program modules are approximately the same size) [4]; we obtain the following equation from Equation (2.25):

$$\epsilon_{\text{opt}} = \frac{\sqrt{K_{a_1}/N + K_{a_2} + K_{a_3}(L/N)}}{\sqrt{C_{m_3}L}} \tag{2.26}$$

For large values of N, the term K_{a_1}/N approaches zero and

$$\epsilon_{\text{opt}} \to \frac{\sqrt{[K_{a_2} + K_{a_3}(L/N)]/C_{m_3}}}{\sqrt{L}} = \frac{\text{constant}}{\sqrt{L}} \tag{2.27}$$

This behavior agrees with the qualitative result suggested in Figure 2.6. That is, as L increases, ϵ_{opt} decreases.

An alternative assumption can be made: L remains constant but N increases (i.e., we are comparing systems of varying program module size). For such situations, as N becomes large,

$$\epsilon_{opt} = \frac{\sqrt{(K_{a_1}/L + K_{a_3})/C_{m_3}}}{\sqrt{N}} + \frac{\sqrt{K_{a_2}/C_{m_3}}}{\sqrt{L}} \to \frac{\sqrt{K_{a_2}/C_{m_3}}}{\sqrt{L}} \qquad (2.28)$$

In other words, for systems of the same L but differing N, the model suggests that the investment in conversion software should be greater for the system with the larger value of N. However, for large values of N, ϵ_{opt} approaches a minimum value.

It is interesting to compare the level of investment for conversion software for two conversions of the same type but differing values of N and L. Let us make the following assumptions:

1. Equation (2.25) yields an acceptable value for ϵ_{opt}.
2. The average program module size is independent of N (the number of programs). That is, L/N is approximately constant.
3. The value of N is large.

For such situations Equation (2.27) is valid and we thus obtain the following ratio:

$$\frac{\epsilon_{opt_1}}{\epsilon_{opt_2}} \to \sqrt{\frac{L_2}{L_1}} = \sqrt{\frac{N_2}{N_1}} \qquad (2.29)$$

We see that the ratio of values for ϵ_{opt} approaches the square root of the inverse ratio of the size of the conversions (measured in total lines or number of programs). If, for example, $L_2 = 2L_1$, then $\epsilon_{opt_2} = \epsilon_{opt_1}/\sqrt{2}$. We can use Equation (2.18) to estimate the relative investment in conversion software for the two optimum cases:

$$\frac{(C_{a_1})_2}{(C_{a_1})_1} = \left(\frac{\epsilon_{opt_1}}{\epsilon_{opt_2}}\right)^\alpha = 2^{\alpha/2} \qquad (2.30)$$

Equation (2.25) was derived by assuming that α is equal to 1, so our relative investment in conversion software should be $2^{1/2} = 1.41$. In other words, increasing the size of the conversion by a factor of 2 implies an increase in the optimum investment in conversion software of about 40%.

An interesting variation in the optimization problem is the reuse of existing conversion software. Clearly, if the cost of developing or obtaining conversion software (i.e., C_{a_1}) is totally applied to a given conversion project, the value for C_{a_1} for a second project of the same type would be zero if the software is reused. If we assume that Equation (2.18) is valid, we see that C_{a_1} is proportional to K_{a_1} and that K_{a_1} appears in Equation (2.24) (i.e., the equation used to compute ϵ_{opt}). By reducing K_{a_1}, we reduce ϵ_{opt}, so even if L and N are the same, the optimum value of ϵ is reduced for the second project. The implication is clear: If conversion software is to be reused, it is worthwhile to budget some funds for upgrading the software. Upgrading the software can accomplish two different objectives:

1. Improve the software from the point of view of function (i.e., reduce ϵ).
2. Improve the software from the point of view of performance (i.e., reduce K_{a_2} and K_{a_3}).

2.7 CONVERSION COST PER LINE

For some situations a feasible method for converting programs is to contract for a service on a per line basis. For smaller systems the bulk of the effort is associated with the conversion and testing of programs. (There might be some additional effort required for conversion of data and job control.) For larger systems the program conversion effort is a smaller percentage of the total job.

Most services will offer two prices. The lower price is for *clean compile* and the higher price is for *full implementation*. The clean compile service brings programs to a level where they pass through the target compiler error-free. The full implementation price includes testing of programs until the program output is correct for each test case agreed upon. Typically, the price for full implementation is two to three times the price for clean compile.

A number of companies offer such services and therefore prices tend to be comparable. A price list from Dataware, Inc., is shown in Table 2.6. This list includes a fairly large selection of conversions with the emphasis on COBOL. Since COBOL is by far the most popular programming language (see Tables 1.3–1.5 in Section 1.3), it is not surprising that fixed price per line services tend to concentrate on COBOL.

It should be emphasized that the prices shown in Table 2.6 include computer charges. If we compare the prices the Table 2.6 to the cost per statement for the RIS data shown in Table 2.1 (Section 2.2), we see that the RIS prices are generally higher even though computer costs are *not* included in the RIS data. The explanation for this apparent paradox is that the RIS data are for complete system conversions, whereas the Dataware prices are for program conversions.

TABLE 2.6   Dataware Prices as of May 1, 1980

From	To	Clean Compile		Full Implementation	
		Per Line	Per Program	Per Line	Per Program
FORTRAN	FORTRAN	$0.40	$40	$0.80	$80
COBOL	COBOL	0.40	40	0.80	80
RPG/RPG II	COBOL	0.50	40	1.25	80
RPG/RPG II	PL/1	0.75	40	1.50	80
Autocoder	COBOL	1.25	40	2.50	80
PL/1	COBOL	1.50	40	3.00	80
Easycoder/Easytran	COBOL	1.25	40	2.50	80
IBM Assembler	COBOL	1.50	40	3.00	80

Source: Dataware, Inc., Tonawanda, N.Y.

One interesting point to note about the data in Table 2.6 is that the prices include a charge per program as well as a charge per line. For example, a COBOL-to-COBOL conversion of 200 lines would cost $200 \times \$0.80 + \$80 = \$240$ for full implementation. Conversion of two 100-line programs would cost $200 \times \$0.80 + 2 \times \$80 = \$320$. The difference is certainly reasonable. It costs more to convert and test two programs of 100 lines than one program of 200 lines.

It is interesting to use the model developed in Section 2.6 to predict the cost of conversion per line. We have already noted that conversions are affected by the economy of scale. That is, as L increases, the cost per line (measured by C_t/L) decreases. We can use the model to explain why in fact this happens. If we divide Equation (2.21) by L, we obtain

$$
\frac{C_t}{L} = \epsilon^{-\alpha} \left(\frac{K_{a_1}}{L} + \frac{N}{L} K_{a_2} + K_{a_3} \right)
$$

$$
+ \frac{N}{L} C_{m_1} + C_{m_2} + C_{m_3} \epsilon_\beta L^{\gamma-1} N^\delta + C_{f_1} N^\eta L^{\nu-1}
$$

(2.31)

If we assume that L/N (i.e., the average size of the individual modules) is approximately constant, then our equation becomes

$$
\frac{C_t}{L} = \frac{Q_1}{L} + Q_2 L^{\gamma-1} + Q_3 L^{\nu-1} + Q_4
$$

(2.32)

The equations for the Q_i's can be obtained by comparing (2.31) and (2.32). The value of C_t/L will decrease with increasing L if $\gamma \leqslant 1$ and $\nu \leqslant 1$. Since observations confirm the fact that C_t/L decreases as L

increases, these conditions for γ and ν are apparently reasonable. Equation (2.32) also yields a lower limit for C_t/L for large values of L:

$$\frac{C_t}{L} \rightarrow Q_4 = \epsilon^{-\alpha} \left(\frac{N}{L} K_{a_2} + K_{a_3} \right) + \frac{N}{L} C_{m_1} + C_{m_2} \qquad (2.33)$$

This equation is a contradiction to the simple formula developed in Section 1.5 but is more reasonable. In Equation (1.3) an exponential relationship between E (which is partially analogous to C_t) and L was assumed. For cases where the exponent is less than 1, $C_t/L \rightarrow 0$ as $L \rightarrow \infty$, which is clearly unreasonable.

2.8 SUMMARY

In this chapter equations were developed for estimating the relative effort (or cost) associated with conversion, reprogramming, and redesign of computer software. In Section 2.4 it was shown that in general, the larger the system, the lower the ratio of conversion to redesign or reprogramming effort. The basis for this conclusion is the fact that conversions can be automated (to some degree) and are therefore affected by the economy of scale. A similar conclusion was noted for project duration; however, the relative improvement was not as dramatic.

In Section 2.5 it was noted that there is an optimum level for investment in conversion tools and aids. As the size of the conversion project increases, clearly this investment should be increased. The arguments developed in Section 2.5 were primarily qualitative. A mathematical model for optimization was described in Section 2.6. Although a number of simplifying assumptions were used to develop the model, some interesting conclusions were obtained from the model.

In Section 2.7 program conversion costs per line were discussed. For some situations it is feasible to contract for conversions on a per line (plus per program) basis. Some computer software companies offer this type of service and one can usually choose between a *clean compile* or a *full implementation* option. (Typically, full implementation costs two to three times as much as clean compile.) It was emphasized that this type of service is different than a total system conversion. For example, the end user still must convert data and job control files, in addition to completing the installation and final system testing. The difference becomes increasingly important as the total system size increases.

The general subject of cost estimation for conversion projects has received increasing attention. The U.S. Federal Conversion Support Center (FCSC) has recently published a document comparing various conversion cost estimating techniques [10]. Boehm states that although the FCSC model has not been fully calibrated and validated, its estimates appear to be reasonable and consistent [9]. Boehm also discusses a technique for estimating an equivalent number of delivered source instructions (EDSI) for conversion projects. Once the EDSI has been calculated, the effort E is estimated using normal program development estimation methods. This approach seems to be quite reasonable for primarily manual conversions (i.e., conversions with a large reprogramming component).

As an example, Boehm considers a 50,000 line FORTRAN program being converted from a UNIVAC 1110 to an IBM 3033. The computed EDSI is 10,500 lines and using his basic model for new program development effort ($E=2.4L^{1.05}$) with L equal to 10.5, a value of E equal to 28 person-months is obtained. This value is significantly less than the 45 person-months computed using Equation (1.3) with L equal to 50. The Boehm estimate should be more accurate because it is based upon an analysis of the problems associated with the specific FORTRAN conversion. Equation (1.3) is an estimate based on a correlation of data from a variety of conversion projects. We can expect to see continuing improvements in the methods for estimating conversion effort and duration as additional data become available.

REFERENCES

1. Rand, N., Rand Information Systems, private communication, August 1980.
2. Oliver, P., "Software Conversion and Benchmarking," *Software World*, Vol. 10, No. 3, pp. 2-11, 1979.
3. Walston, C. E., and C. P. Felix, "A Method of Programming Measurement and Estimation," *IBM Systems Journal*, Vol. 17, No. 1, pp. 54-73, 1977.
4. Schneider, V., "Prediction of Software Effort and Project Duration—Four New Formulas," *SIGPLAN Notices*, Vol. 13, No. 6, pp. 49-59, 1978.
5. Wolberg, J. R., "Comparing the Cost of Software Conversion to the Cost of Reprogramming," *SIGPLAN Notices*, Vol. 16, No. 4, pp. 104-110, April 1981.
6. Brandon, D. H., "Commercial Software," in *Software Portability*, Cambridge University Press, New York, 1977, Chap. VI.D.
7. Wolberg, J. R., "Conversion Tools and the CONVERT Language," *BSO Conversion Symposium Proceedings*, April 1980, pp. IV-1 to IV-9.
8. Wolberg, J. R. and M. Rafal, "The Development and Use of Automatic Converters for Software Conversions," *Proceedings of the ONLINE Conference: Pragmatic Programming and Sensible Software*, Chameleon Press, 1978, pp. 77-92.
9. Boehm, B. W., *Software Engineering Economics*, Prentice-Hall, 1981.
10. Houtz, C., and T. Buschbach, Review and Analysis of Conversion Cost-Estimating Techniques, GSA Federal Conversion Support Center Report No. GSA/FCSC-81/001, Falls Church, VA., March 1981.

VIII. Rule-Based Restructuring Systems

Part VIII concerns automated systems for restructuring which are driven by restructuring rules. These systems are based on the following simple idea: Create a catalog of rules for restructuring software. (One such rule might be, if a variable is defined but never used, remove the variable's definition and notify the programmer.) Each rule has a recognition part, which is used to decide if the rule applies to the software, and a restructuring part, which changes the software if the recognition part is satisfied. An interpreter iteratively finds rules (in the catalog) to apply to the software. The interpreter decides which rule to apply in case more than one rule applies and when to terminate applying rules.

Compared to the automated restructuring tools in Part V (see the papers by M. Lyons and by H. Morgan), rule-based restructuring systems offer several potential advantages:

- By selecting what rules go into the catalog, the user has explicit control over both the structural features to be recognized and what software changes these features induce. In Part V, the cited tools have built-in views of structural improvements, which may or may not be what the user desires.

- The rules in effect are clearly visible in the rules catalog and are not buried inside a program's code.

- Adding/changing/deleting rules from the catalog is easy.

- Rule-based systems appear particularly well-suited to standards enforcement: the rules can be used to detect certain kinds of standards violations and either automatically correct the violation, or flag the violation as deserving further review by programmers.

- The evolutionary modification of the code may be seen by reviewing the effects of single rule applications during a sequence of rule applications.

- New rules, called "meta-rules," about how the rules should be applied may be devised to guide the interpreter.

- The rule-based software architecture is highly related to rule-based systems in artificial intelligence (AI) and could benefit from hardware and software advances in rule-based AI systems.

Rule-based restructuring systems do have limitations, however. If a rule, or a set of rules, cannot be devised to recognize a particular restructuring situation, then other automated/manual means are needed for restructuring (e.g., recognizing functionally obsolete code might be difficult to capture in a rule). If a restructuring situation can be recognized, but an automatic change cannot be easily formulated, then purely automated restructuring cannot be performed. For example, a rule may be devised to recognize excessive intermodular complexity, but one may be hard-pressed to express algorithmically, in the rule, how a large system should be remodularized.

Rule-based systems, as applied to software restructuring, originally grew from rule-based systems for automating software development. These systems are surveyed in the first paper, "Program Transformation Systems" by H. Partsch and R. Steinbruggen. The wide variety of systems presented attests to the research popularity this area enjoys.

The second paper, "Automatic Program Improvement: Variable Usage Transformations" by B. Maher and D.H. Sleeman, gives a specific example of a rule-based restructuring system. The improvement strategy is based on first improving the system syntactically by applying syntactic transformation rules (e.g., to delete unreachable code). The system improves the program's usage of variables by applying variable usage rules (e.g., to delete redundant assignments to the same variable). The design of this rule-based restructuring system is simple; the paper clearly reveals implementation details in building a rule-based system for software restructuring. Also of interest is that the system may be used to improve programs in more than one programming language and the set of syntactic transformation rules is easily changed.

Program Transformation Systems

H. PARTSCH AND R. STEINBRÜGGEN

Institut für Informatik, Technische Universität München, Munich, West Germany

Interest is increasing in the transformational approach to programming and in mechanical aids for supporting the program development process. Available aids range from simple editorlike devices to rather powerful interactive transformation systems and even to automatic synthesis tools. This paper reviews and classifies transformation systems and is intended to acquaint the reader with the current state of the art and provide a basis for comparing the different approaches. It is also designed to provide easy access to specific details of the various methodologies.

Categories and Subject Descriptors: D.1.2 **[Programming Techniques]**: Automatic Programming; D.2.6 **[Software Engineering]**: Programming Environments; D.3.4 **[Programming Languages]**: Processors—*optimization*; F.3.1 **[Logics and Meanings of Programs]**: Specifying and Verifying and Reasoning about Programs—*mechanical verification*; I.1.3 **[Algebraic Manipulation]**: Languages and Systems—*special-purpose algebraic systems*; I.2.2 **[Artificial Intelligence]**: Automatic Programming; I.2.3 **[Artificial Intelligence]**: Deduction and Theorem Proving

General Terms: Algorithms, Design, Documentation, Verification

Additional Key Words and Phrases: Transformational programming, transformation system

INTRODUCTION

"The time is clearly ripe for program-manipulation systems" [Knuth 1976].

Programming is a difficult task characterized by the problem of mastering complexity. There are many steps between the analysis of a problem and its efficient solution. Even between a formal (descriptive) specification of a problem and its accommodation to a given programming environment on a particular machine, a huge gap must be bridged. There is widespread agreement that the difficulties involved in constructing correct programs can only be overcome if the whole task is broken into sufficiently small and formally justified steps. This insight is not restricted to academic circles. Industrial environments also recognize the need for formally justified software and for tools for supporting the development process. The effort to develop a programming environment for the Department of Defense language, Ada,[1] is one example of this recognition.

In any programming methodology—whether it emphasizes a "synthetic" process of deducing the program from its formal specification or a more "analytic" process of deducing properties from the already finished program—pure creativity goes hand in hand with many automatable activities. Substantial support for program

---

[1] Ada is a trademark of the U.S. Department of Defense.

Computing Surveys, Vol. 15, No. 3, September 1983

CONTENTS

---

development can already be expected if the automatable parts are performed by a machine and the programmer is free to concentrate on the creative aspects.

Software development systems are gradually becoming indispensable devices for programming. Within this class a small subclass, that of program transformation systems, is playing an increasingly important role [Pepper 1984].

This paper surveys the present capabilities of such transformation systems and how they actually support programming. This survey is not a tutorial on the methodological background of transformational programming;[2] rather, it provides an over-

view on the state of the art for readers who already have a basic understanding of the transformational programming paradigm.

1. A GENERAL VIEW OF TRANSFORMATION SYSTEMS

Since designers' intentions differ, existing transformation systems cannot be compared readily. In this section we establish a general framework of common criteria by which such systems can be classified and compared. We start by defining, in a deliberately informal way,[3] what we mean by a "transformation system."

1.1 Basic Notions

The word "program" is to be read in its ordinary sense: A *program* is a description of a method of computation that is expressible in a formal language. A *program scheme* is the representation of a class of related programs; it originates from a program by parameterization. Programs, conversely, can be obtained from program schemes by instantiating the schema parameters. In its most general form a *transformation* is a relation between two program schemes P and P'. It is said to be *correct* (or *valid*), if a certain semantic relation holds between P and P'.

The most important semantic relation in this context is *equivalence*. Secondary relations are the *weak equivalence* or the *descendant relation*. In contrast to equivalence, weak equivalence "ignores" undefined situations for P (e.g., program nontermination, given certain input) and assumes the designer does not care what happens to erroneous data. The descendant relation is important if P is a nondeterministic program (if P may generate different results, given the same input); it means that, for the same input, the possible results of P' are included in the set of possible results of P.

In general, arbitrary semantic relations [Broy et al. 1980] could be proposed pro-

---

[2] Introductions to the basic principles of transformational programming can be found in Balzer et al. [1976], Bauer [1976], Burstall and Feather [1978],

Darlington [1979], Loveman [1977], or Manna and Waldinger [1979]; for a comprehensive treatment of the subject see Bauer and Wössner [1982].
[3] A formal treatment of the mathematical foundations may be found in Steinbrüggen and Partsch [1984].

vided they have ordering and monotonicity properties. Ordering properties, such as *reflexivity* and *transitivity*, are required to compose transformations. *Monotonicity* guarantees that the global correctness is not affected by correct local changes.

Transformation rules[4] are partial mappings from one program scheme to another such that an element of the domain and its image under the mapping constitute a correct transformation. They are represented either by some procedure (*procedural rules*) or by a pair of related schemes (*schematic rules*). *Applying a transformation rule* simply means applying the respective mapping. Since this mapping may be partial, *enabling conditions*, that is, predicates over program schemes, are used to restrict the domain of a transformation rule.

Transformational programming is a methodology of program construction by successive applications of transformation rules. Usually this process starts with a (formal) *specification*, that is, a formal statement of a problem or its solution, and ends with an executable program. The individual transitions between the various versions of a program are made by applying correctness-preserving transformation rules. It is guaranteed that the final version of the program will still satisfy the initial specification.

Although the particular emphasis in transformational programming may vary (some may emphasize correctness, others efficiency), the *constructive approach* to program development remains constant. This contrasts, for example, with pure verification approaches, where the question of how to obtain the program to be verified is ignored.

A *transformation system*, finally, is an implemented system for supporting transformational programming. Not only must one learn about technical details (input, output, mode of operation, internal representations, and implementation techniques used) but one must also understand those capabilities (such as automatic rule selection, use of efficiency information in making design decisions, and mechanisms for rule composition) that depend on the specific underlying philosophy.

1.2 A Framework for Classifying Transformation Systems

To compare the various systems, we introduce a multidimensional classification scheme in which each dimension represents a major issue concerning transformation systems. Within the respective dimensions (each discussed in separate subsections below), the range of variation will be marked by identifying characteristic "values" on the respective scale.

1.2.1 Intentions of Transformational Programming

Before we look at different transformational programming goals, a more global distinction among transformation systems should be made. Consider the input to a system. Some systems take as input and manipulate *fixed specifications*. Others take a tentative, incomplete specification and gradually develop it into a complete one. By their very nature, transformations in the latter, *general software development systems*, are only one tool among many, whereas in the former, *proper transformation systems*, they play the dominant role.

In addition to occupying different positions in the software development process, transformations are used to achieve different specific goals. The most common goal is that of *general support for program modification*. This includes the *optimization* of control structures, the efficient *implementation* of data structures, and the adaptation of given programs to particular styles of programming (e.g., applicative, procedural, machine oriented). If modification is not restricted to proper programs but is extended to include program schemes, the system also may be used to formally derive new transformation rules (which are correct by construction). Hence, to some extent, modification also comprises *rule generation*.

A second goal of program transformation is *program synthesis*, the generation of a program from a (formal) description of the

---

[4] Frequently, these are called just *rules* or *transformations*. Sometimes they are also called *source-to-source translations*.

problem. Here the respective systems vary with regard to the formulation of the input. Program synthesis may start from specifications in (restricted) natural language, from examples in some formal language, or from mathematical assertions. (Synthesis by modifying similar programs is a somewhat different approach.)

A third goal is that of *program adaptation* to particular environments. For example, the designer might want to adapt a program written in one language to a related language with different primitives.

Other goals include *program description* (by exhibiting the derivation history or by building up "family trees" of related algorithms) and deduction-oriented *verification* of programs' correctness.

1.2.2 Range of System Support

Of course, each transformation system, whether general or special purpose, has a *component for dealing with transformations.* Usually this component consists of a facility for keeping the (predefined) collection of available transformations, called a catalog, and a mechanism for applying them. Frequently, systems allow this collection to be extended by the definition of new rules, but most systems expect these new rules to be proved by the user. Only a few systems allow the proof or derivation of new rules within the system by means of built-in composition operators. Some systems also provide some form of guidance for selecting rules from the collection.

Nearly all transformation systems are *interactive.* Even the "fully automatic" ones require an initial user input and rely (interactively) on the user to resolve unexpected events. *Input/output facilities* vary with respect to the user's comfort: The spectrum ranges from ad hoc implementation-dependent interfaces to high-level structured command languages. The system's reaction to input may include automatic checks on the "reasonableness" of given commands, as well as incremental interactive parsing using correction mechanisms. Usually the output of the system is filtered and presented to the user in a well-formatted *prettyprinted* form, sometimes even annotated with further information.

Most systems also have some *facility for documenting the development process*—one of the promising aspects of the transformational approach. These facilities include internal preservation of the source program, of final output, and of all intermediate versions. The documentation itself ranges from a simple sequential log of the terminal session (*bookkeeping*) to rather sophisticated database mechanisms. The most clever of these are even able to automatically redo a particular program development starting from a (slightly) changed input—a nontrivial task, particularly if the development is not a simple linear sequence but a graphlike structure (*decision tree*). In this "automatic redo" sense, the documentation facility plays an active part in the process of transformation selection.

Assessment of programs can be supported in qualitatively different ways: The system may incorporate some execution facility, such as an interpreter or a compiler to some target level, or it may utilize aids for "testing," such as symbolic evaluators. Occasionally the system will also have tools for program analysis, either for aiding in the selection of transformation rules or simply for "measuring" the effect of some transformation.

1.2.3 Organization and Types of Transformations

Most systems have a *predefined collection of transformation rules,* which is in some sense extensible. (The PDS approach, described in Section 4.1, in which the user alone supplies the development process with suitable transformations, is a notable exception.) In principle, there are two contrary methods for keeping transformations in the system: the *catalog approach* and the *generative set approach.* The borderline between them is somewhat hazy, and there is an evident tendency to move from the former toward the latter: Recent versions of systems that originally worked with catalogs now experiment with small sets of rules supplemented by suitable tactics or strategic means for generating new, more complex rules from simpler ones.

A *catalog of rules* is a linearly or hierarchically structured collection of transfor-

Computing Surveys, Vol. 15, No. 3, September 1983

mation rules relevant for a particular aspect of the development process. Catalogs may contain, for example, rules about *programming knowledge* (i.e., available solution strategies, such as "a good way to search in an ordered list is by dichotomic search"), optimizations based on *language features*, such as recursion removal or loop fusion, or rules reflecting *data domain knowledge*, such as arithmetic and Boolean algebra, arrays, or sets. Additionally, some systems have catalogs of *efficiency information* or codified knowledge for *automatic data structure selection*. Systems based on the catalog approach are also frequently referred to as *knowledge-based systems*. The main problems of the catalog approach are completeness and structure, in particular, the availability of and the rapid access to individual rules.

By a *generative set* we mean a small set of powerful elementary transformations to be used as a basis for constructing new rules. Since these language-independent principles cannot be complete (in the sense that all imaginable transformations cannot be produced from them), they are used in connection with further knowledge about data structures and the specific programming task. This knowledge is presented to the system as another restricted set of rules about certain object domains. If elementary transformations are additionally coupled with a rather restricted language, a certain restricted kind of completeness may be achieved. In the generative set approach the main problem is to find the order in which to apply these elementary rules to achieve some bigger transformation.

1.2.4 Forms of Transformation Rules

We have already said that a transformation rule, as a (partial) mapping from program to program, can be represented in two ways: in the form of an algorithm, taking a program and producing a new one (*procedural rule*), or as an ordered pair of program schemes (*schematic rule* or *pattern replacement rule*), usually separated by some replacement symbol such as "⇔" for equivalence or "⇒" for descendance. Although the latter, syntax-oriented representation seems better suited to human perception,

it has the disadvantage that it is badly suited for expressing semantic knowledge or global information. Consequently, the schematic representation is used mainly in connection with *local rules*, and the algorithmic form is usually employed for *global rules*.

Typical *locally* applicable rules (*refinement rules*) serve to do the following:

(1) Relate *language constructs* (*syntactic rules*),[5] such as

$$\text{L: if B then S; goto L fi}$$
$$\Leftrightarrow \textbf{while B do S od.}[6]$$

(2) Describe *algebraic properties* relating different language constructs, such as

$$1 + \textbf{if B then } x \textbf{ else } y \textbf{ fi}$$
$$\Leftrightarrow \textbf{if } B \textbf{ then } 1 + x \textbf{ else } 1 + y \textbf{ fi}.$$

(3) Express *domain knowledge* (*domain rules*) in the form of data-type properties, such as

$$\text{pop}(\text{push}(s, x)) \Leftrightarrow s$$

$$\text{(for unbounded stacks } s),$$

or

$$b \wedge b \Leftrightarrow b \quad \text{(for Booleans } b).$$

Global rules, sometimes also called *semantic rules*, make up flow analysis, consistency checks, global cleanup operations, or representation of programming techniques and paradigms, such as the "divide-and-conquer" technique.

There are also hybrids between local and global rules used to codify certain *programming knowledge*. Two common hybrids are the UNFOLD and FOLD rules:

> UNFOLD is the replacement of a call by its body, with appropriate substitutions.
> FOLD is the inverse transformation, the replacement of some piece of code by an equivalent function or procedure call.

Hybrids are also used to represent *implementation details* (*implementation rules*),

---

[5] They even may be used for the formal definition of the semantics of a language [Pepper 1979].

[6] For denoting language constructs we use a self-explanatory ALGOL-like language.

such as "a bounded stack may be represented by an array and an index variable."

1.2.5 Performance of the Transformation Process

All program transformation systems successively apply elementary transformation rules. The systems' differences lie in *user control*, that is, in the amount of work that is required from the user.

Obviously the simplest implementation is one that makes the *user responsible* for every single transformation step. Such an approach is only practical if the system provides some means for building up compact and powerful transformation rules, such as *remove recursion* or *implement data structure*.

Fully automatic systems, on the other hand, enable the selection and application of appropriate rules to be completely determined by the system using built-in heuristics, machine evaluation of different possibilities, or other strategic considerations. Such systems, however, work satisfactorily only for restricted domains of application.

Between the two extremes lie the *semiautomatic systems*, which, for predefined subtasks, work autonomously; however, for unsolvable problems the user becomes responsible. Usually these systems offer the user assistance in evaluating criteria for design decisions, depending either on the program version alone or on some predefined goal as well.

In addition to the different rule selection mechanisms, there are different techniques for *matching*, that is, for identifying the concrete instances of a certain rule. The simplest case is *first-order matching*, where only instances of object variables (*ordinary scheme parameters*) must be identified. If program schemes having both object and function variables are used, *second-order matching* is necessary.[7] Second-order matching is a more flexible and powerful technique, but unlike first-order matching, which is completely mechanizable, second-order matching sometimes needs assistance by the user.

---

[7] For a theoretical treatment of second-order matching, see the work by Huet and Lang [1978].

Matching can be also done in technically different ways. *Pattern-directed invocation*, a technique like that provided by QLISP, where applicable rules are identified if their left-hand sides match some piece of the currently considered program, or *anchored patterns*, which we describe later in Section 5.2.2., are typical examples.

In all systems the set of rules is supplemented by additional "advice" on how to apply them, at least in the form of *enabling conditions* for guaranteeing correct application. Other additions include *strategic conditions*, information for selecting rules that depends on some goal to be achieved; *assertions*, properties of the objects of manipulation; *continuation information*, which rule(s) to try next; and *information about the scope of application*, where in the program to try another rule.

1.2.6 Languages

Language sheds considerable light on a system's abilities. We are less interested in the languages used for implementation, although this is an important factor with respect to portability, but rather in the *kind* (or *style*) *of program* that is treated by the system. Although some systems are conceptually independent of a particular language, each implementation is in the end tied to a particular language.

Depending on the particular purposes of the systems, many conceptually different languages can be used as input. These languages may be separated into *specification languages*, which support the formal statement of problems, and *programming languages*, which are used for formulating solutions to problems. The borderline is hazy, since certain languages, such as the applicative languages of NPL or HOPE, may be associated with either of these categories.

Specification languages range from formalized natural language, over purely descriptive formal languages, such as mathematical notation or predicate logic, languages with both descriptive and operative constructs, such as CIP-L (Section 2.6.1), and fully operational specification languages, such as GIST (Section 2.1.3), to the aforementioned applicative languages, including also recursion equations or algebraic axioms.

For programming languages, a global distinction can be made between functionally oriented ones, such as LISP, and purely procedural ones, such as FORTRAN. Other frequently used programming languages include subsets of ALGOL, Pascal, or PL/I, which allow both applicative and procedural formulations, or particular languages such as EL1, CIP-L, or MENTOL (Section 4.2).

Data structures differ in how they are incorporated into the language: The languages either have fixed data types or provide mechanisms for generating new types.

Which kind of (input) language is used depends on the particular methodology and the specific purpose of the respective system. For the same reason the "output languages" differ. Whereas input and output language will be the same for systems aiming primarily at optimization, they will differ for synthesis systems.

1.2.7 Range of Applicability

From a practical viewpoint, the most interesting aspect of a transformation system is the range of problems it can handle. That this range may be too limited is a main source of criticism of the transformational approach (see Dijkstra [1976a]). In principle, there is no such limitation. However, all the described transformation systems originated in research institutions and, at present, must be considered mainly as experimental tools with restricted abilities.

A precise statement on the relative power of each system is impossible, owing to the lack of detailed technical information. We confine ourselves to giving an impression of each system's capabilities by indicating which examples it has successfully treated.

1.3 About This Survey

It is difficult to contrast transformation systems to related systems such as *general AI systems* [Biermann 1976], *production systems* [Davis and King 1975], *expert systems* [Michie 1979, 1981], *verification systems* [Igarashi et al. 1975], *data structure selection systems* [Low 1978; Schonberg et

al. 1979], or general software development environments [Hesse 1981; Hünke 1981]. As the main criterion for inclusion we have concentrated on systems having a proper *transformation component*. There still remain systems that fall exactly on the borderline, such as Hewitt's PLANNER [Hewitt 1971]. Occasionally, to provide background information, we also report on side developments (within bigger projects), even though they are not transformation systems in the strict sense. Furthermore, to be included in the survey, at least part of the system should actually be *implemented*.[8]

It is difficult to favor any one of the criteria given in the previous section. In contrast to an earlier work [Partsch and Steinbrüggen 1981] on the subject of this paper, we decided here to first distinguish proper transformation systems from general software development systems. Within the transformation systems, we further separated general systems from special-purpose ones. We are fully aware, though, that our classification is arbitrary (as is any other).

Within the respective section on each system, we give a brief summary of its overall performance and then concentrate on its specific properties in detail. Instead of ignoring the nomenclature of each system, we relate it to the notions introduced above, to ease the reader's access to the original literature.

2. GENERAL TRANSFORMATION SYSTEMS

In this section we review some transformation systems that we classify as general systems. They are restricted neither to a particular aspect of the software development process nor to specific kinds of transformation rules. Even though the published material does not explicitly stress their generality, it can be inferred from the basic system concept.

2.1 The SAFE/TI Project at ISI

The activities headed by R. Balzer at the Information Science Institute (ISI) in Los

---

[8] In this respect, we have relied mainly on published information.

Angeles emerged from earlier ideas on automatic programming [Balzer 1973]. ISI's activities aim at machine support for software development and are organized into two projects: The first, SAFE (Specification Acquisition From Experts [Wile et al. 1977; Balzer et al. 1978]), deals with the synthesis of formal specifications from informal ones, and the second, TI (Transformational Implementation) [Balzer et al. 1976], concentrates on the derivation of efficient programs from formal specifications by means of transformations.

2.1.1 The SAFE System

The basis for the SAFE synthesis system is the observation that precise formal and accurate specifications are not only difficult to write by hand, but are also hard to understand owing to the enormous amount of detail. Partial problem descriptions, on the other hand, focus both the writer's and reader's attention on the relevant issues and thus condense a specification. SAFE is an effort to provide a mechanism for resolving the ambiguity introduced into a specification by partial descriptions and for incorporating refinements of, and modifications to, structures produced from the text of a specification.

The input to SAFE is an informal description of the problem and its solution in a natural language, which is parenthesized to avoid parsing problems. This input first passes through a linguistic phase where it is translated into a series of *event descriptors*. These descriptors correspond approximately to procedure definitions that are built from basic actions and relations known to the system as either primitives or domain-specific actions. Typical types of basic event descriptors are *events* from verbs, *objects* and *sets* from nouns and plurals, and *conditionals*, *conjunctions*, and *loops* from verbs with set objects. The planning phase looks at the partial sequencing information contained in the input, then determines the overall operation sequencing for the program outline. In the next phase, *actions* are defined as sequences or refinements of events. And in the final phase, the fine details are resolved by symbolic evaluation (*metaevaluation*) to produce the formal specification.

SAFE tries to find out what the user means. Like an "intelligent reader," it performs a number of elementary tasks, such as finding missing operands, performing implicit coercions, or detecting terminology changes. If any ambiguity cannot be solved automatically, SAFE asks for the user's intention. SAFE tests the "adequacy" of the resulting formal specification by checking heuristics that assess its semantic reasonableness.

Examples handled by SAFE include a message processor and components of a satellite communication system [Balzer et al. 1978].

2.1.2 The TI Project

The TI project provides technologies for automating aspects in the second part of the software development process to bridge the gap between a formal specification and its implementation as an efficient program. Developing an implementation from a specification is seen as a continuous process of applying transformations, either to replace pure specification constructs with algorithmic ones [London and Feather 1981] or to simplify algorithmic constructs. The result of this process is a program in a subset of the specification language GIST (Section 2.1.3), which is automatically translatable into an existing programming language.

The main activity of the transformation process is the programmer's selection of appropriate transformations from a preexisting catalog. If an appropriate transformation does not yet exist in the catalog, the programmer may either extend the catalog or modify the program directly through an interactive editor. In either case the responsibility for the correctness of a transformation rests with the user. The transformations in the catalog [Balzer et al. 1976] include UNFOLD, certain domain-dependent transformations such as $x \in \{y : p(y)\} \Leftrightarrow p(x)$ for sets, different forms of loop merging, rules for conditionals, and substitution of data structures with their representation. In this latter substitution transformation, both the objects and their characteristic operations must be replaced. An interesting aspect of TI with respect to transformation application is *jittering*: TI automatically modifies a program to match a transformation that previously failed to match because of some technical detail.

The system, implemented in INTER-LISP, tries to relieve some of the implementor's burden by providing

- an interactive transformation engine, a mechanism for applying selected transformations to the program being developed (provided by POPART; see Section 2.1.3);
- support for the development process, such as source-text maintenance or *bookkeeping* (see PADDLE, Section 2.1.3), that is, automatic documentation that allows one to redo a development using a modified specification;
- a catalog of transformations reflecting the knowledge of how to implement certain specification constructs or certain optimization techniques;
- a mechanism for translating the fully developed program into some target language.

Examples that have been treated within the TI approach include, among others, several versions of a line justifier [Balzer 1977], a text editor [Balzer et al. 1976], a text compressor [Wile 1981b], the "eight-queens" problem [Balzer 1981b], and a package router [London and Feather 1981].

2.1.3 Further Activities

Most of the tools for developing programs within the TI approach have been produced by Wile's POPART (Producer of Parsers and Related Tools) system [Wile 1981a]. These tools include, notably, a parser, editors, and the system for performing transformations. It should be noted that this system does not depend on a particular language but produces these tools for an arbitrary context-free language.

Currently, transformations are applied sequentially in the TI system. Ideas for imposing some structure on the development, in order to model the developer's

thoughts more appropriately, are condensed in PADDLE (POPART's Development Language) [Wile 1981b]. PADDLE contains primitive commands such as "apply transformation" and a facility for specifying goal structures. These facilities are intended to support a global strategy for program development along a goal/refinement structure. This attempt to impose structure on the collection of transformations contributes to the solution of the catalog-oriented approach's administrative problem. It also supports reimplementation as another benefit. Since POPART is language independent, it can be applied to PADDLE, which means that programs in the development language themselves can be manipulated via POPART.

Work in the TI project also concentrates on a specification language called GIST [Goldman and Wile 1980; Balzer, 1981a], which was developed to

- provide the flexibility and ease of expression necessary for describing the full range of acceptable system behaviors;
- be *wide spectrum*, that is, to be not only a reasonable specification language, but also an implementation language for describing efficient programs whose behavior coincides with the specification. (Here "implementation" is to be understood in an abstract sense, since at a certain level automatic translation is desired.)

A GIST specification is a formal description of valid behaviors of systems. It is composed of a set of states (determined by object types and relations between them), transition between states (defined by asynchronous responses to stimuli also known as actions and demons), and a set of constraints on states and state transitions. GIST's main effort has been to provide formal equivalents of the specificational expressiveness of natural languages. The expressive capabilities of GIST include historical reference to past process states, a relational and associative data model, and an *inference* global declaration for describing relationships among data. Because all constructs in GIST are operational, it can be used for *rapid prototyping* [Balzer et al. 1982; Cohen et al. 1982; Feather 1982a] by allowing operational simulation models of an intended system to be run with test data.

2.1.4 The GLITTER System

Within the TI environment, the GLITTER system (GoaL-directed jITTERer) [Fickas 1982] was designed to partially automate the design process of mapping an abstract program into an efficient, compilable one. In the GLITTER approach, recording a formal machine-usable history of the design process (including design goals and subgoals, competing methods, and selection criteria used to reach an implementation) plays an important role.

Program development with GLITTER begins with the user stating (in GIST) some design goal to a *problem solver*, which in turn either asks the user for details or checks its (extensible) *method catalog*. This catalog of methods for achieving goals contains both source-to-source transformations (*tactical knowledge*) and planning techniques (*strategic knowledge*). If there are several applicable methods, GLITTER uses the *selection rule catalog* to decide which to choose. Methods are ordered not only by the current planning state, but also by postplanning states. The *applier* applies the chosen method, thereby changing the problem state and recording it in the *history*.

The basic methods to be applied are essentially the same as those in the TI approach, methods for mapping specification freedoms, checking applicability conditions, or simplifying by jittering. These simplification methods, unlike the automatic invocation in PADDLE, are user invoked.

The GLITTER system is not fully automatic. The user is expected to guide the overall development by providing development goals for GLITTER to achieve. Besides providing development organization, the user also will probably be asked to supply information that is unavailable to the system and to fill in the missing portions of the respective catalogs.

GLITTER is implemented in Hearsay-III, a framework for constructing knowledge-based expert systems. In addition to implementing numerous toy examples,

GLITTER has been successfully used to develop a controller for a mechanical postal package router. In the router development, the system was able to generate automatically a significant number of steps of the development.

2.2 The PSI System

The PSI system (produced mainly at Stanford [Green 1976, 1977, 1978; Green et al. 1979]) is a large LISP system designed to synthesize efficient programs. PSI takes as its input a specification obtained from a dialogue with the user, which includes natural language or partial traces of computations (with sample input–output pairs being a special case). It is designed as a collection of knowledge-based *experts* for various tasks. One group of experts, the *acquisition group*, is responsible for acquiring specifications from the user. The group consists on an English parse–interpreter, a trace expert, a discourse expert, and an application domain expert, all of which extract information from the dialogue and convert it into program fragments that serve as input for another acquisition expert, the program model builder. This model builder, in turn, produces a complete *program model* and uses that model as its interface to the *synthesis group*, consisting of a coding expert and an efficiency expert.

2.2.1 The Program Model Builder

The main role of PMB (Program Model Builder) [McCune 1977, 1979] is to build a complete and consistent *program model*, an abstract, implementation-independent, annotated program in a high-level language, corresponding to the desires of the user. The inputs to PMB are program fragments, which may be incomplete, ambiguous, inconsistent, and arbitrarily ordered. Building such a complete model is an incremental process of extracting information and then updating a partial model. While updating, PMB also performs appropriate consistency checks to ensure a legal (with respect to the language semantics) and correct (with respect to the user's intention) model. If any problem cannot be resolved within PMB itself, it asks the other acquisition experts or, finally, the user for advice.

PMB's expertise is implemented in IN-TERLISP as a set of approximately 200 procedural rules, scheduled by a rule inter-preter. These rules also include knowledge of program-model equivalence transforma-tions to map equivalent expressions into a canonical form.

2.2.2 The Coding Expert

The coding expert, called PECOS [Barstow 1977c, 1979a] takes an abstract program description produced by PMB and succes-sively refines this description by applying transformation rules that reflect coding knowledge. The description consists of es-sentially two parts:

- a collection of about 400 transformation rules about symbolic programming [Bar-stow 1979c] organized as an extensible knowledge base [Barstow, 1977a, 1977b];
- a task-oriented control structure based on the paradigm of developing programs by successive refinements.

The extensible catalog contains rules of essentially three types: *refinement rules* containing the coding knowledge, *property rules* to specify additional properties of a program description, and *query rules* to an-swer the experts' queries about a descrip-tion, used to ensure the applicability of other rules. The refinement rules represent only the coding knowledge about the par-ticular domain of symbolic programming. Early ideas on how to combine this knowl-edge-based approach with deduction-ori-ented ones can be found in Barstow's work [1979b]. The transformation rules in the catalog deal with general program con-structs such as implementation for itera-tors or correspondences, with particular domains such as data representation or task-specific knowledge, or with properties of the target language such as table-ori-ented implementations for correspond-ences, linked-list or array representations for sets, and rules for enumeration [Bar-stow 1979c; Green and Barstow 1975, 1978].

The development essentially consists of a step-by-step successive refinement of the program description until a running LISP program[9] evolves. Both the algorithm and the data structure are refined interdepen-dently. To drive a refinement, PECOS uses a simple task-oriented control structure. In each cycle a task (*refine, property, query*) is selected, and a rule is applied to the task. While PECOS is working on a given task, it may generate subtasks, which are han-dled in a last-in, first-out manner. When several rules are applicable, the refinement is split, with each rule applied in a different branch of the tree of program descriptions. The root of this tree is the original specifi-cation, the tree's leaves are programs in the target language, and each path from the root to a leaf constitutes a refinement se-quence; thus the entire tree actually repre-sents a family of algorithms [Green and Barstow 1978].

The critical issue in the whole approach is the size of this tree of partially developed programs. To keep the tree to a reasonable size, certain possible refinement steps are rejected and usually only one path is taken, following advice from the user, some heu-ristics, and the automated efficiency expert.

2.2.3 The Efficiency Expert

The purpose of the efficiency expert, LI-BRA [Kant 1977, 1979], is to give advice to the coding expert and thus help make de-sign decisions. LIBRA provides techniques for pruning the tree of partially refined programs and for directing the order of further expansion of the tree. Its expertise is codified in an extensible knowledge base of approximately 100 rules. New rules can be derived semiautomatically from new transformations or can be gained by asking appropriate questions of the user. A typical new rule would be a *planning* rule, derived from the previous analyses of how to make particular implementation decisions. Other examples include rules for grouping related decisions, and rules about scheduling and resource allocation that reflect the impor-tance of a coding decision and of its ex-pected consequence.

---

[9] The program is actually written in a subset of INTERLISP. There have also been experiments with other target languages, such as SAIL [Barstow 1977b].

For each decision not made by planning rules, LIBRA uses flow analysis and incrementally computes upper and lower bounds on the estimated costs. For this cost analysis LIBRA occasionally needs additional information from the user about things such as the number of elements in a set or the probabilities of the alternatives of a branching instruction. From this information LIBRA then computes measures such as the average storage requirement or the average number of times a loop is executed. LIBRA maintains its cost analysis of a program at every level of refinement for comparison between different refinements or branch-and-bound search. In particular, this cost analysis identifies parts that will lead to a bottleneck in the refinement process, so that refinement resources can be concentrated on those parts.

2.2.4 The Synthesis Phase

The synthesis phase of PSI also can be used as an independent subsystem, PSI/SYN, for transforming specifications given in the model builder's formal high-level language [Kant and Barstow 1981]. Here, in contrast to earlier ideas [Barstow and Kant 1976], the roles of PECOS and LIBRA are interchanged: Whereas in the earlier concept PECOS asked LIBRA for its advice, now part of LIBRA's knowledge, the *searching knowledge*, is used in each stage of refinement to call on either the coding rules to generate legal refinements or the cost-estimation rules to provide an evaluation function for the alternative implementations.

2.2.5 Experiences

The examples treated within the PSI efforts all were of moderate size. They comprised number-theoretic algorithms for computing prime numbers [Barstow 1979a; Kant and Barstow 1981], set algorithms [Barstow and Kant 1976], concept formation [Barstow 1979a; McCune 1977], a simple learning program [Kant 1977], a simple retrieval program [Kant 1979], and an algorithm dealing with the reachability of nodes in graphs [Barstow 1979a]. A hypothetical dialogue with the system for synthesizing a sorting program for linked lists

(70 steps, 150 transformations) can be found in work by Green and Barstow [1976]. Later, they approach the sorting problem again [Barstow 1979a; Green and Barstow 1978] and derive a whole family of sorting algorithms.

2.2.6 The CHI System and the Algorithm Design Project

The CHI system (for a collection of individual papers see Green et al. [1982]) is a more recent attempt to use some of the PSI technology, specifically that of PECOS and LIBRA, to build a knowledge-based programming environment. Instead of autonomous experts, though, CHI uses a homogeneous collection of tools sharing common databases. These tools enable the user to query all parts of the environment in a uniform way.

The major system components are

- an object-oriented database of programming knowledge that contains static refinement rules (for implementing sets, mappings, enumerations in terms of lists, arrays, hash tables, etc.) and a dynamic program-refinement workspace;
- the *knowledge-base manager*, a database that enables contexts and multiple versions and that manages the file utilities for storing and loading from disk storage;
- a structure-based editor used to modify programs and synthesis rules;
- an agenda mechanism to control user guidance and heuristic search.

CHI's essential difference from the former PSI system is its use of a more humanly readable wide-spectrum language, called *V*. that covers both high-level program specification and programming knowledge (synthesis rules, synthesis plans, constraints on programs). The primitives in V include sets, mappings, relations, enumerations, and state transformation sequences. Both declarative and procedural statements are allowed, as are facts about program efficiency or algorithm analysis. V is *uniformly extensible*, in that it allows continuous change and development of the objects used in programming.

Synthesis rules can be applied by name, by effect, or by analogy (by indicating a related rule having a similar effect). With respect to naming by effect, CHI shows some analogies to GLITTER (Section 2.1.4).

CHI is a *self-described programming environment*, meaning that the environment itself is described in terms that the modification rules understand. Consequently, the environment may be modified using the tools it, itself, provides.[10] Adding new rules to this system, therefore, does not necessarily imply a decrease in performance due to increased search time, but may even increase performance.

CHI has successfully been used to redevelop the system's rule compiler and has resulted in a program that is ten times shorter than the original one [Green et al. 1982]. Other, less comprehensive examples were several programs of differing complexity for computing even squares.

Strongly connected to the CHI activities is the Algorithm Design project [Green et al. 1982], which is aimed at providing tools to assist the user in the more creative aspects of new algorithms development. As an intermediate result, a set of *methods* has been formalized and partly implemented in CHI. In these methods, algorithm design principles are expressed in the form of *synthesis plans* (or *paradigm algorithms* [Darlington 1981b]). Typical of such principles are *generator incorporation* (usually known as *filter promotion* [Darlington 1981a]), *divide-and-conquer*, and *store versus recompute* (better known as *dynamic programming* [Aho et al. 1974] or *tabulation techniques* [Bird, 1980]).

Examples of problems that the Algorithm Design project has tackled include the *shortest path in a graph* problem and different versions of *prime finding*.

2.3 The Edinburgh School

Whereas the systems described in the previous sections are based on the catalog approach, the systems described below rely on the generative set approach.

2.3.1 The Early Work of Darlington and Burstall

The early work of Darlington and Burstall [Darlington 1972; Darlington and Burstall

1973, 1976] was based on a schema-driven method for transforming applicative recursive programs into imperative ones with improving efficiency as the ultimate goal. The system worked largely automatically, according to a set of built-in rules, with only a small amount of user control. The rules were complex transformations, including recursion removal, elimination of redundant computations, unfolding, and structure sharing. The main objection to this very early system was the incompleteness of the rule set, on one hand, and the difficulty of extension, on the other.

2.3.2 The Work of Burstall and Darlington

On the basis of experiences gained with their first system, in particular the observation that significant improvements can and should be done on an applicative level of formulation, Burstall and Darlington [1975, 1977] implemented a second system. This system, implemented in POP-2, was designed to manipulate applicative programs.

Their second system is a typical representative of the generative set approach and consists of only six rules: *definition, instantiation, unfolding, folding, abstraction,* and *laws* (actually a set of data-structure-specific rules). The basic idea of this system, the *unfold/fold method*, is simple but nevertheless rather powerful. Definition allows the introduction of new functions (in the form of recursion equations), which may be additionally structured using abstraction. After unfolding calls on the right-hand side of the equations, the right-hand sides may be further manipulated using substitution instances (introduced by instantiation) and the laws. These manipulations always try to allow a subsequent folding and thus an independent definition of a new and (it is to be hoped) more efficient function.

The theoretical background of the unfold/fold method—including sophisticated criteria to guarantee total correctness for folding—has been studied by Kott [1978, 1982].

In addition to synthesizing functions defined by implicit equations, the system is designed to improve user-provided func-

---

[10] The problem of correctness preservation is the user's responsibility.

tions. The user presents these functions as an appropriate set of explicit equations, written in a slightly restricted subset of NPL, an applicative language for first-order recursion equations [Burstall 1977]. The output of the system is again a program in NPL, but a less complex one (e.g., tree-like recursion will have been transformed into tail recursion).

The system works largely automatically, using *forced folding*. Within the currently considered equation, the system proposes foldings that the user either accepts or rejects, asking for another proposal. The user's duty is to supply the system with appropriate definitions and to provide clever ideas in the form of *Eurekas*.

The user must also supply laws for the data structures, give explicit reduction rules, preset switches to control the system's search for folds, and allow or disallow generalizations of expressions during the unfold/apply-law/fold process.

Examples of programs that have been treated with this system include algorithms for computing Fibonacci numbers or Cartesian products, an algorithm for diagonal search, a string-matching algorithm [Darlington 1981a], set algorithms [Darlington 1975], and the synthesis of sorting algorithms [Darlington 1978]. Ideas for using the unfold/fold method to develop implementations of abstract types can be found in work by Darlington and Moor [Darlington 1978; Moor and Darlington 1981].

2.3.3 The ZAP System

The ZAP system [Feather 1978a, 1979, 1982b] is based on the Burstall/Darlington system with a special emphasis on software development by supporting large-program transformation. The principle of the system is, again, the fold/unfold method. And the input/target language of the system is the same as in the previous Burstall/Darlington system, NPL.

In contrast to its predecessors, the ZAP system substantially supports the program development by providing the user with advanced means for concisely expressing guidance. It allows the user to write *metaprograms* to be applied to NPL programs,

and thus to direct the transformation of these programs in a high-level, hierarchical fashion. An overall *transformation strategy* is hand-expanded by the user into a set of *transformation tactics* such as *combining*, *tupling*, or *generalization*. These, in turn, are expanded, with some machine assistance, into *pattern-directed transformations* (i.e., transformation rules where the user gives only the approximate form of the expected answer, in the form of a pattern, and the system fills in the missing details). The pattern-directed transformations are commands to ZAP, which the system automatically expands into sequences of elementary manipulations (essentially those of the previous Burstall/Darlington system).

Also new—compared with the former Edinburgh systems—is the possibility of restricting ZAP's search for an applicable rule. The user can specify a context by indicating equations to be used for fold/unfold, lemmas to be used during unfold, and functions that may occur within the answer. For more details on these technical aspects, see the work by Feather [1978a].

Additional features for the convenient use of the system have been incorporated. These include an extended control language, defaults (in particular, certain standard patterns for pattern-directed transformations), a bookkeeping facility (for introducing, testing, and saving program versions, and a mechanism for rerunning developments), and a *discovery* capability, with which the system is able to suggest alternative transformations.

The examples dealt with by the system range from "toy" problems to comprehensive ones such as the telegram problem [Feather 1978b], a small compiler, and a text formatter [Feather 1979]. Preliminary investigation of the use of this approach for supporting maintenance and modifications of programs can be found in joint work by Darlington and Feather [1979].

2.3.4 Recent Developments

A richer metalanguage system, based on Feather's ZAP system and experiences from the Edinburgh LCF project [Gordon et al. 1977], is now used in Darlington's system at Imperial College [Darlington 1981b]. In this system, HOPE, an applicative language based on NPL [Burstall et al. 1980] is used for the formulation of programs to be transformed and also for writing the metaprograms. These metaprograms are composed of *first-level tactics*, the basic rules of the unfold/fold system, out of which can be built the *second-level tactics*, higher level operators, such as *merge loop* or *convert-to-iteration*. Still being researched are ways to express *paradigm algorithms*, such as the general divide-and-conquer paradigm and other general strategies. This concept of unifying the development, maintenance, and modification of ordinary and metalanguage programs is the next step of importance in research on transformational programming. A feeling for this advanced methodology may be obtained by studying the Hammings problem example [Darlington, 1981b].

2.4 Stanford Transformation Systems

The Stanford University work on program transformations, like the Edinburgh activities, can be best understood when broken into different phases, according to the techniques applied and the purposes of the program transformations.

2.4.1 The Work of Dershowitz and Manna

On the basis of their previous work [Dershowitz and Manna 1975], Dershowitz and Manna [1977] implemented a system in QLISP (an extension of INTERLISP with pattern-directed function invocation and backtracking) for modifying programs by using transformations. The basic idea of this approach is to find an *analogy* between the specification of an already constructed program and that of the program to be constructed. This analogy is then used as a basis for transforming the existing program to meet the new specification. This process is performed in three major steps:

(1) First, in a *premodification phase*, the old program is hand-annotated with assertions that constitute its specification. This specification and that of the intended new program are then rephrased (in a user–

system dialogue) to bring out their similarities.

(2) Then, in the *modification phase*, the system discovers the analogy between the old and the new specifications, and presents it to the user in the form of a set of transformations. Some of the transformations must be checked for validity; if valid, they are then applied to the old program. Applying valid transformations might result in unexecutable statements, as could be the case if a variable were replaced by an expression that then showed up on the left side of an assignment. Then the user must rewrite these statements into executable ones.

(3) Finally, in the *postmodification phase*, again performed interactively with the user, code for unachieved parts of the new specification is added and the new program is further optimized, if possible.

The examples treated with the system were simple numerical problems, such as the transformation from "bad" real division to "good" real division and array-manipulation problems, such as the search for the minimal element. More recent theoretical considerations on the same topic can be found in work by Dershowitz [1980, 1981].

2.4.2 The DEDALUS System

The DEDALUS system (DEDuctive ALgorithm Ur-Synthesizer) by Manna and Waldinger [1978a, 1979], earlier referred to as the SYNSYS system [Manna and Waldinger 1977a, 1977b], is also implemented in QLISP. Its goal is to derive LISP programs automatically and deductively from high-level input–output specifications in a LISP-like representation of mathematical–logical notation.

The task of synthesizing a program can be viewed as that of achieving some goal expressed in the specification. By use of meaning-preserving transformations, this goal is modified in steps until nonprimitive constructs of the specification language have been replaced by equivalent LISP constructs.

The truth or falsity of the respective enabling conditions is established using the system's *theorem-proving rules*. If a condition cannot be proved, a conditional expression is introduced by case analysis (*conditional introduction rule*). Superfluous synthesis of conditionals is avoided by using the *redundant-test stategy.*

If, among the consecutive subgoals, the system recognizes an instance of the top-level goal, and if termination is guaranteed, the system introduces a recursive call (*recursion formation rule*, the same as FOLD, described in Section 1.2.4). Similarly, instances of lower level goals trigger the system to introduce and call auxiliary functions (*procedure-formation rule*).

The transformations, QLISP programs, include knowledge about the programming language or programming techniques and rules expressing facts about certain subject domains. In addition to the logical enabling conditions, the transformation rules are supplemented by strategic conditions and ordered to prevent foolish applications.

DEDALUS is able to create a program, a correctness proof, and a proof of termination (via well-founded sets) simultaneously for programs not involving mutual recursion. To achieve a certain subgoal, DEDALUS selects candidate rules by *pattern-directed invocation* (see Section 1.2.5) and tries those rules sequentially, according to their ordering. DEDALUS selects the transformation that best substantiates the termination proof. If no rule applies to a given subgoal, DEDALUS automatically backtracks using the backtracking directly available from QLISP. The synthesis fails if the system runs out of backtracking possibilities and succeeds if the system can achieve all goals. The output of a successful synthesis is a running LISP program.

In addition to describing a not yet implemented *generalization rule*, incorporating the knowledge that a slightly general goal is sometimes easier to achieve than any given particular goal, Manna and Waldinger [1979] also outline how to integrate their earlier ideas about variables, loops, and side effects in program synthesis [Manna and Waldinger 1975, 1978b]. In essence, this integration would lead to an extension of the specification language to allow sequential subgoals and the formulation of side effects. It would also require

extending DEDALUS by corresponding elementary transformations such as the *variable-assignment rule*, rules for the *wp-operator* [Dijkstra 1976b], and further technical rules for coping with the interaction between these new rules and those already in the system. Parts of these additional rules have been implemented in a separate system [Waldinger 1977].

Although based on only a few general principles, the DEDALUS system actually contains more than a hundred individual transformations. By the introduction of new rules, the system can be simply expanded to handle a new subject domain.

DEDALUS is considered by its designers to be a laboratory tool rather than a practical tool. Hence the examples that have been treated by DEDALUS are in some sense toy examples: different versions of the greatest-common-divisor function, the modulo function, some list algorithms (maximum number of elements, intersection of two lists, or relation of one element to all others), and basic set operations, such as union or intersection.

2.4.3 Recent Work

Recently, Manna and Waldinger [1980] have come up with ideas for a new, not-yet implemented, deduction-oriented synthesis system. This new approach regards program synthesis as a theorem-proving task and relies on a method that combines unification, mathematical induction, and transformation rules.

The basic entity in the new system is a structural unit called a *sequent*, consisting of assertion and goal specifications written in first-order logic and output expressions formulated in a LISP-like language. The meaning of such a sequent is that, if all instances of each of the assertions are true, some instance of at least one of the goals is true and the corresponding instance of its output expression satisfies the respective specification.

The system operates by adding new assertions and goals and their corresponding new output expressions to the sequent without changing its meaning. New entries in a sequent can be constructed from existing ones by means of logical rules, such as those for splitting conjunctions or disjunctions, transformation rules, resolution rules for eliminating certain subexpressions, polarity strategies for restricting the resolution rules, and mathematical induction. In addition, rules already available in the DEDALUS system can be used, such as recursion formation rules, generalization, and formation of auxiliary procedures.

This new system has simpler structure and greater flexibility (e.g., in searching for applicable rules) than does the DEDALUS system. Although they exceed the capabilities of the DEDALUS system, the examples that have been treated (quotient of two integers, last element of a list) belong to the same class of toy problems. Recently, a more interesting example, an algorithm for unification [Manna and Waldinger 1981], has been treated along the proposed derivation technique.

2.5 The PUC System

Arsac's system [Arsac 1978] was designed to interactively manipulate imperative programs formulated in a language containing conditionals, iteration with nested exits, and basic assignment and input/output statements. It is currently used at the Institut de Programmation in Paris and was first implemented in SNOBOL at the Pontificia Universidade Catolica (PUC) de Rio de Janeiro.

Transformations are applied sequentially, and the user must indicate both the transformation and the program location at which it is to be applied. If a specified transformation step violates the applicability condition, an error message is displayed and the user is asked for another transformation. Because there is an inverse for each (syntactic) transformation, previous development steps can be restored in the case of a blind alley.

To avoid retrieval problems, the catalog of transformations is deliberately small and does not contain more involved transformations, such as changing data structure representations. The tools for performing transformations, though, are sufficiently flexible and powerful to cope with the more

involved transformations if necessary. There are approximately 50 transformation rules in the system, falling into five categories:

(1) *Syntactic transforms* are source-to-source transformations that preserve the flow of computation and are entirely checked by the system. They were first suggested by Arsac [1974] and were proved to be complete by Cousineau [1976]. A more detailed treatment can be found in the later work of Arsac [1979]. These rules comprise interchanging of the **if–fi** construct and other statements (*simple absorption*), moving statements into and out of loops (*simple expansion, false iteration*), rearrangement of loops (*inversion*), loop unrolling (*repetition*), and reduction of nested loops into single ones (*double iteration*).

(2) *Regular program equations* [Arsac 1977a] form a system of parameterless procedures (*actions*) without local variables, which are connected by terminal calls that may only appear as the last action of a statement body. The rules for solving such regular program equations are substitution, replacement of tail recursion by iteration, and elimination of dead code.

(3) There are two possibilities for dealing with nonterminal recursion, both of which simulate the stack mechanism by explicitly keeping track of the flow of control, either by using a system-generated activation counter or by using a user-defined discriminating predicate.

(4) *Local semantic transforms* are source-to-source transformations that change the flow of computation but rely on local program properties. Defining these transforms is the user's own responsibility, and they can include rules for assignment combination, loop simplification, the removal of unreachable alternatives, and the elimination of redundant tests.

(5) The *editing rules* include *prettyprinting* and unchecked textual modifications.

One strategy for using these basic transformations is to "translate the program into actions, build up a system of regular program equations, and solve that regular system"; this strategy has been applied to recursion removal [Arsac and Kodratoff

1979]. Owing to the possibility of unrestricted textual modification,[11] the system is powerful. Examples that have been treated with the proposed methodology[12] include a sorting program, the Chinese Rings (*Baguenaudier* [Arsac 1978]), permutations in lexicographical order, partitions [Arsac 1979], tree printing, Towers of Hanoi, Fibonacci numbers [Arsac and Kodratoff 1979, 1982], Ackermann's function [Arsac 1977b], and others [Arsac 1977a].

2.6 The Munich CIP Project

A research group directed by F. L. Bauer and the late K. Samelson at the Technical University of Munich also concentrates on the transformational approach to programming (for an overview see work by Bauer and others [Bauer 1976; Bauer and Wössner 1982; Möller et al. 1983]). The project, called CIP (Computer-aided, Intuition-guided Programming), consists of two main parts: the design of a programming language and the development of a program-transformation system.[13]

The project focuses on correctness-preserving, source-to-source program transformations at all levels of formulation, ranging from nonalgorithmic specifications, via purely applicative formulations, to imperative and even machine-oriented styles. This work also includes corresponding transformations on the data structure side.

The algorithmic language, CIP-L [Bauer et al. 1978, 1981a, 1981b], was especially designed for the methodology of transformational programming just described. CIP-L is a *wide-spectrum language* comprising all the aforementioned different styles of programming within one coherent syntactic and semantic frame. It is a *scheme language* (i.e., a language without a fixed set of basic data types) based on a suitably defined, treelike, abstract data type. Moreover, it is an abstract language with several

concrete representations (e.g., ALGOL- or Pascal-like dialects). A small kernel language of CIP-L is defined by a mathematical semantics. All other language constructs are viewed as extensions of that kernel, made by *definitional transformations* [Pepper 1979]. The language is described as a hierarchy of algebraic abstract data types [Broy et al. 1982]: The syntax of the language defines a term algebra, context conditions form predicates in this algebraic theory, and conditional equations (corresponding to transformation rules with enabling conditions) define the semantics. This algebraic language definition not only allows a modular description but also makes it easy to extend the language.

To provide a homogeneous formal basis for the whole transformational approach, the CIP transformation system, too, is founded on an algebraic view of the program-formulating language and is itself specified in a hierarchical algebraic way. This has the particular advantage that both the definition of the system and its implementation are independent of a particular language. The running prototype of the CIP-system operates on abstract trees [Luckmann 1979]. Within this prototype, programs in every language having both an appropriate string-to-tree precompiler and a facility for the tree-to-string retranslation can be manipulated.[14]

The purpose of the CIP system is to manipulate program schemes (of which concrete programs are a special case). Program schemes are terms of the underlying algebraic language definition, with scheme parameters as subterms. This ordinary concept of schemes (see Section 1.1) has been extended by introducing *context parameters* [Steinbrüggen 1980a], which allow the user to mark fragmentary terms (*contexts*), as well as subterms, as replaceable. In this way, whole classes of rules, differing only in varying contexts, can be compressed into a single rule. For example, consider the following rule:

F [if C then A else B fi]
   $\Leftrightarrow$ if C then $F[A]$ else $F[B]$ fi
(where A, B, and C are scheme parameters, and F is a context parameter)

---

[11] The possibility of arbitrary textual modification, in some sense, contradicts the idea of program transformations. By the way, the same remark holds for the TI system (Section 2.1.2) and the Programmer's Apprentice (Section 4.3).
[12] From the literature it is not clear which of the examples have been done with the system.
[13] A prototype transformation system has been specified and implemented by R. Steinbrüggen's group.

[14] Both are provided for the ALGOL dialect of CIP-L.

This rule states the distributivity of the **if**-**then**-**else** construct with anything else. Applied to the statement

$$x := a * \textbf{if } x \geq 0 \textbf{ then } x \textbf{ else } -x \textbf{ fi}$$

it yields

if $x \geq 0$ **then** $x := a * x$
    else $x := a * (-x)$ **fi.**

The reason for considering schemes as manipulation objects is that, since transformation rules themselves consist of three schemes—source template, target template, and enabling condition—they can also be manipulated by the system.

In addition to *rule application* [Erhard 1981], *expansion* and *composition* of transformation rules [Steinbrüggen 1981a] are realized. The basic operations allow the formal derivation of more complex rules from elementary ones within the system.[15] According to the language definition, the set of elementary rules is composed of the following:

- the fundamental rules (such as FOLD or UNFOLD) of the language kernel that are verified with respect to the mathematical semantics;
- the definitional rules for the additional language constructs that hold axiomatically;
- the axioms of the algebraic data types (characterizing certain subject domains) that can be defined within individual programs.

The system has no means for automatically performing transformations. Instead, transformation rules must be selected by the user. This might seem burdensome, but the system offers a metalanguage for formulating transformational algorithms. Despite its expressive poverty (this metalanguage has only a few simple constructs, viz., *union, product, closure*[16]), it provides the full computational power (of a Turing machine [Steinbrüggen 1982]). Nonetheless, to ease the formulation of transformational

---

[15] Occasionally, induction principles fit into this framework too.
[16] Essentially, these are the regular set theory operations. The difference in computational power is due to rule application.

algorithms, an extension to the full CIP-L vocabulary is planned.

To support communication with the user, the CIP system also provides an interactive shell responsible for the user dialogue. In addition to making the aforementioned functions available to the user, this subsystem provides functions for textual program modifications. More details on this subsystem and a sketch of its formal derivation can be found in Riethmayer [1981].

Currently, the means for (automatically) recording the history of a program development are lacking. Early work toward such a capability has been done [Bauer et al. 1977].

The development of the running prototype system has proceeded from prealgorithmic specifications [Steinbrüggen 1980b] to an applicative version and, finally, to a Pascal version, through a half-dozen intermediate stages. The main transitions are documented by program transformations. Because of this, the running system is proved to meet its specifications.

The system has been used to prove parts of its own development [Brass et al. 1982]. Currently, it is being used by students to develop algorithms and to prove, via derivation chains, theorems about abstract types. A new transformation system is currently being developed using the running prototype system [Partsch 1984].

2.7 The SETL Project and Related Activities

The transformational activities in connection with the SETL project [Schwartz 1975a; Dewar et al. 1979a] at the Courant Institute of New York University concentrate on three areas: an optimizer; an interactive, semiautomatic development system; and a verification/manipulation system.

Work on the SETL optimizer is strongly related to transformation systems. Although it is not a transformation system in a strict sense, it does use transformational techniques, particularly for selecting data structures and ensuring efficient data-type representation [Schwartz 1975b; Schonberg et al. 1979, 1981]. By adding type declarations to the program, the user can choose among a variety of ready made implementations for *tuple, set,* and *map* types, which the system provides. If declarations are missing, concrete representations are automatically chosen by the SETL optimizer.

The second contribution to the transformational approach is an experimental interactive system for supporting the semi-automatic development of reliable and efficient software, using source-to-source transformations. This system, RAPTS (Rutgers Abstract Program Transformation System), implemented in SETL by R. Paige [1983] at Rutgers University emphasizes the strict stepwise refinement of programs by successive application of manually selected powerful correctness-preserving transformations. These transformations are based on *finite differencing*, also known as *formal differentiation*, a general form of strength reduction [Paige and Schwartz 1977; Paige 1981; Paige and Koenig, 1982; Sharir 1979a, 1979b, 1981]. If applicable, this technique always improves efficiency. In Paige's system it is strongly coupled with the data-type facilities provided by the input language SETL. Most other features supported by the system are fairly standard. Paige (private communication, 1981) plans to develop program analysis routines to automate the verification of applicability conditions associated with transformations. This task is known to be complex for nonsyntactic transformations. Currently, control-flow and data-flow analyses have been implemented, and type and perturbation analyses are being developed.

The third area of concentration is the SETL verification/manipulation system [Schwartz 1977; Deak 1980, 1981]. It can be briefly characterized as a semantically knowledgeable editor that allows programs to be changed when written in a SETL-like language and annotated with assumptions, if the resulting program remains correct. If the system cannot verify a change, it adds new assumptions to the program, which the user later verifies. This approach is catalog oriented. The catalog contains proof rules (for verifying assumptions) and transformation rules. Typical proof rules include assumption introduction, assertion elimi-

nation, propagation, induction, and proof-checker rules. Transformation rules include expression- or selection-substitution rules, refinement rules (selection refinement, insertion, and deletion), rules for labels and jumps, and some other optimization techniques well known from compiler construction.

Problems that have been dealt with by the SETL project range from the simple to the complex, such as a minimal path in a graph [Schonberg et al. 1979], garbage collection algorithms [Dewar et al. 1979b], and the Cocke–Younger parsing algorithm [Deak 1981]. For a fair comparison with other systems, though, it should be added that even though the latter developments are detailed case studies, they contain a great deal of informal reasoning and thus would require more technical work before they would be treatable by any system. Recently, Paige and Koenig have begun applying program transformations to database transaction optimization [Koenig and Paige 1981; Paige 1982].

3. SPECIAL-PURPOSE SYSTEMS

As mentioned in Section 1, it is difficult to differentiate between general and special-purpose transformation systems. Whereas general transformation systems support various aspects of the transformational approach to software development, special-purpose systems use the transformational concept to achieve a specific goal. All special-purpose systems may be characterized by the particular facet of the transformational activity (e.g., optimization, synthesis, verification, or adaptation) on which they focus and the particular class of programs that they manipulate. Examples of restricted programs include array-manipulating programs, programs specified by algebraic equations, and programs restricted to both a particular language (FORTRAN) and a special application area (numerical algorithms).

3.1 The Irvine SPECIALIST

The Irvine transformation system, called SPECIALIST [Kibler 1978], is implemented in LISP at the University of California at Irvine. On the basis of experiences gained with an earlier system [Kibler et al. 1977] SPECIALIST is restricted in two respects: It deals only with the optimization of executable programs and only in the domain of matrix problems. The input for the system is an ALGOL-like program, bearing *local predicate* constraints on data structures, such as "the matrix used is a diagonal matrix." The target is a simplified ALGOL-like program.

The transformation catalog is extendable and consists of about 50 rules. All the rules are syntactic or semiprocedural, and most are independent of the specific language, ALGOL. In particular, the rules dealing with control constructs are directly transferable to other languages. Most of the rules are simply rewrite rules called *productions*. A few others, such as those for useless-assignment elimination, empty-statement elimination, and constant propagation, need additional enabling conditions. The correctness of the rules in the catalog has been proved by an adaptation of Dijkstra's weakest precondition methodology [Dijkstra 1976b].

The area covered by the transformations concentrates on simplification of matrix computations,[17] although there are also rules specific to other domains (e.g., definitions, axioms, theorems, or optimizations for arithmetic or Boolean algebra). For handling local, temporary information, *dynamic transformations* are defined and used. These dynamic transformations are mainly applied by simple expansion as in, for example,

Diagonal-matrix (x)
$\Rightarrow$ (**if** $i \neq j$ **then** $x[i, j] = 0$ **fi**).

The transformations in SPECIALIST always assume correct, executable program versions. During the development process, SPECIALIST will not modify an algorithm's general strategy. Thus, for example, a transformation from linear search to binary search is impossible. There is no pos-

sibility for treating global constraints, such as "the matrix used is invertible," and none of the optimizing transformations depend on global flow analysis or execution monitors. Global optimization is instead achieved by *chaining* simple local transformations.

Chaining [Kibler 1978] is based on the observation that, within the scope of any special problem field, a successful application of a transformation will provide information for significantly reducing the search space for the next step. By knowing where the last transformation was applied, the scope or *locality* (a node in the internal tree representation) of the next transformation in the program can be limited. The information about which transformation was applied provides hints for possible next-rule candidates. Each transformation is augmented by a list of *directions*. Each direction consists of a relative specification of a new locality, followed by an unordered list of successor rules. Because a reasonable ordering of that list would obviously speed the development process, suitable criteria, such as expense of applicability test, expense of performance, probability of applicability, and user intuition, are still being investigated. A successful transformation application causes the first direction to be tried and the others to be kept on a treelike *agenda* structure to enable directed backtracking, if necessary.

Given a program, local constraints, and a user-specified initial locality, the system automatically produces an optimized program. During this process, up to 90 transformations can be automatically chained without backup or user assistance. The system also provides the user assistance for entering new rules in the catalog. It does so by supporting the incremental derivation of new rule augmenting, using an appropriate list of directions (see above).

Examples that have been treated with Kibler's system concentrate—as do the transformation rules—on matrix computations [Kibler 1978]. A typical example, the development of matrix multiplication given diagonality or symmetry constraints, has been treated in complete detail [Kibler et al. 1977].

---

[17] Rules going beyond matrix problems can be found in earlier Irvine work on transformational programming [Standish et al. 1976a, 1976b].

3.2 An Orsay System

Guiho's system [Bidoit et al. 1979; Guiho et al. 1980] in Orsay (Université Paris-Sud) is also restricted in two ways: (1) As with Kibler's system, it only deals with array-manipulating programs; (2) unlike Kibler's system, it aims only at one specific transformation task, that of synthesis from given specifications, with no effort toward optimization.

The system, which is implemented in LISP, takes as input high-level, nonalgorithmic specifications and produces ALGOL-like recursive programs. Although restricted to arrays, this system is based on the more general approach of algebraically specified abstract data types, and extensions are therefore possible. Typical examples of admissible specifications to the system include "Find index, such that P (index, input) holds," "Test P(input)," "Construct an array such that P(index, input) holds," and combinations of these.

The system employs two kinds of heuristics. The first is based on the interplay between constructors and selectors in abstract data types: Selectors decompose the problem; constructors synthesize a solution. In the special case of arrays, this interaction reduces to: "If the array is empty, then no operation; otherwise, operate on one element and then on the rest of the array." This rule corresponds to the conditional-formation rule in the DEDALUS system, given in Section 2.4.2. The second kind of heuristic deals with general programming knowledge such as *formation of recursive calls* (folding), generalization (used if a direct folding fails), and introduction of subsidiary programs. The system uses first-order matching to detect tail-recursive calls, second-order matching to select transformation rules (a simple keyword detection similar to the pattern-directed invocation described in Section 1.2.5), and a theorem prover, which, although "naive," proved sufficient for the examples it handled.

The examples are, of course, all array based and include those of element insertion, maximal element, test for sortedness, membership test, array reversal, test for identity of two arrays, and computation of two arrays' intersection.

3.3 The ISI AFFIRM System

The AFFIRM system at the Information Science Institute of the University of Southern California (ISI) [Erickson 1981; Gerhart et al. 1980] is based on algebraic data-type specifications having algebraic axioms[18] to characterize sets of objects according to the interrelation of their characteristic operations. AFFIRM is a verification system and not, in the strictest sense, a transformation system. But since algebraic axioms are specific kinds of transformations (see the algebraic view in the CIP project, Section 2.6), the classification of AFFIRM as a special-purpose transformation system seems plausible. In addition to this restricted kind of transformation, AFFIRM also has a limited scope of application: It is primarily an experimental system for the algebraic specification and verification of Pascal-like programs, using algebraically defined abstract types.

The purpose of the system is to help the user prove properties. The system's assistance essentially consists of the axiom applications (considered to be rewrite rules) and support for induction proofs, in which AFFIRM generates the cases of the induction.

Responsibility for the strategy of the proof rests solely with the user. The user must find the right set of axioms, the theorems to be proved, and the lemma structure of the proof. The system makes no effort to find proofs beyond repeatedly applying the axioms until no further rewriting is possible and doing some automatic simplification (mainly in the area of **if–then–else** constructs). However, because the system performs recording, undoing, and redoing of proof steps, it helps the user in the mechanical parts of a proof derivation.

The constituents (called *abstract machines*) of the AFFIRM system belong to several categories. The basic stock of transformations consists of the *rewrite rules*, the

---

[18] These axioms are usually equations, sometimes restricted by certain definedness conditions.

set of rewrite expressions based on the user-defined axioms. For performing transformations, the *specification* provides facilities for creating, modifying, destroying, and listing data-type specifications (including certain well-formedness checks). The *logic* comprises the usual propositional calculus, as well as the more advanced features of skolemization, normalization, unification, instantiation, and *case analysis*, the latter being a transformation to interchange function calls and the **if–fi** construct. The *theorem prover* maintains the treelike proof structure and provides means for interactively moving around the tree and modifying it. The service component includes the *executive*, which handles communication with the user and among the system's constituents, a *verification condition generator*, and *formula input/output*.

The AFFIRM system is strongly influenced by its implementation language, INTERLISP. The rewrite rules are simply translated into LISP functions, the INTERLISP history list acts as a bookkeeping device, and the automatically produced transcript is used as a proof session record. In addition, components such as the parser and structured editors of the implementation system are directly used.

As in the CIP system (Section 2.6), the AFFIRM system's specification and verification follow their own particular theoretical and programming paradigms:

(1) algebraic specification of abstract data types,
(2) verification by rewrites rules.

Of course, this does not mean that AFFIRM has been used to create itself, but rather that the respective proofs had been done by hand along the lines of the incorporated methodology.

Examples of problems treated by AFFIRM include many data-type specifications and proofs of associated properties [Musser 1979; Thompson et al. 1981], some simple problems using induction [Gerhard 1980], different versions of a message system [Gerhart and Wile 1979], and communication protocols [Thompson et al. 1981]. And Lee et al. [1981] report an in-cident in which the system helped in finding a design error in a distributed system.

3.4 The Argonne TAMPR System

The TAMPR (Transformation-Assisted Multiple Program Realization) system [Boyle and Dritz 1974; Boyle 1976; Boyle and Matz 1977] at the Argonne National Laboratory again is a special-purpose transformation system, since its primary goal is to use transformations to adapt numerical algorithms to particular hardware, software, and problem environments. (For a perspicuous outline of the underlying philosophy, see work by Boyle [1980].) TAMPR is designed to abstract from the details of several numerical subroutine packages for slightly different machines or languages and to express their commonality in the form of a *prototype program*, a program from which a set of variant, systematically related mathematical subroutines can be automatically derived. For the derivation of these variants, or *realizations*, sets of schematic transformation rules relating different FORTRAN[19] programs or program schemes are used. These sets of rules are known as *realization functions*. The transformation rules are also called *intragrammatical transformations*[20] because they guarantee syntactic correctness of the transformed program and serve to connect realizations either with the prototype program or with each other.

In the implementation, these transformations are carried out on a representation of the program written in an *applicative* language called *structured FORTRAN*. In detail, a given FORTRAN program is first translated into a parse tree and then into a *canonical abstract form* in structured FORTRAN. The system then applies the transformations to this canonical abstract form. From every intermediate version of the program, TAMPR is able to produce executable FORTRAN. Experiments with other

---

[19] Although the ideas are, in principle, language independent, all the actual work has been done in FORTRAN.
[20] Early ideas, in particular those about implementing intragrammatical transformations, can be found in work by Boyle [1970].

languages, such as PL/I, also have been successfully carried out.

The transformations mainly focus on the transition from Basic Linear Algebra subroutines to in-line FORTRAN code. Typical examples [Boyle and Matz 1977; Boyle 1978, 1981] include some forms of unfolding, loop unrolling, conversion of a complex function to its real counterpart, converting single precision to double precision, and changing two-dimensional arrays into one-dimensional ones. TAMPR has been successfully applied to widely used numerical subroutine packages.

4. GENERAL PROGRAMMING ENVIRONMENTS

There are many general software development systems (for a typical example, see Alberga et al. [1981]; for a comprehensive survey and classification, see Hesse [1981]), but very few of them include a component for program transformations or provide tools for transformational programming. All the systems described in this section are general, rather than special-purpose, systems. When compared with the systems described in earlier sections, they are even more general, in the sense that the performance of program transformations is only a small aspect of the whole system.

4.1 The Harvard PDS

Built on the basis of experiences from the ECL project [Wegbreit 1972; Cheatham and Wegbreit 1972; ECL 1974], the Harvard PDS (Program Development System) [Cheatham et al. 1979b; Cheatham 1981; Townley 1981] is a programming environment consisting of an integrated collection of interactive tools to support definition, testing, and maintenance of large programs or program families whose members must be maintained in synchrony. The PDS puts special emphasis on program derivation from abstract specifications by nontrivial refinements.

The PDS system views a program as a hierarchical collection of modules used to solve a certain programming task. Each module consists of entities such as procedural expressions, data definitions, and

documentation. Relationships among the modules are given by interface specifications whose consistency is checked by the PDS. A module may have several descendants, all of which are considered as refinements of the original parent module. Thus a program is defined at several levels, and a fundamental goal of the PDS is to support this multilevel view of a program by providing appropriate structures and means for maintaining the different program versions.

The PDS constructs and uses a database of facts about a program and its constituents, including a representation of the modules' interdependence and a history of their refinement, organized to enable automatic incremental rederivation, given a modified abstract specification. The interface to the user is provided by the executive of the PDS. Other available components include specification tools, analysis tools such as a symbolic evaluator [Cheatham et al. 1979a], and execution tools.

Refinement of an entity or module can be specified either by an incremental definition/redefinition of the respective entity via its attributes (name, derivation number, time of creation, etc.), by the history mechanism (the set of previously used refinements), or by the rewrite facility, that is, the transformation component of PDS [Cheatham et al. 1981]. In contrast to most of the other systems, which rely on preexisting cataloged transformations, the PDS transformations must be defined by the user.[21] They represent design decisions in the stepwise refinement sequence and, as programs, are encapsulated in modules.

Transformation rules are represented schematically. They consist of a syntactic input pattern (with scheme parameters and iteratable constructs explicitly marked), optionally augmented with a semantic predicate for applicability, and a syntactic output pattern, the *replacement part*.

Transformations are used to introduce nomenclature, implement an abstract notion (notational extension, similar to the

---

[21] From the literature it is not clear whether PDS supports individual user-defined transformation catalogs.

definitional transformations in the CIP system given in Section 2.6) or certain aspects of the behavior of an abstract data type, and derive realizations of an abstract program.

In the PDS, the refinement of an abstract program consists of a series of steps leading from a program and a refinement module to a new program module. The entities in these modules may be divided into named groups to provide local scoping and to control the local application of a transformation. Instructions within the refinement module may specify which rules apply to which entities of the program module. Nesting transformations (in which transformations act as constituents of another transformation's replacement part) enable local transformations to be done by limiting the scope of applicability.

Rule application does not consist of a single replacement step but is performed in repeated passes over the evolving program module until no further rules apply. Transformations that are not intended to be used in the further development of their own "right side" can be marked for solitary application.

Examples of large programs that have already been developed with the PDS include the symbolic evaluator, a family of interpreters for EL-1 (the language of the ECL system), a family of interprocess communication handlers, a formula simplifier, and the PDS itself. Townley has done a detailed development of an efficient algorithm for reducing a deterministic automaton [Townley 1982].

4.2 The MENTOR System

The MENTOR system at INRIA [Donzeau-Gouge et al. 1975, 1980] was also designed for developing "realistic" programs. Its purpose is to realize an interactive programming environment in which the programmer can design, implement, document, debug, test, validate, and maintain programs or modify them for transportation purposes. Although MENTOR is, in principle, independent of language and development methodology, nearly all of the work actually done has focused on Pascal programs [Mélèse 1981]. By bootstrapping a

small system core written in Pascal, MENTOR could be used to do most of its own development[22] and maintenance. In particular, MENTOR was used to develop its transportation from the IRIS 80 to the PDP-10 computer. The authors' philosophy is that a programming environment is a set of specialized interpreters for helping programmers do various computations and rearrangements on their programs. Hence MENTOR is not only extensible but also allows the structured editing of Pascal programs, including simple transformations such as parentheses insertion or *pretty-printing* in different type fonts. In addition, MENTOR allows normalization of Pascal programs (by rearranging declarations or cleaning up scope information) and, of course, different source-level transformations, such as constant propagation, consistent renaming of identifiers, and recursion removal for tail recursion.

MENTOR is a processor designed for manipulating structured data represented by abstract syntax trees. The translation between Pascal programs and abstract syntax trees is done by the system. For driving MENTOR, a special-purpose tree-manipulating language, called MENTOL, is used.

MENTOL is an interactive language designed for editing. It has side-effect-free expressions, commands with side effects, procedures with different calling mechanisms, a sophisticated facility for comments, and a built-in facility for pattern matching. Expressions are used for operations such as selecting and displaying marked subtrees of an abstract syntax tree. Typical commands modify or evaluate the selected subtree. The latter is most important, since, together with the possibility for defining schemes (constructable by commands or input through the parser) and pattern matching, it supports the implementation of transformations in terms of *tree-rewriting* operations. From basic commands, more complex ones can be built by using conventional language features such as sequencing, grouping, bound iteration, and conditional and case statements.

---

[22] From the literature it is not clear which parts have been implemented.

Furthermore, the language provides good debugging aids, including a trace package, an interrupt facility, and file manipulation primitives. Finally, it has its own abstract syntax, which allows a mixed development of both Pascal and MENTOL programs. In particular, it is possible (for experts only) to modify Pascal manipulation programs written in MENTOL.

4.3 The Programmer's Apprentice

The PA (Programmer's Apprentice) [Rich and Shrobe 1978; Rich et al. 1979] is a "knowledge-based editing approach" [Waters, 1982]. As such, it lies between an aid to an improved programming methodology and a knowledge-based automatic programming system.

Programmer and system work together (see "partnership" in GLITTER, Section 2.1.4) during all phases of development and maintenance. The programmer performs the "difficult" tasks such as design and implementation, and the PA acts as a junior partner and critic by keeping track of details and assisting in documentation, debugging, and maintenance.

PA's assistance mainly concentrates on two activities. First, given a LISP program, PA is able to analyze its underlying structure and recognize the structure's known building blocks or *plans*. Second, given an abstract or incomplete description of an algorithm, PA helps fill in details and debug incorrect portions. The result of this second activity is an executable LISP program, together with a layered description of its top-down construction process.

Program structures are represented as plans, conceptual units of behavior that are either primitive or hierarchically composed of other plans. A plan's basic entity is a *segment*, defined by *specs*, formal statements of input expectations and output assertions, based on a relational view of data. The relationship between individual plans are kept by *dependency links* comprising syntactic relations (data and control flow) and semantic relations (knowledge of how the behavior of a plan is inferred from the behavior of its components).

PA's knowledge is embodied in a *plan library*, a hierarchically organized knowledge base[23] of formalized general knowledge about nonnumerical programming. Typical plans include knowledge about the concept of a loop and its specializations into enumeration loops or search loops, or knowledge about general techniques for manipulating trees, lists, arrays, and the like.

On the basis of its understanding of the logical structure of a program, PA is able to reason deductively about plans. In particular, the system can verify that a plan matches some portion of a concrete program, point out bugs by finding discrepancies between its understanding and the actual program operations, and reason about consequences of modifying existing programs by determining what parts are affected by the change.

PA is based on an informal and flexible editing paradigm. The particular knowledge representation by plans allows both synthesis and analysis, and moving from the abstract to the concrete, or vice versa. By producing a low-level plan structure from a given program, the system helps to analyze already written programs. On the other hand, a user may construct a LISP program with assistance from the system, by naming general algorithms (plans from the plan library) and refining their abstract components into LISP code (by naming more concrete plans or filling in literal values).

There is neither a formal specification in the PA approach, nor are the changes required to be correctness preserving. This implies that, within the bounds of plan compatibility, arbitrary changes to a program can be made (see also the PUC system, Section 2.5). It is especially for this reason that PA can be considered a transformation system only in a rather broad sense.

4.4 The Draco System

The Draco System [Neighbors 1980] is a general mechanism for software construc-

---

[23] This knowledge base is similar to that of PECOS, Section 2.2.2, except for the explicit representation of the logical structure of programs.

tion based on the paradigm of "reusable software." "Reusable" here means that the analysis and design of some library program can be reused, but not its code. Draco is an interactive system that enables a user to refine a problem, stated in a high-level problem-domain-specific language, into an efficient LISP program.

Accordingly, Draco supplies mechanisms for defining problem domains as special-purpose domain languages and for manipulating statements in these languages into an executable form.

Initially, Draco contains domains that represent conventional, executable computer languages. On this basis, a hierarchy of new domains may be defined by providing the syntax of the (new) domain language in a Backus-Normal-Form (BNF) -like formalism defining the semantics by appropriate mappings (*refinements*) from the statements in the new language into statements of one or more previously defined languages, and by giving, finally, a set of optimizing (source-to-source) transformations for the new language.[24]

The user may then formulate a specific problem in terms of the new domain language. The transformations allow the user to "strip away generalities" and specialize the general components of the domain language according to his or her own particular use. While guiding a refinement, using the semantic mappings mentioned above, the user may make individual modeling and implementation choices among competing refinements presented by the system or rely on user-defined tactics to guide the semi-automatic refinement process. Design choices have enabling conditions and, if used, make assertions about the resulting program. If these conditions and assertions

ever conflict, backward movement to a safe, nonconflicting earlier development stage is necessary.

The complete refinement history then is a top-down description of the final program. Each schematic transformation rule is given an application code (identifying what it does and how desirable its application is) when it is defined. This code implies a partial order among transformations which is used to build up metarules, rules that relate the rules of a given fixed set to each other.

When a program formulated in terms of the domain language is parsed into the domain's internal tree form, Draco generates, upon request, for each node, an agenda of applicable transformations in the order of application code. The transformation mechanism then allows the application of rules within a user-selected *locale* in an instance of a domain. By providing the metarule mechanism and different application policies, Draco circumvents the need for transformation algorithms (*procedural transformations*).

The interesting aspect of the Draco approach is its way of achieving implementation-independent representation of algorithms: Draco enables the user to define his or her own level of abstraction. This has the additional advantage that powerful transformations are easily expressible. A typical example is given by the domain language for augmented transition networks; in this language, elimination of an unreadable transition state, which is difficult to capture in LISP code, can be simply formulated.

The Draco ideas have been implemented in a prototype system running under TOPS-10 on a DEC PDP-10 computer. However, owing to memory restriction, only small programs can be created using this prototype. An example that has been treated is a program for finding roots in a quadratic equation, originally formulated in a 10-line ALGOL program that was refined into approximately 80 lines of LISP. Another example was a natural language parser specified in the above-mentioned augmented transition networks.

---

[24] This is similar to the CIP approach (see Section 2.6), where a new problem domain can be defined by means of a suitable abstract type; the signature of the type defines the syntax, and the axioms serve as semantic definition as well as transformation rules. The essential difference lies in how the semantics of the new domain are defined. In Draco, an operational definition is given, whereas in the abstract data-type approach of the CIP project an axiomatic, algebraic one (which leaves freedom for various operational realizations) is used.

5. FURTHER ACTIVITIES

In addition to the projects described so far, there are other efforts that, from the present points of view, play only a minor role in the field. Nevertheless, they show some interesting properties and deserve mention.

5.1 Former Systems

The systems described in this section have in common the fact that there is no information about their implementor's current activities.

5.1.1 Haraldsson's System

Haraldsson's system REDFUN-2 [Haraldsson 1974, 1977, 1978], implemented in INTERLISP, is designed to simplify arbitrary LISP programs. This is achieved through the application of many algorithms. Among these, *partial evaluation* [Beckmann et al. 1976] of procedures (in different versions) based on partial information about the variables is most prominent. The concept of partial evaluation (also *mixed computation* [Ershov 1978, 1982]) is simple: If, for example, a function is defined with two arguments but actually depends on only one of them (i.e., the other is constant), it may be changed into an equivalent function with only one argument. Other techniques used are global analysis, β-*expansion* (unfolding), constant propagation, and certain collapsing rules to remove redundant code.

5.1.2 Rutter's System

Rutter's system [Rutter 1977] for improving the efficiency of LISP programs can be seen as a forerunner of Kibler's system, since its main contribution to the research on program transformations is an attempt to automatically chain rule applications. It consists of about 200 language-dependent rules. These rules are stored in a list and sequentially applied to the different program versions; applicable rules are found by binary search, depending on previous successes. The improvement process terminates when no rule is applicable. Some of the optimizations additionally require global flow analysis, the ordering of condi-

tionals, or the choice of data structures, as determined by an *execution monitor*.

5.1.3 Loveman's System

Loveman's ideas [Loveman 1977; Loveman and Faneuf 1975] for a transformation system are partly implemented in the IVTRAN compiler (FORTRAN compiler for ILLIAC-IV). In addition to "classical" transformations such as constant propagation, dead-variable elimination, and code motion, the system also contains about two dozen rules focusing on loop constructs (case splitting, loop unraveling, loop fusion, and interaction between loops and conditionals). Note that this approach, too, allows rules to be augmented with a set of possible-next-candidate rules.

Even more interesting is Loveman's attempt to incorporate transformations designed to execute loops on a parallel machine with a finite number of processors. The techniques used are the *coordinate method* for transforming well-behaved sets of nested loops into concurrent loops for several asynchronously operating processors, the *hyperplane method* for transforming well-behaved sets of nested loops into simultaneous loops for processors operating in a "lock-step" fashion, and *strip mining* for adjusting a given parallel loop to a machine with a fixed number of processors.

5.2 Recent Projects

Although there are now many groups working on program transformations, we shall briefly mention only some of those that recently became active in the field.

5.2.1 The CROPS/Pascal System

The CROPS (Conversational Restructuring, Optimizing, and Partitioning System)/Pascal system [Chusho 1980] is an interactive optimization system implemented in Pascal for Pascal programs that perform matrix computations. The system is characterized by having a generative set of basic rules (*commands*) out of which new rules can be built. Supporting this aspect of the system is a slightly different view of program transformations (*optimization com-*

mands): Transformations are not considered as preverified theorems on programs but rather as interactively specified replacement steps whose correctness must still be verified. However, by hierarchically basing arbitrary commands on more primitive ones, this correctness proof is strongly supported by the system and individual proof techniques are only occasionally needed. More primitive commands include predefined optimization commands; commands for testing, debugging, or verifying optimization commands; and edit commands for line/character manipulating and restructuring. Typical examples of predefined optimization commands include rules for changing the structure of loops (split, merge, move, rotate, expand), renaming variables, moving parts of code, doing expansion, performing strength reduction, and implementing a simple form of symbolic execution.

5.2.2 The IPMS

The IPMS (Interactive Program Manipulation System) [de Rivières 1980] can be characterized as a hybrid of a structured editor and a transformation catalog.

Starting with a functionally correct Pascal program[25] as input, the user gives standard structured editing commands (such as insertion, deletion, movement, or replacement) for modification or optimization. The IPMS attempts to carry out the command by finding a sequence of primitive, correctness-preserving, source-to-source transformations (similar to those in Kibler's system, Section 3.1) that achieves the desired result. Within this sequence, competing applicable rules are chosen in the order in which they appear in the catalog. Infinite sequencing of rules is prevented by a system-defined threshold. In case of failure the program is not altered and the programmer is informed about the difficulties encountered; otherwise, the command is performed and an optimized program version is produced as output.

The rules provided by IPMS are schematic quintuples: name, goal, left-hand-side pattern, right-hand-side pattern, enabling condition. In addition to the usual kind of patterns, one called *anchored pattern*,[26] which requires little or no searching, is used. These anchored patterns contain a bound variable, the *anchor*, which is identified first during matching. The remaining parts of the pattern are then searched for around the anchor. Instead of a right-hand-side replacement pattern, the rules may contain further goals to achieve. Thus IPMS (like GLITTER, Section 2.1.4) addresses both program space and problem space.

The collection of transformation rules is indexed by the editing functions they perform. Accordingly, rules that can perform more than one function have several index terms. For selecting applicable rules, a form of *pattern-directed invocation* (see DEDALUS, Section 2.4.2) is used. If there are enabling conditions, they are checked by inspecting control paths in the program tree leading to and from the site of application. For handling program-specific transformations, that is, transformations depending on values of variables, *dynamic transformations* (where equivalence is ensured by the specific context) are used.

From its conception, but also with respect to its abilities, IPMS is obviously another special-purpose system (see Section 3). Unfortunately, from the literature it is not clear whether the system really has been implemented. However, if it has not been, an implementation could be done straightforwardly, thanks to the technically detailed description given by de Rivières [1980].

5.2.3 The FOO System

The FOO system [Mostow 1981] is a system for AI problem solving by "operationalizing" a problem description stated at the problem-domain level into a procedure. This transformation is done relying only on actions that are executable by a *task agent* in the *task environment*. Roughly speaking, in Neighbors' terminology (see Section 4.4), this is the same as deriving an

---

[25] Actually a subset of Pascal, restricted to basic data types and a few simple control constructs, is used.

[26] There is a similar mechanism in SNOBOL.

operative solution for a problem in terms of already available components. One of the techniques used in the derivation of such a procedure is based on the "pigeonhole principle": A limited number of possible solutions is filtered by conclusions derivable from available facts.

The FOO system is catalog oriented and contains approximately 300 rules. From these, the user repeatedly selects appropriate ones and indicates where in the actual problem expression they should be applied. A selection among competing instantiations of the same rule must be made by the user.

Mostow's work [Mostow 1981] also contains a proposal for automating portions of the operationalization process (which again bears some resemblance to that of GLITTER, Section 2.1.4) by suggesting *means–end analysis* to guide the rule selection. The user provides the left-hand-side pattern of some rule that he or she finally wants to be applied. The *means–end module* then computes the *difference* between the pattern and the current problem expression and uses the computed difference as an index to selecting rules that might help reduce the difference.

5.2.4 Goad's System

Goad [1982] has introduced a system for "special-purpose automatic programming." This system is designed to increase the efficiency of computations by synthesizing, for particular classes of problems defined in ordinary mathematical terms, fast special-purpose programs from more general solutions.

As well as being denoted as relations rather than functions, the original solutions must have the property of *sweep coherence*, meaning that the result depends on two arguments, one of which changes slowly, and one rapidly. The basic idea of the approach may be characterized as a mixture of partial evaluation (Section 5.1.1) and formal differentiation (Paige's system, Section 2.7). By expanding (repeated unfolding, see Section 1.2.4) a partial call of the given solution into its complete decision tree, a special variant of the solution is synthesized and then analyzed

and appropriately modified. This process is repeated for all values of the slowly changing parameter and produces a family of special-purpose programs that covers the original solution.

Of course, to be profitable, a proceeding such as this requires that the effort in constructing the special-purpose programs not exceed the effort in running the original general-purpose program.

On the basis of the general principles, a program for the synthesis of special-purpose priority sorting programs has been implemented in MACLISP on a DEC PDP-10 computer. This program has been applied to the problem of "hidden surface elimination from displays of three-dimensional scenes" and resulted in special-purpose algorithms an order of magnitude faster than the best available general-purpose algorithms.

5.2.5 The Leeds Transformation System

The intention of the LTS (Leeds Transformation System) [Maher and Sleeman 1983] is to transform existing programs into "tidier," better readable, better structured programs. Owing to this restricted area of application, the LTS must also be considered a special-purpose system. On the basis of the observation that programmers vary in what they consider to be an acceptable form of a program, the system is *data driven*, and is independent of a particular language. The class of suitable languages is only restricted to languages without pointers, in which the flow of control is syntactically decidable. The translation between a particular language and the system's internal form is done by respective pre- and postprocessors (see also the CIP system, Section 2.6).

The transformation process is split into three independent phases: In the first phase, controlled by the user, the internal form of the program is restructured using a set of syntactic transformation rules (similar to those in Kibler's system, Section 3.1). By *variable usage transformations*, in the second phase, redundant variables, redundant statements, and loop-invariant statements are automatically eliminated until no further changes can be made (see also the Harvard PDS, Section 4.1). In the third phase, certain structuring features are introduced to replace more basic statements. This *modularization* phase again relies on the user to set appropriate bounds for the search processes involved.

The data-driven view requires that the user supply the system with information on the syntactic structures (language syntax in BNF, tables of language-specific constructs, transformation rules for the redefinition of statements), on statements effecting the flow of control, and on the effect of particular statements on variables.

Since the set of syntactic transformation rules is supplied as data, it is extensible and modifiable. The responsibility for the correctness of the rules rests exclusively with the user (as it did in the PA system, Section 4.3, or in the CHI system, Section 2.2.6). Furthermore, the transformation process assumes syntactically valid programs; programs containing semantic runtime errors are not excluded. Potential uses of the system are the following:

- transforming a program into its structured counterpart (e.g., FORTRAN into RATFOR);
- transforming an existing program to meet an installation standard;
- transforming unsupported features on "imported" programs into those supported by the system;
- optimizing programs in different ways (e.g., "peephole optimization," or transforming high-level constructs into more efficient lower level ones).

Because of the amount of pattern matching and replacement involved with syntactic transformations, the system was implemented in a dialect of SNOBOL called SPITBOL, on a DEC PDP-10 computer. Examples that have been treated include medium-size FORTRAN programs (500–1000 lines of code), numerous ALGOL-60 programs, and some small PL/I programs.

6. PERSPECTIVES FOR THE FUTURE

There is a widespread demand for safe, verified, and reliable software. This demand arises from economic considerations (production of correct chips), ethical reasons (protection of privacy), safety requirements (critical software, as for nuclear power stations), and strategic demands (reliability of weapon systems). Transformational programming can clearly make a valuable contribution toward this goal. But there are additional advantages: Programmers tend to underestimate the complexity of given problems and overrate their own mental capacity. Formal methods, integrated in transformational programming, safeguard against this human tendency. Since an initial problem specification is normally independent of any machine considerations, it can be used for deriving final programs not only for the sequential, storage-programmed, von Neumann computer but also for new architectures such as dataflow machines and array processors, provided that suitable transformation rules are available.

Because of these advantages, many people are enthusiastic about transformational programming as a programming methodology. There are also many people who object to the idea of mechanically supported transformational programming. Some people do not believe that automating the selection of transformations via an artificial intelligence problem solver is feasible and worry that, without such automation, the user would be forced into too much detail. Other people hope to avoid such burdensome detail by accomplishing the development in a few large conceptual steps. If, however, formal rigor really is their goal, transformational programming cannot exist without a computer-implemented transformation system.

As mentioned earlier, today's transformation systems are experimental and the problems they are capable of coping with are still more or less toy problems. However, work is under way worldwide, not only to investigate as yet unsolved theoretical problems, but also to check the methodology's feasibility on medium-size and large problems from many application areas.

In the systems themselves, the trend is away from generalized huge catalogs, and toward individual, problem-oriented subsystems based on small sets of powerful rules allied with advanced metalanguages. Of course, this does not mean that the systems will not support any storing of transformation rules. But, in order to be conveniently manageable, the catalogs must be more specific for certain groups of users and restricted to particular problem domains (e.g., sorting, graph problems, parsing). It is only by this restriction that individual rules can be made powerful enough to become widely accepted, valuable engineering tools.

Among the current approaches to the construction of formally verified software, transformational programming is certainly the most advanced and the most flexible. It already covers several phases of the classical software engineering life cycle and shows promise of covering the remaining ones. Transformational programming is likely to become a standard topic in computer science, analogous to deductive methods in mathematics. Consequently, transformation systems will become integrated parts of future software development support systems.

ACKNOWLEDGMENTS

The authors wish to thank their colleagues from the CIP group, notably, F. L. Bauer, M. Broy, A. Laut, and B. Möller, and the anonymous referees of COMPUTING SURVEYS for critical remarks and helpful suggestions on earlier versions of this paper. Comments by J. Darlington, M. Feather, and B. Paige on their part of the work reported on are also gratefully acknowledged. Special thanks go to R. Bird, R. Hyerle, and ACM's technical editor, R. Rutherford, who improved the English formulation, and to M. Krämer, I. Dippold, and S. Figura for their excellent and speedy typing.

REFERENCES

AHO, A. V., HOPCROFT, J. E., AND ULLMAN, J. D. 1974. *The Design and Analysis of Computer Algorithms.* Addison-Wesley, Reading, Mass.

ALBERGA, C. N., BROWN, A. L., LEEMAN, G. B., JR., MIKELSONS, M., AND WEGMAN, M. N. 1981. A program development tool. In *Proceedings of 8th ACM Symposium on Principles of Programming Languages* (Williamsburg, Va., Jan. 26–28). ACM, New York, pp. 92–104.

ARSAC, J. 1974. Languages sans etiquettes et transformations de programmes. In *Proceedings of 2d International Colloquium on Automata, Languages, and Programming.* Lecture Notes in Computer Science, vol. 14. Springer-Verlag, New York.

ARSAC, J. 1977a. *La Construction de Programmes Structures.* Dunod, Paris.

ARSAC, J. 1977b. Emploi de méthodes constructives en programmation. Un dossier: la fonction d'Ackermann. *RAIRO Theor. Comput. Sci. 11,* 2, 91–112.

ARSAC, J. 1978. An interactive program manipulation system for non naive users. LITP Res. Rep. 78-10, Institut de Programmation, Paris.

ARSAC, J. 1979. Syntactic source to source transforms and program manipulation. *Commun. ACM 22,* 1 (Jan.), 43–54.

ARSAC, J., AND KODRATOFF, Y. 1979. Some methods for transformation of recursive procedures into iterative ones. LITP Res. Rep. 79-2, Institut de Programmation, Paris.

ARSAC, J., AND KODRATOFF, Y. 1982. Some techniques for recursion removal from recursive functions. *ACM Trans. Program. Lang. Syst. 4,* 2 (Apr.), 295–322.

BALZER, R. 1973. A global view of automatic programming. In *Proceedings of the 3rd International Joint Conference on Artificial Intelligence* (Stanford, Calif.), pp. 494–499.

BALZER, R. 1977. Correct and efficient software implementation via semi-automatic transformations. USC/ISI Internal Rep., Information Science Institute, Univ. of Southern California, Marina del Rey.

BALZER, R. 1981a. Final report on GIST. Information Science Institute, Univ. of Southern California, Marina del Rey.

BALZER, R. 1981b. Transformational implementation: An example. *IEEE Trans. Softw. Eng. SE-7,* 1, 3–14.

BALZER, R., GOLDMAN, N., AND WILE, D. 1976. On the transformational implementation approach to programming. In *Proceedings of 2nd International Conference on Software Engineering* (San Francisco, Oct. 13–15). IEEE, New York, pp. 337–344.

BALZER, R., GOLDMAN, N., AND WILE, D. 1980. Informality in program specifications. *IEEE Trans. Softw. Eng. SE-4,* 2, 94–103.

BALZER, R. M., GOLDMAN, N. M., AND WILE, D. S. 1982. Operational specifications as the basis for rapid prototyping. *SIGSOFT Softw. Eng. Notes* (ACM) *7,* 5 (Dec.), 3–16.

BARSTOW, D. R. 1977a. Automatic construction of algorithms and data structures using a knowledge base of programming rules. Ph.D. dissertation, Stanford Univ., Stanford, Calif.

BARSTOW, D. R. 1977b. A knowledge base of organization for rules about programming. *SIGART Newsl.* (ACM) *63,* (June), 18–22.

BARSTOW, D. R. 1977c. A knowledge-based system for automated program construction. *Proceedings of the 5th International Joint Conference on Artificial Intelligence* (Cambridge, Mass.). M.I.T., Cambridge, Mass., pp. 382–388.

BARSTOW, D. R. 1979a. An experiment in knowledge-based automatic programming. *Artif. Intell. 12,* 73–119.

BARSTOW, D. R. 1979b. The roles of knowledge and deduction in program synthesis. In *Proceedings of the 6th International Joint Conference on Artificial Intelligence* (Tokyo, Aug. 20–23). International Joint Council on Artificial Intelligence, Inc., Stanford, Calif., pp. 37–43.

BARSTOW, D. R. 1979c. On convergence toward a data base of programming rules. Paper distributed at *2nd Program Transformation Workshop* (Cambridge, Mass., Sept.).

BARSTOW, D. R., AND KANT, E. 1976. Observations on the interaction between coding and efficiency knowledge in the PSI program synthesis system. In *Proceedings of the 2nd International Conference on Software Engineering* (San Francisco, Oct. 13–15). IEEE, New York, pp. 19–31.

BAUER, F. L. 1976. Programming as an evolutionary process. In *Language Hierarchies and Interfaces,* F. L. Bauer and K. Samelson, Eds. Lecture Notes in Computer Science, vol. 46. Springer-Verlag, New York, pp. 153–182.

BAUER, F. L., AND WÖSSNER, H. 1982. *Algorithmic Language and Program Development.* Springer-Verlag, New York.

BAUER, F. L., PARTSCH, H., PEPPER, P., AND WÖSSNER, H. 1977. Notes on the project CIP: Outline of a transformation system. TUM-INFO-7729, Institut für Informatik, Technische Univ. München, Munich, West Germany.

BAUER, F. L., BROY, M., GNATZ, R., HESSE, W., KRIEG-BRÜCKNER, B., PARTSCH, H., PEPPER, P., AND WÖSSNER, H. 1978. Towards a wide spectrum language to support program specification and program development. *SIGPLAN Not. (ACM) 13,* 12 (Dec.), 15–24.

BAUER, F. L., BROY, M., DOSCH, W., GEISELBRECHTINGER, F., HESSE, W., GNATZ, R., KRIEG-BRÜCKNER, B., LAUT, A., MATZNER, T., MÖLLER, B., PARTSCH, H., PEPPER, P., SAMELSON, K., WIRSING, M., AND WÖSSNER, H. 1981a. Report on a wide spectrum language for program specification and development. TUM-I8104, Institut für Informatik, Technische Univ. München, Munich, West Germany.

BAUER, F. L., BROY, M., DOSCH, W., GNATZ, R., KRIEG-BRÜCKNER, B., LAUT, A., LUCKMANN, M., MATZNER, T., MÖLLER, B., PARTSCH, H., PEPPER P., SAMELSON, K., STEINBRÜGGEN, R., WIRSING, M., AND WÖSSNER, H. 1981b. Programming in a wide spectrum language: A collection of examples. *Sci. Comput. Program. 1,* 73–114.

BECKMANN, L., HARALDSSON, A., OSKARSSON, Ö., AND SANDEWALL, E. 1976. A partial evaluator and its use as a programming tool. *Artif. Intell. 7,* 319–357.

BIDOIT, M., GRESSE, C., AND GUIHO, G. 1979. A system which synthesizes array-manipulating programs from specifications. In *Proceedings of 6th International Joint Conference on Artificial Intelligence* (Tokyo, Aug. 20–23). International Joint Council on Artificial Intelligence, Inc., Stanford, Calif., pp. 63–65.

BIERMANN, A. W. 1976. Approaches to automatic programming. In *Advances in Computers,* vol. 15. Academic Press, New York, pp. 1–63.

BIRD, R. S. 1980. Tabulation techniques for recursive programs. *ACM Comput. Surv. 12,* 4 (Dec.), 403–417.

BOYLE, J. M. 1970. A transformational component for programming language grammar. Rep. ANL-7690, Argonne National Laboratory, Argonne, Ill.

BOYLE, J. M. 1976. An introduction to transformation-assisted multiple program realization (TAMPR) system. In *Cooperative Development of Mathematical Software,* J. R. Bunch, Ed. Dept. of Mathematics, Univ. of California, San Diego.

BOYLE, J. M. 1978. Extending reliability: Transformational tailoring of abstract mathematical software. In *Proceedings of Programming Environment for Mathematical Software* (Pasadena, Calif., Oct. 18–20). ACM, New York, pp. 27–30.

BOYLE, J. M. 1980. Software adaptability and program transformation. In *Software Engineering,* H. Freeman and P. M. Lewis, Eds. Academic Press, New York, pp. 75–93.

BOYLE, J. M. 1981. Practical applications of program transformation. Unpublished manuscript.

BOYLE, J. M., AND DRITZ, K. W. 1974. An automated programming system to facilitate the development of quality mathematical software. In *Information Processing 74.* Elsevier North-Holland, New York, pp. 542–546.

BOYLE, J. M., AND MATZ, M. 1977. Automating multiple program realizations. In *Proceedings of the MRI Symposium.* Computer Software Engineering, vol. 24. Polytechnic Press, Brooklyn, N.Y., pp. 421–456.

BRASS, B., ERHARD, F., HORSCH, A., RIETHMAYER, H.-O., AND STEINBRÜGGEN, R. 1982. CIP-S: An instrument for program transformation and rule generation. TUM-I8211, Institut für Informatik, Technische Univ. München, Munich, West Germany.

BROY, M., PARTSCH, H., PEPPER, P., AND WIRSING, M. 1980. Semantic relations in programming languages. In *Information Processing 80,* S. H. Lavington, Ed. Elsevier North-Holland, New York, pp. 101–106.

BROY, M., PEPPER, P., AND WIRSING, M. 1982. On the algebraic definition of programming languages. TUM-I8204, Institut für Informatik, Technishe Univ. München, Munich, West Germany.

BURSTALL, R. M. 1977. Design considerations for a functional programming language. In *Proceedings of Infotech State of the Art Conference* (Copenhagen). Infotech Ltd., Maidenhead, UK.

BURSTALL, R. M., AND DARLINGTON, J. 1975. Some transformations for developing recursive programs. In *Proceedings of International Conference* on *Reliable Software* (Los Angeles). IEEE, New York, pp. 465–472.

BURSTALL, R. M., AND DARLINGTON, J. 1977. A transformation system for developing recursive programs. *J. ACM 24*, 1 (Jan.), 44–67.

BURSTALL, R. M., AND FEATHER, M. S. 1978. Program development by transformation: An overview. In *Les fondements de la programmation. Proceedings of Toulouse CREST Course on Programming*, M. Armirchahy and D. Neel, Eds. IRIA-SEFI, Le Chesnay, France.

BURSTALL, R. M., McQUEEN, D. B., AND SANNELLA, D. T. 1980. HOPE: An experimental applicative language. Internal Rep., Dept. of Computer Science, Edinburgh Univ., Scotland.

CHEATHAM, T. E., JR. 1981. Overview of the Harvard program development system. In *Software Engineering Environments*, H. Hünke, Ed.

CHEATHAM, T. E., JR., AND WEGBREIT, B. 1972. A laboratory for the study of automatic programming, In *Proceedings of AFIPS Spring Joint Computer Conference* (Atlantic City, N.J., May 16–18), vol. 40. AFIPS Press, Reston, Va., pp. 11–21.

CHEATHAM, T. E., JR., HOLLOWAY, G. H., AND TOWNLEY, J. A. 1979a. Symbolic evaluation and the analysis of programs. *IEEE Trans. Soft. Eng. SE-5*, 4, 402–417.

CHEATHAM, T. E., JR., TOWNLEY, J. A., AND HOLLOWAY, G. H. 1979b. A system for program refinement. In *Proceedings of 4th International Conference on Software Engineering* (Munich, West Germany, Sept. 17–19). IEEE, New York, pp. 53–62.

CHEATHAM, T. E., JR., HOLLOWAY, G. H., AND TOWNLEY, J. A. 1981. Program refinement by transformation. In *Proceedings of 5th International Conference on Software Engineering* (San Diego, Calif., Mar. 9–12). IEEE, New York, pp. 430–437.

CHUSHO, T. 1980. A good program = a structured program + optimization commands. In *Information Processing 80*, S. H. Lavington, Ed. Elsevier North-Holland, New York, pp. 269–274.

COHEN, D., SWARTOUT, W., AND BALZER, R. 1982. Using symbolic execution to characterize behavior. *SIGSOFT Soft. Eng. Notes* (ACM) 7, 5 (Dec.) 25–32.

COUSINEAU, G. 1976. Transformations de programmes iteratifs. In *Programmation*, B. Robinet, Ed. Dunod, Paris. pp. 53–74.

DARLINGTON, J. 1972. A semantic approach to automatic program improvement. Ph.D. dissertation, Dept. of Machine Intelligence, Univ. of Edinburgh, Scotland.

DARLINGTON, J. 1975. Applications of program transformation to program synthesis. In *Proceedings of International Symposium on Proving and Improving Programs* (Arc-et-Senans, France, July 1–3). IRIA, Le Chesnay, France, pp. 133–144.

DARLINGTON, J. 1978. A synthesis of several sort programs. *Acta Inf. 11*, 1, 1–30.

DARLINGTON, J. 1979. Program transformation: An introduction and survey. *Comput. Bull.* (Dec.), 22–24.

DARLINGTON, J. 1981a. An experimental program transformation and synthesis system. *Artif. Intell. 16*, 1–46.

DARLINGTON, J. 1981b. The structured description of algorithm derivations. In *Algorithmic Languages*, J. W. deBakker and H. van Vliet, Eds. Elsevier North-Holland, New York, pp. 221–250.

DARLINGTON, J., AND BURSTALL, R. M. 1973. A system which automatically improves programs. In *Proceedings of 3d International Joint Conference on Artificial Intelligence* (Stanford, Calif.). SRI, Menlo Park, Calif., pp. 479–485.

DARLINGTON, J., AND BURSTALL, R. M. 1976. A system which automatically improves programs. *Acta Inf. 6*, 41–60.

DARLINGTON, J., AND FEATHER, M. 1979. A transformational approach to modification. Paper presented at the 25th meeting of IFIP WG 2.1 (Summit, N.J., Apr.). Available from authors.

DAVIS, R., AND KING, J. 1975. An overview of production, systems. STAN-CS-75-524, Dept. of Computer Science, Stanford Univ., Stanford, Calif.

DEAK, E. 1980. A transformational approach to the development and unification of programs in a very high level language. Courant Computer Science Rep. 22, Courant Institute, New York Univ., New York.

DEAK, E. 1981. A transformational derivation of a parsing algorithm in a high-level language. *IEEE Trans. Softw. Eng. SE-7*, 1, 23–31.

DE RIVIÈRES, J. 1980. The design of an interactive program manipulation system. Master's thesis, Dept. of Computer Science, Univ. of Toronto, Canada.

DERSHOWITZ, N. 1980. The evolution of programs. Ph.D. dissertation, Dept. of Applied Mathematics, Weizmann Institute of Science, Rehovot, Israel; available as Rep. R-80-1017, Dept. of Computer Science, Univ. of Illinois, Urbana Ill.

DERSHOWITZ, N. 1981. The evolution of programs: Program abstraction and instantiation. In *Proceedings of 5th International Conference on Software Engineering* (San Diego, Calif., Mar. 9–12). IEEE, New York, pp. 79–88.

DERSHOWITZ, N., AND MANNA, Z. 1975. On automating structured programming. In *Proceedings of International Symposium on Proving and Improving Programs* (Arc-et-Senan, France, July 1–3). IRIA, Le Chesnay, France.

DERSHOWITZ, N., AND MANNA, Z. 1977. The evolution of programs: Automatic program modification. *IEEE Trans. Softw. Eng. SE-3*, 6, 377–385.

DEWAR, R. B. K., GRAND, A., LIU, S-C., AND SCHWARTZ, J. T. 1979a. Programming by refinement as exemplified by the SETL representation sublanguage. *ACM Trans. Program. Lang. Syst. 1*, 1 (July), 27–49.

DEWAR, R. B. K., SHARIR, M., AND WEIXELBAUM, E. 1979b. On transformational construction of garbage collection algorithms. Paper presented at the 26th meeting of IFIP WG 2.1 (Brussels, Dec.). Available from authors.

DIJKSTRA, E. W. 1976a. Why naive transformation systems are unlikely to work. EWD-636, privately circulated manuscript.

DIJKSTRA, E. W. 1976b. *A Discipline of Programming.* Prentice-Hall, Englewood Cliffs, N.J.

DONZEAU-GOUGE, V., HUET, G., KAHN, G., LANG, B., AND LEVY, J. J. 1975. A structure oriented program editor: A first step towards computer assisted programming. In *Proceedings of International Computing Symposium 1975* (Antibes, France). Also, Lab. Rep. 114, IRIA, Le Chesnay, France.

DONZEAU-GOUGE, V., HUET, G., KAHN, G., AND LANG, B. 1980. Programming environments based on structured editors: The MENTOR Experience. Res. Rep. 26, INRIA, Le Chesnay, France.

ECL 1974. ECL programmer's manual. TR-23-74, Center for Research in Computing Technology, Harvard Univ., Cambridge, Mass.

ERHARD, F. 1981. Programmtransformation im CIP System. Notizen zum interaktiven Programmieren 6, GI Fachausschuss 2, GI, Bonn, West Germany.

ERICKSON, R. W., Ed. 1981. AFFIRM collected papers. Information Science Institute, Univ. Southern California, Marina del Rey.

ERSHOV, A. P. 1978. On the essence of compilation. In *Proceedings of IFIP Working Conference on Formal Description of Programming Concepts* (St. Andrews, Canada, 1977), E. J. Neuhold, Ed. Elsevier North-Holland, New York, pp. 391-420.

ERSHOV, A. P. 1982. Mixed computation: Potential applications and problems for study. *Theor. Comput. Sci. 18*, 41-67.

FEATHER, M. S. 1978a. ZAP program transformation system: Primer and user manual. Res. Rep. 54, Dept. of Artificial Intelligence, Univ. of Edinburgh, Scotland.

FEATHER, M. S. 1978b. Program transformation applied to the telegram problem. In *Program Transformations*, B. Robinet, Ed. Dunod, Paris, pp. 173-186.

FEATHER, M. S. 1979. A program transformation system. Ph.D. dissertation, Univ. of Edinburgh, Scotland.

FEATHER, M. 1982a. Mappings for rapid prototyping. *SIGSOFT Softw. Eng. Notes 7*, 5 (Dec.) 17-24.

FEATHER, M. S. 1982b. A system for assisting program transformation. *ACM Trans. Program. Lang. Syst. 4*, 1 (Jan.) 1-20.

FICKAS, S. F. 1982. Automating the transformational development of software. Ph.D. dissertation, Univ. of California, Irvine.

GERHART, S. L. 1980. Complete and recursion induction in current AFFIRM. Affirm-Memo-33-SLG, Information Science Institute, Univ. Southern California, Marina del Rey.

GERHART, S. L., AND WILE, D. S. 1979. The DELTA experiment: Specification and verification of a multiple-user file updating module. In *Proceedings of Specifications of Reliable Software Conference* (Cambridge, Mass., Apr.). IEEE, New York, pp. 198-211.

GERHART, S. L., MUSSER, D. R., THOMPSON, D. H., BAKER, D. A., BATES, R. L., ERICKSON, R. W., LONDON, R. L., TAYLOR, D. G., AND WILE, D. S. 1980. On overview of AFFIRM: A specification and verification system. In *Information Processing 80*, S. H. Lavington, Ed. Elsevier North-Holland, New York, pp. 343-347.

GOAD, C. 1982. Automatic construction of special purpose programs. Rep. STAN-CS-82-897, Dept. of Computer Science, Stanford Univ., Stanford, Calif.

GOLDMAN, N., AND WILE, D. 1980. A relational data base foundation for process specification. In *Entity Relationship Approach to Systems Analysis and Design*, P. P. S. Chen, Ed. Elsevier North-Holland, New York.

GORDON, M. J., MILNER, R., AND WADSWORTH, C. 1977. Edinburgh LCF. Rep. CSR-11-77, Dept. of Computer Science, Edinburgh Univ., Scotland.

GREEN, C. 1976. The design of the PSI program synthesis system. In *Proceedings of 2d International Conference on Software Engineering* (San Francisco, Calif., Oct. 13-15). IEEE, New York, pp. 4-18.

GREEN, C. 1977. A summary of the PSI program synthesis system. In *Proceedings of 5th International Joint Conference on Artificial Intelligence* (Cambridge, Mass.). M. I. T., Cambridge, Mass., pp. 380-381.

GREEN, C. 1978. The PSI program synthesis system 1978: An abstract. In *Proceedings of 1978 National Computer Conference* (Anaheim, Calif., June 5-8), AFIPS Press, Reston, Va., pp. 673-674.

GREEN, C., AND BARSTOW, D. 1975. Some rules for the automatic synthesis of programs. In *Advance Papers of the 4th International Joint Conference on Artificial Intelligence* (Tbilisi, Georgia, USSR, Sept. 3-8). International Joint Council on Artificial Intelligence, Inc., Stanford, Calif.

GREEN, C., AND BARSTOW, D. 1976. A hypothetical dialogue exhibiting a knowledge base for a program understanding system. In *Machine Representations of Knowledge*, E. W. Elcock and D. Michie, Eds. Wiley, New York, pp. 335-359.

GREEN, C., AND BARSTOW, D. 1978. On program synthesis knowledge. *Artif. Intell. 10*, 241-279.

GREEN, C., GABRIEL, R. P., KANT, E., KEDZIERSKI, B. J., McCUNE, B. R., PHILLIPS, J. V., TAPPEL, S. T., AND WESTFOLD, S. J. 1979. Results in knowledge based program synthesis. In *Proceed-*

ings of 6th International Joint Conference on Artificial Intelligence* (Tokyo, Aug. 20–23). International Joint Council on Artificial Intelligence, Inc., Stanford, Calif., pp. 342–344.

GREEN, C., PHILIPS, J., WESTFOLD, S., PRESSBURGER, T., KEDZIERSKI, B., ANGEBRANNDT, S., MONT-REYNAUD, B., AND TAPPEL, S. 1982. Research on knowledge-based programming and algorithm design—1981. Rep. Kes. U. 81.2, Kestrel Institute, Palo Alto, Calif.

GUIHO, G., GRESSE, C., AND BIDOIT, M. 1980. Conception et certification de programmes a partir d'une décomposition par les données. *RAIRO Inf. 14*, 4, 319–351.

HARALDSSON, A. 1974. PCDB—A procedure generator for a predicate calculus data base. In *Information Processing 74*. Elsevier North-Holland, New York, pp. 375–379.

HARALDSSON, A. 1977. A program manipulation system based on partial evaluation. Ph.D. dissertation, Dept. of Mathematics, Linkoping Univ., Sweden.

HARALDSSON, A. 1978. A partial evaluator and its use for compiling iterative statements in LISP. In *Proceedings of 5th Annual Symposium on Principles of Programming Languages* (Tucson, Ariz., Jan. 23–25). ACM, New York, pp. 195–202.

HESSE, W. 1981. Methoden und Werkzeuge zur Software-Entwicklung: Einordnung und Oberblick. In *Werkzeuge der Programmiertechnik*, G. Goos, Ed., Informatik-Fachberichte, vol. 43. Springer, New York, pp. 113–153.

HEWITT, C. 1971. Desciption and theoretical analysis (using schemata) of PLANNER: A language for proving theorems and manipulating models in a robot. Ph.D. dissertation, Massachusetts Institute of Technology, Cambridge, Mass.

HUET, G., AND LANG, B. 1978. Proving and applying program transformations expressed with second-order patterns. *Acta Inf. 11*, 31–55.

HÜNKE, H., Ed. 1981. *Software Engineering Environments*. Elsevier North-Holland, New York.

IGARASHI, S., LONDON, R. L., AND LUCKHAM, D. C. 1975. Automatic program verification I: Logical basis and its implementation. *Acta Inf. 4*, 145–182.

KANT, E. 1977. The selection of efficient implementations for a high-level language. In *Proceedings of 4th ACM Symposium on Artificial Intelligence and Programming Languages* (Rochester, N.Y., Aug. 15–17). *SIGPLAN Not.* (ACM) *12*, 8 (Aug.)/ *SIGART Newsl.* (ACM) 64 (Aug.), 140–156.

KANT, E. 1979. A knowledge-based approach to using efficiency estimation in program synthesis. In *Proceedings of 6th International Joint Conference on Artificial Intelligence* (Tokyo, Aug. 20–23). International Joint Council on Artificial Intelligence, Inc., Stanford, Calif., pp. 457–462.

KANT, E., AND BARSTOW, D. R. 1981. The refinement paradigm: The interaction of coding and efficiency knowledge in program synthesis. *IEEE Trans. Softw. Eng. 7*, 458–471.

KIBLER, D. F. 1978. Power, efficiency, and correctness of transformation systems. Ph.D. dissertation, Univ. of California, Irvine.

KIBLER, D. F., NEIGHBORS, J. M., AND STANDISH, T. A. 1977. Program manipulation via an efficient production system. In Proceedings of Symposium on Artificial Intelligence and Programming Languages, (Rochester, N.Y., Aug. 15–17). *SIGPLAN Not.* (ACM) *12*, 8 (Aug.)/*SIGART Newsl.* (ACM) 64 (Aug.), 163–173.

KNUTH, D. E. 1974. Structured programming with **goto** statements. *ACM Comput. Surv. 6*, 4 (Dec.), 261–301.

KOENIG, S., AND PAIGE, R. 1981. A transformational framework for the automatic control of derived data. In *Proceedings of 7th International Conference on Very Large Data Bases* (Cannes, France, Sept. 9–11). IEEE, New York, pp. 306–318.

KOTT, L. 1978. About a transformation system: A theoretical study. In *Program Transformations*, B. Robinet, Ed. Dunot, Paris.

KOTT, L. 1982. Unfold/fold program transformations. Res. Rep. 155, INRIA Centre de Rennes, France.

LEE, S., ERICKSON, R. W., AND GERHART, S. L. 1981. Finding a design error in a distributed system: A case study. In *Proceedings of IEEE Symposium on Reliability in Distributed Software and Database Systems* (Pittsburgh, Pa., July 21–22). IEEE Computer Society, Los Alamitos, Calif.

LONDON, P., AND FEATHER, M. 1982. Implementing specification freedoms. Res. Rep. 81-100, Information Science Institute, Univ. of Southern California, Marina del Rey.

LOVEMAN, D. B. 1977. Program improvement by source-to-source transformation. *J. ACM 24*, 1 (Jan.) 121–145.

LOVEMAN, D., AND FANEUF, R. 1975. Program optimization—Theory and practice. In Proceedings of Conference on Programming Languages and Compilers for Parallel and Vector Machines. *SIGPLAN Not. 10*, 3 (Mar.), 97–102.

LOW, J. R. 1978. Automatic data structure selection: An example and overview. *Commun. ACM 21*, 5 (May) 376–385.

LUCKMANN, M. 1979. CIP-Baummodul (Benutzeranleitung). Report, Institut für Informatik, Technische Univ. München, Munich, West Germany.

MAHER, B., AND SLEEMAN, D. H. 1983. Automatic program improvement: Variable usage transformations. ACM *Trans. Program. Lang. Syst. 5*, 2 (Apr.) 236–264.

MANNA, Z., AND WALDINGER, R. 1975. Knowledge and reasoning in program synthesis. *Artif. Intell. 6*, 2, 175–208.

MANNA, Z., AND WALDINGER, R. 1977a. The automatic synthesis of recursive programs. In Proceedings of Symposium on Artificial Intelligence and Programming Languages (Rochester, N.Y., Aug. 15–17). *SIGPLAN Not.* (ACM) *12*, 8 (Aug.)/ *SIGART Newsl.* (ACM) 64 (Aug.), 29–36.

329

MANNA, Z., AND WALDINGER, R. 1977b. The automatic synthesis of systems of recursive programs. In *Proceedings of 5th International Joint Conference on Artificial Intelligence* (Cambridge, Mass., Aug. 22–25). M. I. T., Cambridge, Mass., pp. 405–411.

MANNA, Z., AND WALDINGER, R. 1978a. The synthesis of structure-changing programs. In *Proceedings of 3rd International Conference on Software Engineering* (Atlanta Ga., May 10–12). IEEE, New York, pp. 175–187.

MANNA, Z., AND WALDINGER, R. 1978b. DEDALUS—The DEDuctive Algorithm Ur-synthesizer. In *Proceedings of National Computer Conference* (Anaheim, Calif., June 5–8), vol. 47. AFIPS Press, Reston, Va., pp. 683–690.

MANNA, Z., AND WALDINGER, R. 1979. Synthesis: Dreams ⇒ Programs. *IEEE Trans. Softw. Eng.* SE-5, 4, 294–328.

MANNA, Z., AND WALDINGER, R. 1980. A deductive approch to program synthesis. *ACM. Trans. Program. Lang. Syst. 2*, 1 (Jan.), 90–121.

MANNA, Z., AND WALDINGER, R. 1981. Deductive synthesis of the unification algorithm. *Sci. Comput. Program. 1*, 5–48.

MCCUNE, B. P. 1970. The PSI program model builder: Synthesis of very high-level programs. In Proceedings of Symposium on Artificial Intelligence and Programming Languages (Rochester, N.Y., Aug. 15–17). *SIGPLAN Not.* (ACM) *12*, 8 (Aug.)–*SIGART Newsl.* (ACM) 64 (Aug.), 130–139.

MCCUNE, B. P. 1979. Building program models incrementally from informal descriptions. Ph.D. dissertation, STAN-CS-79-772, Computing Science Dept., Stanford Univ., Stanford, Calif.

MÉLÈSE, B. 1981. MENTOR: L'environnement PASCAL. Tech. Rep. 5, INRIA Centre de Roquencourt, Le Chesnay, France.

MICHIE, D., ED. 1979. *Expert Systems in the Micro Electronic Age.* University Press, Edinburgh, Scotland.

MICHIE, D. ED. 1982. *Introductory Readings in Expert Systems.* Gordon and Breach, New York.

MÖLLER, B., PARTSCH, H., AND PEPPER, P. 1983. Programming with transformations: An overview of the Munich CIP project. Submitted for publication.

MOOR, I. W., AND DARLINGTON, J. 1981. Formal synthesis of an efficient implementation for an abstract data type. Unpublished manuscript.

MOSTOW, D. J. 1981. Mechanical transformation of tasks heuristics into operational procedures. Ph.D. dissertation, Rep. CMU-CS-81-113, Carnegie-Mellon Univ., Pittsburgh, Pa.

MUSSER, D. R. 1979. Abstract data type specification in the AFFIRM system. In *Proceedings of Specifications of Reliable Software* (Cambridge, Mass., Apr. 3–5). IEEE, New York, pp. 47–57.

NEIGHBORS, J. M. 1980. Software construction using components. Ph.D. dissertation, Tech. Rep. 160, Univ. of Calif., Irvine.

PAIGE, R. 1981. Expression continuity and formal differentiation of algorithms. Rep. LCSR-TR-9, Laboratory for Computing Science Research, Rutgers Univ., New Brunswick, N.J.

PAIGE, R. 1982. Applications of finite differencing to database integrity control and query/transaction optimization. In *Advances in Database Theory*, vol. 2, J. Minker, J. M. Nicolas, and H. Gallaire, Eds. Plenum Press, New York.

PAIGE, R. 1983. Transformational programming—Application to algorithms and systems. In *Proceedings of 10th ACM Symposium on Principles of Programming Languages* (Austin, Tex., Jan. 24–26). ACM, New York, pp. 73–87.

PAIGE, R., AND KOENIG, S. 1982. Finite differencing of computable expressions. *ACM. Trans. Program. Lang. Syst. 4*, 3 (July), 402–454.

PAIGE, R., AND SCHWARTZ, J. T. 1977. Expression continuity and the formal differentiation of algorithms. In *Proceedings of 4th ACM Symposium on Principles of Programming Languages* (Los Angeles, Calif., Jan. 17–19). ACM, New York, pp. 58–63.

PARTSCH, H. 1984. The CIP transformation system. In *Program Transformation and Programming Environments*, Pepper, P., Ed. Lecture Notes in Computer Science. Springer-Verlag. New York, to be published.

PARTSCH, H., AND STEINBRÜGGEN, R. 1981. A comprehensive survey on program transformation systems. Rep. TUM I8108, Institut für Informatik, Technische Univ. München, Munich, West Germany.

PEPPER, P. 1979. A study on transformational semantics. In *Program construction*, F. L. Bauer and M. Broy, Eds. Lecture Notes in Computer Science, vol. 69. Springer-Verlag, New York, pp. 322–405.

PEPPER, P., ED. 1984. *Program Transformation and Programming Environments.* Lecture Notes in Computer Science. Springer-Verlag, New York. To be published.

RICH, C., AND SHROBE, H. E. 1978. Initial report on a LISP programmer's apprentice. *IEEE Trans. Softw. Eng. SE-4*, 6.

RICH, C., SHROBE, H. E., WATERS, R. C. 1979. Overview of the programmer's apprentice. In *Proceedings of 6th International Joint Conference on Artificial Intelligence* (Tokyo, Aug. 20–23).

RIETHMAYER, H.-O. 1981. Die Entwicklung der Bedienungskomponente des CIP Systems. Notizen zur interaktiven Programmierung 6, GI-Fachausschuss 2, GI, Bonn, West Germany.

RUTTER, P. E. 1977. Improving programs by source-to-source transformations. Ph.D. dissertation, Univ. of Illinois, Urbana.

SCHONBERG, E., SCHWARTZ, J. T., AND SHARIR, M. 1979. Automatic data structure selection in SETL. In *Proceedings of 6th ACM Symposium on Principles of Programming Languages* (San Antonio, Tex., Jan. 29–31). ACM, New York, pp. 197–210.

SCHONBERG, E., SCHWARTZ, J. T., AND SHARIR, M. 1981. An automatic technique for selection of data representations in SETL programs. *ACM Trans. Program. Lang. Syst. 3,* 2 (Apr.), 126–143.

SCHWARTZ, J. T. 1975a. On programming: An interim report of the SETL project. Courant Institute, New York Univ., New York.

SCHWARTZ, J. T. 1975b. Automatic data structure choice in a language of very high level. *Commun. ACM 18,* 722–728.

SCHWARTZ, J. T. 1977. Correct program technology. Courant Computer Rep. 12, Courant Institute, New York Univ., New York.

SHARIR, M. 1979a. Some observations concerning formal differentiation of set-theoretic expressions. Tech. Rep. 16, Computer Science Dept., Courant Institute, New York Univ., New York.

SHARIR, M. 1979b. Algorithm derivation by transformations. Tech. Rep. 021, Computer Science Dept., Courant Institute, New York Univ., New York.

SHARIR, M. 1981. Formal integration: A program transformation technique. *Comput. Lang. 6,* 35–46.

STANDISH, T. A., HARRIMAN, D. C., KIBLER, D. F., AND NEIGHBORS, J. M. 1976a. The Irvine program transformation catalogue. Dept. of Information and Computer Science, Univ. of California, Irvine, Calif.

STANDISH, T. A., KIBLER, D. F., AND NEIGHBORS, J. M. 1976b. Improving and refining transformations by program manipulation. In *Proceedings of Annual Conference,* (Houston, Tex., Oct. 20–22). ACM, New York, pp. 509–516.

STEINBRÜGGEN, R. 1980a. The use of nested scheme parameters in the system CIP. In *GI-10. Jahrestagung Saarbrücken,* R. Wilhelm, Ed. Informatik Fachberichte, 33. Springer-Verlag, New York. (Extended abstract.)

STEINBRÜGGEN, R. 1980b. Pre-algorithmic specifications of the system CIP. Part 1. Rep. TUM-I8016, Institut für Informatik, Technische Univ. München, Munich, West Germany.

STEINBRÜGGEN, R. 1981. The composition of schemes for local program transformation. In *Proceedings of 3d Hungarian Computer Science Conference* (Budapest, Jan.), M. Arato and L. Varga, Eds. Akademiai Kiado, Budapest, pp. 111–124.

STEINBRÜGGEN, R. 1982. Program development using transformational expressions. Rep. TUM-I8206, Institut für Informatik, Technische Univ. München, Munich, West Germany.

STEINBRÜGGEN, R., AND PARTSCH, H. 1984. Mathematical foundation of transformation systems. Tech. Rep., Institut für Informatik, Technische Univ. München, Munich, West Germany. To appear.

THOMPSON, D. H., SUNSHINE, C. A., ERICKSON, R. W., GERHART, S. L., AND SCHWABE, D. 1981. Specification and verification of communication protocols in AFFIRM using state transition models. RR-81-88, Information Science Institute, Univ. of Southern California, Marina del Rey.

TOWNLEY, J. A. 1981. PDS user's manual. Center for Research in Computing Technology, Harvard Univ., Cambridge, Mass.

TOWNLEY, J. A. 1982. The use of transformations to implement an algorithm. In *Proceedings of International Symposium on Programming* (Turin, Italy, Apr. 6–8). Lecture Notes in Computer Science, vol. 137. Springer-Verlag, New York, pp. 381–406.

WALDINGER, R. J. 1977. Achieving several goals simultaneously. In *Machine Representations of Knowledge,* Machine Intelligence, vol. 8, E. W. Elcock and D. Michie, Eds. Ellis Horwood, Chichester, England, pp. 94–136.

WATERS, R. C. 1982. The programmer's apprentice: Knowledge based program editing. *IEEE Trans. Softw. Eng. SE-8,* 1, 1–12.

WEGBREIT, B. 1971. The ECL programming system. In *Proceedings of AFIPS Fall Joint Computer Conference* (Las Vegas, Nev., Nov. 16–18), vol. 39. AFIPS Press, Reston, Va., pp. 253–262.

WILE, D. 1981a. Program developments as formal objects. USC/ISI Tech. Rep. Information Science Institute, Univ. of Southern California, Marina del Rey.

WILE, D. 1981b. POPART: Producer of parsers and related tools, system builder's manual. USC/ISI Tech. Rep., Information Science Institute, Univ. of Southern California, Marina del Rey.

WILE, D., BALZER, R., AND GOLDMAN, N. 1977. Automated derivation of program control structure from natural language program descriptions. In Proceedings of Symposium on Artificial Intelligence and Programming Languages (Rochester, N.Y., Aug. 15–17). *SIGPLAN Not.* (ACM) *12,* 8 (Aug.)–*SIGART Newsl.* (ACM) 64 (Aug.), 77–84.

Received July 1981; final revision accepted January 1984.

Automatic Program Improvement: Variable Usage Transformations

B. MAHER and D. H. SLEEMAN
The University of Leeds

The design objective of the Leeds Transformation System is to transform existing programs, written in a variety of languages, into "tidier" programs. The total system was conceived of as having three phases: syntactic transformations, variable usage transformations, and synthesizing features. Because programmers vary greatly in what they consider to be a more acceptable form, we have aimed to make the system as data driven as possible. (That also enables us to deal with a variety of programming languages.) The paper reviews the first two phases, reports the second in some detail, and illustrates the use of the system on an ALGOL 60 program.

Redundant assignments, redundant variables, and loop-invariant statements are discovered by means of a novel approach which represents variable usage within a program as a correspondence matrix. Potential enhancements of the system are also discussed.

Categories and Subject Descriptors: D.2.7 [**Software Engineering**]: Distribution and Maintenance—*restructuring*; D.3.4 [**Programming Languages**]: Processors—*optimization*; I.2.2 [**Artificial Intelligence**]: Automatic Programming—*program modification*; *program transformation*; K.6.3 [**Management of Computing and Information Systems**]: Software Management—*software maintenance*

General Terms: Algorithms, Design, Management, Standardization

Additional Key Words and Phrases: Variable usage, correspondence matrix, flow-of-control graph

1. INTRODUCTION

The objective of this work is to provide a software engineering tool: a data-driven transformation system. There are numerous areas in which such a tool would be useful; the major one in our view is in the criticism of working programs. It is good practice for a programmer to look objectively at his program (even though it produces correct results) with a view to making it clearer. Programmers frequently ignore this practice, with the penalty of having to spend extra time understanding the program after it has been left for a period. It is not surprising that this stage is overlooked by some programmers, since standard program methodology omits this "criticism" stage. There are a number of ways in which a program can be criticized; some are mentioned here:

(1) the use of inappropriate constructs;

Authors' present addresses: B. Maher, Computer-Based Learning Project, The University, Leeds 2, England; D. H. Sleeman, Department of Computer Science, Stanford University, Stanford, CA 94304.
Permission to copy without fee all or part of this material is granted provided that the copies are not made or distributed for direct commercial advantage, the ACM copyright notice and the title of the publication and its date appear, and notice is given that copying is by permission of the Association for Computing Machinery. To copy otherwise, or to republish, requires a fee and/or specific permission.
© 1983 ACM 0164-0925/83/0400-0236 $00.75

(2) the use of redundant code;
(3) neglecting to use functions/loops where they are appropriate;
(4) the use of inappropriate data types;
(5) inadequate comments within a program.

This work concentrates on the first three points. The Leeds Transformation System we describe can

(1) restructure programs using a set of transformation rules;
(2) remove redundant assignments, redundant variables, and loop-invariant statements;
(3) generate certain features from more basic statements.

These stages can be considered to be independent, although some "standard" transformations for the first stage require information from the second. The third stage relies on the user to set appropriate bounds for the search process.

The Leeds Transformation System can be used in a number of ways in the "criticism" of programs. For example,

(1) a set of "standard" transformations which improve the readability of a program can be applied to the program [14];
(2) the user can construct his own transformation rules for use on his own program;
(3) a program can be "modularized" using stage three of this system.

An example of a "standard" transformation is removing "jumps around statements": the transformed ALGOL 60 program segment below is considered to be more readable than the original.

Original
```
if a < 10 then goto lp;
a := b;
b := c;
lp:
```
(assuming lp: is only referenced here)

Transformed
```
if not (a < 10) then
  begin
    a := b;
    b := c;
  end;
```

It can be argued that programmers should be taught to use the second alternative instead of the first, but students whose only previous language did not contain compound statements (e.g., FORTRAN) may well continue to employ the first alternative. Additionally, large systems are very tedious and time-consuming to improve manually, but it is clearly very acceptable to apply transformations to such systems at some "off-peak" time, with a resultant saving of time/space when the "transformed" system is subsequently run. Since it is data driven, this system is a powerful tool and has other potential uses. These include

(1) automatically transforming a program into its structured counterpart, for example, FORTRAN to RATFOR;
(2) transforming *existing* programs to an installation standard;
(3) transforming unsupported features on "imported" programs to those supported by the system; and

ACM Transactions on Programming Languages and Systems, Vol. 5, No. 2, April 1983.

333

(4) "optimizing" programs. There are a number of possibilities:

(a) optimization of compiler- (macro-) generated code (as in peephole optimization [1]);
(b) transformation of features into those which a particular compiler optimizes best;
(c) transformation, for reasons of efficiency, of some high-level constructs into their lower level counterparts.

These transformations are carried out at the source level. It is our opinion that removing redundancies in programs improves their *readability*. To date, the system has been used to transform ALGOL 60, American National Standard FORTRAN,[1] and PROLON (a subset of PL/I) programs but would have to be made more efficient, as discussed in Section 5, before it could be used on an everyday basis.

1.1 Overview of the Leeds Transformation System

Earlier systems which performed syntactic transformations [4, 5, 8, 9] dealt only with a single programming language. LTS (Leeds Transformation System) is data driven and so can be used with a class of "algorithmic" programming languages. The structure of the first two phases is given in Figure 1. In order to describe an algorithmic programming language the following data are needed:

(1) the syntactic structures of that language;
(2) the program statements that affect the flow of control;
(3) the effect of particular statements on variables (i.e., definition/reference).

It was assumed, for the variable usage analysis only, that

(1) no pointers were available in the language;
(2) the flow of control could be syntactically distinguished, thereby excluding label variables.

There are a number of points to note:

(1) The syntactic transformation rules are provided as data, and this set can be extended or modified. The set currently used has been extracted from the analysis of numerous student programs; it is not claimed that this set is, or ever could be, complete.

(2) Only programs which are syntactically valid can be transformed. However, programs that generate run-time errors *can* be dealt with. Indeed, tidying up an ill-structured program could be an important first stage in finding run-time errors.

(3) The user or implementer is responsible for ensuring that the transformation rules provided do *not* change the semantics of the transformed program (the system makes no such checks).

(4) Particular characteristics of a language are removed by a preprocessor to the transformation system. For example, the range of a DO loop is made uniform (syntactically) by using "$(" and "$)". (A postprocessor reinstates the transformed program to an appropriate form.)

---

[1] As defined in ANSI X3.9-1966, American National Standard FORTRAN; however, no provision for EQUIVALENCEing statements was made.

ACM Transactions on Programming Languages and Systems, Vol. 5, No. 2, April 1983.

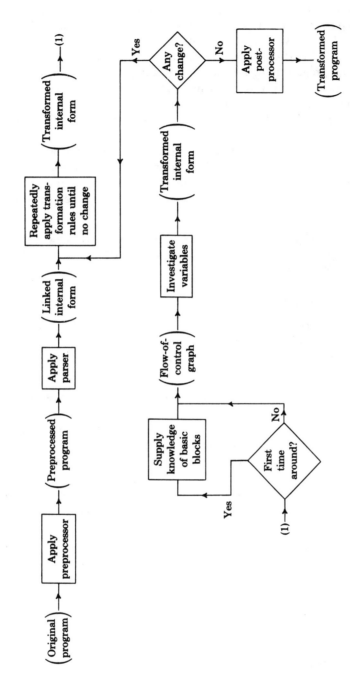

Fig. 1. Overview of system.

(5) The variable usage transformations are applied to the data structure produced by the parser. This phase detects some redundant assignments, redundant variables, and loop-invariant statements.[2]

(6) The three phases of the Leeds Transformation System are operational, and programs in several programming languages, including ALGOL, FORTRAN, and a subset of PL/I, have been transformed. Phase three has been used to "modularize" small FORTRAN and ALGOL programs.

(7) The transformation cycle, as Figure 1 shows, continues until no further changes can be made.

(8) As it is possible that the user-supplied syntactic transformations could lead to infinite loops (where the first transformation would transform a feature and another rule would reverse the transformation), LTS allows the user to specify the maximum number of transformations which are to be applied for the complete run.

Appendix A shows all the transformations, both syntactic and variable usage (VU), applied to an ALGOL program. Analogous transformations have been applied to a FORTRAN program.

Figure 2 indicates the data needed by the various phases. Below, an indication is given of the nature of these data files:

(1) The BNF data file contains the full grammar of the particular language and is used to parse the initial program into a linked list.
(2) The TAB(le) data file describes the particular program language constructs in terms of

   (a) new-block starters (statements that start a new section, e.g., subroutines, blocks);
   (b) complex statements (those statements that themselves contain statements, e.g., the ALGOL **if-then-else** statement);
   (c) designational statements (statements that explicitly change the flow of control);
   (d) the remaining statements of the language, including procedure calls.

(3) The RED(uce) data file redefines some statements of the programming language that are present in the rules.
(4) The RUL(es) data file gives the transformation rules.
(5) The FC (flow-of-control) data file contains information relevant to the second phase and gives the program statements that have significance in building up a flow-of-control graph, that is, labels, jumps, implicit loops, etc.

The RED and the FC databases for ALGOL are given in full in Appendix B, together with a subset of the BNF data for ALGOL.

2. PROGRAM OPTIMIZATION AND DATA-FLOW ANALYSIS

The most common transformations reported in the program optimization literature are redundant-variable elimination, redundant-assignment elimination, com-

---

[2] Variable usage transformations to deal with these cases appear to be common to all the languages we have so far processed and so have been "hard-wired" into the system. However, some variable usage transformation rules have been supplied as data. See Section 4.4.

ACM Transactions on Programming Languages and Systems, Vol. 5, No. 2, April 1983.

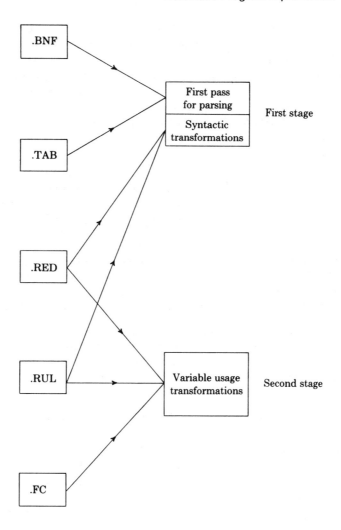

Fig. 2.   Data files provided to each stage.

mon-subexpression identification, loop expansion, variable substitution, and movement of code.

Methods to detect conditions for such optimizations require the flow-of-control graph of a program; this graph depicts the possible data paths through a program. The nodes, or basic blocks, of the flow graph correspond to sections of "straight-line" code. Their effects are summarized as "actions" on variables:

(1) definition: a variable is given a value;
(2) undefinition: a variable becomes undefined;
(3) reference: a variable is referenced.

The basic idea behind data-flow analysis is to propagate information about variable definition and reference along execution paths. This becomes more difficult when the flow graph contains loops, that is, backward links. Among the

ACM Transactions on Programming Languages and Systems, Vol. 5, No. 2, April 1983.

many techniques for performing data-flow analysis [16], we outline the "iterative" technique, proposed by Kildall [11] and improved by Kam and Ullman [10], and the "interval" technique [2, 3, 19]. In this paper, an approach is presented which solves a pertinent subset of the optimizations given above, using a simple and more transparent algorithm.

The "iterative" analysis scheme cycles through the nodes of the flow graph propagating information from each node to its successors or predecessors until no change in the information gathered is found. Let us consider variable substitution, for instance. If there is only one definition of a variable which *reaches* point p and that definition is a constant, then, if there is a reference to that variable at point p, it can be replaced by that constant. To obtain the definitions that reach each point [1], we need for each basic block

(1) the set of generated definitions that reach the end of the block (i.e., the variable associated with that definition is not redefined in the block). Let this set be called GEN(B);

(2) the set of definitions outside of basic block B that define variables that also have definitions in B. Let this set be called KILL(B).

KILL and GEN can readily be found by analyzing the program code. The next step is to compute IN(B), all definitions reaching the point just before the first statement of block B, and OUT(B), the set of all definitions reaching the point just after the last statement of B. Once IN(B) is obtained, then, for any reference to a variable in B, the definitions that reach it are known. There are two sets of equations, *data-flow equations*, that relate IN and OUT:

(1) OUT(B) = (IN(B) − KILL(B)) ∪ GEN(B) (i.e., a definition reaches the end of block B if either it reaches the beginning of B and is not killed by B or it is generated within B);

(2) IN(B) = OUT(P_1) ∪ OUT(P_2) ∪ · · · where P_1, P_2, . . . are predecessors of B (i.e., a definition reaches the beginning of block B if and only if it reaches the end of one of its predecessors)

where "−" is set subtraction and "∪" is set union.

These two equations can be solved "iteratively" starting with IN(B) = ∅ and converging to the proper values of IN and OUT. It has been proved that this method terminates [11].

The "interval" technique reduces flow graphs into unique subgraphs called intervals; these intervals can be considered to be nodes of another flow graph, which can also be reduced into intervals; etc. The basic method relies on the flow graph having the property called "reducibility," although it can be extended to handle irreducible graphs. Each interval has as its first element an interval header, which in turn is used to derive the members of the interval.

The interval technique solves the data-flow equations given earlier for reaching information in two phases [3]. The first computes GEN and KILL for all nodes in each interval, starting with the intervals of the lower order graph and passing information regarding GEN and KILL to the next higher order graph and so on. The first phase also holds information regarding loops, that is, what definitions reach the header of an interval. The second phase computes IN and OUT, processing the graphs from high to low order.

ACM Transactions on Programming Languages and Systems, Vol. 5, No. 2, April 1983.

Data-flow equations can be specified for other data-flow analysis problems which, once solved, contain enough information to make it possible to ascertain whether certain actions can be performed on the program (optimizations) without changing its meaning. Schneck [19] has implemented a FORTRAN-to-FORTRAN optimizing compiler using the interval technique. Other systems such as DAVE [17] *report* redundancies at the source level, assuming they derive from logical errors or misspellings. IPAS (Interactive Programming Advisory System) [9] also uses the iterative technique to detect and remove redundancies in FORTRAN programs.

The method proposed in this paper does not gather information for all nodes and then analyze individual nodes as in the previous methods but rather propagates essential information through the basic blocks by "collapsing" them while continually checking for certain kinds of redundancy. The algorithm is simple and, as such, is transparent to the user. For example, a redundant assignment is taken as a redefinition of a variable before an intermediate reference. The collapsing process gathers information that "could possibly" reach a certain node. In this analysis scheme parallel blocks are collapsed into one block.[3] Each of the parallel basic blocks B_i has associated variable references R_i and definitions D_i. Given two parallel basic blocks B_1 and B_2 with associated variable definitions and references D_1, R_1 and D_2, R_2, a third block B_3 would be created to represent B_1 and B_2. D_3 would comprise the set intersection of D_1 and D_2, and R_3 would comprise the set union of R_1 and R_2; this is discussed in detail in Section 4. A shortcoming of this algorithm is that redundant assignments that occur on *one* branch of a parallel block would not be detected. The variable usage algorithm operates on flow graphs with single-entry loops and a binary graph structure (see Section 5.1.2 for a discussion of "unstructured" graphs).

2.1 Data-Flow Analysis with Procedures

A major difficulty in data-flow analysis is the effect of procedure calls. In the DAVE system mentioned earlier, nonrecursive procedures can be treated by gathering information that crosses procedure boundaries, that is, entries to and exits from the procedure. To handle recursion, an iterative method can be employed [1]. Similarly, Rosen [6, 18] uses an iterative method to calculate which variables are *modified, referenced, and preserved* in procedures.

In LTS, procedures are handled with the following restrictions:

(1) no procedure/label parameters;
(2) calls to procedures are textually identifiable;
(3) entry to a procedure is through the start node of the procedure.

For each procedure a correspondence matrix showing the variables defined and referenced in the procedure body is created. For recursive procedures this correspondence matrix is used in an iterative process.

For unanalyzed procedures (e.g., separately defined procedures) an assumption is made, namely, that each parameter is defined and referenced.[4] Input/Output (I/O) routines are treated as a special case of unanalyzed procedures and are

---

[3] If the flow graph contains alternative branches, as in the case of a program conditional statement, the two paths are considered parallel. The basic blocks for each path are called parallel blocks.
[4] LTS does not handle the case where unanalyzed procedures contain global variables.

ACM Transactions on Programming Languages and Systems, Vol. 5, No. 2, April 1983.

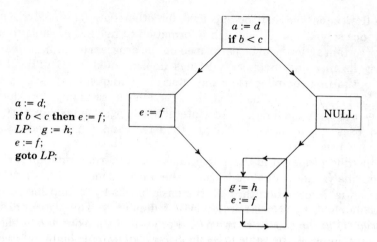

$a := d;$
if $b < c$ **then** $e := f;$
$LP:$ $g := h;$
$e := f;$
goto $LP;$

Fig. 3.   The representation of an alternate statement followed by an explicit loop.

assumed to increment a generated global variable (reflecting the changes to the pointer to the input/output stream). This is a mechanism which prevents transformations on I/O routines from taking place.

3. HOW TO DERIVE THE FLOW-OF-CONTROL GRAPH

The flow-of-control graph reflects the possible paths through the program (sometimes referred to as "data paths"). Such graphs consist of a network of nodes, which themselves consist of a series of sequential statements; that is, nodes do *not* contain any transfer-of-control statements. In this paper, nodes are referred to as basic blocks. The system must know the program statements that affect this flow [2]. Statements have been categorized as follows:

(1) labels: start a basic block;
(2) jumps: end a basic block;
(3) branching statements: terminate a basic block and are linked to two
                                      other basic blocks;
(4) nonbranching statements: form the "body" of basic blocks;
(5) implicit loops: the graph shows the backward pointer;
(6) function/procedure calls: constitute a complete basic block.

For branching (alternate) statements,[5] the conditional expression terminates the current basic block, whereas the branches controlled by the conditional statement are taken to be the start of separate parallel basic blocks. See Figure 3 for an example of how both an alternate statement and a loop are represented.

The FC (flow-of-control) data file indicates the program statements that have significance in building up a flow-of-control graph, such as labels, jumps, and implicit loops. In order to build a flow graph it is necessary to analyze each program statement to obtain the variables that are defined and referenced in it. The additional work required to process "unstructured" flow graphs is discussed in Section 5.1.2.

---

[5] An example of an alternate statement is the ALGOL **if–then–else** statement.

ACM Transactions on Programming Languages and Systems, Vol. 5, No. 2, April 1983.

4. THE CORRESPONDENCE MATRIX APPROACH

Deciding whether the value of variable a is or is not dependent in some way on the value of variable b is formally equivalent to the problem of deciding whether or not there exists a path between a node containing a and a node containing b in a graph. This problem has been solved by graph theorists, who represent the direct connections between the nodes of a graph as elements of a correspondence matrix. The algorithm to determine the "complete" correspondence matrix, which gives all the direct and indirect paths, is the transitive closure algorithm [7]:

Given M_1, compute
$$M_{s+1} = M_s * M_1 + M_1$$
until $M_{s+1} = M_s$.

In this context, a correspondence matrix may be built up by associating the value *true* (1) to the (i, j)th element of the matrix if the jth element depends on element i; otherwise, the value *false* (0) is assigned to that element. For example, given

(1) b depends on c,

(2) c on a,

(3) a on c and b,

M_1 would be

	a	b	c	
a	0	1	1	from (3)
b	0	0	1	from (1)
c	1	0	0	from (2)

The complete correspondence matrix can now be derived using the above formula, and the indirect relationships between a, b, and c inferred.

Since this matrix technique is the basis for identification of loop invariants, the other redundancy algorithms have been developed to work with correspondence matrices.

4.1 Simple Redundancies

As described earlier, one of the objectives is to uncover redundant assignments and redundant variables. To achieve this, the system builds up a correspondence matrix for the basic block, but here, instead of creating *Boolean* matrices, the entries are the *addresses* of the various statements. An assignment is redundant if the defined variable is not referenced prior to another definition of the same variable. Not until the final basic block has been processed is it possible to say whether a *variable* is redundant. If one is dealing with a block-structured language, for "final basic block" read "the last basic block where the variable is in scope."

4.1.1 *Redundancy in a Simple Block.* The correspondence matrix is produced by scanning the basic block sequentially; at each stage a check is made for redundant assignments. See Figure 4 for a detailed example.

In Figure 4c the algorithm notes that there is a second definition of variable a. Therefore, a's column is searched for an entry between 1 and 3 to determine a reference to a. An entry at 2 is found, and so no action is taken. (Figure 4d shows

ACM Transactions on Programming Languages and Systems, Vol. 5, No. 2, April 1983.

341

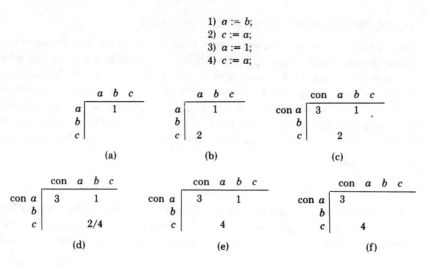

Fig. 4. Basic block redundancy. This figure gives the initial program (each line is uniquely numbered), the corresponding correspondence matrix, and the subsequent matrices produced by the algorithm (con is an abbreviation for constant).

how the system accommodates multiple definitions of variables, in this case c.) In Figure 4d, however, there is no reference to variable c before a redefinition. Therefore, statement 2 is redundant, and both the corresponderce matrix and the program are modified; see Figure 4e. This algorithm iterates until no further redundancies can be discovered; in this case the final correspondence matrix is that shown in Figure 4f. (Once statement 2 is eliminated, statement 1 is also found to be redundant.)

4.1.2 *Redundancy in Sequential Blocks.* In general, at this stage there will be N sequential blocks to be processed.[6] When we combine, say, blocks 1 and 2, it is necessary to know the last references and definitions of all the variables in block 1 and the first references and definitions of all the variables in block 2 (this information is contained in the correspondence matrices). Redundant assignments are then removed from the combined block; that is, they are deleted from what had been the "bottom" of block 1. As with the simple blocks, the combined correspondence matrix is processed until no further redundancies are discovered. The resultant correspondence matrix, $CM_{1/2}$, is then combined in an analogous process with the correspondence matrix for the next block, block 3. (The combined correspondence matrix for blocks i to j is represented as $CM_{i/j}$.) Consider the following example:

B_1
1) $a := b$
2) $a := a + c + b$
3) $b := c$

CM_1

	a	b	c
a	2	1/2	2
b			3
c			

---
[6] The N sequential blocks could arise either if redundant labels appear in the program or from collapsing parallel blocks, as discussed in Section 4.1.3.

ACM Transactions on Programming Languages and Systems, Vol. 5, No. 2, April 1983.

B_2 4) lp: $a := b$ CM_2

	a	b
a		4
b		

B_3 5) $lp1$: $a := a + b$ CM_3

	a	b
a	5	5
b		

On combining CM_1 and CM_2, as there is no reference to variable a between the last definition of a in B_1 (statement 2) and the first definition of a in B_2 (statement 4), statement 2 is therefore redundant and is deleted. When this process is iterated, statement 1 is also found to be redundant. Thus, the final $CM_{1/2}$ is

	a	b	c
a	4		
b		3	
c			

The algorithm then combines $CM_{1/2}$ with the next block, CM_3, giving $CM_{1/3}$:

	a	b	c
a	5	4/5	
b			3
c			

(Statement 4 is *not* redundant as variable a is referenced in statement 5.) Correspondence matrices derived from loops possess an extra row to show variables referenced in the loop; this effectively inhibits assignments which have an earlier reference in the loop from being deleted (by sequential collapse of correspondence matrices) from the loop. For example, given the following basic blocks and respective correspondence matrices, after combining CM_1 and CM_2 only statement 3 is deleted and not statement 2.

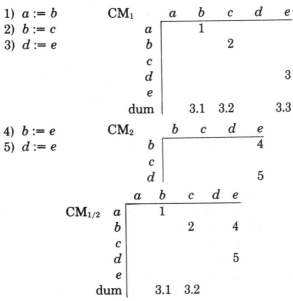

1) $a := b$ CM_1

	a	b	c	d	e
a		1			
b			2		
c					
d					3
e					
dum		3.1	3.2		3.3

2) $b := c$

3) $d := e$

4) $b := e$ CM_2

	b	c	d	e
b				4
c				
d				5

5) $d := e$

$CM_{1/2}$

	a	b	c	d	e
a		1			
b			2		4
c					
d					5
e					
dum		3.1	3.2		

4.1.3 *Producing a Correspondence Matrix from Two Alternate Blocks.* Initially, the two alternate correspondence matrices must be replaced by a single *combined* correspondence matrix. (Once the combined correspondence matrix is produced, it is further combined with other correspondence matrices as described in Section 4.1.2.) In the combined correspondence matrix a variable is only shown as being defined if it is defined on *both* branches (i.e., definitions in the correspondence matrix are the set intersection of the combined definitions from both the correspondence matrices). References from either branch are shown as references by dummy variables. For this algorithm, it is also necessary to indicate for each variable whether a reference occurs *before* the first definition (on either branch) and *after* the last definition (on either branch). Here is an example:

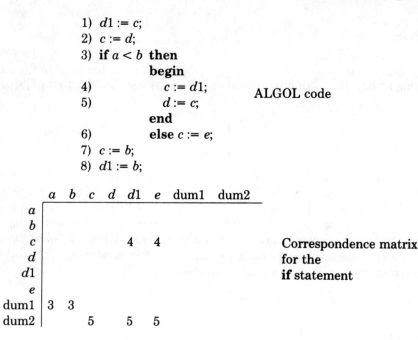

On combining this correspondence matrix with the correspondence matrix which corresponds to the earlier basic block, the algorithm determines that statement 2, "$c := d$", is redundant, and as such it is deleted.

Once a redundancy is noted in alternate blocks, it is necessary to recreate the combined correspondence matrix before the above algorithm is repeated; currently this algorithm is *not* iterated through at this level. Any more redundancies would be discovered on the next complete pass.

4.2 Loop Invariants

The correspondence matrix iteration formula described earlier is used to find loop-invariant *variables*. The variables used to control the execution of a loop are considered to be loop variant.

A *statement* is loop invariant only if all variables that the statement references are loop invariant. Once a loop-invariant statement is found, there is the subsidiary question of whether it can be moved before the loop without affecting the

ACM Transactions on Programming Languages and Systems, Vol. 5, No. 2, April 1983.

program semantics. There are three cases where a loop-invariant statement *cannot* be moved:

(1) when the loop body need not be executed;
(2) when the variable defined in the loop-invariant statement is referenced in the loop body before its definition;
(3) when the loop-invariant statement is on one path of a branching flow graph (i.e., if it is contained in a parallel block).

For case (1), the user has the option to indicate whether to move loop-invariant statements or to *report* them. Case (2) is illustrated by

```
for i := 1 step 1 until 10 do
begin
  g := i + c;
  c := f;
end;
```

Although the statement "$c := f$" is loop invariant, it cannot be moved, as the variable c is needed in the evaluation of the variable g. Case (3) is illustrated by

```
for i := 1 step 1 until 10 do
begin
  g := h + i;
  if g < h then e := d;
end;
```

Although the variables e and d are loop invariant, the loop-invariant assignment "$e := d$" cannot be moved, because its execution depends on g, which is loop variant.

4.2.1 *Loop Invariance in a Simple Block.* If a basic block is enclosed in a loop, then the correspondence matrix is set up as shown in Section 4.1.1, and the redundant variables are determined as described in Section 4.1 and are eliminated. This correspondence matrix is then transformed into a Boolean matrix by replacing all nonzero elements with *true* (1). The algorithm mentioned in Section 4 is applied to this transformed correspondence matrix, and, from the complete correspondence matrix, loop invariance is decided as follows:

(1) All variables whose diagonal elements are *true* are loop variant (dependent); columns in which diagonal elements are *true* are said to be "dependent" columns. That is, a variable whose diagonal element is true is (possibly) changed each time through a loop, in a way dependent on its previous value.

(2) All variables whose elements are *true* in a "dependent" column are loop variant, and the corresponding column(s) are designated as "dependent" column(s). That is, these variables (possibly) change each time through the loop because they are set to a value dependent on a variable that is known to change each time through the loop.

(3) A variable is loop invariant if and only if its entry in each "dependent" column is *false* (0).

Given the program in Figure 5, the algorithm determines that variables a, b, and c are loop variant and that d and e are loop invariant. Therefore, statement "$e := d$" may be removed from the loop and the program modified accordingly.

ACM Transactions on Programming Languages and Systems, Vol. 5, No. 2, April 1983.

345

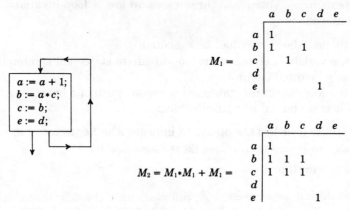

$$M_3 = M_2 * M_1 + M_1, \text{ which equals } M_2; \text{ therefore, } M_2 \text{ is the complete}$$
correspondence matrix.

Fig. 5. This figure shows the initial correspondence matrix with the direct relationships between variables and the final correspondence matrix with all the *indirect* as well as the direct relationships between variables. Note that, as this algorithm does not manipulate constants, they have not been shown in the above correspondence matrices.

4.2.2 *Loop Invariance in Sequential Blocks.* In the majority of situations a loop structure would contain more than one basic block. Two sequential blocks are combined into one block (using the algorithm of Section 4.1.2), and the algorithm of Section 4.2.1 is then applied to this block.

4.2.3 *Loop Invariance in Alternate Blocks.* In this case it is necessary to create two correspondence matrices: first, the "standard" correspondence matrix of Section 4.1.3, which is used to detect redundant assignments and variables, and, second, the loop correspondence matrix, which is used to detect loop-invariant statements (for the tidied-up block). The loop correspondence matrix for a block is the *union* of references and the *union* of definitions in both branches, as there is a possibility of *both* branches being taken. ($\mathrm{LCM}_{i/j}$ is defined as the loop correspondence matrix for blocks B_i to B_j.)

4.3 Processing Procedure Declarations and Activations

In order to analyze the use of variables in a program it is necessary to analyze both procedure declarations and activations. In Section 4.3.1 "nonrecursive" procedures are discussed; recursive procedures are considered in [13]. Consider the following section of ALGOL code and corresponding flow graph:

1) $A := B$;	$\boxed{A := B}$	
2) $P1(A, C)$;	$\boxed{P1(A, C)}$	(assuming no flow-of-control side effects)
3) $A := A + B$;	$\boxed{A := A + B}$	

```
begin
  2) integer a, b, d;
  3) procedure f1(a, b); integer a, b;
  begin
    4) integer c;
    5) c := b + 1;
    6) a := b + c;
  end;
  7) a := 10;
  8) f1(a, b + d);
  9) a := 999;
end
```

Fig. 6.   ALGOL procedure declaration and activation.

One cannot decide if statement 1 is redundant until the definitions/references of all variables affected by the call to $P1$ are known. In Section 4.3.1 an algorithm to accomplish this is outlined.

The algorithm for processing procedures has two stages. The first creates the flow graph for each procedure, noting all other calls to procedures. The second, which is performed at the end of the current program block being processed, analyzes those procedures (to uncover variable usage redundancies in the procedure bodies themselves) that cause no aliasing problems.

4.3.1 *Nonrecursive Procedures.* The ALGOL program given in Figure 6 contains a procedure declaration and its activation (line numbers are given in brackets). The procedure body is treated as a separate section (which would usually be more than one basic block) and is collapsed in the usual way (see Sections 4.1.1–4.2.3). The final correspondence matrix is then re-expressed in terms of formal parameters and local variables. For example, as variable c is local to the procedure $f1$, it would be replaced by $local1$, and other local variables would be replaced by $local2$, $local3$, etc. The formal parameters, a and b, are replaced by $vbl1$, $vbl2$, etc. The correspondence matrix for this procedure is

	con	$local1$	$vbl1$	$vbl2$
con				
$local1$	5			5
$vbl1$		6		6
$vbl2$				

When processing the flow graph, on encountering a procedure call, an "actual" correspondence matrix for the procedure is produced, where the entry associated with the statement number is a number pair: the head being the number of the line which *calls* the procedure and the tail being the corresponding entry in the procedure's correspondence matrix. Parameters called by value are considered to be referenced on entry to the procedure (FORTRAN parameter passing is assumed to be "call by location"; however, functions are assumed to be passed by value). Other parameters are substituted for their respective formal parameters in the procedure's correspondence matrix. That is, on encountering the call to $f1$

ACM Transactions on Programming Languages and Systems, Vol. 5, No. 2, April 1983.

in line 8, the following correspondence matrix is created:

	con	*local*1	*a(vbl*1)	*b(vbl*2)	*d(vbl*2)
con					
*local*1	(8 5)			(8 5)	(8 5)
*a(vbl*1)		(8 6)		(8 6)	(8 6)
*b(vbl*2)					
*d(vbl*2)					

This correspondence matrix is then processed similarly to the ways described earlier. When this correspondence matrix is combined with the correspondence matrix associated with statement 7, "$a := 10$" is found to be redundant. After further combining the correspondence matrix associated with statement 9, statement (8 6) (i.e., line 6 in the procedure) appears to be redundant. However, since this is a procedure correspondence matrix, no action can be taken; this algorithm *could* be extended such that, if *all* the calls to a procedure indicated that particular statements were redundant, then such statements could be removed. Further, to ensure that possible "aliasing" variables are not incorrectly processed, procedure bodies can *not* be analyzed until all their respective calls have been encountered. For example, given the following procedure

$P1\langle$ *formal parameters*: $a, b\rangle$
  1) $a := b + b$;
  2) $c := b$;
  3) $a := b$;

the statement "$a := b + b$" appears to be redundant, as a is not referenced before it is reset. However, a procedure call which contains multiple identical actual parameters, called by reference/name, is recognized as a situation which *could* involve aliasing, and hence the procedure body is not analyzed. Similarly, any procedures called by such a procedure will not be analyzed. Another case where aliasing might appear is when global variables appear both in a procedure body and also as actual parameters for that procedure. If this is so, the procedure body is not analyzed. These are the only aliasing conditions considered in this system; in particular, shared storage areas are not accommodated, and so EQUIVA-LENCE statements in FORTRAN are not handled. As noted in Section 1.1, LTS does not handle pointers; therefore, for indirect addressing, a more sophisticated variable-mapping algorithm would be required.

4.4 Collapsing Loop Structure

A potential optimization, sometimes called loop fusion, is to combine two loops into one. Suppose a program contains two implicit loops, $LOOP_1$ and $LOOP_2$, separated by a number of statements, B_2, all of which contain neither labels nor jumps. The first objective is to relocate the intermediate statements B_2. To achieve this, the algorithm investigates their independence with respect to both loops. The test of independence between, say, $LOOP_1$ and B_2 is as follows: variables referenced before being defined in $LOOP_1$ should *not* be defined in B_2 (and vice versa). If B_2 is found to be independent with respect to $LOOP_1$, then it is moved before $LOOP_1$; otherwise, if it is independent with respect to $LOOP_2$, then it is moved after $LOOP_2$ [12]. If these statements cannot be relocated, then loop collapse is not possible. A more sophisticated algorithm would take into account where the variables in B_2 were used in the rest of the program.

When the loops are adjacent, the following tests are performed:

(1) Determine whether both loop ranges are identical (and do not evaluate functions with side effects).
(2) Determine whether any of the loop-body statements modify their respective control variables.
(3) Determine whether there are any jumps to or from the loop bodies.
(4) Determine whether both loop bodies are independent of each other.

If all these conditions are satisfied, the two loops can be combined.

The transformation rules for these operations are included in the rule set and require both syntactic and variable usage information. See the transformations involved in transforming the programs shown in Appendix A, for instance, A12 and A13. Loops which contain uses of the *same* array will not be transformed, because an entire array is treated as one variable. (At the syntactic level it is not possible to uncover what array element is being referenced.)

4.5 Order of Processing

The flow graph is processed as follows:

(1) Create and process the correspondence matrix for each basic block.
(2) Repeatedly process the most deeply nested loop structure (creating, if necessary, the loop correspondence matrix required to cope with alternate blocks. See Section 4.2.3 and the example in Section 4.6.)
(3) Starting at the initial correspondence matrix, process the correspondence matrices in succession (creating, if necessary, the combined correspondence matrices to represent each pair of alternate blocks. See Section 4.1.3 and the example in Section 4.6.)
(4) Process the final correspondence matrix to uncover redundant variables.

Note that this algorithm is able to cope with embedded alternate statements and implicit loops. In practice, step (1) need not be carried out separately but may be combined with steps (2) and (3).

4.6 An Extended Example

Given a flow graph such as that in Figure 7a, the following processes are carried out.

(1) The individual blocks B_1 to B_{10} are processed to determine redundant assignments (step (1) of Section 4.5).
(2) The loop structure B_2–B_4 is processed, creating $LCM_{2/4}$, which is checked for loop invariants; see Figure 7b (step (2) of Section 4.5).
(3) The loop structure B_1–B_9 is processed, creating $LCM_{1/9}$, which is again checked for loop invariants; see Figure 7c. When $LCM_{1/9}$ is created, the alternate blocks B_6 and B_7 are combined as described in Section 4.2.3 (step (2) of Section 4.5).
(4) The blocks B_2–B_4 are combined sequentially, creating $CM_{2/4}$, which is checked for redundant assignments (step (3) of Section 4.5).

ACM Transactions on Programming Languages and Systems, Vol. 5, No. 2, April 1983.

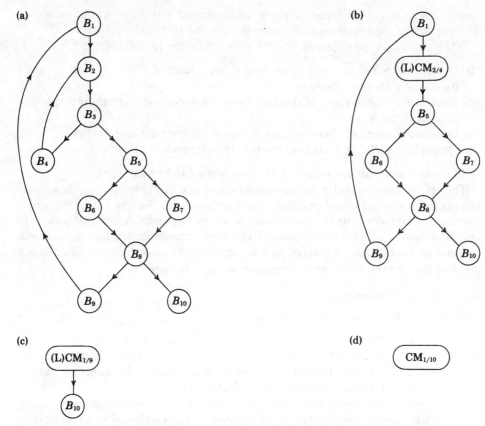

Fig. 7.   The reduction of basic blocks.

(5) The blocks B_1–B_9 are processed, creating $CM_{1/9}$; the alternate blocks B_6 and B_7 are combined as described in Section 4.1.3 (step (3) of Section 4.5).

(6) The blocks $CM_{1/9}$ and B_{10} are combined sequentially, creating $CM_{1/10}$ (see Figure 7d), which is analyzed to uncover redundant variables (step (4) of Section 4.5).

5. RESULTS AND CONCLUSIONS

The first phase of the system, the syntactic transformations, involves a great deal of pattern matching and replacement, and so it was decided that the complete system should be implemented in SNOBOL; in fact, the system has been implemented in SPITBOL [15] for the DECsystem-10. The complete LTS has 2500 lines of SPITBOL code, which occupy 44K of DEC-10 memory. LTS has successfully transformed

(1) a FORTRAN program of 1000 lines—25 transformations applied;
(2) a 500-line FORTRAN program into RATFOR—70 transformations applied;
(3) numerous ALGOL 60 programs;
(4) some small PL/I programs.

ACM Transactions on Programming Languages and Systems, Vol. 5, No. 2, April 1983.

The CPU time needed to accomplish these transformations varied according to the size of the program and the number of transformations applied. For the example given in Appendix A each transformation took on average 2 seconds CPU time. The amount of working storage needed to carry out the variable usage transformations varies depending on the complexity of the flow graph and is of order n^2 where n is the number of variables in the program block. There are a number of ways in which the efficiency of this system might be improved:

(1) using sparse-matrix techniques to reduce the amount of storage required;
(2) adopting a more efficient parsing algorithm that avoids backtracking;
(3) rewriting the system in a noninterpretive language;
(4) having a *prematcher* for syntactic transformation rules that would indicate whether a full match (binding variables and evaluating predicates) would be needed.

5.1 Enhancement of Current System

5.1.1 *User Control of Transformations.* Before the system can be used as an everyday software tool, it is very desirable that a facility be added to allow the user to *inhibit* the use of specified transformations on certain sections of the program. Programmers' views on what constitutes a readable program differ greatly, and so a particular programmer might not want, say, a procedure transformed even though it may contain redundancies.

5.1.2 *"Unstructured" Flow Graphs.* The current variable usage algorithm is able to operate on flow graphs that have a "binary" structure defined as follows:

(1) each node has no more than two predecessors;
(2) for those nodes with two predecessors, these predecessors must have only one successor.

The following graph has a "binary" structure:

The following is an "unstructured" flow graph, as nodes B, C, and G do not comply with the above definition:

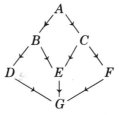

This flow graph would need extra processing before being passed to the variable usage algorithm. This processing would involve creating copies of particular

ACM Transactions on Programming Languages and Systems, Vol. 5, No. 2, April 1983.

nodes, which would be "guarded" to prevent any redundancies being removed from them. However, this limitation could be readily removed.

5.2 Further Work

It is desirable that the system be able to accomplish the following:

(1) simple generalizations;
(2) creating local program blocks (cf. ALGOL 60 blocks).

Often one sees programs written to solve one case of a particular problem when the whole of a range of tasks could be obtained by merely providing the value for a variable during execution. Similarly, in languages which allow the dynamic declaration of arrays, a specific program can be made more general by modifying it so that the size of the array is dependent on the value provided at run time.

The use of local program blocks might allow for a more efficient use of storage, but a program which had a large number of blocks might not be acceptable to a programmer. Programmers frequently attempt to strike a balance between program readability and efficiency on this issue and create a block for variables which are used in the "same section" of the program.

5.3 Summary

Transformation systems usually deal with improving the efficiency or some other predetermined criterion of a program. The first stage of LTS allows the user to control the transformation process. The second phase complements the first by removing and/or reporting, at the source level, redundancies in the program (redundant assignments and variables together with loop-invariant statements). The third stage will complete the program transformation system by presenting the user with a facility to generate features in his program.

APPENDIX A. A TRANSFORMED ALGOL PROGRAM

A1. The Original Program

```
begin
    integer A1, B1, I, J, C1, C2;
    integer array A[0:10], B[0:10];
    I := 10;
    I := 0;
    LP:  READ(A[I]);
    READ(B[I]));
    C1 := I;
    I := I + 1;
    if I ≤ 10 then goto LP;
    C1 := 10;
    A1 := 0;
    B1 := 0;
    A1 := A1;
    I := 0;
    goto LP1;
    J := 0;
    LP1:  C2 := 10;
    A1 := A1 + A[I];
    I := I + 1;
```

ACM Transactions on Programming Languages and Systems, Vol. 5, No. 2, April 1983.

352

```
    if I ≤ 10 then goto LP1;
    for J := 0 step 1 until 10 do
        B1 := B1 + B[J];
    if B1 ≠ 0 then PRINT(A1/B1);
end
```

A2. The Program After Application of the Transformation for an Assignment to the Same Variable

```
begin
    integer A1, B1, I, J, C1, C2;
    integer array A[0:10], B[0:10];
    I := 10;
    I := 0;
    LP:   READ(A[I]);
    READ(B[I]);
    C1 := I;
    I := I + 1;
    if I ≤ 10 then goto LP;
    C1 := 10;
    A1 := 0;
    B1 := 0;
    I := 0;   ←————————
    goto LP1;
    J := 0;
    LP1:   C2 := 10;
    A1 := A1 + A[I];
    I := I + 1;
    if I ≤ 10 then goto LP1;
    for J := 0 step 1 until 10 do
        B1 := B1 + B[J];
    if B1 ≠ 0 then PRINT(A1/B1);
end
```

A3. The Program After Application of the Transformation for Unreachable Code

```
begin
    integer A1, B1, I, J, C1, C2;
    integer array A[0:10], B[0:10];
    I := 10;
    I := 0;
    LP:   READ(A[I]);
    READ(B[I]);
    C1 := I;
    I := I + 1;
    if I ≤ 10 then goto LP;
    C1 := 10;
    A1 := 0;
    B1 := 0;
    I := 0;
    goto LP1;   ←————————
    LP1:   C2 := 10;
    A1 := A1 + A[I];
    I := I + 1;
    if I ≤ 10 then goto LP1;
    for J := 0 step 1 until 10 do
        B1 := B1 + B[J];
    if B1 ≠ 0 then PRINT(A1/B1);
end
```

ACM Transactions on Programming Languages and Systems, Vol. 5, No. 2, April 1983.

353

A4. The Program After Application of the Transformation for Creating an Implicit Loop

```
begin
  integer A1, B1, I, J, C1, C2;
  integer array A[0:10], B[0:10];
  I := 10;
  for I := 0 step 1 until 10 do
  begin
    READ[A(I));
    READ(B[I]);
    C1 := I;
  end;
  C1 := 10;
  A1 := 0;
  B1 := 0;
  I := 0;
  goto LP1;
  LP1:   C2 := 10;
  A1 := A1 + A[I];
  I := I + 1;
  if I ≤ 10 then goto LP1;
  for J := 0 step 1 until 10 do
    B1 := B1 + B[J];
  if B1 ≠ 0 then PRINT (A1/B1);
end
```

A5. The Program After Application of the Transformation for Jumping to the Next Statement

```
begin
  integer A1, B1, I, J, C1, C2;
  integer array A[0:10], B[0:10];
  I := 10;
  for I := 0 step 1 until 10 do
  begin
    READ(A(I));
    READ(B[I]);
    C1 := I;
  end;
  C1 := 10;
  A1 := 0;
  B1 := 0;
  I := 0;
  LP1:   C2 := 10;
  A1 := A1 + A[I];
  I := I + 1;
  if I ≤ 10 then goto LP1;
  for J := 0 step 1 until 10 do
    B1 := B1 + B[J];
  if B1 ≠ 0 then PRINT (A1/B1);
end
```

A6. The Program After Application of the Transformation for Creating an Implicit Loop

```
begin
  integer A1, B1, I, J, C1, C2;
  integer array A[0:10], B[0:10];
  I := 10;
```

```
  for I := 0 step 1 until 10 do
  begin
    READ(A[I]);
    READ(B[I]);
    C1 := I;
  end;
  C1 := 10;
  A1 := 0;
  B1 := 0;
  for I := 0 step 1 until 10 do ⎤
  begin                         ⎥
    C2 := 10;                   ⎬ ←——————
    A1 := A1 + A[I];            ⎥
  end;                          ⎦
  for J := 0 step 1 until 10 do
    B1 := B1 + B[J];
  if B1 ≠ 0 then PRINT(A1/B1);
end
```

A7. The Program After Application of the Transformation for Moving a Loop Invariant

```
begin
  integer A1, B1, I, J, C1, C2;
  integer array A[0:10], B[0:10];
  I := 10;
  for I := 0 step 1 until 10 do
  begin
    READ(A[I]);
    READ(B[I]);
    C1 := I;
  end;
  C1 := 10;
  A1 := 0;
  B1 := 0;
  C2 := 10; ←——————————————
  for I := 0 step 1 until 10 do
    A1 := A1 + A[I];
  for J := 0 step 1 until 10 do
    B1 := B1 + B[J];
  if B1 ≠ 0 then PRINT(A1/B1);
end
```

A8. The Program After Application of the Transformation for Removing a Redundant Assignment

```
begin
  integer A1, B1, I, J, C1, C2;
  integer array A[0:10], B[0:10]; ←——————————
  for I := 0 step 1 until 10 do
  begin
    READ(A[I]);
    READ(B[I]);
    C1 := I;
  end;
  C1 := 10;
  A1 := 0;
  B1 := 0;
  C2 := 10;
```

ACM Transactions on Programming Languages and Systems, Vol. 5, No. 2, April 1983.

355

```
    for I := 0 step 1 until 10 do
      A1 := A1 + A[I];
    for J := 0 step 1 until 10 do
      B1 := B1 + B[J];
    if B1 ≠ 0 then PRINT (A1/B1);
  end
```

A9. The Program After Application of the Transformation for Removing a Redundant Assignment

```
begin
  integer A1, B1, I, J, C1, C2;
  integer array A[0:10], B[0:10];
  for I := 0 step 1 until 10 do
   begin
     READ(A[I]);
     READ(B[I]);  ←——————
   end;
  C1 := 10;
  A1 := 0;
  B1 := 0;
  C2 := 10;
  for I := 0 step 1 until 10 do
    A1 := A1 + A[I];
  for J := 0 step 1 until 10 do
      B1 := B1 + B[J];
  if B1 ≠ 0 then PRINT (A1/B1);
end
```

A10. The Program After Application of the Transformation for Removing a Redundant Assignment

```
begin
  integer A1, B1, I, J, C2;
  integer array A[0:10], B[0:10];
  for I := 0 step 1 until 10 do
  begin
    READ(A[I]);
    READ(B[I]);
  end;  ←——————
  A1 := 0;
  B1 := 0;
  C2 := 10;
  for I := 0 step 1 until 10 do
    A1 := A1 + A[I];
  for J := 0 step 1 until 10 do
    B1 := B1 + B[J];
  if B1 ≠ 0 then PRINT(A1/B1);
end
```

A11. The Program After Application of the Transformation for Removing a Redundant Assignment

```
begin
  integer A1, B1, I, J;
  integer array A[0:10], B[0:10];
  for I := 0 step 1 until 10 do
```

ACM Transactions on Programming Languages and Systems, Vol. 5, No. 2, April 1983.

356

```
begin
  READ(A[I]);
  READ(B[I]);
end;
A1 := 0;
B1 := 0;  ←————————
for I := 0 step 1 until 10 do
  A1 := A1 + A[I];
  for J := 0 step 1 until 10 do
    B1 := B1 + B[J];
  if B1 ≠ 0 then PRINT(A1/B1);
end
```

A12. The Program After Application of the Transformation for Collapsing Implicit Loops

```
begin
  integer A1, B1, I;
  integer array A[0:10], B[0:10];
  for I := 0 step 1 until 10 do
  begin
    READ(A[I]);
    READ(B[I]);
  end;
  A1 := 0;
  B1 := 0;
  for I := 0 step 1 until 10 do
  begin
    A1 := A1 + A[I];      ⎫
    B1 := B1 + B[I];      ⎬ ←————————
  end;                     ⎭
  if B1 ≠ 0 then PRINT(A1/B1);
end
```

A13. The Program After Application of the Transformation for Relocating Statements

```
begin
  integer A1, B1, I;
  integer array A[0:10], B[0:10];
  A1 := 0; ⎫ ←————————
  B1 := 0; ⎭
  for I := 0 step 1 until 10 do
  begin
    READ(A[I]);
    READ(B[I]);
  end;
  for I := 0 step 1 until 10 do
  begin
    A1 := A1 + A[I];
    B1 := B1 + B[I];
  end;
  if B1 ≠ 0 then PRINT(A1/B1);
end
```

No more transformations can be applied.

ACM Transactions on Programming Languages and Systems, Vol. 5, No. 2, April 1983.

B. Maher and D. H. Sleeman

APPENDIX B

B1. RED(uce) Data File

TC = 'if' BOOLEX 'then' STATEMENT
//**then** conditional.

EC = 'if' BOOLEX 'then' STATEMENT 'else' STATEMENT
//**else** conditional.

JUMP = 'goto' DEFLABEL
//Jump.

ASS = VBL ':=' ARITHEX
//Assignment.

STEPASS = VBL ':=' VBL '+' ARITHEX
//Step assignment.

FOR = 'for' VBL ':=' ARITHEX 'step' ARITHEX 'until' ARITHEX 'do'
STATEMENT
//**for** loop.

FOR2 = 'for' VBL ':=' ARITHEX 'while' BOOLEX 'do' STATEMENT
//**for** loop.

FOR3 = 'for' VBL ':=' ARITHEX ',' ARITHEX 'while' BOOLEX 'do'
STATEMENT
//**for** loop.

LABEL = ID ':'
//Label.

B2. FC (Flow-of-Control) Data File

FOR(D, U, U, U, S)
FOR2(D, U, U, S)
FOR3(D, U, U, U, S)
LABEL(D)
JUMP(D)
ASS(D, U)
TC(U, S)
EC(U, S, S)
*

J*JUMPFC	JUMP STATEMENTS
O*ASSFC | ECFC | TCFC	ORDINARY STATEMENTS
L*FORFC | FOR2FC	IMPLICIT LOOP STATEMENTS THAT MAY BE EXECUTED
L1*FOR3FC	IMPLICIT LOOP STATEMENTS THAT ARE ALWAYS EXECUTED
LA*LABELFC	LABEL

Here S represents a statement, D a variable which has a value assigned to it, and U an expression (e.g., the right-hand side of an assignment statement or the Boolean expression of a conditional). FOR, LABEL, etc., are as defined in the RED(uce) data file.

ACM Transactions on Programming Languages and Systems, Vol. 5, No. 2, April 1983.

B3. BNF Data File (A Subset of the BNF Description for ALGOL)

PROCDEC	::= 'procedure' *⟨PROCHEADING⟩* *⟨STATEMENT⟩*
	| *⟨TYPE⟩* 'procedure' *⟨PROCHEADING⟩*
	⟨STATEMENT⟩
FORLIST2	::= *⟨ARITHEX⟩* 'step' *⟨ARITHEX⟩* 'until'
	⟨ARITHEX⟩
FORLIST1	::= *⟨FORLIST2⟩*
	| *⟨ARITHEX⟩* 'while' *⟨BOOLEX⟩*
	| *⟨ARITHEX⟩*
FORLIST	::= *⟨NIL⟩*
	| ',' *⟨FORLIST1⟩*
	| ',' *⟨FORLIST1⟩* *⟨FORLIST⟩*
FOR	::= 'for' *⟨VBL⟩* ':=' *⟨ARITHEX⟩* 'step'
	⟨ARITHEX⟩ 'until' *⟨ARITHEX⟩* *⟨FOR-LIST⟩* 'do' *⟨STATEMENT⟩*
FOR2	::= 'for' *⟨VBL⟩* ':=' *⟨ARITHEX⟩* 'while'
	⟨BOOLEX⟩ *⟨FORLIST⟩* 'do' *⟨STATE-MENT⟩*
FOR3	::= 'for' *⟨VBL⟩* ':=' *⟨ARITHEX⟩* *⟨FORLIST⟩* 'do'
	⟨STATEMENT⟩
GOTO	::= 'goto' *⟨DESIGEX⟩*
LEFTPART	::= *⟨VBL⟩* ':=' | *⟨PROCID⟩* ':='
LEFTPARTLIST	::= *⟨LEFTPART⟩* *⟨LEFTPARTLIST⟩*
	| *⟨LEFTPART⟩*
ASS	::= *⟨LEFTPARTLIST⟩* *⟨ARITHEX⟩*
	| *⟨LEFTPARTLIST⟩* *⟨BOOLEX⟩*
TC	::= 'if' *⟨BOOLEX⟩* 'then' *⟨STATEMENT⟩*
EC	::= 'if' *⟨BOOLEX⟩* 'then' *⟨STATEMENT⟩* 'else'
	⟨STATEMENT⟩
COMHEAD	::= 'begin'
COMTAIL	::= 'end'

ACKNOWLEDGMENTS

We acknowledge conversations with John Darlington (Imperial College, London). We thank the referees for their helpful comments on an earlier draft of this paper and would also like to thank Mrs. Eniko Kortvelyesi (SZAMOK, Budapest) for forcing us to define more precisely the data required by LTS and for formulating the data for a subset of PL/I. One of us, Brian Maher, acknowledges an SRC studentship, which has enabled him to undertake this work.

Finally, we acknowledge countless computer science undergraduates who inadvertently brought this fascinating topic to our attention.

REFERENCES

1. AHO, A.V., AND ULLMAN, J.D. *Principles of Compiler Design.* Addison-Wesley, Reading, Mass., 1978.
2. AHO, A.V., AND ULLMAN, J.D. *The Theory of Parsing, Translation, and Compiling,* vol. 2: *Compiling.* Prentice-Hall, Englewood Cliffs, N.J., 1973, pp. 845–963.

ACM Transactions on Programming Languages and Systems, Vol. 5, No. 2, April 1983.

359

3. ALLEN, F.E., AND COCKE, J.   A program data flow analysis procedure. *Commun. ACM 19*, 3 (Mar. 1976), 137–147.

4. ARSAC, J.J.   Syntactic source to source transforms and program manipulation. *Commun. ACM 22*, 1 (Jan. 1979), 43–54.

5. BAKER, B.S.   An algorithm for structuring flowgraphs. *J. ACM 24*, 1 (Jan. 1977), 98–120.

6. BARTH, J.M.   A practical interprocedural data flow analysis algorithm. *Commun. ACM 21*, 9 (Sept. 1978), 724–736.

7. CHRISTOFIDES, N.   *Graph Theory: An Algorithmic Approach.* Academic Press, New York, 1975, pp. 17–21.

8. DARLINGTON, J., AND BURSTALL, R.M.   A system which automatically improves programs. In Proceedings of the Third International Joint Conference on Artificial Intelligence, 1973, pp. 479–485.

9. GILLETT, W.   An interactive program advising system. In Papers of the ACM SIGCSE–SIGCUE Technical Symposium: Computer Science and Education. Published as joint issue: *SIGCSE Bull. 8*, 1 and *SIGCUE Topics 2* (Feb. 1976), 335–341.

10. KAM, J.B., AND ULLMAN, J.D.   Global data flow analysis and iterative algorithms. *J. ACM 23*, 1 (Jan. 1976), 158–171.

11. KILDALL, G.A.   A unified approach to global program optimization. In Conference Record of ACM Symposium on Principles of Programming Languages, Boston, Oct. 1–3, 1973, pp. 194–206.

12. LOVEMAN, D.B.   Program improvement by source-to-source transformation. *J. ACM 24*, 1 (Jan. 1977), 121–145.

13. MAHER, B.   A Program Transformation System. Ph.D. dissertation, Univ. of Leeds, Leeds, England.

14. MAHER, B., AND SLEEMAN, D.H.   A data driven system for syntactic transformations. *SIGPLAN Notices* (ACM) *16*, 10 (Oct. 1981), 50–52.

15. MCCANN, A.P., HOLDEN, S.C., AND DEWAR, R.B.K.   Macro SPITBOL—DECsystem-10 version. Tech. Rep. 94, Dep. of Computer Studies, Univ. of Leeds, Leeds, England, Dec. 1976.

16. MUCHNICK, S.S., AND JONES, N.D.   *Program Flow Analysis: Theory and Applications.* Prentice-Hall, Englewood Cliffs, N.J., 1981.

17. OSTERWEIL, L.J., AND FOSDICK, L.D.   DAVE—A validation error detection and documentation system for FORTRAN programs. *Softw. Pract. Exper. 6* (1976), 473–486.

18. ROSEN, B.K.   Data flow analysis for procedural languages. *J. ACM 26*, 2 (Apr. 1979), 322–344.

19. SCHNECK, P.B., AND ANGEL, E.   A FORTRAN to FORTRAN optimizing compiler. *Comput. J. 16*, 4 (1973), 322–329.

Received October 1979; revised March 1980, April 1981, and February 1982; accepted May 1982

ACM Transactions on Programming Languages and Systems, Vol. 5, No. 2, April 1983.

360

Annotated References
on Software Restructuring

In addition to the papers of this Tutorial, the reader will find the following references also informative.

Arnold, R.S. *On the Generation and Use of Quantitative Criteria for Assessing Software Maintenance Quality,* Ph.D dissertation, University of Maryland, 1983. Available as dissertation number 8402525 from University Microfilms International, 300 N. Zeeb Rd., Ann Arbor, Mich. 48106.

A straightforward approach to applying software metrics during software maintenance. The emphasis is on how measurements can be used to stimulate concrete actions for improving software maintenance. (The technique may also be used during software development.) A detailed example, using software maintenance data from the NASA Goddard Space Flight Center, is given. This work is much expanded from the paper, "The Dimensions of Healthy Maintenance," by R.S. Arnold and D.A. Parker (*Proceedings of the 6th International Conference on Software Engineering.* Washington, D.C.: IEEE Computer Society, 1982).

Arnold, R.S. A survey of 24 techniques for software restructuring. *Proceedings of the 2nd National Conference on EDP Software Maintenance,* Silver Spring, Md.: U.S. Professional Development Institute, 1984. pp. 402-425.

A survey which lays out a range of restructuring techniques and attempts to qualitatively assess their relative usefulness.

Ashcroft, E. and Manna, Z. The translation of 'goto' programs into 'while' programs, in *Proceedings of the 1971 IFIP Congress.* Amsterdam: North-Holland, 1971. pp. 250-260.

An early software restructuring paper, significant because of its constructive algorithm for transforming any program into a structured program. "Structure" here is in terms of control structures used by the program. This technique was substantially improved in the book by R.C. Linger, H.D. Mills, and R.J. Witt mentioned below.

Baker, B. An algorithm for structuring flowgraphs. *Journal of the ACM,* Vol. 24, no. 1 (January 1977). pp. 98-120.

Presents an algorithm for structuring programs, based on a graph of the program's control flow. The algorithm was used as a basis for the "Struct" tool, available on UNIX for rewriting FORTRAN programs.

Bohm, C. and Jacopini, G. Flow diagrams, Turing machines, and languages with only two formation rules. *Communications of the ACM,* Vol. 9, no. 5 (May 1966). pp. 366-371.

One of the earliest papers on program restructuring, significant because it showed 'goto' statements are not theoretically necessary for creating arbitrary programs. The proof of this was constructive, and at least one commercially available tool has been refined from this algorithm.

Brooks, F. *The Mythical Man-Month.* Reading, Mass.: Addison-Wesley, 1975.

A software engineering classic, but of interest here because it proposes that maintenance must lead to poor software structure (p.123). An empirical fact of the time perhaps, but not a theoretical necessity.

Bush, E. The automatic restructuring of COBOL. *Proceedings of the Conference on Software Maintenance—1985.* Washington, D.C.: IEEE Computer Society, 1985. pp. 35-41.

Outlines RECODER, a proprietary tool for restructuring the control flow of COBOL programs. The restructuring approach is based on first representing a program's logic as a graph of control flow, then successively transforming the graph using proprietary transformations, then using the final control graph to generate the restructured COBOL program. The approach has its historical roots in the work by Bohm and Jacopini (see above). RECODER is available from Language Technology, Salem, Massachusetts.

Canning, R. (ed.) Rejuvenate your old systems. *EDP Analyzer,* Vol. 22, no. 3 (March 1984). pp. 1-16.

An excellent account of some practical case studies for restructuring software. This, and its companion article next, are well worth reading.

Canning, R. (ed.) Tools to rejuvenate your old systems. *EDP Analyzer,* Vol. 22, no. 4 (April 1984). pp. 1-16.

More insightful case studies.

de Balbine, G. Better manpower utilization using automatic restructuring. In Parikh, G. (ed.) *Techniques of Program and System Maintenance,* Cambridge, Mass.: Winthrop, 1982, pp. 217-233.

This work, originally reported in 1975, describes an automated approach to restructuring FORTRAN programs. The idea was first to design S-FORTRAN, a version of

FORTRAN with "structured" constructs. S-FORTRAN serves "both as a target language for restructured programs and as an implementation language for new programs." A structuring engine, consisting of 30,000 lines of Pl/1 code, then restructures a FORTRAN program into a pretty-printed S-FORTRAN version, which may be used during maintenance by programmers. The S-FORTRAN version of a program is compiled by inputting the program to an S-FORTRAN-to-FORTRAN preprocessor prior to compilation by the FORTRAN compiler.

Carlyle, R. E. Can AI save COBOL? *Datamation,* News in Perspective section, September 15, 1985.

Discusses three commercially available tools (Structured Retrofit, SUPERSTRUCTURE, and RECODER) for restructuring COBOL code.

Federal Conversion Support Center, "Software Improvement—A Needed Process in the Federal Government," *Report OSD-81-102,* Federal Conversion Support Center, Falls Church, Va., June 3, 1981. 14 pp.

The earliest report in the Federal Conversion Support Center series on software improvement. This short report discusses why software should be improved and what the goals of software improvement should be.

Federal Conversion Support Center, "Guidelines for Planning and Implementing a Software Improvement Program (SIP)," *Report OSD/FCSC-83/004,* Federal Conversion Support Center, Falls Church, Va., May 1983. 75 pp.

A management-oriented overview for planning a software improvement program. This report is a good summary of the software improvement program.

Federal Conversion Support Center, "Establishing a Software Engineering Technology (SET)," Federal Conversion Support Center, *Report OSD/FCSC-83/014,* Falls Church, Va., May 1983. 105 pp.

A description of software engineering practices, standards, guidelines, and tools that would support and be a part of the software improvement process.

Federal Conversion Support Center, "The Software Improvement Process—Its Phases and Tasks," (two parts), Federal Conversion Support Center, *Report OSD/FCSC-83/006,* Falls Church, Va., July 1983. 229 pp. plus appendices

A detailed management guide to implementing a software improvement program.

Gillin, P. Spaghetti code glut spawns program restructuring services. *Computerworld,* Vol. XIX, no. 4 (Jan. 28, 1985). pp. 1,10.

Discusses three commercially available tools for restructuring COBOL programs. The tools are: a COBOL restructuring service from Language Technology, Inc. (see the paper above by E. Bush), Structured Retrofit from Peat, Marwick, Mitchell & Co., and SUPERSTRUCTURE from Group Operations, Inc.

Higgins, D.A. Structured maintenance: new tools for old problems. *Computerworld* ("In Depth" section), Vol. XV, no. 24 (June 15, 1981).

Concerns how to restructure a program into a structure more easily understood. The idea is, if a program is hard to understand, restructure it into a form more easily understood and then make further restructuring decisions. In this case, the form of the "more easily understood" structure comes from the Warnier-Orr design methodology. This methodology seeks to have a program's structure mirror the structure of the data which the program operates on.

Kapur, G.K. Software maintenance. *Computerworld* ("In Depth" section) Vol. XVII, no. 39 (September 26, 1983). pp. ID/13-ID/22.

This paper presents a software restructuring methodology called a "maintenance reduction plan." The plan involves three phases: a maintenance management audit, a software system audit, and software rehabilitation. The last phase involves (1) improving program format, logic, and documentation, (2) updating all system documentation, and (3) rechecking the quality ratings for program modules to ensure the ratings have improved.

Lawrence, M. An examination of evolution dynamics, in *Proceedings of the 6th International Conference on Software Engineering.* Washington, D.C.: IEEE Computer Society, 1982. pp. 188-196.

An independent critique of the five "laws" of software evolution mentioned by M. Lehman (see below). Software release data from several software systems is presented and analyzed. Except for the first law, little evidence supported the laws.

Lehman, M.M. Programs, life cycles, and laws of software evolution. *Proceedings of the IEEE,* Vol 68, No. 9 (September 1980). pp. 1060-1076.

An informative article on how programs evolve. Five "laws" of program evolution are presented. The paper has a good practical example on how to decide in which direction a system should evolve.

Linger, R.C., Mills, H.D., and Witt, R.J. *Structured Programming: Theory and Practice.* Reading, Mass.: Addison-Wesley, 1979.

A common problem with restructuring approaches that produce a theoretically "structured" program is that the resulting code is hard to understand. The new program's structure is strange and the correspondence between the new program's code and the old code—especially the documentation—may be obscure.

Chapter 4 of this book concerns code readability as well as code structure for its own sake. A mathematically precise definition of a "structured program" is given. A theorem is given, whose constructive proof shows how to transform an arbitrary program into a structured program. (This theorem was first proven in the paper by Mills discussed below.) Then the structured program is restructured for readability. The idea is to start with the giant case statement version of a program, a version which can be mechanically generated (see the paper above by Ashcroft and Manna). Then the case statement is iteratively modified for increased readability. This involves inspecting the cases in the case statement for "islands" of structure, simplifying the case statement by encapsulating the structured islands, and reexamining the program for further simplification.

Chapter 4 is a good place to start for those wanting to build their own tool for restructuring a program's control flow. The IBM Corporation has recently done this, for COBOL programs. The tool is called COBOL Structuring Facility (commercially available in February 1986).

Marsh, R.E. Application maintenance: one shop's experience and organization. *Proceedings of the National Computer Conference,* Vol. 52, Arlington, VA: AFIPS Press, 1983. pp. 145-153.

One of the few papers with any empirical measurements of software restructuring activity. Here restructurings ("preventive maintenance") constituted 2.2% of maintenance requests. The effort expended for each restructuring averaged .9 person-days.

Martin, J. and McClure, C. *Software Maintenance: The Problem and Its Solution.* Englewood Cliffs, N.J.: Prentice-Hall, 1983.

The authors take an all-or-nothing approach to restructuring: don't restructure a hard-to-maintain program, rewrite it instead (p. 12). This may be reasonable advice for poorly structured short code, but may be unrealistic for code many thousands of lines long.

Mills, H.D. Mathematical foundations for structured programming. First written in 1972; reprinted in Mills, H.D., *Software Productivity,* Boston: Little, Brown, and Co., 1983.

Among other results, this paper gives a theorem whose constructive proof shows how to restructure a proper program into a program which uses sequence, if-then-else, and do-until statements along with several logical and selection operators. (A proper program has a control flow graph with exactly one input line and one output line, and for each node in the graph there is a path through the node from the input line to the output line.) This paper supplies some of the mathematical work used by Linger, Mills, and Witt in their book mentioned above.

Parikh, G. Logical retrofit may save millions of dollars in software maintenance. *Proceedings of the 2nd National Conference on EDP Software Maintenance.* Silver Spring, Md.: U.S. Professional Development Institute, 1984. pp. 427-429.

Suggests restructuring software according to the design techniques created by Jean-Dominique Warnier. See J.-D. Warnier's book below.

Parikh, G. and Zvegintzov, N. (ed.) *Tutorial on Software Maintenance.* Washington, D.C.: IEEE Computer Society, 1983.

A good collection of papers and issues on software maintenance. Touches on a wider variety of software maintenance topics (e.g., maintenance management) than the present Tutorial.

Perry, W.E. *Managing Systems Maintenance.* Wellesley, Mass.: Q.E.D. Information Systems, 1981.

Appendix A contains a set of qualitative criteria for deciding when to restructure software. These can be refashioned as quantitative criteria for use in particular software maintenance environments.

Richardson, G.L., Butler, C.W., and Hodil, E.D. Mending crazy quilt systems. *Datamation,* Vol. 30, no. 7 (May 15, 1984). pp. 130-142.

Describes "a rational way of managing the software asset and improving the performance of the maintenance dollar." The paper includes (1) a definition of code quality, (2) how poor quality code undergoing maintenance may be located, and (3) the use and economic justification for tools used to improve code documentation.

Sobrinho, F.G. *Structural Complexity: A Basis for Systematic Software Evolution.* Ph.D dissertation, University of Maryland, 1984. Available from University Microfilms International, 300 N. Zeeb Rd., Ann Arbor, MI 48106.

Among other results, this dissertation proposes a way to partition programs into independent sets of programming language statements. The approach features the development of dependency matrices, which give the probability that a change in one module will affect another module. The point of the partitioning algorithm is to prepare a matrix that captures a measure of the "similarity" of one module to another and which can be used as input to further module clustering algorithms.

Travis, A. J. Re-engineering business systems. *Proceedings of the 3rd National Conference on EDP Software Maintenance.* Silver Spring, Md.: U.S. Professional Development Institute, 1985.

Discusses how restructuring may be used to aid the strategic evolution of an enterprise's data processing capabilities. To re-engineer a system, the approach suggests performing bottom-up analysis, to quantitatively assess the code's state; performing top-down planning, to ensure the system is restructured consistent with anticipated enterprise needs; and performing bottom-up implementation, to restructure code in the current system before enhancing the system (e.g., migrating a file system-based system to one which uses a data base). The approach is implemented for COBOL using the proprietary tools PATHVU (for calculating software metrics and displaying code complexity) and Structured Retrofit (for restructuring COBOL code). The tools are available from Peat, Marwick, Mitchell & Co., Chicago, Illinois.

Warnier, J-D. *Program Modification.* Boston: Martinus Nijhoff, 1978.

Discusses how to modify programs already designed by using Warnier's program design methodology. (Warnier's methodology designs a program to reflect the hierarchical structure of the data the program operates on.) Changes to a program are first evaluated as to their impact on input data structure, then the program is modified. Other modification principles are given in case the input data is not affected by a proposed change.

Weinberg, G. Worst-first maintenance, in Parikh, G. (ed.) *Techniques of Program and System Maintenance.* Cambridge, Mass.: Winthrop, 1982.

Recommends improving the roughly 20% of modules involved in 80% of the discovered software problems in a system.

Yourdon, E. *Techniques of Program Structure and Design.* Englewood Cliffs, N.J.: Prentice-Hall, 1975.

Presents the control-flow restructuring techniques of the boolean variable approach and the duplication of coding approach. An example of the Ashcroft-Manna giant case statement approach (see reference above)—called the state variable approach by Yourdon—is also presented.

Zvegintzov, N. Immortal software. *Datamation,* Vol. 30, no. 9 (June 15, 1984). pp. 170-180.

A survey of issues on software aging. Perhaps the most interesting question posed here is, what is the "optimal" amount of software restructuring for a system?

Author Biography

Dr. Robert S. Arnold is a member of the technical staff at the MITRE Corporation in McLean, Virginia. Prior to this, in 1983, he taught professional seminars in software maintenance, software testing, design techniques, C, and UNIX. In 1981-82 Dr. Arnold analyzed 8 years of software maintenance data on 10 software projects from NASA/Goddard Space Flight Center in Greenbelt, Maryland. In 1980 he worked with Sperry Univac Corp. in Austin, Texas, and used a fourth generation language to help create a hospital data processing system. In 1976 and 1977, Dr. Arnold worked under Dr. E.F. Codd at the IBM/San Jose Research Laboratory, California, on RENDEZVOUS, a natural language front end to a relational data base system.

Dr. Arnold is a member of the IEEE Working Group on a Standard for Software Quality Metrics. He was Program Co-Chair of the Conference on Software Maintenance-1985 (CSM-85) and a Session Chair at the 1985 Hawaii International Conference on Systems Sciences. He was Editor of the Workshop Record for the 1983 Software Maintenance Workshop, the first software maintenance workshop sponsored by the IEEE Computer Society.

Dr. Arnold received his Ph.D in computer science from the University of Maryland in 1983. His dissertation, "On the Generation and Use of Quantitative Criteria for Assessing Software Maintenance Quality," gave software maintenance managers an easy-to-follow, systematic way to transform quantitative data on the software maintenance process into concrete suggestions for improving that process. From 1977-1980 he did graduate work at the University of Texas at Austin. He received his M.S. in computer science from Carnegie-Mellon University in 1977. He received his B.A. "with highest distinction" in mathematics and computer studies from Northwestern University, Evanston, Illinois, in 1975.

Dr. Arnold is a member of Phi Beta Kappa, Phi Kappa Phi, ACM, SIGSOFT, and the IEEE Computer Society.